**SAP PRESS e-books**

Print or e-book, Kindle or iPad, workplace or airplane: Choose where and how to read your SAP PRESS books! You can now get all our titles as e-books, too:

- By download and online access
- For all popular devices
- And, of course, DRM-free

Convinced? Then go to www.sap-press.com and get your e-book today.

Migrating to SAP S/4HANA®

SAP PRESS is a joint initiative of SAP and Rheinwerk Publishing. The know-how offered by SAP specialists combined with the expertise of Rheinwerk Publishing offers the reader expert books in the field. SAP PRESS features first-hand information and expert advice, and provides useful skills for professional decision-making.

SAP PRESS offers a variety of books on technical and business-related topics for the SAP user. For further information, please visit our website: www.sap-press.com.

Baumgartl, Chaadaev, Choi, Dudgeon, Lahiri, Meijerink, Worsley-Tonks
SAP S/4HANA: An Introduction
2017, 449 pages, hardcover and e-book
www.sap-press.com/4153

Anil Bavaraju
SAP Fiori Implementation and Development (2nd Edition)
2017, 615 pages, hardcover and e-book
www.sap-press.com/4401

Christensen, Darlak, Harrington, Kong, Poles, Savelli
SAP BW/4HANA: An Introduction
2017, 427 pages, hardcover and e-book
www.sap-press.com/4377

Michael Jolton, Yosh Eisbart
SAP S/4HANA Cloud: Use Cases, Functionality, and Extensibility
2017, approx. 350 pp., hardcover and e-book
www.sap-press.com/4498

Frank Densborn, Frank Finkbohner, Jochen Freudenberg,
Kim Mathäß, Frank Wagner

Migrating to SAP S/4HANA®

Editor Will Jobst
Acquisitions Editor Hareem Shafi
German Edition Editor Janina Karrasch
Translation Lemoine International, Inc., Salt Lake City, UT
Copyeditor Yvette Chin
Cover Design Graham Geary
Photo Credit Shutterstock.com/413666632/© Carlos Caetano
Layout Design Vera Brauner
Production Graham Geary
Typesetting III-satz, Husby (Germany)
Printed and bound in the United States of America, on paper from sustainable sources

ISBN 978-1-4932-1448-8

© 2017 by Rheinwerk Publishing, Inc., Boston (MA)
1st edition 2017
1st German edition published 2017 by Rheinwerk Verlag, Bonn, Germany

Library of Congress Cataloging-in-Publication Control Number: 2017025848

All rights reserved. Neither this publication nor any part of it may be copied or reproduced in any form or by any means or translated into another language, without the prior consent of Rheinwerk Publishing, 2 Heritage Drive, Suite 305, Quincy, MA 02171.

Rheinwerk Publishing makes no warranties or representations with respect to the content hereof and specifically disclaims any implied warranties of merchantability or fitness for any particular purpose. Rheinwerk Publishing assumes no responsibility for any errors that may appear in this publication.

"Rheinwerk Publishing" and the Rheinwerk Publishing logo are registered trademarks of Rheinwerk Verlag GmbH, Bonn, Germany. SAP PRESS is an imprint of Rheinwerk Verlag GmbH and Rheinwerk Publishing, Inc.

All of the screenshots and graphics reproduced in this book are subject to copyright © SAP SE, Dietmar-Hopp-Allee 16, 69190 Walldorf, Germany.

SAP, the SAP logo, ABAP, Ariba, ASAP, Concur, Concur ExpenseIt, Concur TripIt, Duet, SAP Adaptive Server Enterprise, SAP Advantage Database Server, SAP Afaria, SAP ArchiveLink, SAP Ariba, SAP Business ByDesign, SAP Business Explorer, SAP BusinessObjects, SAP BusinessObjects Explorer, SAP BusinessObjects Lumira, SAP BusinessObjects Roambi, SAP BusinessObjects Web Intelligence, SAP Business One, SAP Business Workflow, SAP Crystal Reports, SAP EarlyWatch, SAP Exchange Media (SAP XM), SAP Fieldglass, SAP Fiori, SAP Global Trade Services (SAP GTS), SAP GoingLive, SAP HANA, SAP HANA Vora, SAP Hybris, SAP Jam, SAP MaxAttention, SAP MaxDB, SAP NetWeaver, SAP PartnerEdge, SAPPHIRE NOW, SAP PowerBuilder, SAP PowerDesigner, SAP R/2, SAP R/3, SAP Replication Server, SAP S/4HANA, SAP SQL Anywhere, SAP Strategic Enterprise Management (SAP SEM), SAP SuccessFactors, The Best-Run Businesses Run SAP, TwoGo are registered or unregistered trademarks of SAP SE, Walldorf, Germany.

All other products mentioned in this book are registered or unregistered trademarks of their respective companies.

Contents at a Glance

PART I Basic Principles

1 SAP S/4HANA—Requirements and Benefits 25
2 SAP S/4HANA versus the Traditional SAP Business Suite 75
3 Cloud, On-Premise, and Hybrid Scenarios 99
4 Preparing the Migration to SAP S/4HANA 133
5 SAP Activate 157
6 Trial Systems and Model Company 179

PART II Migrating to SAP S/4HANA in the Cloud

7 Migrating to the Public Cloud 193
8 Integrating SAP S/4HANA Cloud into the System Landscape 241

PART III Migrating to SAP S/4HANA On-Premise

9 Installing and Configuring SAP S/4HANA On-Premise or in the Private Cloud 311
10 System Conversion 329
11 New Implementation of Single Systems 377
12 Landscape Transformation 457
13 Integrating SAP S/4HANA, On-Premise, into the System Landscape ... 503

PART IV Assessing the Transformation Scenarios

14 Selecting Your Migration Scenario 527

Dear Reader,

With a team like this, you know your migration is off to a good start:

Frank Densborn, product manager for SAP S/4HANA Data Migration.

Frank Finkbohner, delivery manager for the SAP S/4HANA Cloud data migration content.

Dr. Jochen Freudenberg, head of the Development Landscape Management Architecture department.

Kim Mathäß, product manager for SAP S/4HANA data management and migration.

Frank Wagner, product expert within SAP S/4HANA product development.

This team has the expertise you need for your SAP S/4HANA migration project. They are passionate about providing you with the know-how you need to ensure a smooth migration process.

What did you think about *Migrating to SAP S/4HANA*? Your comments and suggestions are the most useful tools to help us make our books the best they can be. Please feel free to contact me and share any praise or criticism you may have.

Thank you for purchasing a book from SAP PRESS!

Will Jobst
Editor, SAP PRESS

willj@rheinwerk-publishing.com
www.sap-press.com
Rheinwerk Publishing · Boston, MA

Contents

Preface 15
Introduction 17

PART I Basic Principles

1 SAP S/4HANA—Requirements and Benefits   25

1.1	**Future Business Challenges**	26
	1.1.1 Digitization of Business Processes	27
	1.1.2 Trends of the Digital Transformation	30
1.2	**The Pledge of SAP S/4HANA**	37
	1.2.1 Simplification of the Functionality	37
	1.2.2 Simplification of the Data Structure	40
	1.2.3 Simplified User Interfaces	43
	1.2.4 Simplified Analyses	45
1.3	**Business Functions in SAP S/4HANA**	46
	1.3.1 Accounting	47
	1.3.2 Logistics	52
	1.3.3 Human Resources	57
	1.3.4 Procurement	64
	1.3.5 Marketing	68

2 SAP S/4HANA versus the Traditional SAP Business Suite   75

2.1	Comparing the Available Solutions: SAP S/4HANA and the Digital Core	75
2.2	**Simplification**	79

Contents

2.3	The New Data Model and the SAP HANA Database	81
	2.3.1 SAP HANA	83
	2.3.2 The Data Model	84
	2.3.3 Handling Existing Data	87
	2.3.4 Sizing	87
2.4	SAP Fiori User Interfaces	88
	2.4.1 Technological Changes	90
	2.4.2 Operating Concept	91
2.5	Interfaces	95
2.6	SAP S/4HANA Embedded Analytics	96

3 Cloud, On-Premise, and Hybrid Scenarios   99

3.1	Overview of Operating Models	100
	3.1.1 On-Premise Operating Model	100
	3.1.2 Cloud Operating Model	100
	3.1.3 Hybrid Operating Model	103
3.2	The SAP S/4HANA Product Family	104
	3.2.1 SAP S/4HANA, On-Premise	105
	3.2.2 SAP S/4HANA Cloud	109
	3.2.3 SAP HANA Enterprise Cloud	113
3.3	Comparing the Operating Models	115
	3.3.1 Hardware, Software, Operation, and Maintenance	115
	3.3.2 User Interfaces	117
	3.3.3 Functional Scope and Supported Country Versions	118
	3.3.4 Options for Enhancement	120
	3.3.5 Payment Model and Runtime	120
	3.3.6 Model for Migration to SAP S/4HANA	121
3.4	Extensibility in SAP S/4HANA	122
	3.4.1 Side-by-Side Enhancements	124
	3.4.2 In-App Enhancements	126
	3.4.3 Checking Custom Enhancements When Migrating to SAP S/4HANA	132

4   Preparing the Migration to SAP S/4HANA   133

4.1	Basic Considerations	133
4.2	The Three Migration Scenarios	139
	4.2.1 New Implementation of SAP S/4HANA	140
	4.2.2 System Conversion to SAP S/4HANA	146
	4.2.3 Landscape Transformation with SAP S/4HANA	153

5   SAP Activate   157

5.1	SAP Activate Content	158
	5.1.1 SAP Best Practices	160
	5.1.2 Guided Configuration	165
	5.1.3 SAP Activate Methodology	173
5.2	SAP Activate Phases	174

6   Trial Systems and Model Company   179

6.1	Trial System in the SAP Cloud Appliance Library	179
6.2	SAP S/4HANA Fully-Activated Appliance	182
6.3	Solution Scope of the Model System	185
6.4	Enterprise Structure of the Model Company	188

PART II   Migrating to SAP S/4HANA in the Cloud

7   Migrating to the Public Cloud   193

7.1	Setting Up SAP S/4HANA Cloud	193
	7.1.1 Discover Phase: Configuring the SAP S/4HANA Cloud Trial System	194
	7.1.2 Explore Phase: Configuring the SAP S/4HANA Cloud Starter System	195

		7.1.3	Realize Phase: Configuring the SAP S/4HANA Cloud Quality Assurance System	204
		7.1.4	Deploy Phase: Configuring the SAP S/4HANA Cloud Production Systems	208
	7.2	Configuring SAP S/4HANA Cloud		210
	7.3	Migrating Data to SAP S/4HANA Cloud		213
		7.3.1	Available Migration Objects	214
		7.3.2	Data Migration Using the SAP S/4HANA Migration Cockpit	216

8   Integrating SAP S/4HANA Cloud into the System Landscape — 241

8.1	Integration with SAP Ariba Solutions		241
	8.1.1	Integration Scenarios in Procurement and Accounts Payable	242
	8.1.2	License Prerequisites and Provision of SAP Ariba System Accesses	249
	8.1.3	Executing an Integration Project with SAP Activate	249
	8.1.4	Integration Settings in SAP S/4HANA Cloud	252
	8.1.5	Configuration in SAP Ariba	266
	8.1.6	Testing the Integrated Business Processes and Going Live	272
	8.1.7	Outlook	273
8.2	Integration with SAP SuccessFactors		274
	8.2.1	Configuration in SAP S/4HANA Cloud	279
	8.2.2	Configuration in SAP Cloud Platform Integration	282
	8.2.3	Configuration in SAP SuccessFactors Employee Central	283
8.3	Integration with SAP Hybris Marketing Cloud		284
	8.3.1	SAP Hybris Marketing Cloud Data Model	289
	8.3.2	Integration with SAP ERP Systems	291
	8.3.3	Importing Data from External Systems	296
	8.3.4	Importing Data from Social Media	302
	8.3.5	Integration of SAP Hybris Cloud for Customer Systems	306

PART III Migrating to SAP S/4HANA On-Premise

9 Installing and Configuring SAP S/4HANA On-Premise or in the Private Cloud — 311

9.1	Installation	313
9.2	System Configuration	318
9.3	Setting Up the Frontend Server for SAP Fiori User Interfaces	322
	9.3.1 On-Premise Installation of the Frontend Server	324
	9.3.2 SAP Fiori Cloud	325

10 System Conversion — 329

10.1	Overview of the System Conversion Project	329
	10.1.1 System Conversion Process	332
	10.1.2 System Group Conversion	334
10.2	Converting Single Systems	337
	10.2.1 System Requirements	338
	10.2.2 Simplification List	340
	10.2.3 Maintenance Planner	344
	10.2.4 Prechecks	346
	10.2.5 Adapting Custom Developments	348
	10.2.6 Database Sizing for SAP S/4HANA	362
	10.2.7 Using Software Update Manager	363
	10.2.8 Migrating to SAP Fiori User Interfaces	370

11 New Implementation of Single Systems — 377

11.1	Data Migration Phases	378
	11.1.1 Data Analysis	380
	11.1.2 Mapping	382
	11.1.3 Implementation	383

	11.1.4	Testing	384
	11.1.5	Data Validation	384
	11.1.6	Data Cleansing	386
	11.1.7	Productive Load and Support	386
11.2	Supported Migration Objects		387
11.3	Rapid Data Migration		390
	11.3.1	Tools	390
	11.3.2	Architecture	392
	11.3.3	Migration Content	396
	11.3.4	Connecting to Source Systems	405
	11.3.5	Data Profiling	408
	11.3.6	Field Mapping	411
	11.3.7	Value Mapping and Conversion Tables	419
	11.3.8	Data Validation	426
	11.3.9	Importing Data	430
	11.3.10	Monitoring	432
	11.3.11	Optimizing IDoc Performance	434
11.4	SAP S/4HANA Migration Cockpit		437
11.5	SAP S/4HANA Migration Object Modeler		441
	11.5.1	Edit Source Structures	445
	11.5.2	Display Target Structures	448
	11.5.3	Display Structure Mapping	449
	11.5.4	Edit Field Mapping	450
	11.5.5	Technical Functions	451
	11.5.6	Advanced Activities	452
11.6	Comparison of Migration Tools		453

12   Landscape Transformation   457

12.1	The Three Transformation Scenarios		458
12.2	Carrying Out a Transformation Project		459
	12.2.1	Preanalysis and Planning	462
	12.2.2	Blueprint and Project Team	462
	12.2.3	Test Runs	464

	12.2.4	Production Conversion	466
	12.2.5	Support after Go-Live	467
12.3	System Consolidation		467
12.4	Company Code Transfer		476
12.5	Transformation to Central Finance		482
	12.5.1	Implementing SAP S/4HANA Central Finance	483
	12.5.2	Global Parameters	487
	12.5.3	Master Data	493
	12.5.4	Mapping, Error Handling, and Initial Data Load	498

13 Integrating SAP S/4HANA, On-Premise, into the System Landscape — 503

13.1	Integration with SAP Ariba Solutions		503
	13.1.1	Integrated Business Processes with SAP Ariba Solutions and SAP S/4HANA	503
	13.1.2	Technical Integration of SAP S/4HANA with SAP Ariba	506
13.2	Integration with SAP ERP HCM and SAP SuccessFactors		509
	13.2.1	ALE Integration with SAP ERP HCM	510
	13.2.2	Integration of SAP ERP HCM within the SAP S/4HANA Instance	511
	13.2.3	Integration with SAP SuccessFactors Employee Central	513
	13.2.4	Synchronizing Employee Data with Business Partners	519
13.3	Integration with Existing SAP Systems		521

PART IV Assessing the Transformation Scenarios

14 Selecting Your Migration Scenario — 527

14.1	Overview of Procedures and Input Helps		527
14.2	Creating Your Own Roadmap		530
	14.2.1	Initial Scenario: Single System	534

13

		14.2.2	Initial Scenario: Decentralized System Landscape	539
		14.2.3	Sample Roadmaps	542
14.3		**The Most Important Criteria for Your Decision**		546
14.4		**Conclusion**		549

The Authors	551
Index	555

Preface

The world economy is currently undergoing a transformation. With increasing frequency, technological innovations are launched that exert drastic influence in our daily lives. The Internet, with its heightened interoperability of persons, products, and services, substantially impacts your enterprise and business processes. To consider this interoperability, you must reassess traditional business models and adapt your business processes if required. Exponential data growth requires innovative approaches for data storage and processing. In terms of system landscape, the requirements for outsourcing business processes to the cloud keep changing, but access to your systems via mobile devices ensures future viability. As the market leader for business software, we consider it our responsibility to help our customers, whatever the status their existing system landscapes may be, and support them in addressing the challenges of this digital transformation.

With SAP S/4HANA, SAP provides a modern ERP suite that uses the in-memory technology of SAP HANA to overcome the technical limits of traditional databases. SAP S/4HANA can become the digital core of central, mission-critical business processes such as accounting, logistics, procurement, and sales and distribution. The design of SAP S/4HANA is based on the following core aspects: simplification of the application, in particular simplification of data structures; simplification of the user experience through role-based user interfaces in SAP Fiori; *embedded analytics*; *machine learning*; and a *cloud-first approach* for developing new functions and business processes.

SAP S/4HANA allows customers to select the appropriate operation option for their business processes: running the business processes on-premise, operating entirely in the cloud, or outsourcing only selected parts of the business processes to the cloud and running other parts on-premise—SAP S/4HANA ensures flexibility. Since its introduction in 2015, more than 6,300 customers have chosen SAP S/4HANA. In 2017, the central question for our customers is no longer *if* they migrate to SAP S/4HANA but *how* to perform the migration to gain the maximum benefit from it.

This book describes the different operating models and the migration scenarios to SAP S/4HANA in detail. We hope to enable readers to assess the corresponding scenarios and thus plan their migration to SAP S/4HANA more efficiently. In the context of the various SAP S/4HANA migration scenarios, we'll illustrate different options for defining your own pace for the migration and thus protecting the investments made into your existing system landscape.

Sven Denecken
Senior Vice President and Chief Product Owner for SAP S/4HANA Cloud

Rudolf Hois
Vice President and Chief Product Owner for SAP S/4HANA, On-Premise

Introduction

SAP S/4HANA, short for *SAP Business Suite 4 SAP HANA*, is SAP's next-generation application suite. SAP S/4HANA is targeted both at existing customers who use SAP ERP or the traditional SAP Business Suite and also at new customers who have never used an SAP solution before.

Regardless of your situation—if you want to use SAP S/4HANA, this book is your guide to migrating to SAP S/4HANA. We'll familiarize you with all critical areas of the new SAP S/4HANA system and describe how to migrate to SAP S/4HANA using individual migration scenarios to illustrate the process.

In this context, we won't just introduce the basic options for the tools provided by SAP; we'll also support you during the migration process by illustrating typical usage scenarios. Our goal is to provide optimal support and find the best way to make SAP S/4HANA work for you—irrespective of whether you want to use SAP S/4HANA in the cloud or on-premise and irrespective of your existing ERP system. This book describes different operating models for SAP S/4HANA and explains the differences in the migration processes of the various models. <small>On-premise or in the cloud?</small>

You'll also learn how to convert your existing SAP system to SAP S/4HANA, how to implement a new SAP S/4HANA system and transfer your data to this system, and how to transform an existing landscape into an SAP S/4HANA landscape. SAP has defined three ways to SAP S/4HANA: <small>Scenarios</small>

- New implementations of SAP S/4HANA
- System conversions to SAP S/4HANA
- Landscape transformations with SAP S/4HANA

Furthermore, in this book, we'll discuss how to integrate this new system into your existing IT landscape and address the required modifications. The goal of this book is to illustrate and explain the necessary processes in detail. After introducing the basic principles of SAP S/4HANA, we'll discuss all aspects of the migration scenarios and of the integration with SAP S/4HANA Cloud and SAP S/4HANA, on-premise. You will be provided with step-by-step descriptions of the different migration scenarios, and their differing requirements and implementations are compared using real-life examples. <small>Integration</small>

This book will also equip you with decision-making criteria and the necessary knowledge. By the end, you'll be the person with the know-how to decide which method is ideal for your migration to SAP S/4HANA.

Who This Book Is For

Because this book provides a holistic overview of migrating to SAP S/4HANA, we have targeted various groups of readers. For making decisions and choosing the appropriate migration scenario, this book supports *IT managers* and *administrators* who will integrate SAP S/4HANA. However, because we also go into detail, this book also supports *SAP consultants* who manage SAP S/4HANA migration projects for customers or in their own organization and *project leads* who want to get an overview of the individual methods and tools. All these groups can use the instructions in this book as a guide to implementing their own migration projects.

Previous knowledge

Because SAP S/4HANA is a completely new business suite, you do not require any previous SAP ERP knowledge for this book. However, if you want to reproduce the migration scenarios in this book, you should have a basic understanding of SAP NetWeaver. For more information on SAP NetWeaver, SAP HANA, and data migration in SAP systems, or for a detailed business overview of SAP S/4HANA, refer to the other specialized SAP PRESS books.

Release status

This book describes all procedures and methods for *SAP S/4HANA, on-premise, 1610* and *SAP S/4HANA Cloud 1702*, the latest releases as this book was going to press. If you use higher versions, the screenshots shown in this book might deviate slightly from your screen views. However, we assume that the basic steps for migrating to SAP S/4HANA will stay the same in higher releases.

> **Terminology**
>
> The term *SAP S/4HANA migration* in this book is the generic term for the various scenarios of the migration to SAP S/4HANA. So this term not only refers to data migration and data transfer from legacy IT systems or SAP production systems; it also refers to the conversion of individual systems or the transformation of system landscapes.

Structure of This Book

This book is structured into four parts. The following summarizes the content of these parts and the individual chapters for better orientation.

Part I: SAP S/4HANA—Basic Principles

The first part of the book contains descriptions of the most important basic concepts, which will be necessary for you to make a decision for or against a specific installation and migration scenario. This part is also relevant to IT managers and IT employees in organizations that have not yet decided on a concrete migration plan but want to get more information about the various options. We'll explain the various deployment options for SAP S/4HANA: in a public cloud, on-premise, and as a hybrid model. Finally, you'll learn how to prepare the migration to SAP S/4HANA and explore the steps of a new implementation method for SAP S/4HANA.

Chapter 1, "SAP S/4HANA—Requirements and Benefits," provides a basic overview of SAP S/4HANA and illustrates the benefits of this new solution. In this context, we'll also cover the transformation of traditional business models—a result of the digital transformation—and we'll describe digitalization challenges that enterprises face today and will face in future. You'll get to know SAP S/4HANA's technological and business features to address these challenges.

Requirements and benefits

Chapter 2, "SAP S/4HANA versus the Traditional SAP Business Suite," introduces the basis differences between SAP S/4HANA and the SAP Business Suite and positions the new solution into the SAP product portfolio. In this chapter, we'll also explain the reasons for these differences and discuss the relevant options for your IT department and business processes. We'll also describe the relevance of these changes for your SAP S/4HANA migration plan.

Differences between SAP S/4HANA and the SAP Business Suite

SAP S/4HANA is available in different deployment models. These options include an implementation in the private cloud or public cloud, on-premise in your data center, and using a hybrid approach. **Chapter 3**, "Cloud, On-Premise, and Hybrid Scenarios," conveys a fundamental understanding of these operating models and introduces the deployment options within the SAP S/4HANA product family. This chapter also describes the differences between the individual models in detail.

Cloud, on-premise, and hybrid

Preparing for migration

After explaining the basic principles of SAP S/4HANA, **Chapter 4**, "Preparing the Migration to SAP S/4HANA," introduces the procedures for migrating to SAP S/4HANA and describes the concrete steps that you need to consider in the project planning process. The last part of the book then looks back at these descriptions and summarizes the advantages and disadvantages of the various scenarios under different conditions.

Implementation methodology

Introduced with SAP S/4HANA, SAP Activate is a new method for implementing SAP software and is designed to support customers migrating to SAP S/4HANA. **Chapter 5**, "SAP Activate," introduces this successor to the ASAP and SAP Launch implementation models.

Model company

Chapter 6, "Trial Systems and Model Company," concludes the first part of the book. In this chapter, we'll cover the available trial systems and introduce the model company provided by SAP S/4HANA. The model company is comprised of a preconfigured system including customizing (such as predefined company codes and organizational structures) and sample data. The model company helps you identify the requirements and prerequisites for your migration.

Part II: Migrating to SAP S/4HANA Cloud

Public cloud

The second part of the book provides a step-by-step description of the different migration scenarios for SAP S/4HANA Cloud. In this part, we'll discuss the tools and procedures for the data migration and for integration with other systems.

Migration

A cloud solution offers new opportunities of organizing and financing the IT in your enterprise. **Chapter 7**, "Migrating to the Public Cloud," shows how you can deploy SAP S/4HANA in a public cloud. In this chapter, we'll discuss the things you should consider when implementing a cloud solution, which tools are available for the data migration in SAP S/4HANA Cloud, and the individual steps of the migration.

Integration with the system landscape

Chapter 8, "Integrating SAP S/4HANA Cloud into the System Landscape," describes how to integrate an SAP S/4HANA Cloud system with other SAP cloud solutions such as SAP Ariba or SAP SuccessFactors and how to embed SAP Hybris Marketing Cloud into your existing SAP system landscape. In this chapter, we'll illustrate how to connect your systems and which interfaces you should use for this purpose.

Part III: Migrating to SAP S/4HANA, On-Premise

After focusing on the standalone SAP S/4HANA Cloud solution in the second part, the third part of the book concentrates on SAP S/4HANA, on-premise, which can also be hosted in a private cloud. This version features additional migration scenarios, which are introduced in this chapter in detail with relevant usage scenarios. This part also illustrates the differences of operating in a public cloud and discusses the various integration options for SAP S/4HANA, on-premise.

On-premise or private cloud?

When migrating to SAP S/4HANA, on-premise, you'll either install a new SAP S/4HANA system or transform an existing SAP system. **Chapter 9**, "Installing and Configuring SAP S/4HANA On-Premise or in the Private Cloud," describes the necessary steps for installing backend and frontend servers and for installing the system.

Installation and configuration

Chapter 10, "System Conversion," introduces the first scenario for migrating to SAP S/4HANA, on-premise: a system conversion. Converting an existing SAP Business Suite system enables you to migrate to SAP S/4HANA without having to install a new system. This chapter describes the general process (from the planning phase to the actual conversion), the individual steps required, and the necessary technical tools.

System conversion

Chapter 11, "New Implementation of Single Systems," then details the various migration tools for new implementations (greenfield approach) of a new SAP S/4HANA, on-premise system. In this chapter, we'll introduce SAP S/4HANA migration cockpit, SAP S/4HANA migration object modeler, and SAP Data Services including SAP Best Practices Content (Rapid Data Migration) on the basis of real-life examples. In addition, we'll discuss the general procedure of a data migration project to SAP S/4HANA.

New implementation

Chapter 12, "System Landscape Transformation," addresses the third migration scenario, landscape transformation, and its corresponding procedure. Furthermore, we'll provides detailed information on a critical use case for SAP S/4HANA: Central Finance.

Landscape transformation

Finally, **Chapter 13**, "Integrating SAP S/4HANA, On-Premise, into the System Landscape," details various integration options for SAP S/4HANA, on-premise, especially integration with SAP Ariba, SAP SuccessFactors, and existing SAP systems.

Integration

Introduction

Part IV: Assessing the Migration Scenarios

The last part of the book analyzes which scenario is ideal for *your enterprise*. The appropriate strategy for migrating to SAP S/4HANA depends on your initial situation. This part provides you with decision-making criteria and examples for each individual migration scenario.

Selecting a migration scenario

Chapter 14, "Selecting Your Migration Scenario," summarizes the advantages and disadvantages of the individual migration scenarios and compares them. This chapter discusses core decision criteria between choosing a new implementation or a system conversion. Landscape transformation is a special case because it can be combined with both scenarios. Ultimately, however, your choice among these scenarios will be based on business requirements.

Information boxes

The highlighted boxes in this book contain information that is good to know and useful but outside the context. To help you immediately identify the type of information contained in the boxes, we have assigned symbols to each box:

- [»] Boxes marked with this symbol contain information about *additional topics* or important content that you should note.

- [!] This icon refers to *specifics* that you should consider. It also *warns* about frequent errors or problems that can occur.

- [Ex] *Examples*, which are highlighted with this icon, refer to real-life scenarios and illustrate the functions described.

- [o] Text passages highlighted with this icon summarize thematic relationships *at a glance*.

We hope that this book proves to be a good reference and guide for your migration to SAP S/4HANA. We wish you an enjoyable read and hope you can use the insights gained from reading this book in real life.

Frank Densborn, Frank Finkbohner, Jochen Freudenberg,
Kim Mathäß, Frank Wagner
and our integration experts **Andreas Muno** and **Markus Trapp**

PART I
Basic Principles

Chapter 1
SAP S/4HANA—Requirements and Benefits

Increasing digitalization and interoperability in the economy doesn't just impact industrial production processes. This chapter explains how SAP S/4HANA addresses the requirements of the digital transformation.

Enterprises have always had to deal with technological changes and innovations. Since the 1970s (since the so-called industrial revolution), automation has increasingly become prevalent in production. Since computers have been introduced and electronics and information technology have been used in production, previously manual process steps are now performed by machines.

The interoperability of products, processes, and infrastructures in real time has led to another critical change in industrial production processes, introducing a fourth stage of industrial revolution. All areas of the value chain, such as supply, production, delivery, customer service, and maintenance, are linked via the Internet, and information on each individual step is available in real time. The *Internet of Things* (IoT), as well as data and services, entail a holistic digitalization of the traditional industries, which can be summarized by the concept *Industry 4.0*.

_{The 4th industrial revolution—Industry 4.0}

As shown in Figure 1.1, in the past, people and enterprises had about a hundred years to migrate to the next industrial level. After industrialization, mass production, and automation, Industry 4.0 now leads to global and extensive changes in production processes, business models, technologies, the world of work, and people's everyday lives.

This paradigm shift, which is often referred to as *digital transformation*, offers opportunities and risks for new business models and existing value chains. Established enterprises can increase the efficiency of existing business models or develop new ones. Enterprises that ignore transformation

_{Opportunities and risks}

risk being forced out of business by more innovative enterprises because their own business processes remained too stagnant.

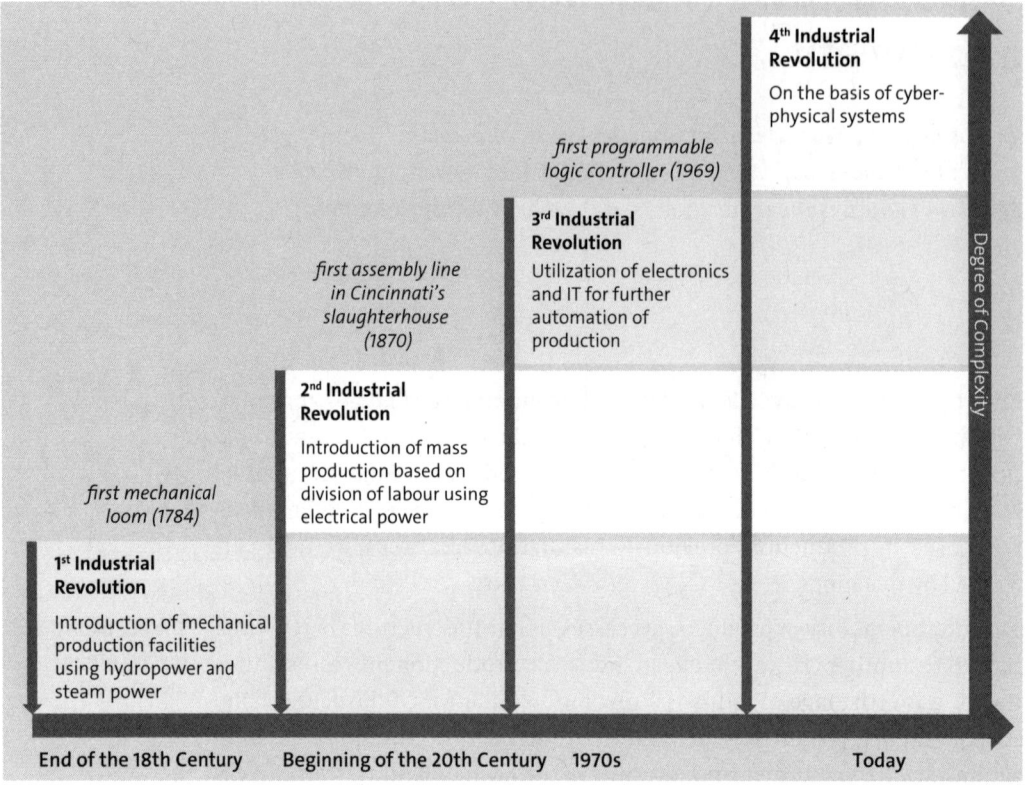

Figure 1.1 Levels of the Industrial Revolution

This chapter first addresses these opportunities and risks in detail. Section 1.2 then introduces the solutions offered by SAP S/4HANA to take advantage of the digital transformation. Section 1.3 describes individual SAP S/4HANA components for marketing, procurement, logistics, finances, and human resources.

1.1 Future Business Challenges

The 2000s also involved changes requiring enterprises to adapt their business models. In comparison to the previous industrial revolutions, the radical character and speed of the latest digital transformation are specific and new. In the past, changing business models often led to large enterprises acquiring small enterprises; today, in the digital economy, dynamic enterprises acquire slow, passive enterprises. Product suppliers that had been previously unknown can become market leaders in no time at all and can thus turn established industries upside down.

1.1.1 Digitization of Business Processes

Today's business processes are influenced by the increasing penetration of IT, which forces enterprises with traditional business processes to rethink their business processes and adapt them to the digital transformation. Table 1.1 lists some examples of how traditional business processes have changed over the last years.

Examples of digital transformations

Enterprises	Traditional Business Processes	Digital Business Processes
Airlines	Order processing via travel agencies	Online order processing
	High-quality service	No services
	Departure/arrival at central airports	Departure/arrival at provincial airports
Fashion enterprise	Outsourced production in Asia	Backsourcing of the production to Southern Europe
	Design cycles of several months	Collections changing every week
	Fashion retail in specialized shops	Distribution via online channels
Company for heating systems	Thermostats for heating systems in households and enterprises	Thermostats including integration into smart home technology
	High quality and holistic server portfolio	Proactive Maintenance Schedules
		Portfolio of additional products for smart home technology

Table 1.1 Comparison of Traditional and Digital Business Processes of Various Industries

Enterprises	Traditional Business Processes	Digital Business Processes
Taxi company	Assignment of taxi services via telephone	Taxi order via smartphones
	Cash payment	Automatic payment by credit card
Tool manufacturer	Tools for construction companies	Site management including leasing tools at fixed prices per month (including repair and maintenance services)
	High-quality and holistic server portfolio	24/7 last-mile delivery service of tools to the site
	On-premise retailer	Online order processing
Guitar manufacturer	Standard production	Additional custom shop as distribution channel for customized guitars
	Outsourced production to low-cost countries	High-price segment with production in home country

Table 1.1 Comparison of Traditional and Digital Business Processes of Various Industries (Cont.)

Level of digitalization

How high the pressure for changing traditional business processes actually depends on the segment in which the enterprise operates. Table 1.2 shows various industries categorized into the following groups:

- **Enterprises with a high level of digitalization**
  Enterprises in industries with conditions strongly supporting digitalization with regard to processes, value chains, investments for digitalization, and integration of digitalization into the business strategy

- **Enterprises with an average level of digitalization**
  Enterprises in industries with conditions moderately supporting digitalization

- **Enterprises with a low level of digitalization**
  Enterprises in industries in which digital processes only play a minor role

High Level of Digitalization	Average Level of Digitalization	Low Level of Digitalization
■ Enterprises in the information and communications technology (ICT) sector ■ Knowledge-based service providers	■ Finance and insurance sector ■ Retail ■ Energy and water supply ■ Mechanical engineering ■ Chemical and pharmaceutical industry ■ Transport and logistics ■ Automotive industry	■ Healthcare ■ Other manufacturing

Table 1.2 Evaluation of Industries Based on Their Level of Digitalization

Organizations that do not adapt to the changes resulting from the digital transformation will be massively impaired by their own business processes. In today's world, customers want to buy products whenever and wherever they want. Organizations using processes that do not meet this requirement will vanish from the market if they do not adapt their processes to this market condition.

The increasing digital transformation comprises three types of changes for business models:

Types of transformation

- Existing traditional business models can be complemented by the digital transformation.
- Existing traditional business models can be superseded by the digital transformation and replaced by digital business processes.
- The digital transformation can allow for business models that would not be possible without the digital transformation.

If the existing traditional business model is complemented by the digitalization, usually the enterprise can keep or even reinforce its market position. Take, for example, optimizing machine tools and production facilities. For example, if sensor technology costs can be reduced, the enterprise can measure the maintenance requirements for a production machine and only take maintenance actions when actually required. In this case, the digital transformation supports and improves an existing traditional business

Complementing business processes

model. The existing product and service portfolio is extended to ensure future business growth.

Replacing business processes
In some areas, traditional business models might be superseded by the digital transformation and replaced by digital business processes. This digitalization can radically change the rules of the market, often referred to as *disruptive transformation* or *disruptive innovation*.

Radical change can also open traditional sales markets for new enterprises. Who would have thought that a manufacturer of Wi-Fi routers would add radiator thermostats and switchable outdoor outlets to its product portfolio? Using online services provided by the router manufacturer, customers can control the thermostats in their homes or control their garden sprinklers via the Internet. Traditional providers of radiator thermostats, as well as new competitors entering the market, can respond to this digital transformation and also provide Internet-based smart home products. Some providers go a step further and use the connected radiator technology to involve maintenance technicians and calculate maintenance schedules proactively.

New business processes
One example of a business model that has been made possible by the digital transformation is *crowdsourcing* or *crowdfunding*. For crowdsourcing, project tasks are distributed across Internet users via Internet platforms. For crowdfunding, investors are found who want to (partly) invest in a project. The interaction of these actors has been made, not only possible, but economic and efficient by the Internet, thus forming the basis for these business models.

The digital transformation provides a wide range of options for creative business actions, and certain themes, such as focus on the customer and the quality of the infrastructure, have come to the fore. Focusing on the end consumers and their benefits is becoming a key success factor.

1.1.2 Trends of the Digital Transformation

Business and technical trends
In the context of digital transformation, the business and technical trends shown in Figure 1.2 play a major role. The following sections discuss each of these trends in greater detail.

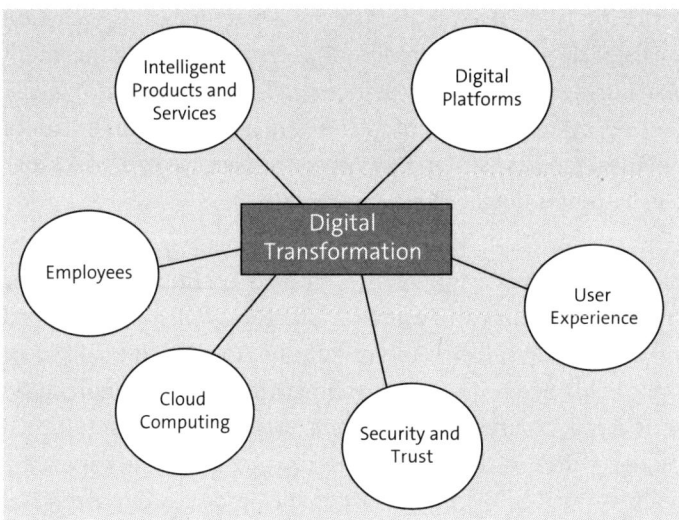

Figure 1.2 Trends of the Digital Transformation

Smart Products and Services

Increasing interoperability and the development of rapid sensor technology have transformed every device and machine into an information hub. Also called the *Internet of Things* (IoT), these capabilities have changed established value chains and industrial production processes. Previous business models focused on the quality, price, and delivery times of products; in the digital world, personalized products and services with additional benefits (*smart products* and *smart services*) have become increasingly important.

Internet of Things

The following three examples illustrate how the digital transformation can change established value chains and production processes:

Smart products and services

- **Smart maintenance**

    In smart service processes, sensor data can be used to predict the maintenance status of machines. The goal is to optimize maintenance processes by performing maintenance actions only when the status of the machine makes maintenance necessary. If this capability is supported by IT, not only will you be able to measure the current status of a machine, but you'll also be able to predict, based on historical data, when the machine is likely to break down, a capability known as *predictive analytics*.

Smart automation is involved if a sensor on a machine or a prediction triggers a spare parts procurement in the ERP system. This enhancement of traditional business models also demonstrates how production facilities and the ERP system of the enterprise can converge. You'll benefit greatly from these smart maintenance processes because your machines will function better for longer.

- **Digital farming**
Digital production processes have also entered traditional industries such as farming. A tractor can become a data hub, which—if equipped with the corresponding sensor—can determine how much fertilizer or seed different fields need. Harvesters can become data collectors, used by agricultural machinery manufacturers to supplement traditional business models with additional services. Conversely, mobile harvesters can also be integrated into smart maintenance processes. Agricultural machinery can be centrally monitored, and smart maintenance periods can be determined so that harvest processes run smoothly.

- **Lot Size One**
Let's say a guitar manufacturer adds custom products to its standard product portfolio. For selected, high-price guitars, a customer can compose their own individual guitar (selection of the wood type, shape of the guitar neck, integrated pickups, individual artificial aging of the guitar, etc.). Providing these individual pieces requires a highly flexible structure in production processes regarding order processing. In the context of digitalization, this kind of production is an individual production till the lot-size of one ("unit-of-one"). An interesting dimension of unit of one products is that these highly emotional products involve a relationship to the guitar maker. The enterprise's website introduces customers to the guitar makers who design these individual products. These individual production processes have been made possible by the easy customer communication facilitated by the Internet. In general, decreasing the number of units with increasingly changing orders, and consequently increasing setup times for machines, are a digitalization trend that many organizations should take into account.

These examples illustrate how interoperability increases automated, software-based value chains and supplements and supports traditional business processes with corresponding services. In the future, value chain elements will be increasingly connected across the involved enterprises. The communication between the individual steps of an end-to-end business process will increasingly take place in *real time*. Correspondingly, the need for standards in the context of Industry 4.0 will increase, which is also demonstrated by the publication of DIN SPEC 91345 as a standard for the "Reference Architecture Model Industrie 4.0 (RAMI4.0)" in April 2016.

Platforms

Compared to both new and modified value chains, digital platforms are a completely different business model. Some examples of digital platforms include:

- The Apple iTunes App Store on which independent providers offer apps for iPhones and iPads
- The Amazon Marketplace into which independent retailers and their products are integrated into Amazon's product portfolio
- Airbnb, a platform for leasing and letting accommodations in private homes
- Uber, an online agency service for transport services
- Industry-specific platforms such as First4Farming, a technology platform that connects participating enterprises in the farming industry

Examples of digital platforms

Digital platforms, the Internet, and the cloud are inextricably intertwined. Search and purchasing processes are performed online; customers can order products using any mobile end device anytime. Digital platforms enable external providers to be a part of the value chain without having a specific technology infrastructure. The platform provider is responsible for the operation and maintenance of the infrastructure but also defines the rules and costs for using the platform.

Characteristics of digital platforms

Digital platforms follow a completely different approach than traditional value chains. While the focus is on the product in the traditional economic world, platforms turn their attention to infrastructure services. For example, the services provided by Airbnb and Uber (only) consist of connecting users with providers of accommodations in private homes and of private taxi services, respectively. Digital platforms provide service providers with simplified access to digital real-time markets and cloud technologies. Many providers could not offer their services without the platform.

Focus on services

Human Capital

Need for flexible employees

The migration to digital business processes requires highly qualified employees. If you want to support highly flexible and customer-specific production processes, you'll need highly flexible employees supported by critical information and data. Your employees' specific capabilities, especially their flexibility, are key factors of the digital transformation. Enterprises need to support their employees with more flexible working hours, home office options, the required infrastructure, and flextime.

E-learning

The increasing requirements of flexible and complex business models additionally require further employee qualifications. To ensure continuous development, enterprises must integrate modern qualification approaches that are based on digital technologies. For example, specific e-learning courses (so-called *massive open online courses*, MOOCs) convey knowledge through videos and forums and allow trainers and students to communicate with each other and establish communities. The significance of employee qualifications must also be reflected in the context of a shortage of skilled workers, which is seen as a barrier to digitalization by many large enterprises.

User Experience

The wide usage of smartphones, tablets, smart TV, the Internet, messenger services, and emails generally affect the customers' expectations for user interfaces. Today's customers, who order products and services on the Internet, have the same high expectations for all the user interfaces they encounter.

Business model focusing on the user experience

The assignment of taxi services via smartphone apps has created a new business model, which replaces traditional taxi companies using radio communication to assign taxi services. In both cases, the customer orders a taxi. However, why is this (often quoted) example of the digitalization of business models successful and interesting? Because of the excellent user experience created by the taxi app on the customer's smartphone. The central feature of this experience is that an attractive order process (with an interactive map that displays taxis nearby) is linked with an attractive payment process. The app is so easy that you can simply leave the taxi after the ride and don't have to do anything, because the invoice is paid via credit card details specified earlier. This example illustrates that digital business processes also differentiate themselves from each other by means of the user experience. Digital business processes will only be successful if they create outstanding user experiences.

Thus, with the digital transformation, all enterprises need to focus on the consumer. The technology is not as important as the value added by the digital business process for the customer. The interface that supports the business process plays a major role for user acceptance.

Focus on consumers

Cloud Computing

Another digitalization trend is that IT services and business processes are outsourced to the cloud. An increasing number of cloud offerings enables you to overthink the tasks of your internal IT department. For example, specific services that cannot be efficiently provided by your own IT department can be outsourced to cloud providers. The data centers of cloud providers can usually respond more efficiently and flexibly to workload fluctuations that require computing and memory capacities to be flexible and adaptable. In addition, the costs of these flexible adaptations to fluctuations are easier to calculate. If you outsource services to external cloud providers, you don't necessarily have to support the new employee skills required by the digital transformation, which we mentioned in the "Human Capital" section earlier.

Flexible IT and costs

If you consider the impact of cloud computing on business processes, speed and flexibility play a major role. For example, an enterprise that outsources new business processes to the cloud, which results in shorter implementation cycles, can respond more quickly and more flexibly to changing market conditions. Cloud computing also enables enterprises to redefine business processes. A growing number of cloud offerings allows enterprises to standardize business processes and outsource them to the cloud if they do not have to differentiate themselves from competitors in this area. Enterprises do not necessarily have to run their online shop themselves, and you can use common Internet trading standards as a guide. In contrast, core business processes might emerge where you might want to, or have to, differentiate yourself from your competitors. Perhaps you want to implement highly specialized and individual business processes that are not compatible with the standardized processes in the cloud.

Impact on business processes

In this case, you'll usually want to run these business processes yourself within your enterprise.

Security and Trust

On the one hand, the increasing interoperability of value chains and the collection of large data volumes, using sensors that have become cheaper and cheaper, allow for new and supplementary business models. On the other hand, these developments also present security risks, which business organizations must address.

Security in the cloud One of the greatest barriers to cloud solutions is security, which must be considered when designing the applications. While monitoring production facilities was once rather an enterprise-specific topic, in the context of smart maintenance processes, the system can be opened up to network access, which requires the corresponding security measures.

Digital business processes also place stricter requirements on security and the protection of the collected data. You must ensure that, in the relevant business processes, only authorized and authenticated partners can communicate with each other. Modern IT security and encryption systems can ensure security for this communication but must be tailored for this purpose.

Employee qualifications For data security, the employee qualifications again play an important role. To innovate and ensure the competitive edge of your enterprise, your employees need to be qualified in cybersecurity. The digital skills of your employees regarding the handling and disclosure of data must be supported. What good is a modern cybersecurity concept if your employees use the same, insecure password for all systems?

Higher security standards Outsourcing business processes to the cloud can be the ideal solution for cybersecurity, because reliable cloud providers usually have higher security standards than the IT department in many organizations can ensure. Centrally managed cloud environments can also provide the benefits of backup and recovery processes.

The users' trust In the context of digital transformation, the success of an enterprise also depends on the users' trust. Customers will turn away from an enterprise that cannot ensure personal data is protected. But users' trust is not limited to data security; customers might also consider ethics and values when assessing a business model. Would customers prefer a taxi app if they knew that the drivers were treated more fairly and that a higher share of revenue was used for car inspections? Possibly!

1.2 The Pledge of SAP S/4HANA

SAP S/4HANA is a real-time ERP suite that can form the *digital core* of a business. SAP S/4HANA is completely based on SAP HANA, an in-memory platform, and provides SAP Fiori as an intuitive, role-based user interface that is structured on advanced design principles. Two deployment options are available for SAP S/4HANA: on-premise and SAP S/4HANA Cloud.

Section 1.3 describes the business processes integrated in SAP S/4HANA and discusses how SAP S/4HANA can support various business departments in mastering the digital challenges we detailed in the previous section.

This section summarizes to what extent the basic design of SAP S/4HANA meets the requirements of the digital transformation. The aim of SAP S/4HANA is to help enterprises address the challenges resulting from the digital transformation. SAP S/4HANA enables customers to map new digital business models in addition to their traditional business models. SAP S/4HANA is SAP's answer to the increasing complexity of the digital world. SAP S/4HANA simplifies functions, data structure, user experience, and analyses to meet the requirements for benefiting from interoperability, the Internet of Things, or big data.

Support for the digital transformation

1.2.1 Simplification of the Functionality

One of the characteristics of ERP software is that their functionality grows over the years. New business trends are often integrated into the latest version of an ERP software. Initially provided mappings of business requirements are supplemented and extended, and new applications are launched.

However, in real life, this natural and useful software growth often produces multiple functions for identical or similar requirements. In addition, technological trends and different programming languages make their way into ERP software versions.

This business and technical variety leads to complexity. For example, different technologies generate different requirements for maintenance processes. Redundantly mapped business requirements make promoting innovation difficult. If identical functions are provided in various areas, new business trends need to be integrated into all the different areas. Finally, this functional redundancy has a negative effect for all customers because the development resources of the software provider are required at various areas and are not available for other tasks, which decelerates the innovation cycle of the functions provided.

With SAP S/4HANA, SAP is committed to the *principle of one*, which means that, in SAP S/4HANA, a business requirement is mapped only on one target architecture.

One mapping per requirement

An example of the principle of one in action in SAP S/4HANA is the credit management function. In SAP ERP, two credit management types have emerged over the last years: on the one hand, SAP Credit and Risk Portfolio Management (SD-BF-CM) and, on the other hand, the advanced version, SAP Credit Management (FIN-FSCM-CR), which was introduced to SAP ERP at a later stage. The advanced SAP Credit Management version, which provides a wealth of functions, enables you, for example, to integrate external credit information providers. Because SAP Credit Management is SAP's preferred target architecture for credit management, only SAP Credit Management is integrated as a function into SAP S/4HANA. Future innovations will also only take into account this function.

Simplification of the system landscape

Another example of the principle of one is the simplification of existing system landscapes. In the 2000s, *best of breed* was a trend in the software development sector and would signify that the best possible solution was provided for each application area. Due to this trend, separate solutions were developed for some application areas and operated in separate systems, which then had to be integrated with the enterprise's ERP system. SAP also followed this approach by developing separate planning, sales, and purchasing systems. Not all of the functions that are provided in these separate solutions are also available in SAP ERP.

SAP S/4HANA provides some of these previously outsourced application areas. Thus, migrating to SAP S/4HANA additionally offers the ability to consolidate linked business processes into one system and thus simplify the system landscape and save IT costs.

> **Production Planning, Detailed Scheduling, and Purchasing Functions** [Ex]
>
> An example would be Production Planning and Detailed Scheduling (PP/DS). This function enables you to generate proposals for in-house production or external procurement to cover product requirements. In the past, PP/DS has been provided within SAP Advanced Planning and Optimization (SAP APO). SAP APO is an independent solution that can be integrated and operated with SAP ERP. As of SAP S/4HANA 1610, customers can also use the integrated Production Planning and Detailed Scheduling function in SAP S/4HANA.
>
> Another example in this context is the mapping of purchasing functions from SAP Supplier Relationship Management (SAP SRM) in SAP S/4HANA or in the cloud-based SAP Ariba solution. Integrated warehouse management functions in SAP S/4HANA can supersede warehouse management systems that previously ran in parallel.

When migrating to SAP S/4HANA, you should evaluate the options for simplifying your system landscape and how you can benefit from this simplification. You can also optimize your landscape after migrating to SAP S/4HANA because the existing integration scenarios are usually also available with other on-premise solutions. For more information, refer to SAP Note 2376061 (SAP S/4HANA 1610: Process Integration with SAP on-premise Solutions).

A third example of the principle of one is that previously industry-specific functions that operated independently are merged in SAP S/4HANA. For example, SAP S/4HANA 1610 provides functions from SAP Retail and from SAP Discrete Industries and Mill Products (DIMP). Figure 1.3 gives you an idea of how the industry solutions are mapped in SAP S/4HANA.

Merging industry-specific functions

In addition to the examples mentioned, future SAP S/4HANA releases are supposed to integrate further industry solutions that can currently only be operated separately.

The benefits from simplifying the functionality, however, also have consequences that customers should be aware of when migrating to SAP S/4HANA. Customers using Credit and Risk Management (SD-BF-CM) must know that this function is not available in SAP S/4HANA and that migrating to the new SAP Credit Management (FIN-FSCM-CR) function needs to be considered.

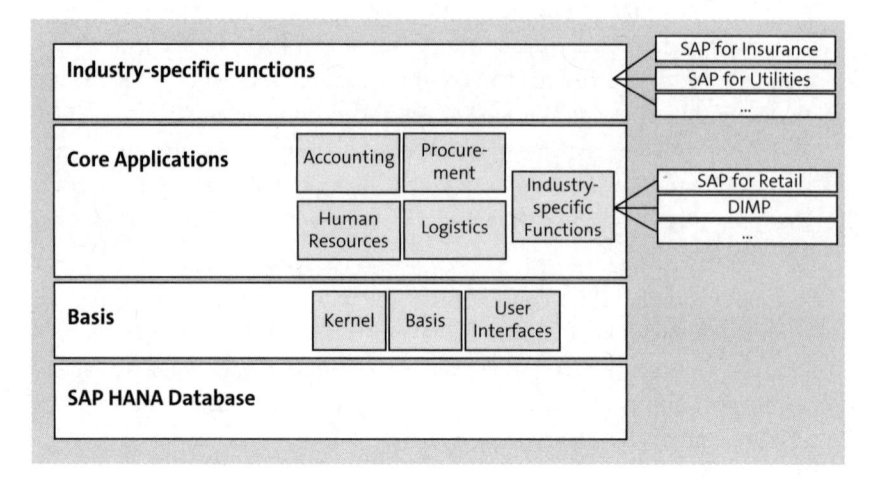

Figure 1.3 SAP S/4HANA: Shared Industry Solutions

> **Checking the Availability of Solutions**
>
> Before migrating to SAP S/4HANA, you should check whether the solutions you use are available in SAP S/4HANA or whether you might have to migrate to new solutions.

For more information on customizing functions in the context of migrating to SAP S/4HANA and on the relevant support provided, refer to Chapter 10.

1.2.2 Simplification of the Data Structure

In 2011, SAP introduced the new SAP HANA in-memory database, which supplements the technical framework of traditional databases. Previously, data was mainly stored on hard disks due to the limited capacity of memory; now that this limitation is no longer valid, you can use other programming methods for applications that run on in-memory databases. SAP S/4HANA leverages these new options and optimizes business applications in such a way that the potential of the SAP HANA database is fully exploited. For example, the table structure for data storage is optimized.

1.2 The Pledge of SAP S/4HANA

As shown in Figure 1.4, tables in the different application areas of SAP S/4HANA were modified in such a way that aggregates in tables can be omitted.

Thanks to the increased access speed of in-memory databases, data no longer needs to be stored redundantly, which was necessary before for performance reasons. For more technical details on how the SAP HANA database allows for these optimizations of the data models, refer to Chapter 2, Section 2.3.

At this point, you might ask yourself what the benefit of a simplified (technical) data structure is for the customer. We'll use two examples to demonstrate the benefits: one example from inventory management and one example from accounting.

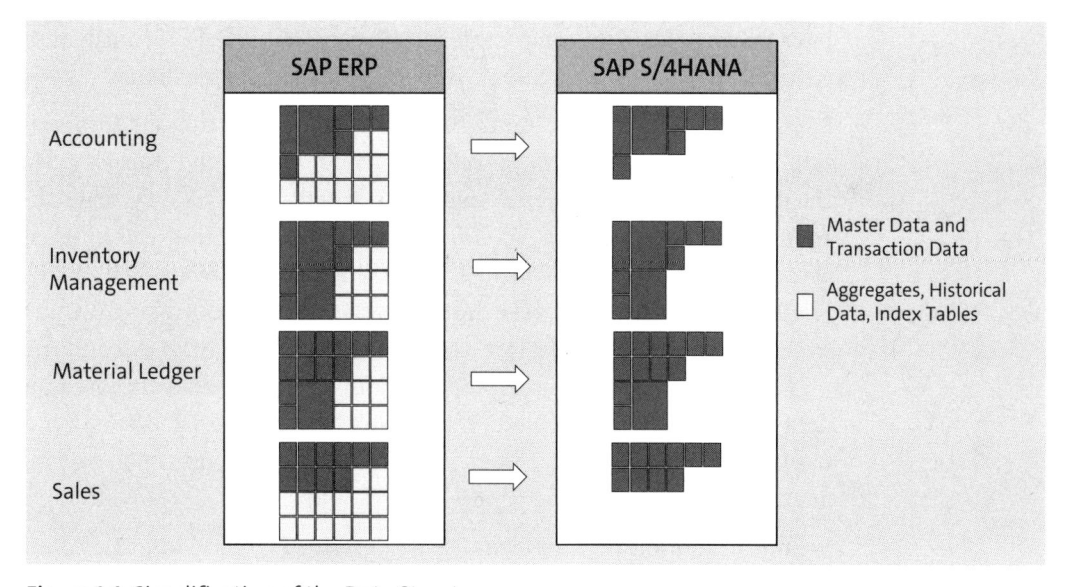

Figure 1.4 Simplification of the Data Structure

Determining the current material stock is rather complex, both from the business perspective and from the technical perspective. In addition to the physical inventory, you must also consider the planned goods receipts and issues at any given time. In SAP ERP's software architecture, this process was based on traditional databases. Consequently, the inventory management tables contained aggregates to optimize the performance for the determination of the current material stock. To avoid data deviations, the

Simplifications in inventory management

material stock has to be locked when new goods receipts or issues are posted. Parallel goods receipts and issues have to wait until the other process is completed. With the SAP HANA inventory management function, the SAP HANA in-memory database enables you to write goods receipts and issues of a material directly to a large material stock table without having to form aggregates (table MATDOC). Because goods receipts and issues now directly update stock information, the delay from locks, which were previously necessary, is minimized. As a result, a simplified data structure in inventory management also supports a higher data throughput.

Simplifications in accounting

The technical conditions of traditional databases in SAP ERP led to a software architecture that distributes the data across various tables and structures and consequently also stores data redundantly. This redundancy is a problem for the programs used to conduct financial closings because they have to consolidate this data content. This process involves reconciliation tasks that make it difficult and time-consuming to map line items.

SAP HANA enables you to centralize this previously distributed information in SAP S/4HANA in the so-called *Universal Journal* and thus simplify the process. SAP S/4HANA provides a central table (table ACTDOCA) that consolidates all line item data. As a result, external accounting and internal accounting are always reconciled, which ensures that reconciliations or real-time integrations between SAP Financials (FI) and Controlling (CO), as well as between General Ledger Accounting (FI-GL) and Asset Accounting (FI-AA), are no longer required. Reports from all components are based on data from the same documents. This consolidation of the data in one database allows for shorter closing cycles. You can create reports and analyses anytime during the posting period.

We must mention that the benefits we described from a simplified data structure also have effects that you should be aware of when migrating to SAP S/4HANA. Customers that convert their SAP ERP system to SAP S/4HANA, on-premise, have to check their existing customer-specific program code. If your custom code refers to data structures and SAP entities that change in SAP S/4HANA, you might have to carry out adaptations during the migration. So-called *compatibility views* were provided that maintain read access to obsolete SAP ERP data structures. However, if data is written to data structures that are no longer available in SAP S/4HANA, you'll have to adapt the code.

> **Checking References to SAP ERP Data Structures**
> Before migrating to SAP S/4HANA, check whether your custom developments refer to SAP ERP data structures that were modified for SAP S/4HANA.

1.2.3 Simplified User Interfaces

With the new user experience (UX) with SAP Fiori, SAP meets the requirements of the digital transformation for advanced user interfaces. SAP Fiori is an intuitive user interface that has been developed according to advanced design principles. Available on all end devices (mobile devices, desktop, tablet), SAP Fiori allows for role-based user experiences that can be compared to the user experience of consumer apps. Chapter 2, Section 2.4, addresses the technical differences between SAP Fiori and SAP GUI and the operating concept behind the new interfaces.

SAP's new way of thinking about user interface design has already been recognized with awards. Who would have thought that possible when thinking of traditional SAP ERP interfaces? SAP Fiori 2.0, which is based on SAP S/4HANA, won the Red Dot Award 2015. According to the committee, "The SAP Fiori 2.0 – Next Generation Business Software concept takes the personalized, responsive, and simple user experience to the next level."

Red Dot Award

Another excellent example of SAP's UX strategy is the *SAP Consumer Insight 365* app, which won the Red Dot Award 2016 and the User Experience Award 2014. SAP Consumer Insight 365 is a data service that provides users with holistic and precise insights into consumers' behaviors at physical locations. The app allows you to know, for example, the demographic characteristics of the visitors to a store or at an interesting location. This information is based on nearly real-time mobile data and indicates consumers' backgrounds, including their age, their gender, and what mobile devices they use. Figure 1.5 illustrates an example of a modern SAP user interface.

SAP Consumer Insight 365

You can find a list of available SAP Fiori apps in the *SAP Fiori apps reference library*. By choosing Fiori apps for SAP S/4HANA you can display the SAP Fiori apps that are available for SAP S/4HANA.

SAP Fiori apps reference library

1   SAP S/4HANA—Requirements and Benefits

Custom SAP Fiori applications   Officially released SAP Fiori apps additionally enable enterprises or SAP partners to develop custom SAPUI5-based SAP Fiori applications using the *SAP Web IDE*.

This browser-based toolkit can be found on the SAP Cloud Platform and includes an integrated development environment. This option for developing custom user interfaces is extremely important for SAP customers. In today's SAP Business Suite, about 50% of the interfaces that are used by SAP customers are custom developments.

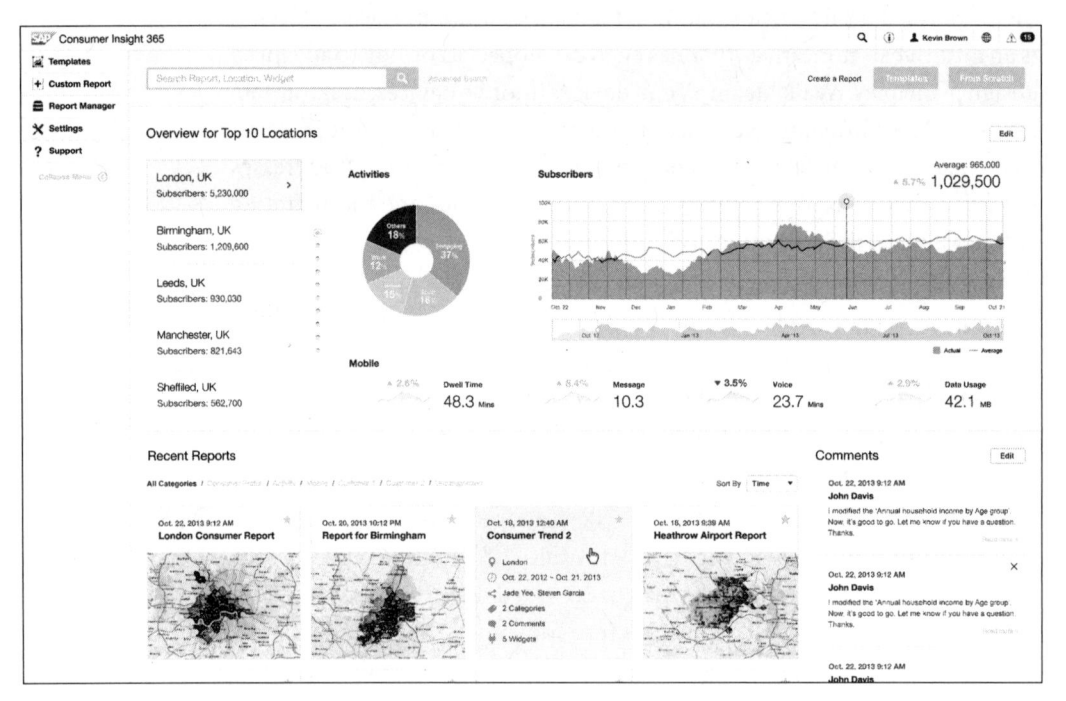

Figure 1.5 SAP Consumer Insight 365

> **Additional Information**
>
> You can find further information for redesigning the SAP UX using SAP Fiori under *https://www.sap.com/products/fiori.html*.
>
> For more information on SAP Fiori 2.0, go to *https://experience.sap.com/skillup/sap-fiori-2-0-the-ideal-overview/*.
>
> You can access the SAP Fiori apps reference library at *https://fioriappslibrary.hana.ondemand.com/sap/fix/externalViewer/*.

1.2.4 Simplified Analyses

In an increasingly complex world, you require increasingly more detailed information for your decision-making processes. Providing precise analytical data has always been a challenge and has become more and more important in the last two years. For example, 85% of the participants in "Analytics That Work: Deploying Self-Service and Data Visualization for Faster Decisions" (*https://hbr.org*, March 2016), a Harvard Business Review study, mentioned the increasing relevance of analytical data as the basis for decisions. Most participants (93%) thought that analytical data will be even more relevant in the next two years. The community using analytical data has also changed. Previously, strategic departments were the main users, but today, operational departments increasingly have to justify their decisions with analytical data.

Relevance and user community of analytical data

Consequently, the number of users of analytical data has increased, which also affects how this data is collected and made available. Traditionally, the IT department of the enterprise was responsible for collecting the data, and the data was usually provided in custom reports. If these reports did not exist, they were requested. For custom reports, the SAP Business Suite with its ABAP-based reports was ideal.

Provisioning type for analytical data

But these reports are actually not fast, not user-friendly, and not available to all user groups. To meet increasing requirements, advanced analytical tools need to enable end users without specific IT knowledge to create new analyses. New visualizations have to be optimized, and complex data and data structures must be presented in a simple format.

Another concern is how data that is supposed to be analyzed is distributed across multiple sources. Today, reports are often based on data that is distributed across ABAP reports, Excel files, or embedded Business Warehouses (BW). Creating a report can entail a time-consuming process of generating analyses and standardizing complicated visualizations of the results.

Distribution of data

The analytical functionality provided by SAP S/4HANA is referred to as *SAP S/4HANA embedded analytics*. This function enables users (not just experts for analytical data evaluations but any user) to create and carry out real-time analyses based on SAP S/4HANA application data. Standard reports and analytical SAP Fiori apps are also delivered with SAP S/4HANA. The analytical data can be displayed via the new SAP Fiori launchpad, which is

SAP S/4HANA embedded analytics

based on SAP Fiori technology. Chapter 2, Section 2.6, discusses the technical details of this approach.

> **Additional Information**
>
> You can find more information and examples of analytics under *https://experience.sap.com/skillup/sap-fiori-2-0-a-primer-on-embedded-analytics/* or in the SAP Fiori apps reference library under *https://fioriappslibrary.hana.ondemand.com/sap/fix/externalViewer/*.

1.3 Business Functions in SAP S/4HANA

As a modern digital ERP suite, SAP S/4HANA forms the core of the central business processes for accounting, logistics, human resources, procurement, and marketing. Customers can use SAP S/4HANA, on-premise, or SAP S/4HANA Cloud. Figure 1.6 illustrates the central business processes, which are briefly described in this section.

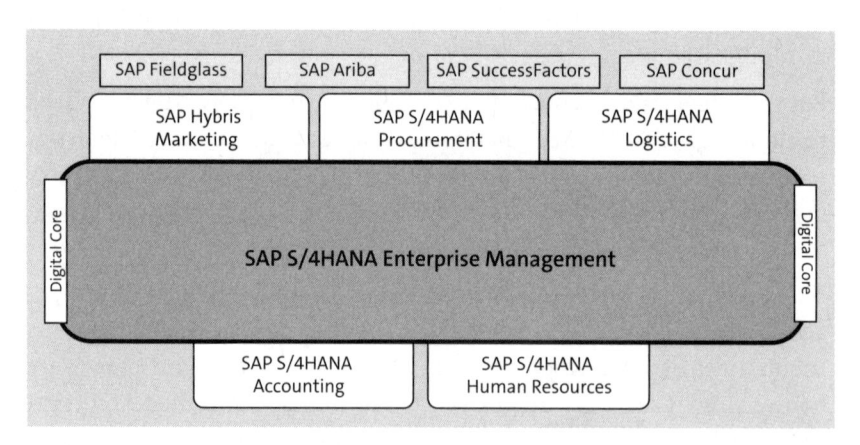

Figure 1.6 Central Business Processes in SAP S/4HANA

Central business processes
The SAP S/4HANA business functions that are introduced in the following sections only highlight some of the supported functions in SAP S/4HANA. These examples demonstrate how SAP S/4HANA supports customers in meeting the requirements of the digital transformation. You can find a

description of all SAP S/4HANA functions in the SAP documentation on SAP S/4HANA (*http://help.sap.com/s4hana*). Remember that these functions require different SAP S/4HANA licenses.

> **Additional Information**
>
> For more information on SAP SuccessFactors, go to *www.successfactors.com*.
> For more information on SAP Ariba, go to *www.ariba.com*.
> For more information on Concur, go to *www.concur.com*.
> For more information on SAP Fieldglass, go to *www.fieldglass.com*.

1.3.1 Accounting

In accounting, digitalization has rapidly increased the number and complexity of postings to systems. The transition from standardized, bulk processes to personalized products and services to made-to-order processes triggers the creation of various documents, which are then used in cost centers, asset accounting, or profit and loss statements. The increasing number of processes that need to be performed through the ERP system places an extreme workload on traditional ERP systems.

Requirements of the digital transformation

In general, SAP S/4HANA can map all business processes as you would expect from an advanced accounting system. The simplified data structures in accounting, supplemented by intuitive SAP Fiori-based user interfaces, enable a completely different working experience. Figure 1.7 shows the core functions of accounting that SAP S/4HANA maps.

Functions

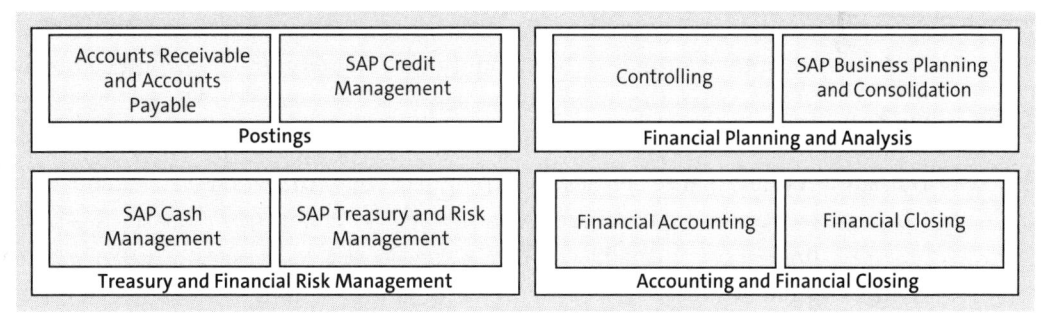

Accounts Receivable and Accounts Payable	SAP Credit Management	Controlling	SAP Business Planning and Consolidation
Postings		Financial Planning and Analysis	
SAP Cash Management	SAP Treasury and Risk Management	Financial Accounting	Financial Closing
Treasury and Financial Risk Management		Accounting and Financial Closing	

Figure 1.7 SAP S/4HANA: Accounting

We cannot introduce all accounting functions of SAP S/4HANA here, but we can discuss some special functions in the following sections.

Accounting and Financial Closings

Finances in general The financial functions in SAP S/4HANA support all transactions that are relevant for accounting in the logistics and human resources components of SAP S/4HANA. In financial accounting, transactions are posted in real time via automatic account determination. As a result, all logistic quantity transactions (goods receipts, stock withdrawals, etc.) and of value-based accounting updates have identical statuses.

Universal Journal As described in Section 1.2.2, how data is stored has been optimized and adapted in SAP S/4HANA for accounting. The Universal Journal consolidates previously distributed information, and as a result, external accounting and internal accounting are always reconciled, which allows for shorter closing cycles. You can create reports and analyses anytime during the posting period. Of course, common accounting standards such as International Financial Reporting Standards (IFRS) or United States Generally Accepted Accounting Principles (US-GAAP) are still supported but can be executed much more efficiently in SAP S/4HANA and can consequently be executed several times in one period. As a result, you can shift from monthly closings to weekly or even daily closings and perform dynamic simulations.

Parallel accounting In addition to the legal accounting requirements, the SAP S/4HANA accounting function also meets modern requirements such as the mapping of parallel accounting in general ledger accounting. Thus, you'll be able to close a company code according to various accounting standards. For example, a German subsidiary of a US group can prepare a period-end closing both according to the accounting standards of the US parent company (US-GAAP) and according to the German Commercial Code (Handelsgesetzbuch, HGB).

Central Finance Central Finance enables you to connect your distributed system landscape to a centralized SAP S/4HANA finance system. In this scenario, a central finance system is added to the existing system landscape, thus allowing for a general, cross-system reporting structure. With Central Finance, you can migrate to SAP S/4HANA without facing interruptions in the existing system landscape, which might consist of a combination of SAP systems with different releases and non-SAP systems. For more information on Central Finance, refer to Chapter 3, Section 3.2.1.

Financial Planning and Analysis

The optimized data structure in SAP S/4HANA is the basis for flexible real-time analyses and evaluations to support your daily tasks. In combination with the SAP S/4HANA role concept, end users can navigate from an overview analysis to individual documents for specific tasks and use these details to make operational or strategic decisions. The necessary reports and analyses as well as simulation tools are available to meet your various requirements.

SAP Business Planning and Consolidation (BPC) for S/4HANA is a flexible and user-friendly solution for financial planning in enterprises. With regard to content, the functions for financial planning cover planning tasks for profit and loss statements and liquidity planning. For example, from the strategic revenue goals of a group, you can drill down to profit center level or view costs that were planned at the cost center level summarized at the enterprise level. In contrast to previous solutions for financial planning, planning is carried out in real time without master and transaction data being replicated to an additional planning tool. This capability and the integrated planning model with one plan data persistencyallow for short and frequent planning cycles and fast simulations across multiple planning phases.

SAP Business Planning and Consolidation

BPC for S/4HANA is integrated in SAP S/4HANA. A separate installation as an add-in is not necessary. The solution provides predefined templates and planning functions, which create excellent user experiences due to its intuitive Microsoft Excel add-in. The integrated planning function supports the following scenarios with the corresponding planning content, for example:

- Balance sheet planning
- Profit and loss statement planning
- Market segment planning
- Profit center planning

You should first work with the provided content to get to know the available functions. Of course, the corresponding functions for modifying

1 SAP S/4HANA—Requirements and Benefits

the content according to your customer-specific requirements are also available.

Controlling The controlling functions of SAP S/4HANA enable you to view the costs that are incurred within the organization (actual data) but also to prepare cost planning (planned data). Using the appropriate SAP Fiori apps for comparing actual data to planned data, you can determine deviations in data and then control your operational processes accordingly. Figure 1.8 shows an example of a profit and loss statement.

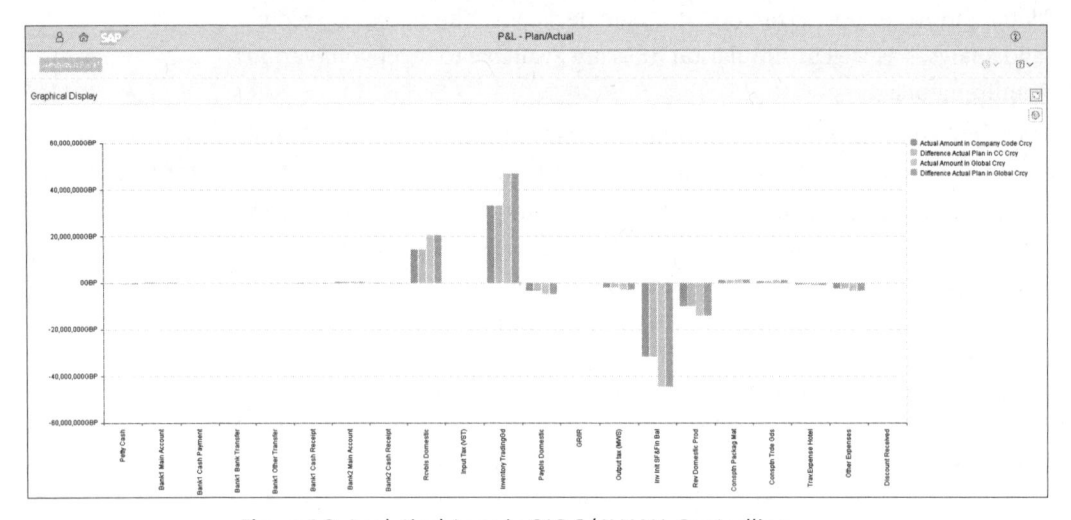

Figure 1.8 Analytical Apps in SAP S/4HANA Controlling

Treasury and Financial Risk Management

SAP Cash Management SAP Cash Management in SAP S/4HANA enables the finance department or the liquidity management department to centrally manage cash and liquidity. Real-time analyses can provide a cash manager with an overview of liquidity, credit lines, risk as well as cashflow and foreign currency risks analyses. Liquidity analyses can be evaluated based on a key date and on financial data that has already been entered, parked, or planned for accounting purposes. SAP Cash Management functions are supplemented by a central bank management component for managing bank accounts and processing approval workflows for setting up new bank accounts or changing existing bank accounts. For SAP Cash Management, you'll need a separate license.

SAP Treasury and Risk Management in SAP S/4HANA provides multiple solutions designed to analyze and optimize the business processes related to an enterprise's financial tasks. These solutions include:

SAP Treasury and Risk Management

- **Transaction Manager**
  The financial transactions that are mapped in the Transaction Manager are B2B transactions between your enterprise and banks, financial institutions, brokers, or similar institutions.

- **Market Risk Analyzer**
  The Market Risk Analyzer (TRM-MR) component of SAP Treasury and Risk Management is designed for global risk management of insurance policies and organizations.

- **Credit Risk Analyzer**
  This component of SAP Treasury and Risk Management enables you to measure, analyze, and control default risks.

- **Portfolio Analyzer**
  The Portfolio Analyzer (FIN-FSCM-TRM-PA) component supports calculating and monitoring the ROI of your financial assets.

Postings

SAP S/4HANA enables you to manage the accounting data of your vendors and customers. The corresponding accounting documents are automatically posted from the related sales and purchasing business transactions to the new, simplified accounting data structure. This provides electronic, and thus automated, support for all common methods of payment as forms. The solution maps all advanced collaboration scenarios as supported in the cloud-based Ariba Network solution—also for invoice processing and accounting in SAP S/4HANA.

Accounts payable/receivable

SAP Credit Management in SAP S/4HANA provides functions for credit standing checks and credit limit checks for business partners to minimize the risks of payment defaults. For existing customers, you can define rules for credit standing checks and thus automate order processes. For new customers, you can integrate external providers of credit information via a dedicated interface. SAP Credit Management supports a heterogeneous system landscape and enables you to consolidate credit-related decisions in the system landscape.

SAP Credit Management

> **Additional Information**
>
> For more information on SAP S/4HANA, refer to the SAP documentation: *https://help.sap.com/sfin*.
>
> For more information on SAP S/4HANA Central Finance, refer to SAP Notes 2148893 (Central Finance: Implementation and Configuration) and 2154420 (SAP Landscape Transformation Replication Server for Central Finance). SAP Note 1972819 provides further information on how to set up SAP Business Planning and Consolidation (BPC) for SAP S/4HANA.

1.3.2 Logistics

Requirements of the digital transformation

As described in Section 1.1 the digital transformation places new requirements on logistics and production processes. Highly personalized products, digital supply chains, and new service-oriented business models in the spare parts and repairs processing area (so-called *aftermarket business models*) arise from the digital transformation. The ERP systems that are integrated in these digital business processes need to support these models.

Functions

Figure 1.9 shows the core logistics functions of SAP S/4HANA. Again, we cannot introduce all the logistics functions in SAP S/4HANA. In general, SAP S/4HANA enables you to map all common business processes of logistics management in enterprises. The following sections discuss only some special functions in detail.

Supply Chain Management

Inventory management

In SAP S/4HANA, the principle "No posting without a document" also applies to inventory management. To meet the increasing posting requirements of enterprises in the digital world, data storage processes for inventory management were also simplified in SAP S/4HANA as already described in Section 1.2.2. Various SAP Fiori apps support plant controllers in analyzing stock quantities and can warn them about future material bottlenecks.

SAP Fiori apps allow you to monitor items with reduced inventory turns and to track the shelf-life of products in real time, as new user interfaces enable users to work much more efficiently.

1.3 Business Functions in SAP S/4HANA

Asset Management
- Maintenance
- Environment, Health, and Safety

Manufacturing
- Material Requirements Planning
- Production Planning and Detailed Scheduling (PP/DS)

Research and Development/Engineering
- SAP Product Lifecycle Management and SAP Project System
- SAP Engineering Control Center
- SAP Portfolio and Project Management

Sales and Service
- Sales and Distribution
- Shipping
- Customer Service

Supply Chain
- General Logistics
- Inventory Management
- SAP Extended Warehouse Management (EWM)

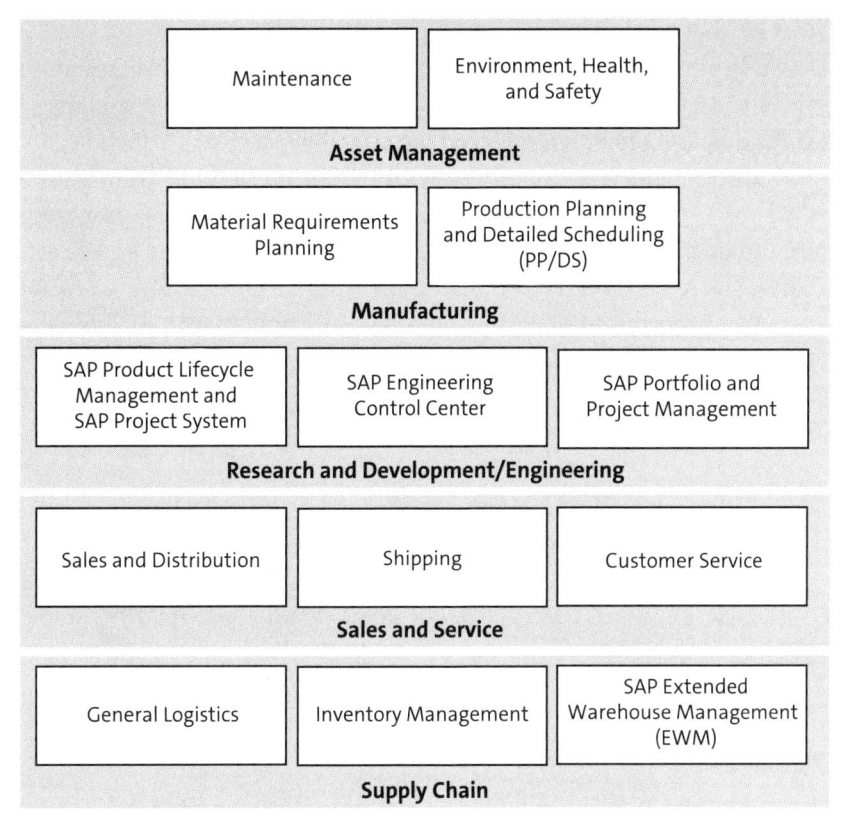

Figure 1.9 Logistics in SAP S/4HANA

The global availability check (*Advanced Available to Promise*, aATP) in SAP S/4HANA provides advanced functions for availability checks. In addition, managing delivery quotas across multiple levels, new backorder processing methods, and interactive rescheduling methods ensure that high-priority customers are served first when a bottleneck exists.

Global availability check

SAP Extended Warehouse Management (EWM) provides advanced warehouse functions, which are now also integrated in SAP S/4HANA with SAP S/4HANA 1610. Available functions include automation via storage retrieval systems, task and work optimization, and the usage of mobile end devices without requiring a separate system. In this context, you can also optimize your system landscape when migrating to SAP S/4HANA. However, you can also still run SAP EWM separately.

SAP Extended Warehouse Management

Sales and Service

Optimized processes

Digital business processes aim to automate the standard processing of sales and service orders as much as possible and optimize the handling of exceptions. Therefore, in addition to providing standard functions for order and delivery processing, SAP S/4HANA focuses on the optimization of the processes for handling exceptions. An optimized SAP Fiori user interface can enable your sales employees to get an overview of a bottleneck, analyze the reasons for the bottleneck, and trigger solutions. Figure 1.10, for example, shows the SAP Fiori app for sales order fulfillment and illustrates various exceptions for order processing.

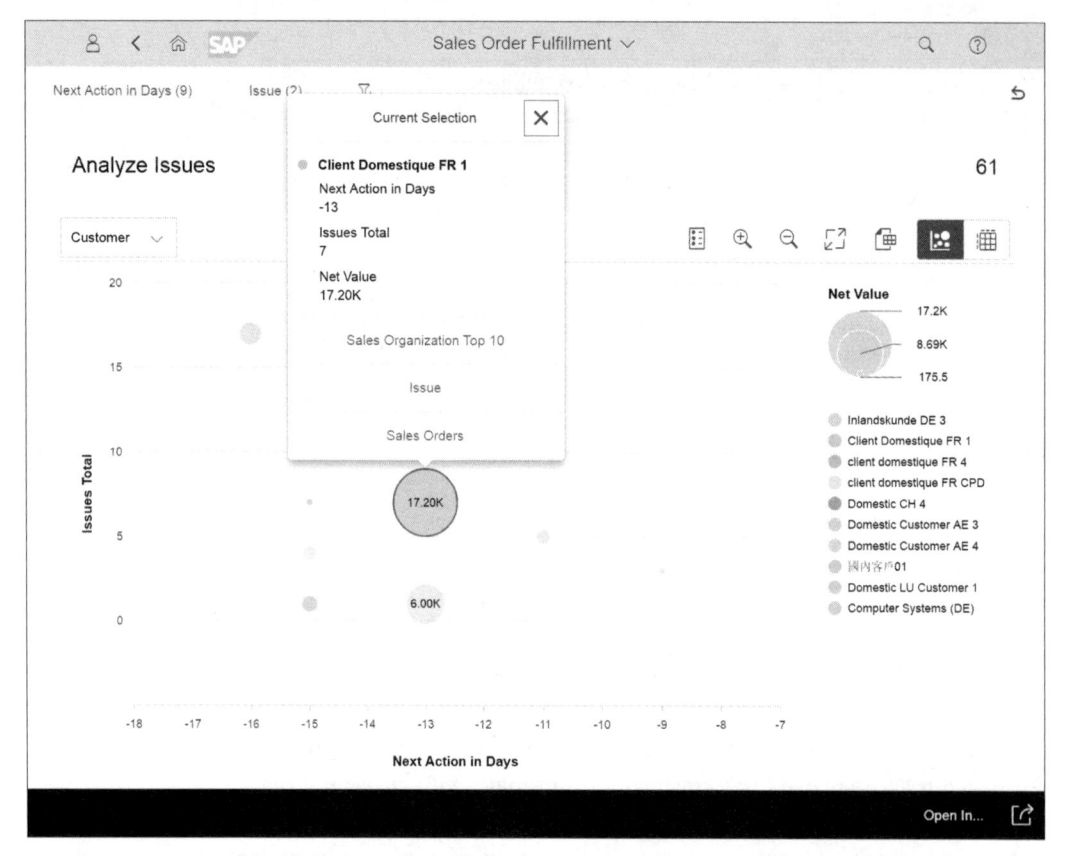

Figure 1.10 Analysis of Order Processing Exceptions in SAP S/4HANA

1.3 Business Functions in SAP S/4HANA

Production and Material Requirements Planning

SAP S/4HANA 1610 provides dedicated functions for production planning and detailed scheduling. These functions can be specifically used to plan critical products, for example, products with long replenishment lead times or products that are produced using bottleneck resources. Previously, these functions were provided in separate planning systems such as SAP Advanced Planning and Optimization (SAP APO). Migrating to SAP S/4HANA will simplify your system landscape.

Production planning and detailed scheduling

To consider the actual production status in production planning in SAP S/4HANA, you can integrate SAP S/4HANA with SAP Manufacturing Execution (MES) or other manufacturing execution systems. This integration enables production processes to be confirmed in the SAP S/4HANA system, where you can then create the required production orders, planned orders, and maintenance orders.

SAP Manufacturing Execution

Research, Development, and Engineering

The digital transformation affects the areas of research and development (R&D) and engineering in two ways: with the trend towards personalized products and with the need to carry out a large number of change projects and manage these projects efficiently.

To meet these requirements, SAP S/4HANA provides standard functions for SAP Product Lifecycle Management (PLM) and SAP Project System (PS) but also additional specialized functions such as SAP Engineering Control Center and SAP Portfolio and Project Management. Let's start by introducing the two specialized solutions.

SAP Product Lifecycle Management and SAP Project System

The trend towards personalized unit of one products increases product variety and complexity. Correspondingly, providing product information across the entire product lifecycle and supporting the decisions of all involved business departments by supplying holistic product data are required. For this purpose, SAP Engineering Control Center, the add-on for SAP S/4HANA, offers functions that support processes from development to the actual production of a product. SAP Engineering Control Center enables you to integrate data from computer-aided design (CAD) solutions into a central data source. Today, complex devices often consist of mechanical, electronic, and software components. Thanks to SAP Engineering Control Center, the corresponding authoring tools for each kind of

SAP Engineering Control Center

1   SAP S/4HANA—Requirements and Benefits

component can be merged, allowing a holistic 360° view of the product data.

SAP Portfolio and Project Management

The digital transformation also increases the number of change projects in enterprises. Correspondingly, software requirements increase to better and more efficiently support these projects with regard to managing, controlling, and integrating internal and external employees. In addition to the traditional standard functions for project management, SAP S/4HANA provides SAP Portfolio and Project Management 1.0 as a customized solution for project and portfolio leads and members. Instead of leading to complex data aggregations and batch processes for project monitoring and controlling tasks, SAP Portfolio and Project Management enables real-time access to the relevant data for accounting or human resources. SAP Fiori-based user interfaces allow for project monitoring and provide an overview of upcoming project milestones, project tasks, and reoccurring problems. The role-based approach of SAP Fiori apps solves the problem where different interfaces are required by users who use project functions versus those who rarely have to perform project-related tasks.

Asset Management and Healthcare

SAP S/4HANA Asset Management

SAP S/4HANA Asset Management enables you to analyze and evaluate asset data that is based on machine or sensor data in real time. You can thus make decisions and create forecasts in a timely manner to minimize downtimes.

SAP S/4HANA Environment, Health, and Safety (EHS)

The SAP S/4HANA Environment, Health, and Safety (EHS) functions support your enterprise in managing your business processes in the environment, health, and safety sector. These functions use real-time data to help EHS experts perform the following tasks:

- Controlling operational risks
- Occupational safety
- Conformity with integrated solutions for managing accidents or chemical data
- Assessing operational risks
- Occupational health and monitoring of exposures
- Adherence to legal requirements
- Emissions management

> **Additional Information**
>
> For more information on the *Advanced Available to Promise* in Supply Chain Management, go to *https://blogs.sap.com/2016/11/12/s4hana-1610-use-case-series-1b-advanced-availability-to-promise-tech-view/*.
>
> For more information on SAP EWM, go to *https://help.sap.com/ewm*.
>
> For a video showing how you can accelerate exception handling in order processing in SAP S/4HANA, go to *https://www.youtube.com/watch?v=mO87IYOn75U*.
>
> SAP Note 2381624 and 2382787 describe implementing and using production planning and detailed scheduling. For more information on SAP Manufacturing Execution (MES), go to *https://www.sap.com/products/execution-mes.html*.

1.3.3 Human Resources

The digital transformation does not only impact production processes. Advanced human resources processes face the following challenges:

Requirements of the digital transformation

- The increasing flexibility of the business processes must entail more flexible working hours and working time models.
- If business models change quickly, you'll also have to quickly adapt the goals of the individual employees to correspond the new strategic goals of the business.
- In a global market for qualified employees, enterprises can no longer ignore digital media for recruitment.
- Enterprises must strive to find and engage qualified employees. Enterprises need to know which skills individual employees have and which skills are missing in the enterprise to stay ahead of competitors in the digital world.
- Furthermore, advanced compensation systems have to consider the increasing demands on employees.
- Enterprises want to create a viable and innovative environment for their employees and managers. For this purpose, the software for human resources (HR) processes should be as intuitive as possible and provide for a compelling user experience.

1   SAP S/4HANA—Requirements and Benefits

The trend of outsourcing business processes to the cloud is particularly reflected in human resources. Increasing cost pressure and the options provided by digital learning platforms or online ratings make enterprises outsource their business processes to the cloud, in particular in the HR area.

SAP SuccessFactors   In SAP S/4HANA, cloud-based functions in SAP SuccessFactors can map the target architecture for HR. SAP S/4HANA maps core HR functions and comprehensive talent management functions such as recruiting, application management, onboarding, learning management, performance management, and succession management in the cloud. Standardized integration scenarios and a unified user interface, which is based on SAP Fiori, ensure the technical and functional integration of human resources processes.

Figure 1.11 provides an overview of the functions provided by SAP S/4HANA and SAP SuccessFactors.

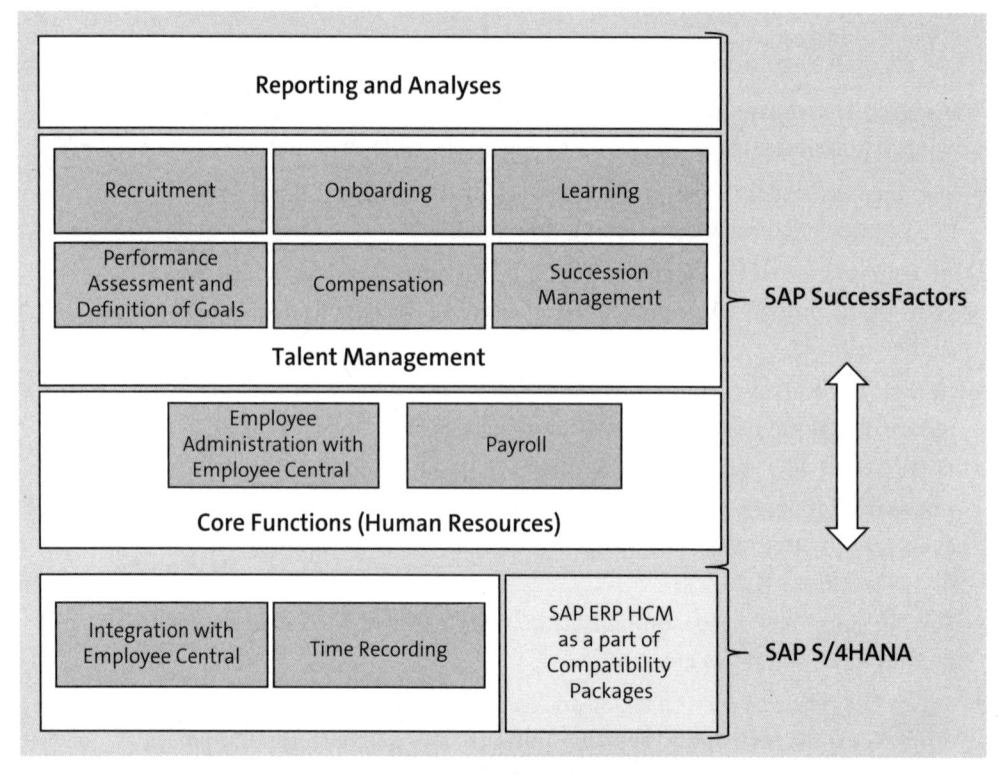

Figure 1.11 Human Resources in SAP S/4HANA

Human Resources Functions with SAP S/4HANA

In SAP S/4HANA, on-premise, you cannot use the traditional SAP ERP HCM functions as you know them from SAP ERP. However, you'll have access to the new time recording function, which can be used for project settlement processes in particular, and access to SAP SuccessFactors Employee Central for integrating employees.

The SAP Fiori app for time recording enables you to enter times for specific activities to settle and invoice projects. You can also record times for tasks that are not related to projects, for example, for administration tasks, trainings, or travel. Managers can approve or reject time sheets that employees have submitted for approval.

Time recording

Integrated with *SAP SuccessFactors Employee Central*, SAP S/4HANA provides access to the employee master data managed. You'll be able to use the employee data required for carrying out processes such as project planning and project time recording to create customer invoices or to invoice and reimburse travel costs. Replicating employee data from SAP SuccessFactors Employee Central to SAP S/4HANA is based on standardized service Application Programming Interfaces (APIs).

Integrating employees

In SAP S/4HANA, the *SAP S/4HANA compatibility packages* provide familiar functions as you know them from SAP ERP. After migrating to the SAP S/4HANA, on-premise, these functions are still available but are not the target architecture from the technological perspective. For more information on the SAP S/4HANA compatibility packages, refer to Chapter 3, Section 3.2.1.

Traditional HCM functions

For human resources in SAP S/4HANA, on-premise, the following SAP ERP HCM functions are available, for example:

- Core HR functions (such as personnel administration and organizational management)
- Payroll
- Talent management
- Time recording

In general, customers who use the SAP ERP HCM functions already on their SAP ERP system (either installed together on one system or as a separate SAP ERP HCM system integrated with SAP ERP) can continue to use them after their migration to SAP S/4HANA, on-premise. Please note the entries for SAP ERP HCM in the SAP S/4HANA simplification list. However, for SAP, the future of HR business processes is in the cloud. SAP SuccessFactors functions are target architecture for human resources management in the future.

> **Gradual Migration with Compatibility Packages**
> The functions delivered with the compatibility packages, and thus SAP ERP HCM, allow you to migrate to the target architecture gradually.

Core Functions of SAP SuccessFactors Employee Central

Among others, SAP SuccessFactors provides the following functions:

- **Talent management**
  SAP SuccessFactors Employee Central provides a unified view of employee data across regions, cost centers, and employees. SAP SuccessFactors Employee Central offers functions for managing organizations and personnel administration. Functions for personnel events like hiring, changing positions, and rehiring are supported. In addition, employees and managers will have access to self-service interfaces to change personal data, display salary information, and trigger administrative measures or salary increases. With SAP SuccessFactors Employee Central, you can make core HR processes more efficient, and your employees will benefit from increased ease of use.

- **Payroll**
  You can carry out payroll processes using the employee master records from SAP SuccessFactors Employee Central with SAP Payroll, a solution hosted by SAP. The payroll system retrieves cost center data from the SAP S/4HANA accounting solution and employee master data from SAP SuccessFactors Employee Central. As a result, functions from both are available for SAP Payroll, supporting for example, settlement activities, legal reports, and bank transfers; posting payroll results, and configuring wage types.

Talent Management Using SAP SuccessFactors Recruiting

Recruitment

SAP SuccessFactors Recruiting is a function for efficient recruitment—from selecting the applicants to hiring them—so that your enterprise can engage qualified talent for the right positions. SAP SuccessFactors Recruiting provides various communication tools, which your HR department and the recruiting business department can use to exchange information. For example, the HR department and the business department can interactively exchange a checklist with the required skills, which accelerates the selection process considerably.

The *Career Site Builder* function of SAP SuccessFactors Recruiting enables HR managers to easily design, implement, and manage career portals in the form of consumer apps.

Career Site Builder

SAP SuccessFactors Recruiting's onboarding functions support onboarding processes for new employees. Newly hired employees will have online access to the forms they need on their first day at work. Other business departments can be centrally informed about new employees so that the IT and security departments, for example, can be involved in a timely manner.

Onboarding functions

Performance Assessment and Definition of Goals

SAP SuccessFactors Performance & Goals allow managers to define employee goals with the new strategic goals of the business in mind. Using these functions, team leaders can determine general goals and inform their employees.

Performance and goal functions

The user interfaces help managers objectively assess the performance of their employees. Managers have access to an overview of all assigned employees and can view and adapt their assessments anytime. Continuous performance management allows for regular feedback for employees and for a focus on coaching. CEOs can compare and assess employees to determine high performers and potential managers.

Compensation

SAP SuccessFactors Compensation Management supports HR managers and employees in planning and distributing budgets, adapting compensation to business results, and defining a transparent wage policy. With SAP SuccessFactors Compensation Management, you can ensure that salaries comply with budgets. Integrated reports will help you meet compliance guidelines, and performance-based comparisons of employees across the entire organization ensure that employees are paid fair salaries based on performance. You can also use this function to manage bonus payments.

SAP SuccessFactors Compensation Management

Intuitive user interfaces simplify editing and managing individual salary components, such as basic salary, and variable salary components. Variable Pay is a salary component which depends on an employee's performance. Top managers usually have a smaller fixed pay and with the opportunity for variable pay. For example, this could be depending from the success of the company (e.g. measured by the level of the share price).

Succession and Development Planning

SAP SuccessFactors Succession & Development

The functions in SAP SuccessFactors Succession & Development support HR managers in recruiting and promoting talent and in establishing successors for all important positions. HR managers will have access to an overview of the talent in the enterprise; can quickly identify vacancies and possible personnel gaps; and can provide for suitable replacements using the integrated tools, reports, and search functions, which can also accommodate external applicants.

Development

SAP SuccessFactors Learning

Modern organizations need employees who develop continuously to meet the requirements of the digital transformation. SAP SuccessFactors Learning supports HR managers in providing training and further education opportunities to employees as well as professional development options to senior managers. From their workstations, employees can access training materials via tablets or smartphones. You can manage and update courses and propose new training courses. Learning achievements are recorded in analyses and reports.

Workforce Analytics and Workforce Planning

HR reporting

SAP SuccessFactors Workforce Analytics visualizes personnel data and key figures. *SAP SuccessFactors Workforce Planning* provides analyses and reports for personnel planning. This data enables you to determine the current skills of a team and identify the skills required for future projects.

Deployment Variants

Cloud, on-premise, or hybrid

Figure 1.12 illustrates three ways HR functions in SAP S/4HANA can be deployed:

1. **Cloud scenario**
   The first variant is to deploy all solutions in the cloud. The integration between SAP S/4HANA Cloud and SAP SuccessFactors ❶ allows you to run financial and logistics processes, together with the HR management functions, in the cloud.

2. **Hybrid scenario**
   The second variant is a hybrid scenario in which you run the financial and logistics processes in SAP S/4HANA, on-premise, and integrate these processes with the functions of SAP SuccessFactors in the cloud ❷.

3. **On-premise scenario**
   The third variant is a strictly on-premise scenario. After migrating to SAP S/4HANA, you can continue to use traditional HCM functions—either by installing SAP S/4HANA together with SAP HCM ❸a or, alternatively, by connecting a separate SAP ERP HCM system ❸b.

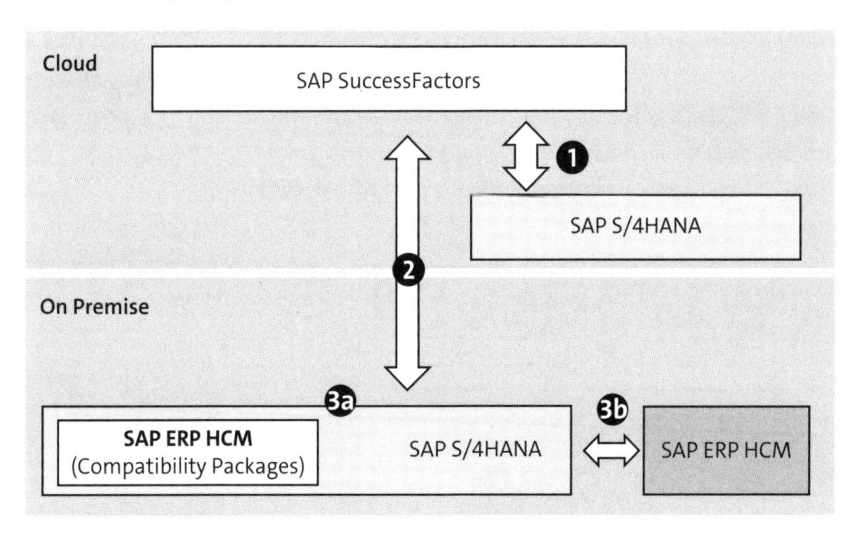

Figure 1.12 Deployment Variants for Human Resources Functions with SAP S/4HANA

Additional Information

For more information on SAP SuccessFactors, go to:

- *https://www.successfactors.com*
- *https://www.sap.com/products/human-resources-hcm.html*

1.3.4 Procurement

Requirements of the digital transformation
As part of the digital transformation, more and more devices and machines are becoming linked information hubs. Advanced machines and devices use sensors to report their maintenance requirements to ERP systems and thus increase the need for automation in the purchasing department, where most of an enterprise's costs are incurred. Consequently, material requirement processes need to be automated. Digitalization will automate all processes that can be mapped by algorithms. Buyers will increasingly focus on strategic tasks and only process deviations from defined business process. To make efficient strategic decisions or exceptional decisions, buyers need to be supported by qualified data and information.

Functions
The procurement function in SAP S/4HANA maps all common purchasing processes—from strategic processes to operational processes: purchase order handling for direct and indirect materials and services, goods movements, invoices (including the transfer to accounting), etc. SAP S/4HANA's preconfigured integration with the cloud-based Ariba Network and with SAP Fieldglass solutions optimizes electronic and interactive processes with suppliers and assists the management of external employees. Figure 1.13 shows the procurement functions of SAP S/4HANA.

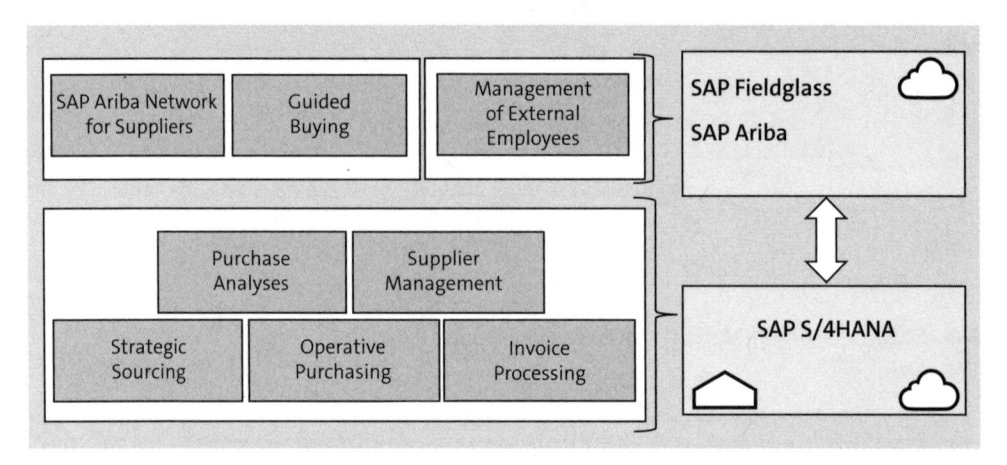

Figure 1.13 Procurement with SAP S/4HANA

Operative Purchasing

Automated functions
SAP S/4HANA eases the workload of operational buyers and significantly optimizes standard processes. The functions include the following:

- Automated purchase order creation based on order requirements
- Purchase order handling for direct and indirect materials as well as service procurement including the corresponding confirmation processes
- Catalog-based material procurement based on self-service processes
- Completely electronic communication with suppliers (optional)
- Integration with Ariba Network for optimizing the collaboration with suppliers

Strategic Sourcing

To automate operational purchasing, you'll have to lay a foundation in strategic sourcing. SAP S/4HANA enables you, for example, to specify the sources of supply for the required products and services in corresponding purchasing contracts. This determination ensures that the right products are automatically ordered with the right price from the right supplier for material requirements planning (MRP). The monitoring of the purchasing contracts assures that the relevant release quantities and target quantities are available anytime and that actions can be taken if required.

Foundation for automation

Invoice Processing

SAP S/4HANA also enables you to map the processing of all incoming invoices. In addition to invoices for purchase orders from the SAP S/4HANA system, you'll be able to map incoming invoices created with Ariba Network or SAP Fieldglass. The goal of this function is to increasingly automate invoice verification processes for standard invoices so that buyers only have to process invoices that deviate from the usual purchase orders (e.g., with regard to items, quantities, or price).

Supplier Management

SAP S/4HANA provides various functions for classifying suppliers on the basis of attributes and master data. You can evaluate suppliers according to different factors (compliance with agreed prices or scorecards).

Analyses in Purchasing

With SAP S/4HANA, buyers can analyze data in real time without using separate data warehouses. Some of the available analyses, based on SAP Fiori, include the following:

Embedded analytics

1   SAP S/4HANA—Requirements and Benefits

- **Supplier analyses**
  Supplier on-time delivery, price variance, and quantity variance

- **Purchasing contract analyses**
  Unused contracts and expiring agreements

- **Spend analyses**
  Purchasing spend and contract leakage

Procurement overview

These analyses enable buyers to make operational and strategic decisions based on up-to-date data. Figure 1.14 shows an SAP Fiori app for the procurement overview in purchasing.

Figure 1.14 SAP Fiori App for the Procurement Overview

Guided Buying

Efficient workflow

Guided buying processes walk buyers through the system to help them make the right purchase decision according to business requirements in an efficient manner. Ultimately, guided buying processes save buyers from non-value-adding tasks and are based on existing SAP Ariba catalogs and enterprise-specific *policies* that are easy to maintain. With guided buying, you can also define budget policies for material groups or define the logic behind approval workflows.

Ariba Network for Suppliers

The Ariba Network for suppliers is a cloud-based platform that supports collaboration with your suppliers of materials or services. Figure 1.15 illustrates the electronic processes between buyer and supplier that can be integrated with Ariba Network.

Communication with supplier systems

In SAP S/4HANA, the integration with Ariba Network is already preconfigured. From the technical perspective, Ariba Network is the central interface to the supplier and converts data into the data formats that the relevant supplier supports. For example, PDF forms can be filled out and exchanged via email or in specific data formats such as EDIFACT (Electronic Data Interchange for Administration) or ANSI X12 (American National Standards Institute Accredited Standards Committee X12).

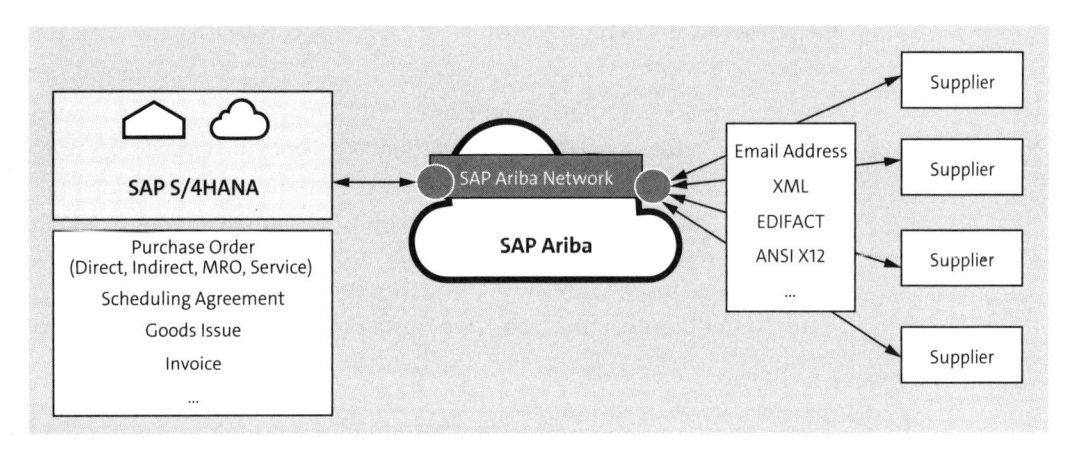

Figure 1.15 Collaboration Processes with Ariba Network

Management of External Employees

Because business processes are constantly changing, enterprises increasingly rely on external employees. By hiring external employees, temporary skills gaps can be closed, and peak loads can be balanced. The cloud-based SAP Fieldglass solution provides functions for service procurement processes and for managing these external employees. Based on preconfigured integration with SAP S/4HANA, master data, such as cost centers, internal orders, or organizational data, is exchanged, and invoice processing, including for the invoices of external employees, can be automated.

SAP Fieldglass

1   SAP S/4HANA—Requirements and Benefits

1.3.5   Marketing

Requirements of the digital transformation

SAP Hybris Marketing Cloud is the marketing component in the SAP S/4HANA world. Over the last ten years, the volume of online sales has grown significantly. In the past, customers regularly went to stores or retailers to do their shopping; today, more and more purchases are made via the Internet. In the early days, customers were loyal to their retailer, and customers and vendors often knew each other by name; in the era of the anonymous Internet, customer loyalty is volatile. Prices and offers can be compared within minutes, and purchase decisions are made more quickly. While previously you directly told your retailer when you weren't satisfied with the service or product, criticism is now distributed millions of times across social platforms such as Facebook or Twitter. Irrespective of what enterprises think of social media, they can't avoid being present in these media—even if the only reason is to respond to criticism and take the appropriate actions.

Therefore, marketing department must fulfill more requirements than a decade ago. Before, a postcard at Christmas and a note for special sales campaigns once or twice a year was sufficient to satisfy and retain your customers. Today, you have to analyze and categorize your customers and their needs in much more detail to make customer-specific marketing campaigns successful. Previously, you watered the entire garden with enough water for all flowers; now, you have to water every flower with the exact amount of water that flower needs to flourish.

> [»]   **SAP S/4HANA Marketing Cloud Becomes SAP Hybris Marketing Cloud**
>
> As of SAP S/4HANA Cloud 1702, *SAP S/4HANA Marketing Cloud* is called *SAP Hybris Marketing Cloud*. Because this change had not been completely implemented at the time of this writing, some figures still display the obsolete name, SAP S/4HANA Marketing Cloud. Because the change will be introduced with version 1702, we'll use the product name current up to version 1611, i.e., SAP S/4HANA Marketing Cloud, when we explicitly refer to version 1611.

Best practices

SAP Hybris Marketing Cloud is the cloud variant of the SAP on-premise product *SAP Hybris Marketing*. The cloud solution contains predefined best practices, which are available for the on-premise solution as *rapid-deployment*

1.3 Business Functions in SAP S/4HANA

solutions (RDS), which allows for a rapid deployment of the cloud solution. For more information on the best practices for these solutions, go to *https://rapid.sap.com/bp/#/BP_CLD_MKT*.

You configure, enhance, and manage SAP Hybris Marketing Cloud via the SAP Fiori user interface. As a result, your customers and employees don't need to familiarize themselves with common SAP tools. Thus, even customers who have never used SAP software can quickly get accustomed to SAP Hybris Marketing Cloud, considerably reducing the cost of training and internal support. Figure 1.16 shows the initial page interface for SAP Hybris Marketing Cloud.

SAP Fiori user interface

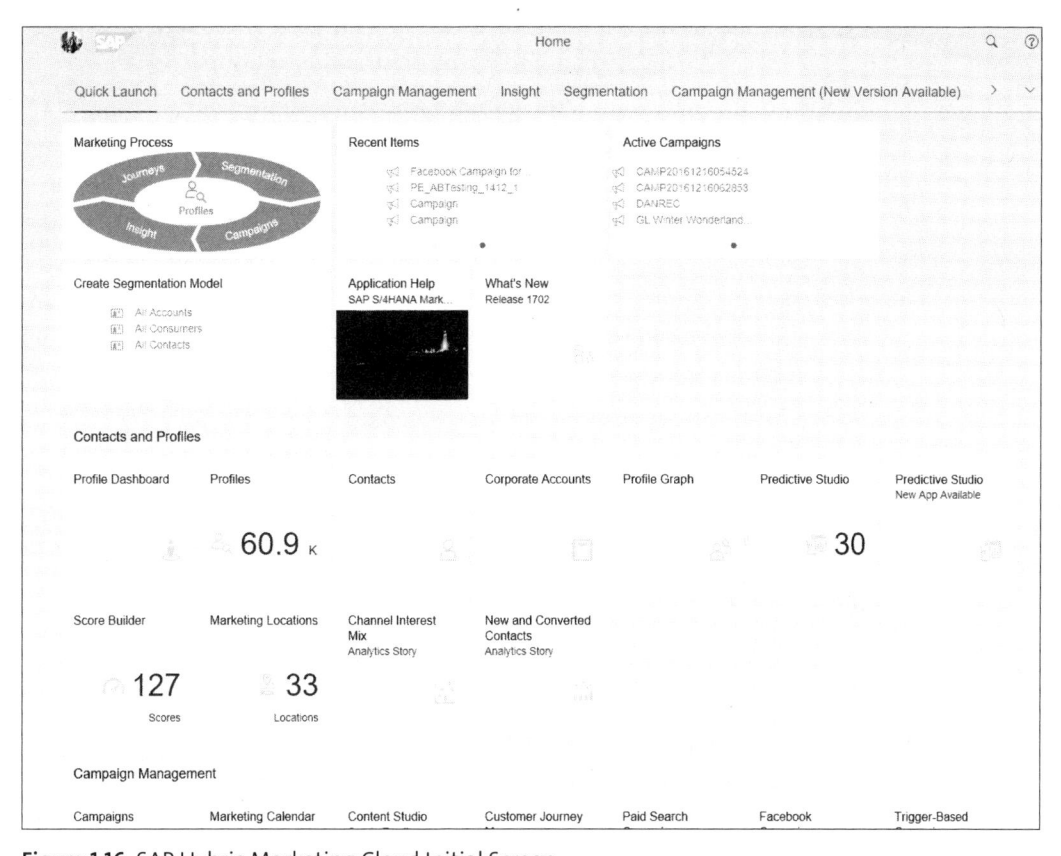

Figure 1.16 SAP Hybris Marketing Cloud Initial Screen

You can set up the entire system in a guided *self-service configuration* process. You don't have (and you don't need) direct access to the technical

Easy self-service configuration

69

infrastructure. The standardized interfaces for integrating certain business processes from *SAP Hybris Commerce* or *SAP Hybris Cloud for Customer,* for example, are provided, which allows for end-to-end scenarios across multiple lines of business. Social networks such as Facebook and Twitter are integrated via their public interfaces. For more information, see Chapter 8, Section 8.3.

Benefits of the SaaS solution

The benefits of cloud-based software as a service (SaaS) solution in contrast to the on-premise variant or private cloud solution include the following examples:

- The effort of implementing a solution (for example, purchasing and setting up the technical infrastructure) are omitted or reduced by a cloud-based SaaS but are required by the on-premise solution.
- The time period until the solution *goes live* is shorter.
- In contrast to the on-premise solution, less technical knowledge and training is necessary to develop the corresponding technical skills. Technical knowledge (e.g., of SAP HANA, SAP GUI) is not required for the cloud solution.
- Due to automatic updates to the latest version every quarter, you are automatically provided with the latest functions of, and enhancements for, the solution.
- SAP is entirely responsible for the deployment of the solution and also provides the infrastructure.

However, in contrast to the on-premise solution, the flexibility and extensibility of an SaaS solution is reduced due to the system design. However, in most cases, this lack of flexibility is offset by the benefits.

Functions

By default, SAP Hybris Marketing Cloud comprises the application areas shown in Figure 1.17. The following sections introduce these areas in detail.

Consumer and Customer Analytics

On the basis of big data, information on end consumers, customers, or contacts, as well as their interests, is collected from various channels and analyzed. As a result, you can determine the interests of your customers. Then, based on these insights, you can offer products and solutions in a targeted manner and develop more targeted marketing campaigns, which reduces costs and increases the chance for success.

1.3 Business Functions in SAP S/4HANA

Consumer and Customer Analytics			SAP Hybris C4C / SAP Hybris C4S / SAP ERP / SAP Hybris Commerce / SAP Hybris Convert
Contacts and Profiles	Target Groups	Segmentation	
Sentiment Engagement	Forecast Studio		
Customer Behavior Analysis	Score Builder	Campaigns	Twitter, Gigya, Sprinklr, Google AdWords, Facebook, SurveyMonkey
Customer Visit History	Query Browser	Segmentation and Campaign Management	

Marketing Resource Management			
Budget Planning	Analysis/Planning	Marketing Calendar	SAP ERP / Any Other System
Programs	Expense Management		

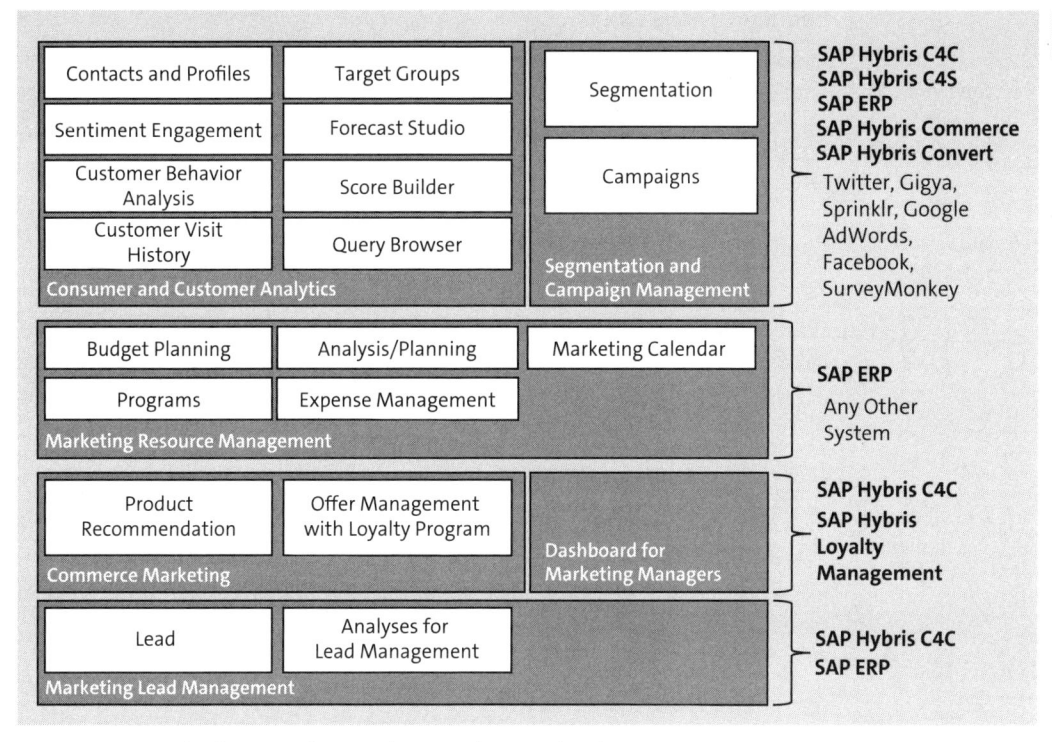

Commerce Marketing			
Product Recommendation	Offer Management with Loyalty Program	Dashboard for Marketing Managers	SAP Hybris C4C / SAP Hybris Loyalty Management

Marketing Lead Management			
Lead	Analyses for Lead Management		SAP Hybris C4C / SAP ERP

Figure 1.17 Standard Scope of SAP Hybris Marketing Cloud

Segmentation and Campaign Management

The insights gained from big data can help you categorize customers into groups so that marketing campaigns can be optimized. You can address existing and potential customers via email and social media in a targeted manner. So, the insights gained can more quickly generate actions.

In addition to emails, you can also address customers and prospects via marketing campaigns using targeted advertisements in Facebook. Newsletters and incentive-driven campaigns can be managed via subscriptions. The External Campaign scenario enables you to plan and prepare campaigns in SAP Hybris Marketing Cloud and run them in a different external system.

Facebook

In *paid search campaigns*, you use *paid searches* to place banners in search engines such as Google, Yahoo, and Bing. In this way, you can draw the attention of prospective customers to your products and solutions.

Paid search

71

Commerce Marketing

Product recommendations and loyalty programs

Product recommendations enable you to recommend products during a customer interaction in any channel in real time. Offer management in *loyalty programs* uses insights from loyalty analyses of your customers to offer products and product categories in a targeted manner.

Marketing Resource Management

Budget management

You can use the Marketing Resource Management function to plan your marketing budgets and costs according to various criteria. The marketing calendar provides an overview of all ongoing and scheduled marketing activities.

Marketing Executive Dashboard

Quick overview in the dashboard

The Marketing Executive Dashboard provides a quick overview of the success of the various marketing instruments used. Information on specific key performance indicators (KPIs) can include, for example, brand awareness, distribution channels, and sentiment in social media.

Marketing Lead Management

360° customer view

The Marketing Lead Management function helps you acquire new customers and manage leads that have been acquired via marketing campaigns. Marketing experts can define and manage *lead score* and *lead stages* rules without needing support from business and data analysts. Thus, SAP Hybris Marketing Cloud is a fully integrated multichannel marketing solution that provides a 360° customer view.

[»]
> **Free SAP S/4HANA Marketing Cloud Trial Version**
>
> The following link (case sensitive) navigates you to a 30-day trial version of SAP S/4HANA Marketing Cloud:
>
> *http://bit.ly/TryTheMarketingCloud*
>
> As of this writing, the free trial version includes the following scenarios:
>
> - Customer Profiling
> - Segmentation and Campaign Management
> - Lead Marketing
> - Commerce Marketing

- Marketing Resource Management
- Marketing Analytics

You can test all functions here:

https://www.hybris.com/en/downloads/free-trial/hybris-marketing/901

SAP Documentation for SAP Hybris Marketing Cloud

You can find the SAP documentation for SAP S/4HANA Marketing Cloud on the SAP Help Portal at *https://help.sap.com/s4hana*. Choose your edition, e.g., **SAP S/4HANA Cloud 1611**. Then, navigate to **Product Assistance** and select your language for the **SAP User Assistance**. In SAP User Assistance, choose **Cloud Editions** • **SAP S/4HANA Marketing Cloud** to display the **SAP Documentation**.

You can find the SAP documentation for SAP Hybris Marketing Cloud on the SAP Help Portal at *https://help.sap.com/mkt*. Choose your version, e.g., **1705** and select your language. Then, navigate to Application Help and choose **SAP Hybris Marketing Cloud** to display the **SAP Documentation**.

Chapter 2
SAP S/4HANA versus the Traditional SAP Business Suite

How are SAP S/4HANA and SAP ERP related? What is SAP's "new digital core"? Perhaps you've already asked yourself these and similar questions. In this chapter, we'll tackle these basic questions and explain the role of SAP S/4HANA in SAP's product portfolio.

SAP offers various enterprise resource planning (ERP) products. The most important ones are SAP ERP, including its various Enhancement Packages (EHPs); SAP Business Suite on SAP HANA; and the new SAP S/4HANA solution. This chapter describes the similarities and differences between traditional products and SAP S/4HANA. We'll first discuss the key areas and goals of each product and then explain the important concepts behind the new solution: its simplification concept, its new data model, and the underlying SAP HANA database, as well as the new SAP Fiori user interface (UI). Finally, we'll address integrating SAP S/4HANA into your system landscape, reviewing changes on existing interfaces. Based on the information in this chapter, you'll be able to assess and plan your migration to SAP S/4HANA.

2.1 Comparing the Available Solutions: SAP S/4HANA and the Digital Core

For several decades, SAP has been the market leader for business software, known especially for its applications in core business areas and for its ERP products in particular. The most popular SAP ERP products are SAP R/3, SAP R/3 Enterprise, and SAP ERP (including its various EHPs). How does SAP S/4HANA fit into this portfolio? To answer this question, let's look in detail at core business processes, and which conflicting requirements your business application faces.

2 SAP S/4HANA versus the Traditional SAP Business Suite

Core business processes

Core business processes form the backbone of any enterprise. On top of the standard processes implemented by the software vendor, usually enhancements are added to meet enterprise-specific requirements, i.e., developing new and advanced business processes, strengthening customer relationships, optimizing goods movements, and more.

One of the characteristics of core processes is their high level of stability at first glance. If you take a closer look at these processes, you'll see that now, they undergo changing requirements and expectations as well. The supporting software solution must therefore be able to take into account new perspectives and issues. Otherwise, the software solution no longer supports business processes but instead hinders them.

Pressure for change

In addition to this process-related pressure for change, another pressure for change is driven by technical requirements: As with other technical products, technological innovations enable new design approaches for ERP systems. Such a technological innovation allowed SAP to develop SAP R/3, the successor to SAP R/2. This new system used the client's server architecture for the first time and thus permitted new usage patterns.

In-memory SAP HANA technology

The new SAP in-memory database, SAP HANA, was the next technological innovation: In the past, software solutions had to compensate for slow access to physical data storage media when users worked with large data volumes. Thanks to the in-memory database, this compensation is no longer necessary, opening up a new realm of possibilities for the architecture of data models and related processes.

Future challenges

As a user of an ERP solution, the question you should ask yourself is: How can I benefit from an advanced software solution? To answer this question, you should consider the dimension of time: How will the requirements for my business processes change in future? SAP asked itself these questions, and we saw, from analyzing these conflicting requirements, that SAP could only meet future challenges if they revise the application core.

Even if the traditional ERP architecture can cover the current processes in an enterprise, in a few years, this architecture will probably no longer be sufficient, if you look at the future trajectory of data volumes. In this context, compare the examples in Figure 2.1 and Figure 2.2, which are taken from a study conducted by Cisco, a telecommunications company (*http://www.cisco.com/c/en/us/solutions/collateral/service-provider/visual-networking-index-vni/vni-hyperconnectivity-wp.html*). According to these examples, the volume of the global Internet Protocol (IP) data traffic will triple, and data volumes for machine-to-machine communication will increase six fold within the next five years.

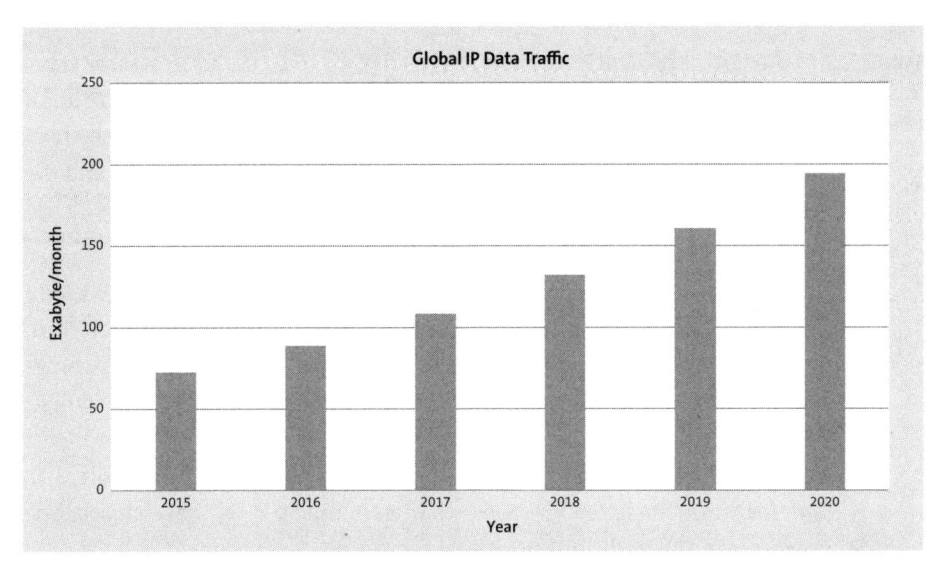

Figure 2.1 Predicted Growth of the Global IP Data Traffic (Source: Cisco Systems, Inc.)

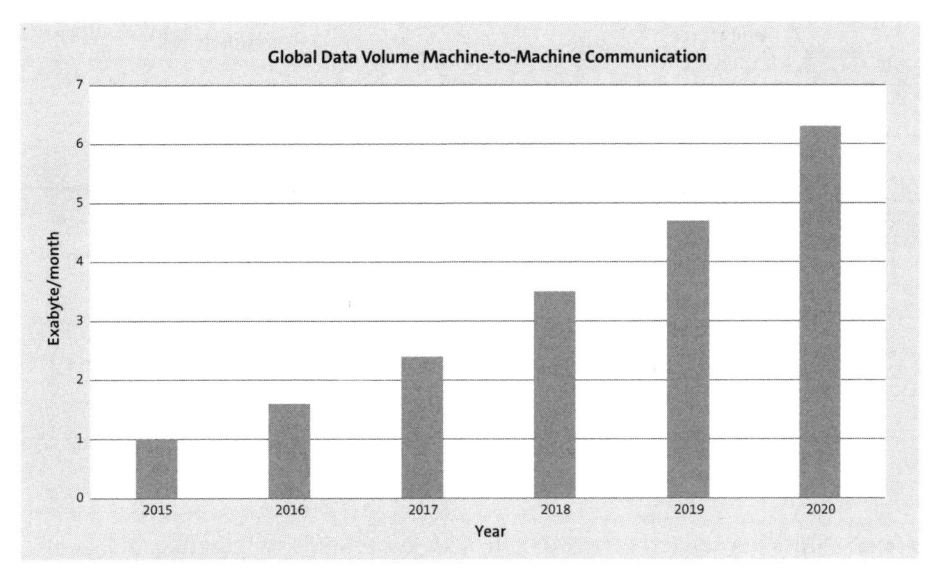

Figure 2.2 Predicted Data Volume for Machine-to-Machine Communication (Source: Cisco Systems, Inc.)

2   SAP S/4HANA versus the Traditional SAP Business Suite

Growing data volume Application architectures from the 1990s can no longer process these data volumes with the performance your business requires. Thus, SAP would offer suboptimal solutions had it ignored this basic architectural change.

More holistic value chains In addition, expectations about the scope of *end-to-end processes* have risen: Process chains have become increasingly longer. The extension of process chains is indicated by the fact that the direct interaction between the manufacturer and the end customer has taken on a bigger role and the fact that various distribution channels continue to merge (a famous example is *omnichannel retail*).

For this reason, SAP has redistributed the functions of its applications. In addition to SAP ERP for core business processes, the traditional SAP Business Suite contained further standalone solutions such as SAP Customer Relationship Management (CRM), SAP Supplier Relationship Management (SRM), or SAP Supply Chain Management (SCM). Because these products were positioned separately, some functions overlapped. By default, SAP S/4HANA now includes processes that were mapped by these standalone processes in the traditional SAP Business Suite.

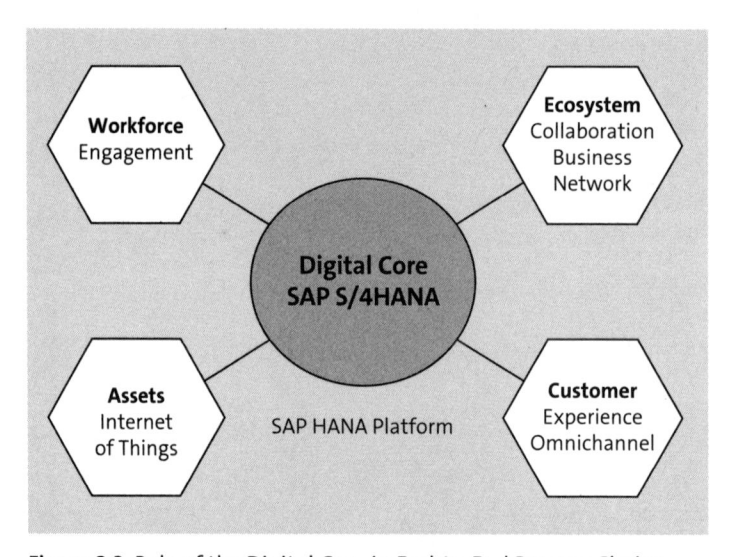

Figure 2.3 Role of the Digital Core in End-to-End Process Chains

New digital core SAP's new *digital core*, SAP S/4HANA, is designed to integrate and supplement default processes with core processes (see Figure 2.3). Compared to the traditional SAP Business Suite where the integration between SAP ERP and other applications usually had to be implemented specifically, SAP S/4HANA provides the major benefit of these functions integrated fully with each other.

Many enterprises want to gear up for these challenges, and SAP S/4HANA enables you to lay a technical foundation for mastering these challenges. The solution can be rolled out gradually, that is, the individual components can be implemented when your business processes require them, thanks to the compatibility between SAP S/4HANA and SAP ERP. Chapter 4 discusses options for a gradual transition in more detail.

2.2 Simplification

The rise of the so-called *digital natives*—the generation that has grown up with advanced digital technologies—as employees fundamentally changes the requirements for IT business systems: More and more employees expect to access IT systems *anytime*, *anywhere*, and from *any device*. Furthermore, application interfaces should be intuitive and guide users (if possible via artificial intelligence), thus allowing users to focus on the content-related solution to their business issues.

Expectations of digital natives

SAP S/4HANA meets these requirements with the new *user interface* (UI) architecture and with adapted development policies for this UI, which is accessed via browser-based apps on a frontend server. The name of this new UI concept is *SAP Fiori*, which we'll discuss in more detail in Section 2.4.

New SAP Fiori UI concept

These newly designed user interfaces are only a part of the overall *simplification* that SAP wants to implement with SAP S/4HANA. However, SAP S/4HANA's simplification goes deeper. Simplifications and optimizations of data models form the foundation for this new concept. On this basis, access to data is considerably enhanced in comparison to the traditional suite. For example, you'll have access to embedded data analysis functions, which are described in Section 2.6. Business applications are then built on these technical simplifications, and SAP has merged functions from various areas of the traditional SAP Business Suite into SAP S/4HANA.

While alternative solutions for similar business processes have emerged over time, SAP today focuses on the applications that have gained the highest customer acceptance. Some applications in the traditional SAP

Reducing alternative implementations

79

2 SAP S/4HANA versus the Traditional SAP Business Suite

Business Suite were replaced or will be replaced by others as demonstrated in Section 2.2.

In most cases, adapting these implementations is mainly technical and does not require time-consuming projects on the customer side. However, depending on the individual structure of your system, further activities might be required. Usually, you can flexibly schedule these activities, because the traditional functionality will still be available for some time.

> **Note: Simplification List for SAP S/4HANA**
>
> SAP provides a complete list of the functional simplifications in the *simplification list for SAP S/4HANA*. When planning your migration to SAP S/4HANA, you should always refer to the following list:
>
> *http://bit.ly/v1448083*

New product

The following conclusions can be drawn from the simplification: SAP S/4HANA is a new product and not a new version of SAP ERP. SAP S/4HANA also covers all core business processes but follows a new approach and is based on a different technical architecture.

Thus, SAP currently provides two lines of products for core business processes:

- The *traditional line of products*, which consists of the core SAP ERP applications and EHPs as well as SAP CRM, SAP SCM, and SAP SRM, will be maintained at least until 2025 and is compatible with all common databases.

- The *new line of products*, SAP S/4HANA, which has a completely revised architecture, forms the basis for future innovations. This line of products is exclusively available on the SAP HANA in-memory database.

> **SAP S/4HANA and SAP ERP**
>
> SAP S/4HANA refers to a separate line of products that is available in parallel to the line of products of the traditional SAP Business Suite. SAP S/4HANA is an alternative implementation of the business functionality.

Thus, changing to SAP S/4HANA means that you'll switch to a different product family. Chapter 3, Section 3.2, introduces the members of this new product family. While migrating to a higher version within a product family is implemented via upgrades, changing to a new product family usually requires a new implementation (see Figure 2.4). For SAP S/4HANA, SAP also provides the option of converting an existing SAP ERP system into an SAP S/4HANA system. Chapter 4 defines in more detail the different technical options for changing to the new product family.

Changing the product family

Product family	Product version

Classic SAP Business Suite: SAP ERP → SAP ERP Enhancement Packages

Migration: Conversion or new implementation

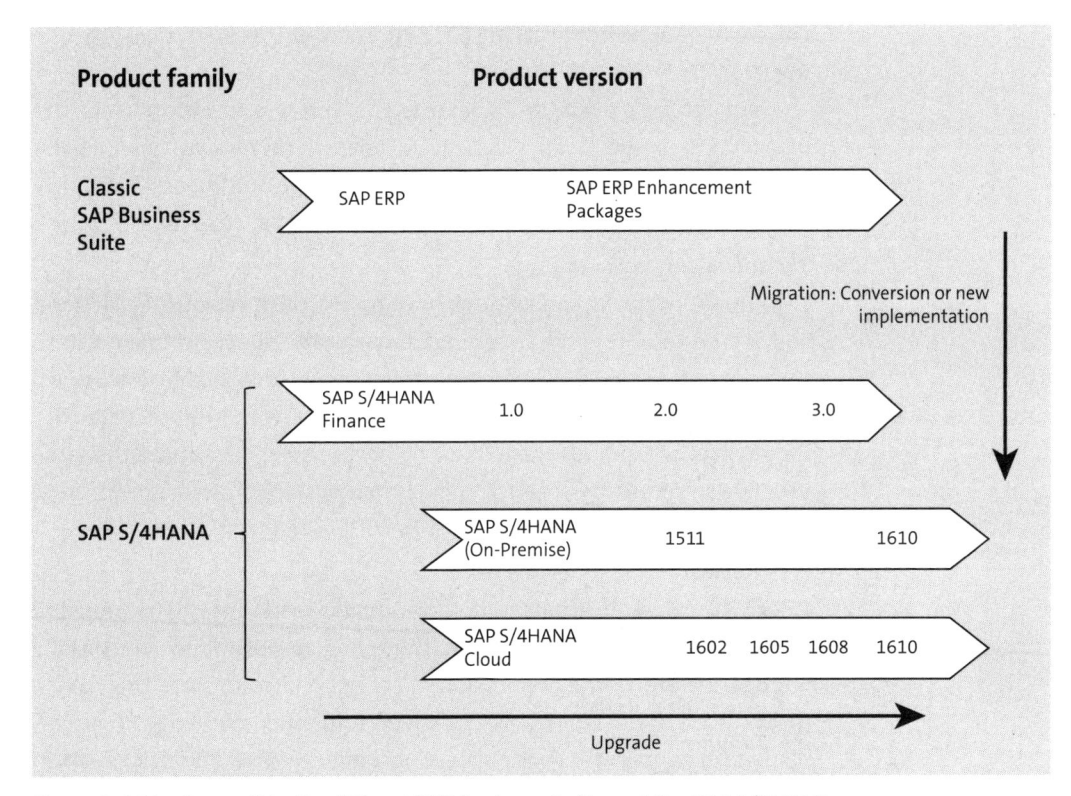

SAP S/4HANA:
- SAP S/4HANA Finance: 1.0, 2.0, 3.0
- SAP S/4HANA (On-Premise): 1511, 1610
- SAP S/4HANA Cloud: 1602, 1605, 1608, 1610

Upgrade →

Figure 2.4 Versions of the Traditional SAP Business Suite and the SAP S/4HANA Product Family

2.3 The New Data Model and the SAP HANA Database

Traditional databases are based on designs that were developed decades ago. The technical conditions, as well as the usage requirements, during this time differed from today's expectations. Traditional databases have been enhanced, but their ability to adapt to new challenges is limited due to compatibility reasons.

Limitations of traditional databases

From the perspective of business application software, traditional databases lead to critical limitations and can complicate or even hinder the simplification, acceleration, and integration of business processes. The following characteristics of traditional databases can be obstructive, for example, when redesigning your business processes:

- **Online transaction processing (OLTP) versus online analytical processing (OLAP)**
  Users of database solutions have to decide whether they want to analyze data (OLAP) or update data (OLTP). However, in many situations, a combination of both views makes sense, for example, for forecasts and simulations or for making decisions on the basis of real-time data.

- **Technical restrictions**
  Traditional business applications have to deal with various restrictions, which complicate things for users. Examples include locks that occur so that only one user can work on a data set at a time, which slows down processes. Another factor is the delay resulting from internal data editing processes. Updates carried out by other users, or even by the same user, are sometimes written to the relevant system tables with considerable delay.

- **Integration**
  In traditional applications, raw data is usually first internally prepared and consolidated via *aggregates*. These aggregates follow the specific logic of the individual application. If other applications use this data, a delay occurs. Furthermore, you'll require semantic knowledge of the corresponding application aggregate. Consequently, the data first needs to be translated into the data model of the other application. For this purpose, interfaces must be available or must be developed.

  Integration on the basis of such an architecture thus has disadvantages with regard to costs (development and maintenance of the interfaces) and with regard to lacking real-time access.

Over the last few years, new database architectures have been developed, so-called *in-memory databases*. SAP S/4HANA is completely based on this kind of database: SAP HANA. The following sections describe the characteristics of SAP HANA and describe why no other in-memory database is currently compatible with SAP S/4HANA.

In-memory database

2.3.1 SAP HANA

If you take a look at hardware development in the few last years, you'll see that two basic changes arose at the turn of the millennium: On the one hand, multicore processor architectures emerged and, with them, the option of substantial parallelization. On the other hand, memory evolved from being relatively expensive and limited into being widely available.

Due to the memory restrictions with regard to availability (i.e., price and addressability), the data in software architectures was mainly stored on the hard disk, and only some data was stored in the memory. Accessing in traditional databases was limited by hard disk processing speeds. In in-memory databases, the hard disk is only used to store, archive, and restore data. The data itself is permanently kept in the main memory.

Data permanently stored in the main memory

In contrast to other in-memory databases, SAP HANA has further unique characteristics: SAP HANA is not only an ideal generic database but has also been optimized for business applications due to SAP's holistic experiences with this kind of applications.

Optimization for business software

The key result of SAP's experience is that the data in SAP HANA is stored in column-based tables, while the data in other databases is stored in row-based tables (see Figure 2.5). Why is this relevant?

Column-based database

In business applications, most data is accessed "per column": Usually, the values of a field or a selection of fields are selected and edited (e.g. names of a set of employees or prices of a selection of goods). Rarely is an entire set of rows required (i.e. all attributes of an employee or of a good). If SELECT statements are executed using column indexes, much smaller volumes of data need to be processed. Moreover, the values in the columns can usually be easily compressed—in particular under the conditions given for business applications, which consist of similar data.

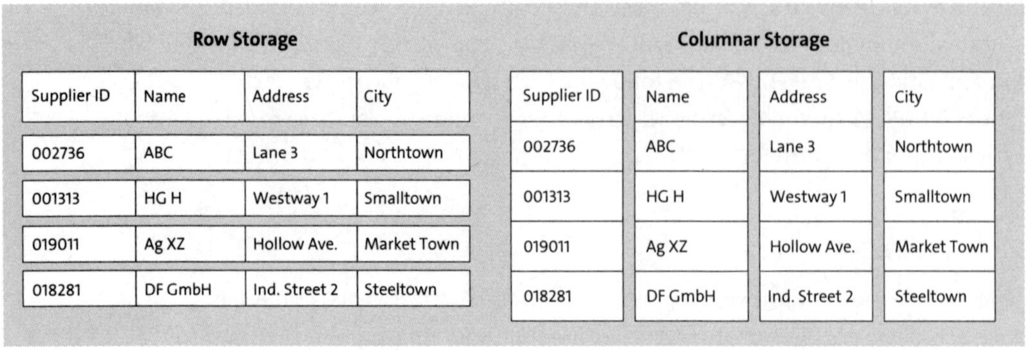

2   SAP S/4HANA versus the Traditional SAP Business Suite

Row Storage				Columnar Storage			
Supplier ID	Name	Address	City	Supplier ID	Name	Address	City
002736	ABC	Lane 3	Northtown	002736	ABC	Lane 3	Northtown
001313	HG H	Westway 1	Smalltown	001313	HG H	Westway 1	Smalltown
019011	Ag XZ	Hollow Ave.	Market Town	019011	Ag XZ	Hollow Ave.	Market Town
018281	DF GmbH	Ind. Street 2	Steeltown	018281	DF GmbH	Ind. Street 2	Steeltown

Figure 2.5 Comparison of Row-Based and Column-Based Data Storage

Parallelization   Another benefit of SAP HANA is that this database has been optimized in such a way that the main business data operations can be executed with high performance. For this purpose, SAP HANA uses multicore CPUs (central processing units) for parallelization. In addition, algorithms are optimized using assumptions about the types of updates, inserts, and deletions that are carried out frequently and should consequently be the focus for high performance.

2.3.2   The Data Model

Optimization of the data models for the database   SAP S/4HANA is designed to fully exploit the benefits of SAP HANA described in the previous section. With this focus on SAP HANA, the following consequences arise for the data models in SAP S/4HANA:

- Aggregates are omitted.
- Existing ABAP Dictionary tables are redesigned.
- Code is pushed down.

The following sections discuss each of these consequences in greater detail.

Omission of Aggregates

Disadvantages of aggregates   To compensate for poor speed of traditional databases, data was previously consolidated in *aggregate tables*. The applications then accessed these aggregate tables to read the data. However, these aggregates had the following disadvantages: Due to the consolidation, entries in the aggregate tables always lagged behind entries in the original tables. This delay increases with the growth of the volume of data that needs to be processed.

Another disadvantage is that the aggregation uses assumptions of the content as a prerequisite for consolidation. As a result, processing this data from a different perspective is usually not possible without reworking the aggregation and thus can be a rather complicated task. For this purpose, you'll have to use the original data, which reduces processing speed.

Figure 2.6 shows an example of a target architecture with a simplified data model for sales documents after migrating from SAP ERP to SAP S/4HANA.

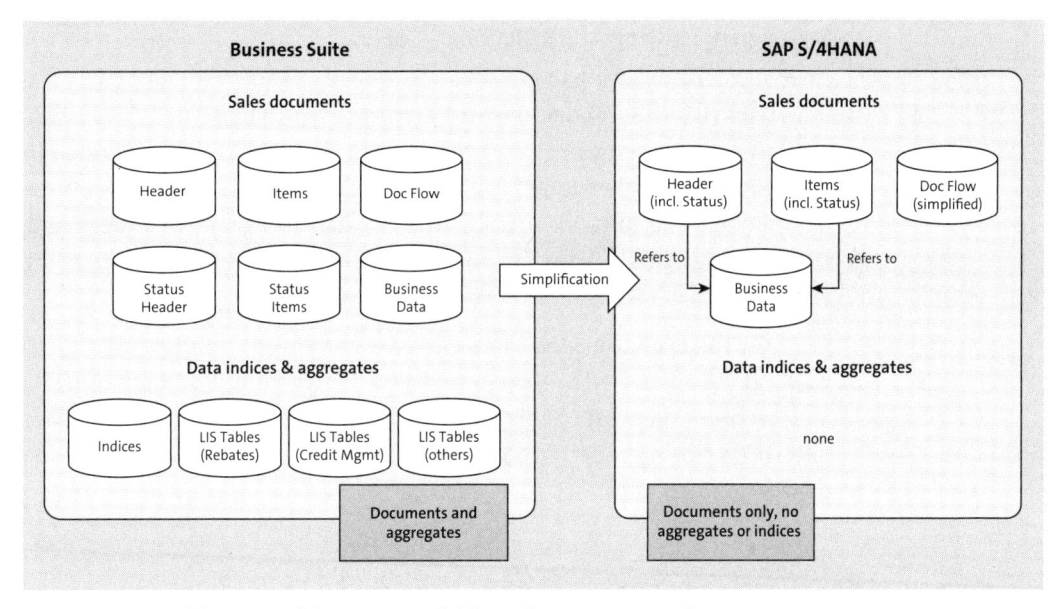

Figure 2.6 Simplification of the Data Model for Sales Documents (Target Architecture)

The usual aggregate tables were omitted in this case. All new SAP HANA-optimized applications directly access the original data.

Note that the aggregates continue to exist in the new data model: The database can emulate the tables in real time. For this purpose, SAP S/4HANA provides predefined *database views*. These views simulate the aggregates in real time so that existing applications that have not been optimized for SAP HANA can be deployed smoothly.

Database views

> **[o] Accessing the Traditional Data Model**
> SAP S/4HANA includes compatible database views, which allow you to access the data model of the traditional SAP Business Suite.

As a result, you'll still have read access to existing custom developments, such as reports, and you can usually still use these reports without needing adaptations to the new data model. Chapter 10, Section 10.2.5, describes how you can check your existing code for compatibility with SAP S/4HANA.

Redesign of Existing ABAP Dictionary Tables

Optimizing the data architecture
In addition to omitting aggregates, the example shown in Figure 2.6 also illustrates that the architecture for the storage of original data is also partly optimized. In this context, you must keep in mind that the data models in SAP ERP had been developed over several decades. On the one hand, these data models had to be compatible with all databases; on the other hand, rigid changes would have led to problems with SAP ERP EHP upgrades, which were promised and expected to be easy to use.

With the focus on the SAP HANA database and the clear differentiation to existing products, SAP S/4HANA now also allows for redesigning the data architecture in general. In this process, data storage is further optimized for SAP HANA, for example, to enhance the compression rate or optimize the general performance.

Code Pushdown

Another innovation in SAP S/4HANA is that procedures can be directly transferred to the database. In the traditional SAP Business Suite, the ABAP kernel decoupled the application from the database to ensure compatibility to any type of database. Consequently, the raw data first had to be loaded from the database and then concatenated in the application to carry out complex, data-intensive selections and calculations.

Optimizing the application code
In SAP S/4HANA, some data-related processes are pushed down to the database itself, which accelerates the entire process, which is known as *code pushdown*. Code pushdown can be executed either in ABAP using Open SQL or via SAP HANA content created in SAP HANA Studio.

How does this affect existing custom code enhancements? Because existing Open SQL data access still works, you can continue to use existing enhancements and only have to adapt them in exceptional cases. However, these codes do not exploit the full potential of SAP S/4HANA. Thus, when you plan to migrate to SAP S/4HANA, you should check which custom codes should be rewritten and optimized. Because you can address custom code at any time after migrating SAP S/4HANA, you'll enjoy greater flexibility in planning.

2.3.3 Handling Existing Data

How do these changes to the data model affect planning a migration? The good news is that you'll only have to take into account a small portion of these data model changes because SAP S/4HANA provides database views with all the necessary compatibility (see "Omission of Aggregates" in Section 2.3.2). However, when planning your migration project, you'll have to bring your existing data into the new data models. Depending on the technical migration scenario selected (Chapter 3 and Chapter 4 introduce the individual scenarios), different technical procedures are used to *convert the data*. Usually, these procedures include *execution of program after import* (XPRA) or *after import methods* (AIMs). Regardless of the scenario you choose, converting the technical data will take some time.

Converting data for the new data models

How much time this conversion needs mainly depends on the volume of the data to be converted. For this reason, you should check what existing data can be archived before migrating to SAP S/4HANA. In this way, you can reduce the volume of the data to be converted and thus minimize the conversion runtime. Thanks to SAP S/4HANA's built-in compatibility mode, applications contain read modules that allow you to read archived data.

2.3.4 Sizing

If you want to implement a new SAP S/4HANA system or convert an existing SAP ERP system to SAP S/4HANA, you'll have to consider the following issues:

Sizing depends on the size of the database

- **The sizing rules for SAP S/4HANA systems and for SAP ERP systems differ**
  Analyzing hardware requirements (*sizing*) for modern systems follow different conditions and rules than sizing systems based on traditional

databases. The main reason for this difference is that SAP HANA stores data in random-access memory (RAM), which requires different sizing requirements. The new SAP HANA data architectures and embedded data compression algorithms routinely achieve data compression rates of 3 to 5 on average.

- **Random-access memory = twice the compressed data volume**
  As a rule of thumb, SAP recommends calculating twice the compressed data volume for the RAM volume. Because sizing strongly depends on your specific conditions (for example, on the compression rate that can be achieved), SAP recommends running a sizing report in your existing SAP ERP systems. For more information on sizing, see *http://service.sap.com/sizing*.

In summary, the SAP HANA database is more closely linked to implementing application functions than other databases in previous years. This close link is the only way for applications to sufficiently benefit from the advantages of the database. This close relationship is probably also why SAP S/4HANA is currently only available for SAP HANA. The in-memory databases of third-party providers sometimes follow other approaches and require alternative implementations.

2.4 SAP Fiori User Interfaces

SAP developed its traditional SAP Business Suite applications assuming that users access the ERP system using a specifically assigned frontend computer. The component used for this frontend access is *SAP GUI*. Through a time-consuming process, SAP GUI had to be installed at all workstations in the enterprise because the applications could only be used with the appropriate and latest version of SAP GUI on the user's desktop computer.

Role-based portals In the 2000s, SAP wanted to provide users with role-based access to the increasingly complex business processes. For this purpose, central portals were successfully implemented, allowing users access via a browser. Connections to the SAP ERP system were established through dedicated frontend applications deployed on the central portal.

New UI concept Despite this progress, the interfaces in the SAP ERP systems seem to be outdated—in particular if you compare them to the omnipresent interfaces of smartphones, tablet computers, and modern computers. SAP S/4HANA is based on a completely new UI concept called *SAP Fiori*, which combines technological changes with newly designed user concepts.

SAP Fiori comprises three different types of apps, which differ with regard to their focus and requirements for the infrastructure:

- **Transactional apps**
  These apps enable you to perform transactional tasks such as creating leave requests for employees. Transactional apps provide focused views for users to interact with business processes and solutions.

- **Fact sheets**
  Fact sheets display context information and the most important aspects of central objects (for example, a purchase info record fact sheet provides information about the purchase info record business object). From a fact sheet, you can drill down to detailed information about the relevant object.

- **Analytical apps**
  With analytical apps, you can monitor relevant key figures in real time and use them to make decisions.

You can find a list of available SAP Fiori apps in the *SAP Fiori apps reference library*. By choosing **SAP S/4HANA** or **SAP S/4HANA Cloud**, you can display the SAP Fiori apps that are available for SAP S/4HANA.

SAP Fiori apps reference library

Thus, when migrating to SAP S/4HANA, you should consider implementing SAP Fiori. To facilitate this migration, SAP has ensured the compatibility of the new product: You can still use SAP GUI to access applications. However, users can only access the traditional SAP ERP applications via SAP GUI but not the newly developed SAP S/4HANA functions, which run on SAP Fiori.

> **Flexible User Access**
>
> SAP S/4HANA, on-premise, also enables users to access traditional transactions via SAP GUI.

This compatibility allows for a gradual migration: Chapter 4 goes into further detail.

2.4.1 Technological Changes

One major change with SAP Fiori is that no GUI component is locally installed. A web browser is used to access the SAP S/4HANA system, eliminating the time-consuming process of setting up local SAP GUI installations.

Cross-device access Consequently, users can basically use any Internet-enabled device to access SAP applications and are not bound to their workstations but can use a smartphone or tablet to access the SAP system. For this purpose, the SAP S/4HANA application instances are supplemented by a central *frontend server* as shown in Figure 2.7.

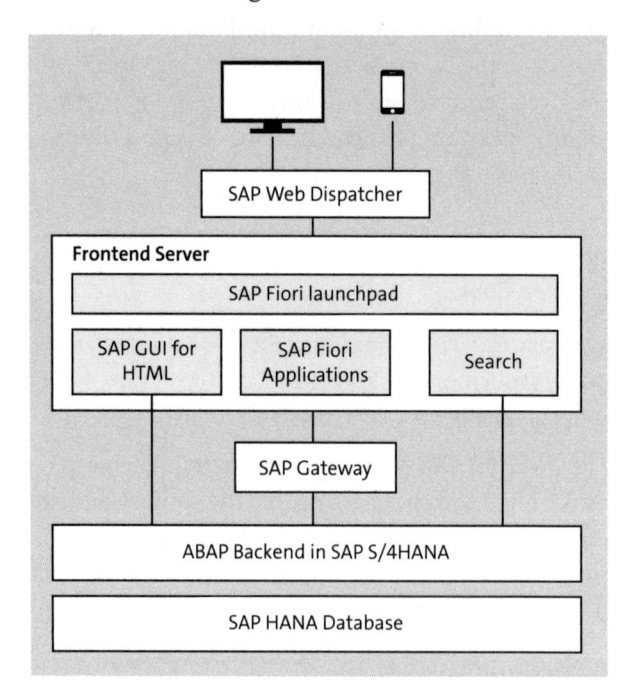

Figure 2.7 Architecture of SAP S/4HANA

SAP Web Dispatcher establishes the connection to the frontend server. On the frontend server itself, you can find the SAP Fiori launchpad and the SAP Fiori applications. These main components of the frontend server are complemented by an installed search function and *SAP GUI for HTML*, which is available for compatibility reasons. *SAP Gateway* is responsible for distributing the browser requests of the frontend server across your various application systems (backend systems). You can implement SAP Gateway separately or as a part of the frontend server.

Although you can install the frontend server on the central instance, in most cases, you should install the frontend server separately as a central frontend hub. SAP recommends installing the frontend server on the central instance (*embedded*) only for single-system landscapes, such as proof of concept installations or small production systems. Figure 2.8 illustrates the basic distribution of the required system instances.

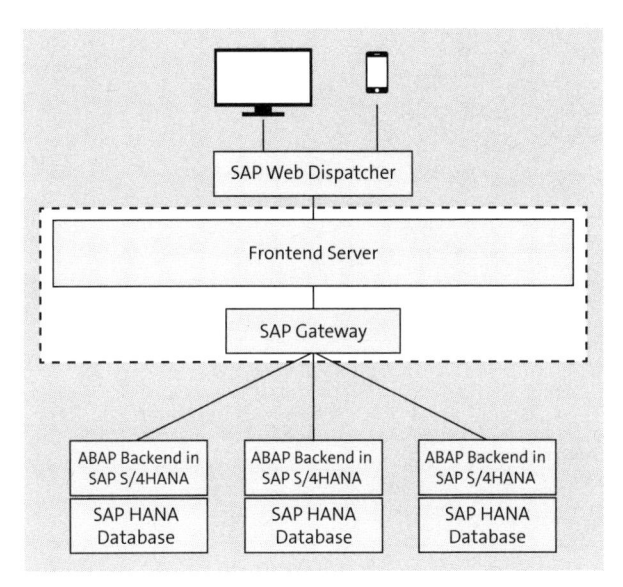

Figure 2.8 Connecting an SAP Fiori Frontend Server to an SAP System Landscape

2.4.2 Operating Concept

The operating concept behind SAP Fiori can be summarized in one word: simplicity. With SAP Fiori, SAP provides simplified access options for all users. You've already come across one element of this simplified access: access from any end device.

In addition, the structure of applications is simplified: The *SAP Fiori launchpad* (see Figure 2.9) replaces the SAP Easy Access menu of the traditional SAP Business Suite. The launchpad consists of tiles used to access applications.

SAP Fiori launchpad

2 SAP S/4HANA versus the Traditional SAP Business Suite

	SAP		Home		
ick Launch	Contacts and Profiles	Insight	Marketing Executive Dashboard	Segmentation	Campaign
	13.5 K				
Predictive Studio	Predictive Studio New App Available	Score Builder	Marketing Locations	Channel Interest Mix Analytics Story	
3		2 Scores	0 Locations		
New and Converted Contacts Analytics Story					
Insight					
Behavior Insight	Sentiment Engagement	Customer Journey Insight			

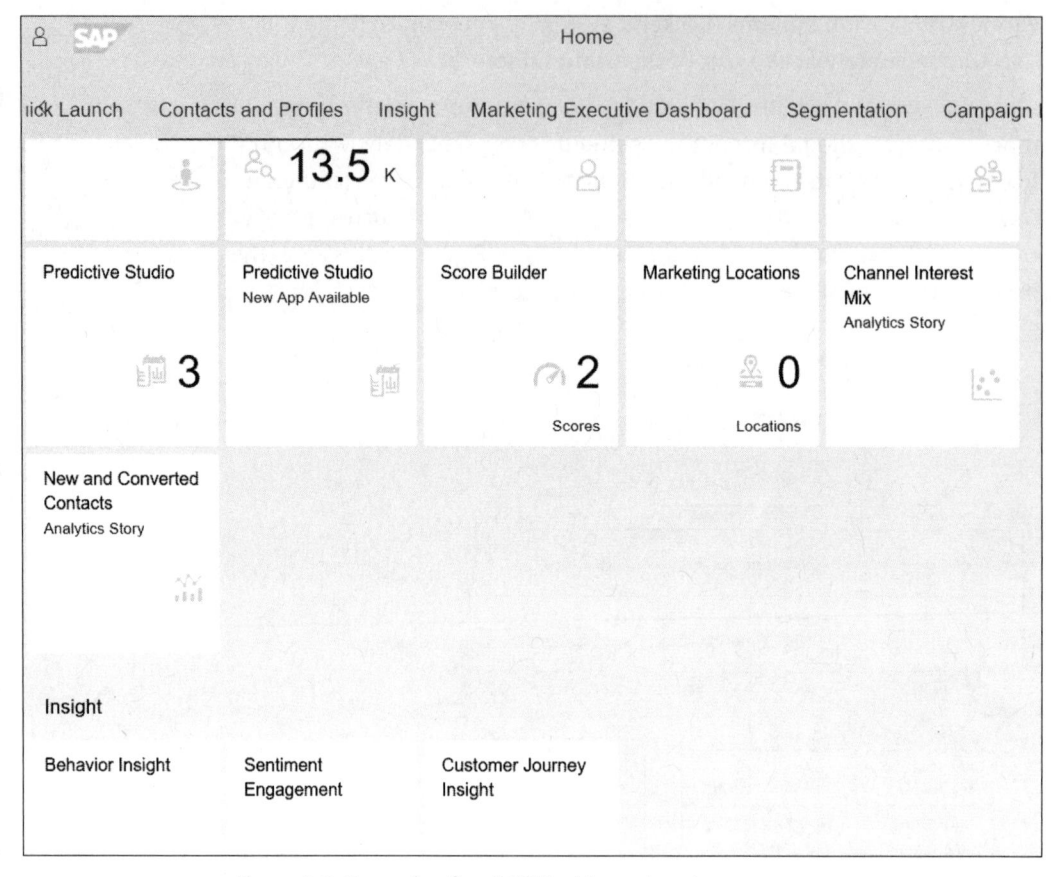

Figure 2.9 Example of an SAP Fiori Launchpad

Live tiles with relevant KPIs The launchpad also includes so-called *live tiles*, which display relevant information from underlying applications, such as aggregated key performance indicators (KPIs). As a result, users can determine directly from the SAP Fiori launchpad which applications require direct intervention.

Tiles are assigned to *launchpad groups*, which allows for a transparent tile structure and also enables users to directly access a group of tiles via the dropdown menu ⌄ in the upper right area of the screen.

Access control via SAP Fiori user roles The availability of the tiles in the launchpad depends on the centrally assigned roles of the users. These roles are specific *SAP Fiori roles* that must not be confused with authorization roles in a traditional SAP Business Suite solution. Thus, when migrating to SAP S/4HANA, you should factor in sufficient time for planning or adapting your enterprise-specific role structure. In SAP S/4HANA, applications are more focused on actual work processes and try to guide users more effectively through this process than previously. You'll also have a lot of freedom to customize the predefined design. These changes are dynamic: Settings, such as filters, affect the displayed results and available process options in real time.

In addition to a modern design for applications, including a completely new structure and order of screen elements, a search function has also been implemented. Users can search for any keywords such as long texts, parts of key numbers, names, and much more. The search is carried out across various business objects and even across system boundaries, and the results include matches related to the keyword. This powerful search function eliminates a disadvantage of the previous SAP interface, which usually only permitted users to search for individual field values via [F4] help.

Comprehensive search functions

If users still have questions about how to use applications, a newly designed documentation system supports self-help options: The so-called *X-ray documentation approach* enables users to click on the areas about which they want more information. This help system navigates the user to the relevant documentation.

Help function

Of course, you can also extend the SAP Fiori user interfaces. In contrast to extending SAP Business Suite, you usually don't have to write any code to extend an SAP Fiori user interface: What's called *key-user extensibility* allows users to add custom fields, hide or display objects, modify structures, or supplement the calculation logic, for example. Only enhancements that cannot use key-user extensibility require you to write the new code.

Enhancements

Officially released SAP Fiori apps can enable your enterprise or SAP partners to develop custom SAPUI5-based SAP Fiori applications using the *SAP Web IDE*. The browser-based toolkit can be found on the SAP Cloud Platform and includes an integrated development environment. Developing custom user interfaces is extremely important for most SAP customers. In today's SAP Business Suite, about 50% of the interfaces used by SAP customers are custom developments.

Finally, you can assign a custom *theming* to your user interface to map the corporate identity on the screen (consider your company's color scheme and logo).

> **Additional Information**
>
> You can find further information for redesigning the SAP user experience (UX) using SAP Fiori at the following website:
>
> - https://www.sap.com/products/fiori.html
>
> For more information on SAP Fiori 2.0, go to the following website:
>
> - https://experience.sap.com/skillup/sap-fiori-2-0-the-ideal-overview
>
> You can find a video covering design concepts at the following website:
>
> - https://www.youtube.com/watch?v=NSq40zfuyll
>
> You can access the SAP Fiori apps reference library at the following website:
>
> - https://fioriappslibrary.hana.ondemand.com/sap/fix/externalViewer
>
> For more information on SAP Web IDE, go to the following website:
>
> - https://www.sap.com/developer/topics/sap-webide.html
>
> For more information on the development guidelines for SAP Fiori 2.0, go to the following website:
>
> - https://experience.sap.com/documents/sap-fiori-2-0-administration-and-developer-guide.pdf

Accessing traditional transactions

All elements mentioned in this section are only available with the newly designed SAP S/4HANA. If you want to access traditional SAP ERP applications, you'll have to follow the usual approaches. However, if required, you can also provide the traditional transactions in the SAP Fiori launchpad.

Gradual introduction

In summary, we can make the following statements: You can convert an SAP ERP system to SAP S/4HANA without directly implementing SAP Fiori across the entire system landscape. However, in this case, you won't benefit from SAP S/4HANA's significantly simplified applications and can only use the traditional SAP Business Suite applications. Thus, your SAP S/4HANA implementation project should minimally include a gradual introduction of the SAP Fiori UI concept. Because the SAP Fiori concept is role-based, you can easily select individual business areas and employee groups for conversion. Because of the benefits provided by SAP Fiori, SAP S/4HANA Cloud can only use SAP Fiori UIs.

> **Gradual Introduction**
> The new SAP Fiori UI concept is controlled on the basis of roles and can thus be introduced gradually.

2.5 Interfaces

So far, this chapter focused on the SAP S/4HANA innovations that affect a single system. If you migrate from an existing SAP ERP system to SAP S/4HANA, this SAP ERP system is usually integrated into a system landscape or has been enhanced with custom or third-party applications. What do you have to take into account in these cases?

First, you should determine how the system has been integrated or enhanced:

- **Integration via SAP Process Integration (PI) or SAP Process Orchestration (PO)**
  Existing integration that flows through the SAP PI or SAP PO middleware can be kept. SAP S/4HANA is compatible with SAP PI and SAP PO. To integrate new or significantly changed SAP S/4HANA applications, you might have to implement additional integration content.

- **Integration via authorized interfaces**
  You can continue to use authorized interfaces such as Business Application Programming Interfaces (BAPIs). In SAP S/4HANA, implementations of these interfaces are adapted to the new data model if required. This compatibility, again, refers to traditional application scenarios only.

- **Proprietary integration**
  If you have implemented custom access options or interfaces, you'll have to analyze whether you can continue to use them in SAP S/4HANA. When implementing the new data model, SAP took into account compatibility, but some adaptation work may still be required. Chapter 4 describes how to determine this.

- **Third-party applications**
  If you use third-party applications, you should contact your software provider for more information on their compatibility with SAP S/4HANA.

Depending on the result of this analysis, you may have to include follow-up measures in the planning of your migration project. In summary, the more strictly you followed SAP's recommendations for the implementation and the more modification-free enhancements or standard interfaces you use, the less follow-up work is required. Chapter 8 and Chapter 13 explain in detail how to integrate SAP S/4HANA into an existing landscape.

2.6 SAP S/4HANA Embedded Analytics

The analytical functionality provided by SAP S/4HANA is referred to as *SAP S/4HANA embedded analytics*. This function enables users (not just analytical data experts but any users) to create and carry out real-time analyses based on SAP S/4HANA application data. Standard reports and analytical SAP Fiori apps are also delivered by SAP S/4HANA. The analytical data is displayed via the new SAP Fiori launchpad, which is based on SAP Fiori technology.

CDS views — Technically, SAP S/4HANA embedded analytics functions are based on the core data services (CDS) views of the ABAP layer in SAP S/4HANA. These CDS views are database views organized in a *virtual data model* (VDM). On the basis of these CDS views, users can run queries on transactional data in real time. For these queries, users can either use default views, enhance existing views, or create new views based on the relevant application tables.

In addition to fast customization of analytical queries, SAP S/4HANA's simplified data structures considerably enhance the creation of queries in real time. Because aggregates have been omitted and data redundancy is thus eliminated, users do not have to know the aggregation logic and can build their queries on the data of the native tables.

Analytical data in SAP Fiori — Analytical data is usually displayed via SAP Fiori interfaces. Various user interfaces and use cases are provided for different user groups (end users, key users, and developers). As shown in Figure 2.10, end users are provided with analytical analyses that are adapted to the role and use case, but tools and functions for analytics key users are also available to enable them to create their own queries.

2.6 SAP S/4HANA Embedded Analytics

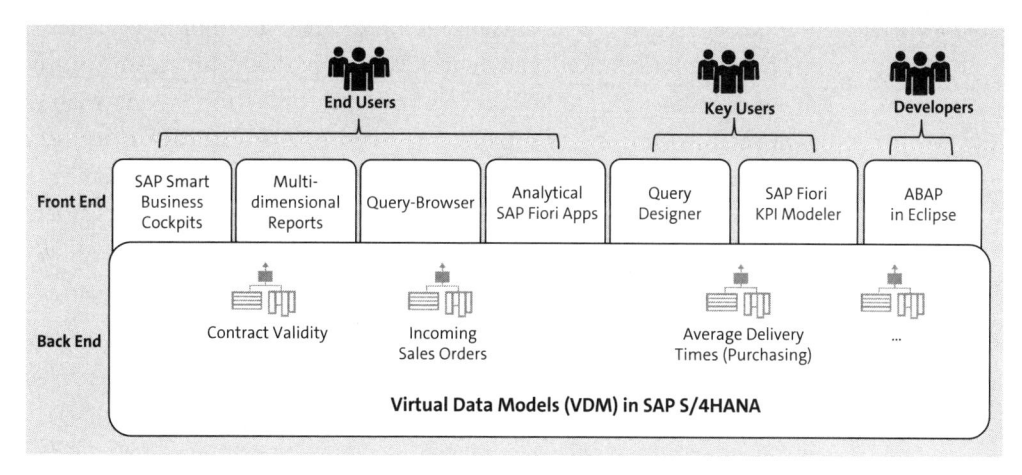

Figure 2.10 SAP Embedded Analytics: Different User Roles

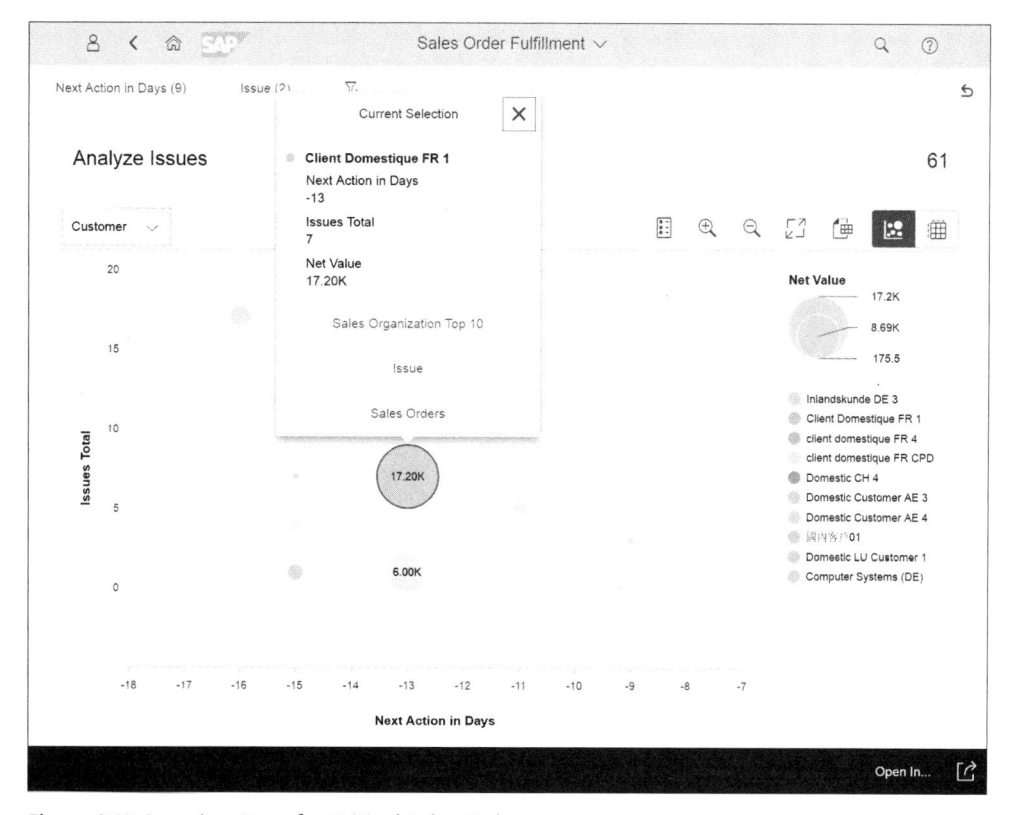

Figure 2.11 Overview Page for Critical Sales Orders

Example: critical sales orders

Let's look at an example of a user role, an internal sales employee, to illustrate how the integration of analytical data supports the processing of critical sales orders. The SAP Fiori app for sales order fulfillment enables employees to process exceptions for sales orders. Critical orders (e.g., orders where the promised delivery date cannot be kept) are displayed in an overview page (see Figure 2.11). From this page, end users can navigate to the relevant detail views and analyze the reason for the delay individually for each critical order.

> **Additional Information**
>
> You can find more information and examples of analytics at *https://experience.sap.com/skillup/sap-fiori-2-0-a-primer-on-embedded-analytics/* or in the SAP Fiori apps reference library at *www.sap.com/fiori-apps-library*.

Chapter 3
Cloud, On-Premise, and Hybrid Scenarios

You can use SAP S/4HANA in various cloud-based and on-premise editions. But what are the differences between these operating models? And what are the differences between the individual SAP S/4HANA editions?

When migrating to SAP S/4HANA, you'll have to make some basic decisions. You'll have to select the type of system landscape and decide which SAP S/4HANA functions you want and how they are supposed to be used (see Figure 3.1). First, you'll need to choose whether you want to run SAP S/4HANA *on-premise* (i.e., the software runs on your enterprise's hardware); in the *cloud* (i.e., the software is leased and hosted by a provider); or as a *hybrid scenario* (i.e., some parts of the business scenarios are outsourced to the cloud, other parts are kept on-premise). Furthermore, you'll have to decide whether you want to leverage the migration process to redesign your own business processes (*greenfield approach*) or whether to keep existing business processes (*brownfield approach*).

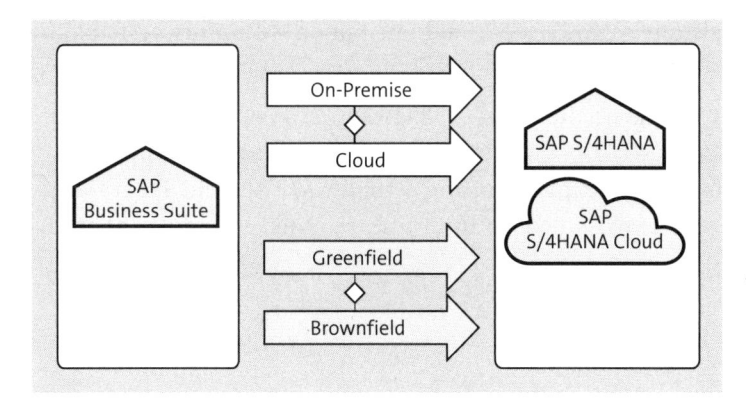

Figure 3.1 Strategic Decisions for Migrating to SAP S/4HANA

3 Cloud, On-Premise, and Hybrid Scenarios

This chapter covers the basic options for and differences between the various operating models and provides you with the basic information required to make these necessary decisions. First, we'll provide an overview of the operating models and define critical concepts. Then, we'll introduce and compare the individual editions of the SAP S/4HANA product family.

Usually, an enterprise wants to customize its business processes. In addition to business configuration settings, individual enhancement options can be an essential way for an enterprise to differentiate itself from competitors. The last section of this chapter describes in detail SAP S/4HANA's enhancement concepts.

3.1 Overview of Operating Models

To enable you to choose an SAP S/4HANA operating model, the following section describes the basic characteristics of the different operating models. Section 3.3 then compares the operating models.

3.1.1 On-Premise Operating Model

Full control of hardware and software

Usually, the on-premise operating model refers to using software that a customer has purchased and runs and manages on hardware owned by the customer. As a result, the customer is in full control of the hardware and software, of mission-critical application data, and of software maintenance schedules. Moreover, the customer achieves maximum flexibility with regard to custom enhancements and integration with other systems (in-house solutions or external systems).

But the customer is also fully responsible for the availability of the software as well as access, security, and system stability. In addition to the costs for hardware and software, powerful and complex ERP systems incur further costs for the IT experts needed to introduce, manage, and maintain the software.

3.1.2 Cloud Operating Model

Leasing software and services

In cloud operating models, a customer does not operate or manage the software himself but rather engages a service provider for this purpose. The software and the corresponding services are leased for a defined period of time in the cloud operating model. Hardware and operating system software are not required on-premise. The enterprise's IT staff can thus focus on other tasks.

Internet access is usually necessary to access the solution, and users can access the cloud software from anywhere and in most cases also via mobile end devices. One of the major benefits of the cloud operating model is the associated cost transparency. The infrastructure of cloud-based software is shared by multiple customers.

However, to ensure efficient operation, individual customers can only impact the maintenance cycles and schedules of the cloud software to a limited extent. Thus, usually the customization options in the cloud operating model are more limited than in the on-premise operating model. Another issue that needs to be analyzed specifically in each case is data security (*cloud security*). In general, the data security standards and processes of trustworthy cloud providers are higher or more extensive than the security infrastructure of the average enterprise.

Limited scope for intervention

How to evaluate the cloud operating model, however, also significantly depends on the service and deployment models used. Figure 3.2 provides an overview of these service and deployment models, which are based on the definitions from the *National Institute of Standards and Technology* (NIST, https://www.nist.gov).

Service and deployment models

For service models, the following three categories are differentiated:

Service models

- **Software as a Service (SaaS)**
  In the case of the software as a service (SaaS) model, customers use the applications of a provider, which are operated on a cloud infrastructure. Typically, customers access these applications via the Internet using a web browser. In the SaaS model, the provider is responsible for managing and controlling the cloud infrastructure. Besides user-specific configuration settings, customers do not have any functions for managing or controlling the software.

  In addition to the SAP S/4HANA public cloud editions, the following SAP solutions fall into this category: SAP SuccessFactors, SAP Hybris Marketing Cloud, SAP Ariba, Concur, and SAP Fieldglass.

3   Cloud, On-Premise, and Hybrid Scenarios

- **Platform as a service (PaaS)**
  In the platform as a service (PaaS) model, application developers are provided with programming languages and tools as a service. As in the SaaS model, the provider is responsible for managing and controlling the underlying cloud infrastructure. The customers manage their applications, which they have built on the basis of the development environment provided. One example of this model is SAP Cloud Platform (previously SAP HANA Cloud Platform (SAP HCP)).

- **Infrastructure as a service (IaaS)**
  Infrastructure as a service (IaaS) refers to a service that provides users with access to computing power, data storage, and network capacity. In this model, the customers control the applications and operating systems used and usually also install them themselves. Nevertheless, the provider is again responsible for controlling and managing the cloud infrastructure. SAP HANA Enterprise Cloud (SAP HEC) (see Section 3.2.3) belongs to this category.

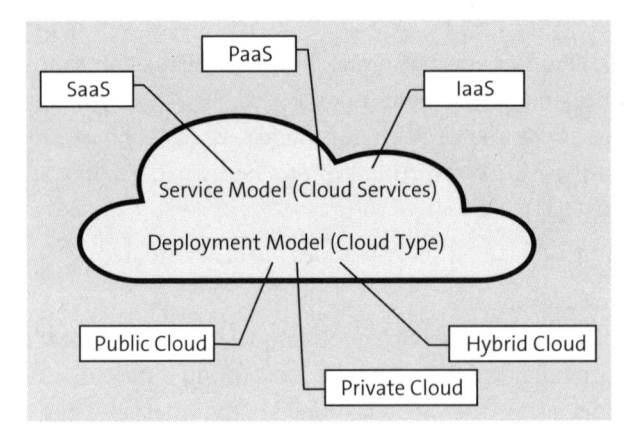

Figure 3.2 Service and Operating Models in the Cloud

Deployment models

For the *cloud deployment models*, we differentiate between three types:

- **Public cloud**
  In the case of public clouds, services and applications are publicly available and can generally be used by everyone. Usually, users share the resources of the cloud infrastructure, which is provided by an external provider.

- **Private cloud**
  In a private cloud, the cloud infrastructure is deployed for specific customers or only one customer. The cloud infrastructure can be deployed by a department of the enterprise or by an external provider. The same applies to operating a private cloud. If the cloud is operated in-house, the transition to the on-premise operating model is different. The transition should take into account how flexible and scalable you need the IT infrastructure to be, how business applications will be accessed via the Internet, or how regularly programs should be updated automatically.
- **Hybrid cloud**
  A combination of public cloud and private cloud is referred to as a *hybrid cloud*. In this case, part of the IT infrastructure is operated on-premise, while other services are provided by an external public cloud provider.

3.1.3 Hybrid Operating Model

In hybrid operating models, some parts of the business scenario are operated on-premise, and some parts are operated in the cloud. Hybrid operating models enable you to combine the characteristics of the on-premise operating model and the cloud operating model. For example, core areas of your enterprise, where you want a high degree of control and a high level of flexibility, can be operated on-premise, while other enterprise areas can be operated in the cloud because common industry standards are sufficient.

> **Hybrid Structures in Human Resources**
>
> An example of an enterprise area in which business processes are largely outsourced to the cloud is human resources (HR). As described in Chapter 1, SAP's target architecture for HR business processes is the cloud. With the SAP SuccessFactors solution portfolio, SAP enables HR departments to outsource to the cloud functions such as workforce administration or managing job candidates and applications, employee performance, or talent.

Hybrid scenarios can also make sense based on the organizational structure of an enterprise. For example, you might want to run global business processes at headquarters on-premise, while the regional business processes at your subsidiaries can be standardized and outsourced to the cloud.

Integration requirements

With regard to technology and content, a combination of on-premise processing and cloud-based processing poses specific requirements for integrating the various solutions used, as shown in Figure 3.3.

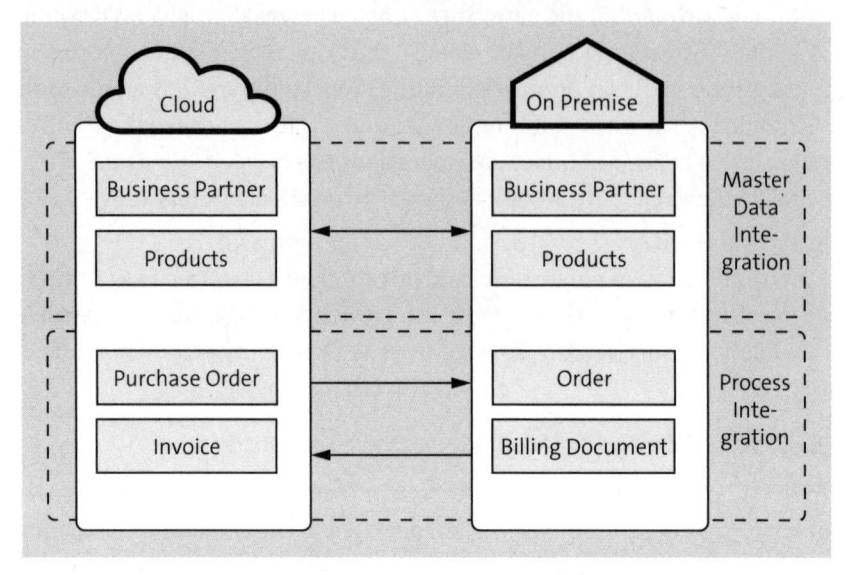

Figure 3.3 Integration in Hybrid Scenarios

Therefore, when choosing an operating model, you should consider your specific requirements regarding master data and process integration. For more information on the integration scenarios for the various SAP cloud solutions, see Chapter 8.

3.2 The SAP S/4HANA Product Family

Customers can choose between multiple editions of the SAP S/4HANA product family. Figure 3.4 shows members of the SAP S/4HANA product family currently available.

On-premise and cloud editions

In general, we differentiate between the on-premise editions and the cloud editions. However, all members of the SAP S/4HANA product family are based on the same program code. End users will only see differences between the editions due to the different user interface (UI) concepts. SAP S/4HANA Cloud only provides SAP Fiori-based user interfaces, while the SAP S/4HANA, on-premise, allows you to continue to use the traditional interfaces based on SAP GUI for Windows. SAP S/4HANA Enterprise Management Cloud (Private Option) is a *private managed cloud solution*, that is, a hosted service, in SAP HANA Enterprise Cloud (SAP HEC) and is a combination of the on-premise deployment model and the cloud deployment model.

```
SAP S/4HANA Cloud
    SAP S/4HANA Enterprise Management (Private Option)
    SAP Hybris Marketing Cloud
    SAP S/4HANA Enterprise Management
    SAP S/4HANA Professional Services Cloud
    SAP S/4HANA Finance Cloud

SAP S/4HANA
    SAP S/4HANA
    SAP S/4HANA Finance

Digital Core SAP S/4HANA
```

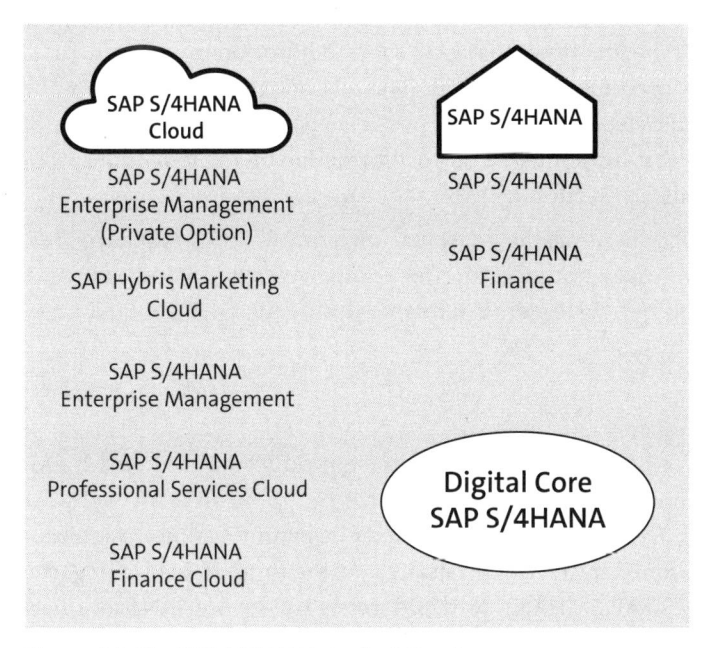

Figure 3.4 The SAP S/4HANA Product Family

3.2.1 SAP S/4HANA, On-Premise

In SAP S/4HANA, on-premise, customers operate the software in their own system landscape. They are responsible for purchasing the necessary hardware, for installing and managing the software, and for maintaining the system (for example, implementing software changes). Currently, SAP S/4HANA is available in two on-premise editions:

- SAP S/4HANA Finance
- SAP S/4HANA

SAP S/4HANA Central Finance is an additional on-premise variant that enables global financial processes as a complementary instance for the operational systems in the system landscape.

SAP S/4HANA Finance

First product from the SAP S/4HANA product family

Released in 2014, SAP S/4HANA Finance was the first product from the SAP S/4HANA product family (at this time, SAP S/4HANA Finance was called the *SAP Simple Finance Add-on for SAP Business Suite powered by SAP HANA*). The data structures in the accounting area in SAP S/4HANA Finance were adapted to fully exploit the potential of SAP HANA's in-memory database technology for the first time. Thanks to this modification to data structures in accounting, processes in Financials (FI) and Controlling (CO) can now be processed in one step, which was not possible before in SAP ERP because of high resource consumption. For more information on the individual product innovations, see Section 3.3.1.

Latest available version

At the time of this writing, the latest version is SAP S/4HANA Finance 1605. At present, SAP does not plan to offer another version of SAP S/4HANA Finance. If required, customers can migrate from SAP S/4HANA Finance to a newer version of SAP S/4HANA.

SAP S/4HANA

The digital core

In November 2015, the second on-premise product was launched: SAP S/4HANA. Then referred to as *SAP S/4HANA 1511, on-premise*, or *S/4HANA Enterprise Management*, this version added further innovations in addition to those mentioned in the financials area. At the time of this writing, the latest version is SAP S/4HANA 1610. SAP refers to SAP S/4HANA as a new *digital core* for enterprise software. Figure 3.5 shows this digital core including the relevant innovations that cover various *lines of business* (LOBs).

SAP Ariba SAP S/4HANA Finance	SAP SuccessFactors SAP Fieldglass SAP S/4HANA Human Resources	SAP Ariba SAP Fieldglass SAP S/4HANA Sourcing & Procurement	SAP S/4HANA Supply Chain	SAP S/4HANA Manufacturing

SAP S/4HANA Enterprise Management (Digital Core)

SAP Hybris Marketing	SAP S/4HANA Sales SAP Hybris	SAP Hybris Service	SAP S/4HANA Asset Management	SAP S/4HANA Research and Development

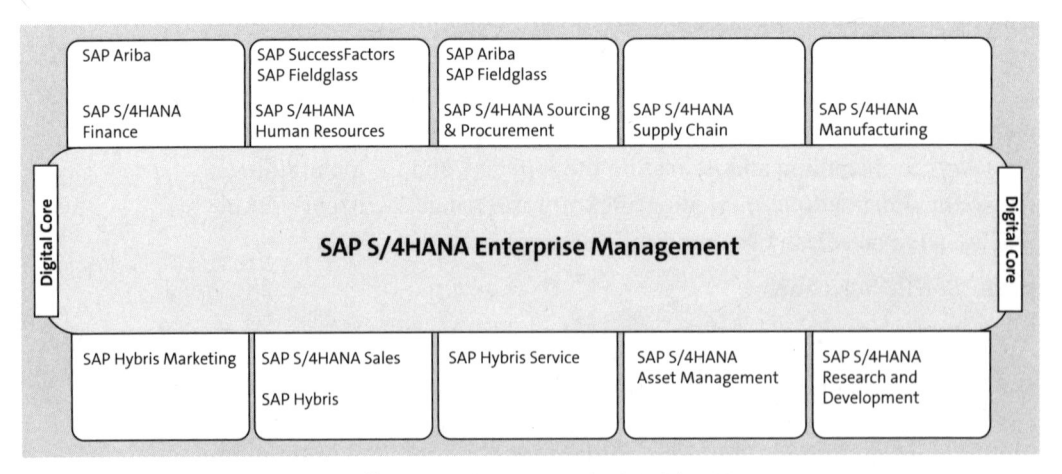

Figure 3.5 Different Business Areas in SAP S/4HANA

3.2 The SAP S/4HANA Product Family

For more information on product innovations in the individual business areas, see Section 3.3.

SAP S/4HANA is supplemented by functions from so-called *compatibility packages* (see Figure 3.6).

Compatibility packages

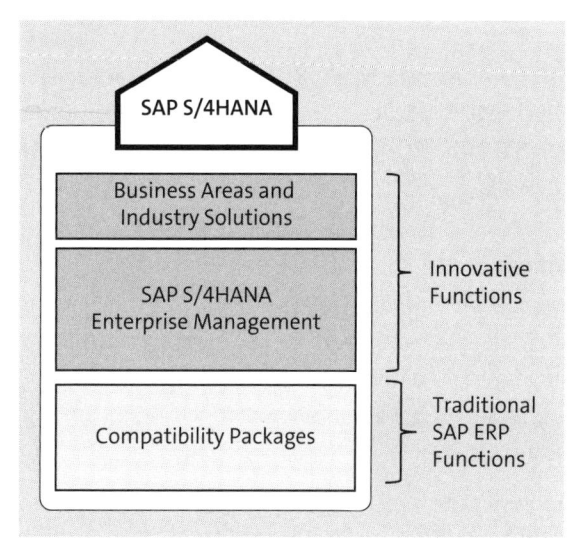

Figure 3.6 SAP S/4HANA Compatibility Packages

Compatibility packages provide functions with the traditional design you are familiar with from SAP ERP—functions, for example, for human capital management (SAP ERP HCM), for warehouse management (SAP ERP WM), or for transport management (LE-TRA). After migrating to SAP S/4HANA, these functions are still available in the same format (for example, the data model is not adapted, and the user interfaces also remain the same). However, these functions are not the target architectures from the technological perspective. For example, the target architecture for human capital management is SAP SuccessFactors; for warehouse management, SAP Extended Warehouse Management (SAP EWM); and for transport management, SAP Transportation Management (SAP TM). Consequently, compatibility packages provide functions that give you the option of continuing to use traditional functions to map these specific business requirements after you migrate to SAP S/4HANA.

3   Cloud, On-Premise, and Hybrid Scenarios

> **Gradual Migration to the Target Architecture**
>
> Compatibility packages enable you to choose whether you want to migrate directly to the target architecture in these subareas or whether you'd rather continue using the traditional functions.

Useful life   The useful life of the functions covered by the compatibility packages is restricted. Up to the end of 2025, you can continue to use these functions in the traditional format. After 2025, the license for their usage in SAP S/4HANA will no longer be valid.

SAP S/4HANA Central Finance

For distributed system landscapes   SAP S/4HANA Central Finance is a variant of SAP S/4HANA. In this variant, customers can connect their distributed system landscapes to a central SAP S/4HANA Finance system. Figure 3.7 demonstrates an example of a combination of SAP and non-SAP systems in which financial documents are replicated in SAP S/4HANA Central Finance.

> **More Information on SAP S/4HANA, On-Premise, Editions**
>
> For further information on SAP S/4HANA Finance, see SAP Help at *https://help.sap.com/sfin*. The "SAP S/4HANA Compatibility Scope Matrix," attached to SAP Note 2269324, lists the functions mapped by compatibility packages.
>
> For more details on SAP S/4HANA Central Finance, see SAP Notes 2148893 (Central Finance: Implementation and Configuration) and 2154420 (SAP Landscape Transformation Replication Server for Central Finance).

Postings from FI and CO are submitted from existing operational source systems to the complementary Central Finance system. The *SAP Landscape Transformation Replication Server (SAP SLT Replication Server)* is responsible for replicating the actual data from the decentralized source systems to the Central Finance system after the data has been initially exchanged. Optionally, a central master data system (e.g., SAP Master Data Governance (SAP MDG)) can ensure the relevant financial master data is distributed.

3.2 The SAP S/4HANA Product Family

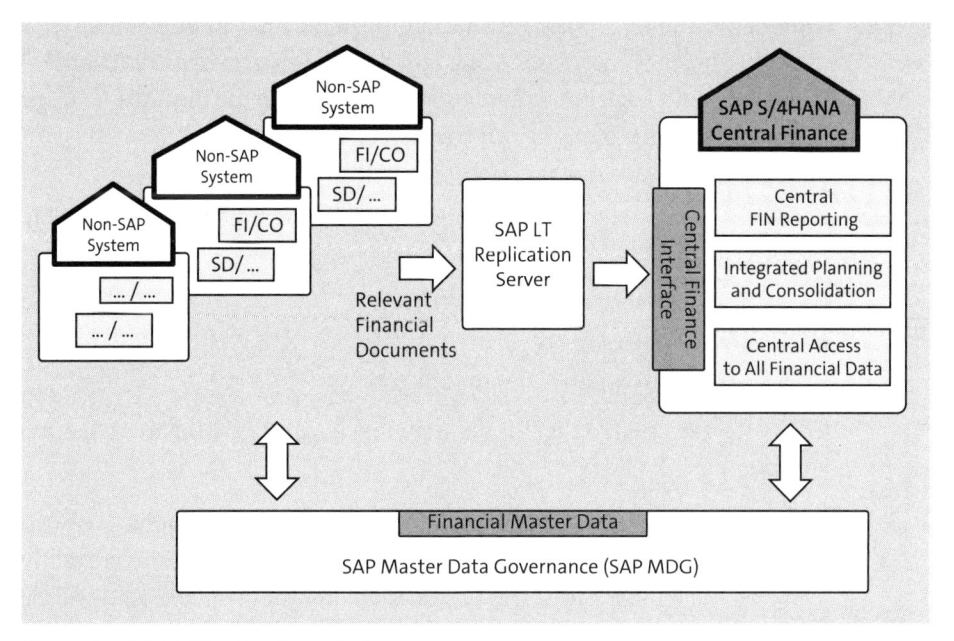

Figure 3.7 SAP S/4HANA Central Finance

3.2.2 SAP S/4HANA Cloud

In SAP S/4HANA Cloud, SAP operates and maintains the software. Customers access their SAP S/4HANA Cloud systems from any network with Internet access using a browser and a unique, customer-specific URL. Multiple types of end devices are supported.

Sophisticated security procedures such as the *Transport Layer Security* (TLS) encryption procedure secure the communications between customers and the SAP S/4HANA Cloud system. In addition to this technical procedure, the following security and quality principles apply to SAP S/4HANA Cloud:

- Business data is stored in data centers according to the highest security standards.
- Customers may share physical hardware, but their data is always stored separately.
- Users requiring access to business data have to authenticate themselves, and their identity needs to be verified by user and access management.
- Customers always remain the owners of their respective customer data.

Security

3   Cloud, On-Premise, and Hybrid Scenarios

Implementation   After deploying an SAP S/4HANA Cloud system, you can implement your necessary business processes using the *SAP S/4HANA Guided Configuration* to guide you through implementation. Then, you can use the SAP S/4HANA migration cockpit to migrate the necessary data from your legacy system to the SAP S/4HANA Cloud system.

Available editions   Currently, four public cloud editions with differing functions are available for SAP S/4HANA:

- SAP S/4HANA Professional Services Cloud
- SAP S/4HANA Finance Cloud
- SAP S/4HANA Enterprise Management Cloud
- SAP Hybris Marketing Cloud (previously, SAP S/4HANA Marketing Cloud)

You can integrate these cloud editions with other SAP cloud solutions such as SAP Ariba or SAP SuccessFactors. Figure 3.8 shows the editions currently available, including *SAP S/4HANA Manufacturing Cloud*, and that will be introduced soon. For more information on planned functions, refer to the SAP S/4HANA Cloud roadmap.

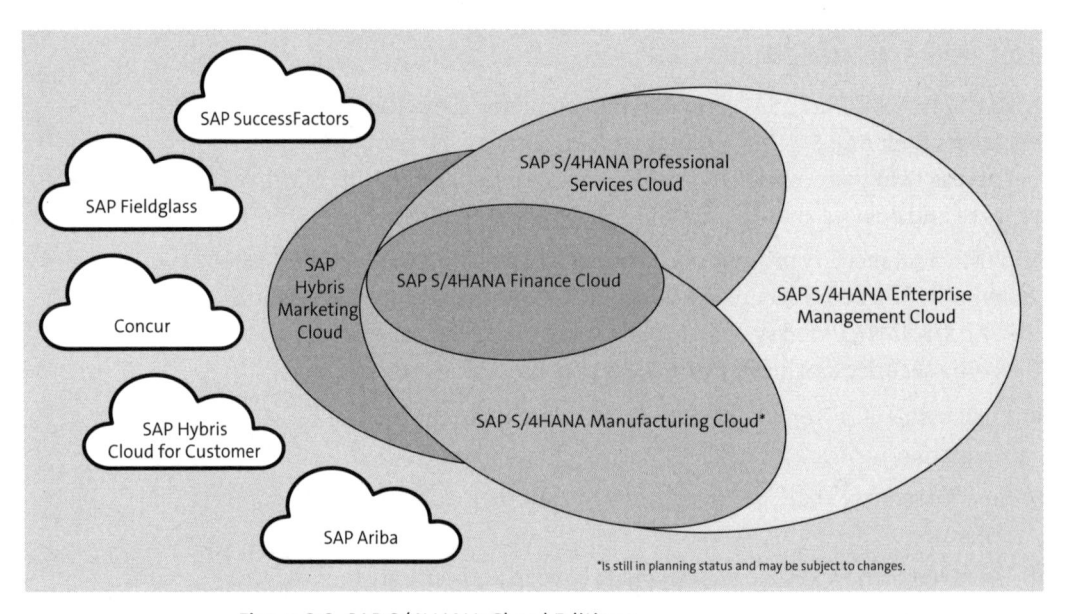

Figure 3.8 SAP S/4HANA Cloud Editions

SAP S/4HANA Professional Services Cloud

SAP S/4HANA Professional Services Cloud is a public cloud edition that maps project management functions. SAP S/4HANA Professional Services Cloud allows you to manage both internal projects and customer projects. The projects are integrated with order handling, project billing, and accounting, thus fulfilling end-to-end process scenarios.

Project management

Innovations in SAP S/4HANA Professional Services Cloud include the following examples:

Product innovations

- **Resource management**
  Integration of internal and external resources for project staffing
- **Project analyses**
  Analysis of the profitability of projects based on costs and revenues
- **Project purchasing**
  Project-related purchasing
- **Integration with other SAP solutions**
  Integration with various SAP and non-SAP systems, for example, a native integration with SAP SuccessFactors Employee Central, SAP Jam, and SAP Ariba is possible.

At the time of this writing, SAP S/4HANA Professional Services Cloud 1611 is the latest version.

Latest available versions

SAP S/4HANA Finance Cloud

SAP S/4HANA Finance Cloud is a public cloud edition that focuses on business processes in accounting. SAP S/4HANA Finance Cloud integrates internal sales and purchasing processes with accounting and supports business processes with connections to SAP SuccessFactors and SAP Ariba.

Accounting

Innovations in SAP S/4HANA Finance Cloud include the following examples:

Product innovations

- **Principle of a one-tier system**
  A shared Universal Journal for FI and CO postings optimizes business processes.
- **Optimization of financial closings**
  A *soft financial close* allows you to simulate period-end or year-end closings at any time, which helps ensure transparency during the current business year.

- **Integration with SAP SuccessFactors**
  Integration with the SAP SuccessFactors HCM Suite links the accounting processes to innovative HR processes.

At the time of this writing, the latest version was SAP S/4HANA Finance Cloud 1611.

SAP S/4HANA Enterprise Management Cloud

All business processes
SAP S/4HANA Enterprise Management Cloud is a public cloud edition that enables you to map all business processes of an enterprise (i.e., sales, manufacturing, and purchasing), as well as financial functions, in the cloud. You can implement the following end-to-end processes with SAP S/4HANA Enterprise Management Cloud:

- Project management
- Planning and procurement
- Order handling
- Period-end closing
- Invoice processing
- Payment processing
- Profitability and cost analysis

Thus, SAP S/4HANA Enterprise Management Cloud is the most comprehensive edition of SAP S/4HANA in the cloud. Consequently, you can also integrate your business processes with SAP SuccessFactors, SAP Ariba, SAP Fieldglass, SAP Hybris, and Concur in this edition. At the time of writing, the latest version was SAP S/4HANA Enterprise Management Cloud 1611.

SAP Hybris Marketing Cloud

Marketing
Until SAP S/4HANA 1611, SAP Hybris Marketing Cloud was called the *SAP S/4HANA Marketing Cloud*. A public cloud edition that focuses on marketing functions, SAP Hybris Marketing Cloud is designed for SAP customers who want to map campaigns or customer analyses in real time using a cloud-based software solution.

You can integrate SAP Hybris Marketing Cloud with other SAP S/4HANA solutions or operate it as a standalone solution.

Among others, SAP Hybris Marketing Cloud provides the following product innovations:

Product innovations

- **Customer analyses in real time**
  Based on the system's real-time data, smart analyses can be generated for your decision-making processes, including predictive analyses of customer behavior or trend analyses. Web analyses examine customer behavior when navigating websites in real time.

- **Personalized customer experience**
  You can selectively approach customer groups via traditional sales channels or online and target them with personalized product offers and recommendations.

- **Flexible marketing**
  You can control marketing activities from planning and budgeting to coordination and implementation as well as develop marketing plans with budget management and cost monitoring in real time.

- **Integration with other SAP solutions**
  You can integrate SAP Hybris Marketing Cloud with various SAP and non-SAP systems. SAP Best Practices for integration are also available (for example, to exchange cost data between SAP ERP and SAP Hybris Marketing Cloud).

At the time of this writing, the latest version was SAP S/4HANA Marketing Cloud 1611. As of version 1702, the name changes to SAP Hybris Marketing Cloud.

> **Additional Information**
>
> More information on the SAP S/4HANA Cloud editions is available at *http://help.sap.com/s4hana*. You can find the roadmap for SAP S/4HANA Cloud at *www.sap.com/s4roadmap-cloud*.

3.2.3 SAP HANA Enterprise Cloud

Another variant is to deploy SAP S/4HANA as a *managed cloud solution*, that is, as a hosted service, in SAP HANA Enterprise Cloud (SAP HEC). In this variant of the private cloud deployment model, customers can individually choose between infrastructure and application management services.

Managed cloud

Depending on the scope of the selected services, a managed cloud, an *IaaS* offering, can operate more like an on-premise operating system or can operate more in the cloud.

In this context, SAP HEC supplements the SAP S/4HANA editions and links infrastructure services and application services. Customers can either solely use the cloud infrastructure or additionally outsource the operation and maintenance of the SAP S/4HANA software. You can use all functions of the SAP S/4HANA, on-premise, with this operating variant.

Application management services

Customers can also flexibly select the application management services provided by SAP HEC. For example, 24/7 service desk operations, internal notification processing, transportation tasks (e.g., implementing SAP Notes), job management, authorization management, print management, or interface administration can be outsourced to service providers. SAP HEC is not only provided by SAP but is also available from selected service partners, such as IBM or Hewlett Packard Enterprise.

SAP S/4HANA Enterprise Management Cloud (Private Option)

Private cloud option

The private cloud option for SAP S/4HANA Enterprise Management Cloud is a variant that meets specific enhancement and security requirements. For example, customers are provided with private cloud enhancement options that go beyond the scope of the options of the public cloud editions. Customers have dedicated systems and do not share system resources. In this cloud edition, customers can also better influence the frequency of software and content updates and have them implemented only once a year, for example. With regard to functions and supported country versions, the private option for SAP S/4HANA Enterprise Management Cloud corresponds to the SAP S/4HANA, on-premise.

> **Additional Information**
>
> For more information on SAP HANA Enterprise Cloud, go to *https://www.sap.com/products/hana-enterprise-cloud.html*. A list of external service partners who operate SAP HANA Enterprise Cloud is available as well.
>
> For more information on the application management services, go to *https://www.sap.com/germany/services/application-management.html*.

3.3 Comparing the Operating Models

This section describes the individual characteristics of the respective operating models in detail and compares how the corresponding editions of the SAP S/4HANA product family meet these criteria.

3.3.1 Hardware, Software, Operation, and Maintenance

The most obvious difference between the on-premise and cloud editions is the fact that you operate, maintain, and manage the SAP S/4HANA, on-premise, editions yourself, while SAP carries out these tasks in the public cloud editions. Public cloud editions are available as SaaS operating models. All SAP S/4HANA Cloud editions are operated at different data centers located in various countries and regions around the world.

Operation

Table 3.1 lists the differences in detail.

SAP S/4HANA, On-Premise	SAP S/4HANA Cloud	
■ The customer owns and maintains the hardware. ■ The customer is responsible for installing, operating, maintaining, and managing the applications.	■ SAP or selected service partners provide the hardware and infrastructure. ■ Depending on the service level agreement, the customer and SAP or selected service partners install the applications. ■ Depending on the service level agreement, the customer and SAP or selected service partners operate and maintain the applications.	Private Cloud: SAP S/4HANA Enterprise Management Cloud (Private Option)

Table 3.1 Overview of Hardware, Software, Operation, and Maintenance of the SAP S/4HANA Editions

3   Cloud, On-Premise, and Hybrid Scenarios

SAP S/4HANA, On-Premise	SAP S/4HANA Cloud	
	<ul><li>Hardware and infrastructure are located at SAP.</li><li>When the system is handed over, the applications are fully installed.</li><li>SAP operates, maintains, and manages the applications.</li></ul>	**Public Cloud:** SAP S/4HANA Professional Services Cloud/ Finance Cloud/ Enterprise Management Cloud/SAP Hybris Marketing Cloud

Table 3.1 Overview of Hardware, Software, Operation, and Maintenance of the SAP S/4HANA Editions (Cont.)

Hardware in the public cloud

For each public cloud edition, the hardware can be obtained in different packages, depending on the number of users and the required size of the SAP HANA database storage. For example, customers can choose from four SAP HANA database storage packages: from 512 gigabytes up to 2048 gigabytes. When the cloud system is handed over, the applications are fully installed. For the public cloud editions, SAP is responsible for operating, monitoring, and maintaining the system (implementing enhancements and upgrades).

Maintenance cycles in the public cloud

The maintenance cycles are set as follows:

- **Hotfix collection**
  A hotfix collection is implemented every two weeks.

- **Release upgrade**
  Upgrades to the next SAP S/4HANA Cloud release are implemented quarterly. Upgrades contain new functions as well as hotfix collections.

- **Emergency patch**
  Critical corrections for a specific customer system, if required, are implemented as soon as possible.

Differences in the managed private cloud

In the managed private cloud, customers can customize the scope of the required hardware and the supported services to a large extent. For the hardware, you can choose between a two-tier or three-tier landscape (public cloud editions consist of a two-tier system landscape). From the services available, you can choose implementation services (requirements analysis, implementation, data migration, go live) and operation services (incident, problem, and change management and application monitoring). Similar to SAP HEC, customers have influence in when maintenance cycles are scheduled for SAP S/4HANA Enterprise Management Cloud (Private Option).

> **Additional Information**
>
> You can find further information on this topic in the SAP Agreements at *https://www.sap.com/about/agreements.sap-cloud-services-customers.html*.

3.3.2 User Interfaces

In all SAP S/4HANA editions, the role-based approach of SAP Fiori is the basic target UI technology. Thus, the public cloud editions are completely designed for this target architecture. In individual cases, public clouds also use other web-based SAP technologies, such as Web Dynpro, in addition to SAP Fiori. In the on-premise edition and the private cloud edition, you can also use SAP GUI for Windows in addition to the web-based UI technologies (see Table 3.2). SAP GUI-based transactions that can no longer be executed in SAP S/4HANA, on-premise, are included in the simplification list for SAP S/4HANA (see Chapter 10, Section 10.2.2). You should use the SAP Fiori launchpad as the central entry platform for end users in all SAP S/4HANA editions.

UI technology

SAP S/4HANA, On-Premise	SAP S/4HANA Cloud	
■ Web technologies ■ SAP GUI for Windows	■ Web ■ SAP GUI for Windows	Private Cloud: SAP S/4HANA Enterprise Management Cloud (Private Option)
	■ Web	Public Cloud: SAP S/4HANA Professional Services Cloud/Finance Cloud/Enterprise Management Cloud/SAP Hybris Marketing Cloud

Table 3.2 The UI Technologies of the SAP S/4HANA Editions

> **Gradual Migration to the SAP Fiori Target Architecture**
>
> Because traditional user interfaces are still supported, gradual migration to SAP S/4HANA is feasible.

3.3.3 Functional Scope and Supported Country Versions

The on-premise and public cloud editions of SAP S/4HANA are based on the same program code line. Consequently, the same data models and product innovations are available. However, the editions vary with regard to their functional scope, the supported country versions, and the options for customizing the business processes (see Table 3.3).

SAP S/4HANA, On-Premise	SAP S/4HANA Cloud	
<ul><li>Scope of SAP S/4HANA 1610</li><li>63 countries with SAP Standard localization</li><li>Process flexibility according to on-premise configuration options</li></ul>	<ul><li>Scope of SAP S/4HANA 1610</li><li>63 countries with SAP Standard localization</li><li>Process flexibility according to on-premise configuration options</li></ul>	Private Cloud: SAP S/4HANA Enterprise Management Cloud (Private Option)
	<ul><li>Scope of SAP S/4HANA Cloud 1611</li><li>14 countries with SAP Standard localization</li><li>Process flexibility according to cloud scenarios and the guided configuration approach of the public cloud</li></ul>	Public Cloud: SAP S/4HANA Professional Services Cloud/ Finance Cloud/ Enterprise Management Cloud/ SAP Hybris Marketing Cloud

Table 3.3 The Functional Scope and Supported Country Versions of the SAP S/4HANA Editions

On-premise and private cloud
The on-premise versions and the private cloud edition have the same business functions and support the same country versions. The complete

functional ERP scope is supported in 63 countries with the standard SAP localization. To adapt these SAP S/4HANA editions to your specific requirements, all the traditional configuration options are still available in the Implementation Guide (IMG).

The functional ERP scope provided in the public cloud editions is smaller than the function scope of the on-premise edition. For example, compatibility packages (see Section 3.2.1) are not available in the public cloud editions. The supported functional scope is based on the best practices content of the corresponding public cloud edition, which has been deployed as preconfigured. At present, the 4 public cloud editions of SAP S/4HANA support up to 19 countries with SAP standard localization. Table 3.4 lists the supported country versions for SAP S/4HANA Cloud 1611.

Public cloud

SAP S/4HANA Enterprise Management Cloud	SAP S/4HANA Finance Cloud	SAP S/4HANA Professional Services Cloud	SAP Hybris Marketing Cloud
14 countries: Australia, Belgium, Canada, China, France, Germany, Great Britain, Hungary, Japan, Netherlands, Philippines, Singapore, Switzerland, USA		19 countries: The 14 countries listed on the left plus Brazil, Hong Kong, Luxembourg, Singapore, United Arab Emirates	International
10 languages English, German, French, Spanish, Japanese, Russian, Portuguese, Chinese (Simplified), Dutch, Hungarian			

Table 3.4 Supported Country Versions in the Four Public Cloud Editions (as of SAP S/4HANA Cloud 1611)

Additional Information

For more details on the functional scope and supported country versions, see **Feature Scope Description** in SAP Help (*http://help.sap.com/s4hana*) and the globalization area (*http://service.sap.com/globalization*).

3 Cloud, On-Premise, and Hybrid Scenarios

3.3.4 Options for Enhancement

Cloud editions

Basically, you can use the key-user enhancement tools and enhancement options, which are based on SAP Cloud Platform, in all editions of the SAP S/4HANA product family (see Table 3.5). In SAP S/4HANA Enterprise Management Cloud (Private Option), you can additionally carry out further adaptations through ABAP programming. With these adaptations, modification-free enhancements are possible, which can be used for Business Add-Ins (BAdIs) and user exits.

On-premise editions

You can also modify SAP objects in the on-premise editions, but we don't recommend doing this considering the increasing costs for future release changes. Section 3.4 describes the SAP S/4HANA enhancement options in detail.

SAP S/4HANA, On-Premise	SAP S/4HANA Cloud	
<ul><li>Traditional enhancement options through ABAP programming</li><li>Usage of the key-user enhancement tools for S/4HANA</li><li>Enhancements based on SAP Cloud Platform</li></ul>	<ul><li>Selected enhancement options through ABAP programming</li><li>Usage of the key-user enhancement tools for S/4HANA</li><li>Enhancements based on SAP Cloud Platform</li></ul>	**Private Cloud:** SAP S/4HANA Enterprise Management Cloud (Private Option)
	<ul><li>Usage of the key-user enhancement tools for S/4HANA</li><li>Enhancements based on SAP Cloud Platform</li></ul>	**Public Cloud:** SAP S/4HANA Professional Services Cloud/ Finance Cloud/Enterprise Management Cloud/SAP Hybris Marketing Cloud

Table 3.5 The Enhancement Options for the SAP S/4HANA Editions

3.3.5 Payment Model and Runtime

Variants of SAP S/4HANA, on-premise, still offer the traditional license and maintenance model, while the public cloud editions are provided via a cloud subscription model with flexible runtimes (see Table 3.6). The actual

3.3 Comparing the Operating Models

costs for the subscription model depend on the number of users, the application scope used, and the hardware packages selected.

SAP S/4HANA, On-Premise	SAP S/4HANA Cloud	
▪ License and maintenance fee	▪ Flexible model (license and maintenance fee or subscription) ▪ Customers can contribute existing SAP licenses	Private Cloud: SAP S/4HANA Enterprise Management Cloud (Private Option)
	▪ Subscription with flexible runtimes	Public Cloud: SAP S/4HANA Professional Services Cloud/Finance Cloud/Enterprise Management Cloud/SAP Hybris Marketing Cloud

Table 3.6 The Payment Models and Runtimes of the SAP S/4HANA Editions

3.3.6 Model for Migration to SAP S/4HANA

With SAP S/4HANA, on-premise, customers can choose either the brownfield approach or the greenfield approach. In other words, you can either convert an existing SAP ERP system into an SAP S/4HANA system or install a completely new SAP S/4HANA system.

Brownfield or greenfield approach

Migrating to SAP S/4HANA Cloud always entails a new installation of the system. The business processes supported in SAP S/4HANA Cloud are implemented according to best practices, and the required master and document data is transferred to the cloud system (see Table 3.7).

SAP S/4HANA, On-Premise	SAP S/4HANA Cloud	
▪ Brownfield or greenfield approach	▪ New installation with subsequent data migration	Private Cloud: SAP S/4HANA Enterprise Management Cloud (Private Option)

Table 3.7 The Migration Scenarios for the SAP S/4HANA Editions

SAP S/4HANA, On-Premise	SAP S/4HANA Cloud
	Public Cloud: SAP S/4HANA Professional Services Cloud/Finance Cloud/Enterprise Management Cloud/SAP Hybris Marketing Cloud

Table 3.7 The Migration Scenarios for the SAP S/4HANA Editions (Cont.)

For more information on new implementations or on converting single systems, see Part II and Part III of this book.

3.4 Extensibility in SAP S/4HANA

Every enterprise is unique, not just in the specifications for its products or services, but in its employees, its goals, and thus its business process structures. In the ideal case, business software supports such uniqueness and the resulting differences because these details differentiate the enterprise from its competitors.

Previous SAP enhancement options

To date, SAP has supported differentiation to the greatest extent possible with its software: SAP provided released interfaces and disclosed the source code of the entire application. Moreover, SAP offered SAP NetWeaver Application Server ABAP, which is a development environment in the application system. SAP provided several options for integration with other applications, for example, using SAP Process Orchestration (PO). With this portfolio, SAP has created an optimally customizable solution with scalable enhancement options. Third-party providers also appreciate this extensibility and can deliver supplementary functions for standard SAP solutions. When planning your migration to SAP S/4HANA, you should always pay attention to the solution's extensibility.

Extensibility put to test

In SAP S/4HANA, SAP has emphasized this extensibility, which has been adapted according to SAP's simplification philosophy for products. Particular attention was paid to allowing customization without comprehensive programming knowledge but also provide the flexibility required for significant enhancements. In SAP S/4HANA, these concepts were improved. Doing so, disadvantages coming from extending the standard software to individual requirements are minimized. In the past, the high degree of flexibility in SAP ERP could lead to risks that had to be considered individually in each specific case: Comprehensive enhancements entailed projects involving several parties within the enterprise and sometimes implementation partners as well. This, an enhancement could take some time before it could actually be used. When enhancements were implemented, the next risk was in the operation of the software: During the lifecycle of the software, hotfixes and planned updates to the default software are usually installed. Testing modified and custom developments in this constantly updating software lifecycle can involve a great deal of effort.

Consequently, the extensibility in SAP S/4HANA has been adapted to accelerate the implementation of enhancements and reduce the costs of these enhancements. In particular, modifying the default SAP code can be avoided in most cases. For this purpose, SAP S/4HANA provides tool-based enhancement options in the applications themselves, as well as platform-based enhancement options outside the software product. These functions support the following characteristics:

New extensibility concepts

- **Scaled extensibility**
  The default software can be customized at various levels. For example, end users can personalize their user interfaces and implement their own (restricted) enhancements. Selected experts can be authorized to implement further enhancements that affect the processes of multiple users. At the top level, you can customize the entire application in an implementation project.

- **Scaled lifecycle**
  You can loosely couple enhancements. While enhancements can exchange data with SAP S/4HANA and are merged on the user interface, they can also perform independent software maintenance cycles.

- **Openness**
  SAP S/4HANA includes a vast array of open interfaces, so partners can implement existing enhancements or offer their own enhancements.

Extensibility of SAP S/4HANA
You can customize SAP S/4HANA using various enhancement procedures.

3   Cloud, On-Premise, and Hybrid Scenarios

To implement this extensibility, SAP follows two approaches:

- *Side-by-side enhancements*
- *In-app enhancements*

Both approaches complement each other and can be combined. Figure 3.9 compares the two enhancement approaches. These approaches are described in detail in the following sections.

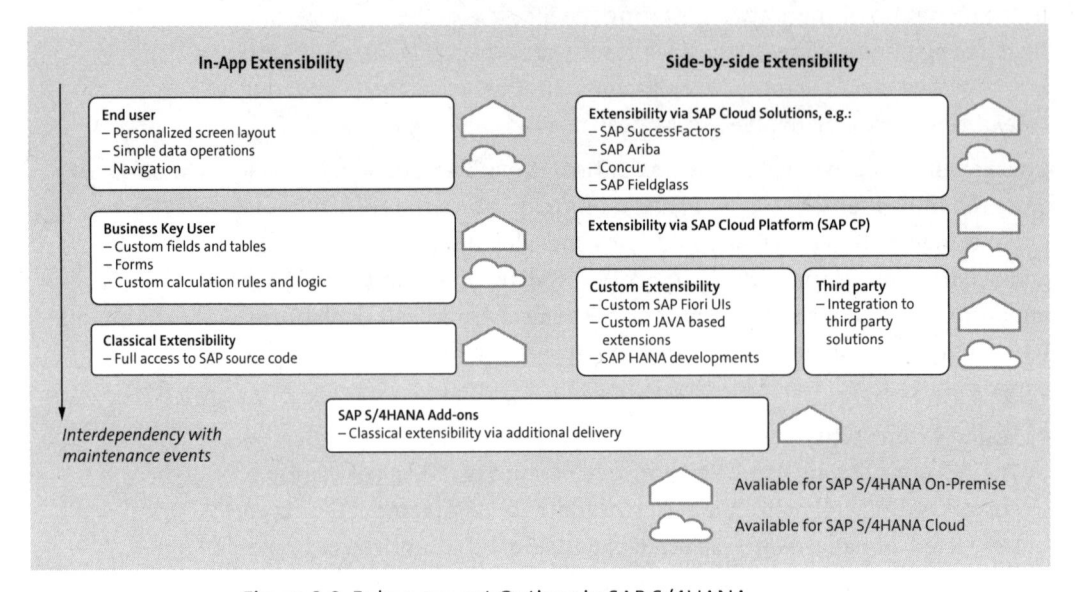

Figure 3.9 Enhancement Options in SAP S/4HANA

The in-app and side-by-side approaches involve various levels. The deeper the level, the greater the impact on the software lifecycle. Not all options are available in all deployment options (see Section 3.3.4).

3.4.1   Side-by-Side Enhancements

SAP Cloud Platform

The characteristic of side-by-side enhancements is that they use *SAP Cloud Platform* (previously, SAP HANA Cloud Platform [SAP HCP]). SAP Cloud Platform is a PaaS solution from SAP. In addition to the SAP HANA database, this solution contains comprehensive tools for developing, testing, integrating, and operating the software. As a PaaS product, the technical operation of SAP Cloud Platform is ensured by SAP, which reduces the workload on the internal IT department. By default, each new release of SAP software is ready for integration with SAP Cloud Platform.

Enhancements on this platform can be carried out using various implementation approaches, such as Java code, HTML5 commands, and SAP HANA database queries. SAP Cloud Platform does not provide an ABAP development environment. Consequently, this enhancement approach is particularly suited to developing custom user interfaces and integrating additional steps into SAP Standard business processes.

> **Side-by-Side Enhancements**
> The enhancement options based on SAP Cloud Platform are ideal for creating custom user interfaces or additional business process steps.

User Interfaces

The SAP Fiori user interfaces are written with HTML5 and are based on central SAP libraries (SAPUI5). The software development process for HTML5 applications differs from the development in ABAP, which is the language used to implement the SAP S/4HANA application logic. Therefore, SAP S/4HANA does not contain a development environment for HTML5. Instead, SAP provides an optimized development environment for SAP Fiori user interfaces via SAP Cloud Platform. In addition to development tools such as an editor, this also includes tools for packaging and deploying the user interfaces developed.

Development environment for SAPUI5

Business Processes

SAP S/4HANA enables you to supplement existing business processes with your own business logic and data. In most cases, you'll only need to adjust the SAP Standard processes to your specific business requirements. In some cases, however, your processes deviate so much from those of your competitors that this deviation can no longer be mapped by in-app enhancements. SAP Cloud Platform is the ideal enhancement solution here, allowing you to build complex custom applications using Java and then integrate them with SAP S/4HANA. Communication with the platform is via web services.

Additional Java applications

3   Cloud, On-Premise, and Hybrid Scenarios

Integration infrastructure

The PaaS solution already contains the required integration infrastructure for both cases: a central integration middleware with SAP HANA Cloud Connector and SAP Gateway for integration with SAP Fiori. Consequently, SAP Cloud Platform is the optimal basis for enhancements—not only for SAP S/4HANA but also for other applications in the landscape.

Released interfaces

Extending SAP S/4HANA via the SAP Cloud Platform uses SAP's APIs (Application Programming Interfaces), including the following:

- New SAP S/4HANA interfaces:
    - REST (Representational State Transfer) web services
    - SOAP (Simple Object Access Protocol) web services
    - OData (Open Data Protocol) web services
- Traditional SAP interfaces
    - Business Application Programming Interfaces (BAPIs)
    - Intermediate Documents (IDocs)

The traditional interfaces are included for compatibility reasons and only released for the enhancement of SAP S/4HANA, on-premise. The number of interfaces released is continuously increasing.

3.4.2   In-App Enhancements

In-app enhancements are striking because of their simplicity: These enhancements are implemented in the same system, connections to other systems are not necessary, and latency is reduced. Furthermore, you can use the existing application as a base and use the powerful ABAP Dictionary, which contains the Core Data Services (CDS), to create table views, for example.

Enhancements without developer knowledge

You don't necessarily require any development know-how for enhancements. The following enhancement options are available to users (with increasing capabilities):

- *End-user extensibility*
- *Key-user extensibility*

The key-user extensibility in particular provides the options shown in Figure 3.10.

3.4 Extensibility in SAP S/4HANA

| Extensions End User A | Extensions End User B | Extensions End User C | Extensions End User D |

| Expert Extensibility |

| (Global) Adaption of UIs | Custom forms | Custom reporting and data analysis |

| Custom fields |

| Custom tables | Custom application logic (code based) |

| Classic extensibility (on-premise only) |

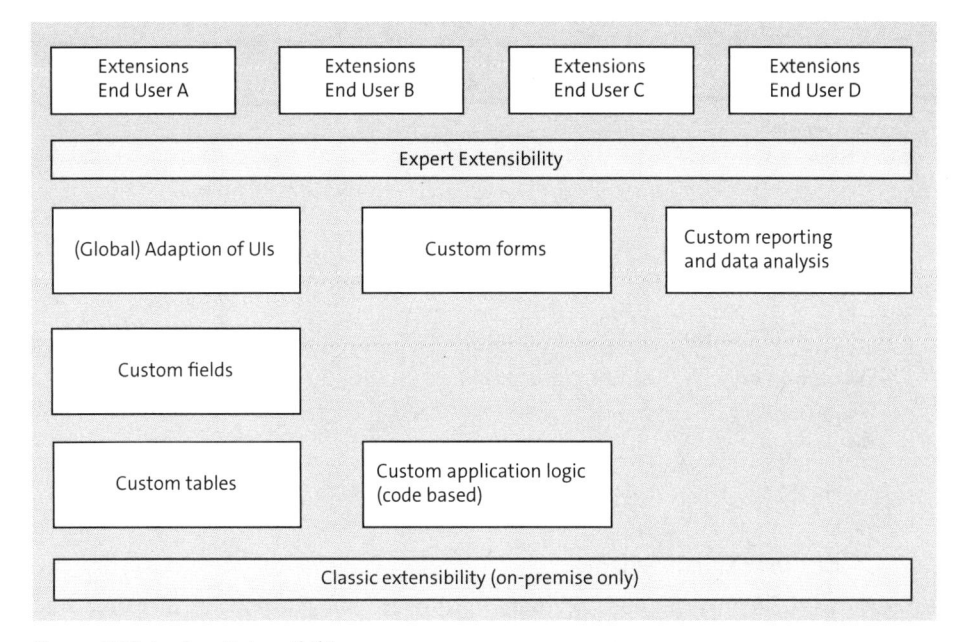

Figure 3.10 In-App Extensibility

Enhancements carried out by central key users impact all users of the system, who can in turn make specific adaptations. The traditional extensibility of the ABAP source code is only available on-premise and is mainly included for compatibility reasons.

End-User Enhancements

End-user enhancements can be implemented directly in SAP Fiori applications. These enhancements are user-specific and do not affect other users of the SAP S/4HANA system. Simple enhancements include customizing screen layouts or selection fields, simple column operations, and basic settings for object-based navigation. These enhancements can only be carried out in specifically prepared applications, and you can access enhancements via the cogwheel icon in the application (see Figure 3.11). You can even customize the cogwheel icon in most SAP Fiori screens.

User-specific customization

3 Cloud, On-Premise, and Hybrid Scenarios

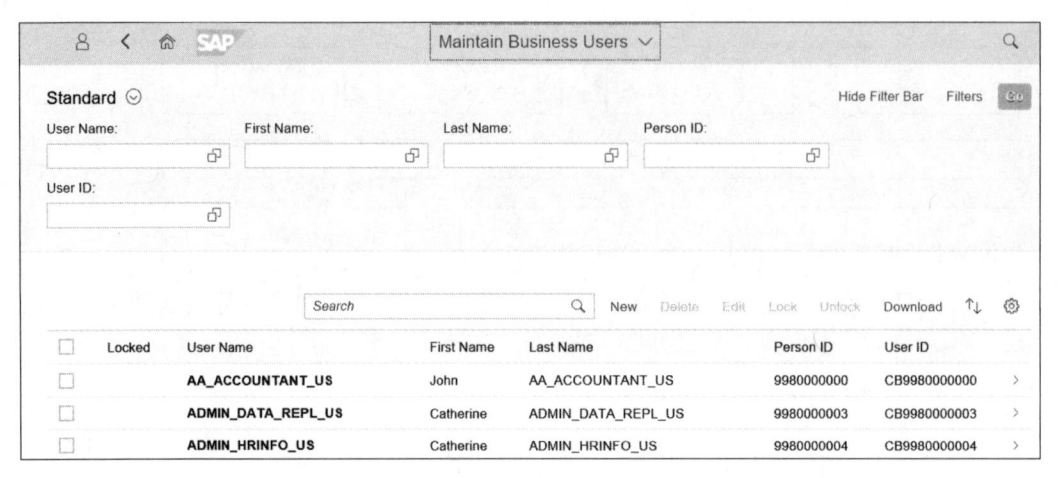

	Locked	User Name	First Name	Last Name	Person ID	User ID	
☐		AA_ACCOUNTANT_US	John	AA_ACCOUNTANT_US	9980000000	CB9980000000	>
☐		ADMIN_DATA_REPL_US	Catherine	ADMIN_DATA_REPL_US	9980000003	CB9980000003	>
☐		ADMIN_HRINFO_US	Catherine	ADMIN_HRINFO_US	9980000004	CB9980000004	>

Figure 3.11 End-User Enhancements for User Interfaces

Key-User Enhancements

Modeling — SAP also provides enhancement options that can partially be implemented using modeling procedures, which is useful when customizing user interfaces or supplementing custom fields or tables. In a new enhancement mode, you only require basic development know-how to modify the calculation logic without directly changing the application code. One of the advantages of this method is that you don't have to adapt enhancements manually when maintaining your SAP software. As a result, operating costs are reduced compared to traditional, code-based enhancements. In contrast to end-user enhancements, key-user enhancements affect all system users. Remember that a specific authorization is required for these key-user enhancement options. This authorization needs to be defined in the application catalog SAP_CORE_BC_EXT and assigned in accordance with the application role.

> **[o] Benefits of Key-User Enhancements**
>
> Key-user enhancements use modeling rules that will not need subsequent adaptations for maintenance operations.

Enhancement options — Key-user enhancement options are selected via SAP Fiori tiles, which are predefined by SAP. Among others, the following options are provided:

- **Customizing user interfaces**
  Similar to end-user customization, you can change the layout of SAP Fiori applications. Examples include hiding fields, renaming identifiers, rearranging blocks, and creating selection variants. These activities do not require any development know-how. To customize a user interface, in the application that you want to change, select the user icon in the upper left of the screen 👤 first. You can then change the user interface using the **Adjust UI** 🔧 icon.

- **Field extensibility**
  In the business contexts provided for that purpose, you can define additional fields for the application to use (see Figure 3.12). Select the **User-defined fields and logic** tile in the **Extensibility** group on SAP Fiori launchpad. These fields are not only displayed on the user interface but can also be stored in the SAP data model and are thus available in the database views, for searches, and for other operations.

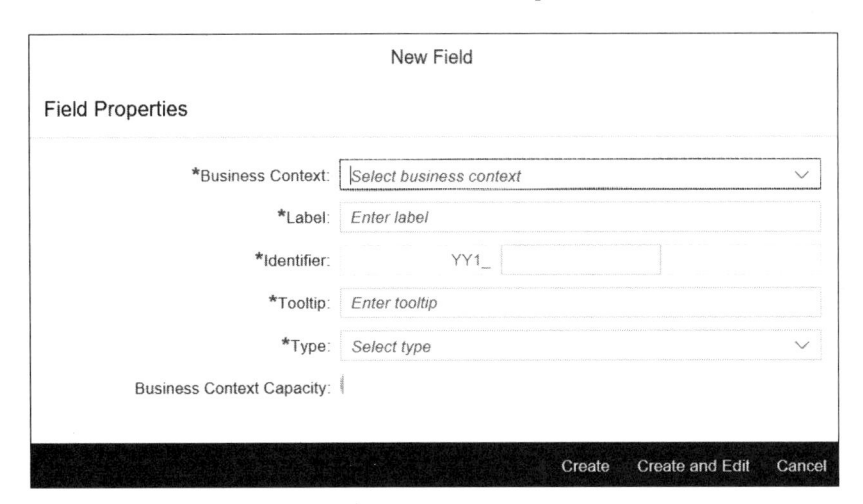

Figure 3.12 Extensibility of Fields

- **Table extensibility**
  Besides new fields, you can also define and use custom tables in SAP S/4HANA. Similar to custom fields, custom tables are created within SAP S/4HANA and integrated into user interfaces. The application then exchanges data with the tables. A custom table is a special kind of user-defined business object.

- **Business objects**
  You can define specific business objects for your enhancements. Business objects are sets of tables between which you define relationships. In addition, you can point an interface to access this newly created business object. Doing so enables you, for example, to access these business objects when specifying calculation logic. To access business objects, select the tile **User-defined business objects** in the **Extensibility** group.

- **Adjusting the calculation logic**
  You may often find it necessary to check the meaning of entered or displayed data, to specify defaults, or to trigger exception handling. Another example of calculation logic adjustments are specific calculation procedures that are not provided in the SAP Standard. In these cases, additional logic can be inserted in the relevant applications. The logic is defined in a code-based implementation via a web editor (see Figure 3.13).

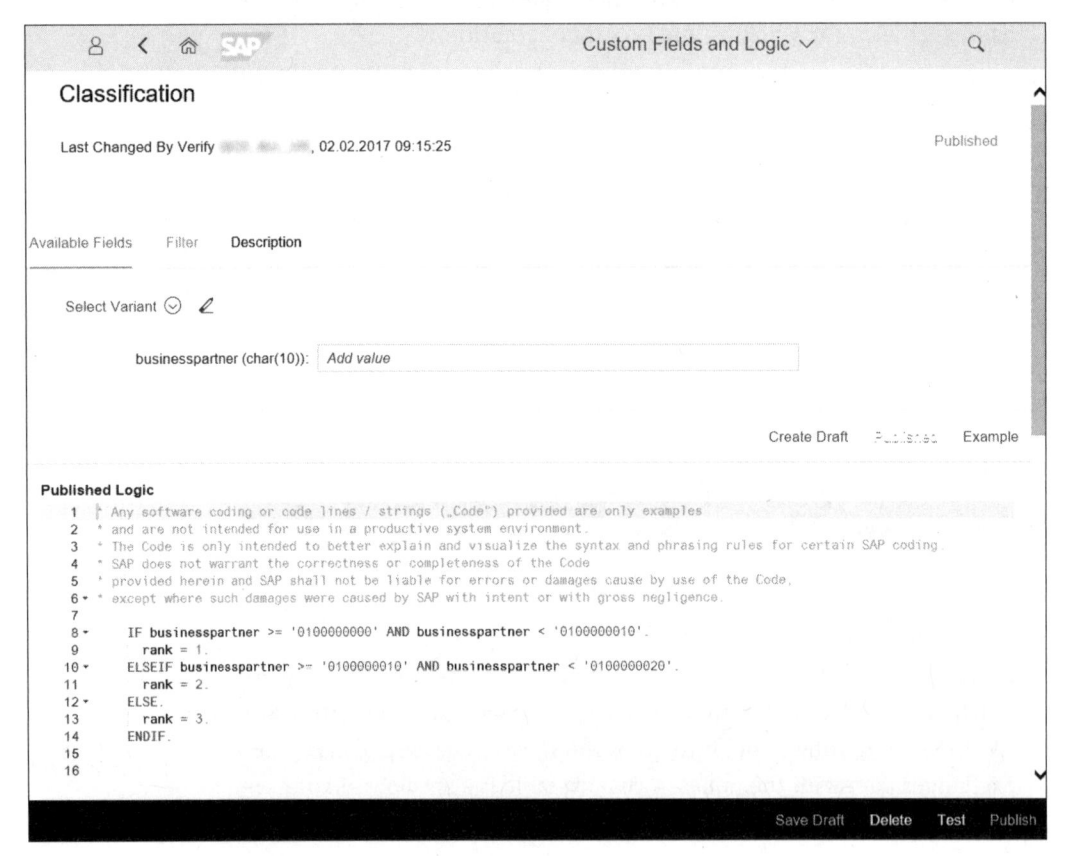

Figure 3.13 User-Defined Fields and Logic

In the editor, the syntax is simplified in comparison to traditional ABAP, so that detailed ABAP know-how is not required. For this adaptation, use the tile **User-defined fields and logic** in the **Extensibility** section. However, you will require some development know-how to do so. Compared to traditional enhancement options, you'll be provided with numerous commands and instructions in this tile. You can also save these enhancements and export them to other systems.

> **[«] Transport of Enhancements**
>
> In general, key-user enhancements should be implemented and tested in a quality assurance system first. To transport verified enhancements to the production system, you can follow this export and import procedure: After developing your enhancement, select the tile **Manage software collections** in the **Extensibility** group. Next, assign your enhancement to a software collection, which you can then export.
>
> Now, in the target system, select the tile **Import software collection** in the **Extensibility** group where can import the previously exported enhancement.
>
> Note that export and import should be carried out by a software logistic administrator, and as a result, this activity requires specific roles with access to the application catalogs SAP_CORE_BC_SL_EXP (for exporting) and SAP_CORE_BC_SL_IMP (for importing).

> **[«] Additional Enhancement Options**
>
> Further options are available in addition to the described enhancement options. For more details, see the section on extensibility in the product documentation at *http://bit.ly/v1448031*.

Traditional Extensibility

In SAP S/4HANA, on-premise, you can still enhance or even modify the ABAP source code using the tools from the traditional SAP Business Suite, such as the ABAP Workbench. While this approach offers the maximum freedom to develop your own custom enhancements, interactions regarding maintenance operations in the system will often be necessary: When

ABAP enhancements

implementing new SAP corrections, you'll always have to adjust your enhancements to the SAP Notes. As a result, you need to install corrections in close cooperation with your development department.

In addition to these more formal enhancement options, SAP S/4HANA also provides comprehensive applications for defining custom data analyses or creating custom forms.

3.4.3 Checking Custom Enhancements When Migrating to SAP S/4HANA

When you plan to migrate to SAP S/4HANA, you should analyze existing adaptations to the current system:

- **End-user customization**
  Individual end-user adaptations are lost when you migrate to SAP S/4HANA. Users will have to then customize the new product again, as described in the previous section.

- **Generic enhancements for all users**
  Generic enhancements that are effective for all system users can be implemented when migrating to the new product. The appropriate procedure for this implementation depends on the operating model selected for SAP S/4HANA. You should generally implement these enhancements using the key-user enhancement options, which will result in fewer follow-up costs and which simplify the maintenance of the enhancements.

If the source system is an SAP source system, you should run SAP's *custom code check* first. This check identifies custom code in the existing system and generates a task list. Chapter 4, Section 4.2.2, and Chapter 10, Section 10.2, discuss this check in detail.

Chapter 4
Preparing the Migration to SAP S/4HANA

This chapter introduces the three migration scenarios covered in this book.

Which steps should you consider when planning your migration project to SAP S/4HANA? How does SAP support you? Can the migration be compared to an upgrade within the SAP ERP product family? This chapter answers these questions. Furthermore, we'll introduce three possible migration scenarios: a new implementation, a system conversion, and a landscape transformation. The last chapter of the book, Chapter 14, then looks back at these scenarios and summarizes their advantages and disadvantages under different conditions.

4.1 Basic Considerations

Migrating to SAP S/4HANA offers many benefits, but to ensure a smooth migration, you must be aware of your specific reasons for migrating. Consequently, you should not plan to migrate to SAP S/4HANA as an update or upgrade of an already implemented solution. The functional and business scope of SAP ERP and SAP S/4HANA are similar, but this migration will introduce a new digital core to your enterprise that ensures future competitiveness.

Upgrade or product implementation?

You should (at least) answer the following questions, which will be discussed in more detail later on in this section:

What needs to be taken into account?

- **Which target status do you want to achieve?**
  What position is SAP S/4HANA supposed to take in your system landscape? Do you want to execute a proof of concept, or do you want to use SAP S/4HANA immediately in production? Can you use the migration as

an opportunity to optimize how your processes are mapped in the enterprise software?

- **Which operating model suits you?**
  Do you want to run SAP S/4HANA at your own data center or through a hosting service? Or, do you want to use SAP S/4HANA as a software-as-a-service model?

- **What is the initial situation?**
  What is the current product version of your source system? What is the quality of the data in your source system? How strictly do you leverage the SAP Standard, and how many custom enhancements exist? Do you want to use a system as a template?

- **Which users do exist?**
  How many users exist, and how are they distributed? Which user groups are expected to benefit from the implementation of SAP S/4HANA?

- **How is the solution to be used?**
  Which business scenarios and transactions are to be used? How are these requirements distributed across your users?

- **What is your defined time frame?**
  Within what period of time is the project supposed to be completed? Which milestones need to be reached and when?

- **Do you need support?**
  What kind of support do you need? What is your budget? Which services do you expect to purchase and which services can be provided in-house?

Preparing for the coming decades

The more aware you are of the significance of SAP's digital core, the more added value SAP S/4HANA can usually generate: The basic concept of SAP S/4HANA is its pledge to prepare enterprises for the challenges of the coming decades. Restricting yourself to a purely technical update of existing systems and landscapes would be an inadequate simplification. You should analyze whether your processes have grown as well as whether your system landscape will be sustainable in the future or whether its structure is obsolete and should thus be adjusted.

Technical and process-oriented parts

Thus, when migrating to SAP S/4HANA, you'll have to consider at least two parts of the implementation: the purely technical part and the process-oriented part (see Figure 4.1).

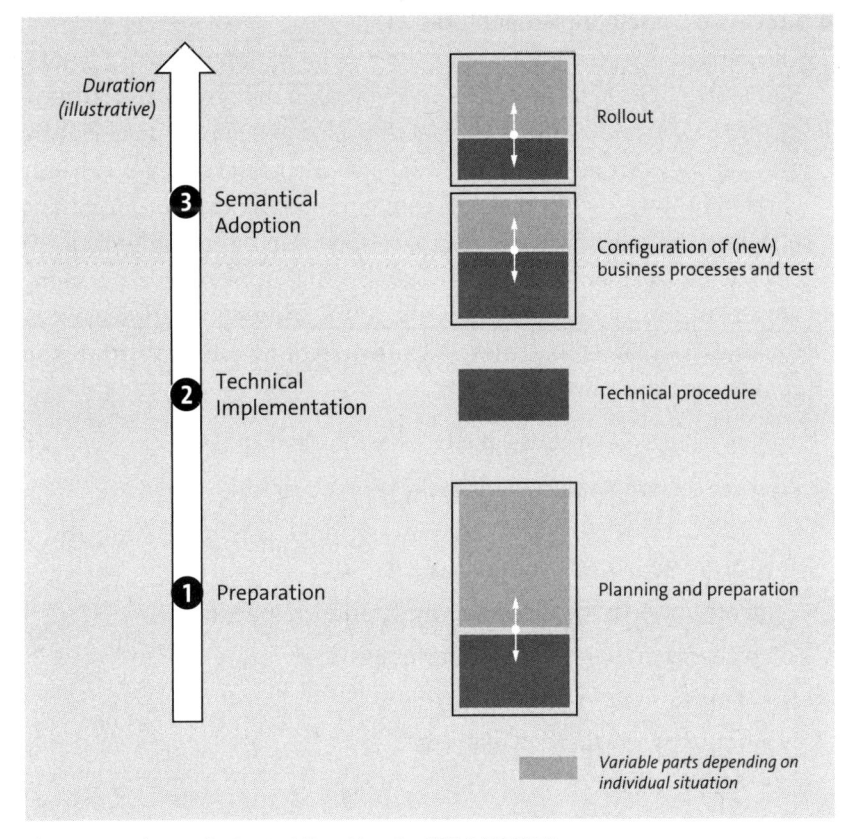

Figure 4.1 The Main Parts Migrating to SAP S/4HANA

- **Technical implementation**
  The technical implementation of a migration mainly includes migrating the database to SAP HANA, replacing the program code, adapting data models to the SAP S/4HANA data model, and implementing the frontend server for SAP Fiori interfaces. Your existing custom code might also have to be technically adapted.

  These activities generally do not depend on the scope of subsequent use in production and can easily be implemented using the relevant tools and can therefore be technically controlled and supported. Thus, SAP provides a comprehensive portfolio of tools for planning and carrying out this technical implementation.

- **Process-oriented implementation**
  The process-oriented implementation of a migration refers to adapting how existing business processes are mapped in the system and to introducing new applications. These modifications to business processes are only partially carried out in the system itself. In most cases, you can only enter indicators, such as changed configuration information. Regarding planning, however, you'll have to perform far more comprehensive change management steps. These steps include, for example, designing your new changed business process, configuring necessary measures, training users, assigning roles and authorizations, pilot operation, and converting the production system.

Tasks in the individual phases

The following tasks can be assigned to these outlined phases:

❶ Preparation (preparatory steps in the source system):
- Analysis of existing business process implementation; comparison with SAP S/4HANA innovations
- Identification of the necessary integration scenarios
- Prechecks in the source system, for example:
  - Functions used
  - Industry-specific enhancements
  - Custom code
  - Third-party enhancements
- Implementation of necessary preparatory conversions in the source system

❷ Technical implementation:
- Installation of SAP S/4HANA
  - SAP HANA database
  - SAP S/4HANA applications
- Adaptation of the technical infrastructure
- Customizing

❸ Process adaptation:
- Adaptation of custom programs in SAP S/4HANA
- Development of new or enhanced business processes to leverage the innovations in SAP S/4HANA

- Adaptation of integration scenarios
- Customization of SAP Fiori interfaces

The time and effort required for the process-oriented implementation—depending on the initial situation and target status—can account for either a small or a large part of the overall process. Thus, we recommend dividing the migration project into the three phases we just described because the process-oriented implementation, in particular the implementation of new business processes, does not have to be carried out in parallel to the technical migration.

> **Process Migration and Technical Migration as Separate Steps**
>
> In general, you can plan the introduction or migration of your business processes independently from the technical migration.

Figure 4.2 shows one possible approach for introducing SAP S/4HANA to your enterprise: In the project, you prepare and implement new functions in batches, while the users continue to use the existing functions.

Parallel project phases

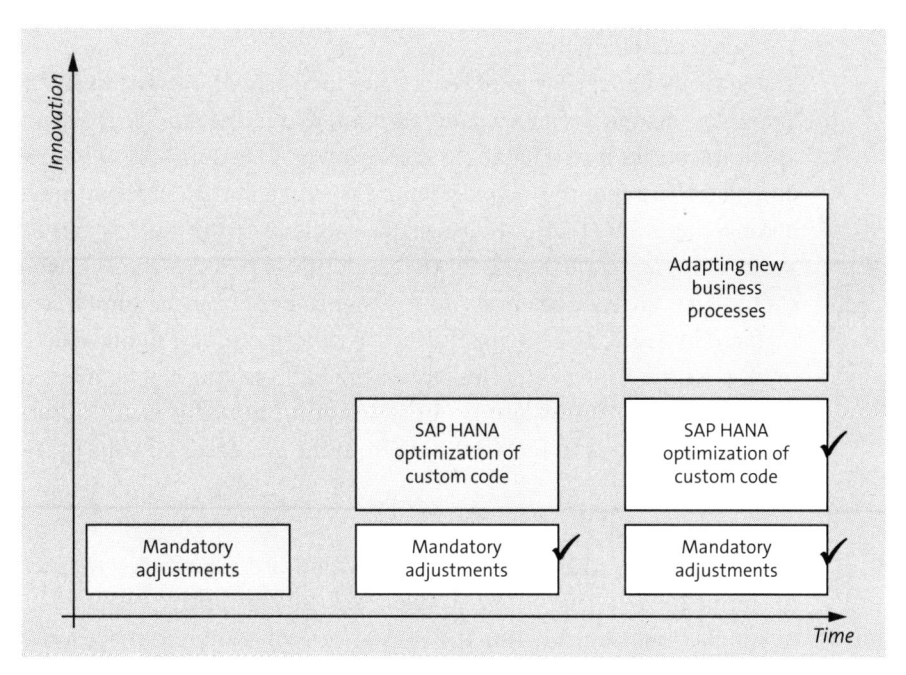

Figure 4.2 Parallel Preparation and Implementation of New Functions

A prerequisite for optimal project planning is knowing the desired target state. While this prerequisite might sound rather trivial at first, SAP S/4HANA migration projects often fail to describe the goal of the migration in detail and rely on vague statements like "implementation of SAP S/4HANA."

Analyzing the trade-off at an early stage

Migrating to SAP S/4HANA has a general trade-off that you should be aware of, in particular if your initial state includes an SAP ERP system or SAP landscape: The more properties of the source system you decide to keep unchanged (e.g., configuration, custom code, or applications), the simpler the (technical part) of the migration project. However, the benefit that can be derived from SAP S/4HANA in this case might also be reduced because the major benefits from SAP S/4HANA are optimized business processes, simplified user interfaces, and greater flexibility for future requirements.

Therefore, you should always analyze this trade-off. Possible analysis criteria include the following:

- **Type of usage**
  Is the target system used for production, or do you want to execute a proof of concept first? In the latter case, you should carry out a greenfield implementation with selective data transfers.

- **Total cost of ownership**
  SAP S/4HANA enables you to reduce the total cost of ownership (TCO). Examples include a reduced *data footprint*, that is, the storage space for application data in the database is reduced (see Section 4.2.2). Another dimension are reduced requirements for your internal IT department because local SAP GUI installations at employee workstations can be avoided. If your explicit goal for the migration is to lower the TCO, you should also analyze where custom enhancements can be omitted or replaced by SAP S/4HANA applications. Furthermore, you should examine the extent to which multiple existing ERP systems can be merged into one SAP S/4HANA system. In addition to the reduced TCO, users benefit from access to real-time data from the systems that were previously separated.

- **Operating model**
  Is SAP S/4HANA to be operated in the cloud or on-premise? The two operating models have different characteristics that need to be analyzed. In simple terms, outsourcing the system administration to the cloud is attractive, especially for standard business processes.

- **Target landscape**

  How is the entire landscape supposed to change? Are systems to be consolidated? Are systems to be separated (e.g., financial accounting and material requirements planning)? How is the existing architecture to be adjusted?

Remember that you usually also have to set up and configure the front-end servers for SAP Fiori, which are required for the new SAP S/4HANA functions.

SAP recommends a methodology with six phases for project planning and implementation: *discover, prepare, explore, realize, deploy,* and *run*. This methodology is called *SAP Activate*, which we'll describe in detail in Chapter 5.

<small>SAP implementation methodology</small>

When referring to migration activities in this book, we assume that you have already opted for SAP S/4HANA. We'll assume the discovery phase—during which enterprise priorities are identified, the target architecture is defined, the business case is optimized, and a readiness check is carried out—has already been successfully completed. Our focus is on the technical implementation of the migration and less on process-oriented implementation. We assume that you have selected and defined the characteristics of the business process scope in a separate business implementation project.

> **Preparation with Trial Access**
>
> If you have not completed the discovery phase yet, you should test an SAP S/4HANA system. For this purpose, SAP provides trial access to a cloud instance of SAP S/4HANA that is only valid for a limited time. For more information on these trial systems, see Chapter 6.

4.2 The Three Migration Scenarios

SAP has defined several technical scenarios for the introduction of SAP S/4HANA and also provides the corresponding tools. When planning the migration, you should select the scenario that meets your individual requirements best. The following sections introduce the individual scenarios and describe the advantages and disadvantages of each approach.

4   Preparing the Migration to SAP S/4HANA

Part III then discusses the different scenarios in detail. Three basic scenarios for the migration to SAP S/4HANA exist (see Figure 4.3):

- New implementation of SAP S/4HANA
- System conversion to SAP S/4HANA
- Landscape transformation with SAP S/4HANA

The landscape transformation also includes the steps of the first two scenarios and complements them to further benefit from SAP S/4HANA.

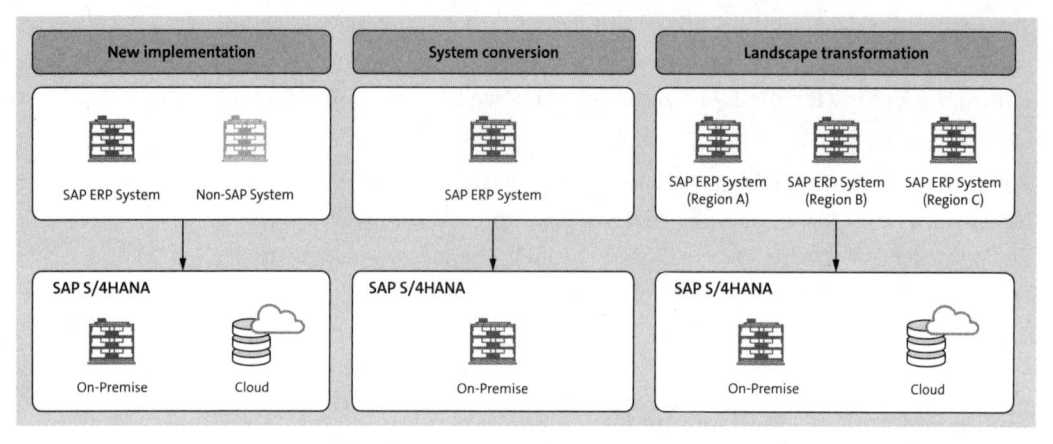

Figure 4.3 The Three Scenarios for the Migration to SAP S/4HANA

Except for the system conversion, all three scenarios allow you to choose whether you want to implement SAP S/4HANA as a software as a service (SaaS) in the cloud or as an on-premise implementation (see Chapter 3, Section 3.1).

4.2.1   New Implementation of SAP S/4HANA

Installing a new system

From the technical perspective, this scenario is based on a completely new installation of SAP S/4HANA. In this scenario, we'll use the *Software Provisioning Manager* (SWPM) to download and set up an SAP S/4HANA system from the available SAP installation media, creating a new system with a new System Identification (SID). In addition to this ABAP instance, a frontend server is also installed, which will be the central hub for operating the SAP Fiori user interface.

4.2 The Three Migration Scenarios

At first, the new system is delivered with a standard configuration. You'll then have to adapt the configuration to meet the requirements of the business processes you want to implement.

Customizing

The new system can be fed data from a source system, using the *SAP S/4HANA migration cockpit*, a tool that has been developed for SAP S/4HANA. Whether the data is from an SAP system or from a non-SAP system does not matter. When the data has been transferred, you can replace the source system with the SAP S/4HANA system (see Figure 4.4).

Data migration

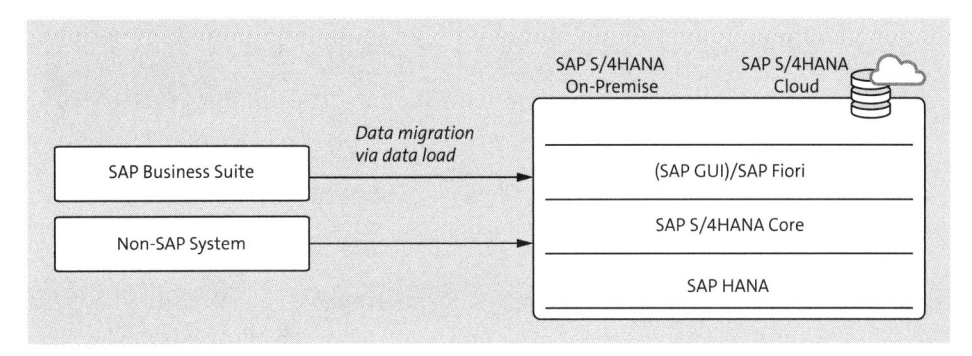

Figure 4.4 New Implementation of SAP S/4HANA

SAP provides predefined models for the data transfer, so-called *migration objects*. These objects regularly get updated or new objects added with new SAP S/4HANA versions. Table 4.1 lists which migration objects are supported at the time of this writing (SAP S/4HANA Cloud 1611 and SAP S/4HANA 1610, on-premise).

Supported migration objects

For more details on using migration objects, see Chapter 7, Section 7.3.1, (for cloud editions) and Chapter 11, Section 11.2 (for on-premise editions).

Supported Migration Objects When Using the Migration Cockpit		
Activity Price	Exchange Rate	Bill of Materials (BOM)
Internal Order	Inventory Balances	Work Center
Profit Center	Material Master	Routing

Table 4.1 Supported Migration Objects for Data Migration Using the SAP S/4HANA Migration Cockpit

Supported Migration Objects When Using the Migration Cockpit		
Bank Master	Material – Long text	Equipment
Customer	Purchasing Info Record	Maintenance Task List
Supplier	Purchase Order	Functional Location
Accounts Receivable (Customer) Open Item	Pricing Condition	Characteristic
Accounts Payable (Vendor) Open Item	Contracts (Purchasing)	Class
Fixed Assets incl. Balances	Source List	Commercial Project Management (CPM)

Table 4.1 Supported Migration Objects for Data Migration Using the SAP S/4HANA Migration Cockpit (Cont.)

Default data fields, the format, and—if available—relationships or references to other business objects are defined for each of the business objects in migration objects.

Following the simplification concept, only the most important data fields of each object are already activated in this predefined content. If needed, you can optionally display additional fields, if available in the SAP Standard. Custom fields (in custom namespaces) can also be supplemented. For on-premise implementations, you would use the SAP Landscape Transformation (LT) Migration Object Modeler (LTMOM) transaction for this purpose; for cloud solutions, please contact the SAP service team.

Overview of the migration project

The selected migration objects are transferred to the project view of the SAP S/4HANA migration cockpit. In the cockpit, at any time during the data transfer, you'll be able to see what object data still has to be loaded and for which objects the migration has been completed.

The source system data is formatted manually as required. If data needs to be cleansed (for example, if duplicates need to be identified and eliminated), you should address these issues before migrating the data. The cleansed data from the source system is stored in a file in a format defined by SAP. The relevant templates are provided by default.

4.2 The Three Migration Scenarios

In the next step, this file is uploaded. Basic inconsistencies in the data that is planned to be imported to the target system or conflicts in the configuration are determined by tools and can be eliminated. Then, the data transfer from the source system is complete. Figure 4.5 illustrates these steps.

Uploading to SAP S/4HANA

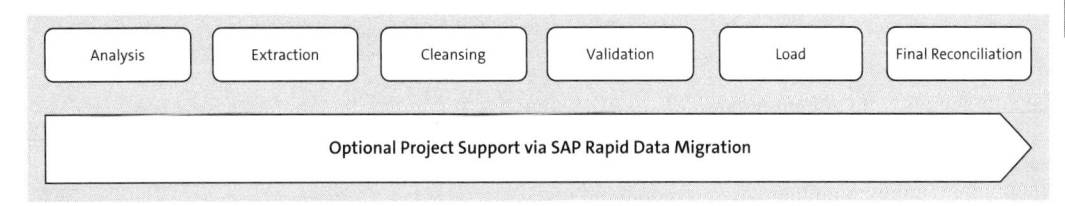

Analysis → Extraction → Cleansing → Validation → Load → Final Reconciliation

Optional Project Support via SAP Rapid Data Migration

Figure 4.5 Steps for the Data Transfer to SAP S/4HANA in the Case of a New Implementation

The result is a system that corresponds to the SAP Standard as much as possible and does not contain any obsolete data. Table 4.2 demonstrates how this procedure focuses on master data and only a small amount of transactional data is transferred.

The SAP S/4HANA migration cockpit replaces the *Legacy System Migration Workbench* (LSMW), which was used in SAP R/3 and SAP ERP systems. SAP S/4HANA no longer supports this tool. LSMW still exists but rarely makes sense to use it and should be used at your own risk.

For the planned new implementation project, which data you want to transfer is decisive: If data objects have requirements that are not part of the content provided, you cannot transfer them with the SAP S/4HANA migration cockpit.

For more specific data transfers, you should use *SAP Data Services*, a tool for extracting and loading data. SAP Data Services is included for all SAP HANA users who have an SAP HANA license. Optionally, SAP offers a license extension for SAP Data Services, which supports modifying and improving data quality and data cleansing. Consisting of a central Data Services server and a local frontend for modeling, SAP Data Services also provides migration content that is more comprehensive than in the SAP S/4HANA migration cockpit (see Table 4.2). However, using SAP Data Services requires more technical effort and key-user know-how than using the SAP S/4HANA migration cockpit.

SAP Data Services

Migration Objects When Using SAP Data Services		
Activity Prices	Fixed Assets	Profit Centers
Activity Type Groups	Functional Location	Purchase Orders*
Activity Types	GL Balances*	Purchasing Info Records
Bank Master	GL Open Items*	Purchasing Requisitions*
Batch	Inspection Methods	Reference Operation Set
Bill of Materials (BOM)	Inspection Plans	Routings
Business Partner	Internal Order*	Sales Orders*
Characteristic Master	Inventory Balance*	Scheduling Agreements*
Class Master	Master Inspection Characteristics	SD Pricing
Configuration Profiles for Material	Material External Customer Replenishment	Secondary Cost Elements
Contracts*	Material Master	Service Master
Cost Center Group	Material Master Classification	Source List
Cost Centers	Material QM Inspection Type	Statistical Key Figures
Credit Memo*	Object Dependency	Supplier Invoice*
Customer Invoice Billing*	Open Deliveries*	Vendor Open Items (AP)*
Customer Open Items (AR)*	Order Reservation*	Work Breakdown Structure
Equipment	Planned Independents Requirements*	Work Centers
Exchange Rates	Profit Center Groups	

The objects marked with * are transactional data; the other objects are master data.

Table 4.2 Supported Migration Objects When Using SAP Data Services

Recall that the migration procedure we described creates a new system with a new SID that contains (selected) data from the source system. In most cases, this new system or the new multi-tier system landscape (involving development, test, and production systems) needs to be integrated into the overall landscape.

Chapter 8 and Chapter 13 provide further information on integration in SAP S/4HANA. Chapter 7 and Chapter 11 discuss the new implementation scenario and the relevant tools.

> **Checklist for New Implementation**
>
> Let's summarize the individual steps for new implementations:
>
> 1. Determining the target status: operating model and distribution of the instances. You can carry out new implementations for on-premise implementations, for SAP HANA Enterprise Cloud (SAP HEC), and in the public cloud.
> 2. Identifying the desired new functions
> 3. Verifying the functions currently used via the simplification list (*http://help.sap.com/s4hana_op_1610*). Take into account the number of users for each function.
> 4. For existing SAP ERP systems: Precheck in simulation mode (see SAP Note 2182725)
> 5. Analyzing custom enhancements using the custom code migration worklist (*http://bit.ly/v1448043*). You usually have to newly implement existing custom programs in SAP S/4HANA Cloud. For more information on new enhancements for SAP S/4HANA Cloud, see Chapter 3, Section 3.4.
> 6. For on-premise editions only: Sizing (*https://service.sap.com/sizing*)
> 7. Adjusting input planning, verifying the migration scenario
> 8. If possible, data cleansing and archiving in the source system
> 9. Setting up the target system
> 10. Starting the SAP S/4HANA migration cockpit and transferring data
> 11. Checking the result
> 12. For on-premise editions only: Setting up the frontend servers for SAP Fiori
> 13. Delta configuration
> 14. Final tests
> 15. Roll-out of new processes for users

4.2.2 System Conversion to SAP S/4HANA

SAP ERP system as a base

In this scenario, we'll take an existing SAP ERP system and convert this system into an SAP S/4HANA system in several steps (see Figure 4.6). The SID, the customization, and the existing data of the source system are kept in this procedure. When selecting this scenario, you should cleanse your data *before* you convert the system. Note that this scenario is *not* an upgrade because the existing system belongs to a different product family.

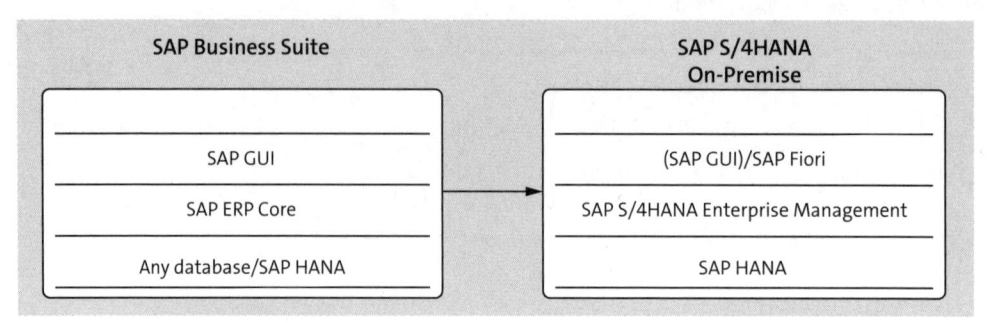

SAP Business Suite	SAP S/4HANA On-Premise
SAP GUI	(SAP GUI)/SAP Fiori
SAP ERP Core	SAP S/4HANA Enterprise Management
Any database/SAP HANA	SAP HANA

Figure 4.6 System Conversion to SAP S/4HANA

[»] **Data Footprint and Archiving**

SAP S/4HANA features a considerably reduced data footprint, meaning that the data in the SAP HANA database occupies less storage space than in common SAP ERP systems on traditional databases. SAP HANA's improved compression algorithms are already considered in SAP's official sizing recommendations.

However, in the case of system conversions, these sizing rules usually do not apply to the target system because the storage requirements are temporarily higher than in newly implemented systems. More memory is needed because SAP keeps your data to avoid data loss. Consequently, data is temporarily kept redundantly in the target system: in both the new data models of SAP S/4HANA and in the obsolete tables of the SAP ERP system.

Therefore, the target system needs to be sufficiently sized initially. After the conversion, you can delete redundant data manually. First, however, you should check whether the data has been successfully converted.

> To effectively size the target system (providing sufficient but not too much memory), you should analyze what data in the source system can be archived. You'll be able to access these archives from SAP S/4HANA. Another benefit is that the runtime of actual conversion will also be reduced. However, you should not archive active data. Your planning should additionally consider that the archiving routines in the SAP S/4HANA target system still have to be adjusted to the new data models so that the target system can also archive future data.
>
> In addition, you can use the *data aging* option, which is integrated into SAP HANA. This method moves data that is not actively used from the SAP HANA memory and could be considered a kind of preparatory step for archiving: Hot data is stored in the SAP HANA memory; cold and historical data is stored in the archive.

Before you convert your system, you must analyze the source system in detail. The simplification list provided by SAP contains all relevant changes that affect available SAP ERP functions: omitted functions, significantly modified applications (or application architectures), and nonstrategic functions (see Figure 4.7). The latter refers to functions that are available in SAP S/4HANA but that SAP no longer recommends. Because SAP doesn't plan to enhance or maintain these functions in the future, you should only use these functions during the transition phase. **Simplification list**

For simplification reasons, SAP provides numerous automatic *prechecks*. These prechecks answer the following questions about your system: **Prechecks**

- Are the technical system requirements met?
- Are functions used that are will no longer be available in the target system in the same form?
- Is incompatible software used, such as add-ons that have not been released for SAP S/4HANA (yet)? Incompatible software must be uninstalled from the source system, or you must find a compatible version for SAP S/4HANA. Please contact the add-on's manufacturer for further information in this case.
- Are your custom enhancements compatible with SAP S/4HANA?

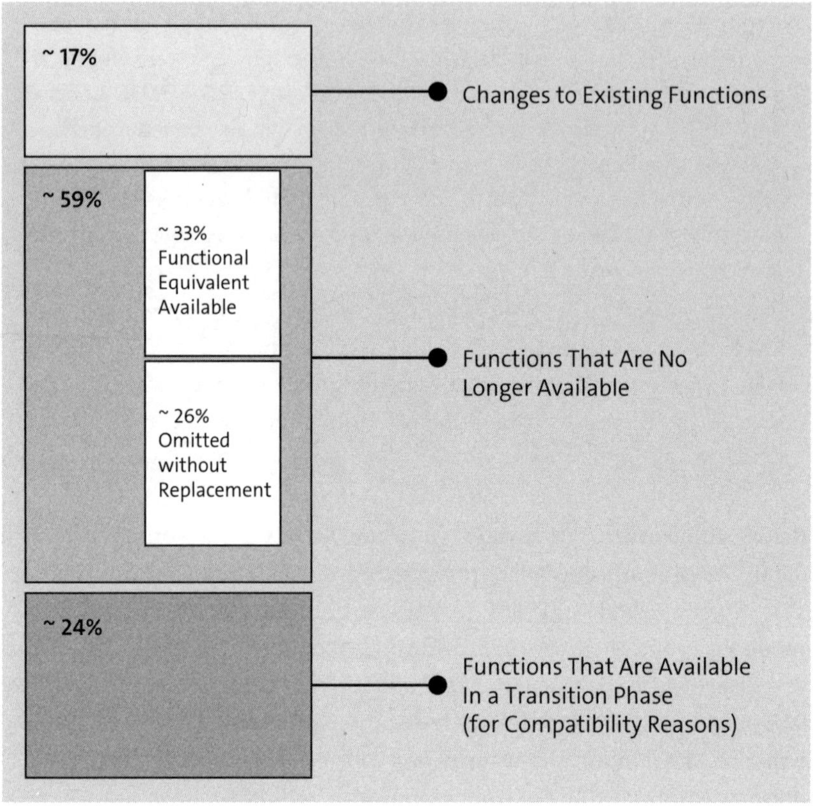

4   Preparing the Migration to SAP S/4HANA

```
~17% ─── Changes to Existing Functions

~59%
  ~33% Functional Equivalent Available
  ~26% Omitted without Replacement
  ─── Functions That Are No Longer Available

~24% ─── Functions That Are Available In a Transition Phase (for Compatibility Reasons)
```

Figure 4.7 Functions from SAP ERP Expected Change or Depreciated

The results of these checks can considerably impact project scoping. We therefore recommend running these checks at the beginning of the conversion project so you can accurately estimate the overall project scope. To run a simulation, you can select the **Simulation Mode** in the prechecks (see Figure 4.8).

Results of the checks

The results of the checks are categorized as follows:

- Positive results (green)
- Warnings (yellow)
- Errors that hinder a conversion (red)

4.2 The Three Migration Scenarios

SAP S/4HANA Pre-Transition Checks

○ Check Class Consistency Check
● Pre-Transition Check Results
○ Display Application Log

☑ Simulation Mode

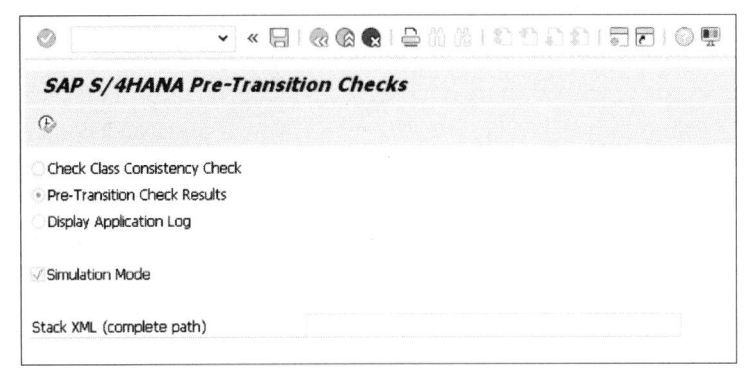

Stack XML (complete path)

Figure 4.8 Initial Screen of the Prechecks for Preparing the SAP S/4HANA Conversion

Warnings do not prevent the technical implementation of the conversion from continuing. However, because these warnings might lead to data loss under certain conditions, you should also analyze warnings in detail. An example of the results of these prechecks is shown in Figure 4.9.

S/4HANA Pre-Transition Check Results

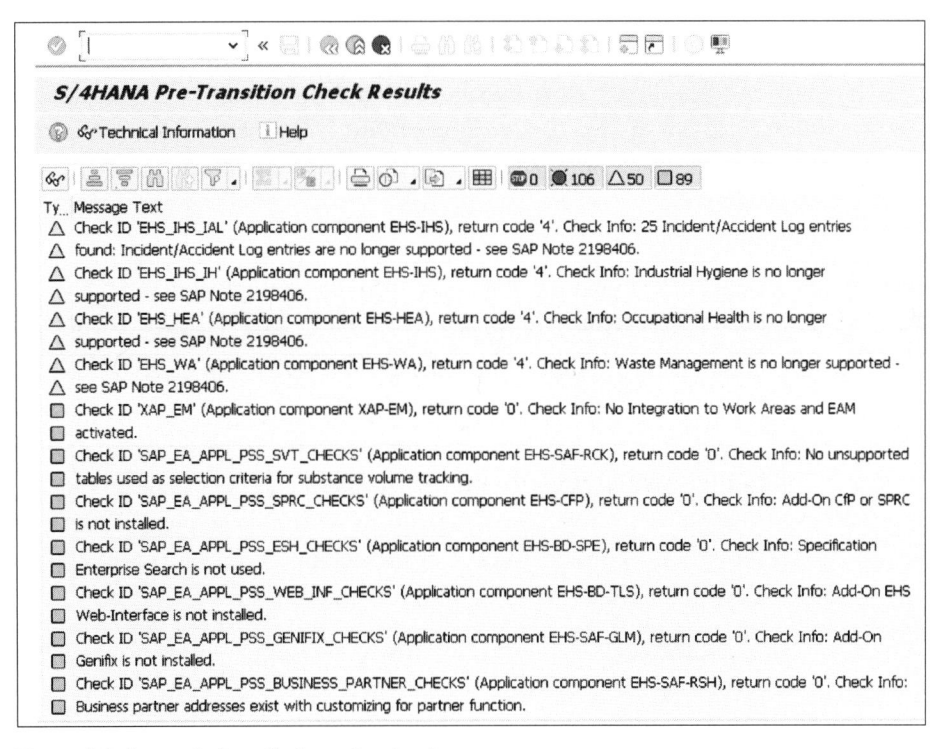

Ty.. Message Text
△ Check ID 'EHS_IHS_IAL' (Application component EHS-IHS), return code '4'. Check Info: 25 Incident/Accident Log entries
△ found: Incident/Accident Log entries are no longer supported - see SAP Note 2198406.
△ Check ID 'EHS_IHS_IH' (Application component EHS-IHS), return code '4'. Check Info: Industrial Hygiene is no longer
△ supported - see SAP Note 2198406.
△ Check ID 'EHS_HEA' (Application component EHS-HEA), return code '4'. Check Info: Occupational Health is no longer
△ supported - see SAP Note 2198406.
△ Check ID 'EHS_WA' (Application component EHS-WA), return code '4'. Check Info: Waste Management is no longer supported -
△ see SAP Note 2198406.
☐ Check ID 'XAP_EM' (Application component XAP-EM), return code '0'. Check Info: No Integration to Work Areas and EAM
☐ activated.
☐ Check ID 'SAP_EA_APPL_PSS_SVT_CHECKS' (Application component EHS-SAF-RCK), return code '0'. Check Info: No unsupported
☐ tables used as selection criteria for substance volume tracking.
☐ Check ID 'SAP_EA_APPL_PSS_SPRC_CHECKS' (Application component EHS-CFP), return code '0'. Check Info: Add-On CfP or SPRC
☐ is not installed.
☐ Check ID 'SAP_EA_APPL_PSS_ESH_CHECKS' (Application component EHS-BD-SPE), return code '0'. Check Info: Specification
☐ Enterprise Search is not used.
☐ Check ID 'SAP_EA_APPL_PSS_WEB_INF_CHECKS' (Application component EHS-BD-TLS), return code '0'. Check Info: Add-On EHS
☐ Web-Interface is not installed.
☐ Check ID 'SAP_EA_APPL_PSS_GENIFIX_CHECKS' (Application component EHS-SAF-GLM), return code '0'. Check Info: Add-On
☐ Genifix is not installed.
☐ Check ID 'SAP_EA_APPL_PSS_BUSINESS_PARTNER_CHECKS' (Application component EHS-SAF-RSH), return code '0'. Check Info:
☐ Business partner addresses exist with customizing for partner function.

Figure 4.9 Example Results from Prechecks

SAP has made these prechecks available via SAP Notes (see SAP Note 2182725). Prechecks are imported into the source system, where you'll run the check, meaning you can carry out prechecks independently of the technical conversion project. To be safe, the conversion routine additionally requests that you run the prechecks to avoid converting systems that have not been checked.

Custom code checks

Custom code checks deviate from the procedure described above. To check custom code, an SAP NetWeaver system is connected to the source system, and the custom code is then analyzed in this SAP NetWeaver system. In this way, unnecessary workload is diverted away from the source system. The result of these checks is a *custom code migration worklist*, which lists adaptations to your custom code recommended by SAP.

Adjusting the source system

After the checks have been carried out, you should eliminate the abnormalities found in your source system. Otherwise, the conversion might not run smoothly. After implementing all corrections, you can verify the system readiness by checking the system again.

Carrying out the conversion

If the prechecks do not indicate any abnormalities, you can initiate the next conversion phase. Call the *Maintenance Planner* via the SAP Support Portal (*https://apps.support.sap.com/sap/support/mp*). Then, enter the desired target status—the selected version of SAP S/4HANA in our case—in the Maintenance Planner. You then carry out the actual technical system conversion using a version of the *Software Update Manager* (SUM) that has been optimized for SAP S/4HANA.

Standard or downtime-optimized

You can choose how the technical conversion should be carried out. SAP provides two procedures for this:

- Using default, predefined procedures, SAP will try to balance resource consumption, downtime, and overall runtime.

- A procedure with optimized downtime converts larger data volumes into the SAP S/4HANA data format while the system is in production operation, which reduces the downtime. The price you pay is increased resource consumption and sometimes a longer runtime for the technical conversion.

At present, the conversion with optimized downtime option is only available for source systems that do not run on SAP HANA. You can optimize additional requirements in individual projects. If you strive for a *near-zero downtime*, SAP recommends involving SAP consultants in the conversion project.

The technical conversion usually involves the following three steps:

Conversion steps

1. **Migrating the database to SAP HANA**
   Your source system database does not have to be SAP HANA. In this case, the SUM enables you to also convert the database to SAP HANA, which is referred to as the *Database Migration Option* (DMO).

2. **Implementing new repository objects**
   The software is updated to the new SAP S/4HANA versions.

3. **Converting the data**
   The data of the source system is transferred to the target system using its new storage options.

After you have successfully implemented the technical conversion, you might have to perform some application-specific tasks.

The system is ready for use again—but only with the functional scope of the legacy system. The new SAP S/4HANA functions are available in the system but usually still have to be configured. To simplify this configuration, SAP provides predefined content in SAP Best Practices.

Configuring the new functions

From a Single System to a Landscape

The conversion steps we described must be performed in *all* systems of the landscape, i.e., at least in the development, test, and production systems. To overcome the resulting downtime, you can generate a temporary copy of the landscape. Please note that, in this case, you probably won't be able to transport code or configuration changes between systems on the source product version and the new SAP S/4HANA systems. This limitation also applies to SAP corrections. These limitations arise because the code (custom code and SAP code) and configuration tables differ. We recommend adjusting the landscapes manually.

Thus, you should also divide the project into two phases and focus on the technical conversion of the system first. You can then introduce new or changed processes on the converted system in a second step.

The possible target SAP S/4HANA versions depends on the source product version. Usually, you can select between multiple target releases. When

Prerequisites

4   Preparing the Migration to SAP S/4HANA

begin a conversion, SAP HANA doesn't have to be already implemented in your source system. You also do not need to implement the versions of SAP S/4HANA sequentially when transitioning to a higher version. In general, a source system running on SAP ERP 6.0 or higher is sufficient, as shown in Figure 4.10. Chapter 10 provides more details on conversion paths.

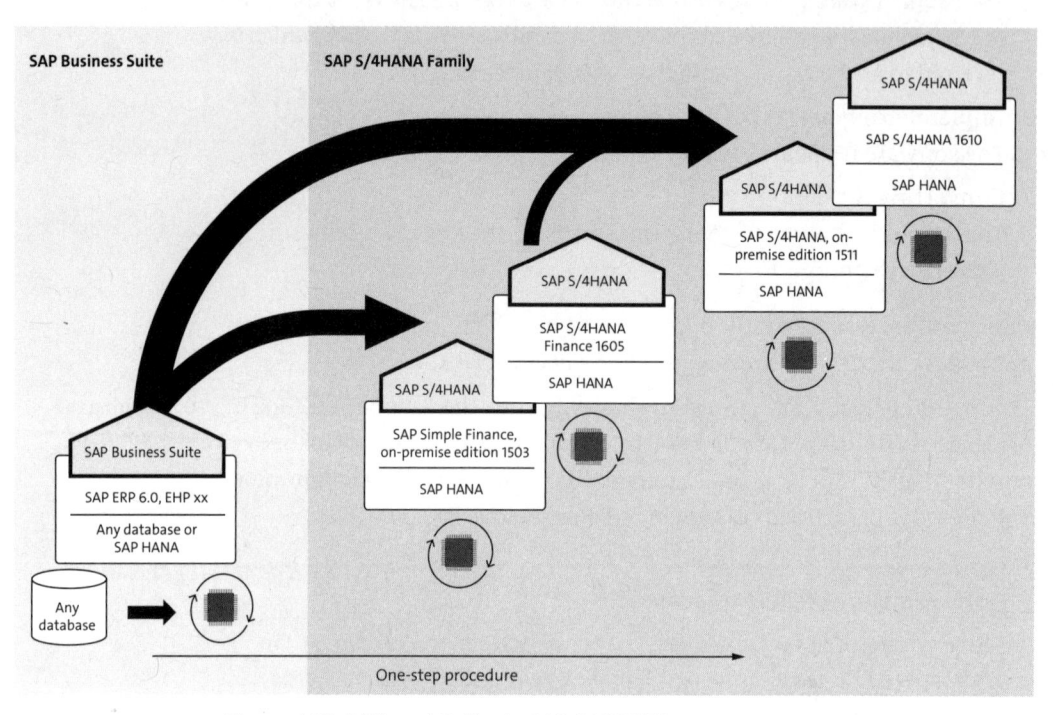

Figure 4.10 Different Paths to SAP S/4HANA

> **Conversion Checklist**
>
> The following list summarizes the individual steps for a system conversion:
>
> 1. Determining the target status: operating model and distribution of the instances. The system conversion can only be carried out for on-premise implementations or for SAP HANA Enterprise Cloud (SAP HEC).
> 2. Identifying the desired new functions
> 3. Verifying the functions currently used via the simplification list. Take into account the number of users for each function.
> 4. Running prechecks in simulation mode and custom code checks (*http://bit.ly/v1448041*)

5. Sizing
6. Adjusting capacity planning for the project and confirmation of the migration scenario
7. If possible, data cleansing and archiving in the source system
8. Planning your system conversion in the Maintenance Planner (*http://bit.ly/v1448042*)
9. Selecting the standard conversion or the conversion with optimized downtime in the SUM, adjusting sizing if required
10. Executing the maintenance transaction
11. Checking the result
12. Setting up the frontend servers for SAP Fiori
13. Delta configuration
14. Roll-out of the new processes for the users

4.2.3 Landscape Transformation with SAP S/4HANA

Landscape transformation refers to a migration scenario in which various SAP ERP systems are integrated into a shared SAP S/4HANA system (see Figure 4.11). You might choose a landscape transformation to benefit the most from SAP S/4HANA's real-time data processing: Only if all data is kept in one database can the system use this data with highest efficiency. Another benefit is that data no longer needs to be replicated. SAP S/4HANA's efficient compression algorithms and its high speed can handle the volume of data that previously would have been spread out to multiple traditional systems.

Data in a shared database

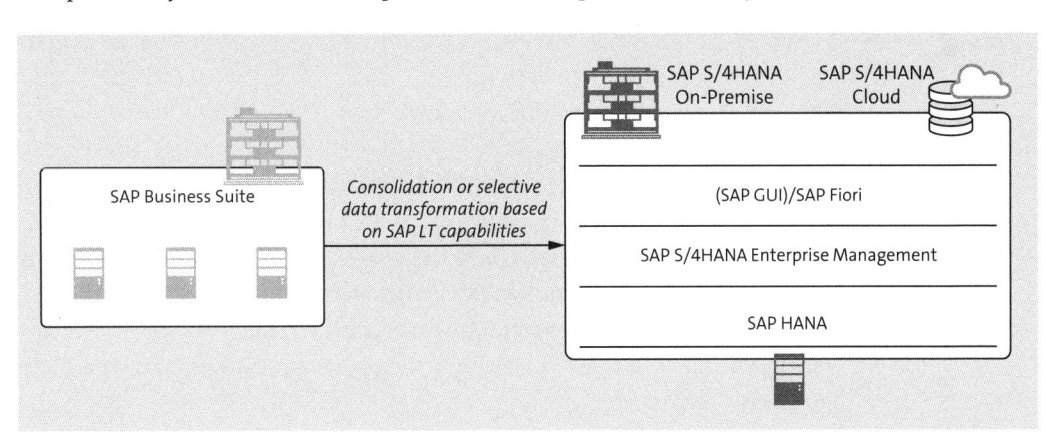

Figure 4.11 Landscape Transformation

4   Preparing the Migration to SAP S/4HANA

Two subprojects The landscape transformation process consists of two subprojects. In the first part, the master system is prepared. As described in the previous two sections, the master system is either a new implementation of an SAP S/4HANA system or a system conversion. The latter scenario is implemented if the landscape contains an SAP ERP system that can be used as the basis for the other systems. The configuration and process specifications should be optimized and up-to-date in this system. When planning this first step, take into account the guidance for new implementations and system conversions described in the previous two sections.

Selecting the data extraction method After you've implemented an SAP S/4HANA master system, you still need to transfer the data from your other systems in the landscape to this system. First, determine the required data extraction method. Figure 4.12 illustrates common methods:

- Consolidation of several complete systems
- Transfer of selected company codes
- Transfer of selected business processes

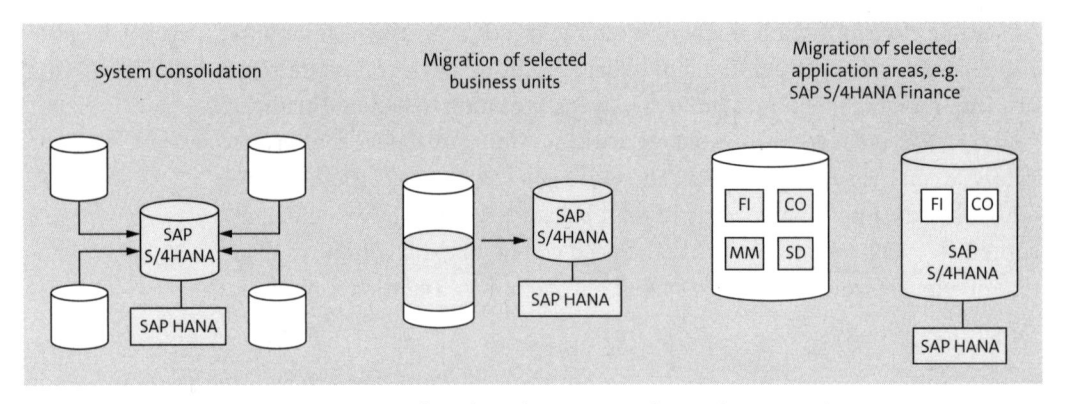

Figure 4.12 Examples of Landscape Transformation Scenarios

SAP Landscape Transformation (SLT) Regardless of data extraction method, the data from (several) SAP ERP versions is read and written to the SAP S/4HANA system. In this process, this data will need to be translated into the new SAP S/4HANA data model using *SAP Landscape Transformation* (SLT). However, you cannot use SLT for continuous data replication, just for one-time data transfers only, as in this scenario. SAP has equipped SLT with the right conversion logic for the new SAP S/4HANA data model.

154

Landscape transformations are also possible for non-SAP systems if you are willing to accept some constraints. In this case, however, you should consider using SAP Data Services as described in the new implementation scenario. The specific tool you use depends on your individual situation.

Non-SAP source systems

The individual realizations in a landscape transformation are highly specialized projects. In addition to the technical support, SAP and other service providers can offer specialized consulting and implementation services for these scenarios. Chapter 12 further describes landscape transformations in detail.

Chapter 5
SAP Activate

SAP Activate is the key to successfully adopting SAP S/4HANA and has been designed for this specific purpose. SAP Activate replaces the previous implementation models of AcceleratedSAP (ASAP) and SAP Launch and combines best practices, configuration, and methodology.

SAP Activate is a new method for implementing SAP software. Designed for the new SAP S/4HANA business solution, SAP Activate assists with new implementations (*greenfield*), conversions of existing SAP Business Suite systems (*lift & shift*), and transformations of system landscapes (see Chapter 4, Section 4.2). The SAP Activate approach includes best practices for business processes, guided configuration, and implementation methodology.

The SAP Activate framework follows the classic waterfall model, i.e., phases are carried out in succession. Usually, the individual project phases do not overlap. When a new phase begins, the previous phase has been completed successfully and must be confirmed before the next phase can proceed. The innovation of SAP Activate is its continuous lifecycle management, which enables you to execute individual phases again when running an update.

SAP Activate answers the following questions and is thus an integral part of adopting SAP S/4HANA:

- How can I implement SAP S/4HANA successfully?
- Where can I find a task list for implementing SAP S/4HANA?
- How can I quickly execute a proof of concept for SAP S/4HANA?
- Where can I find best practices for SAP S/4HANA?

Key questions

The following sections answer these questions by describing the concept behind and the individual phases of SAP Activate.

5   SAP Activate

5.1   SAP Activate Content

Successor of ASAP SAP Activate is the successor to the former ASAP implementation method. The *AcceleratedSAP (ASAP)* model was designed for SAP R/3 in the 1990s and replaced and standardized traditional procedures for software implementations. Then and now, the underlying concept has been using a standardized method to provide all customers with the knowledge gained from previous projects. Consequently, ASAP combined proven business best practices and project management methods. This approach, new at the time, defined a procedure that could be implemented more quickly than previous procedures. However, standardization also reduced flexibility in some cases. Over time, ASAP has been further enhanced (the latest version, ASAP 8, was introduced in 2013) and can be used for new implementations, software enhancements (e.g., with new components), and upgrades.

Successor of SAP Launch The successor of ASAP is SAP Activate, which was first introduced with SAP S/4HANA. Designed for both on-premise implementations and cloud solutions, SAP Activate is not only the successor to ASAP but also to *SAP Launch*, which had been used for SAP Cloud solutions (for example, SAP SuccessFactors or SAP Ariba) until now. In addition to best practices and methodology, SAP Activate also offers guided configuration and thus takes simplification and standardization a step further. SAP Activate provides general procedures and tools but also allows you to use nonstandard procedures.

Goals of SAP Activate The desired *business value* is a faster, more intuitive software implementation—whether on-premise or in the cloud. Innovations will be available more quickly throughout the entire product lifecycle. SAP partners can also use and extend this model.

Figure 5.1 provides an overview of the three components of SAP Activate: SAP Best Practices, guided configuration, and the methodology.

> **Goals of SAP Activate**
>
> In summary, the goals of SAP Activate are the following:
>
> - Simplifying the adoption of SAP S/4HANA with a combination of SAP Best Practices, methodology, and guided configuration

- Delivering predefined business processes that are optimized for SAP S/4HANA
- Deploying best practices for transformation, migration, integration, and configuration of SAP S/4HANA

SAP Activate results in a faster, less service-intensive initial implementation and eases subsequent maintenance of SAP S/4HANA for all SAP S/4HANA customers, irrespective of implementation method selected (see Chapter 4, Section 4.2). The benefits are an accelerated *time to value* and a lower *total cost of ownership*.

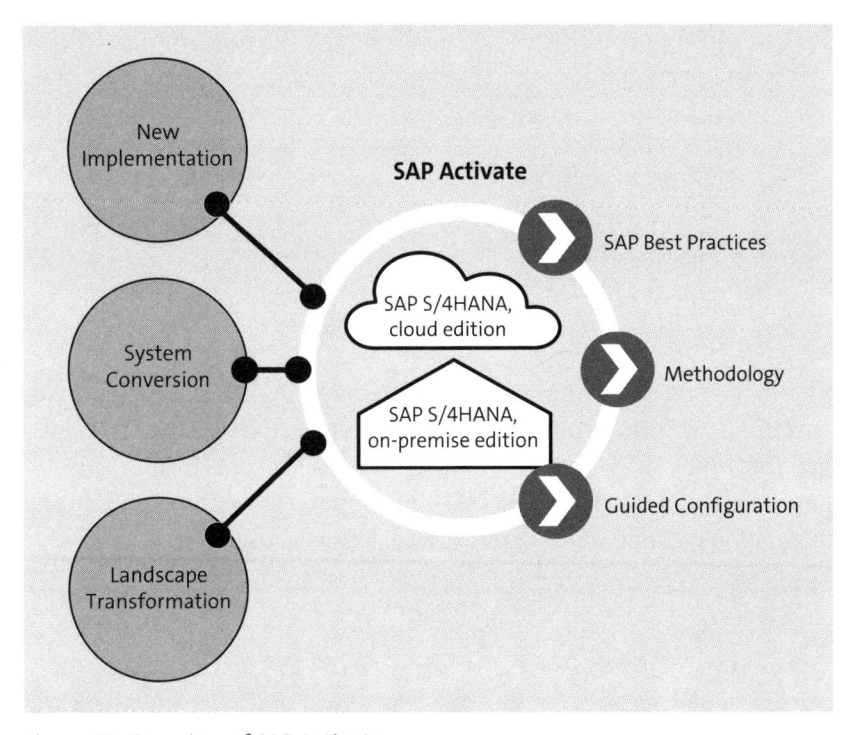

Figure 5.1 Overview of SAP Activate

The following sections introduce the SAP Activate modules, which are also shown in Figure 5.2: best practices for SAP S/4HANA (*SAP Best Practices*), tools for a guided configuration, and the new methodology of SAP Activate.

Modules

5 SAP Activate

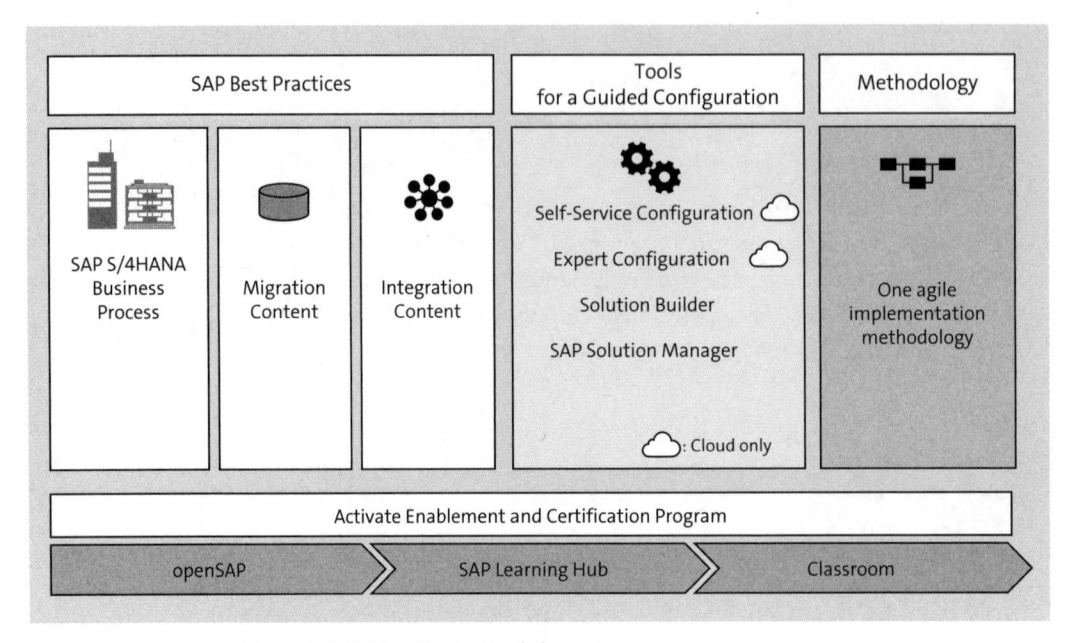

Figure 5.2 SAP Activate Modules

5.1.1 SAP Best Practices

Best practices
SAP Best Practices contains integrated, ready-to-use business processes optimized for SAP S/4HANA, and the SAP Best Practices package is an integral part of the software. Furthermore, SAP Best Practices includes a reference solution in the cloud (a so-called *trial system*) as well as migration and integration content, which is always available to all users.

> [»] **Trial System**
>
> You can test SAP Best Practices by using the free SAP S/4HANA Cloud system as a trial system. With the trial system, you can choose between your own on-premise system hosted by a cloud provider and an SAP S/4HANA Cloud system that you share with other users. You don't have to pay any license fees for the trial period, only the incurred hosting costs if you use the on-premise system. You can access the system at the following link: *www.sap.com/s4hana-trial*.

> This trial access enables you to get a first impression of SAP S/4HANA's new functions and the new SAP Fiori user interface. The guided tours through the provided best practices scenarios can be useful. For more information on the trial systems, see Chapter 6.

SAP Best Practices was introduced in *SAP Business All-in-One* (*BAiO*, previously *MySAP All-in-One*) more than ten years ago. SAP Best Practices was a preconfigured SAP solution based on a standard SAP ERP system (or on a standard SAP CRM system for SAP CRM Best Practices).

SAP Business All-in-One

The difference between a BAiO system and an SAP ERP system was that BAiO included customizing that was specifically preconfigured for medium-sized enterprises. As a result, systems that strictly followed the SAP Standard could be implemented successfully and quickly and could be operated more easily by small and medium-sized enterprises (SME). The individual best practices were available in packages via the SAP Service Marketplace for free. All users can download these packages via their S-user accounts. Moreover, these best practices also laid the foundation for specific SAP partner industry solutions.

The next step involved the development of the concept for large enterprises (LE) in the form of *rapid-deployment solutions* (RDS). The difference between SAP Activate and previous SAP Best Practices and Rapid Deployment Solutions is that SAP Activate includes all best practices as part of the SAP S/4HANA product in the standard system and in SAP S/4HANA Cloud while in case of RDS the package had to be deployed to the system first.

Rapid Deployment Solutions

Figure 5.3 provides an overview of existing SAP Best Practices for the following areas:

Existing SAP Best Practices

- User experience (e.g., SAP Fiori Overview Pages, OVP)
- Analyses (e.g., predefined reports and dashboards)
- Business processes (e.g., predefined business processes in the different components and for several industries)
- Migration (e.g., for migrating either SAP or non-SAP systems to SAP S/4HANA)
- Integration (e.g., for integration with SAP SuccessFactors, SAP Hybris Cloud for Customer (C4C), SAP Ariba, and SAP Hybris Marketing Cloud)

5 SAP Activate

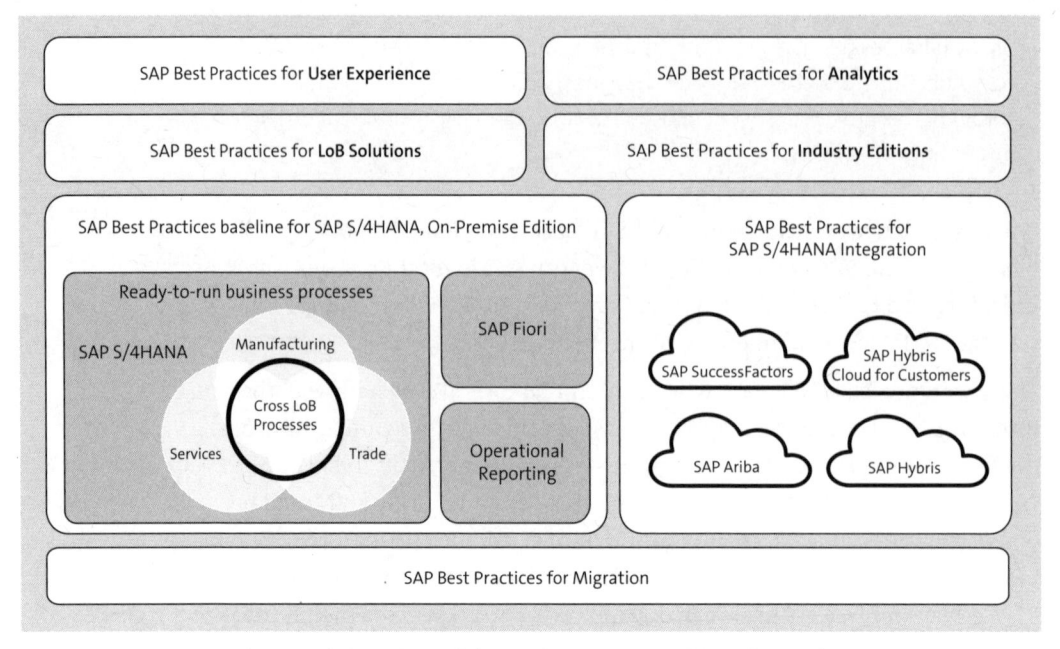

Figure 5.3 Overview of the Various Best Practices of SAP S/4HANA

Chapter 7, Section 7.3, describes using SAP Best Practices for migrating to SAP S/4HANA Cloud, and Chapter 11 explains using SAP Best Practices for migrating to a traditional on-premise SAP S/4HANA or implementing SAP S/4HANA on a private cloud. You can find detailed examples of integration best practices in Chapter 8 and Chapter 13 for on-premise and private cloud variants, respectively.

> **[»] SAP Fiori Best Practices**
>
> You can download SAP Best Practices for implementing and enhancing custom SAP Fiori interfaces for free at: *https://rapid.sap.com/bp/RDS_FIORI*.

With SAP Best Practices, you can breathe life into every SAP S/4HANA system from the start. Instead of starting with an empty system, you can use the configuration and the customizing of a *model company* as an example (see Chapter 6). The entire SAP Best Practices package in SAP Activate is specifically designed and optimized for SAP S/4HANA and shares with the historical best practices only its name. For example, the best practices processes use the SAP Fiori user interface by default whenever possible, and best practices for building your own SAP Fiori applications are also available.

The central part of SAP Best Practices for SAP S/4HANA is the so-called *baseline*, which contains ready-to-use business processes for basic SAP components (e.g., for financial accounting in SAP Financials [FI]) for every enterprise. Localizing this baseline is much more than adapting the logon language and translating the documentation. SAP Best Practices include content on individual countries, for example, for financial closings according to International Financial Reporting Standards (IFRS) closings according to United States Generally Accepted Accounting Principles (US-GAAP) in the United States or German Commercial Code (HGB, German-GAAP) in Germany.

Baseline

In the FI area, SAP Best Practices are available for the following business processes, for example:

Examples of SAP Best Practices

- Accounting and financial closings
- Asset accounting
- Accounts payable
- Accounts receivable
- Internal orders
- Profitability and cost analysis
- Period-end closing

An integral part of SAP Best Practices are *test scripts* (previously business process documents [BPDs]) and *process diagrams*. Figure 5.4 shows a process diagram for processing an order in SAP S/4HANA Cloud and Ariba Network. Chapter 8, Section 8.1, provides more information on the integration between these two systems.

Process diagrams

5   SAP Activate

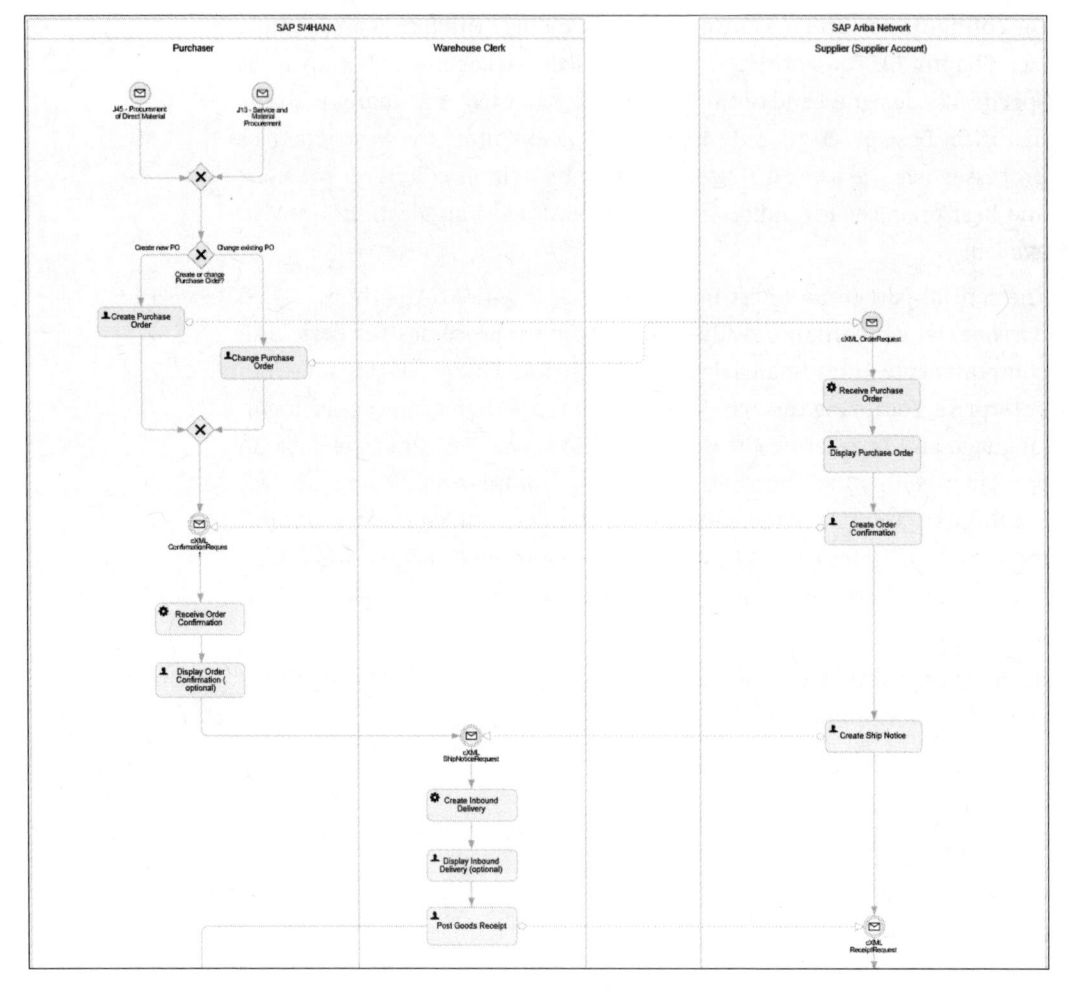

Figure 5.4 Example Process Diagram from SAP Best Practices: Procurement Process

> **SAP Best Practices Explorer**
>
> You can find more information on best practices in the SAP Best Practices Explorer at *http://rapid.sap.com/bp*. The following links provide direct access to the best practices for the individual editions:
>
> - SAP S/4HANA, on-premise:
>   *http://rapid.sap.com/bp/BP_OP_ENTPR*
> - SAP S/4HANA Enterprise Management Cloud:
>   *http://rapid.sap.com/bp/BP_CLD_ENTPR*

- SAP S/4HANA Finance Cloud:
  http://rapid.sap.com/bp/BP_CLD_FIN
- SAP S/4HANA Professional Services Cloud:
  http://rapid.sap.com/bp/BP_CLD_PROJ_SERV

In the individual package, select the appropriate version (localization) from the dropdown list. Then, you'll have access to all the SAP S/4HANA content for your solution by navigating to the relevant SAP S/4HANA subcategory, including overview documents and presentations, general documents such as documentation and SAP Notes, information on so-called *scope items* (Section 5.1.2 will provide more information on scope items), and a content library with the relevant content. In addition, you'll have access to demos that demonstrate individual best practices processes in detail and to familiarize you with the new user interfaces in SAP S/4HANA.

While anybody can use the SAP Best Practices Explorer to obtain information on SAP Best Practices, you'll have to log on and have specific user access provided by SAP (S-user or C-user) to download SAP Best Practices and obtain more detailed information.

5.1.2 Guided Configuration

The *guided configuration* provided by SAP Activate contains tools to guide you through a new implementation as well as common extensions after the go-live. For this purpose, SAP Fiori is a new user interface concept that addresses both technical users and end users. This new concept considerably accelerates the adoption of SAP S/4HANA, which is critical for SAP S/4HANA Cloud solutions in particular.

Implementation and enhancement tools

When introducing the individual components, we'll discuss tools for both the cloud versions and the on-premise editions. We will point out when individual functions are currently only available for SAP S/4HANA Cloud (and not yet for SAP S/4HANA 1610, on-premise).

The guided configuration is a completely new approach to implementing a software system and was introduced with SAP S/4HANA for the first time. In the long run, the guided configuration will replace customizing tools such as the *Implementation Guide* (IMG), which was introduced in SAP R/3. Like the IMG, the guided configuration can be used during the initial implementation phase or later on when new functions are installed and

Successor of IMG

activated. The role concept and the user interface concept in the guided configuration are based on SAP Fiori.

Procedure The procedure is business process-oriented and guides the user step by step through all necessary tasks. You can set up and modify business processes and, if required, further adapt the IMG of your on-premise system. All settings are tracked in the *SAP Solution Manager* to create a configuration history, thus ensuring that you can always trace and undo changes. These change data records are also used for future configurations and delta configurations for extensions and upgrades.

Scope items SAP Solution Manager can be used for monitoring, support, and operation and contains the configuration documentation provided by SAP, SAP Best Practices process models, and implementation guidelines. All SAP Best Practices listed in Section 5.1.1 are modeled as so-called *scope items*. Scope items are components of SAP Best Practices. Examples from *accounting* include the *accounts receivable* and *accounts payable* scope items.

Building blocks SAP builds these scope items using *building blocks*, which are displayed in the Solution Builder next to the scope items. In SAP S/4HANA, on-premise, systems, you can create your own business processes or adjust the predelivered SAP processes, and if you use the SAP Implementation Guide, you won't even need custom code. SAP partners can also develop custom or industry-specific best practices and implement them for you.

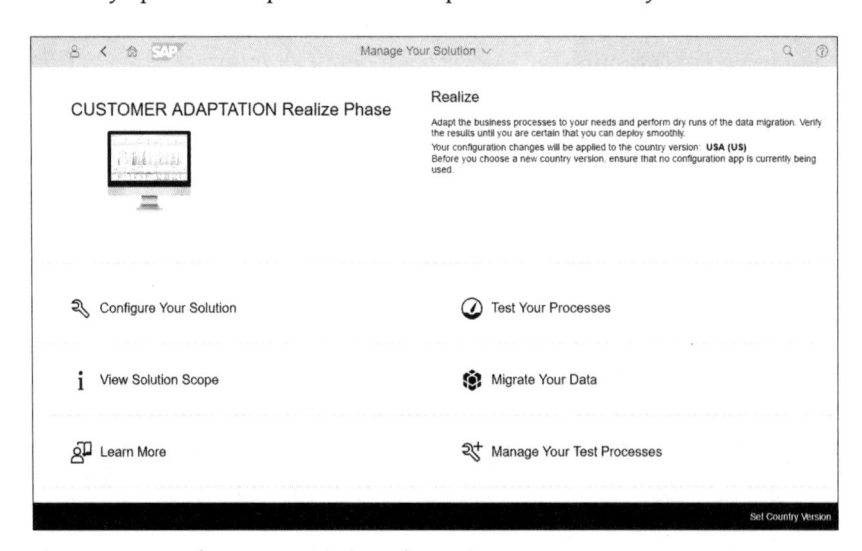

Figure 5.5 SAP S/4HANA Guided Configuration

First, let's look at a default case without any extensions. Figure 5.5 shows the entry screen of the **Manage Your Solution** SAP Fiori app, which includes the steps for configuring a SAP S/4HANA Cloud system in the realize phase (see Section 5.2). The individual functions of this app are described in the following sections.

Manage Your Solution app

Solution Scope

The **View Solution Scope** function displays the business processes that have been activated in your SAP S/4HANA system. This function provides you with a detailed overview of the entire system quickly and easily. This feature also presents possible processes, such as additional integration scenarios or new processes that may suit your solution. Figure 5.6 shows an example of the scope of the SAP S/4HANA Cloud solution.

View Solution Scope function

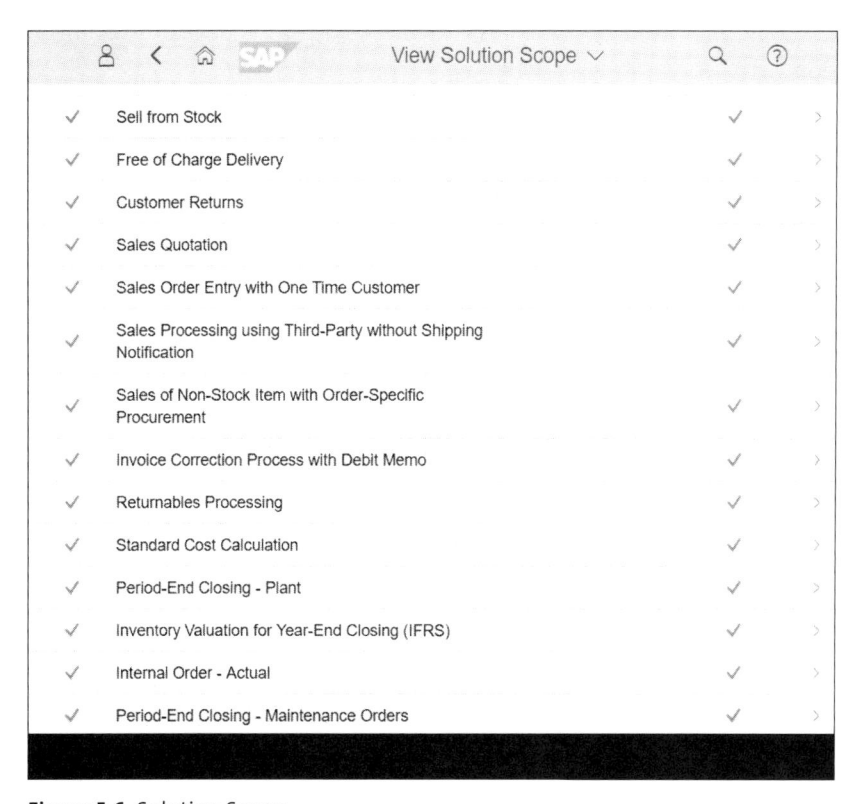

	View Solution Scope	
✓	Sell from Stock	✓
✓	Free of Charge Delivery	✓
✓	Customer Returns	✓
✓	Sales Quotation	✓
✓	Sales Order Entry with One Time Customer	✓
✓	Sales Processing using Third-Party without Shipping Notification	✓
✓	Sales of Non-Stock Item with Order-Specific Procurement	✓
✓	Invoice Correction Process with Debit Memo	✓
✓	Returnables Processing	✓
✓	Standard Cost Calculation	✓
✓	Period-End Closing - Plant	✓
✓	Inventory Valuation for Year-End Closing (IFRS)	✓
✓	Internal Order - Actual	✓
✓	Period-End Closing - Maintenance Orders	✓

Figure 5.6 Solution Scope

View Solution Scope enables you to navigate to the documentation and view details about the individual scope items. Also starting from here, you can easily make the relevant configuration settings for the selected scope. Let's take a closer look at this function.

Self-Service Configuration (Currently Only Available for SAP S/4HANA Cloud)

Configure Your Solution function

Users can use the **Configure Your Solution** function to navigate to the so-called *self-service configuration*, where you can tailor the preconfigured processes to meet your requirements with the help of a wizard.

Figure 5.7 shows an example of how purchasing processes can be configured. The self-service configuration only provides settings that correspond to the relevant phase (see Section 5.2) and preselected scope. End users can use the application to make basic settings, such as changes to organizational structures or master data.

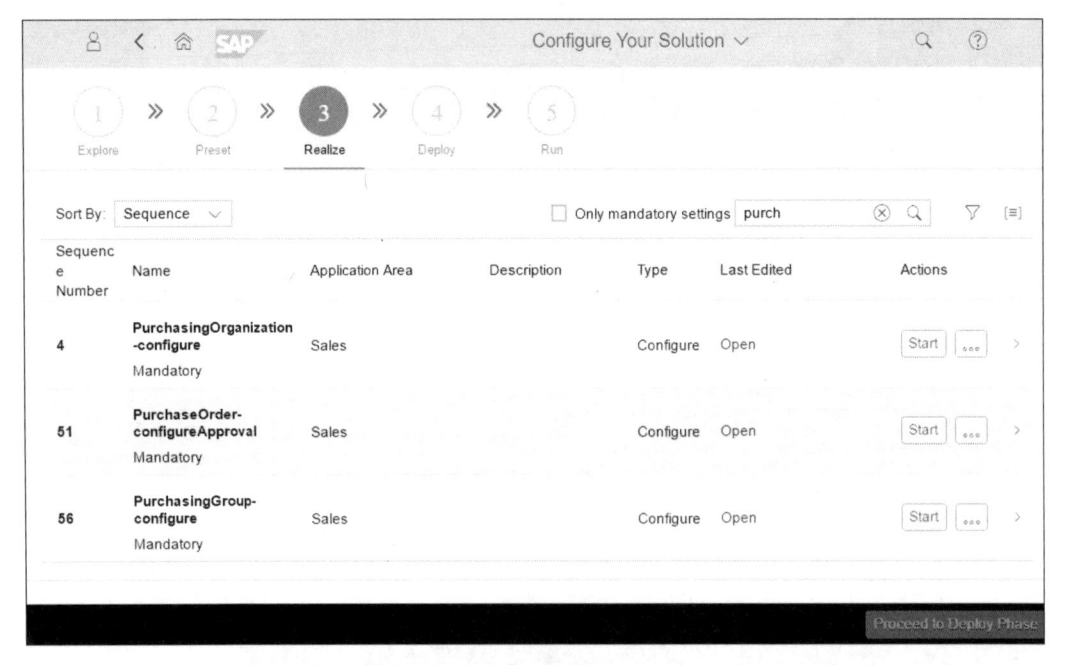

Figure 5.7 Self-Service Configuration

5.1 SAP Activate Content

[Ex]

Adjusting Threshold Values Retroactively

In an enterprise, the employees can order office and IT supplies, such as computer equipment, using a purchasing self-service function in SAP Ariba. Let's say one of the managers realizes that too much money is being spent for procuring office and computer supplies. He discovers that the system is configured in such a way that—provided that the necessary authorizations exist—an approval workflow is only triggered if a purchase order value of $100 is reached. This configuration was made to simplify processes. The manager can now change the threshold value to $50 to trigger the approval workflow more often (see Figure 5.8).

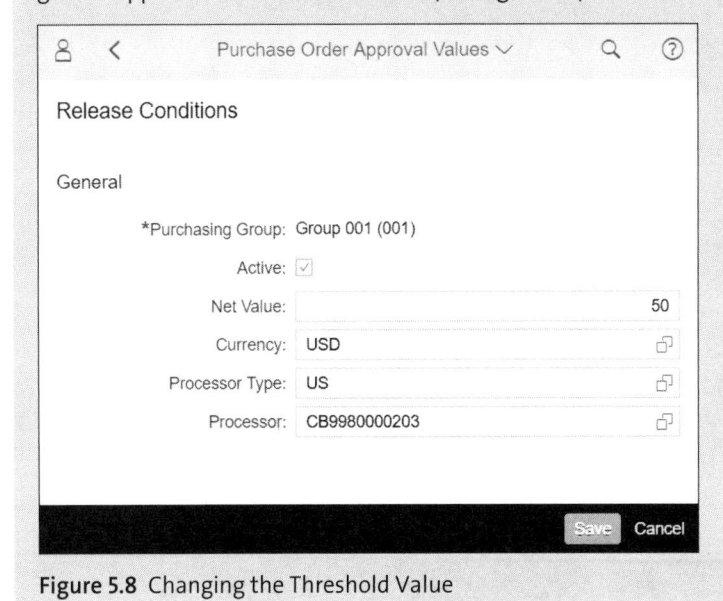

Figure 5.8 Changing the Threshold Value

This self-service configuration tool is not suited to setting up or changing entire business processes; you would use the SAP Service Center for this kind of expert configuration. You can run automated tests to analyze how changing the self-service configuration will affect your SAP S/4HANA system.

Automated Test (Currently Only Available in SAP S/4HANA Cloud)

With the **Test Your Processes** function, end users and IT experts can test configuration changes. This tool enables you to run automated tests based

Test Your Processes function

on test scripts provided by SAP Best Practices that you can fill with test data. After changing the threshold value in the self-service configuration, for example, a manager can run an automated test for an order process with a purchase order value of $49 or $50 to check whether the approval workflow has been triggered or not. Figure 5.9 shows the SAP Fiori application for testing order processes in this scenario. The automated test documents its activities and supports creating, changing, executing, and managing test schedules.

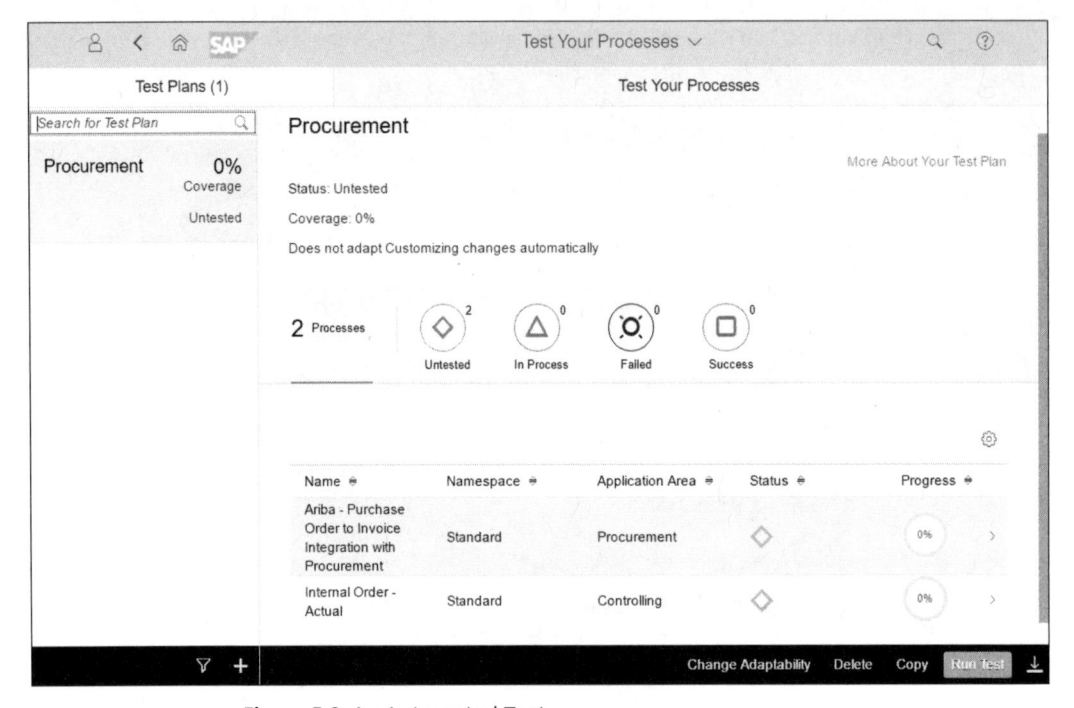

Figure 5.9 An Automated Test

| Manage Your Test Processes function | You can manage your test processes via the **Manage Your Test Processes** app (shown in Figure 5.10). With this app, you can select which processes are supposed to be available for tests, change old test cases, and create new tests. You can either manually create new process steps or use system records to create new process steps. |

5.1 SAP Activate Content

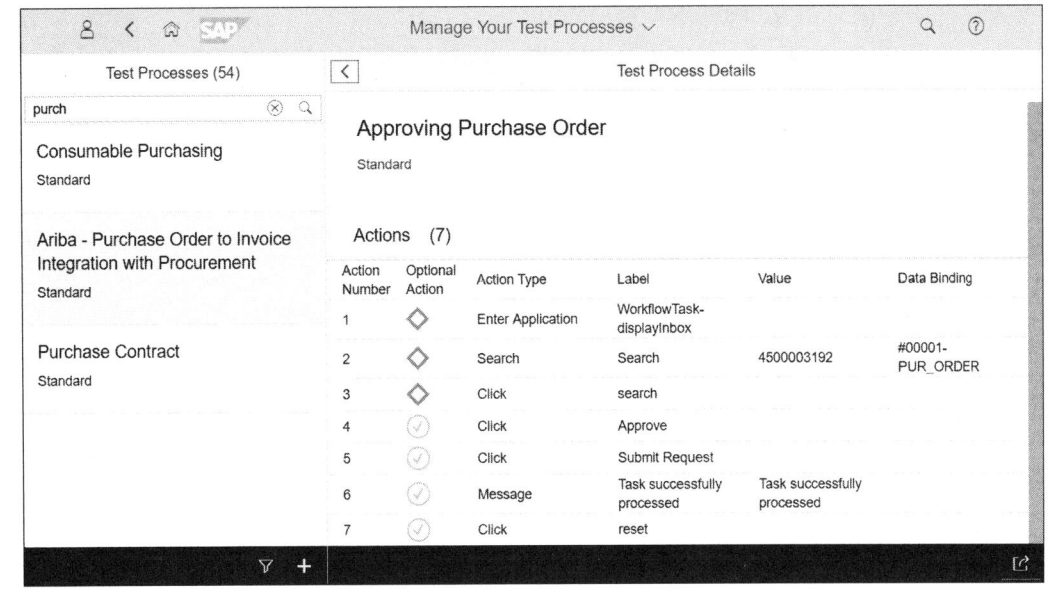

Figure 5.10 Manage Your Test Processes

SAP S/4HANA Migration Cockpit

The **Migrate Your Data** function calls the SAP S/4HANA migration cockpit for new SAP S/4HANA implementations. This tool is described in detail in Chapter 7, Section 7.3, for SAP S/4HANA Cloud and in Chapter 11, for SAP S/4HANA, on-premise.

Migrate Your Data function

> **Planning the Data Migration at an Early Stage**
>
> Experience from previous SAP S/4HANA migration projects has shown that you should be familiar with data migration tools, such as the SAP S/4HANA migration cockpit and migration templates, and with the subject of data migration in general at an early stage. The earlier you can clarify critical issues (if possible, already during the prepare phase), the more smoothly the data migration will run and the more likely strict deadlines will be met.

5   SAP Activate

Embedded Training Material

Access to further information

Instead of classic classroom training, SAP S/4HANA includes online learning content directly integrated into the **Learn More** function of the **Manage Your Solution** app by means of the SAP Learning Hub. Depending on the user role and phase, learning content is provided dynamically. In addition, all SAP Fiori interfaces provide a context-sensitive `F1` help, which goes far beyond the scope of the obsolete `F1` help in SAP ERP. Figure 5.11 shows this help for various buttons and screen elements.

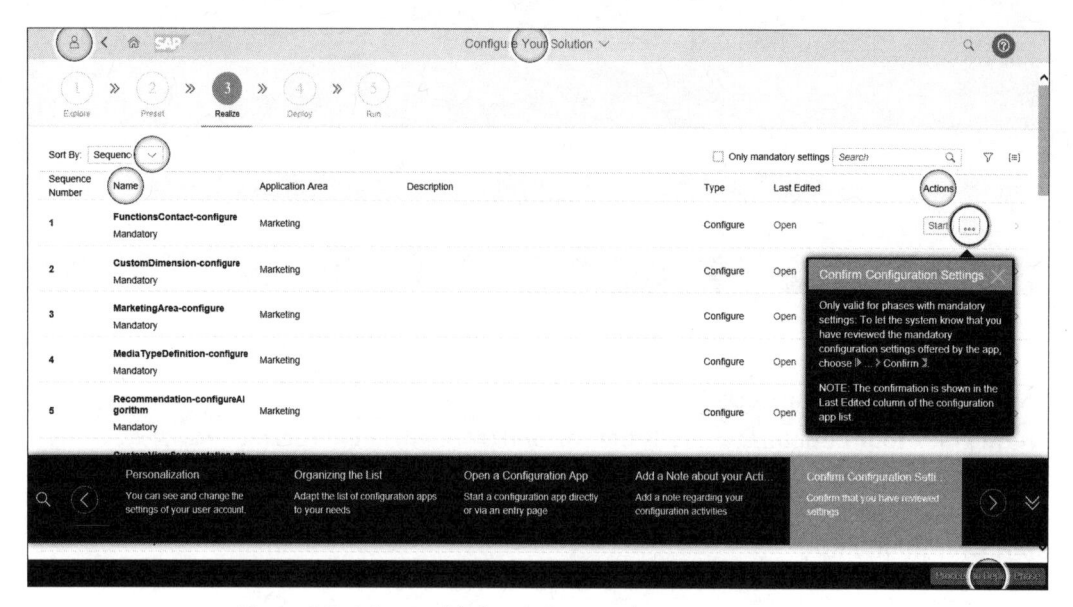

Figure 5.11 Advanced (F1) Help in SAP S/4HANA

> **openSAP Courses**
>
> openSAP is a learning platform developed by SAP and offered in cooperation with the Hasso Plattner Institute (HPI) in Potsdam, Germany. Based on massive open online courses (MOOCs), which differ from other e-learning models in how participants engage with each other, the online presentation approach uses concepts that have been tried and tested in traditional classroom training. These courses are held completely online and can be accessed via computers and mobile devices.

> Learning units, which are divided into weekly units and can be viewed with video, form the largest portion of the learning content. Self-tests, which enable you to check your learning progress, and user forums, which allow participants to exchange information, round out the learning platform. Each course ends with a test, and if you pass the test, you'll receive a certificate. However, the most important thing is that openSAP courses are free of charge.
>
> The various units of the courses introduce SAP S/4HANA and SAP Activate in videos and demos. At present, the following two courses are available:
>
> - Implementation of SAP S/4HANA:
>   http://open.sap.com/courses/s4h4
> - Find Your Path to SAP S/4HANA:
>   http://open.sap.com/courses/s4h5

The **Learn More** function is the central entry point to the SAP S/4HANA learning content. The content also offers role-based onboarding features for new users, including interactive demos. You can use this content to access the fee-based e-learning platform, SAP Learning Hub.

SAP Learning Hub

5.1.3 SAP Activate Methodology

The methodology of SAP Activate is based on the best practices introduced in Section 5.1.1, and you can use the best practices for both on-premise and cloud implementations of SAP S/4HANA. In this context, we'd like to point out that SAP Activate is the first solution to establish a common methodology for implementing cloud, hybrid, and on-premise systems. Moreover, SAP partners and experienced customers can leverage the SAP Activate methodology without having to utilize SAP consulting services.

Which Components or Tools Are Part of the Methodology?

The SAP Activate methodology provides so-called *accelerators* for each phase of the implementation project (see Section 5.2) and for each workspace. These accelerators include templates, questionnaires, checklists, guidelines, and tools to help you implement or upgrade SAP quickly. Templates, for example, enable you to find deltas, develop the architecture, or determine activities that are required for the go-live.

To Which Situation is the Methodology Best Suited?

Basically, the SAP Activate methodology promotes a holistic approach, irrespective of the deployment model (on-premise, cloud, or hybrid) and the scenario (new implementation, system conversion, or landscape transformation; see Chapter 4, Section 4.2). In addition, the methodology is scalable, which means that you can use SAP Activate for smaller projects or customers as well as for large enterprises.

Who Benefits from the Methodology?

Everybody responsible for implementation tasks can use the methodology. Of course, SAP Consulting utilizes SAP Activate as the default procedure, but SAP partners can also use SAP Activate to easily and successfully implement SAP S/4HANA for customers.

5.2 SAP Activate Phases

Using the scenario for a new implementation as an example, this section introduces the individual phases of the SAP Activate methodology. We'll take a closer look at the phases of a typical SAP S/4HANA project. The individual SAP Activate phases cover simple cloud implementations as well as complex installations of on-premise systems.

Four phases

The following four phases are based on redesigned ASAP and SAP Launch methods:

1. **Prepare**
   In this phase, you'll initiate and plan your SAP S/4HANA project, including quality gates and risk plans. You'll also set up the system landscape and determine the best practices for predefined business processes.

2. **Explore**
   In this phase, you'll explore SAP S/4HANA's features and compare them to your requirements. In so-called *fit-to-gap workshops* (or *fit-to-standard workshops* for SAP S/4HANA Cloud), you'll meet with an SAP representative in person to define the target configuration and possible SAP Best Practices extensions.

3. **Realize**

   You'll configure and enhance the SAP S/4HANA system according to the requirements you prioritized in the previous phase. The configuration and subsequent adaptations are implemented in short cycles to allow for regular validations and to obtain feedback from business departments. This phase also includes structured system tests and migration activities.

4. **Deploy**

   The new SAP S/4HANA system is about to go live, so you'll carry out some final preparations for the cutover to prepare the system, the users, and the data for production. Then, the new system will go live and replace the legacy system.

For SAP S/4HANA projects, these four phases are divided into various activities. The type of activity depends on the deployment model selected (cloud, i.e., software as a service (SaaS), or on-premise, which also includes private cloud or hybrid scenarios). Figure 5.12 and Figure 5.13 demonstrate the concepts that SAP uses in the SAP Activate methodology for these individual activities.

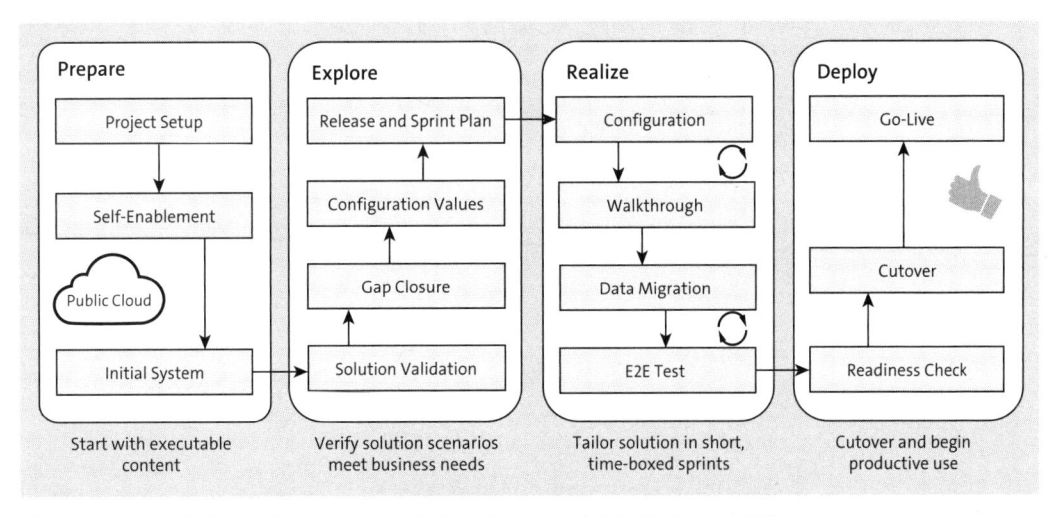

Figure 5.12 SAP Activate Phases and Activities for SAP S/4HANA Cloud Editions

5   SAP Activate

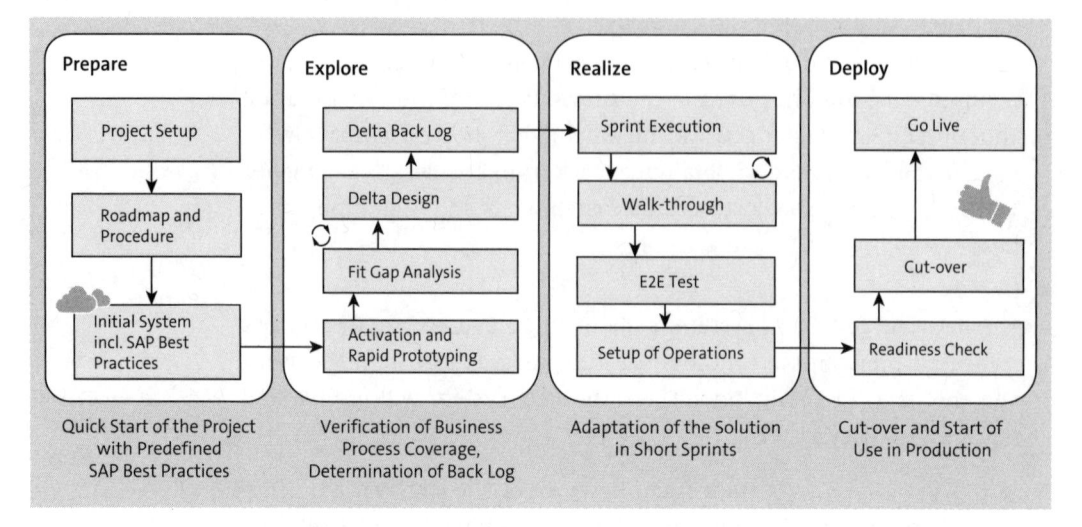

Figure 5.13 SAP Activate Phases and Activities for SAP S/4HANA, On-Premise

> **Roadmap Viewer**
>
> With the Roadmap Viewer, SAP provides an externally accessible portal for SAP Activate and thus an entry point for the implementation of SAP S/4HANA—on-premise or in the cloud. The following link introduces the SAP Fiori interface and displays the described phases and their individual steps: *http://go.support.sap.com/roadmapviewer*.
>
> The Roadmap Viewer provides the following functions:
>
> - *General Methodologies*: roadmaps for SAP Activate
> - *SAP S/4HANA*: cloud and on-premise roadmaps for analyzing the scope of the solution
> - *SAP HANA Technology Platform*: guidelines for the implementation of the SAP HANA platform
> - *SAP Solution Manager*: roadmaps for SAP Solution Manager 7.2, which is not required for using SAP S/4HANA but is recommended by SAP
>
> The roadmaps are continuously updated and can be useful companions for your journey to SAP S/4HANA, regardless of what scenario you selected (see Chapter 4, Section 4.2).

5.2 SAP Activate Phases

Ideally, you can combine SAP Activate with the SAP Solution Manager because SAP Activate is fully integrated into SAP Solution Manager 7.2: SAP Activate provides SAP Best Practices directly within the SAP Solution Manager, and the SAP Solution Manager is the ideal platform for carrying out fit gap analyses to log requirements and changes.

SAP Solution Manager

Figure 5.14 illustrates the individual phases and necessary steps for a system conversion (top) and for a new implementation (bottom).

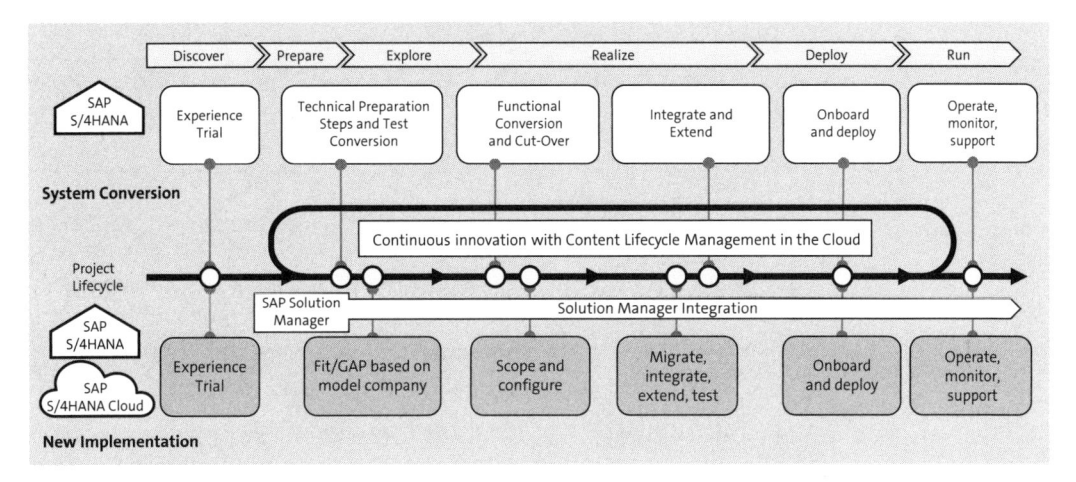

Figure 5.14 SAP Activate Phases

The following list is an example of the steps needed for a new implementation of SAP S/4HANA, on-premise:

Sample process

1. **Preparing the system landscape**
   – Preparing the trial system for SAP Best Practices
   – Preparing the three-tier system landscape consisting of development, test, and production systems
   – Preparing SAP Solution Manager 7.2
2. **Carrying out a fit gap analysis, based on best practices reference processes, with SAP Solution Manager 7.2**
   – Evaluating the target scope using the SAP Best Practices bill of materials (BOM) in in-person workshops
   – Determining your requirements using SAP Activate tools

177

3. **Selecting the solution scope and activating the content in the development client**
   - Importing the reference content
   - Selecting the solution scope
   - Activating the selected solution scope using Solution Builder
4. **Configuration and transport management**
   - Delta configuration after initial activation using the Implementation Guide
   - Additional customizing in SAP Client 000 (beyond SAP Best Practices), for more information see Chapter 6, Section 6.3.

> **Up-to-Date Information**
>
> To provide further and up-to-date information on the SAP Activate methodology and the individual phases, SAP has created an interactive page in the *SAP Jam* platform. SAP Jam allows SAP customers, SAP partners, and SAP employees to exchange information and experiences in forums and shared workspaces and to provide further information.
>
> You can access the open SAP Jam group by registering your email address at *http://bit.ly/SAPActivate*. (Please note the URL is case sensitive.) You'll receive an invitation to the SAP Jam space and have access to methodology content, discussion forums, and the *social collaboration* space.
>
> Like all new concepts, and due to SAP S/4HANA updates, SAP Activate is also subject to updates and enhancements. The following sources provide further information and are continuously updated:
>
> - The official SAP landing page is the entry point to SAP Activate. You can find it at *www.sap.com/activate*.
> - You can find more information in the "SAP Best Practices Reference Guide for SAP Activate", which you can find at *http://bit.ly/S4BPRefguide*. (Please note the URL is case sensitive.)

Chapter 6
Trial Systems and Model Company

The SAP Activate methodology also includes a model company with preconfigured customizing that is based on SAP Best Practices. The model company can help you get started and is ideal for testing and determining the appropriate migration strategy.

The previous chapter introduced SAP Activate as the framework for implementing SAP S/4HANA, and Chapter 5, Section 5.1.1, provided an overview of SAP S/4HANA's reference system, the so-called *model company*, which is a trial system in the cloud. This chapter now introduces this model company and its application options, which go far beyond the scope of common trial systems. The preconfigured system is already customized, containing, for example, predefined company codes, organizational structures, and sample data. The system is based on SAP Activate and SAP Best Practices and helps you identify your requirements for the migration to SAP S/4HANA and your prerequisites.

The model company in SAP S/4HANA replaces the obsolete *world template* in SAP Business Suite and is thus a comprehensive enhancement for SAP S/4HANA particularly because SAP Best Practices is now an integral part of SAP S/4HANA.

6.1 Trial System in the SAP Cloud Appliance Library

Both SAP customers and SAP partners can access the *trial system*, SAP S/4HANA's reference solution in the cloud. The trial system contains the model company as well as corresponding sample data and scenarios.

Trial system

Accessing the Trial System
You can configure the SAP S/4HANA trial system via the following link: *www.sap.com/s4hana-trial*.

6 Trial Systems and Model Company

SAP Cloud Appliance Library — The trial system is provided in the *SAP Cloud Appliance Library* (SAP CAL). SAP CAL delivers preconfigured software systems in a cloud-based solution on demand. You can start and use these systems in your own SAP CAL cloud space.

IaaS concept — This cloud computing option allows you to lease computing infrastructures instead of purchasing your own hardware. The underlying scalable concept follows the *infrastructure as a service* (IaaS) model. SAP CAL provides an online platform for managing your SAP systems, which can be hosted by any IaaS cloud provider (for example, Amazon or Microsoft).

Available versions — Two options are available for you to explore the world of SAP S/4HANA using the trial system:

- **SAP S/4HANA Cloud Trial**
  This variant enables you to create a user with 14-day test access to a preconfigured SAP S/4HANA Cloud demo system. All users share one system, but SAP CAL manages access to the system. This public cloud variant, or SaaS (*software as a service*) in the cloud, behaves like a "real" SAP S/4HANA Cloud system. Part II of this book discusses this type of SAP S/4HANA system in more detail.

  The system is shared by all users and is ready to use. You can execute demo scenarios using wizards. You can use the system to get familiar with SAP S/4HANA's functions and the SAP Fiori user interface. However, you cannot change the configuration of this system and cannot run through migration scenarios because administrative functions are restricted. One advantage of this variant is that it is completely free because no hosting costs are incurred.

- **SAP S/4HANA Trial**
  For this variant, you can use a 30-day test license to create a complete SAP S/4HANA, on-premise, system in the private cloud (which is hosted by a cloud provider). More appropriately, you "instantiate" rather than "create" the system, which is a copy of the model company that we'll discuss throughout this chapter. The test license is free, but you'll have to pay hosting fees for the cloud provider you choose. Because this trial system is *your* system, you can view and change all functions (including customizing). You can also access the system via SAP GUI.

  The system is based on the *SAP S/4HANA Fully-Activated Appliance* for SAP S/4HANA 1610, on-premise, at the time of this writing. Like SAP

S/4HANA, the underlying trial system is continuously enhanced and updated to map additional functions.

> **Setting up Your Access to the Trial System**
>
> As you read Part II and Part III, we recommend activating the corresponding trial system to better understand our explanations by running through the scenarios in the model company in the SAP S/4HANA system.

The SAP S/4HANA Fully-Activated Appliance allows you to run an entire SAP S/4HANA, on-premise, landscape as a trial system either in *Amazon Web Services* (AWS) or in *Microsoft Azure*. You will require an account for the cloud provider. Figure 6.1 shows the SAP S/4HANA Fully-Activated Appliance in SAP CAL.

Amazon Web Services and Microsoft Azure

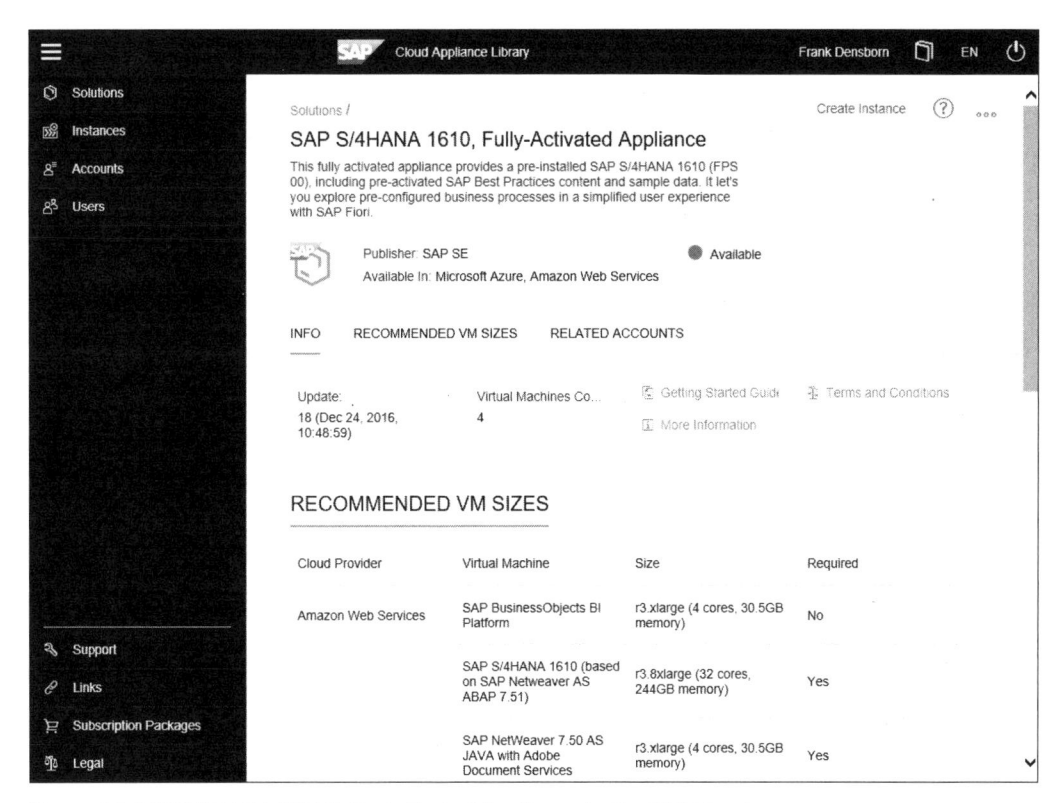

Figure 6.1 SAP S/4HANA 1610 Fully-Activated Appliance in the SAP Cloud Appliance Library

Benefits The benefits of using the SAP CAL landscape are its scalability and availability: You can define various sizes for the virtual systems (i.e., different memory and disk sizes) and thus easily scale the landscape. Furthermore, you can stop, start, and use your system as required. Actual costs involve hourly fees for activated systems only (in addition to the low basic costs for each instance). If needed, you can deactivate a system and then (re)activate it later on.

While this system is deployed within a few hours with the cloud approach, you can also implement this appliance on-premise in your data center within one or two days. In addition to a trial system, this method also allows you to deploy a sandbox system for a proof of concept, for example, or as a development system in your future SAP S/4HANA landscape. The following section discusses these options in more detail.

6.2 SAP S/4HANA Fully-Activated Appliance

Appliance A *software appliance* is a compressed system, similar to a large ZIP file (SAP S/4HANA 1610 Fully-Activated Appliance is about 100GB), which you can easily extract to a common system. The software appliance contains all the settings and properties that were enabled when the original system was set up.

The software appliance behaves like a system copy of a SAP S/4HANA system, including ABAP code, SAP HANA database, SAP Best Practices, and technical SAP Fiori configuration. The SAP HANA database is bundled with the SAP S/4HANA software, including the frontend server for SAP Fiori, SAP Gateway.

In addition, the appliance contains demo scenarios and sample data for the model company. You can therefore easily use it for sandbox systems, for proofs of concept, and for the fit-to-gap or fit-to-standard analyses provided by SAP Activate (see Chapter 5, Section 5.2).

Figure 6.2 illustrates the SAP S/4HANA Fully-Activated Appliance concept.

Basis for the production system Customers and SAP partners can use the preconfigured appliance as a starting point. You can also continue using the appliance after the 30-day trial period if you purchase licenses for SAP S/4HANA and the SAP HANA database.

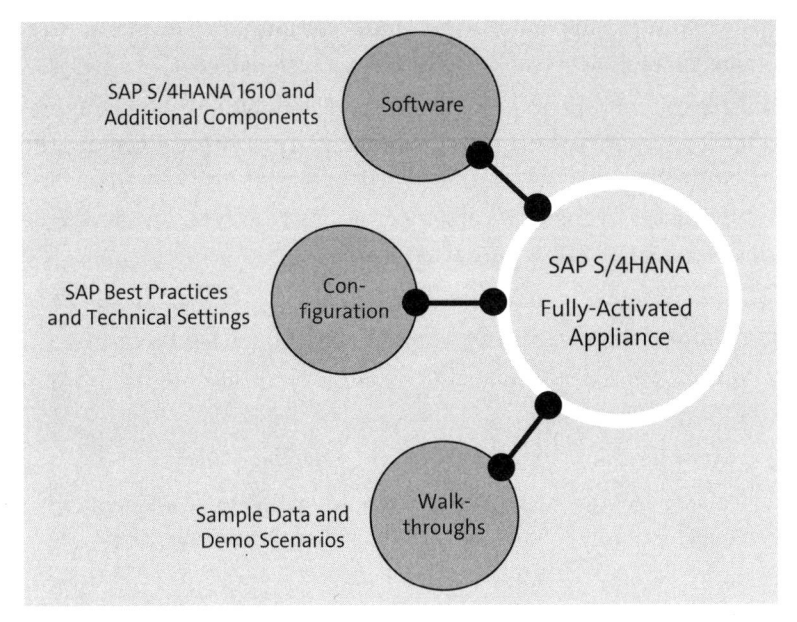

Figure 6.2 SAP S/4HANA Fully-Activated Appliance Concept

You have two options for using the SAP S/4HANA Fully-Activated Appliance:

Using the appliance

- **SAP Cloud Appliance Library**
  SAP CAL allows you to use the appliance in a hosted cloud solution (IaaS). Creating your SAP S/4HANA Fully-Activated Appliance instance to logging on to the system for the first time should only take one or two hours. Hosting will cost only a few dollars per hour when the system is active. Some cloud providers give you a starting credit when creating your account. This option includes a 30-day test license for the SAP S/4HANA system and SAP CAL. After that period, you'll have to purchase a license for SAP S/4HANA, on-premise, and SAP CAL (via *subscription*).

  SAP CAL contains a detailed description of how to set up the solution as well as blogs and forums in which you can get support. You'll also get information on using the appliance beyond the 30-day trial period.

- **On-premise installation**
  You can also install the SAP S/4HANA Fully-Activated Appliance on your own hardware easily. You'll only need hardware that is supported by the appliance and a Linux operating system. All other components are

installed with the appliance. (The Linux version must meet SAP's requirements for a successful installation of a system copy.)

Thanks to the concept of the appliance, you'll be able to utilize your preconfigured system within one to two days. You can either download the installation files from the Internet or order a Blu-ray disk with these files. The appliance is free, even if you order the disk. However, you'll need the corresponding SAP full or partial licenses.

> **Further Information on the Appliance in SAP CAL and On-Premise**
>
> You can find detailed information (including a quick guide to using SAP CAL) at the following link:
>
> *https://www.sap.com/cmp/oth/crm-s4hana/s4hana-on-premise.html*
>
> The following SAP Notes contain further information on the system requirements for the on-premise installation and on the order process:
>
> - For SAP Partners: SAP Note 2041140
> - For customers: SAP Note 2202234

Deployment scenarios

The following deployment scenarios are available for the SAP S/4HANA Fully-Activated Appliance:

- **Sandbox system**
  Sandbox systems may require more time for testing than the 30-day trial period. You might also want to keep the results of testing in the sandbox system, which makes a separate license for the product necessary. With the reference system, you can considerably reduce the initial effort required for setting up the system and is thus the ideal starting point for a sandbox system even if you use it beyond the 30-day trial period. You can start with the appliance and then customize the solution with your own master data, organizational structures, etc., according to SAP Best Practices. For this purpose, a hosting subscription of a cloud provider in SAP CAL is the best option, because you don't have to deploy any hardware.

- **Proof of concept**
  The appliance is an ideal proof of concept (PoC) system because it is preconfigured and can be implemented easily. Because you'll be using a specific copy of the SAP S/4HANA system, you can customize the system as required and extend the solution scope to accelerate your PoC.

- **Development system**
  From a technical perspective, you can also run the appliance as a development system in the production landscape later on. However, SAP does not recommend this system for SAP S/4HANA landscapes, for the following reasons:
  - All languages are installed and enabled in the system. (This does not apply to your production system.)
  - Depending on your licenses, additional license costs might be incurred (for example, for SAP Integrated Business Planning and SAP Master Data Governance [MDG], which are part of the appliance).
  - In contrast to SAP recommendations for production landscapes, SAP Gateway is installed as the frontend server for SAP Fiori in the same system. (SAP recommends separating the frontend server from the backend to make it easier to independently maintain your systems and implement patches.)

> **Cost Overview**
> For an overview of the costs that will be incurred and the licenses that may be required to use the SAP S/4HANA Fully-Activated Appliance, follow the link under "SAP S/4HANA 1610 Appliance – License & Cost Drivers" at *https://blogs.sap.com/?p=406099*.

> **Appliance as a First Step to SAP S/4HANA**
> You can use the trial system and the appliance to get started with SAP S/4HANA. If you then decide to migrate to SAP S/4HANA, you can transfer the settings you made in the trial system to the production landscape.

6.3 Solution Scope of the Model System

The SAP S/4HANA 1610 Fully-Activated Appliance consists of four virtual machines bundled in one instance. The appliance comprises the following components:

- SAP S/4HANA 1610, on-premise (ABAP backend including SAP HANA database and SAP Gateway as the frontend server for SAP Fiori)

185

- SAP NetWeaver Application Server Java (with Adobe Document Services, ADS)
- SAP Best Practices (depending on the client, all SAP Best Practices that are available in SAP S/4HANA 1610 are already enabled)
- SAP Fiori (with its extensibility interfaces and additional available fields)
- SAP Screen Personas
- SAP Extended Warehouse Management (SAP EWM)
- Content for various scenarios in interactive demos

The following components are optional and are only available in SAP CAL (not in on-premise installations of the SAP S/4HANA Fully-Activated Appliance):

- SAP BusinessObjects BI platform (with predefined reports)
- Microsoft Remote Desktop (for easy access to frontend tools and SAP Fiori)
- All 14 localizations in the reference clients (Germany, USA, Australia, Belgium, Canada, China, Switzerland, France, Great Britain, Hungary, Japan, Netherlands, Philippines, and Singapore)

Figure 6.3 provides an overview of the software components of the SAP S/4HANA Fully-Activated Appliance.

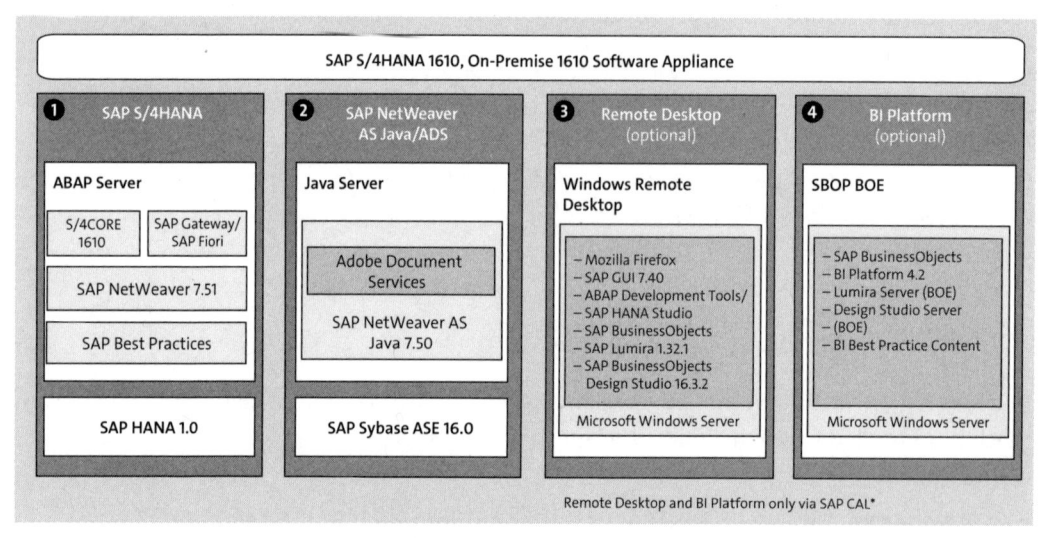

Figure 6.3 SAP S/4HANA Fully-Activated Appliance Components

6.3 Solution Scope of the Model System

The SAP S/4HANA Fully-Activated Appliance contains six preconfigured clients with different flavors of the SAP Best Practices content:

Preconfigured clients

- **Client 000**

  The *master client* is the default client of all SAP S/4HANA systems and is delivered by the appliance without any changes. You can use Client 000 as the starting point for your activities if you want to implement SAP S/4HANA without SAP Best Practices, and it serves as a reference client for comparison of the predelivered customizing with the empty product.

- **Client 100**

  Client 100 is the trial client and includes SAP Best Practices for SAP S/4HANA already activated as well as sample data, processes, and scenarios for the USA and Germany. Client 100 also maps complete business processes of the model company.

  This client serves as the starting point for exploring SAP S/4HANA. The system is already completely preconfigured and filled with data (master and transaction data), so you can start immediately and use a model company with company code 1710 for the USA or company code 1010 for Germany.

- **Client 200**

  All technical activities for activating SAP Best Practices have been executed in this client, but SAP Best Practices have not been activated yet. Thus, you can carry out activating SAP Best Practices yourself using the scope that is relevant to you and possibly restrict it. You can also test the activation.

  Client 200 is a preactivation client that already contains the SAP Fiori launchpad configuration (and is therefore ideal for comparisons if you want to activate SAP Fiori launchpad).

- **Client 300**

  This client is the default reference client for SAP Best Practices. Client 300 is a copy of the master client in which SAP Best Practices is enabled for all 14 localizations in SAP S/4HANA 1610, on-premise. You can view what the system looks like after you have implemented the best practices.

  You can use Client 300 as a reference because this client is not preconfigured. However, as a result, this client doesn't contain demo data, placing it between Client 000 and Client 100 in terms of completeness.

- **Client 400**

  Client 400 is the SAP Business Warehouse (SAP BW) client and contains preactivated content for SAP Integrated Business Planning (IBP) for Finance. This client is used only indirectly to support SAP Best Practices that include IBP, which is based on SAP BW.

- **Client 500**

  Similar to Client 300, Client 500 is a reference system for SAP Best Practices. The difference with Client 300 is that all configurations (including configurations that are not relevant to SAP Best Practices) are copied from the master client.

  You can use this client for fit-to-gap or fit-to-standard workshops because not only can it be used for comparisons with the default content in SAP Best Practices but also for comparisons with the complete Customizing of Client 000.

Integration — By default, the SAP S/4HANA Fully-Activated Appliance is not integrated with SAP Ariba, the SAP Financial Services Network, or the Vertex system. However, you can carry out these integrations yourself. You'll need the corresponding licenses and logon data for the external systems. For more information on this, see Chapter 13.

6.4 Enterprise Structure of the Model Company

Plants and areas — Figure 6.4 shows the enterprise structure of the model company in SAP S/4HANA, on-premise. Placeholder **xx** stands for different country codes. Example country codes include the following:

- 10 = Germany (DE)
- 11 = Great Britain (UK)
- 17 = USA (US)
- 29 = Canada (CA)
- 30 = Australia (AU)

Plant xx10, which is marked with an asterisk, can be copied (for example, to xx20) and then be used for transfers.

6.4 Enterprise Structure of the Model Company

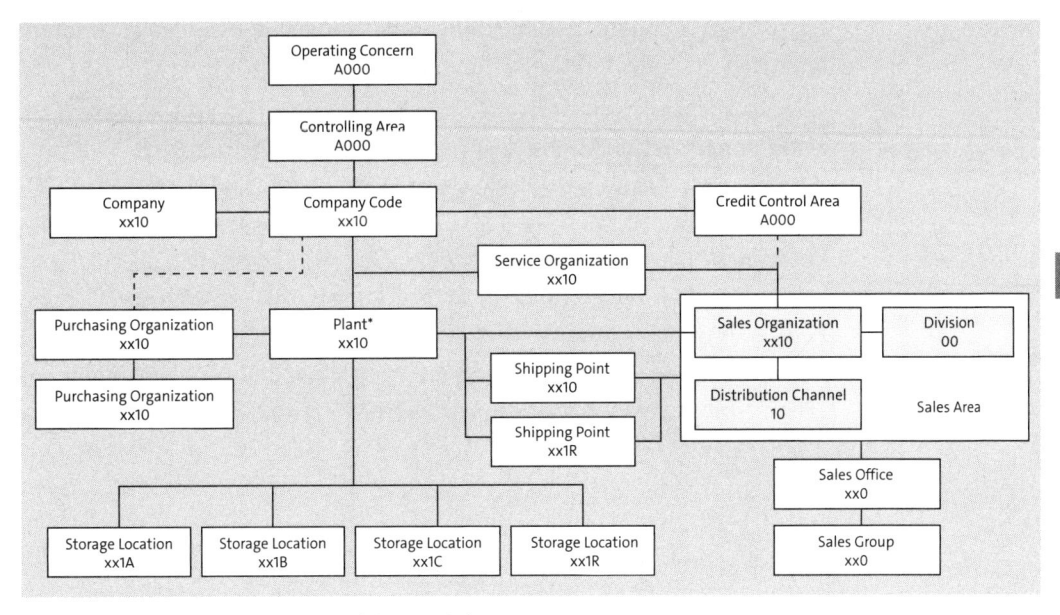

Figure 6.4 Enterprise Structure of the Model Company

If you use the model company, you'll start your implementation of SAP S/4HANA directly. You don't need to start with a fully enabled solution, but you can activate the business processes that you actually need to use in batches. Business processes from various areas can be activated and executed together.

Flexible process activation

You can then run a fit-to-gap or fit-to-standard analysis in the context of the SAP S/4HANA workshop. In this way, all parties involved in the SAP S/4HANA project will receive an overview of the implementation project and develop a migration strategy at an early stage. The idea is to adjust the default model company only if you can achieve a unique selling proposition for your enterprise by doing so. In all other cases, you should adhere or revert to the default settings instead of replicating your legacy system. Generally, you may have decided to deviate from the default settings in your legacy system when the necessary functions were not available in the SAP system. The goal of the fit-to-gap workshop is to understand the functions of the SAP S/4HANA system, validate the solution, and tailor it to your requirements using SAP Best Practices within the SAP S/4HANA system.

Fit gap analysis

189

Possible gaps should be determined and bridged, a completely different approach than the traditional implementation blueprint.

> **Reference System for Preparing the Migration with this Book**
>
> The reference system with the model company described in this chapter can be useful throughout the book. Part II discusses migrating to SAP S/4HANA in a public cloud (the SaaS model), and Part III addresses migrating to SAP S/4HANA, on-premise, or migrating to SAP S/4HANA in a private cloud (hosting).
>
> At this point, the migration road diverges. If you are not sure yet which deployment model (cloud or on-premise) suits your requirements best, read Chapter 7 first.

PART II
Migrating to SAP S/4HANA in the Cloud

Chapter 7
Migrating to the Public Cloud

A cloud solution offers new opportunities for organizing and financing the IT in your enterprise. This chapter introduces SAP S/4HANA Cloud and describes the various SAP S/4HANA Cloud migration scenarios.

How can I access an SAP S/4HANA cloud instance? What do I need to consider when setting up the solution? How do I transfer existing data to the public cloud or an SaaS (software as a service) system?

The first section of this chapter discusses these and similar questions. The second section provides a brief overview of how to configure an SAP S/4HANA cloud system. The third section describes migrating to such a cloud system. While this chapter focuses on migrating to a public cloud, Chapter 11 covers migrating to a private cloud solution.

> **SAP Hybris Marketing Cloud**
>
> As a satellite system used to replicate data from external sources, SAP Hybris Marketing Cloud is not discussed in this chapter. For more information on integration with SAP Hybris Marketing Cloud, see Chapter 8, Section 8.3.

7.1 Setting Up SAP S/4HANA Cloud

If you select a cloud operating model, you can expect to use the software in production rather quickly. To implement your cloud operating model, you should take a closer look at the characteristics of SAP S/4HANA Cloud. Chapter 3, Section 3.1.2 and Section 3.2.2, introduced the basic characteristics of SaaS solutions, their differences from on-premise operating models, and the various SAP S/4HANA public cloud editions.

If you opt for SAP S/4HANA Cloud, you'll access the system via a central URL, which you'll usually receive via email with further access information. With this URL, users can log on to the system and use the applications via a web browser.

New implementation

Migrating to SAP S/4HANA Cloud involves a new implementation of the system. For technical reasons, you cannot convert an existing on-premise system to an SaaS solution. The compatibility functions offered in the on-premise editions mainly serve this system conversion purpose. Consequently, when migrating to the SaaS solution, you'll follow the data transfer scenarios described in detail in Section 7.3.

7.1.1 Discover Phase: Configuring the SAP S/4HANA Cloud Trial System

Trial level

SAP provides various levels for SAP S/4HANA Cloud. The easiest level to reach is the *trial level*, which we introduced in Chapter 6, Section 6.1. Figure 7.1 shows the welcome screen of the corresponding trial system. When you click on the **Start your free trial now** button, you'll be prompted to enter some details. Afterwards, you'll be provided with a system user and access details.

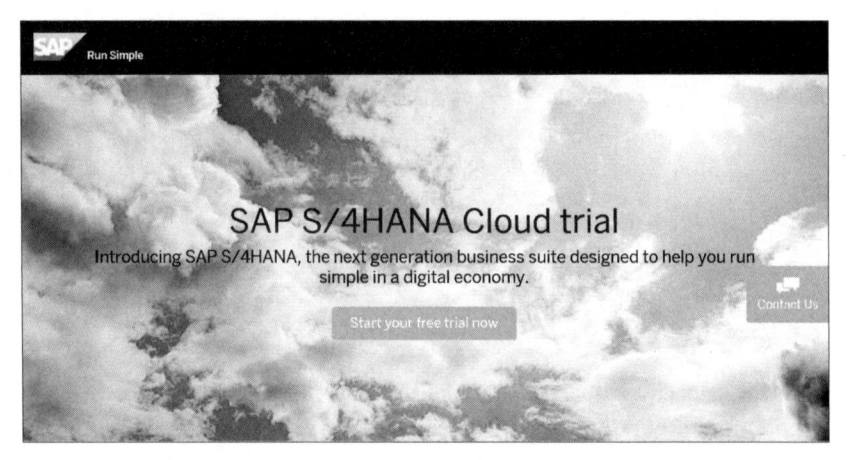

Figure 7.1 Welcome Screen for SAP S/4HANA Cloud Trial

The trial system is preconfigured and contains predefined business roles from which you can select. You'll share the system with other customers.

The trial system will give you your first impressions of the navigation, the user interface, and the design of SAP S/4HANA Cloud. You cannot use the trial system to set up your own SAP S/4HANA Cloud system. A separate instance is required for your own SAP S/4HANA Cloud system. The trial system is an optional offer from SAP, and you won't have to purchase or use SAP S/4HANA Cloud when using the trial system.

7.1.2 Explore Phase: Configuring the SAP S/4HANA Cloud Starter System

You'll purchase SAP S/4HANA Cloud from SAP sales representatives. If you entered your data for the trial access, a sales representative should contact you at some time. You can also contact the sales team directly, using the contact buttons on the website or in the system.

Once you agree to the contract, you can start migrating to SAP S/4HANA Cloud. Your migration project will be divided into the four phases of the SAP Activate implementation method, which we introduced in Chapter 5, Section 5.2. In the first phase, you'll explore the trial system. Figure 7.2 illustrates the project phases for your journey to SAP S/4HANA Cloud.

SAP Activate phases

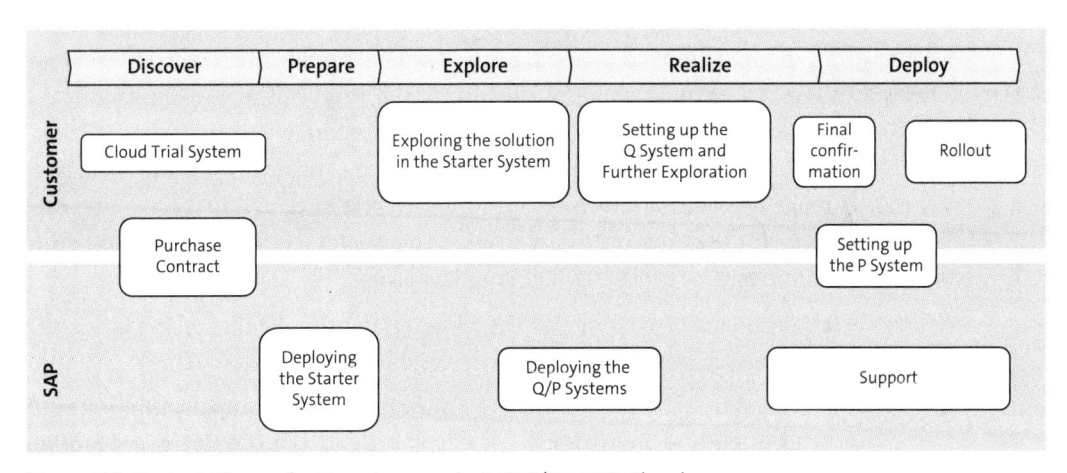

Figure 7.2 Project Phases for Your Journey to SAP S/4HANA Cloud

When you purchase SAP S/4HANA Cloud, SAP will provide a *starter system* that has the following two goals:

Starter system

- The starter system allows you to explore SAP S/4HANA Cloud in more detail than the trial system. You should not miss this opportunity to thoroughly test the business scope for your specific requirements. This phase is therefore referred to as the *explore phase*.

- The starter system also allows you to define your own environment: In the starter system, you'll assign roles, configurations, users, and the integration with other systems.

The following sections further describe how to configure the starter system. Because at first you'll only have a technical user, the general procedure involves the following steps:

1. Creating the administrator
2. Logging off from the system and logging on again as the administrator
3. Modeling roles using templates
4. Maintaining employees and assigning roles
5. Logging on with the created personal users
6. Setting up and using the system

Assigning Users for the Administrator and Key User

Creating the administrator user

In the first step, you should receive several emails from SAP, at least two. One of the emails contains the technical user; the other email contains the corresponding password. With this information, you'll create an administrator and define administrator access. With this administrator, you'll later make all necessary technical settings. Of course, you'll first have to create users for the employees involved in the implementation project to define your business processes (i.e., your key users).

1. Log on to the system with the technical user by clicking on the link in the first email. Enter your user name and password.

2. The start screen of the SAP Fiori launchpad will be displayed. In our example shown in Figure 7.3, we navigated to the **Contacts and Profiles** group. The header line displays the selected group and its adjacent groups.

3. First, you must ensure that the employee master data is maintained for you and your project team. Select the **Maintain Employees** tile in the **Employee—Master Data** group (see Figure 7.4).

7.1 Setting Up SAP S/4HANA Cloud

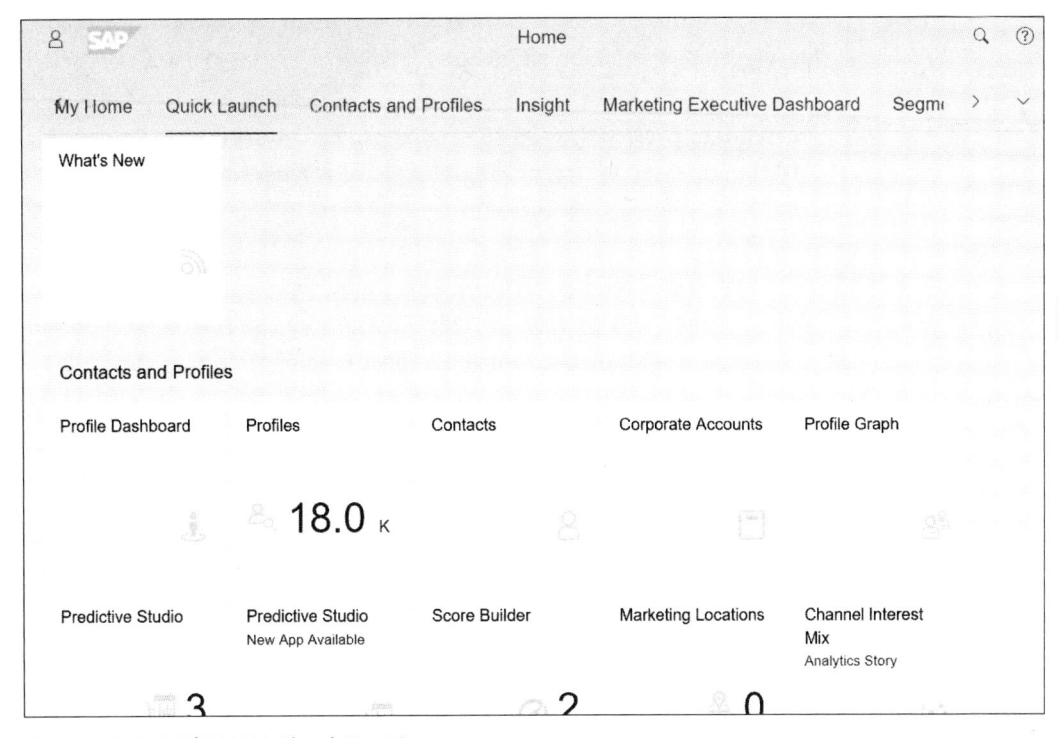

Figure 7.3 SAP S/4HANA Cloud Start Screen

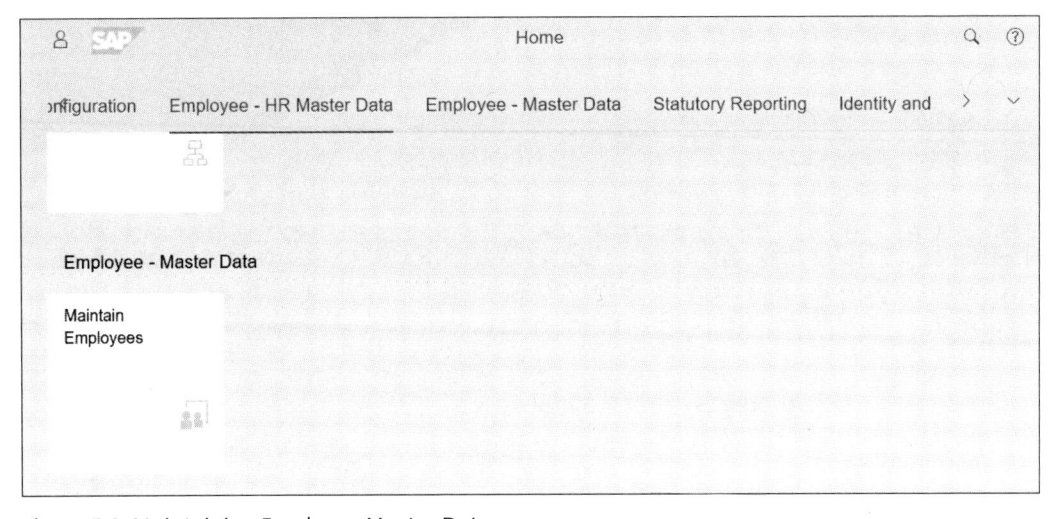

Figure 7.4 Maintaining Employee Master Data

197

7 Migrating to the Public Cloud

> [»] **Navigation in SAP Fiori Launchpad**
>
> The start screen (SAP Fiori launchpad) is divided into launchpad groups. The currently selected group is underlined in the header line. You can navigate to other groups by scrolling to the desired group or using the dropdown menu ✉ at the top right.

4. On the next screen (see Figure 7.5), you'll maintain the required user master data, at least for the administrator(s). Alternatively, you can import user data lists using the **Import Employees** tile in the **Employees—HR Master Data** group. We always recommend creating users with your personal user and reserving the technical user for initial access only.

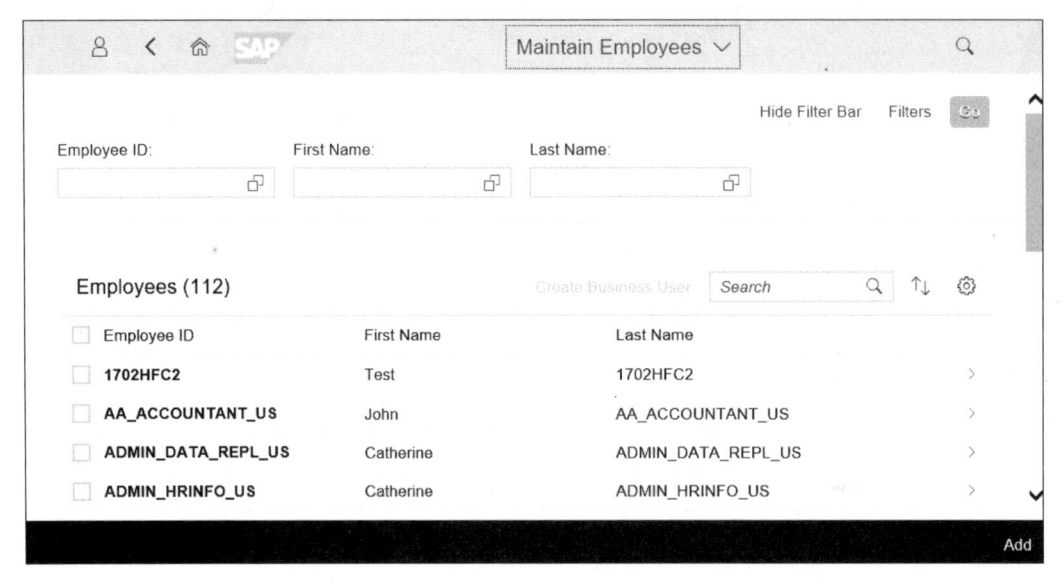

Employee ID	First Name	Last Name
1702HFC2	Test	1702HFC2
AA_ACCOUNTANT_US	John	AA_ACCOUNTANT_US
ADMIN_DATA_REPL_US	Catherine	ADMIN_DATA_REPL_US
ADMIN_HRINFO_US	Catherine	ADMIN_HRINFO_US

Figure 7.5 User Maintenance Entry Screen in SAP S/4HANA Cloud

> [»] **Alternative User Maintenance**
>
> In some SAP S/4HANA Cloud versions, you might not be able to maintain the users directly. In this case, an SAP service employee will have to create the user master data. Open an SAP Support ticket in the SAP Message

> Component XX-S4C-SRV with the subject "User Creation in the Starter System." Attach a list with the required master data to the message. The following fields are available:
>
> - **Email Address**: for example, name@XX.com
> - **Login Name**: for example, FirstnameLastname
> - **Country Code**: for example, US
> - **Family Name**: for example, "last name"
> - **Gender Code**: 1 = male, 2 = female
> - **Given name**: for example, "first name"
> - **Home Address Country Code**: for example, US
> - **Company Code**: company ID
> - **Cost Center**: cost center
>
> For more information, see the Roadmap Viewer at *http://bit.ly/v1448071*.

Assigning Roles for Administrators and Key Users

In the next step, you must assign the administrator role to the administration user:

1. Log on to the system with the newly created user.
2. Select the **Maintain Business Users** tile in the **Identity and Access Management** group.
3. In the next dialog box, assign the desired roles to the selected user, which is the SAP_BR_ADMINISTRATOR administrator role in our example (see Figure 7.6). If the administrator is also expected to maintain employee data, assign the role SAP_BR_ADMINISTRATOR_HRINFO.

Now you can use the administrator. Log on to the system as the administrator and assign roles to your key users.

Please note that the starter system supports only a small number of users because the starter system is designed to explore SAP S/4HANA in detail and to test alternative configurations. As a result, the starter system only provides a few roles. You'll usually create key users in the systems of the next project phase. Section 7.1.3 discusses this phase in more detail. Ensure that you have assigned administrator rights to at least one user.

7 Migrating to the Public Cloud

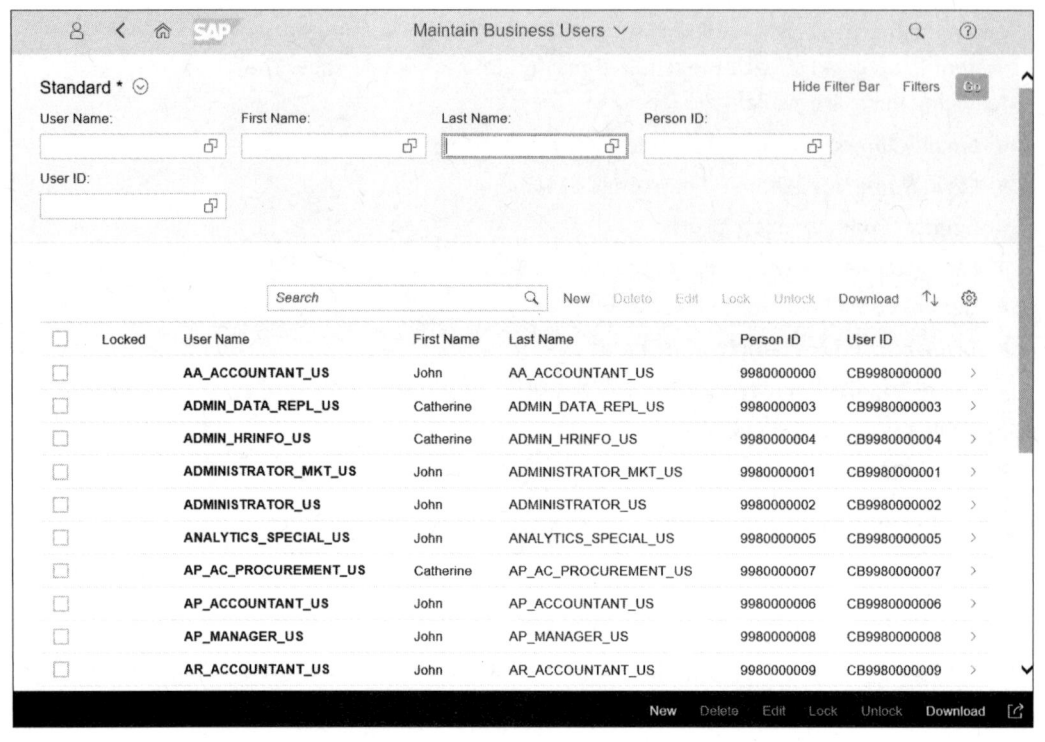

	Locked	User Name	First Name	Last Name	Person ID	User ID	
☐		AA_ACCOUNTANT_US	John	AA_ACCOUNTANT_US	9980000000	CB9980000000	>
☐		ADMIN_DATA_REPL_US	Catherine	ADMIN_DATA_REPL_US	9980000003	CB9980000003	>
☐		ADMIN_HRINFO_US	Catherine	ADMIN_HRINFO_US	9980000004	CB9980000004	>
☐		ADMINISTRATOR_MKT_US	John	ADMINISTRATOR_MKT_US	9980000001	CB9980000001	>
☐		ADMINISTRATOR_US	John	ADMINISTRATOR_US	9980000002	CB9980000002	>
☐		ANALYTICS_SPECIAL_US	John	ANALYTICS_SPECIAL_US	9980000005	CB9980000005	>
☐		AP_AC_PROCUREMENT_US	Catherine	AP_AC_PROCUREMENT_US	9980000007	CB9980000007	>
☐		AP_ACCOUNTANT_US	John	AP_ACCOUNTANT_US	9980000006	CB9980000006	>
☐		AP_MANAGER_US	John	AP_MANAGER_US	9980000008	CB9980000008	>
☐		AR_ACCOUNTANT_US	John	AR_ACCOUNTANT_US	9980000009	CB9980000009	>

Figure 7.6 Entry Screen for Role Assignment Maintenance

Importing Users to the SAP Cloud Identity Tenant

Authenticating users Please note that personal users must also be authenticated to access the cloud system via an *identity provider* (IDP). For SAP S/4HANA Cloud, SAP provides its own identity provider by default: *SAP Cloud Identity*. SAP Cloud Identity automatically provides a tenant for each SAP S/4HANA Cloud installation. Figure 7.7 illustrates this user identification architecture. Of course, you can also use another identity provider. However, we assume that you'll use SAP Cloud Identity for this example. You'll receive separate access data for this SAP Cloud Identity tenant.

You'll have to create each user in these two systems: In the SAP S/4HANA Cloud system, you'll define the user master data and the various roles for business application authorizations. The cloud identity provider authenticates the users. You must not confuse these two systems.

7.1 Setting Up SAP S/4HANA Cloud

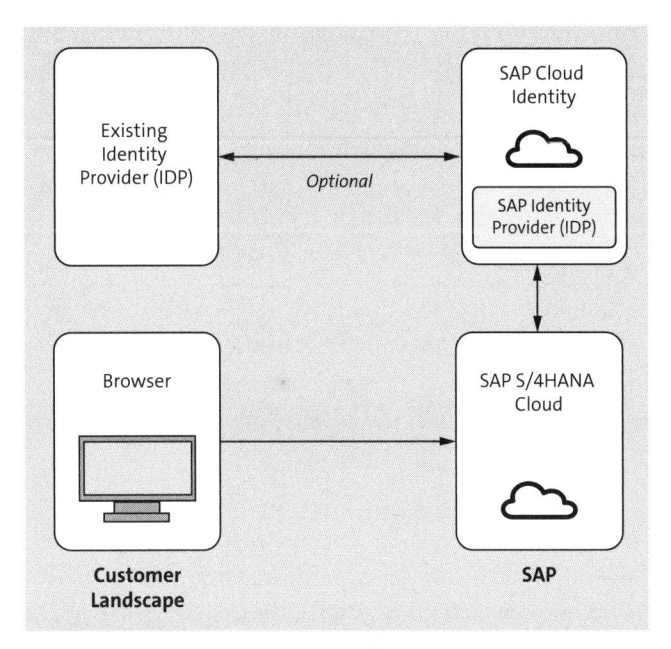

Figure 7.7 User Authentication Architecture

To enable authentication, authorized users must be made known to the cloud identity provider. For data security reasons, only you are allowed to access the identity provider; thus, you'll have to import your users to the identity provider during the implementation project. You'll export the employee master data from SAP S/4HANA Cloud and import this data to the cloud identity provider. Table 7.1 provides an overview of the necessary steps in the two systems.

	Creating Employee Master Data	Exporting Data from SAP S/4HANA	Importing Data to the Cloud Identity Provider
Action	**Maintain Employees** tile	▪ **Maintain Business Users** tile ▪ Select the necessary users ▪ Select **Download**	▪ **Import Users** tile ▪ Upload file ▪ Send email to users
System	SAP S/4HANA Cloud	SAP S/4HANA Cloud	Cloud identity provider

Table 7.1 Maintaining Master Data in the SAP S/4HANA Cloud System and the Cloud Identity Provider

7 Migrating to the Public Cloud

Technical and personal users

From now on, you should always use your personal user when working in the system. After creating personal users with administrator rights and making them known in SAP Cloud Identity, log off from the technical user. Then, log on to the system with the administrator user to make further settings. Alternatively, you can also use a key user to carry out configurations.

> **User Administration Options**
>
> SAP S/4HANA provides various options for managing and authenticating users. Choosing your preferred option is an SAP S/4HANA implementation subproject. Because access to the system is a basic prerequisite for essential migration project steps, let's look at the various options next.
>
> Three user administration models exist for implementing SAP S/4HANA Cloud:
>
> - **Embedded user administration**
>   The simplest option is to use the basic user administration that is already integrated into SAP S/4HANA Cloud. In this model, SAP Cloud Identity contains a specific IDP. This option enables you to maintain basic user master data. SAP S/4HANA does not support advanced human resources (HR) scenarios.
>
> - **Integration of human resources with SAP SuccessFactors**
>   SAP recommends using SAP SuccessFactors for all HR aspects and scenarios. You can integrate SAP SuccessFactors with SAP S/4HANA. If you create employee master data in SAP SuccessFactors, this data will be automatically replicated in SAP S/4HANA, and users will be created based on this data. Then, you'll only have to assign the relevant business roles to these users in SAP S/4HANA. In this scenario, authentication takes place in SAP SuccessFactors.
>
> - **Alternative IDP solution**
>   Alternatively, you can integrate SAP S/4HANA with any third-party IDP solution. This option is designed for customers who already use other user administration solutions. Instead of using the embedded IDP, SAP Cloud Identity will request that the alternative identity provider authenticate the users.
>
> In this book, we focus solely on the first model: basic embedded user administration.

Configuring Business Processes

Users configuring business processes in the system need to have the role SAP_BR_BPC_EXPERT (Configuration Expert – Business Process Configuration). In the **Manage Your Solution** app, this role lets you change the system configuration using the **Configure the Solution** function. This step is described in Section 7.2.

Managing your solution as a process expert

Data Migration

You should test basic data migration aspects in the starter system. As a result, you'll get insights into your data import processes, data quality, and the interaction between data and configuration. For SAP S/4HANA Cloud, data is imported via the SAP S/4HANA migration cockpit.

Testing the data transfer

1. Log on to the system with the administrator user.
2. Select the **Manage Your Solution** tile in the **Full Implementation** group.
3. Select the **Migrate Your Data** function.
4. Perform the steps described in Section 7.3.

Transition to the Realize Phase

Transitioning to the next project phase is an explicit step in the system: You'll have to confirm that you have completed the explore phase in the app **Manage Your Solution**. Only then will you be provided with production systems. You have various options for this transition:

Completing the explore phase

- Select the **Manage Your Solution** tile in the **Full Implementation** group. This tile is the central entry point to the basic system configuration. In the **Manage Your Solution** app, select **Configure Your Solution**. The current phase of your system will be displayed. In the lower right-hand corner of the detail screen, you can trigger the phase shift (see Figure 7.10 later in this chapter).

- Alternatively, you can contact the SAP Service team by opening an SAP Support ticket with the subject "Request Quality System" in the SAP message component XX-S4C-SRV and requesting the transition to the realize phase.

When the phase of the system is changed, configuration will be "frozen" and can no longer be modified. However, the system is still available for test operations.

7 Migrating to the Public Cloud

Quality assurance and production system

Based on the starter system, SAP will now configure the quality assurance system for your production landscape and also create a production instance. Both systems are connected, which means that changes in the quality assurance system can be transferred to production. The production system is only available when the test system has been successfully configured.

> **[»] System Types**
>
> To use SAP S/4HANA in production, SAP generally recommends multisystem landscapes. Consequently, a two-system landscape is used for SAP S/4HANA Cloud. The quality assurance system (or *QA system*) in this two-system landscape enables you to make changes to the system without directly affecting operational production processes. You can implement and test configuration changes, new functions, or customer-specific enhancements in the QA system. Modifications are transferred to production using the SAP transport system only if these modifications have successfully passed the testing phase.

Choosing the time for transition

After SAP has created the quality assurance system, you'll receive an email with access data for this system. Before the production system is activated, you'll be asked to check the correct configuration of the systems. Only when you confirm the configuration will the production system activated in your landscape. You have two options for your implementation project:

- **Configuration in the starter system**
  You'll implement your project in the starter system and have the configurations transferred from this system to production. In this case, you can activate the production landscape in a timely manner.

- **Configuration in the quality assurance system**
  You'll change rather quickly from the starter system to the realize phase. In this case, you'll send the confirmation immediately to SAP. You'll then implement the configurations and specific settings in the QA system directly.

7.1.3 Realize Phase: Configuring the SAP S/4HANA Cloud Quality Assurance System

The starter system is mainly designed to familiarize yourself with SAP S/4HANA as well as identify and determine your individual customization.

The starter system is not released for production. Production requires the final SAP S/4HANA Cloud systems as provided in the realize phase. In these systems, you'll then define the final values and settings and create users for all employees.

The goal of this section is to prepare the system for initial usage in such a way that data from the legacy system can be imported to the cloud system. The following activities are required to prepare the system:

Steps of the realize phase

1. Importing or creating employee master data and setting up the authentication
2. Implementing the basic system configuration
3. Transferring data from the legacy system

To complete these preparatory steps for the system, you'll have to carry out further activities, such as setting up print control and selecting the relevant business processes. However, in this book, we won't discuss how to identify and define these processes. We assume that the necessary business processes have already been specified.

Importing Employee Master Data

Log on to the quality assurance system as an administrator. Use the **Maintain Employees** tile in the **Employee—Master Data** group to create all employees manually or forward a file with employee master data to the SAP Service Center. This procedure corresponds to the procedure in the explore phase, which we discussed in Section 7.1.2.

As in the starter system, you can also only create a limited number of employees in the quality assurance system. You must ensure that the master data for the key users is maintained. Key users are users who configure the system in the implementation project or are responsible for enhancements, tests, and maintenance.

Creating key users

Assigning Key User Roles

In contrast to the procedure in the starter system, you should assign key users differentiated user roles in the quality assurance system in the following way:

1. Log on to the system with the administrator user. Select the **Maintain Business Users** tile in the **Identity and Access Management** group.

205

2. In the next dialog box, assign the desired roles to the selected users. As shown in Figure 7.8, **MAINTENANCE_PLAN_US** user has the specific business role **Maintenance Planner** for maintenance tasks in addition to the generic **Employee** role that is assigned to all employees.

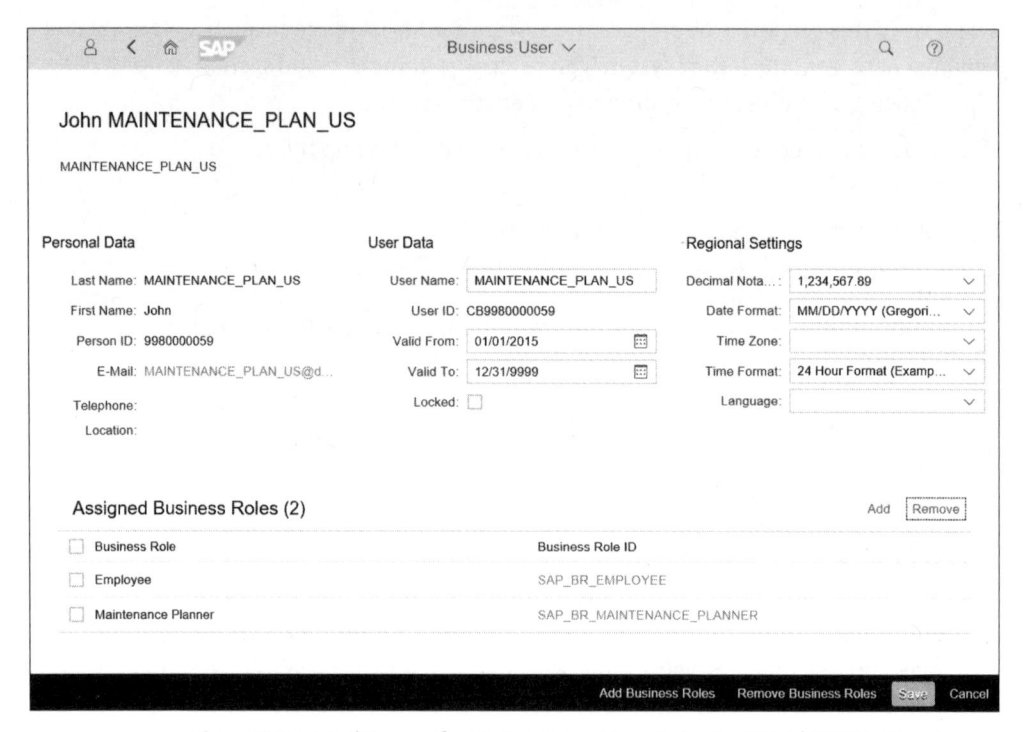

Figure 7.8 Detail Screen for Maintaining User Roles in SAP S/4HANA Cloud

Ensure that you have assigned administrator rights to at least one personal user.

Importing Users to the SAP Cloud Identity Tenant

Please note that, in the quality assurance system, personal users must also be authenticated to access the cloud system. Make your quality assurance system users known to SAP Cloud Identity by downloading the user list from the quality assurance system and importing it to the cloud identity provider. The steps correspond to the procedure in the starter system as described in Section 7.1.2.

Basic System Configuration: Defining Business Processes

Key users are responsible for defining business processes. After logging on as a key user, select the **Manage Your Solution** tile in the **End to End Implementation** group on the start screen. In this application, you'll select which business processes should be available in the system, which we discussed in detail in Section 7.2 under "Configuring Business Processes."

> **Quality Assurance and Production System Consistency** [«]
>
> Please note that the quality assurance system is used as the central template for generating the production system. You should therefore ensure that the business processes in the quality assurance system have been configured as required. The configuration in the production system should not differ from the configuration in the quality assurance system.
>
> For production, the quality assurance system also plays a central role in avoiding unpredicted effects to production, for example, from maintenance operations. You can also use the QA system to test future adaptations of the system usage, such as the implementation of additional functions, before transferring these adaptations to production. You can find more information on this in Section 7.2.

Data Migration

In the starter system, you only tested basic processes. Because the quality assurance system plays a major role for production, this system should be filled with sufficient data to test the defined business processes.

The quality of the data migration must also be ensured because your data and its configuration are interdependent. During the implementation project, you'll usually need to adjust the selection of the transferred data to the defined configuration values, and vice versa. So when migrating to SAP S/4HANA, you should also use the quality assurance system as the test system for the data migration.

As with the starter system, data is also migrated using the SAP S/4HANA migration cockpit as described in more detail in Section 7.1.2 and in Section 7.3.

7.1.4 Deploy Phase: Configuring the SAP S/4HANA Cloud Production Systems

Ensure that the quality assurance system has been fully implemented and that all acceptance tests have been passed successfully. Otherwise, you should not enter the final phase. With this last step, you will change over completely to production.

Requesting the production system — You request the production system in the same way as you requested the quality assurance system (see Section 7.1.3). Because you'll want to transfer your quality assurance system settings to production, open an SAP Support ticket in the SAP message component XX-S4C-SRV with the subject "Configuration Transport to P-System." SAP will then prepare the production system. The configuration and key user configuration from the quality assurance system is used.

> [!] **Quality Assurance System Lock**
>
> When planning the project, take into account that the quality assurance system is locked when the production system is generated to avoid unintentional changes.

Now, let's perform the basic implementation steps for the last time.

Importing Employee Master Data

Creating all production users — Log on to the production system as the administrator and create users for your employees using the **Maintain Employees** tile by importing the employee master data again, as described in Section 7.1.3. Ensure that you have created all employees in the production system.

You should follow a two-level approach when assigning roles and authorizations in the production system: First, you'll provide key users with access to the system. Those key users can then verify that all settings in the system are correct for the last time. Then, you'll provide all users with access to the system.

Assigning Roles for Key Users

In the **Maintain Business Users** dialog box, assign the desired roles to the users. Ensure that you have assigned differentiated roles to the users. Also, ensure that you have assigned administrator rights to at least one personal user.

Importing Key Users to the SAP Cloud Identity Tenant

Import key user data to the SAP Cloud Identity tenant to grant access to the system. Key users can then migrate the data and test the system for the last time. Immediately contact the SAP Service Center via the SAP message component XX-S4C-SRV if you encounter inconsistencies in the production system.

Data Migration

Data from the quality assurance system is not transferred directly to the production system on purpose to avoid having to import all data to the quality assurance system. You should therefore plan to migrate the data manually.

The previous steps also included data migration tests in the quality assurance system. The related test results are considered, and the settings for the data migration (filter criteria, custom fields, etc.) in the quality assurance system are copied for the data migration. Section 7.3.2 describes this procedure in detail.

Previously tested data migration

Assigning Roles to Business Users

Now, use the administrator user to assign the desired roles to all system users in the **Maintain Business Users** app. Again, ensure that you have assigned differentiated roles to the users.

Importing Users for Business Users to the SAP Cloud Identity Tenant

If you have received positive feedback from your key users, complete the user data with all employees in the cloud identity provider. With this step, all your users will gain access to the system.

> **Steps for Implementing Any Cloud System**
> The following steps for the technical implementation are performed in every SAP S/4HANA Cloud instance:

> - Creating employee master data
> - Assigning roles
> - Defining authorized users in the cloud identity provider
> - Defining business processes
> - Migrating data
> - Confirming transition to the next phase
>
> SAP provides a useful online checklist for these steps, which you can find in the Roadmap Viewer. For the technical steps described in this book, "Technical Architecture & Infrastructure" is of particular relevance at http://bit.ly/v1448072.

7.2 Configuring SAP S/4HANA Cloud

Customizing

As we mentioned in previous sections, you'll have to configure your system by defining the *Customizing*. Although mentioned in Section 7.1, this section describes this step in more detail. In general, configuration is a separate subproject. In our example, we'll use the configuration item `CustomerClassification-configure` to demonstrate the required steps for configuration. This configuration item defines the classes into which you'll categorize your customers. SAP provides classes A, B, and C. In this example, we will add class D to the customer classes. If you use another customer classification in your enterprise or want to change the preconfigured names, perform the following steps:

1. Navigate to the **End to End Implementation Experience** group and start the **Manage Your Solution** app (see Figure 7.9).

2. Then, select the **Configure Your Solution** function.

3. The system now displays an overview of the individual configuration apps (see Figure 7.10). Depending on the project phase (*explore*, *prepare*, *realize*, or *deploy*), different configuration apps are available. In the first two phases, you can usually access all configuration applications. As shown in Figure 7.10 and Figure 7.11, our sample configuration is in the fourth phase, **Deploy**, and only a few configuration apps are displayed.

7.2 Configuring SAP S/4HANA Cloud

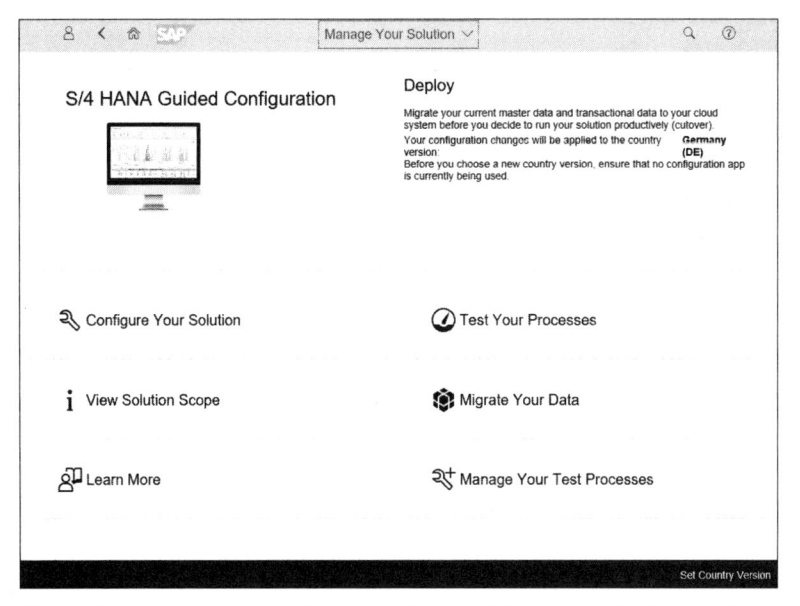

Figure 7.9 "Manage Your Solution" and the SAP S/4HANA Guided Configuration

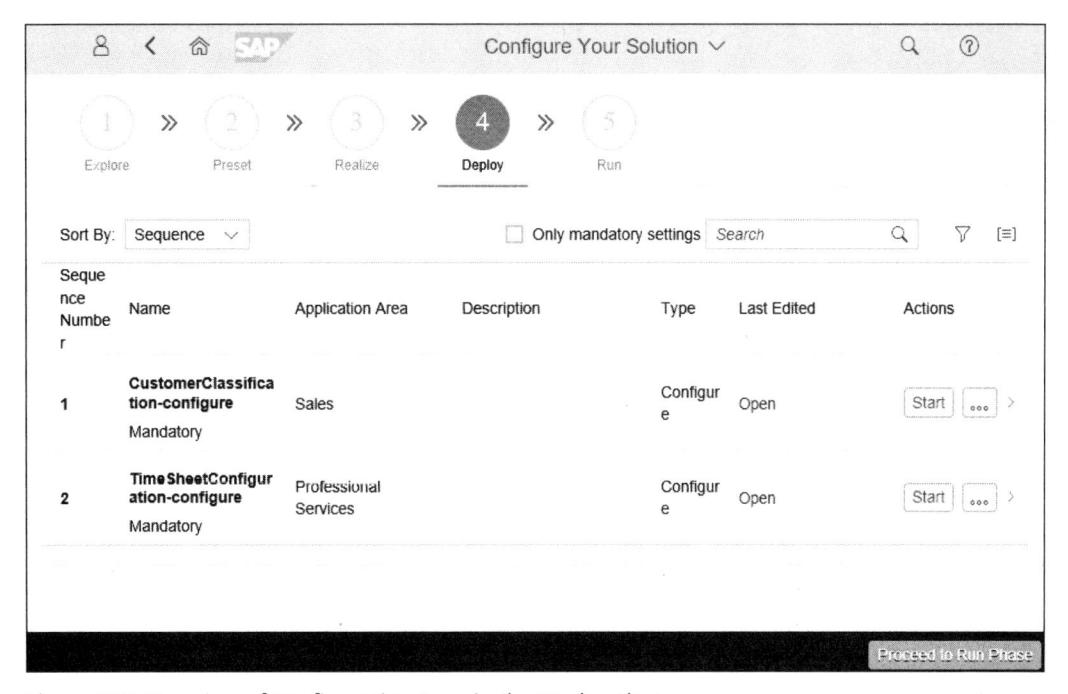

Figure 7.10 Overview of Configuration Apps in the Deploy Phase

7   Migrating to the Public Cloud

> [»] **Activating Help Texts for Configuration Apps**
>
> You can use the help button [?] at the top right next to the search button to activate the help texts for this screen. The system will then highlight the areas for which help texts are available. By clicking on the help button again, you'll deactivate the help texts. Figure 7.11 shows the overview screen with help texts enabled.

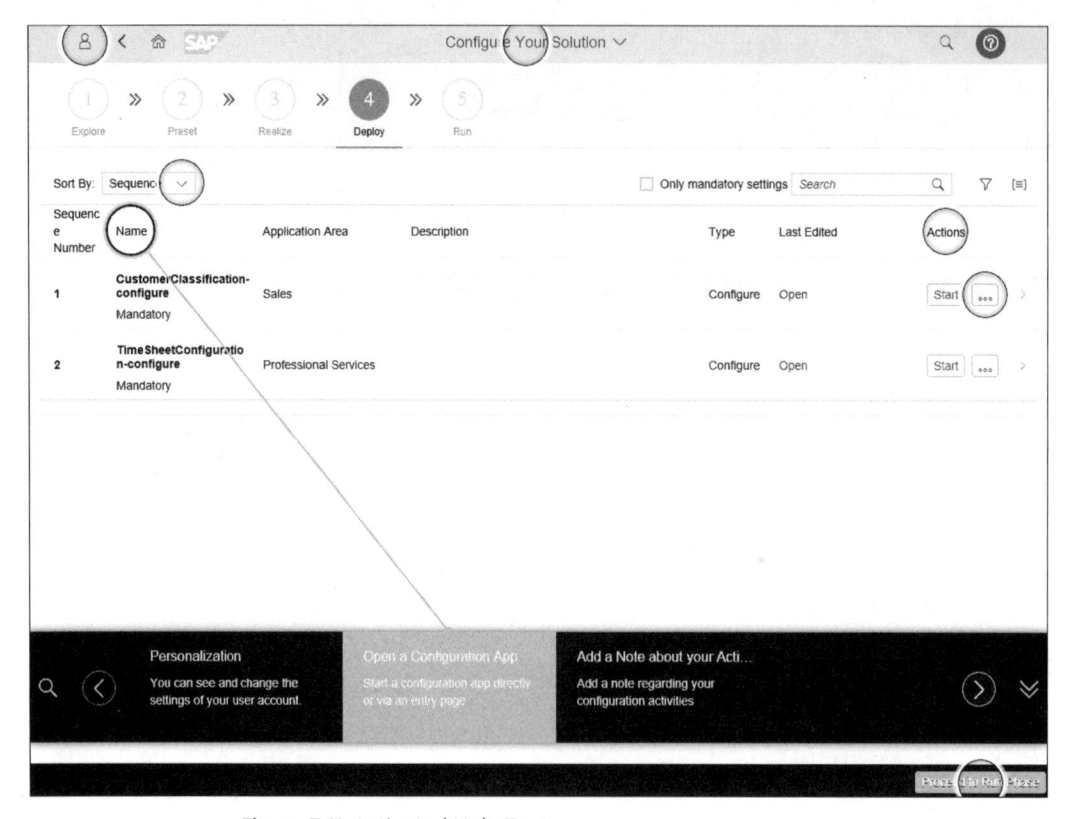

Figure 7.11 Activated Help Texts

4. Select the desired configuration app, **CustomerClassification-configure**, and click on **Start**.

5. Next, in the detail overview screen (shown in Figure 7.12), you'll add further items, customer classes in our example, using the link **Add**.

212

7.3   Migrating Data to SAP S/4HANA Cloud

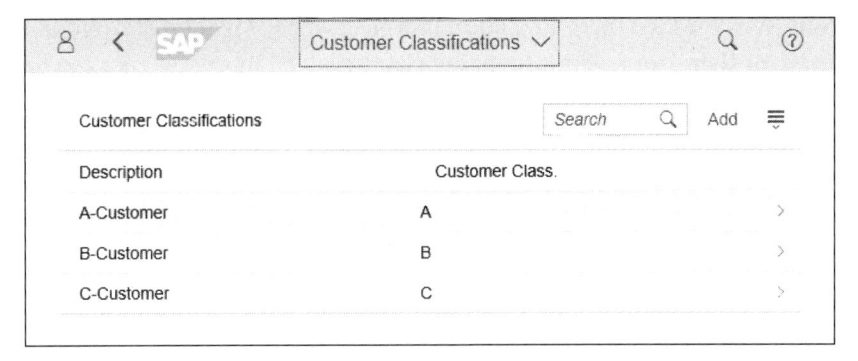

Figure 7.12 Detail Screen of the Configuration App for Customer Classification

6. In the following entry screen, enter an additional **Customer Class** and its **Description** and save these values using the **Save** button (see Figure 7.13).

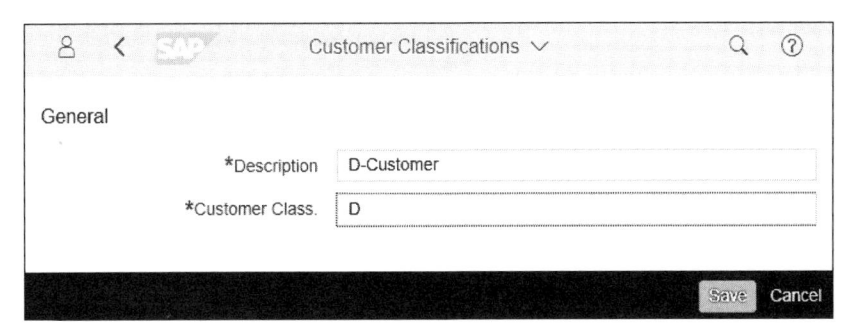

Figure 7.13 Adding a Value to a Configuration Item

You have now maintained a new customer class, and the system returns you to the detail screen, which displays an overview of all customer classes. You can maintain further customer classes or use the back button to return to the configuration app overview.

7.3   Migrating Data to SAP S/4HANA Cloud

Migrating to SAP S/4HANA Cloud differs from migrating to SAP S/4HANA, on-premise, because the known migration tools, such as Legacy System Migration Workbench (LSMW), SAP Data Services (Rapid Data Migration), Migration Workbench (MWB), etc., cannot be used. Either corresponding

7 Migrating to the Public Cloud

SAP Fiori apps for these migration tools (e.g., for LSMW and MWB) don't exist, or there are no corresponding cloud-enabled interfaces that can be called from external sources to migrate data (e.g., for SAP Data Services).

SAP S/4HANA Migration Cockpit

When migrating data to SAP S/4HANA Cloud, you'll use the *SAP S/4HANA migration cockpit*. As of SAP S/4HANA 1610, the SAP S/4HANA migration cockpit is also available for SAP S/4HANA, on-premise (see Chapter 11, Section 11.4).

7.3.1 Available Migration Objects

Migration objects for the cloud

Table 7.2 lists the migration objects that the SAP S/4HANA migration cockpit supports for each cloud edition (as of Version 1611). This list is restricted to the following SaaS cloud solutions that are available for SAP S/4HANA Cloud 1611. The individual cloud editions are abbreviated in Table 7.2 as follows:

- SAP S/4HANA Finance Cloud: FC
- SAP S/4HANA Professional Services Cloud: PSC
- SAP S/4HANA Enterprise Management Cloud: EMC

Migration Object	Area	FC	PSC	EMC
Activity Type	CO	X	X	X
Cost Center	CO	X	X	X
Activity Price	CO			X
Internal Order	CO	X		X
Profit Center	FI	X	X	X
Bank Master	FI	X	X	X
Customer	FI, SD	X	X	X
Supplier	FI, MM-PUR	X	X	X
Accounts Receivable (Customer) Open Item	FI	X	X	X
Accounts Payable (Vendor) Open Item	FI	X	X	X

Table 7.2 Migration Objects Supported by the SAP S/4HANA Migration Cockpit for SAP S/4HANA Cloud Editions

Migration Object	Area	FC	PSC	EMC
Fixed Assets incl. balances	FI-AA	X	X	X
G/L Account Balance	FI	X	X	X
G/L Account Open Item	FI	X	X	X
Exchange Rate	FI	X	X	X
Inventory Balances	MM-IM			X
Material Master	LO-MD	X	X	X
Material – Long Text	LO-MD	X	X	X
Purchasing Info Record	MM-PUR	X	X	X
Purchase Order	MM-PUR	X	X	X
Pricing Condition	SD, CO, MM-PUR	X	X	X
Contracts (Purchasing)	MM-PUR	X	X	X
Source List	MM-PUR			X
Sales Order	SD	X		X
Batches	QM, SD, PP-PI			X
Bill of Material (BOM)	PP			X
Work Center	PP, QM			X
Routing	PP			X
Equipment	PM			X
Maintenance Task List	PM			X
Functional Location	PM			X
Characteristic	CA			X
Class	CA			X
Commercial Project Management (CPM)	CA-CPD		X	

Table 7.2 Migration Objects Supported by the SAP S/4HANA Migration Cockpit for SAP S/4HANA Cloud Editions (Cont.)

Calling the latest object list With every SAP S/4HANA Cloud release, the number of supported migration objects and their functions change. For example, if a new SAP Best Practices package for business processes is available or if existing best practices are enhanced, new migration objects are created, and existing migration objects are adapted. However, these changes always depend on the function of the released data migration interfaces. The *test script* lists the migration objects that are available for the individual releases:

1. To access the script, go to *https://rapid.sap.com/bp/BP_CLD_ENTPR*.
2. Navigate to the **Data Management** scope item group in the **Solution Scope** section.
3. **Data Migration to SAP S/4HANA from File** contains the **Test Script** at **Details**. You can find an overview of migration objects in Chapter 2, Section 2.3.

Excel templates The data that you want to migrate needs to be transferred in predefined Excel files in the *Microsoft Excel XML Spreadsheet 2003* file format. You can download the Excel templates for each migration object using the migration cockpit.

7.3.2 Data Migration Using the SAP S/4HANA Migration Cockpit

Migration project Technically, the SAP S/4HANA migration cockpit is based on the Migration Workbench (MWB), and the delivered template for migration projects is created as an MWB project. When creating a customer project in the SAP S/4HANA migration cockpit, the objects of this template are copied to a customer-specific MWB project. You can generate and start this copy only with the SAP S/4HANA migration cockpit.

Assigning Roles for the Migration

Technical role To use the SAP S/4HANA migration cockpit in the cloud, the user that performs the migration (migration user) must have the technical role SAP_BR_BPC_EXPERT (Configuration Expert – Business Process Configuration).

Application roles In addition, you'll require further roles to import or validate the individual migration objects. These roles (as of Version 1611) are listed for each migration object in Table 7.3.

7.3 Migrating Data to SAP S/4HANA Cloud

Migration Object	Application Role	Application Role ID
Activity Type	SAP_BR_CONTROLLER	Controller
Cost Centers	SAP_BR_CONTROLLER	Controller
Rate	SAP_BR_CONTROLLER	Controller
Internal Order	SAP_BR_CONTROLLER	Controller
Profit Center	SAP_BR_CONTROLLER	Controller
Bank Master	SAP_BR_CASH_MANAGER	Cash Manager
Customer	SAP_BR_BUPA_MASTER_SPECIALIST	Master Data Specialist – Business Partner Data
Supplier	SAP_BR_BUPA_MASTER_SPECIALIST	Master Data Specialist – Business Partner Data
Accounts Receivable (Customer) Open Item	SAP_BR_AR_ACCOUNTANT	Accounts Receivable Accountant
Accounts Payable (Vendor) Open Item	SAP_BR_AP_ACCOUNTANT	Accounts Payable Accountant
Fixed Assets incl. Balances	SAP_BR_AA_ACCOUNTANT	Asset Accountant
G/L Account Balance	SAP_BR_GL_ACCOUNTANT	General Ledger Accountant
G/L Account Open Item	SAP_BR_GL_ACCOUNTANT	General Ledger Accountant
Exchange Rate	SAP_BR_GL_ACCOUNTANT	General Ledger Accountant
Inventory Balances	SAP_BR_INVENTORY_MANAGER	Inventory Manager

Table 7.3 Required Business Roles for the SAP S/4HANA Migration Cockpit

Migration Object	Application Role	Application Role ID
Material Master	SAP_BR_PRODMASTER_SPECIALIST	Master Data Specialist – Product Data
Material – Long Text	SAP_BR_PRODMASTER_SPECIALIST	Master Data Specialist – Product Data
Purchasing Info Record	SAP_BR_PURCHASER	Purchaser
Purchase Order	SAP_BR_PURCHASER	Purchaser
Pricing Condition	SAP_BR_PRICING_SPECIALIST SAP_BR_PRICING_SPECIALIST_PRSV	Pricing Specialist Pricing Specialist – Professional Service
Contracts (Purchasing)	SAP_BR_PURCHASER	Purchaser
Source List	SAP_BR_PURCHASER	Purchaser
Sales Order	SAP_BR_SALES_MANAGER	Sales Manager
Batches	SAP_BR_QUALITY_TECHNICIAN	Quality Technician
Bill of Material (BOM)	SAP_BR_PRODN_ENG_DISC	Production Engineer – Discrete Manufacturing
Work Center	SAP_BR_PRODN_ENG_DISC	Production Engineer – Discrete Manufacturing
Routing	SAP_BR_PRODN_ENG_DISC	Production Engineer – Discrete Manufacturing
Equipment	SAP_BR_MAINTENANCE_PLANNER	Maintenance Planner
Maintenance Task List	SAP_BR_MAINTENANCE_PLANNER	Maintenance Planner
Functional Location	SAP_BR_MAINTENANCE_PLANNER	Maintenance Planner
Characteristic	SAP_BR_BOM_ENGINEER	BOM Engineer

Table 7.3 Required Business Roles for the SAP S/4HANA Migration Cockpit (Cont.)

7.3 Migrating Data to SAP S/4HANA Cloud

Migration Object	Application Role	Application Role ID
Class	SAP_BR_BOM_ENGINEER	BOM Engineer
Commercial Project Management (CPM)	SAP_BR_PROJ_MANAGE_COMM	Project Manager – Commercial Services

Table 7.3 Required Business Roles for the SAP S/4HANA Migration Cockpit (Cont.)

> **Latest Role Overview**
>
> Because the business processes and roles in new releases are constantly being revised and updated, see the respective chapter of the test script mentioned in Section 7.3.1 to obtain an overview of the roles that are available in your release.

As an administrator user, you'll assign to the relevant migration user the business roles for which you require a specific migration object.

Creating Projects

You can call the SAP S/4HANA migration cockpit via SAP Fiori launchpad:

1. First, navigate to the **End to End Experience** group (see Figure 7.14).

Calling the SAP S/4HANA migration cockpit

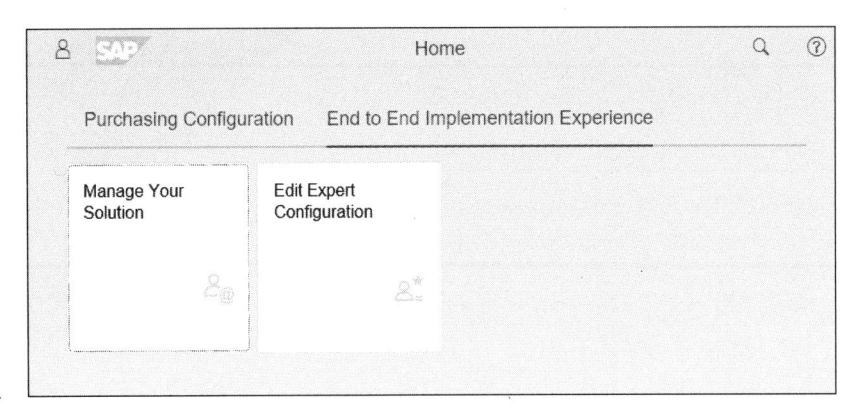

Figure 7.14 Tiles in the "End to End Experience" Group

219

7 Migrating to the Public Cloud

2. The **Manage Your Solution** tile takes you to the configuration view that we discussed in Section 7.2.
3. Choose **Migrate Your Data**, which will take you to the migration cockpit.

> **SAP S/4HANA Migration Cockpit Help**
>
> You can find the SAP S/4HANA migration cockpit help at *http://help.sap.com/s4hana*. Select your edition and navigate to **Product Assistance**. Next, select the language in which you'll read the information. To access the help for cloud solutions, go to **SAP S/4HANA Cloud • Generic Information • Implementation Tools • Migrate Data**.

Overview of the migration objects

The initial screen of the SAP S/4HANA migration cockpit displays all available migration objects that have been created so far. Of course, when you open the SAP S/4HANA migration cockpit for the first time, the list will not contain any projects, as shown in Figure 7.15. In this overview screen, you can **Create**, **Delete**, or **Open** projects.

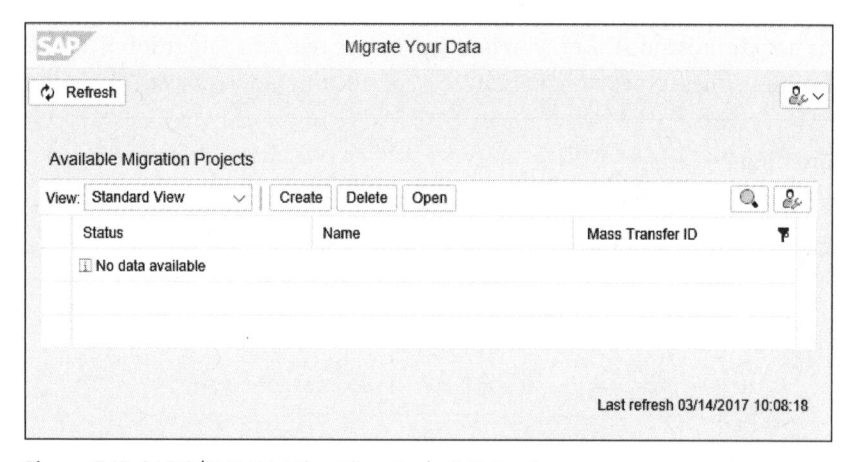

Figure 7.15 SAP S/4HANA Migration Cockpit Entry Screen

> **Before Creating a Project, Log on with the Correct Language**
>
> Before you create a migration project using the migration cockpit, you have to use the appropriate language to log on to the migration cockpit. The SAP S/4HANA migration cockpit only displays migration projects that have been created in the logon language. If you log on in English, the

project is created with English descriptions. So this project is only displayed if the logon language is English.

You can use the personalization function at the top right of the list to filter the list view. If the system displays too many projects, for example, you can apply the filter to the project name and have the system display only the projects you want to view. Next to the personalization function, you can find the search function , which lets you search the list for projects.

Filter and search

When you click on the **Create** button, the **Create Migration Project** dialog box will open (see Figure 7.16).

Creating projects

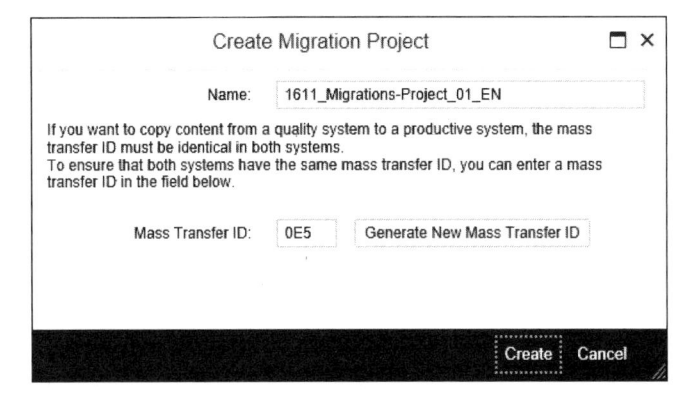

Figure 7.16 Creating a Migration Project

In the **Name** field, assign a name to the migration project. The system automatically determines the **Mass Transfer ID**. When you click on the respective button, the system generates a new ID. If you click on **Create**, the default migration object provided by SAP is copied, and the system will display the project overview, as shown in Figure 7.17.

> **Mass Transfer ID**
>
> The mass transfer ID is a technical key used for the technical name of the newly created migration project (MWB project and MWB subproject) and is unique. The technical name is suffixed with the mass load ID and is thus ZSIN_MIG_<mass transfer ID>. In SAP S/4HANA Cloud, you only need this information if a service employee must solve an issue occurring in the

7 Migrating to the Public Cloud

> backend. For example, if the mass transfer ID is 005, the MWB migration project is created with the technical name `ZSIN_MIG_005`. The service employee, who can access the backend, could then analyze problems that might occur in the MWB.

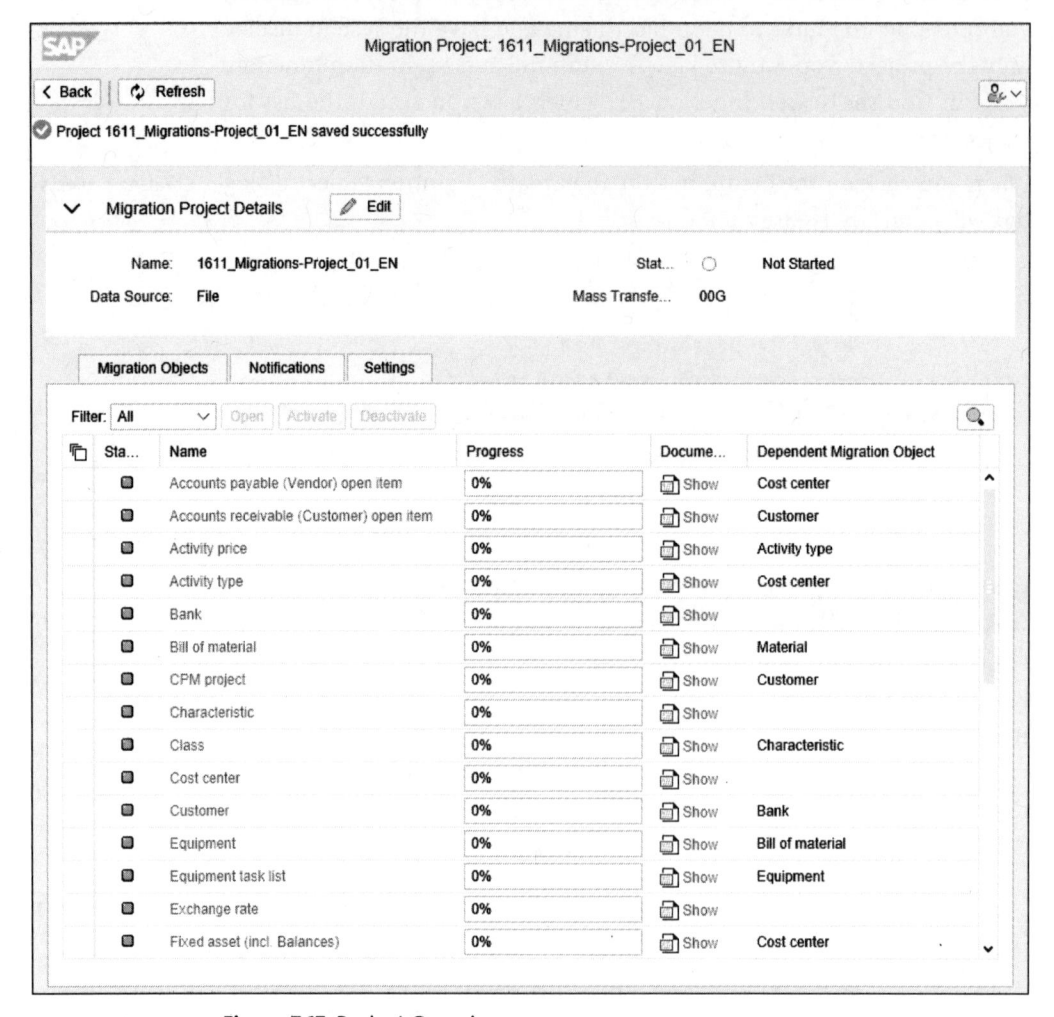

Figure 7.17 Project Overview

Project overview   The project overview lists migration object details such as **Name**, **Data Source**, **Status**, and **Mass Transfer ID** at the top. You can change the name using the **Edit** function.

The migration object list contains the following information:

- **Status** (traffic light colors): This column indicates the status of the migration object. A red traffic light icon indicates an error.
- **Name:** This column shows name of the migration object.
- **Progress:** This column shows the progress of the object migration. If the migration object has not yet been generated, the progress will be 0%.
- **Documentation:** To display the documentation for a migration object, you can use the **Show** function in the column of the object.
- **Dependent migration object:** This column contains related objects that are predecessors of this migration object and have to be migrated or created manually in advance.

Figure 7.18 shows example documentation for a migration object, which contains the following information:

- The **Component** or SAP **Area** of the migration object.
- The **Business Object Type** indicates whether the object is a master data or transaction data object.
- The **Business Object Definition** provides a brief description of the object.
- The **In Scope** specification defines what cloud edition contains the object
- **Out-of-Scope** indicates which cloud edition does not contain this migration object and what restrictions you might have to face during the migration.
- The **Structure Support per Edition** section lists the transfer structures for each edition (cloud [CE] and on-premise [OP]). A plus sign means that that edition's structure is supported; a minus sign means that the transfer structure is not included in the solution scope of that edition.
- **Prerequisites** lists all predecessors of the migration object that need to be migrated in advance as well as further settings that you have to make before the actual migration process.
- **Mapping Instructions** provides additional information for mapping your source data and populating the migration file.
- The **Tasks** section contains detailed instructions that you should follow.
- **Post-processing** lists follow-up activities that you might have to perform after the migration or indicates which tile and user role (for migration into a cloud edition) or transaction (for migration into an on-premise

Migration object documentation

system) you can use to validate the migrated data. Usually, you'll also need the cloud business role to load the data, which should be assigned to the user performing the data migration.

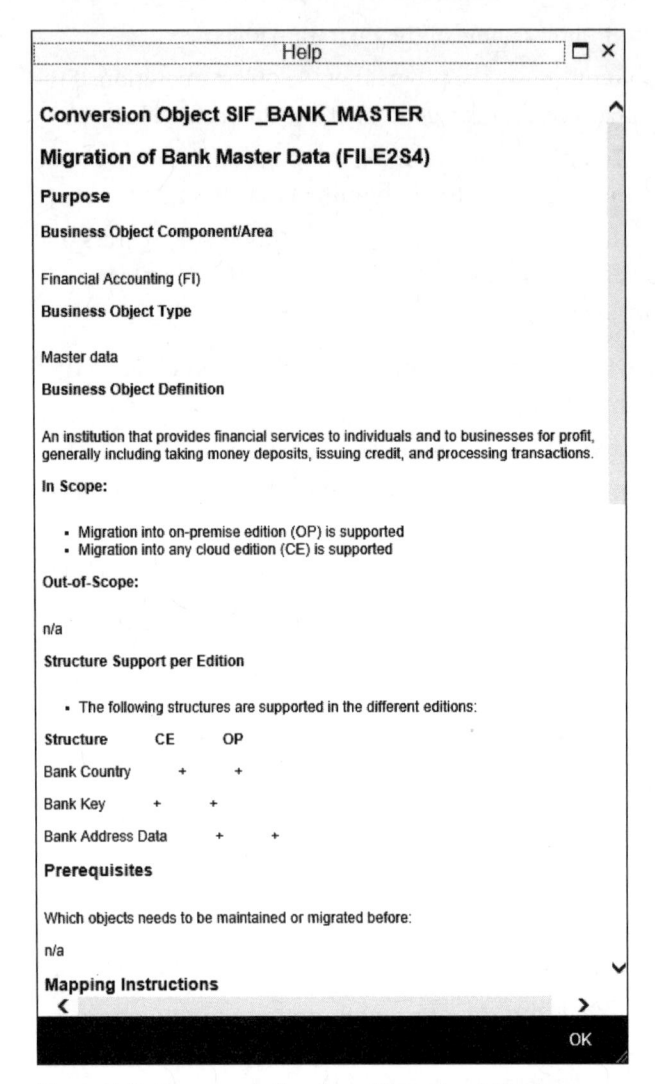

Figure 7.18 Documentation for a Migration Object

- **Version and Release Note** indicates for which editions the object has been released, lists the latest release, and names the release in which the object was delivered for the first time.

7.3 Migrating Data to SAP S/4HANA Cloud

- **Main Changes and Additions in This Release** lists all changes and enhancements in this release.

> **Migration Objects for Phased Rollouts**
>
> A *phased rollout* is a gradual system implementation where business processes and/or organizational units of an (existing) system are added. The rollout thus comprises individual, successive phases.
>
> If you plan to execute a phased rollout, using several separate migration projects might make sense. You should follow this approach particularly if multiple data sources exist. You can then maintain the conversions that are described later in "Validating Data" section regardless of the data source. The "Converting Values" section explains how to export conversions maintained in another project to a new project. If you work with newer releases, you'll also benefit immediately from the adjustments and enhancements of the migration objects delivered by SAP.

Copying Migration Objects

When you have created the project, all migration objects are activated. Before you begin migrating a specific migration object, you should first deactivate all unnecessary migration objects by selecting all migration objects that you don't need and choosing **Deactivate**. The status of these objects will change from **Started** to **Inactive**.

Deactivating objects that are not used

To migrate the data of a specific migration object, select the desired object in the list. The system then displays the dialog box shown in Figure 7.19; confirm by clicking **OK**.

Migrating data

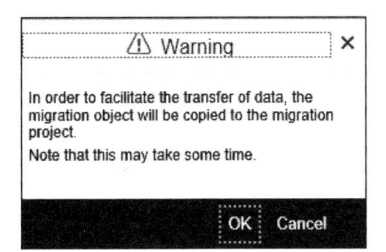

Figure 7.19 Copying a Migration Object

The predefined mappings and conversion rules of SAP Best Practices migration content will be copied to the migration object of the migration project

Copying mappings and rules

225

that was created in the customer namespace. Depending on the connection quality and the object's scope, this process might take some time. When the copying is successful, the progress bar in the migration object list will show 5% completion.

Downloading Migration Templates

Excel file in XML format

The system then displays a detailed overview of the copied migration object (shown in Figure 7.20). Select **Download Template** to download the migration template for this object. As mentioned earlier, the migration template will be in the *Microsoft Excel XML Spreadsheet 2003* file format, and you can open and populate the template using Microsoft Excel as of Version 2003 or Apache OpenOffice (a free spreadsheet program).

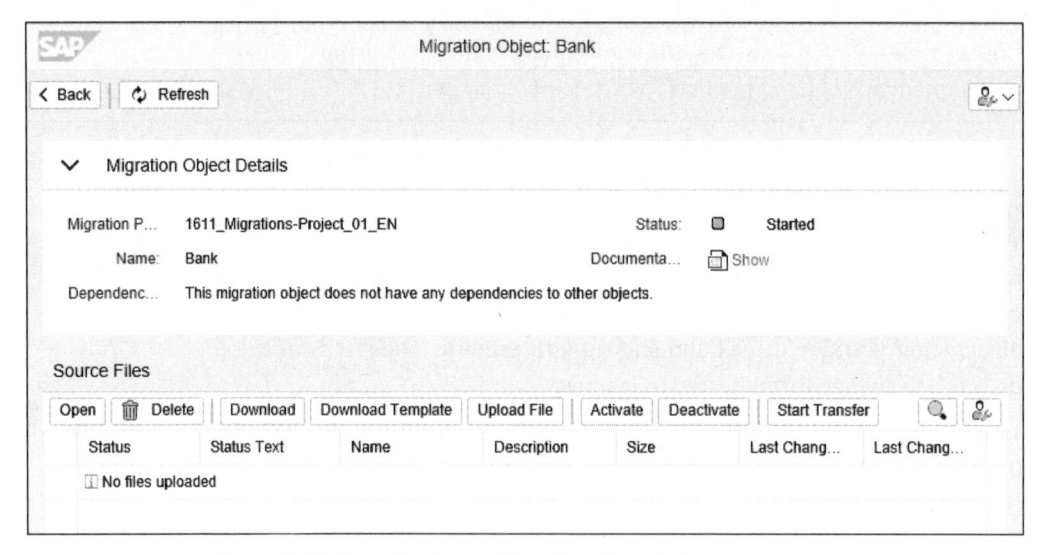

Figure 7.20 Downloading a Migration Template

> **Edition-Dependent View of Migration Templates**
>
> As of Release 1611, the system displays an additional dialog box (shown in Figure 7.21) after you have chosen **Download Template**. In this dialog box, enter the specific *view* for your migration template. The view that you require depends on your SAP S/4HANA Cloud edition. Individual SAP Best Practices business processes are implemented differently depending on

7.3 Migrating Data to SAP S/4HANA Cloud

the edition. As a result, these views only display structures and fields that are actually used in that cloud edition.

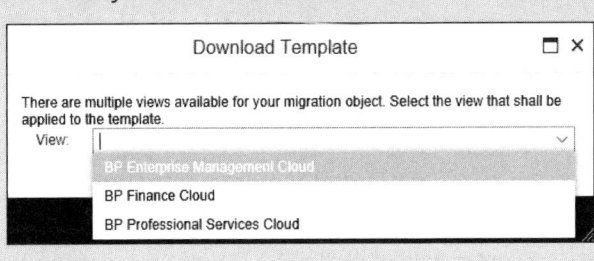

Figure 7.21 Selecting the Migration Template View

After the download, the migration template should have the .xml file extension. For security reasons, Internet browsers always store files of specific file types (for example, .exe) without the extension. Some browsers also store XML files without the .xml extension. If the file type of the downloaded file is "file" and the .xml extension is missing, simply add the extension. Note that—depending on the settings of your file explorer of your operating system—the file explorer might not display extensions of known file types although the extensions physically exist. In addition, make sure that the download was not canceled by a popup blocker.

Adding the XML file extension

The migration template usually consists of several spreadsheets, which reflect the individual transfer structure of the migration object. Initially, rows 4 through 6 are hidden and contain technical information on the object. If you expand row 8 (with the field descriptions), you can view further information for each field, which you might need to map your source data. Mandatory fields and key fields are marked with an asterisk (*) at the end of the field name. The **Field list** spreadsheet contains a list of all fields used for each structure and information on whether the structures and fields are mandatory. Figure 7.22 shows the template file for the **Material** migration object.

Spreadsheet structure

[!] **Only Use Downloaded Templates**

For compatibility reasons, please only use a template that you have downloaded from the latest release to migrate your data. You cannot upload templates from earlier releases. The load program only accepts templates from the release to which they are supposed to be uploaded. Because the

227

7 Migrating to the Public Cloud

migration objects in all releases are always adapted to business process changes, this mechanism ensures data integrity.

Because the templates are XML files with a specific format and an internal structure, you should additionally consider the following:

- Custom XML templates generally cause data loading errors.
- If you copy data to fields in the XML file using the cache or clipboard, for example, this data should only be copied as values without formatting or text. If you are unsure about the formatting, first copy the data to a text editor (e.g., Notepad) and then from the text editor to the XML file.

If you adhere to these rules, you shouldn't have any problems with the file.

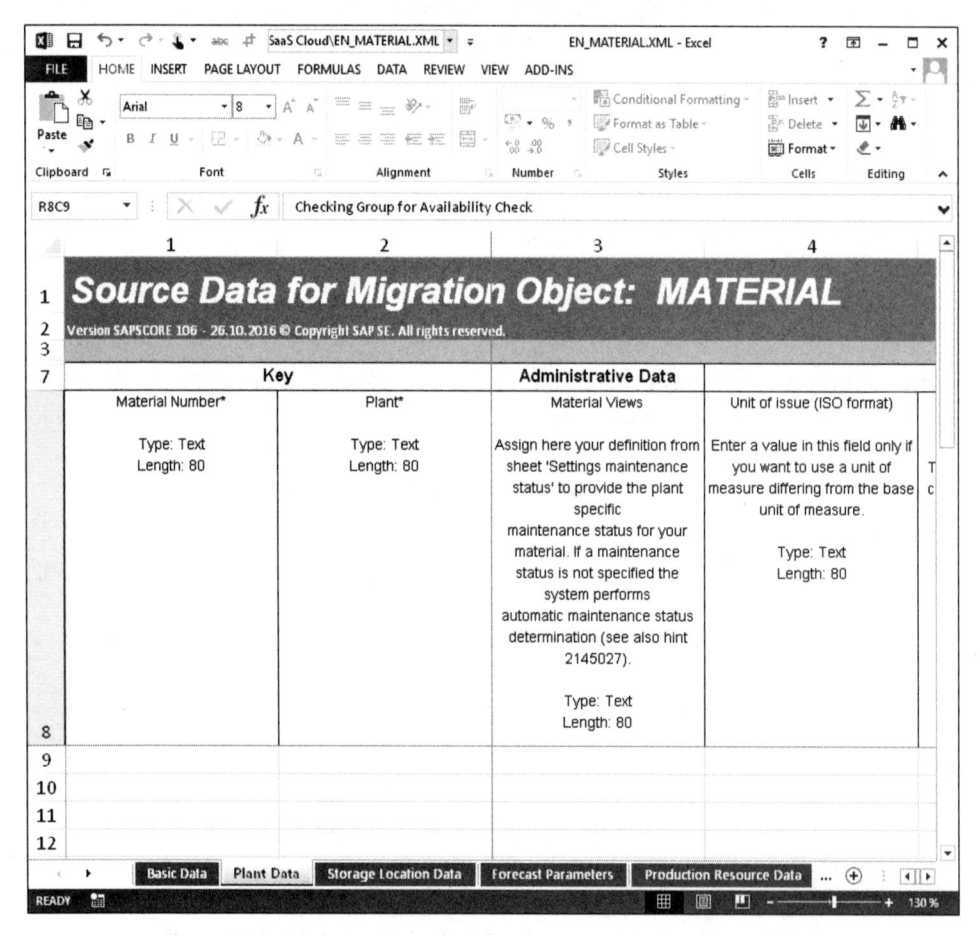

Figure 7.22 Migration Template for the Material Migration Object

The key fields in the individual spreadsheets define the relationship between the header structures and substructures of an object. As a result, a key record must exist in the spreadsheet of the superior structure for each substructure record. Otherwise, the migration cockpit will display an error message.

Key fields

> **Determining Mandatory Structures in Templates**
>
> The migration template contains so-called *mandatory structures*. These structures (spreadsheets) must contain records and must not be empty. All other structures are optional and do not have to be populated. For example, in the **Purchase order** object, the header structure and the item structure are mandatory. In the **Customer** object, only the top-level structure (**General Data**) is mandatory. Structures that are indicated as mandatory structures are marked with **(mandatory)** in the **Field List** spreadsheet, for example, **General Data (mandatory)**.
>
> However, you do not have to fill mandatory fields and key fields in optional spreadsheets if you don't want to use these structures. For example, if you don't want to migrate optional long texts in an object, you don't have to make any entries in this spreadsheet. Leave this spreadsheet blank.

Loading the Migration File into the Staging Area

Once you have populated the migration file, import this file to the SAP S/4HANA migration cockpit by choosing **Upload File**. In the dialog box that opens, select the file on your local computer or from a network path. Enter a meaningful **Description** and an optional **Comment** (as shown in Figure 7.23). The description is mandatory because you can upload multiple files, and you'll need to clearly identify the files after the upload. Files are stored in the *staging area* of the SAP HANA database.

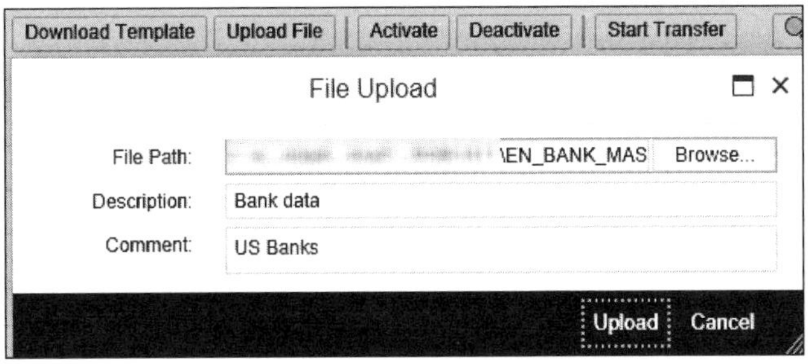

Staging area

Figure 7.23 Uploading a Migration File

7   Migrating to the Public Cloud

Next, click **Upload** to upload the file to the staging area. Figure 7.24 shows a list of the uploaded migration files that you can use for migration.

> [!] **All Activated Files Are Loaded**
>
> If you only want to upload one file, you should deactivate all other files. You also should assign different names to the files to simplify troubleshooting. If errors occur in a file, for example, incorrect key relationships between individual spreadsheets, the system will display the name of the defective file. If several files with the same name are enabled, you cannot know for sure which file is defective and will have to check all activated files.

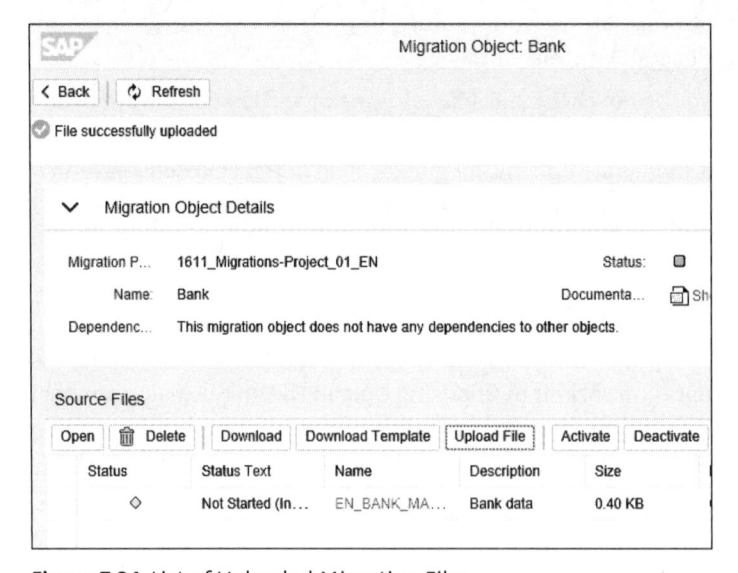

Figure 7.24 List of Uploaded Migration Files

Source file list   The list shows the file status, the file name, the description, the file size, and the name of the user who uploaded the file. You can use the following functions for the files:

- **Open:** The system displays the file content, and you can modify **Name**, **Description**, and **Comment** using **Edit**.
- **Delete:** The file is deleted. You can only delete files that have not been processed yet.

7.3 Migrating Data to SAP S/4HANA Cloud

- **Activate/Deactivate**: Only files that have the status **(Not Started) Active** are migrated in the order of the list. These functions let you control which uploaded files you want to import to the target system.

You cannot edit the file content in the cloud (as of Version 1611). However, you can use **Edit** to change the **Name**, **Description**, and **Comment**. In Figure 7.25, you can see an example of an uploaded file after **Open** has been used.

Opening and editing files

> **[!] Upper Physical Limit of Files**
>
> Migration files should not be too big (<200MB). We cannot specify an exact number of data records or a file size because the file size depends on the migration object and the data that is maintained in the file. In general, you should divide large files into several small files. Make sure that the structural integrity of the files is retained. (Records with dependent key relationships need to be in the same file.)

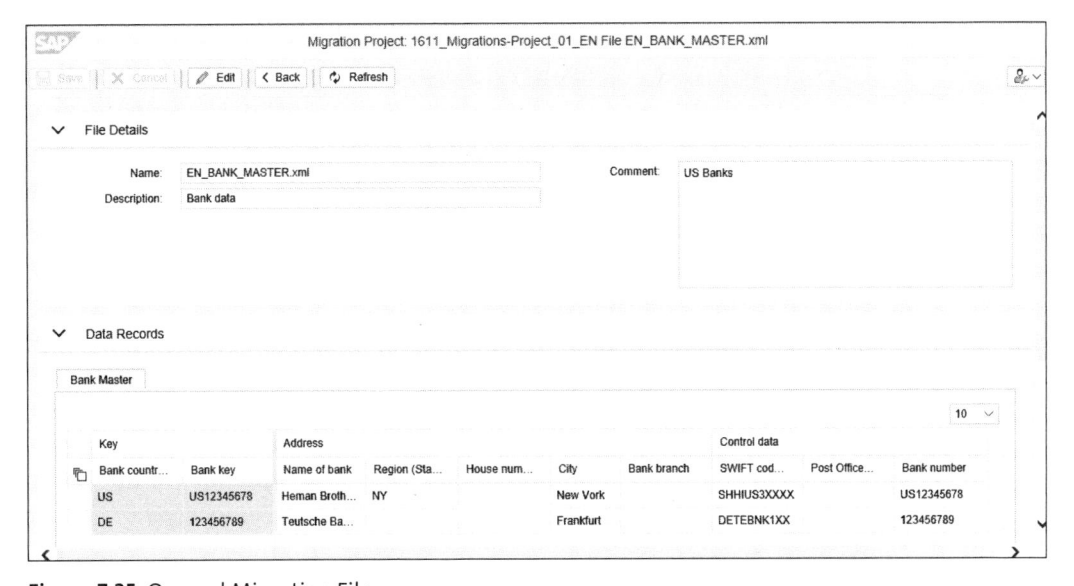

Figure 7.25 Opened Migration File

Start Transfer starts the migration of all active source files. Remember to activate the files in advance. The migration is a *guided process* that consists of the following steps:

Transferring migration files

231

1. **Validate Data**: The data and conversion values are validated.
2. **Convert Values:** In this step, you maintain the conversion tables.
3. **Simulate Import:** This step is only necessary if the interface (i.e., BAPI, function module) used for the migration contains simulation logic, which enables you to simulate transfers in advance.
4. **Execute Import:** With this step, the data is migrated to the system.

You can navigate between the individual steps using the **<Previous** and **Next>** buttons.

Validating Data

Status AUTO
Usually, no conversion values of source data values are maintained for target data values in the first run, and the system displays, depending on your SAP S/4HANA version, one of the following error messages: "The applied combination of translation has status AUTO." or "Information required: specify mapping values in step 'Convert Values.'" This error message indicates new values in the file for which no conversion has been defined so far. These values are automatically added to the relevant conversion table as new values that need to be converted. The source value is used as the target value and abbreviated if too long. As shown in Figure 7.26, you can find individual messages about the data validation step at the bottom of **Notifications from Validation**. Use the **Priority** field to filter by message type.

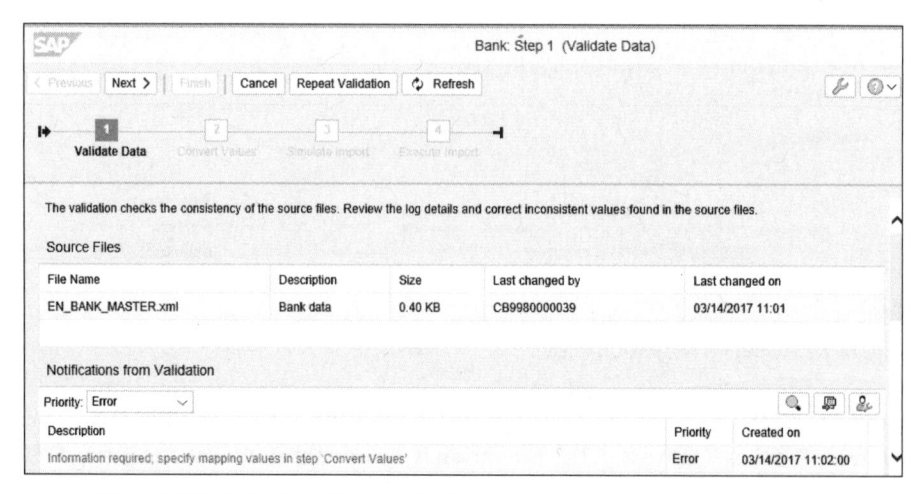

Figure 7.26 Validate Data: Results List

7.3 Migrating Data to SAP S/4HANA Cloud

With **Next>**, you trigger the next step: **Convert Values**.

Converting Values

The **Convert Values** step is somewhat more complex. While the other steps usually output a log after their execution, the missing conversions are maintained in a specific dialog box. Figure 7.27 shows an example of a list of missing conversions.

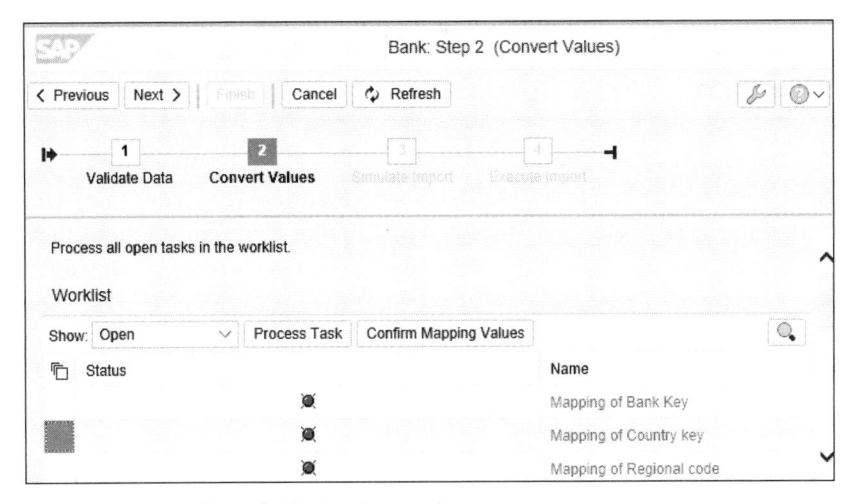

Figure 7.27 Overview of Missing Conversions

Open conversions, i.e., conversions that are not fully maintained, are marked with a red traffic light icon in the **Worklist**. You can maintain the missing conversion either by selecting the corresponding entry in the **Name** column or by selecting the row and clicking on **Process Task**. The system then displays the dialog box for maintaining the conversions. Figure 7.28 shows sample conversion values.

> **Confirming All at Once**
> Alternatively, you can select all open conversions in the overview list and use **Confirm Mapping Values** to confirm all unconfirmed conversion values at once. However, avoid this function if you are not sure whether all values in the source file to be converted already have a target value.

233

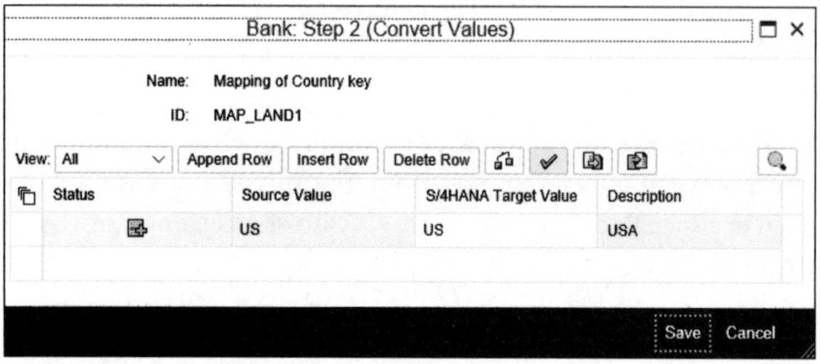

Figure 7.28 Dialog for Maintaining Conversions

Maintain conversions
All conversion values that are still open and have not been confirmed yet have a green plus sign in the **Status** column. Maintain the values to be converted in the last column, S/4HANA **Target Value**. You can use the system value help to select valid values. The target value fields are usually linked to value tables, and the system displays an error messages if you enter an invalid value, for example, "Parameter S/HANA Target value: XX is not a valid value for domain LAND1." The status symbol changes from a red circle to a green square only if you enter a valid value.

After you have maintained all target values, select the rows of values that have not been confirmed yet (green plus sign) and confirm the conversion values using the **Confirm Value** button (green checkmark). Now, all confirmed values are marked with a green square in the **Status** column. Afterwards, click on **Save**, which closes the dialog box. Maintain all open conversions in the worklist one by one until the list is empty. Conversions are always related to projects, which means that conversions used by several objects need to be maintained only once and are available for all objects of a project.

[»]

Exporting and Importing Conversions

The **Export** function lets you store all conversions in a CSV file. The first row of the file contains the technical name of the conversion, the second row contains the column headings, and the following rows contain the values. Column headings and values are separated by semicolons (;) and enclosed in double quotes (").

You can then save this file for documentation purposes, for example, or upload the file into other systems using the function **Import**. As a result,

7.3 Migrating Data to SAP S/4HANA Cloud

you'll only have to maintain large and complex conversions once and can forward the list as an Excel file to the person responsible. If you work with multiple migration projects in a phased rollout, you can also exchange the conversions between individual projects.

If the worklist is empty, clicking on **Next>** navigates you to the next step, **Simulate Import**. You can view completed conversions by selecting **All** or **Completed** in the **Show** field.

The dialog box for setting fixed values only provides the functions **Check**, **Export**, and **Import**, as shown in Figure 7.29, which demonstrates a fixed posting date for inventory balances. In this dialog box, you can set the fixed value and then select **Save**, which will confirm the fixed value automatically.

Fixed values

Fixed Default Values

SAP provides a default value for some fixed values. To view these fixed values, you should set **All** in the **Show** dropdown list of the worklist.

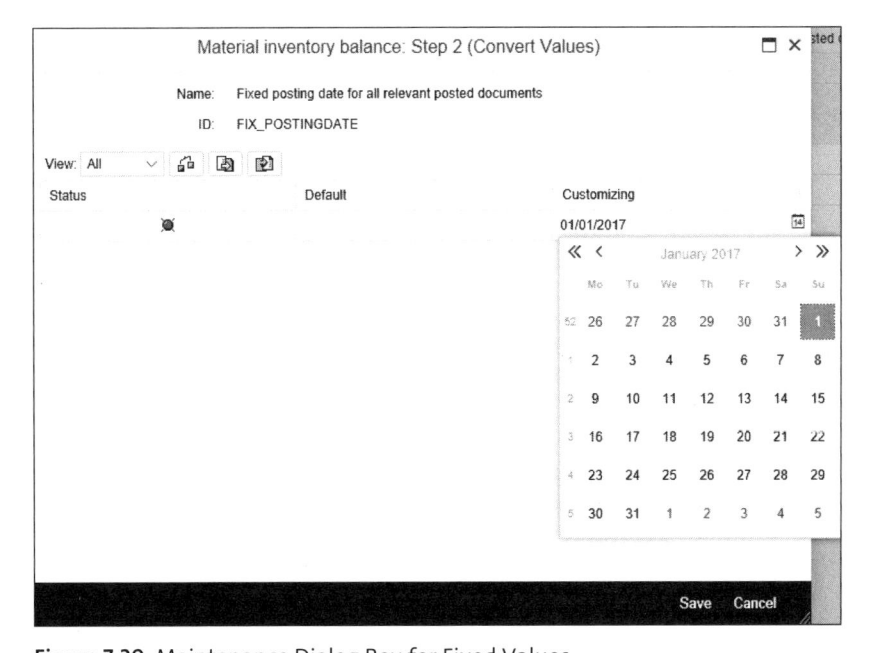

Figure 7.29 Maintenance Dialog Box for Fixed Values

7   Migrating to the Public Cloud

Simulating the Import

As mentioned earlier, this step is displayed only if the import interface provides for a simulation. Depending on the number of data records, a simulation might take some time because the entire interface loading process is executed—except for the import itself. The result of such a simulation is shown in Figure 7.30.

Results list   Initially, the system only displays messages in the **Error** category. If you select **All** in the **Priority** dropdown list, you can view all system messages, including success messages and warnings. As shown in Figure 7.31, if you click on the error text, the system displays the long text of an error message—if long text is maintained.

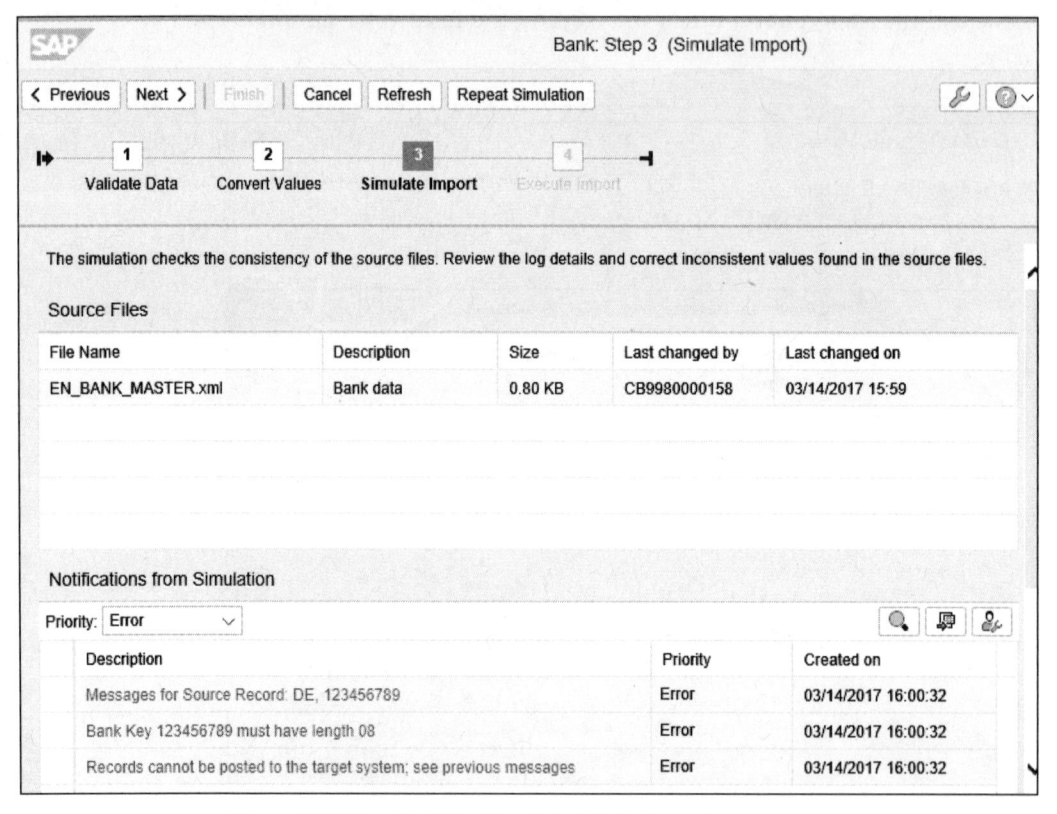

Figure 7.30 Result of the Simulated Data Import

7.3 Migrating Data to SAP S/4HANA Cloud

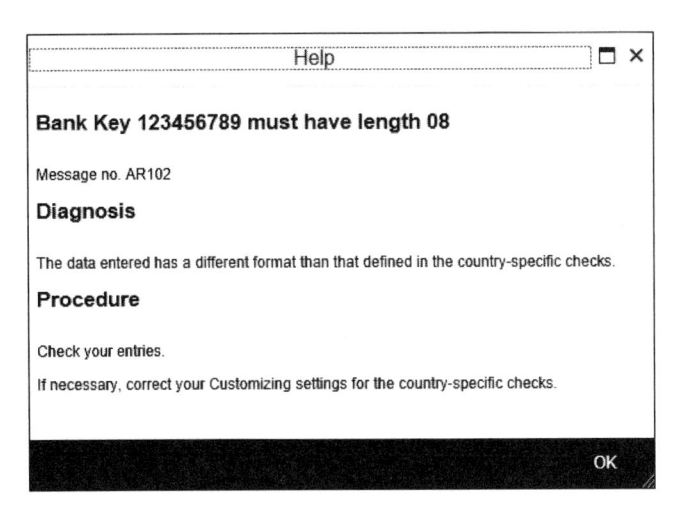

Figure 7.31 Long Text of an Error Message

In our example, an incorrect target value has been maintained and must be corrected. Go back to **Convert Values** either via the status overview or using the **<Previous** button. You'll be taken to the worklist of the completed conversions, where you can correct the faulty target value. Now, use **Next>** or **Simulate Import** to return to the simulation. You can restart the simulation using the **Repeat Simulation** function. The end result should not include any error messages.

Editing error messages

Usually, only the following warning is displayed: "Test migration <technical name of the migration object copied>: no extended validations, no updates in receiver system." This message means that no enhanced checks and updates were done in the receiver system. Finally, you can start the real import via **Next>**.

Executing the Import

As in the previous steps, the data import is executed directly and can be executed as a batch job if required. To execute the data import, select **Run in Background** in the dialog box shown in Figure 7.32.

Importing as batch job

Execution as a batch job is an asynchronous procedure. You can determine the status of the import by clicking on the **Refresh** button regularly.

237

7   Migrating to the Public Cloud

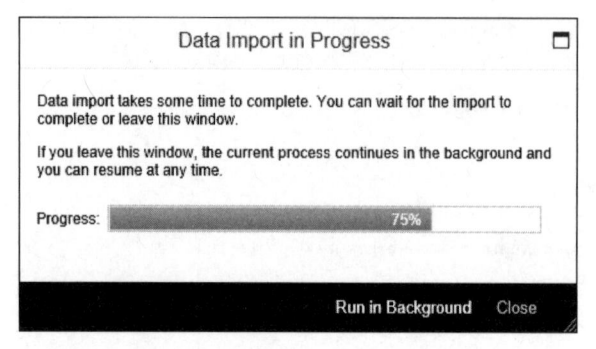

Figure 7.32 Execute Import

Results list   When completed, the system will display a final screen as shown in Figure 7.33. If the data has been migrated successfully, the message overview should only list information messages or warnings.

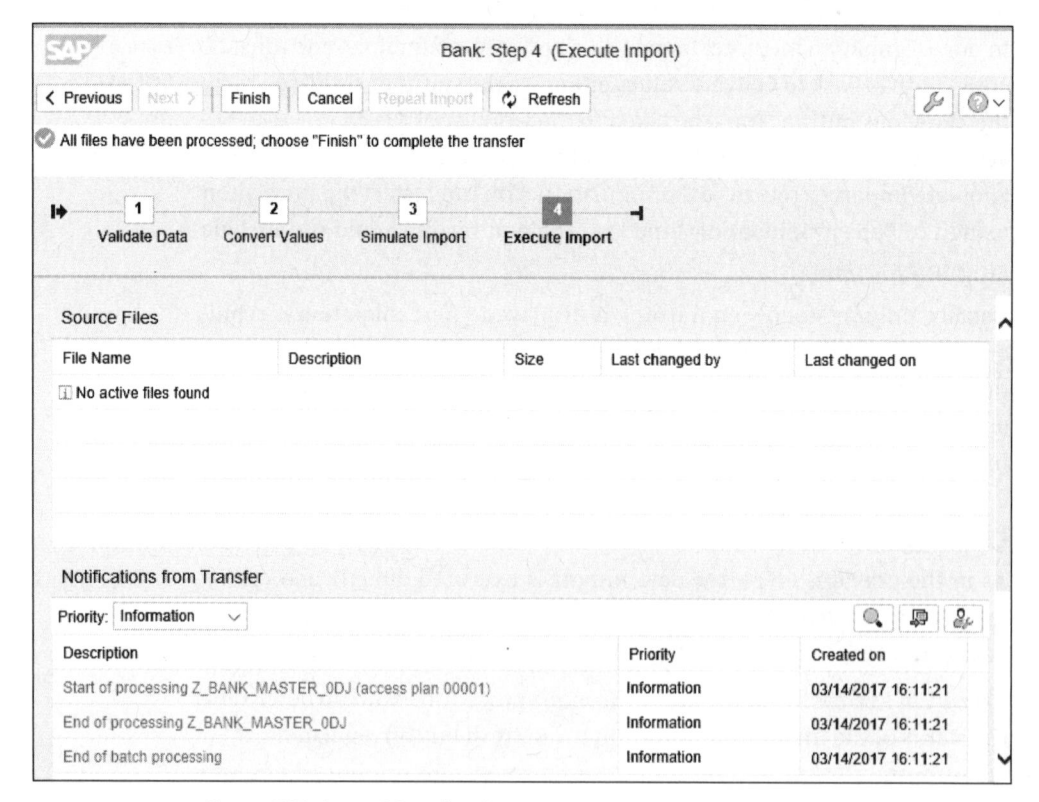

Figure 7.33 Import Results List

7.3 Migrating Data to SAP S/4HANA Cloud

Click **Finish** to complete the data migration for this object. As shown in Figure 7.34, the file receives the status **Finished**, and the migration object then has the status **Finished**.

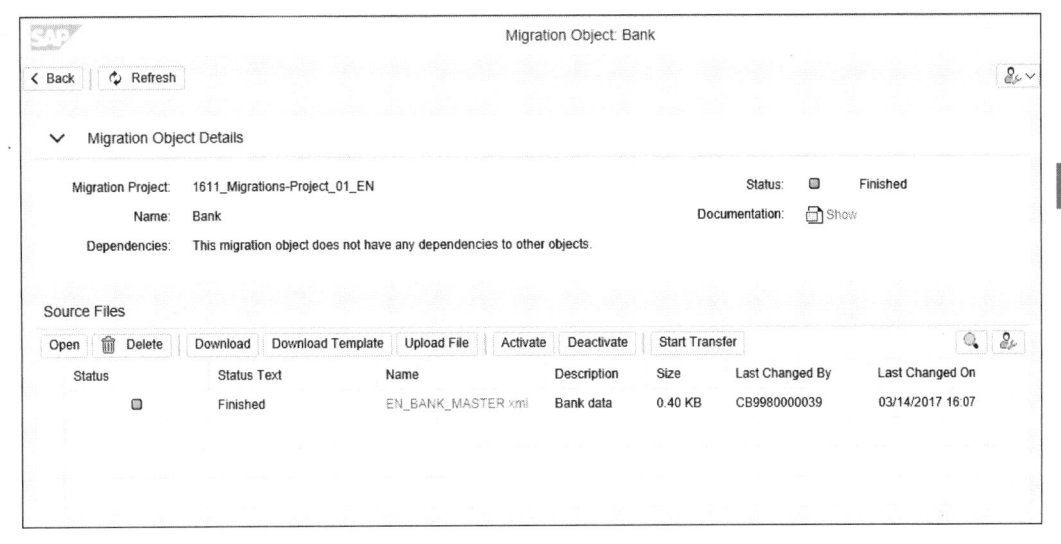

Figure 7.34 Migration Object Finished

The migration object overview screen now shows that the project's **Progress** is 100%.

> **Demo Video for the SAP S/4HANA Migration Cockpit**
>
> You can find a demo of the SAP S/4HANA Migration Cockpit in SAP S/4HANA Cloud at the YouTube channel "SAP Digital Business Services" (https://www.youtube.com/user/SAPSupportInfo) with the title "SAP S/4HANA, Cloud Editions: Migrate Your Data." The demo has the following URL: https://www.youtube.com/watch?v=2FgEwx7ZhUM. You can find another demo for the SAP S/4HANA Migration Cockpit with the title "SAP S/4HANA Migration Cockpit" at https://www.youtube.com/watch?v=fwSHoWiZSEw. Both demos are based on SAP S/4HANA Cloud 1605. The procedure in the more recent releases differs only slightly from the procedure described here.

Chapter 8
Integrating SAP S/4HANA Cloud into the System Landscape

This chapter describes how to integrate an SAP S/4HANA Cloud system with other SAP cloud solutions, such as SAP Ariba and SAP SuccessFactors, and how to embed SAP Hybris Marketing Cloud into your existing system landscape.

Customers cannot directly manipulate and access cloud solutions, which is why cloud solutions meet higher security requirements than on-premise solutions. Due to these high security requirements, network protocols (Remote Function Calls, RFC) and integration procedures (database replication) as you know them from the on-premise world are not available or only available to a limited extent.

Consequently, integration plays a major role in cloud-based system landscapes. This chapter addresses some basic questions about integration:

- What systems can I integrate?
- How are they integrated?
- Where can I find additional information?

First, this chapter discusses integration with SAP Ariba, a business-to-business (B2B) marketplace where enterprises can manage their transactions with each other. The second section describes integration with a cloud-based SAP SuccessFactors solution. The last section covers the various SAP Hybris Marketing Cloud integration options.

8.1 Integration with SAP Ariba Solutions

Why might you want to extend your SAP S/4HANA Cloud procurement operations with SAP Ariba solutions? What are the benefits? In today's digital economy, customers expect to be perceived and valued as individuals. Custom-made and made-to-order production has become the norm but

Relevance of SAP Ariba

8 Integrating SAP S/4HANA Cloud into the System Landscape

still must be as fast and comprehensive as mass production. Chapter 1, Section 1.1.2, mentioned this trend, while Chapter 1, Section 1.3.4 introduced the SAP Ariba functions that can support you in the digital transformation. SAP Ariba solutions help you automate operational procurement functions so you can re-focus your resources on strategic procurement functions such as sourcing new suppliers for new material and services, and negotiating better contracts.

8.1.1 Integration Scenarios in Procurement and Accounts Payable

Integration scenarios

For sourcing, procurement, and financials, you can add applications from the SAP Ariba portfolio to the digital core of SAP S/4HANA Cloud via various integration scenarios (see Figure 8.1).

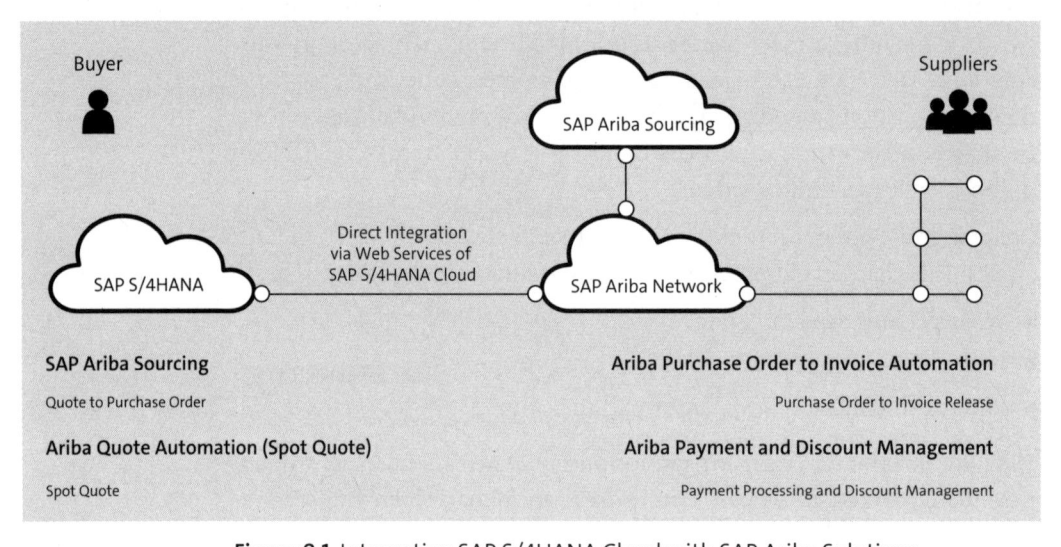

Figure 8.1 Integrating SAP S/4HANA Cloud with SAP Ariba Solutions

Integrating *SAP Ariba Sourcing* adds a professional RFx application and supplier network to SAP S/4HANA Cloud for sourcing and procurement processes. With the other business scenarios, instead of adding applications, you automate the digital exchange of documents via the Ariba Network. These other scenarios are Ariba Purchase Order to Invoice Automation (an integrated process chain from purchase order to supplier invoice) and Ariba Payment and Discount Management (an integrated process chain for payment and managing dynamic discounts for early payments).

8.1 Integration with SAP Ariba Solutions

In SAP S/4HANA Cloud, you can activate all of these scenarios separately, and the SAP Ariba subscription model allows you to select among these scenarios as well. The following sections introduce these scenarios with the units that can be activated in SAP S/4HANA Cloud, called *scope items*. For each scope item, we'll provide schematic process diagrams and tables explaining message types, which you'll need to activate and set up for the corresponding processes or process steps.

Scenario activation

Integrated Sourcing with SAP Ariba Sourcing

If the system is supposed to find sources for purchase requisitions from SAP S/4HANA Cloud, the digital core of SAP S/4HANA Cloud focuses on suppliers whose master data already exists in the system. But what if you want to find new suppliers? In this case, SAP Ariba Sourcing is the ideal solution, possibly the largest independent supplier network, connecting you with more than 2.5 million subscribing companies.

Supplier network

The process begins in SAP S/4HANA Cloud with a purchase requisition to which no supplier has been assigned (yet) (see Figure 8.2).

Process flow

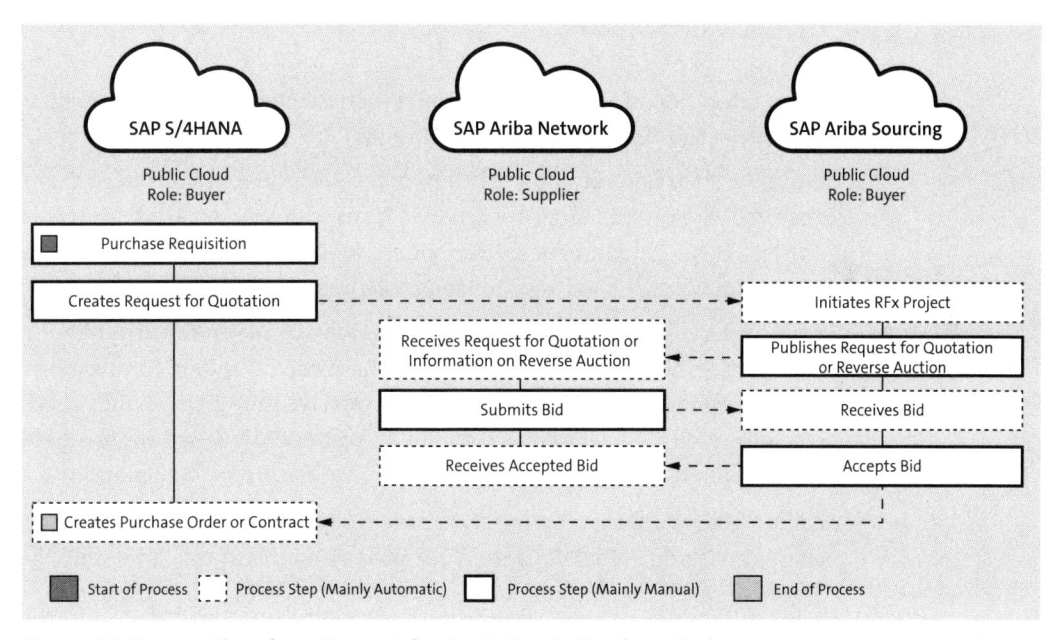

Figure 8.2 Process Flow from Request for Quotation to Purchase Order or Contract with SAP Ariba Sourcing

243

8   Integrating SAP S/4HANA Cloud into the System Landscape

The system uses the purchase requisition to create a request for proposal, which is automatically forwarded to SAP Ariba Sourcing, where it is displayed as a new activity in the sourcing expert worklist. The sourcing expert issues an invitation to bid. When the bidding process is successfully completed, the accepted bid is returned to SAP S/4HANA Cloud. SAP S/4HANA Cloud automatically converts the quotation into a purchase order or a contract.

Message types   For the business process from sourcing request to purchase order or contract creation to be established you would must activate the related message types in the SAP S/4HANA Cloud Customizing (scope item 1A0). Table 8.1 lists the message types for this process.

Message Type in cXML	Direction	Meaning
QuoteRequest	Outbound	Request to submit a quotation
QuoteMessage	Inbound	Quotation/bid

Table 8.1 Message Types for SAP Ariba Sourcing (Scope Item 1A0) and Spot Quotes (Scope Item 1L2)

Automated Document Exchange from Purchase Order to Supplier Invoice with Ariba Network (Including Spot Quotes)

If you want to scale your procurement processes, you must automate them. The process of exchanging documents, from approved purchase orders in SAP S/4HANA Cloud to released supplier invoices (scope item J82), offers a good framework for scaling your sourcing processes (see Figure 8.3).

Process flow   You can send purchase orders to suppliers who can then confirm the purchase orders via Ariba Network and send advance shipping notifications. When the goods have been received, you can have the system send a goods receipt notice to the supplier through Ariba Network. Based on this data, your supplier sends you their invoice.

Ariba Network checks whether the invoices correspond to the original purchase order and actual delivery. Your procurement expert can define the granularity of this check by using tolerance limits for deliveries above or below a threshold are accepted. If the verified supplier invoices are submitted in SAP S/4HANA Cloud, these invoices can usually be released for payment immediately (and automatically). Ariba Network then notifies the supplier of a status change in the invoice.

8.1 Integration with SAP Ariba Solutions

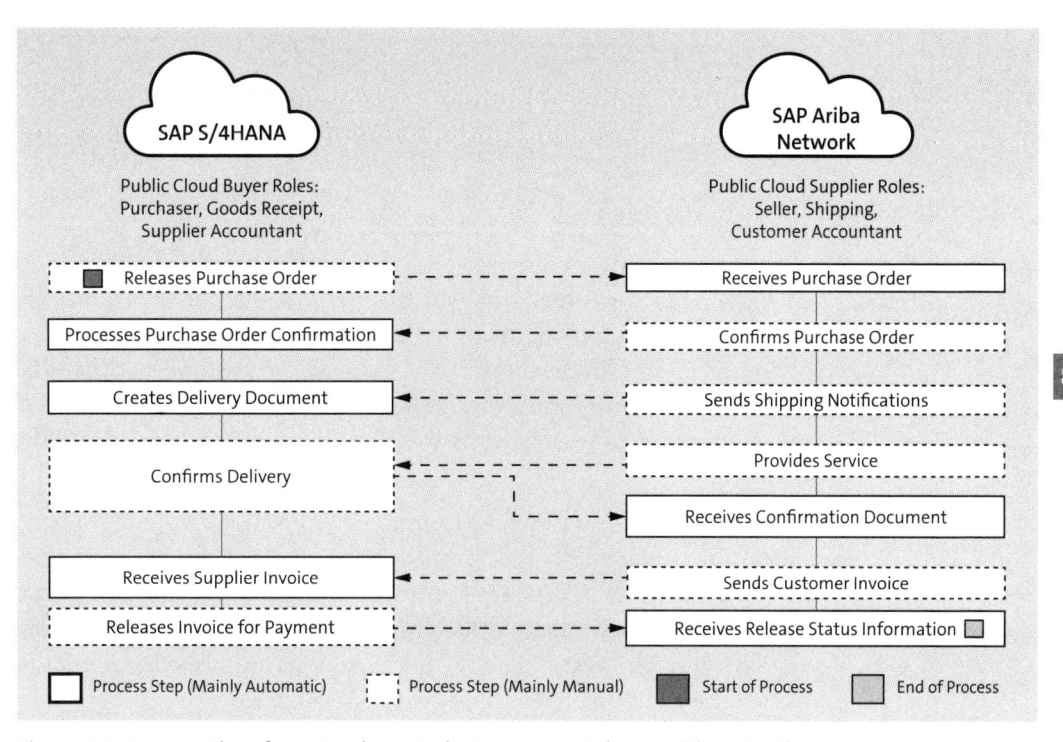

Figure 8.3 Process Flow from Purchase Order to Invoice Release with SAP Ariba Commerce Automation

Table 8.2 lists the message types for this process.

Message Type in cXML	Direction	Meaning
OrderRequest	Outbound	Send purchase order
ConfirmationRequest	Inbound	Process purchase order confirmation
ShipNoticeRequest	Inbound	Receive shipping notification
ReceiptRequest	Outbound	Send confirmation of goods receipt
InvoiceDetailRequest	Inbound	Receive supplier invoice
CopyRequest.InvoiceDetailRequest	Outbound	Send copy of (paper) invoice or automatic Evaluated Receipt Settlement (ERS)

Table 8.2 Message Types for the Process Flow from Purchase Order to Invoice Release with SAP Ariba Commerce Automation

Message Type in cXML	Direction	Meaning
StatusUpdateRequest	Outbound	Send status update of the invoice document (release for payment)

Table 8.2 Message Types for the Process Flow from Purchase Order to Invoice Release with SAP Ariba Commerce Automation (Cont.)

Spot quote   The so-called spot quote process (scope item 1L2, Ariba Quote Automation) allows buyers to automate the process of inquiring suppliers for prices of specific material or simple services. The supplier with the lowest price will be awarded automatically. This way, material infotypes can be easily updated, and ad-hoc purchase orders without contracts can be implemented at the best price.

This procedure is similar to the RFx process: SAP S/4HANA Cloud converts a request for a purchase order to a specific type of request for quotation. SAP Ariba automatically requests specific suppliers to submit their quotations. You can define whether the lowest bid submitted within a specified time will automatically update the infotype or create a purchase order or whether the quotation needs to be accepted manually.

Message types   The message types that you need to enable for spot quotes in SAP S/4HANA Cloud and Ariba Network are the same for SAP Ariba Sourcing (see Table 8.1); however, the subscription for SAP Ariba Commerce Automation covers the spot quote functionality. No subscription to SAP Ariba Sourcing is required for its use.

[»]   **Additional Information**

For more information on SAP Ariba spot quote or quote automation, go to:

- https://www.ariba.com/solutions/solutions-overview/procurement/sap-ariba-spot-buy
- https://www.slideshare.net/Ariba/quote-automation-faster-supplier-identification-and-bid-execution-for-your-procurement-needs

Managing Dynamic Discounts and Sending Electronic Remittance Advices with Ariba Network

If there are no discrepancies between a purchase order and an invoice, document processing can be further automated. You can use Ariba Network to notify suppliers automatically when invoices are released for payment. Based on the terms of payment specified in the document and on the discount rules defined in Ariba Discount Management, the system creates a time-optimized and interest-optimized payment proposal and notifies the relevant supplier (see Figure 8.4).

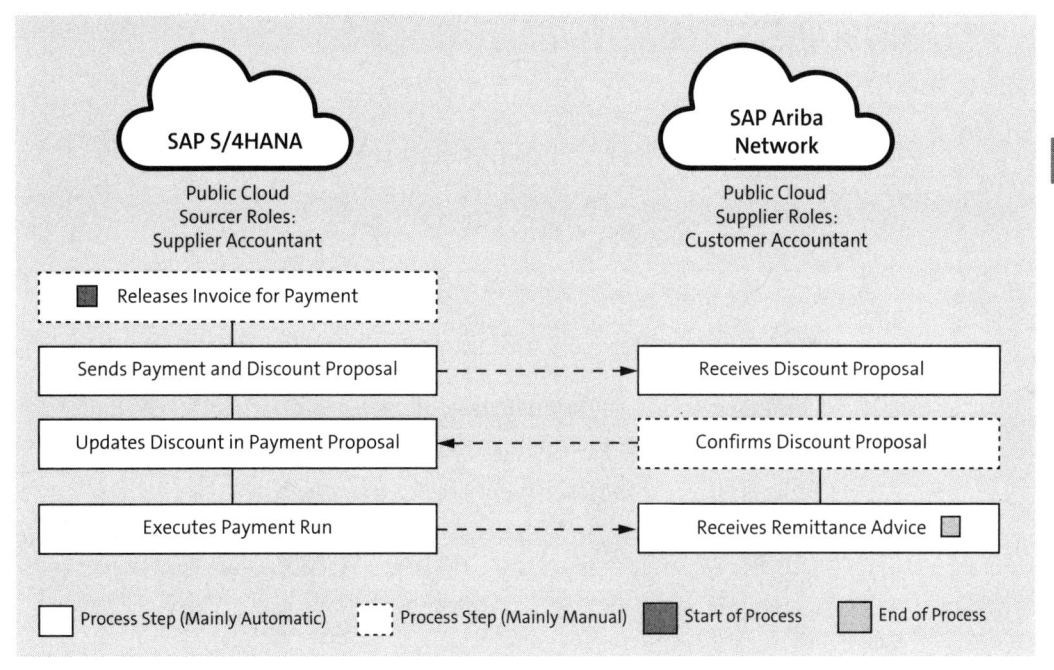

Figure 8.4 Process Flow from Payment Processing to Discount Management with SAP Ariba Payables, Discounting Capabilities

You can define the terms of payment for each supplier individually in *Ariba Discount Management* or for each supplier, supply contract, or purchase order in SAP S/4HANA Cloud. If purchase orders are retrieved in SAP S/4HANA, the system copies the agreed terms of payment to the purchase order document. The payment program then optimizes the date of payment for incoming invoices considering these terms of payment. As a result, if your supplier offers discounts for early payment, the system compares the benefits of the discounted early payment with the liquidity situation and the interest rates that could be achieved or had to be paid within the period until the invoice is due (see Figure 8.5).

Verifying terms of payment automatically

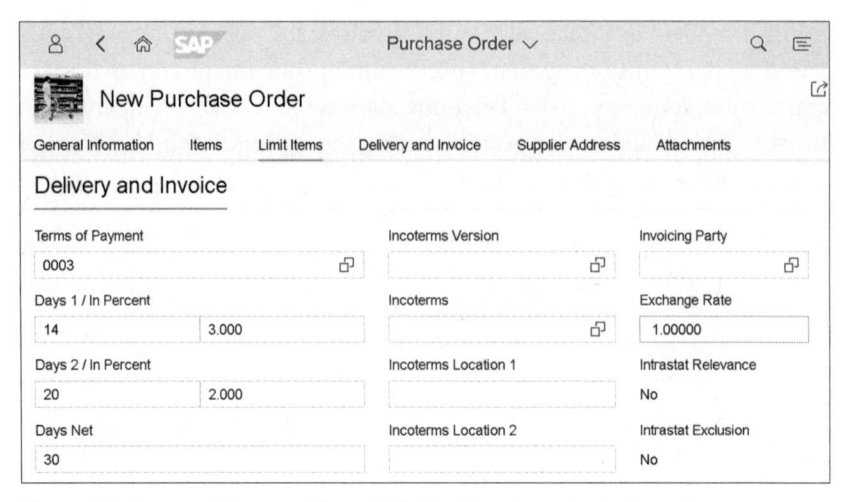

8 Integrating SAP S/4HANA Cloud into the System Landscape

Figure 8.5 Terms of Payment in an SAP Fiori Purchase Order Form in SAP S/4HANA Cloud

Compared to the traditional static predefined discount levels, SAP Ariba Discount Management offers dynamic, declining discounts.

Table 8.3 lists the message types for this process.

Message Type in cXML	Direction	Meaning
PaymentProposalRequest	Outbound	Send payment proposal (with cash discount)
CopyRequest.PaymentProposalRequest	Inbound	Receive response to payment proposal with cash discount
PaymentRemittanceRequest	Outbound	Send remittance advice
PaymentRemittanceStatusUpdateRequest	Outbound	Send status update for payment

Table 8.3 Message Types for Payment Processing and Discount Management with SAP Ariba Payables, Discounting Capabilities

> **Additional Information**
>
> For more information on Ariba Discount Management, go to:
>
> - *http://bit.ly/v1448081*
> - *http://bit.ly/v1448082*

8.1.2 License Prerequisites and Provision of SAP Ariba System Accesses

To support end-to-end business processes between SAP S/4HANA Cloud and SAP Ariba, you need to subscribe to both. However, you don't need a license for the integration. Table 8.4 lists the scope items of the various scenarios for which additional subscriptions are required.

Subscriptions

Scope Items	SAP Ariba Sourcing	SAP Ariba Commerce Automation	SAP Ariba Payables
SAP S/4HANA Enterprise Management Cloud	1A0	J82 and 1L2	19O
SAP S/4HANA Professional Services Cloud	–	J82	19O
SAP S/4HANA Finance Cloud	–	J82	19O

Table 8.4 Integration Scenarios, Licenses, and Possible Combinations in SAP Ariba Solutions

8.1.3 Executing an Integration Project with SAP Activate

With SAP S/4HANA, SAP has changed its implementation method from ASAP to SAP Activate (see Chapter 5). With SAP Activate, the integration of processes differs from the traditional integration method. SAP S/4HANA Cloud is designed to be easily and quickly integrated with SAP Ariba and SAP Fieldglass solutions. Activating integrated business processes is not much more complex than activating internal processes in SAP S/4HANA Cloud. However, this requires a systematic SAP Activate approach for the project.

Integration project or simple activation?

Like with every software implementation, you should carefully plan and implement the project for integrating with SAP Ariba solutions. Each SAP S/4HANA Cloud edition provides reference content for the preconfigured model company (see Chapter 6) as well as testable reference content for the business processes that are integrated with SAP Ariba. The integration itself will also require configuration.

Prepare phase

In the explore phase, based on the predefined solution scope of the selected SAP S/4HANA Cloud edition, you can determine in which areas

Explore phase

249

the reference solution meets your requirements and where you might have to enhance the solution. If unsure whether an existing business process should be integrated with SAP Ariba as part of the solution scope, this phase is ideal for finding out which sourcing processes and with which business partner group a digital collaboration in Ariba Network makes sense. The project team should involve senior sourcing managers as well as sourcing experts and employees in accounts payable.

Prioritization
Prioritize activating the scope items and the included process steps according to the value you expect them to add. Usually, automating incoming invoices is the first message type that is implemented, followed by upstream purchase orders to ensure a consistent document flow. The next most commonly automated items include remittance advices, purchase order confirmations, shipping notifications, discount management, and the two message types for RFx processes. Of course, you can change the order of activation as required to optimally map your business priorities.

[o] **Implementing Integration Scenarios Successively**
As you start integrating with SAP Ariba solutions, you can always activate more message types or add other SAP Ariba solutions later on.

Realize phase
In the realize phase, you set up, test, and progressively optimize the solution scope in several steps.

SAP Best Practices
You can find the basic instructions for integrating with SAP Ariba in SAP Best Practices, which is delivered with SAP S/4HANA Cloud. You can find SAP Best Practices in the SAP Best Practice Explorer (*https://rapid.sap.com/bp*) by choosing one of the following menu paths:

- SAP S/4HANA • Cloud • SAP Best Practices for SAP S/4HANA Professional Services Cloud
- SAP Best Practices for SAP S/4HANA Enterprise Management Cloud
- SAP Best Practices for SAP S/4HANA Finance Cloud.

Here, scope items are divided into groups based on the relevant business area. Scope items are predefined in the system but must be activated. You may also have to make further settings if necessary to your enterprise or to digitally exchange documents with individual suppliers.

8.1 Integration with SAP Ariba Solutions

The scope item integrating with *Ariba Payment and Discount Management* (scope item 19O) is included in the **Finance** scope item group. Scope items integrating with *SAP Ariba Sourcing* (scope item 1AO) for *Purchase Order to Invoice Automation* (scope item J82) and for *Quote Automation* (scope item 1L2) are contained in the **Sourcing and Procurement** scope item group. In the following sections, we'll explain the individual steps for activating these scope items.

Scope items

In the SAP S/4HANA Cloud starter system, integration with SAP Ariba applications is already configured. You'll only have to verify and adapt the settings where your business data deviate from SAP's standard. Process diagrams describe the scope of the scope items and configuration instructions in detail. You'll need to create the scope items manually in the SAP Ariba or SAP S/4HANA buyer account.

Starter system

Your quality assurance system (QA system) will fewer default settings than your starter system because you remain fully responsible for your enterprise structure, the settings, and your master data (for example, for suppliers).

Quality assurance system

The following sections describe the default settings for the starter system, which you'll verify, enhance if required, and copy to the QA system including the adaptations made. Contact the SAP employees and SAP Ariba employees assigned to your project to transport your settings to the production landscape and obtain information on enterprise-specific settings.

Basic Integration Steps

This list includes the basic steps for the integration; multiple iterations are possible:

1. Enter customer-specific connection data in SAP S/4HANA Cloud and SAP Ariba.
2. Check the default integration settings in SAP S/4HANA Cloud in the starter system and in the buyer's user account in SAP Ariba.
3. Validate and enhance default settings and test process integrity using the provided reference data and test scripts.
4. Replicate and adapt the settings for your enterprise in the QA system.
5. Test the process integrity in the QA system again.
6. If the test result is positive, transport the settings to the production system or make specific settings (for example, for system, client data, master data, and output control) in the production system.

8 Integrating SAP S/4HANA Cloud into the System Landscape

8.1.4 Integration Settings in SAP S/4HANA Cloud

First, implement the following settings in the SAP S/4HANA Cloud starter system:

1. Log on to SAP S/4HANA Cloud as the administrator and create a user with the preconfigured expert role for business network settings (SAP_BR_CONF_EXPERT_BUS_NET_INT). Log on to the system as this user.

2. On the start screen, SAP Fiori launchpad displays various groups, for example, **Communication Management**, **Output Control**, **Full Implementation**, and **Business Network—Integration Configuration** (see Figure 8.6).

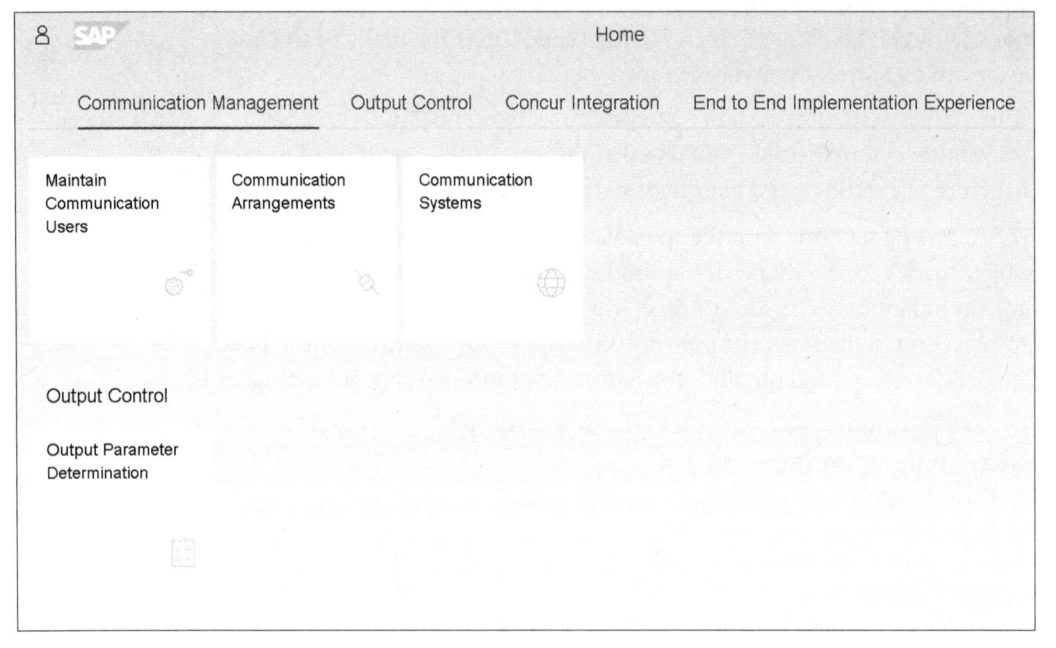

Figure 8.6 Start Screen of the Network Configurator in SAP Fiori Launchpad

3. Open the **Communication Agreements** tile in the **Communication Management** group. Enter "Ariba" in the search field. Check whether the scenario SAP_COM_0032 with the SAP Ariba communication system is enabled (see Figure 8.7).

4. Click on the entry and, in the screen that opens, check whether the **Service Status** in the **Outbound Services** section is enabled (see Figure 8.8). Copy the entry number into the **My System** field at **Shared Data**.

8.1 Integration with SAP Ariba Solutions

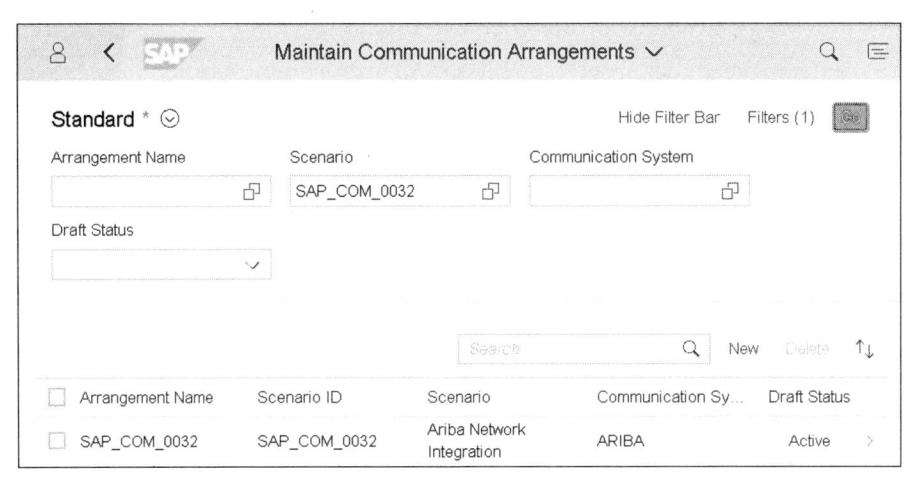

Figure 8.7 Communication Arrangement for Scenario SAP_COM_0032 (Ariba Network Integration)

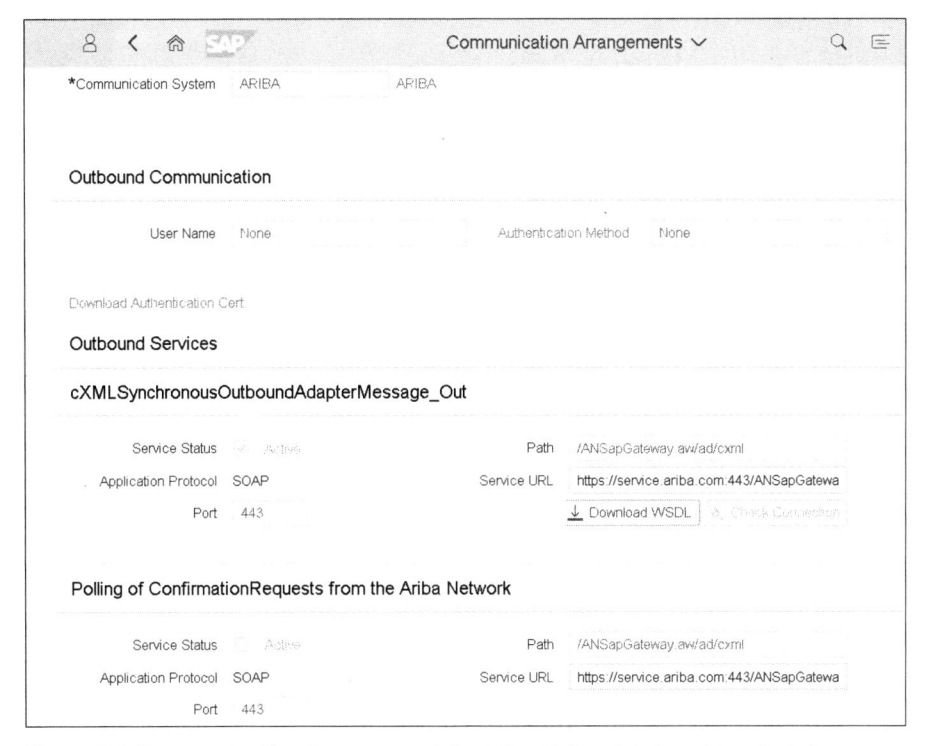

Figure 8.8 Communication Arrangement for Ariba Network Integration: Details

8   Integrating SAP S/4HANA Cloud into the System Landscape

Setting Up the System Communication with SAP Ariba

If not already set up, you can set up SAP Ariba communication in your system yourself.

1. Open the **Communication Systems** app and check that no entry for **ARIBA** exists. Click on the **New** button (see Figure 8.7).
2. Enter "ARIBA" for **System ID** and **System Name** and then click on **Create** (see Figure 8.9).

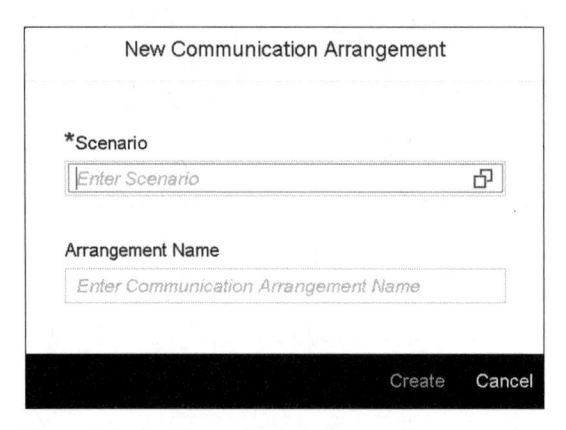

Figure 8.9 Creating a System Connection

3. In the header data, enter "service.ariba.com" for the **Host Name**.
4. Return to the SAP Fiori launchpad and open the **Logon Information and End Points** tile in the **Business Network—Integration Configuration** group (see Figure 8.10).

Ensure that at least one **Ariba Network ID** exists (see Figure 8.11). If you use SAP Ariba Cloud as the central instance for procurement activities with your suppliers across the group, you only need one network ID. However, you can also have separate IDs for each procurement organization.

In the trial system, the **Trial Account** column should have a checkmark. The trial, starter, and Q-system's network ID should end with "-T" for tests, as you may want to avoid exchanging test data with your actual suppliers.

8.1 Integration with SAP Ariba Solutions

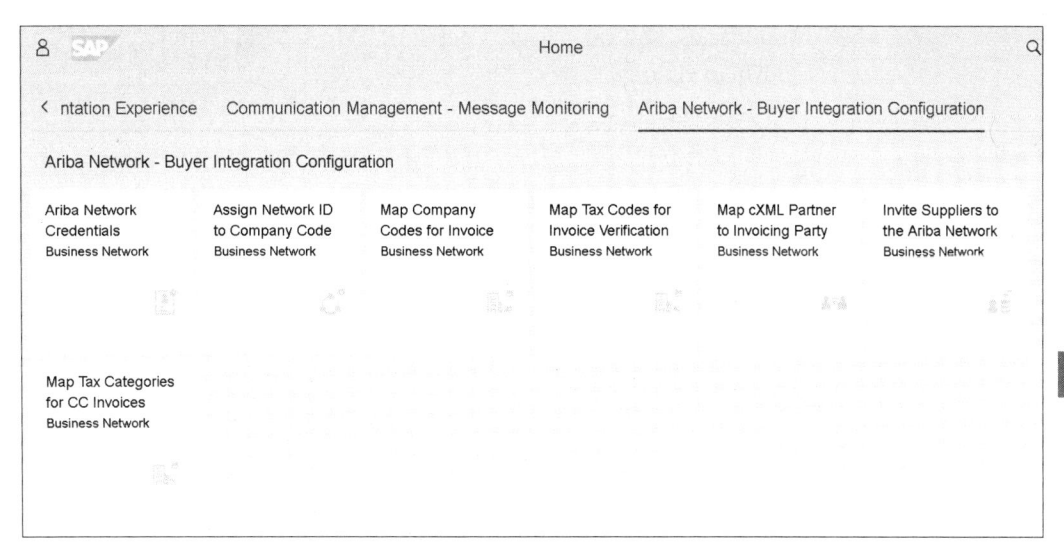

Figure 8.10 Group "Business Network—Integration Configuration"

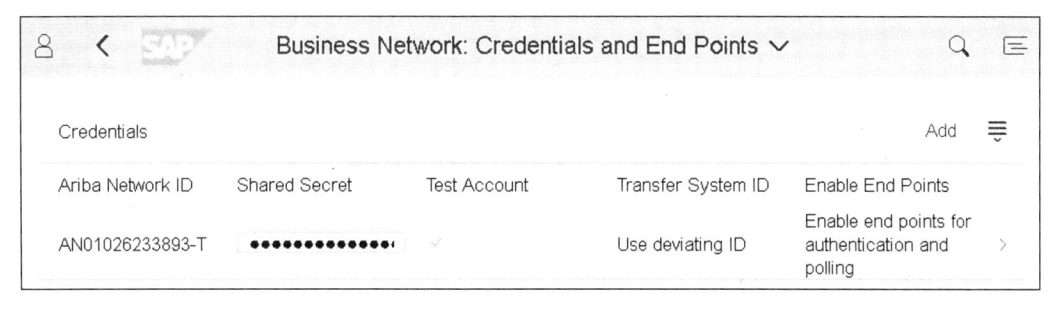

Figure 8.11 Business Network: Logon Information and End Points

5. In **Business Network—Integration Configuration • Assign Network ID to Company Code**, you can assign a network ID to each company code of the suppliers you want to collaborate with via Ariba Network. A company code can also contain only one supplier with which you want to communicate using Ariba Network. The aspects of individual suppliers for each company code will be discussed later on. However, you can assign a specific Ariba Network ID to each company code. If you have a centralized procurement organization that crosses company code

boundaries, you can assign a network ID to several company codes, as shown in Figure 8.12.

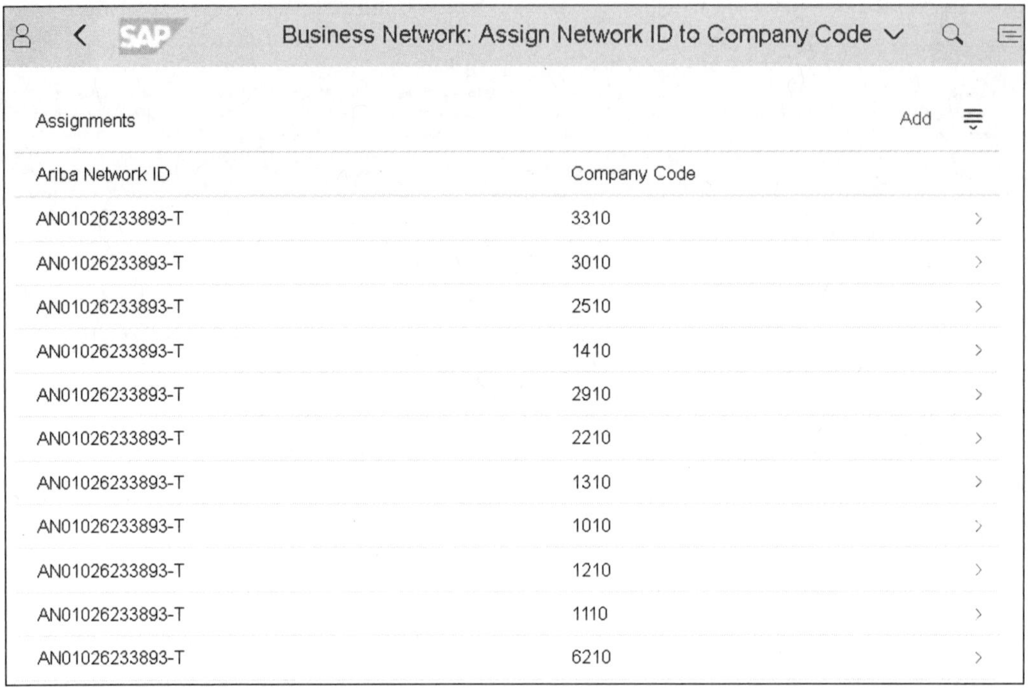

Ariba Network ID	Company Code
AN01026233893-T	3310
AN01026233893-T	3010
AN01026233893-T	2510
AN01026233893-T	1410
AN01026233893-T	2910
AN01026233893-T	2210
AN01026233893-T	1310
AN01026233893-T	1010
AN01026233893-T	1210
AN01026233893-T	1110
AN01026233893-T	6210

Figure 8.12 Assigning the Network ID to Company Codes

Activating scope items
The scope items for the SAP Ariba integration describe tested and true business processes. The following checks illustrate the activation scope of your starter system and provide you with background information on the default settings. Of course, you don't have to implement all scope items immediately, nor use all of the message types of the individual scope items. For example, if you only want to use the SAP S/4HANA Cloud functions that are integrated with SAP Ariba Sourcing, you don't have to configure specific settings for invoice verification.

Business Network: Assigning Company Codes for Invoice Verification

Maintaining suppliers and company codes
If you want to receive incoming supplier invoices electronically via Ariba Network, open the **Company Codes for Invoice Verification** app. To the list

of suppliers with which you communicate via the network, add the relevant entries. Both suppliers and company codes must already exist as master data in SAP S/4HANA Cloud. The **Name of My Enterprise in cXML** column should contain the field value via which all suppliers identify your enterprise in the **BillTo** field (see Figure 8.13). In your starter system, reference suppliers and company codes are already maintained.

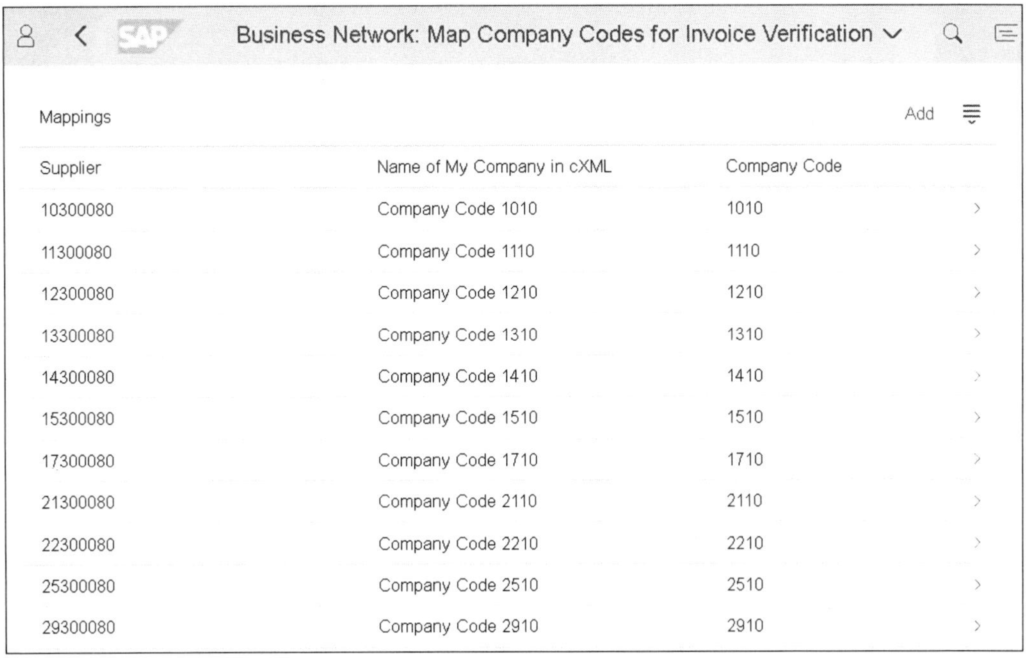
Business Network: Map Company Codes for Invoice Verification
Mappings
Add

Supplier	Name of My Company in cXML	Company Code
10300080	Company Code 1010	1010
11300080	Company Code 1110	1110
12300080	Company Code 1210	1210
13300080	Company Code 1310	1310
14300080	Company Code 1410	1410
15300080	Company Code 1510	1510
17300080	Company Code 1710	1710
21300080	Company Code 2110	2110
22300080	Company Code 2210	2210
25300080	Company Code 2510	2510
29300080	Company Code 2910	2910

Figure 8.13 Assigning Company Codes for Invoice Verification

Business Network: Assigning Tax Codes for Invoice Verification

The **Tax Codes for Invoice Verification** app already contains the tax codes for the selected company codes for all suppliers and SAP Ariba tax categories. With the assignment, the tax codes from the supplier invoices transferred by SAP Ariba are determined and forwarded to SAP S/4HANA Cloud. If you expect to receive incoming supplier invoices electronically via Ariba Network, verify that the settings in the Tax Codes for Invoice Verification app has the settings shown in Figure 8.14.

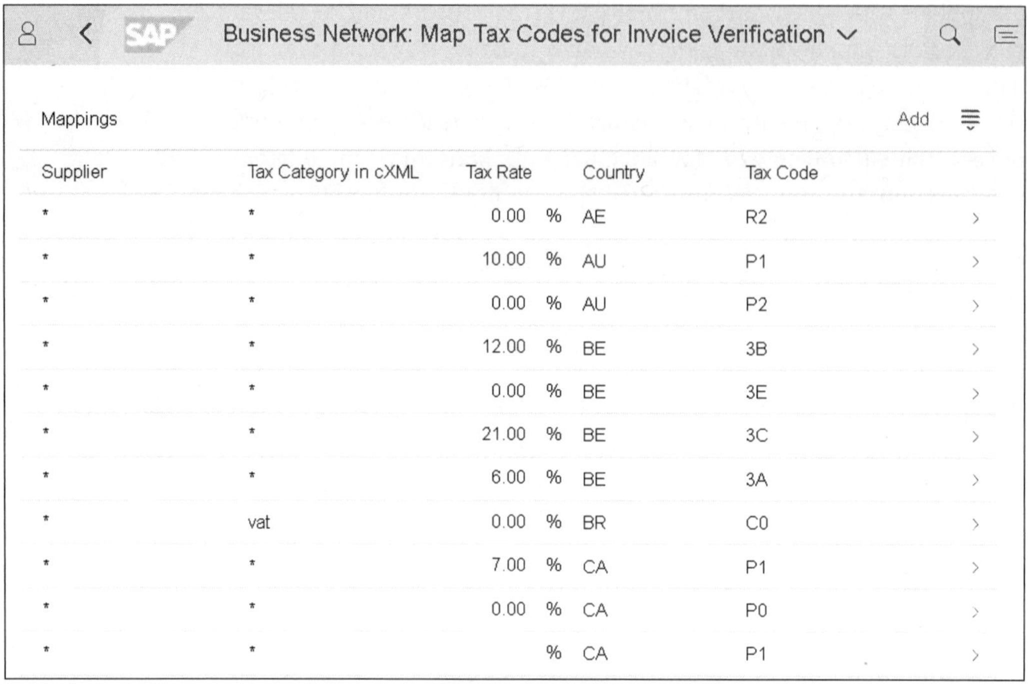

8   Integrating SAP S/4HANA Cloud into the System Landscape

Mappings					Add	
Supplier	Tax Category in cXML	Tax Rate		Country	Tax Code	
*	*	0.00	%	AE	R2	>
*	*	10.00	%	AU	P1	>
*	*	0.00	%	AU	P2	>
*	*	12.00	%	BE	3B	>
*	*	0.00	%	BE	3E	>
*	*	21.00	%	BE	3C	>
*	*	6.00	%	BE	3A	>
*	vat	0.00	%	BR	C0	>
*	*	7.00	%	CA	P1	>
*	*	0.00	%	CA	P0	>
*	*		%	CA	P1	>

Figure 8.14 Assigning Tax Codes for Invoice Verification

Business Network: Assigning cXML Item "Partner" to Invoicing Parties

Deviating invoicing party

Suppliers can outsource their invoicing processes to other organizations, like their parent company, or a third-party service providers to whom they ceded their claims. Only in this case do you configure the deviating invoicing party and maintain the assignments.

Maintain the vendor ID from SAP Ariba in the **cXML Item "VendorID"** under **"From" > "Credential"** field, as shown in Figure 8.15. Maintain the external ID of the invoicing party from SAP Ariba in **Name of the cXML Item "InvoicePartner" (Role "From")**. Assign the invoicing party ID in SAP S/4HANA Cloud. With **Reverse Assignment**, you can select whether you want to have the system send outgoing documents and status updates to the supplier instead of to the invoicing party.

8.1 Integration with SAP Ariba Solutions

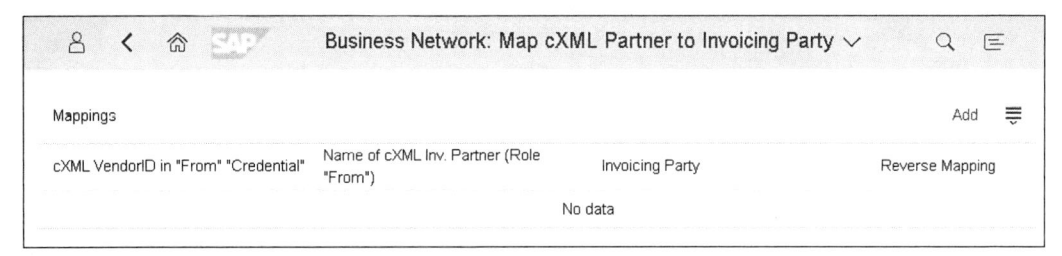

Figure 8.15 Assigning the cXML Item for Deviating Invoicing Parties for Invoice Verification

Inviting Suppliers to Ariba Network

Only enter suppliers from SAP S/4HANA Cloud in the **Suppliers for Quick Enablement** list (as shown in Figure 8.16) with which you want to collaborate via Ariba Network in future and who are not registered yet.

Supplier quick enablement

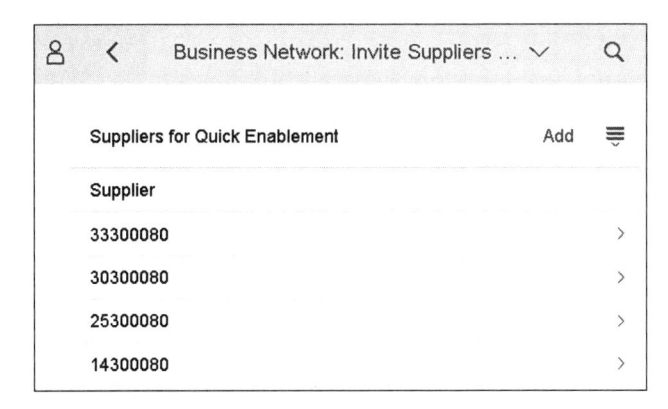

Figure 8.16 Inviting Suppliers from SAP S/4HANA Cloud to Ariba Network

If you add a supplier to this list and send a purchase order, invoice copy, or payment proposal for the first time, the system automatically creates a user account in Ariba Network on the behalf of this supplier. SAP Ariba then contacts the respective supplier on your behalf to electronically integrate the supplier into the network (*supplier quick enablement*). For this integration, the supplier's master data in your SAP S/4HANA Cloud list must contain the correct email address.

You then invite the registered suppliers in Ariba Network for collaboration and assign them to your Ariba Network IDs. If you partner with suppliers that are already registered in the network, you don't have to list them here.

259

8   Integrating SAP S/4HANA Cloud into the System Landscape

> [»] **Usage Fees for Suppliers**
>
> SAP Ariba charges suppliers a usage fee. In some industries, the legal conditions for purchasing organizations can prohibit charging suppliers additional fees for using electronic payment transactions or digital sourcing networks. In these cases, SAP Ariba allows procurement organizations to pay these supplier fees. Consult your SAP Ariba sales representative if this applies to your enterprise.

Control Parameters for Invoice Verification

Automatic document processing

If you expect to receive incoming invoices or credit memos from your suppliers in Ariba Network, you can specify control parameters so that these incoming documents are processed automatically. You can define document types for Ariba Network to use to process incoming digital documents in SAP S/HANA Cloud. Furthermore, you can determine how SAP S/4HANA Cloud will process deviations between the values expected by SAP S/4HANA Cloud and the documents received by the network.

Check indicators

In your starter system, the settings shown in Figure 8.17 are set by default for all company codes and suppliers. However, you can further specify these settings for the individual suppliers and company codes and differentiate between the various document types. Under **Logistics Invoice Verification with Purchase Order Reference**, you can define the following using **Correction Indicators**:

- In the case of unresolved issues, the incoming invoice is parked and needs to be processed manually (Indicator 1). The invoice is stored with the incoming data as well as with the values the system expected and needs to be processed manually.

- In the case of unresolved issues, the draft of the incoming invoice is parked with the invoice header data (Indicator D for Draft). The draft must be processed manually in the **Manage Supplier Invoice** app.

- If no indicator is set, the invoice is posted as it is received and blocked for payment in the case of deviations.

On this screen, the check indicators prevent invoice documents from being posted in SAP S/4HANA Cloud if the values on the document deviate from the expected values. The sending supplier in Ariba Network identifies documents that cannot be posted based on the updated statuses of the related outgoing invoices.

Logistics Invoice Verification Without Purchase Order Reference lets you determine how the system will react if the purchase order reference number in incoming invoices is missing or invalid. **Processing Indicator: Do Not Process** rejects incoming invoices. Ariba Network sends an invoice status update message to the supplier.

Processing invalid invoices

With **Park Invoice**, the invoice document is created with the **Parked** status in SAP S/4HANA. A parked invoice must be processed manually later. If you select **Create Invoice Draft**, the system creates the draft of an incoming invoice in SAP S/4HANA. You'll then have to manually process this draft in the **Manage Supplier Invoice** app later.

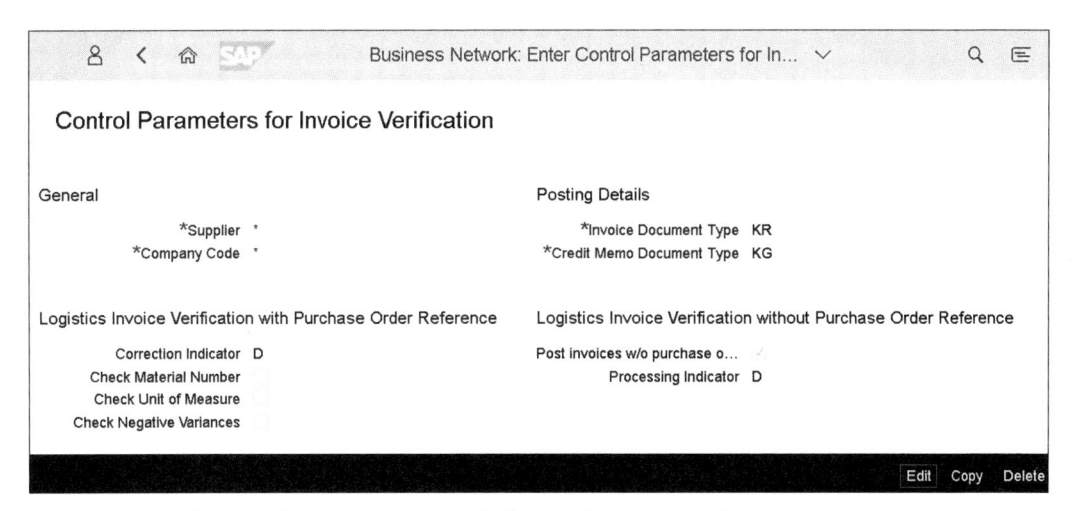

Figure 8.17 Configuring the Business Network: "Control Parameters for Invoice Verification"

Assigning Tax Categories for Invoice Copies

You must specify tax categories for invoice copies (see Figure 8.18) only for suppliers to which you send invoice copies via Ariba Network. You would send electronic invoice copies if you received incoming invoices in paper format, scanned them, and now consider the digital version as the valid reference for further processing. Similarly, you would send electronic invoice copies if you issued invoices to yourself on the basis of incoming deliveries

8   Integrating SAP S/4HANA Cloud into the System Landscape

(also called *evaluated receipt settlement*, ERS) and wanted to inform the supplier via individual credit memo documents.

In your starter system, the table for tax indicators is already filled with default values, but these indicators are not assigned to any suppliers. If required, you can make generic assignments using an asterisk or copy and modify assignments for selected suppliers.

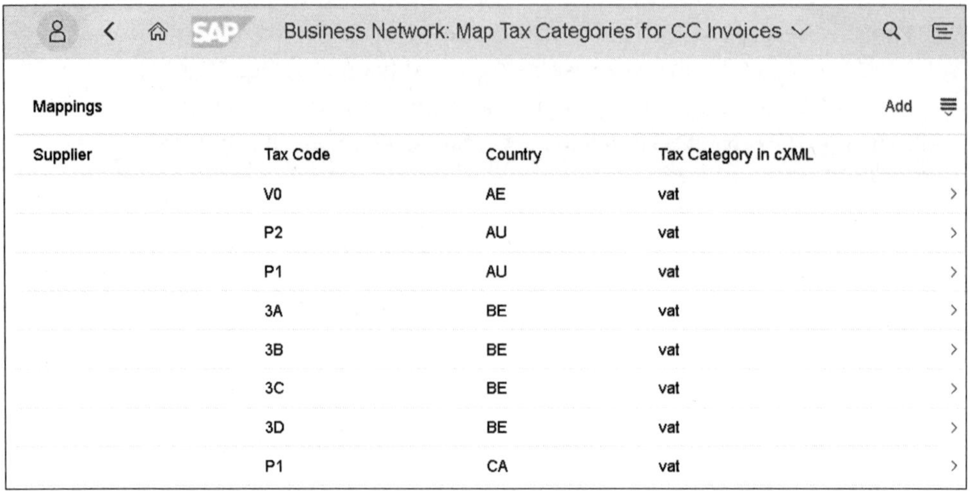

Supplier	Tax Code	Country	Tax Category in cXML
	V0	AE	vat
	P2	AU	vat
	P1	AU	vat
	3A	BE	vat
	3B	BE	vat
	3C	BE	vat
	3D	BE	vat
	P1	CA	vat

Figure 8.18 Configuring the Business Network: "Assign Tax Categories for Invoice Copies"

Message Control

Output Parameter Determination Only outbound message types require you to maintain output parameters. In the **Output Parameter Determination** app, you can check and supplement the corresponding entries. The guides for the relevant scope items describe this configuration in detail. In the **Full Implementation** group (see Figure 8.6), you can activate the desired message types in the **Manage Your Solution** app. The settings you make in this app can be transferred from the quality assurance system to the production system.

1. Select the **Configure Solution** function in the **Manage Your Solution** app. Enter "Network" in the search field on the right (see Figure 8.19).

2. If the system displays **Business Network—Configure Message Types**, confirm this entry by clicking on the **Start** button.

8.1 Integration with SAP Ariba Solutions

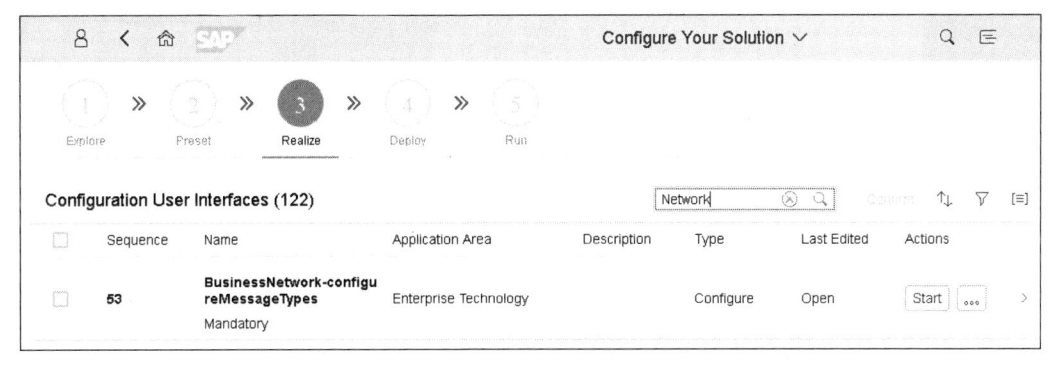

Figure 8.19 Configure Your Solution Business Network: Display Message Types

3. Now, select the message types that you want to activate and mark them as **Enabled** (see Figure 8.20).

Component ID	Object Type	cXML Message Type	Message Direction	Mapping version	cXML version	Active
BNS-ARI-SE-ERP	Accounting Document	CopyRequest.PaymentProposalRequest	IN	V001	1.2.030	>
BNS-ARI-SE-ERP	Accounting Document	PaymentProposalRequest	OUT	V001	1.2.030	>
BNS-ARI-SE-ERP	Accounting Document	PaymentRemittanceStatusUpdateRequest	OUT	V001	1.2.030	>
BNS-ARI-SE-ERP	Purchase Order	ConfirmationRequest	IN	V001	1.2.030	>
BNS-ARI-SE-ERP	Purchase Order	OrderRequest	OUT	V001	1.2.030	>
BNS-ARI-SE-ERP	Inbound Delivery	ShipNoticeRequest	IN	V001	1.2.030	>
BNS-ARI-SE-ERP	Goods Movement	ReceiptRequest	OUT	V001	1.2.030	>
BNS-ARI-SE-ERP	Sales Order	ConfirmationRequest	OUT	V001	1.2.032	>
BNS-ARI-SE-ERP	Sales Order	OrderRequest	IN	V001	1.2.032	>
BNS-ARI-SE-ERP	Incoming Invoice	CopyRequest.InvoiceDetailRequest	OUT	V001	1.2.030	>
BNS-ARI-SE-ERP	Incoming Invoice	InvoiceDetailRequest	IN	V001	1.2.030	>
BNS-ARI-SE-ERP	Incoming Invoice	StatusUpdateRequest	OUT	V001	1.2.030	>
BNS-FG-SE-ERP	Incoming Invoice	InvoiceDetailRequest	IN	V001	1.2.030	>
BNS-FG-SE-ERP	Incoming Invoice	StatusUpdateRequest	OUT	V001	1.2.030	>
BNS-ARI-SE-ERP	Outbound Payment Advice	PaymentRemittanceRequest	OUT	V001	1.2.030	>
BNS-ARI-SE-ERP	Outbound Delivery	ShipNoticeRequest	OUT	V001	1.2.032	>
BNS-ARI-SE-ERP	Quote	QuoteMessage	IN	V001	1.2.030	>
BNS-ARI-SE-ERP	Request for Quotation	QuoteRequest	OUT	V001	1.2.030	>
BNS-ARI-SE-ERP	Outbound Invoice	InvoiceDetailRequest	OUT	V001	1.2.032	>

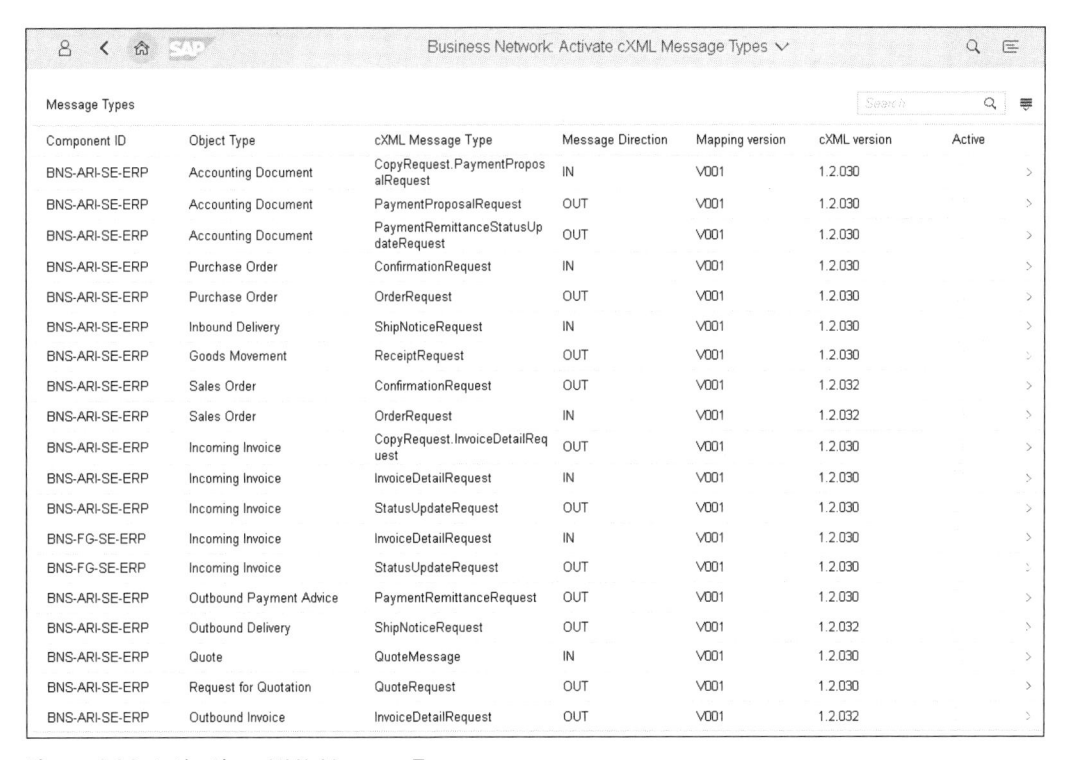

Figure 8.20 Activating cXML Message Types

4. After you have saved your activation, you can enter a comment for your configuration status by clicking on the button with the three dots next to the **Start** button and entering your comments.

[»] **Message Types Sorted According to Process Logic**

The system does not list the **Object Types** and **cXML Message Types** in the table according to the business process order. Table 8.5 lists the cXML message types according to their process logic sorted by scope items. (The component ID, mapping, and cXML version are static in our example and thus not mapped redundantly.)

Scope Item with ID	Object Type	cXML Message Type	Meaning	In/Out
1L2 SAP Ariba Sourcing Integration (scope item 1A0) and Quote Automation	RFx	QuoteRequest	Request to submit a quotation	Out
	Quotation	QuoteMessage	Quotation/bid price	In
J82 Purchase Order to Invoice Automation	Purchase order	OrderRequest		Out
	Purchase order	ConfirmationRequest	Order confirmation	In
	Delivery	ShipNoticeRequest	Shipping notification	In

Table 8.5 Scope Items, Business Objects, Message Types, Meaning, and Transfer Direction from the SAP S/4HANA Cloud Perspective

Scope Item with ID	Object Type	cXML Message Type	Meaning	In/Out
	Goods movement	ReceiptRequest	Goods receipt document	Out
	Incoming invoice	InvoiceDetailRequest		In
	Incoming invoice	CopyRequest. InvoiceDetailRequest	Invoice copy	Out
	Incoming invoice	StatusUpdateRequest	Status update of the invoice (unlocked)	Out
190 Payment and Discount Management	Accounting document	PaymentProposalRequest	Payment proposal (with cash discount)	Out
	Accounting document	CopyRequest. PaymentProposalRequest	Response to payment proposal with cash discount	In
	Outbound remittance advice	PaymentRemittanceRequest	Remittance advice	Out
	Accounting document	PaymentRemittanceStatusUpdateRequest	Status update for payment	Out

Table 8.5 Scope Items, Business Objects, Message Types, Meaning, and Transfer Direction from the SAP S/4HANA Cloud Perspective (Cont.)

8   Integrating SAP S/4HANA Cloud into the System Landscape

Now, the configuration is complete on the SAP S/4HANA Cloud side. Let's take a closer look at your SAP Ariba instance in the following sections.

8.1.5   Configuration in SAP Ariba

Activating the network

To configure SAP Ariba, you should have the following details for your SAP Ariba buyer account at hand: your logon information (user and password), your Ariba Network ID, and the so-called *shared secret* for secure communication between Ariba Network and SAP S/4HANA Cloud. If you have an SAP Ariba Sourcing subscription, have the corresponding logon information and shared secret data ready.

SAP Ariba provides the relevant information when you register your enterprise as a buyer at Ariba Network. Now, log on as the administrator for your buyer account in SAP Ariba (at *https://buyer.ariba.com*). Go to **Administration** (see Figure 8.21). Next, select **Configuration** to navigate to the configuration overview shown in Figure 8.22. Depending on your selected subscriptions, your configuration list might be shorter.

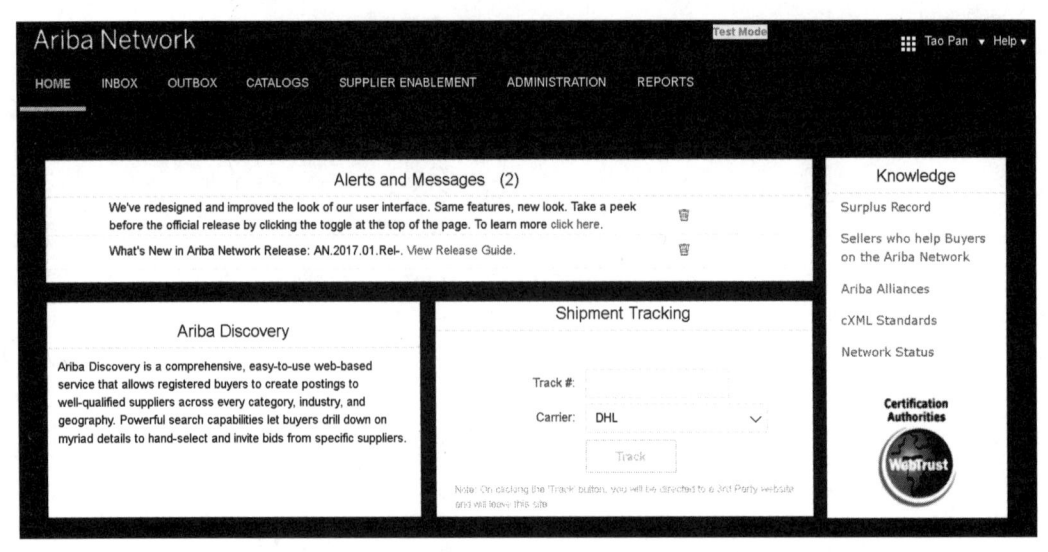

Figure 8.21 Buyer User Account Entry Screen in Ariba Network

Ariba Network

Configuration

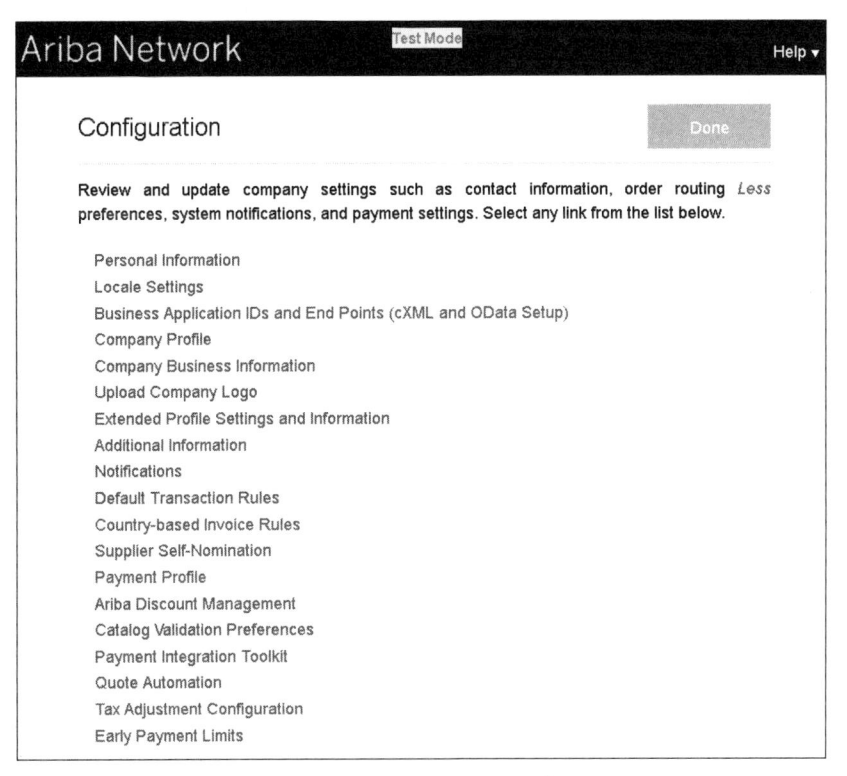

Review and update company settings such as contact information, order routing preferences, system notifications, and payment settings. Select any link from the list below.

- Personal Information
- Locale Settings
- Business Application IDs and End Points (cXML and OData Setup)
- Company Profile
- Company Business Information
- Upload Company Logo
- Extended Profile Settings and Information
- Additional Information
- Notifications
- Default Transaction Rules
- Country-based Invoice Rules
- Supplier Self-Nomination
- Payment Profile
- Ariba Discount Management
- Catalog Validation Preferences
- Payment Integration Toolkit
- Quote Automation
- Tax Adjustment Configuration
- Early Payment Limits

Figure 8.22 Configuration Overview in Ariba Network

Basic Settings for SAP Ariba Sourcing (Scope Item 1A0) and Ariba Quote Automation (Scope Item 1L2)

In the system ID list, select **Create**. Create an entry with the **System ID** and enter the **Unique Address ID** "Ariba". This entry refers to SAP Ariba Sourcing. Save your settings.

On the **System Ids** list, select the entry you just created and then **Endpoints**. In the end point list, select **Create**. Close the popup message regarding the transfer of existing cXML structures. On the **Configure End Point** screen, enter "S/4HANA" in the **End Point ID** field. Select the **cXML** integration type. Select the **Shared Secret** authentication method, and enter your secret. Save your entries.

Creating end points

8   Integrating SAP S/4HANA Cloud into the System Landscape

Now, create an additional sourcing end point in the end point list. Enter the "Sourcing" end point ID (see Figure 8.23). Select the **cXML** integration type. Select the **Shared Secret** authentication method and enter the shared secret for sourcing. Enter the profile URL:

https://s1-eu.ariba.com/Sourcing/cxmlchannel/<ANID>

<ANID> refers to the Ariba Network ID of your buyer account. Do not confuse this URL with the URL of your SAP Ariba Sourcing instance.

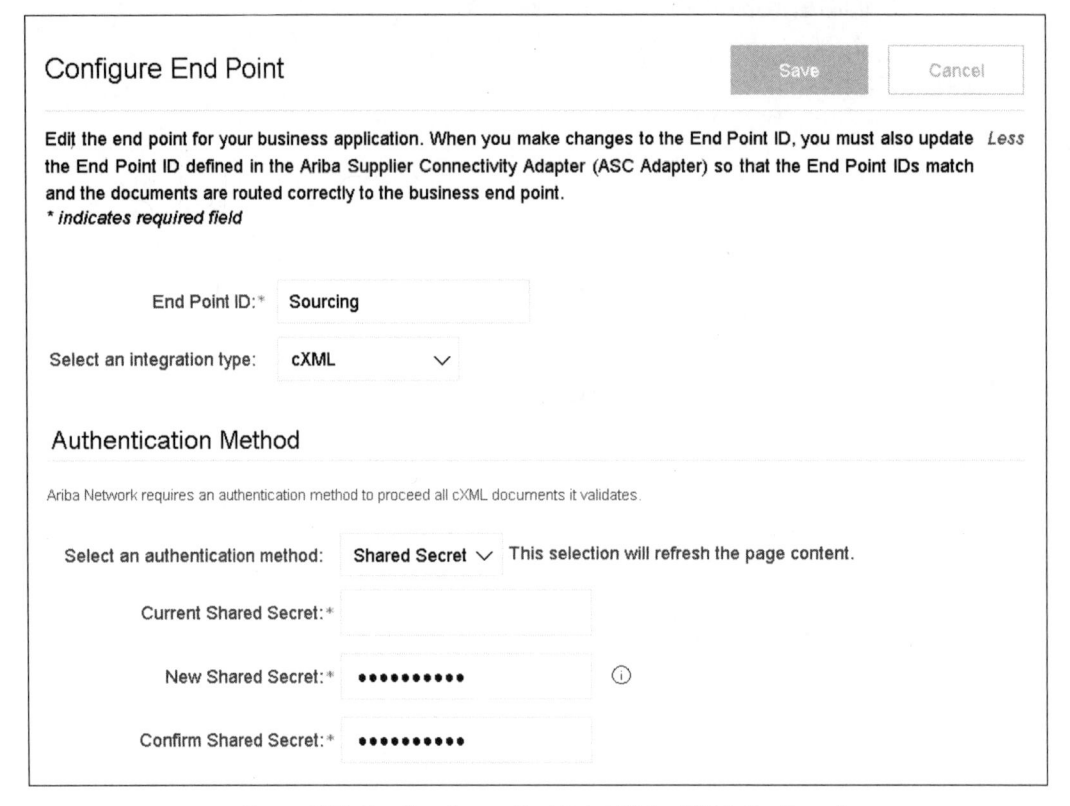

Figure 8.23 Configuring an End Point ID for SAP Ariba Sourcing

Select the checkbox **Yes, I want to receive documents through the POST method instead of through the cXML GetPending method**. Enter the following in the **Post URL** field:

https://s1-eu.ariba.com/Sourcing/cxmlchannel/<ANID>

This URL schema applies to customers in Europe. For countries in the Americas, it may look like *https://s1.ariba.com/Sourcing/cxmlchannel/ <ANID>*. Save your entries.

On the end point list, select the "Sourcing" end point ID as **Default**.

Configuring Ariba Purchase Order to Invoice Automation (Source Item J82) and Ariba Payment and Discount Management Integration (Source Item 190)

If you've followed the SAP Ariba Sourcing settings we've described so far in this section, skip this section and go to the next section, "Defining Transaction Rules."

Profile URL and post URL

On the **Configuration** screen, select one of the following options (depending on your SAP Ariba account settings):

- cXML Setup
- Business Application IDs (cXML and OData Setup)
- Business Application IDs and End Points (cXML and OData Setup)

Now, maintain the profile URL and the post URL. If your system does not display the screen for maintaining these URLs but instead the **List of System IDs**, click on the **System ID** of your SAP S/4HANA Cloud system. If the system still does not display the screen for maintaining URLs, select the **End Point** tab on the **Manage Business Application ID <System ID>** screen and then the end point ID for which you want to specify the settings.

The **Profile URL** section (see Figure 8.24) contains the **Profile URL** field. Delete any existing entries in this field. The **Post URL** section includes the **Yes, I want to receive documents through the POST method instead of through the cXML GetPending method** checkbox, which should not be selected. Save your entries.

Defining Transaction Rules

To create transaction rules, select the **Default Transaction Rules** option on the **Configuration** screen (see Figure 8.25).

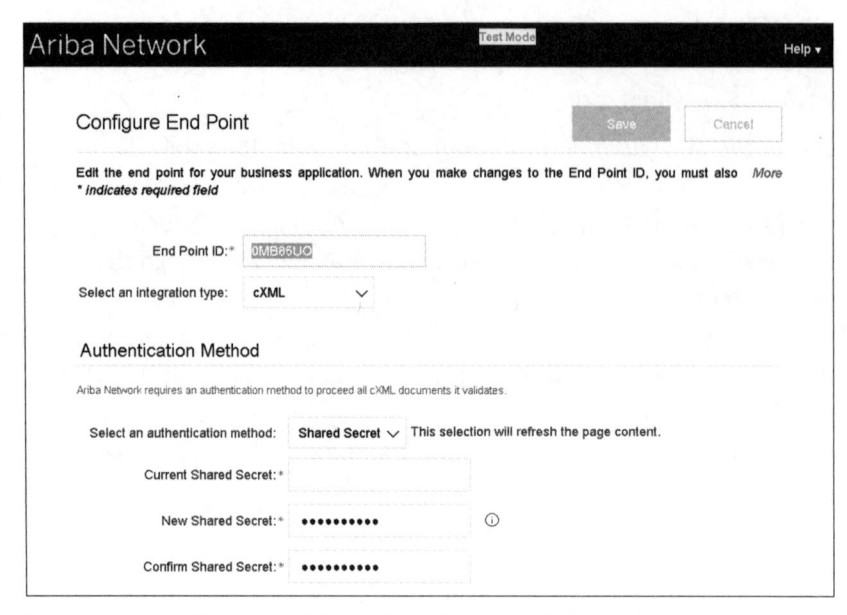

8   Integrating SAP S/4HANA Cloud into the System Landscape

Figure 8.24 Configuring End Points from Purchase Order to Payment (Scope Items J82 and 19O)

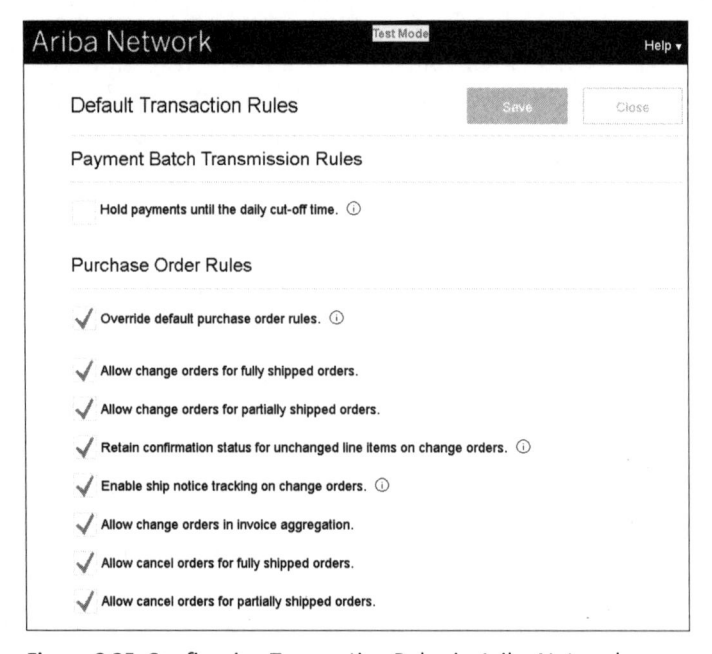

Figure 8.25 Configuring Transaction Rules in Ariba Network

> **Invoice PDF**
>
> If you want to receive electronic invoices including an invoice PDF, contact the SAP Ariba Service Center by following these steps: In the header area of the buyer account, select **Help • Contact Support**. Then, select your language and **Create Online Service Request** under **Contact Ariba Customer Support**. Ask Ariba to make the following setting under **PDF Generation**: Activate "Generate an invoice copy as PDF attachment to the invoice."

Making Suppliers Available in Ariba Network

Your suppliers must be registered in Ariba Network and must be willing to exchange data with your enterprise. To make your suppliers available in Ariba Network, log on to Ariba Network at *http://buyer.ariba.com* with your buyer account. On the **Supplier Enablement** tab, select **Active Relationships**. If you can find the desired supplier in the **Current Suppliers** table, proceed to the following section.

If you cannot find the desired supplier, you'll have to create the business relationship in SAP Ariba by following these steps:

Activating business relationships

1. Select **Search for Suppliers**.
2. Select the appropriate search criteria and click on **Search**.
3. Select the desired supplier. Click on **Action, Add to Selected Suppliers**.
4. Check the supplier profile. You can also download the profile.
5. In the **Selected Suppliers** overview, select the desired supplier and open the entry.
6. Request a business relationship by clicking on **Request a Relationship**.

The supplier must accept this request before you can exchange documents electronically in Ariba Network.

Assigning Supplier Indicators

Supplier master data in SAP S/4HANA Cloud uses IDs as indicators. The same supplier can exist in various ERP systems with different IDs. In this section, we'll assign supplier IDs from SAP S/4HANA Cloud and further systems in Ariba Network on the basis of their Ariba Network ID.

1. First, log on to your buyer account in Ariba Network and select the **Supplier Enablement** tab. Select **Active Relationships**. Find the desired supplier.
2. On the **Edit Preferences for Supplier: <Name of Your Supplier>** screen, select **Enter supplier identifiers for the procurement application** and click on **Add**.
3. If you integrate various SAP S/4HANA Cloud instances or additional ERP systems, select one of your systems and the corresponding supplier ID in this system (for example, 0010300080 in the starter system) in the **Add Supplier Unique Key** dialog box.
4. For SAP S/4HANA Cloud single systems, the first field contains the supplier ID (for example, 0010300080 in the starter system). Save by clicking on **Save**.

Repeat these steps for all the suppliers with which you want to exchange documents electronically through SAP Ariba. Be sure to include all suppliers in all of your SAP S/4HANA Cloud systems and ERP systems. Save your entries on the **Edit Preferences for Supplier: <Name of Your Supplier>** screen.

8.1.6 Testing the Integrated Business Processes and Going Live

Test scripts   You can test the integrated business processes in your starter system and quality assurance system using the test scripts provided. You can find these test scripts in the SAP Best Practices directory, the SAP Best Practices Explorer, at *http://rapid.sap.com/bp* (see Figure 8.26).

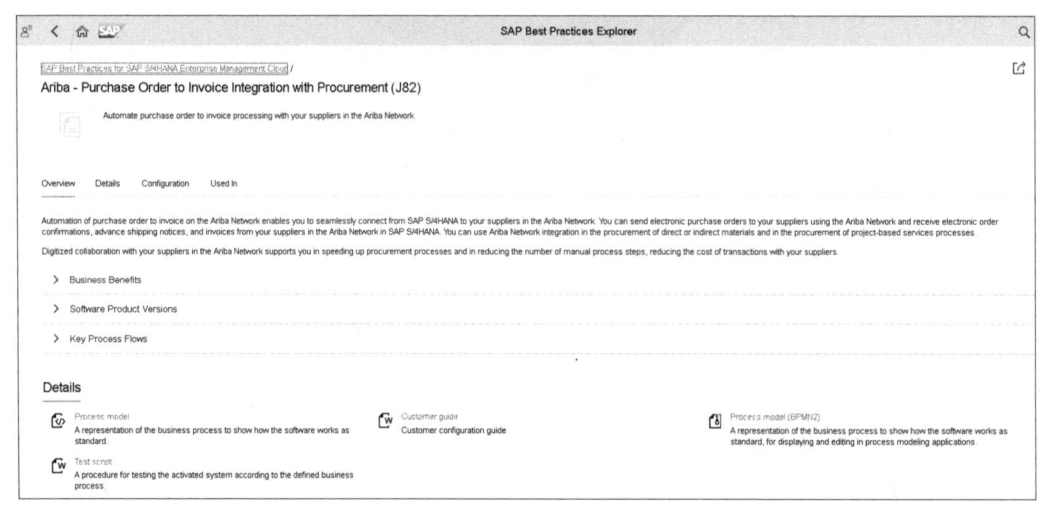

Figure 8.26 Test Scripts and Process Diagrams in the SAP Best Practices Explorer

The test scripts and process diagrams in SAP Best Practices are designed to help users with limited experience get started with the processes and to facilitate testing. Of course, you can also add custom supplier master data, specific materials, or deviating process settings to the test scripts.

After you have completed all tests successfully, have SAP transport the settings that were introduced when we discussed output control in Section 8.1.4 to the production system. All other configurations are set up manually later on.

When you start collaborating with your suppliers in the production system in Ariba Network, you should first communicate the individual processes in detail. The invested effort pays off quickly. In advance, you should discuss with a limited number of suppliers which transactions you want to execute and define your expectations regarding message types, processes, and response times (service-level agreements). For the first few transactions, stay in close contact with your suppliers until the processes have been established successfully on all sides.

Close coordination during the implementation phase

8.1.7 Outlook

Having supply chains coordinated by SAP software is not new at all, just think of *SAP Supply Chain Management* (SCM) and *SAP Supplier Network Collaboration* (SNC). However, because SAP Ariba was added to the SAP product portfolio, and due to the enhanced capabilities from Ariba Network, integration between SAP Ariba and the SAP Business Suite made sense.

Rapid deployment solutions

Since May 2016, SAP has provided a rapid deployment solution for integration with SAP Ariba, which also includes the integration of the *Ariba Collaborative Supply Chain* (CSC): *SAP Ariba Solution Integration for SAP Business Suite* (*https://rapid.sap.com/bp/RDS_ARI*). This integration scenario shows how three end-to-end CSC business processes are implemented: scheduling agreement releases, picking, and subcontracting.

For both SAP S/4HANA, on-premise, and SAP S/4HANA Cloud, these processes should be made available at a later stage. If you require SCC processes activated before they become generally available, please contact your SAP or SAP Ariba sales representative.

8 Integrating SAP S/4HANA Cloud into the System Landscape

SAP Ariba Procure-to-Pay

SAP S/4HANA Cloud covers procurement processes that can be executed by all employees in the enterprise (*Employee Self-Service Procurement, Requisitioning*, scope item 18J). You might already be using SAP Ariba Buying and Invoicing with your SAP ERP system, for example, using the *Ariba Procure-to-Pay Integration for SAP Business Suite* rapid deployment solution (*http://service.sap.com/bp/RDS_ARIBA_P2P*). SAP plans to provide an integration scenario for SAP Ariba Buying and Invoicing in early 2018.

> **Helpful Information Sources**
>
> The contextual help in SAP S/4HANA [?] can answer your questions regarding configuring applications. As with all SAP Ariba integration projects, the SAP Ariba help and support pages are also useful:
>
> - SAP Help: *http://help.sap.com/s4hana*
> - Go SAP page for SAP S/4HANA Cloud: *https://www.sap.com/products/s4hana-erp/cloud.html*
> - Go SAP page "Integration for SAP S/4HANA Cloud with SAP Solutions": *https://www.sap.com/products/s4hana-erp/cloud.integration.html*
> - SAP Support: *http://support.sap.com*. At SAP Support, you can enter tickets by using the "SV-CLD-SINT" component for integration-related content, such as SAP Best Practices, or by using the "BNS-ARI-SE-ERP" component for the functionality and configuration of the SAP Ariba integration.
> - Support for SAP Ariba applications: contextual menu within the applications themselves and at the following page: *http://support.ariba.com*.
> - SAP Community: *http://www.sap.com/community/topic/s4hana.html*
> - Ariba User Community: *http://connect.ariba.com*
> - SAP Cloud Professional Services: *https://www.sap.com/services/cloud-services-consulting.html*

8.2 Integration with SAP SuccessFactors

No human resources in SAP S/4HANA Cloud

SAP allows you to integrate SAP S/4HANA Cloud with SAP SuccessFactors Employee Central in nearly all SAP S/4HANA Cloud editions. One exception is SAP Hybris Marketing, which we'll discuss in detail in Section 8.3.

SAP S/4HANA Cloud does not cover any HR processes, so an external HR system needs to be integrated. SAP SuccessFactors Employee Central is SAP's solution for cloud-based personnel administration.

Of course, you can also import employee data from files. This scenario is ideal for trial systems but less suited for production systems. SAP provides a specific application importing employee data (see Figure 8.27), which you can find as a tile (**Import Employees**) on the SAP Fiori launchpad for administrators.

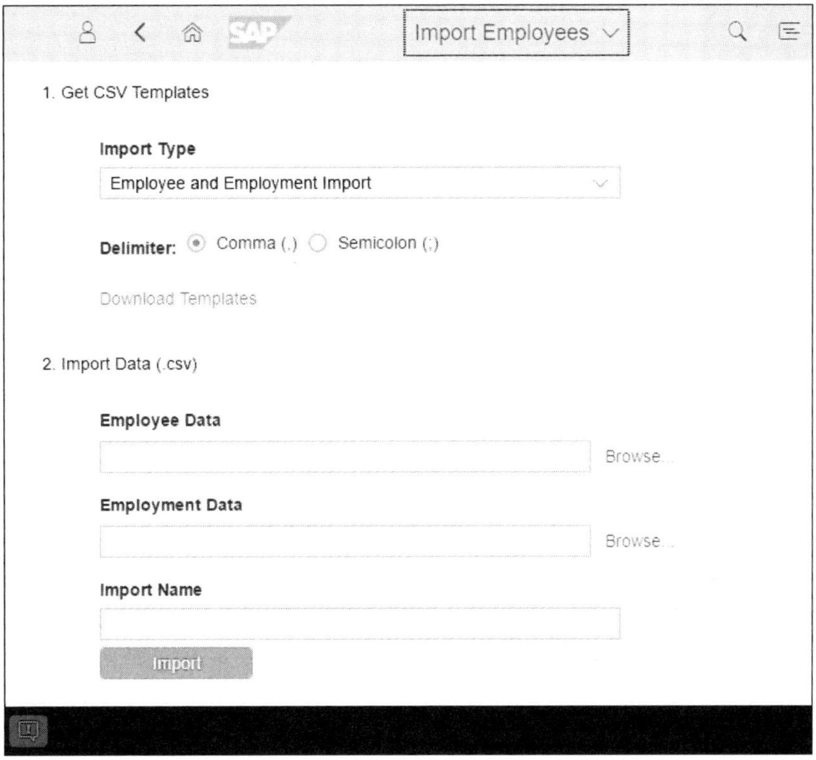

Importing employee data

Figure 8.27 Importing Employee Data from a File

SAP SuccessFactors Employee Central is always integrated with SAP S/4HANA Cloud via middleware, i.e., software that maps individual data fields to each other and initiates the data transfer. The middleware in this case is *SAP Cloud Platform Integration*, which is available to all SAP S/4HANA Cloud customers. See Figure 8.28.

Middleware

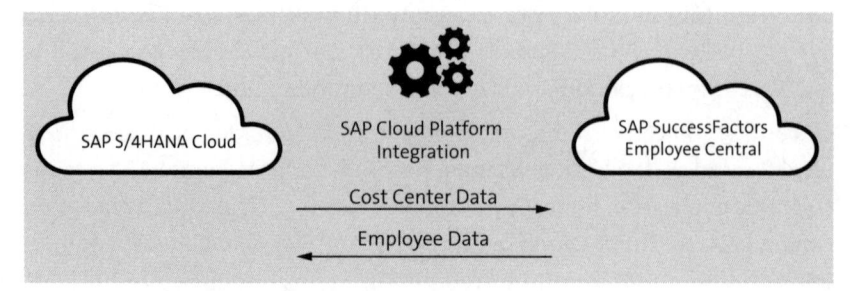

8   Integrating SAP S/4HANA Cloud into the System Landscape

Figure 8.28 SAP Cloud Platform Integration

> **SAP Cloud Platform Integration**
>
> SAP Cloud Platform Integration is used to integrate web-based applications. You can build and run these integration scenarios on the *SAP Cloud Platform* (previously, *SAP HANA Cloud Platform*, HCP). The platform is hosted in SAP Cloud. The integration via SAP Cloud Platform Integration is the preferred method for SAP S/4HANA.
>
> For more information, go to *https://help.sap.com/cloudintegration*.

Integration variants

This integration comes in two variants:

- Integration managed by SAP
- Integration managed by the customer

In the first case, SAP initiates the integration in the background in coordination with the customer. SAP will configure SAP S/4HANA Cloud, SAP Cloud Platform Integration, and SAP SuccessFactors Employee Central. This variant is ideal for customers who want to introduce SAP S/4HANA Cloud and SAP SuccessFactors Employee Central in an integrated system landscape quickly. Changes or adaptations are not possible with this variant.

The second variant is ideal for customers who have already used SAP S/4HANA Cloud or SAP SuccessFactors Employee Central on a production system for some time and want to integrate them with each other. Due to certain prerequisites in the data models of the two systems, you might need to adapt the default integration; for example, the length of some fields in SAP SuccessFactors Employee Central fields may need to be mapped to SAP S/4HANA Cloud fields. These adaptations can be required in the middleware and in SAP SuccessFactors Employee Central. To give customers or SAP implementation partners more freedom for adaptations, SAP provides the *Employee Central Integration* communication scenario (SAP_COM_0001).

The business functions of the two variants are the same. Employee-related data (for example, pictures) are transferred from SAP SuccessFactors Employee Central to SAP S/4HANA Cloud and cost centers, and vice versa.

Table 8.6 provides an overview of the system requirements (new implementation of SAP S/4HANA Cloud or live systems) for which SAP manages an integration variant.

Availability of integration variants

Scenario	Managed by SAP	Managed by Customer	Managed by Customer	Managed by Customer	Managed by Customer
SAP S/4HANA Cloud	New	Production	New	Production	New
SAP SuccessFactors Employee Central	New	New	Production	New	Production
SAP Cloud Platform Integration	New	New	New	Production	Production

Table 8.6 Overview of Selection Scenarios

Figure 8.29 and Figure 8.30 illustrate partial aspects of these transfer methods in detail. You can find additional process diagrams for this integration in the documentation of your SAP S/4HANA Cloud edition integration, but these two figures are the most important ones. They describe the integration process in detail, including replication or data flow and the individual process steps in the middleware.

Process diagrams for data exchange

You can create or change employee data in SAP SuccessFactors Employee Central. The middleware will initiate the data transfer of these changes to SAP S/4HANA Cloud, and the relevant employee data records will be updated or created. In SAP S/4HANA Cloud, the employee data records are mainly used as business partners in the "Employee" role. Consequently, these changes are also made in the business partner data.

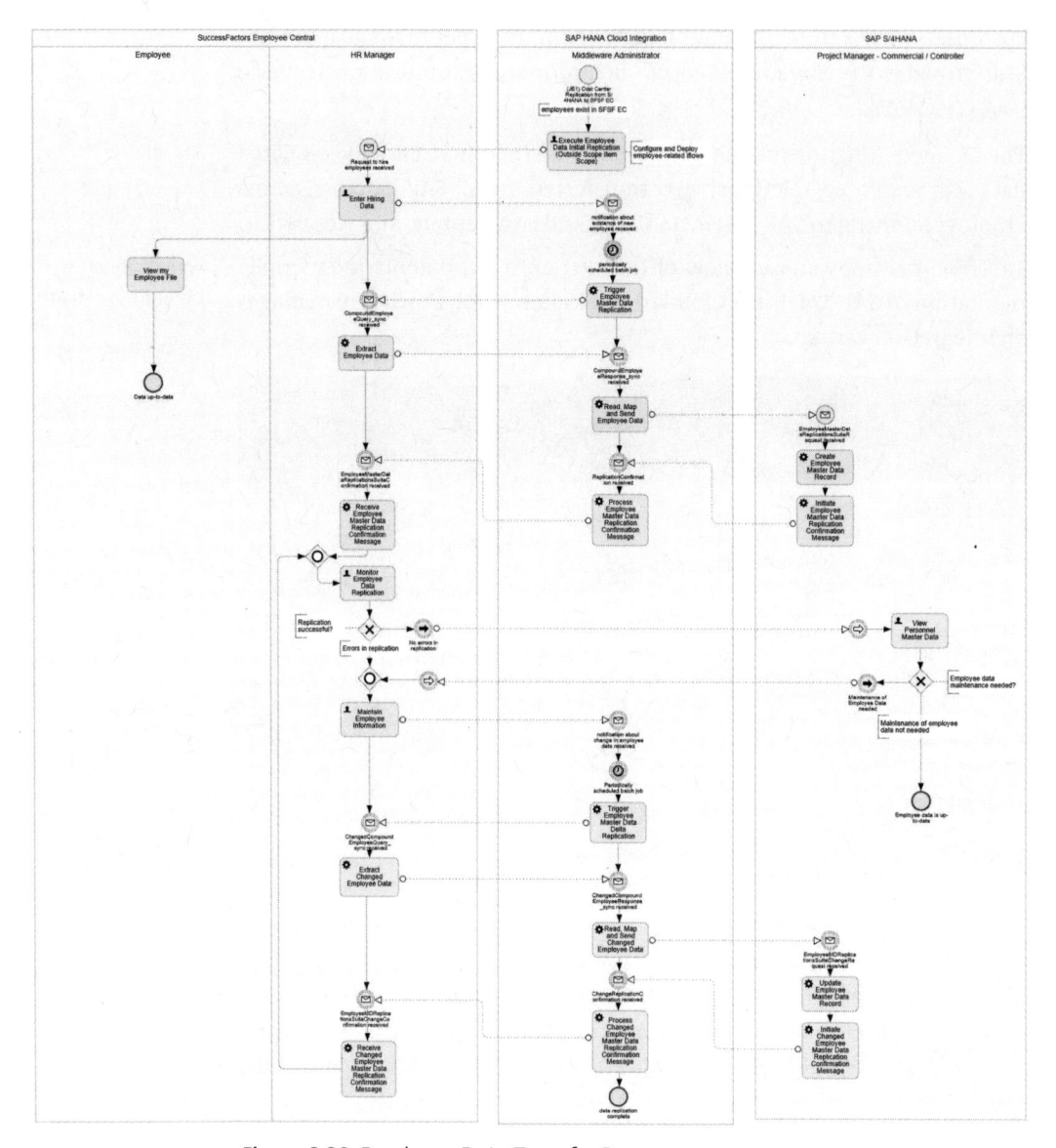

8   Integrating SAP S/4HANA Cloud into the System Landscape

Figure 8.29 Employee Data Transfer Process

SAP SuccessFactors Employee Central always needs the latest cost center information from your financial system. These cost centers are therefore transferred from SAP S/4HANA Cloud where they are maintained in the employee data records. Together with the employee data, the assignments of employees to cost centers are then imported to the SAP S/4HANA Cloud system.

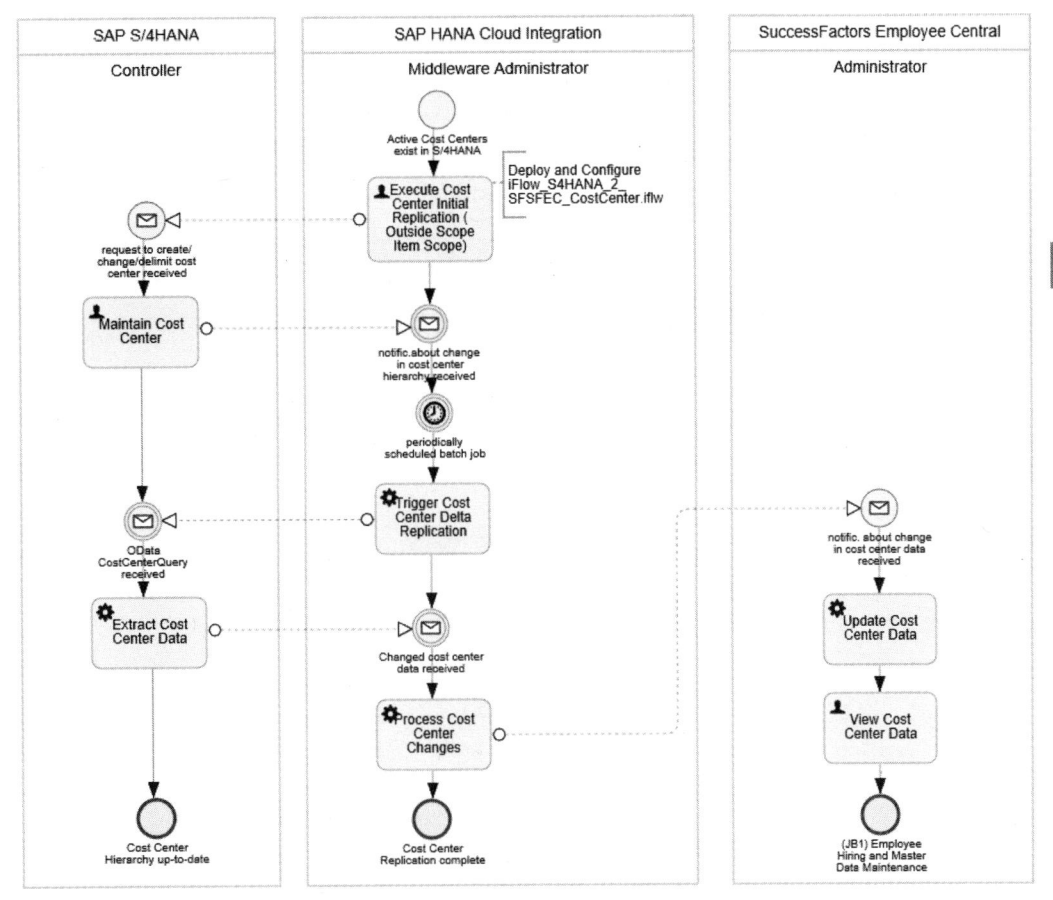

Figure 8.30 Cost Center Transfer from S/4HANA Cloud to SAP SuccessFactors Employee Central

The following sections describe the configuration of this integration.

8.2.1 Configuration in SAP S/4HANA Cloud

To set up the communication between the systems, SAP S/4HANA uses so-called *communication scenarios*, which contain specific configuration parameters, for example, the interface to be used, and other settings. A

Communication scenarios

8   Integrating SAP S/4HANA Cloud into the System Landscape

prerequisite is that all systems involved must be ready for integration, for example, the required certificates have been imported, etc.

Creating a communication user
The first step is to create a communication user. SAP Fiori's communication administration applications, in particular in the **Maintain Communication Users** app (see Figure 8.31), allow you to create and manage communication users. Under **Certificate**, upload your client certificate for SAP Cloud Platform Integration, which you obtained with your administration user for SAP Cloud Platform Integration.

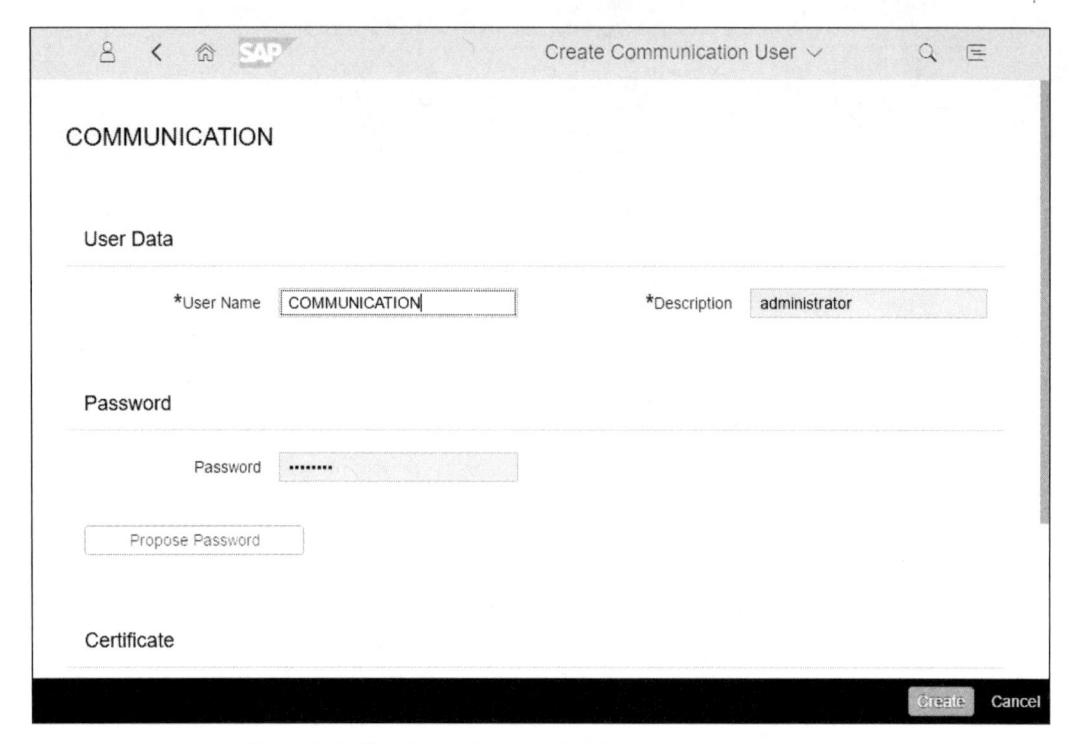

Figure 8.31 Creating a Communication User

Creating a communication system
The next step is to create the communication system. The respective app is also available in the communication administration.

1. First, assign a system ID and system name in the **Create Communication Users** app and click on **Create**.
2. Now, maintain additional fields in **Technical Data**, such as the host name, the client number, and so on.

3. In **User for Inbound Communication**, find the communication user that you created in the previous step.
4. In **Authentication Method**, select the authentication method with SSL client certificates. Also select this method for the user for outbound communication. Now, the communication system is configured.

In the final step, you'll maintain the communication agreement, again in a specific application:

Maintaining a communication agreement

1. To create a new agreement, you must select a communication scenario. For communication scenario for integrating with SAP SuccessFactors Employee Central is SAP_COM_0001 (employee integration).
2. Next, select the communication system you just created and keep the name of the communication user that you maintained earlier (see Figure 8.32).

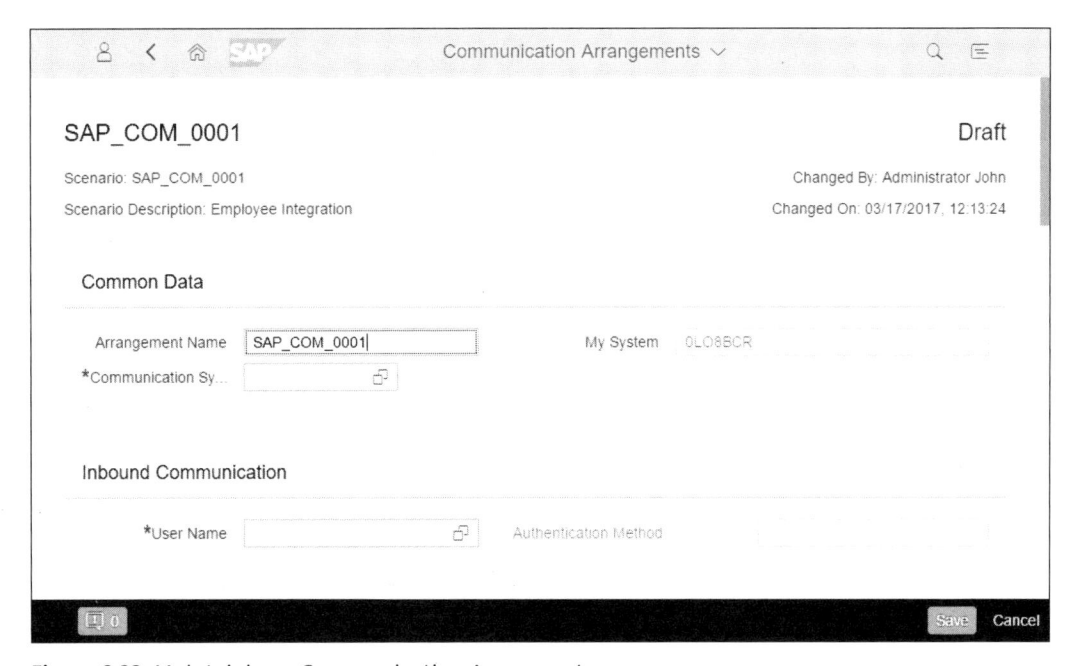

Figure 8.32 Maintaining a Communication Agreement

Now, the configuration in SAP S/4HANA Cloud is complete.

8.2.2 Configuration in SAP Cloud Platform Integration

To be able to adjust Integration Flows (IFlows) in SAP Cloud Platform Integration, Eclipse needs to be installed. In addition, you'll need a key store explorer tool to ensure a secure data transfer by using a digital *key*. (Eclipse is also available as freeware.)

Required authorizations

To implement the configuration, you'll require specific authorizations (as shown in Table 8.7).

Application	Role
<your_tenant_id>iflmap	ESBMessaging.send
<your_tenant_id>tmn	AuthGroup.IntegrationDeveloper
<your_tenant_id>tmn	AuthGroup.BusinessExpert
<your_tenant_id>tmn	AuthGroup.Administrator
<your_tenant_id>tmn	ESBMessaging.send

Table 8.7 Authorizations for Middleware Configuration

SAP provides predefined IFlows in the SAP Content catalog for the integration. The detailed documentation lists which packages or IFlows you need to use.

[»] **Additional Information on Integration Packages**

You can find the integration packages for employee assignments and the related configuration guide in the SAP API Business Hub at *https://cloudintegration.hana.ondemand.com*.

Narrow the search in the catalog, for example, by entering the search string "employee."

To access the SAP API Business Hub, you'll need an SAP Community Network user account (*https://www.sap.com/community.html*) to log on.

You must copy every IFlow to the customer-specific work center where the IFlow is configured, for example, data field mappings. To copy IFlows, you'll have to maintain the address of the target system and the address of the source system. After that, the IFlows in SAP Cloud Platform Integration are activated.

8.2.3 Configuration in SAP SuccessFactors Employee Central

To avoid adaptations in SAP Cloud Platform Integration or of the used IFlows, you should adapt the data model in SAP SuccessFactors Employee Central. Table 8.8 shows some examples. You can find a detailed list in the documentation.

Data Range in Employee Data	Field	Restriction
Contact Information • Telephone Details	Country code	Do not enter leading zeros, for example, only 1 for the U.S.
HR Data • Address	City	Max. length = 40
	Country (USA, AUS)	Max. length = 40
	ZIP code	Max. length = 10

Table 8.8 Adjusting the SAP SuccessFactors Employee Central Data Model

In SAP SuccessFactors Employee Central, you'll create a user with the role SFAPI, which needs to be equipped with certain rights. This user is only used in the SAP SuccessFactors interface and is necessary in order to establish a connection between the middleware and SAP SuccessFactors Employee Central. Of course, this user also requires a password. If you set "-1" as the maximum password age in SAP SuccessFactors Employee Central, the password will never expire. When a password expires, the connection is interrupted.

SFAPI role

Now, you'll have to define your SAP S/4HANA Cloud system as the target system for employee data replication. You can specify the target system in the administration environment of your SAP SuccessFactors instance under **Manage Data**. You can also create a new replication system if one does not exist yet (see Figure 8.33).

Additional Information on the Configuration

You can find more details on the configuration in the documentation for your communication scenario in SAP S/4HANA Cloud.

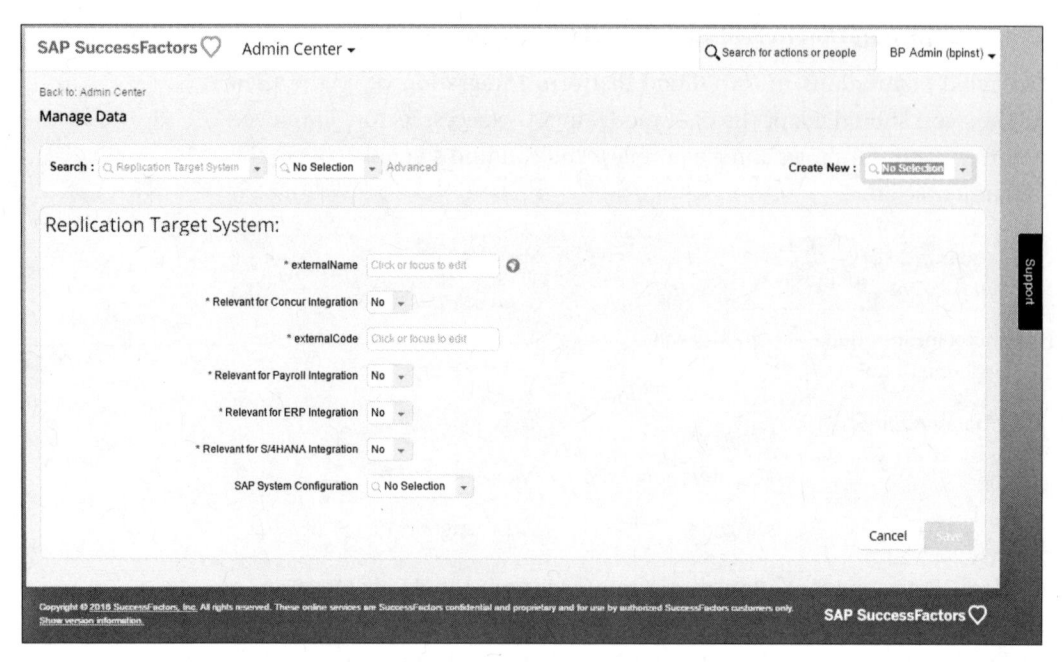

8   Integrating SAP S/4HANA Cloud into the System Landscape

Figure 8.33 Creating the Replication Target System

8.3   Integration with SAP Hybris Marketing Cloud

Marketing platform in the cloud
SAP Hybris Marketing Cloud (until Release 1611, called *SAP S/4HANA Marketing Cloud*; see Chapter 3, Section 3.2.2) is the cloud-based variant of *SAP Hybris Marketing*. As a marketing platform, SAP Hybris Marketing Cloud is not a primary system but a satellite system without its own primary data for customer analysis. As a result, SAP Hybris Marketing Cloud requires efficient integration with upstream systems or other data sources, which constantly provide the system with up-to-date master data and transaction data for analysis purposes.

Released APIs
The system is connected to other systems via released Application Programming Interfaces (APIs). These APIs are based on web service technologies, such as SOAP and OData. SAP HANA database tables cannot be accessed directly. At the time of this writing, direct access via RFC (Remote Function Call) function modules was also not possible. However, SAP plans to make this possible in the future.

8.3 Integration with SAP Hybris Marketing Cloud

You can implement the following SAP Hybris Marketing Cloud integration scenarios in your system landscape by using predefined interfaces (SAP Best Practices content and standard apps):

- Integrating with an SAP ERP system
- Loading defined data objects of other systems as files via the Secure File Transfer Protocol (SFTP)
- Loading defined data objects from other systems as CSV files using an app (see Section 8.3.3)
- Loading data from social networks like Twitter and Facebook
- Integrating with SAP Hybris Cloud for Customer

Table 8.9 lists the available inbound integrations for S/4HANA Marketing Cloud 1611.

Import to the marketing cloud

Type of Data	Data Content	Technology
Loyalty data	Activities of loyalty program members, including sales, via *SAP Hybris Loyalty Management*	*Representational State Transfer* (REST)
	Import/export quotations	OData
Market data and events	Cookie-based user data and interactions	CSV file/OData
	Prospects: contact data, corporate account data	CSV file/OData
	Secondary data of corporate accounts, contacts, and consumers	CSV file/OData
Sales and service data	Contacts and corporate accounts, leads and opportunities, telephone calls, appointments, and visits from *SAP Hybris Cloud for Customer* (C4C) and *SAP Hybris Cloud for Service* (C4S)	OData via SAP Cloud Platform Integration

Table 8.9 Available Inbound Integration with SAP Hybris Marketing Cloud

Type of Data	Data Content	Technology
	Customers and contacts, sales documents (sales orders, etc.) from SAP ERP	OData via SAP Cloud Platform Integration
	Consumer data and sales documents from *SAP Hybris Commerce*	OData via *SAP Hybris Data Hub*
	Contacts, interactions, and sales documents from non-SAP solutions	CSV file/OData
Financial data	Spend of campaigns	SOAP via SAP Cloud Platform Integration
Industry data	Import of offers from *SAP Promotion Management for Retail*	OData
Social media, Internet, etc.	Social posts (tweets) from Twitter's public API	OData via SAP Cloud Platform Integration
	Social posts from Facebook fan pages	OData via SAP Cloud Platform Integration
	Sprinklr data	OData
	Clickstream data from SAP Hybris Commerce	*SAP Event Stream Processor* (EPS)/OData
	User profiles, marketing attributes, and marketing permissions via Gigya	OData
	Evaluated clickstream data from SAP Hybris Conversion	OData
Enhancements	Marketing permissions and contact data from customer websites and landing pages	REST
Digital channels	Import of survey results from *SurveyMonkey*	CSV

Table 8.9 Available Inbound Integration with SAP Hybris Marketing Cloud (Cont.)

Table 8.10 lists the available outbound integrations for SAP S/4HANA Marketing Cloud 1611.

Export from SAP S/4HANA Marketing Cloud

Type of Data	Data Content	Technology
Social channels	Social campaigns and custom audiences to Sprinklr, Facebook, and Instagram	REST
Digital channels	Export of surveys to SurveyMonkey	OData
	Export of *Google AdWords*	REST, SAP Cloud Platform Integration
Personalized commerce	Product recommendations and personalized content to SAP Hybris Commerce	OData via SAP Hybris Data Hub
Sales automation	Leads, sales tasks, telephone calls, and appointments to SAP Hybris Cloud for Customer (C4C)	OData via SAP Cloud Platform Integration
Emails	Emails via Amazon's email service provider and SAP Mobile Services	REST
SMS	SMS to SAP SMS365	REST
Enhancements	Data of target group members to arbitrary *campaign execution solution*	OData via SAP Cloud Platform Integration
	Create customer-specific actions and subsequent objects via *Open Campaign Channel* into any business solution	OData via SAP Cloud Platform Integration

Table 8.10 Available Outbound Integration with SAP Hybris Marketing Cloud

8   Integrating SAP S/4HANA Cloud into the System Landscape

> [»] **Information on Integration with Other Systems**
>
> For more information on the integration of SAP Hybris Marketing Cloud (until releases 1702) with other systems, go to the SAP Help Portal at *https://help.sap.com/s4hana*.
>
> 1. First, choose your cloud edition, e.g., SAP S/4HANA Cloud 1611.
> 2. Navigate to **Product Assistance** and select your preferred language for **SAP User Assistance**.
> 3. In SAP User Assistance, choose **Cloud Editions • SAP S/4HANA Marketing Cloud** to display the **SAP Documentation**.
> 4. If you now navigate to the bottom on the left side of the menu tree, you'll find additional entries, for example:
>   – Integration with SAP ERP
>   – Integration with SAP Hybris Cloud for Customer
>   – Integration with search engine advertising and SAP HANA Cloud Integration
>
> Starting release 1705 the navigation path changed, as seen below:
>
> 1. Go to the SAP Help Portal at *https://help.sap.com/mkt*.
> 2. Navigate to **Application Help** and select **SAP Hybris Marketing Cloud**
> 3. In the Documentation you can select your **Language** and the **Version** via the selection boxes in the upper right area.
> 4. Navigate to **System Setup and Integration** for additional Information on **Integration** and **Import and Export of Data**.
>
> For more information on SAP Best Practices for integrating SAP Hybris Marketing Cloud, go to *https://rapid.sap.com/bp/BP_CLD_MKT*. Navigate to **Solution Scope** and view the scope item groups for **Integration** and **Data Load**. You'll also find further information on the integrations that we did not mention.

Middleware   SAP Cloud Platform Integration and SAP Hybris Commerce, data hub (see Figure 8.34) are the preferred integration platforms (middleware) for accessing SAP Hybris Marketing Cloud.

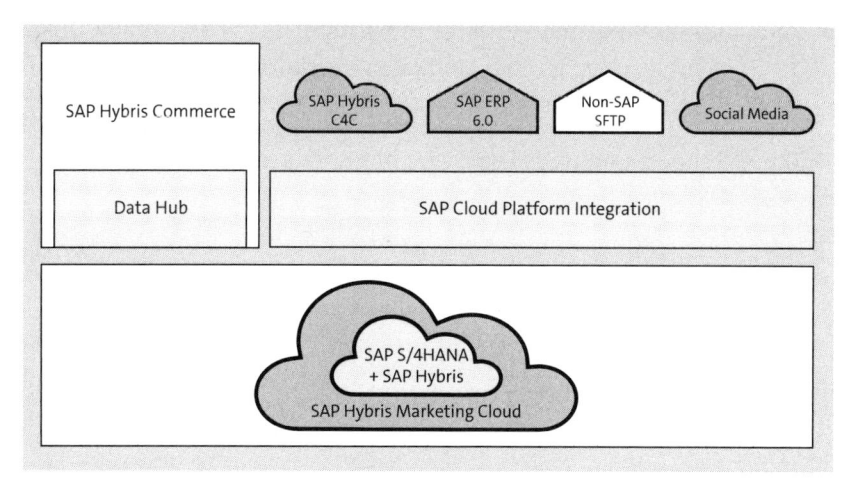

Figure 8.34 Middleware for Integration with SAP Hybris Marketing Cloud

8.3.1 SAP Hybris Marketing Cloud Data Model

The SAP Hybris Marketing Cloud data model is reduced to marketing-relevant business objects, which we'll describe briefly in the following list. The integration packages and some of the additional information are available in English only:

- *Corporate accounts*: data that refers to legal entities or enterprises.
- *Contacts*: individuals in contact with the enterprise.
- *Interactions*: communications between enterprises and contacts. Texts (content) of interactions are automatically evaluated by integrated SAP HANA text analyses when they are saved, enabling you to analyze sentiment, for example.
- *Account team members*: users that are assigned to a team that is responsible for a marketing campaign of a customer.
- *Products and product categories*: categorization of a product, for example, candy bars, sports cars, pens, etc.
- *Interests*: categorization of interactions, for example, by product names, enabling you to consolidate and analyze various interactions (such as support requests or messages on a Facebook fan page).
- *Brands*: words used separately or in combination to uniquely identify a product. They are assigned to a product.

Data model objects

8   Integrating SAP S/4HANA Cloud into the System Landscape

- *Tags*: these are assigned to interests to analyze interactions. They can be a part of social posts or other kind of interactions and are normally created by the SAP HANA Text Analysis engine.

Figure 8.35 shows a simplified overview of the data model.

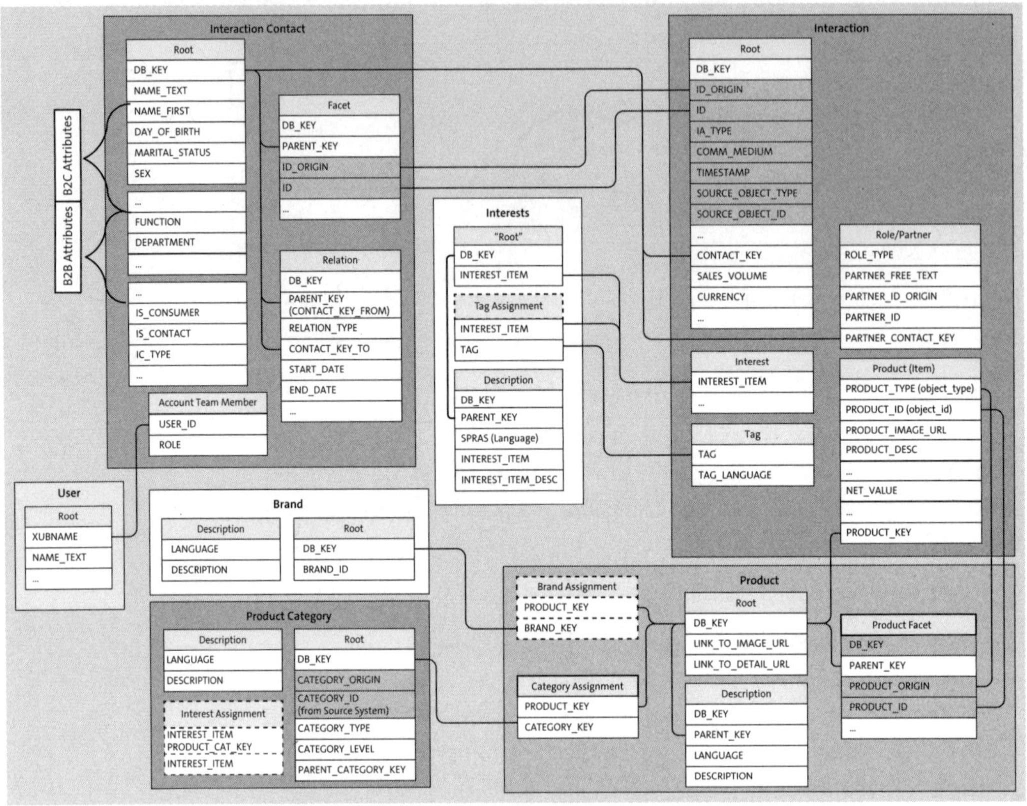

Figure 8.35 SAP Hybris Marketing Cloud Data Model

Contact types	Contacts and corporate accounts are stored in a table and distinguished by their interaction contact type (IC_TYPE). For the sake of simplicity, we refer to both individual contacts and corporate accounts as *contacts*. Contacts can have relationships with each other and can be assigned to interactions.
Interactions	Interactions have a specific type (e.g., **Email**, **Order**, **Social_Posting**, etc.) and can be assigned to products. You can also assign *interests* and *tags* to interactions. You can also link interests and tags.

290

You can assign products to a product category and a brand to simplify later analysis of interactions for future marketing campaigns. In turn, product categories can be assigned to interests. Again, you can also link interests and tags. These links allow you to create versatile interest networks upon which to build your marketing campaigns.

Products

> **[Ex] Analyzing a Sales Order**
>
> For example, a *sales order* is mapped as an interaction with product items. To focus on possible customers for certain products with a targeted marketing campaign, you can now analyze interactions in a targeted manner. For example, you can identify the customers that your company has had an interaction with during a specific period and that are assigned to certain tags and/or interests. If customers bought specific products within the last six months and provided product feedback in social networks or via emails, you can reach these customers with a targeted marketing activity.

8.3.2 Integration with SAP ERP Systems

SAP Hybris Marketing Cloud constantly needs up-to-date customer and product master data as well as sales orders. Ideally, in existing SAP system landscapes, this data comes from an *SAP ERP 6.0* system.

SAP ERP integration

For SAP S/4HANA Marketing Cloud 1611, the following SAP ERP integration scenarios are provided by SAP Cloud Platform Integration:

- SAP ERP Order and Business Partner Integration
- SAP ERP Actual and Committed Spend Integration

Both scenarios use IDocs on the SAP ERP side and OData services on the SAP Hybris Marketing Cloud side for the data integration.

> **[«] Additional Information on OData Services**
>
> For more information on the OData services used, see the SAP Help Portal at *https://help.sap.com/mkt*. Choose your **Version**, e.g., 1702. Navigate to **Integration** and download "Data Management Upload Interfaces."

These so-called *out of the box integrations* provide entire integration workflows, including extraction, mapping, transformation, import, and monitoring.

Out of the box scenarios

8   Integrating SAP S/4HANA Cloud into the System Landscape

[»]
> **Information on SAP ERP Integration Packages**
>
> You can find the *SAP Hybris Marketing Cloud – SAP ERP Actual and Committed Spend Integration* and *SAP Hybris Marketing Cloud – SAP ERP Order and Business Partner Integration* integration packages as well as the corresponding configuration guide in the SAP API Business Hub at *https://cloudintegration.hana.ondemand.com*. Choose **Integration** and then narrow the search with the search string "Marketing Cloud."
>
> To access the SAP API Business Hub, you'll need an SAP Community user account as described in Section 8.2.2.
>
> Figure 8.36 shows all integration packages available for SAP Hybris Marketing Cloud 1611 in the SAP API Business Hub.

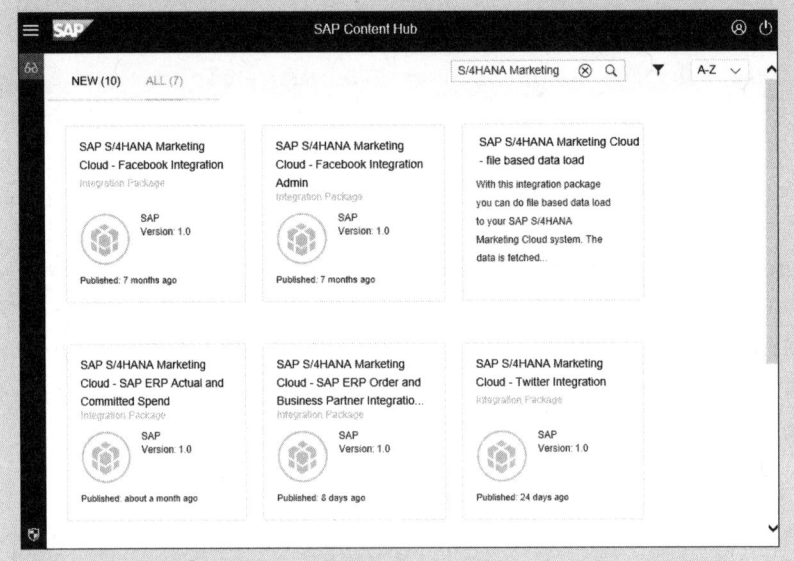

Figure 8.36 Available Integration Packages in the SAP API Business Hub

In the following sections, we'll discuss the two SAP ERP integration scenarios in more detail.

SAP ERP Order and Business Partner Integration

This scenario includes the usage of *quotations*, *orders*, and *returns* as well as the related *business partner* data from SAP ERP in SAP Hybris Marketing Cloud.

8.3 Integration with SAP Hybris Marketing Cloud

The master data and sales documents are transferred from the SAP ERP system to the marketing cloud using IDocs. The IDoc types and OData services listed in Table 8.11 are used to transfer the data.

IDocs and OData services used

Data Class	IDoc Type (Source)	OData Service (Target)
Customer master data	Master data: DEBMAS06 Address data: ADRMAS03 and ADR3MAS03	CUAN_BUSINESS_PARTNER_IMPORT_SRV
Sales orders	COD_REPLICATE_SALES_ORDER01 total	CUAN_BUSINESS_DOCUMENT_IMP_SRV
Actual spend and committed spend data	CUAN_ERP_MARKETING_SPEND	CUAN_ACTUAL_IMPORT_SRV

Table 8.11 Interfaces Used for SAP ERP Order and Business Partner Integration

> **IDoc COD_REPLICATE_SALES_ORDER01**
>
> To use IDoc COD_REPLICATE_SALES_ORDER01 for sales orders, you must use SAP ERP 6.0 EHP4 or higher as the source system. In addition, the *SAP Hybris Cloud for Customer 2.0 integration with SAP ERP* add-on, which is also referred to as the *C4C add-on*, must be installed on this SAP ERP system. The minimum version is SAPK-60024INCODERINT. For more information, see the integration guide for the relevant integration package.

The IDoc structures and fields of the SAP ERP customer data are mapped to the OData service CUAN_BUSINESS_PARTNER_IMPORT_SRV, and the sales orders are mapped to the OData service CUAN_BUSINESS_DOCUMENT_IMP_SRV and imported to the Marketing Cloud using SAP Cloud Platform Integration.

Figure 8.37 shows a schematic diagram of this integration scenario.

8   Integrating SAP S/4HANA Cloud into the System Landscape

SAP Cloud Platform Integration
Integration Flow

SAP ERP 6.0

IDoc

Sales Orders
COD_REPLICATE_SALES_ORDER01

Customer Master Data
DEBMAS06

Customer Addresses
ADRMAS03 (Organization) and
ADR3MAS03 (Person)

OData

SAP S/4HANA + SAP Hybris
SAP Hybris Marketing Cloud

Contacts
CUAN_BUSINESS_PARTNER_IMPORT_SRV

Interactions
CUAN_BUSINESS_DOCUMENT_IMP_SRV

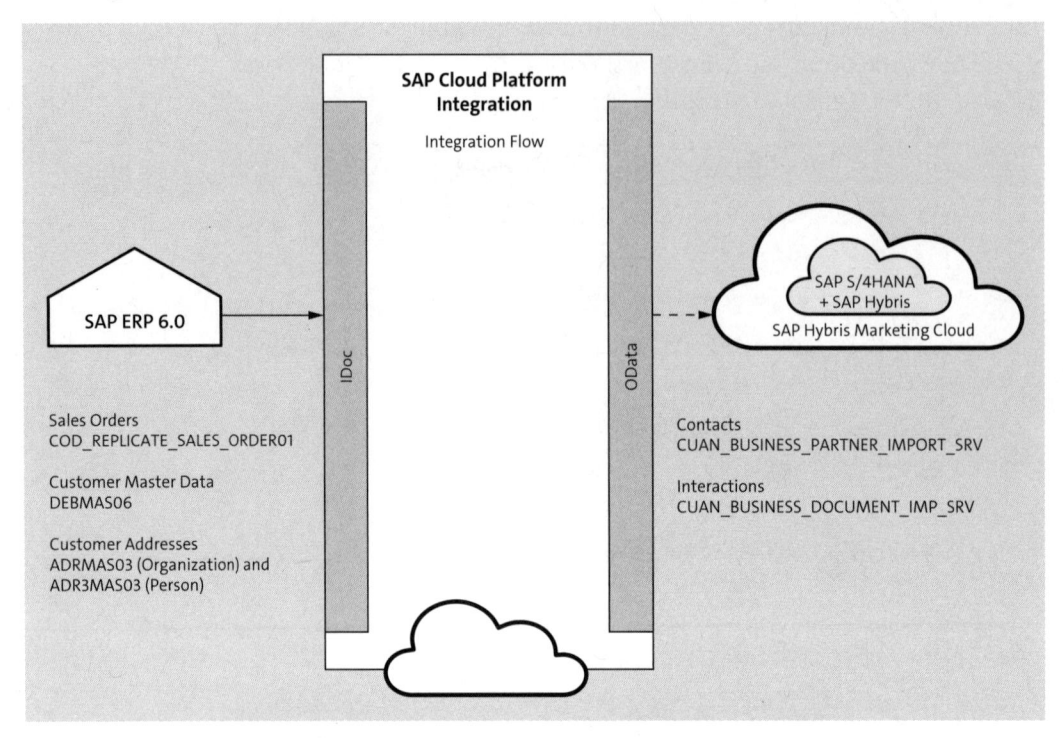

Figure 8.37 SAP ERP Order and Business Partner Integration

SAP ERP Actual and Committed Spend Integration

Marketing spend data — This scenario includes exporting spend data from SAP Hybris Marketing Cloud to SAP ERP and importing actual spend and committed spend data from SAP ERP to SAP Hybris Marketing Cloud. Campaigns and spend items that were created and released in SAP Hybris Marketing Cloud are exported and created as projects and WBS elements in SAP ERP. The reverse proxy technology is used here.

In contrast, actual spend and committed spend data is exported from the SAP ERP system and imported to SAP Hybris Marketing Cloud. The data can be imported to SAP Hybris Marketing Cloud using SAP Cloud Platform Integration or SAP Process Integration (PI) (see Figure 8.38).

8.3 Integration with SAP Hybris Marketing Cloud

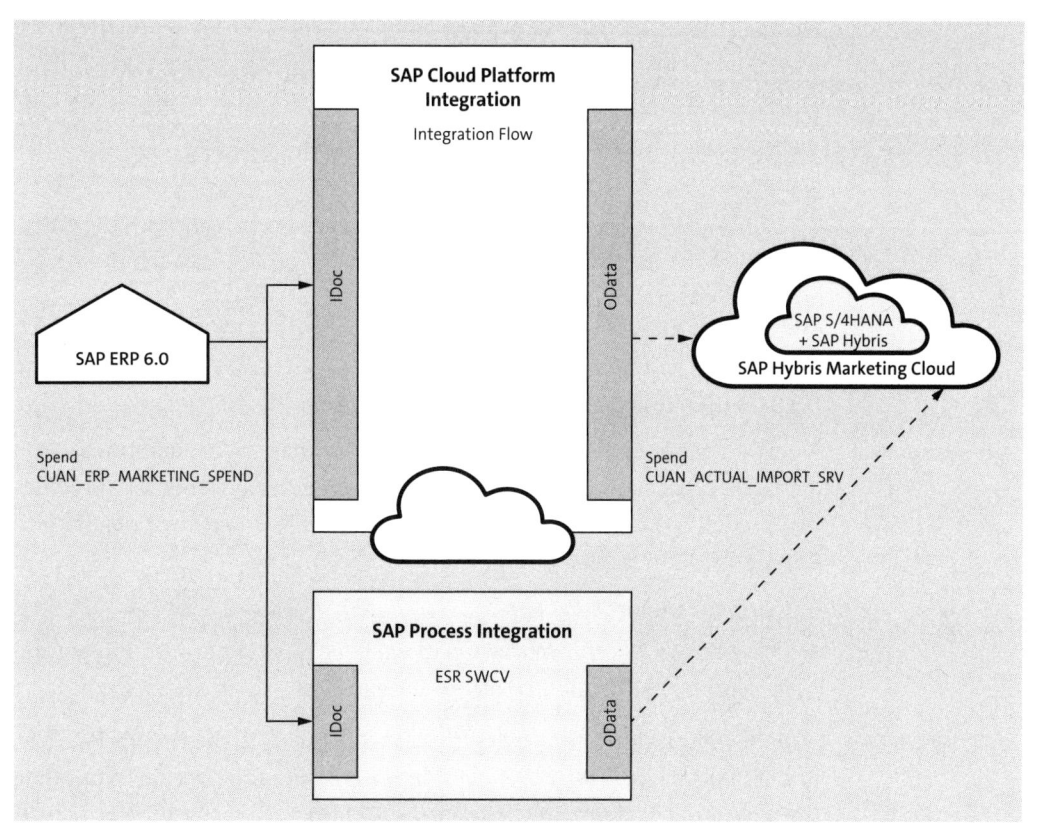

Figure 8.38 SAP ERP Actual and Committed Spend Integration

The integration solution allows you to enter and manage marketing campaigns, marketing plans, and relevant budgets centrally in one system. The central calendar in SAP Hybris Marketing Cloud enables you to better reconcile marketing activities, thus facilitating and accelerating planning processes. You'll be able to monitor your marketing spend data nearly in real time and thus accelerate your strategic decision-making processes.

To integrate the spend data from the SAP ERP system to SAP Hybris Marketing Cloud, the IDoc type and OData service listed in Table 8.12 are used.

Data Class	IDoc Type (Source)	OData Service (Target)
Actual spend and committed spend	CUAN_ERP_MARKETING_SPEND	CUAN_ACTUAL_IMPORT_SRV

Table 8.12 Interfaces Used for SAP ERP Actual and Committed Spend Integration

295

8 Integrating SAP S/4HANA Cloud into the System Landscape

The spend data is extracted in IDoc `CUAN_ERP_MARKETING_SPEND` and the structures and fields of the IDoc are mapped in OData service `CUAN_ACTUAL_IMPORT_SRV` in SAP Hybris Marketing Cloud.

> **[»] IDoc CUAN_ERP_MARKETING_SPEND**
>
> To use the IDoc `CUAN_ERP_MARKETING_SPEND`, you must work with the C4C add-on as described in the previous section, "SAP ERP Order and Business Partner Integration."

8.3.3 Importing Data from External Systems

Data management objects

SAP ERP does not have to be the source of your master data and transaction data; you can also import data using files from other systems. SAP provides two predefined methods to import data as *data management objects* into SAP Hybris Marketing Cloud:

- Using the **Import Data** app
- Using the *SAP Hybris Marketing Cloud – file based data load* integration package from SAP Cloud Platform Integration

Importing CSV files

Like the integration package described in Section 8.3.2, the two options also use OData service `CUAN_IMPORT_SRV`. In both cases, you'll extract your data from external systems to predefined CSV files with a specified structure. You can download sample files using the **Import Data** tile (in the first case) or via the info page for the integration package in the SAP API Business Hub (in the second case). While the **Import Data** app is suited for importing data to the system ad hoc, the solution using SAP Cloud Platform Integration is designed for permanent interfaces.

> **[»] CSV Files**
>
> CSV (*comma-separated values* or *character-separated values*) files store table-type data in the text format. CSV files are widespread in the IT world and are used as the import and export format for numerous systems and applications.

The "Import Data" App

In SAP S/4HANA Marketing Cloud 1611, you can import the following data management object data using the **Import Data** app (see Figure 8.39):

Importing data with the app

- Corporate accounts
- Contacts
- Account team members
- Product categories
- Products
- Interests
- Interactions
- Marketing locations
- Marketing beacons
- Subscriptions

The following data can also be imported:

- Custom business objects
- Brands
- Custom dimensions
- Actual and committed spend
- Survey responses
- Campaign success

For other data, different OData services are used than `CUAN_IMPORT_SRV`.

> **Additional Information on OData Services**
>
> You can find more information on the OData service used in the app at *https://help.sap.com/mkt*. Choose your **Version**, for example, 1702. Navigate to **Integration** and download the following document:
>
> - *Data Management Upload Interfaces Guide*
>
> Or, navigate to **System Setup and Integration** and choose **Import and Export of Data**. There you will find the section **Import of Data Using an OData Service**.

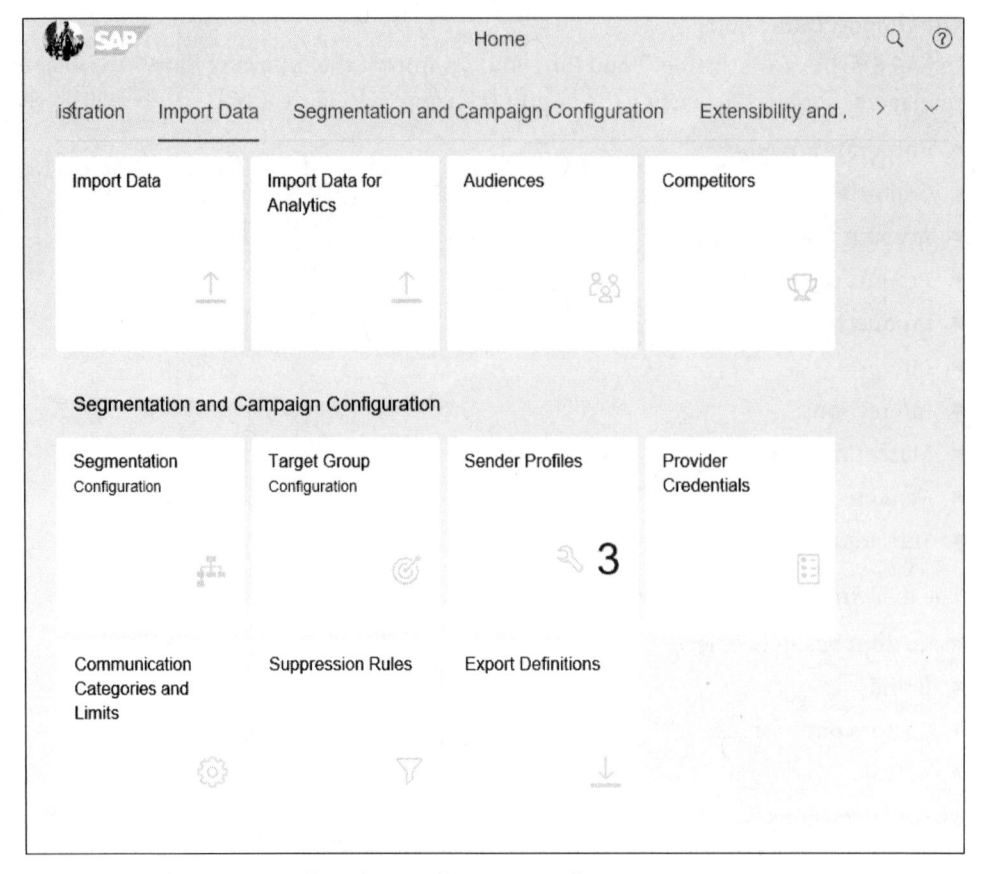

8   Integrating SAP S/4HANA Cloud into the System Landscape

Figure 8.39 Calling the App "Import Data"

Importing data management objects

Perform the following steps to import the data management objects to your system:

1. Choose the **Import Data** tile.
2. Then, select your desired data management object, for example, **Contacts** ❶ (see Figure 8.40).
3. Download the sample file to your local computer using **Download CSV Template** ❷.
4. Edit the file or format your source data.
5. Select your CSV file for the target system from your local computer using **Browse** ❸.

6. **Import** your file ❹.

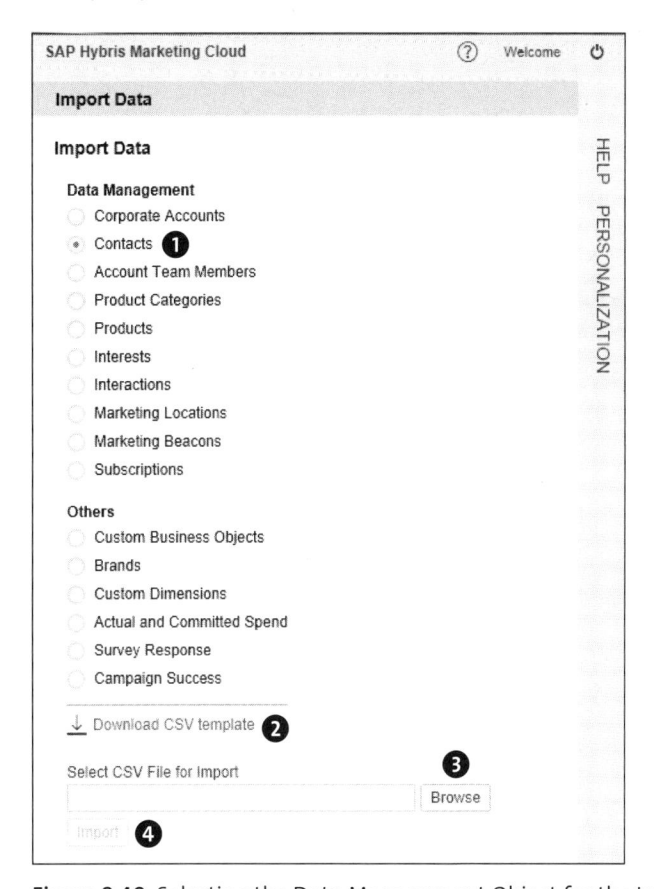

Figure 8.40 Selecting the Data Management Object for the Import

Importing Data with the SAP Hybris Marketing Cloud Integration Package

The *SAP Hybris Marketing Cloud – File Based Data Load* integration package in Version 3.0 enables you to import data management objects with SAP Cloud Platform Integration via SFTP.

> **Secure File Transfer Protocol (SFTP)**
> SFTP is an alternative to the Secure Shell (SSH) for the *File Transfer Protocol* (FTP), which enables encryption.

8 Integrating SAP S/4HANA Cloud into the System Landscape

Version 3.0 lets you import the following objects to SAP Hybris Marketing Cloud:

- Accounts
- Contacts
- Interactions
- Interactions with multiple products

Figure 8.41 illustrates the different processes of the integration package in the SAP Content Hub.

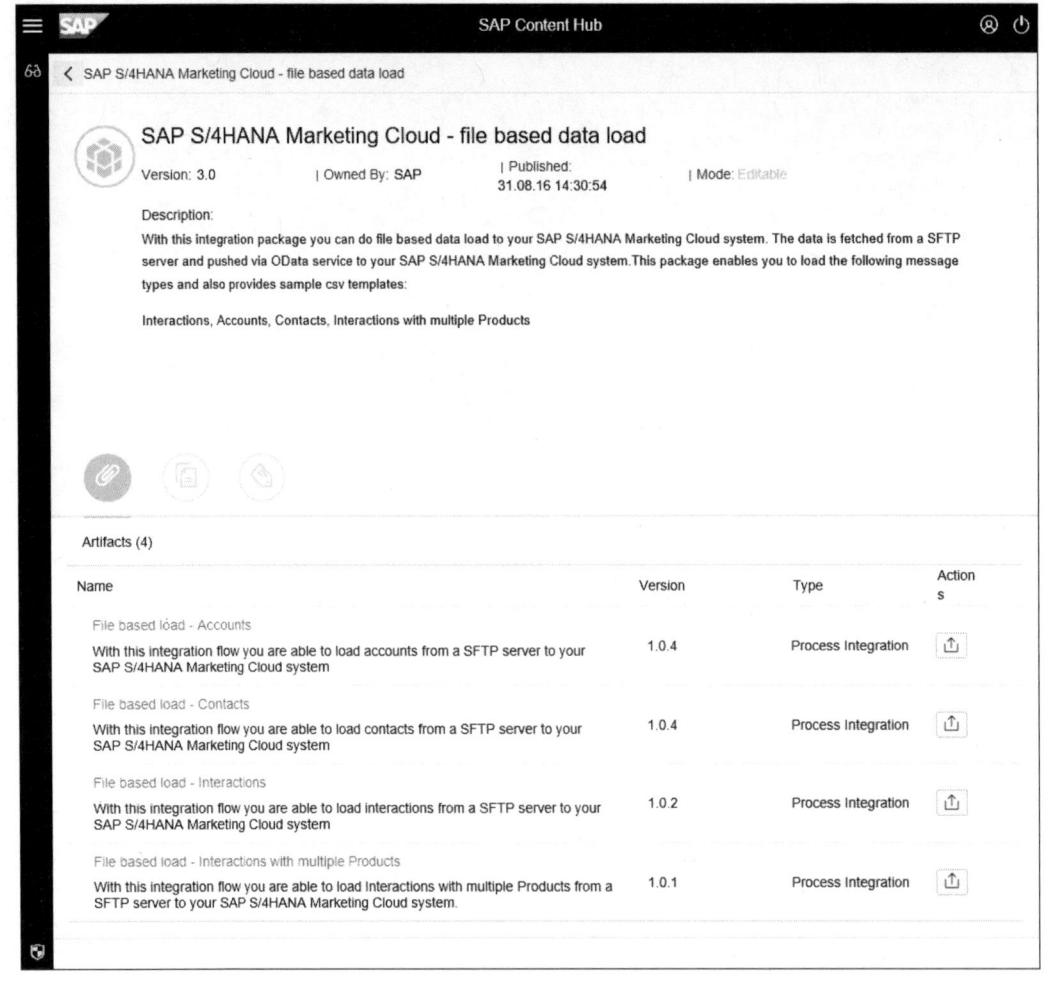

Figure 8.41 Integration Processes for Importing Data via Files

8.3 Integration with SAP Hybris Marketing Cloud

As when you use the app, the data must be in the specified CSV format. Within SAP Cloud Platform Integration, these files are mapped to the data structures and fields of OData service CUAN_IMPORT_SRV. The files are then read by an SFTP server, and the OData service sends the files to SAP Hybris Marketing Cloud. Figure 8.42 illustrates this process.

Integration flow

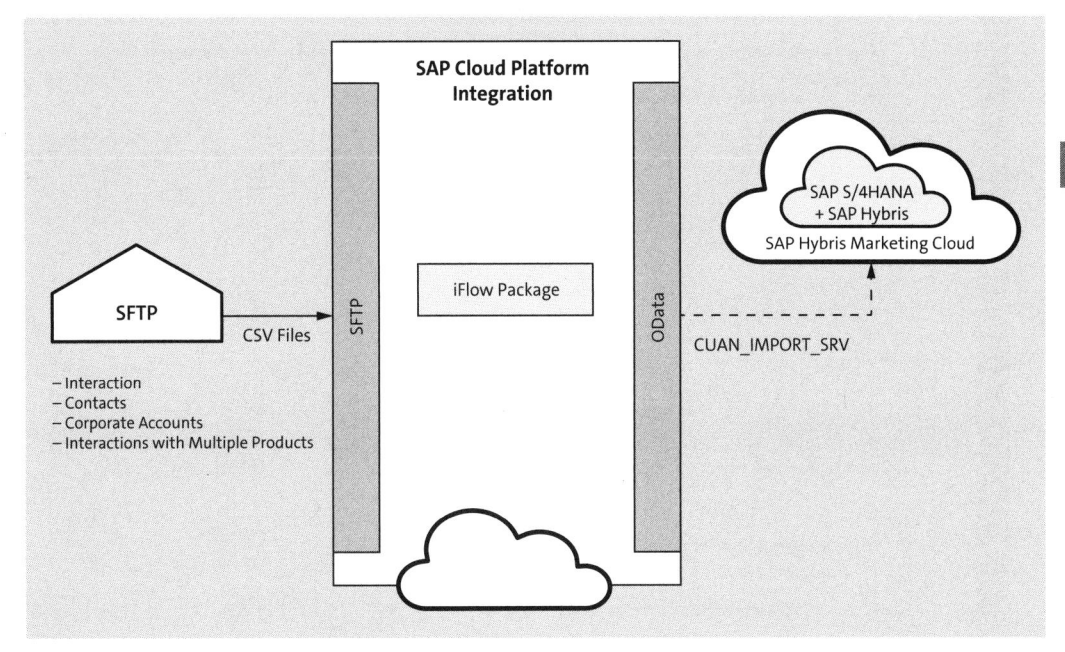

Figure 8.42 Integration of External Systems via Files

> **Additional Information on the Integration Package**
> You can find the integration package in the SAP API Business Hub at *https://cloudintegration.hana.ondemand.com*. Limit the number of the displayed packages in the search screen by entering "Marketing Cloud."

Figure 8.43 shows the various documents that are available for the package:

- The **Best practice configuration guide** listing the necessary configuration steps
- Sample files for the individual data objects (**CSV examples**)
- Description of the individual data objects **Mapping details**

Documents in the SAP API Business Hub

301

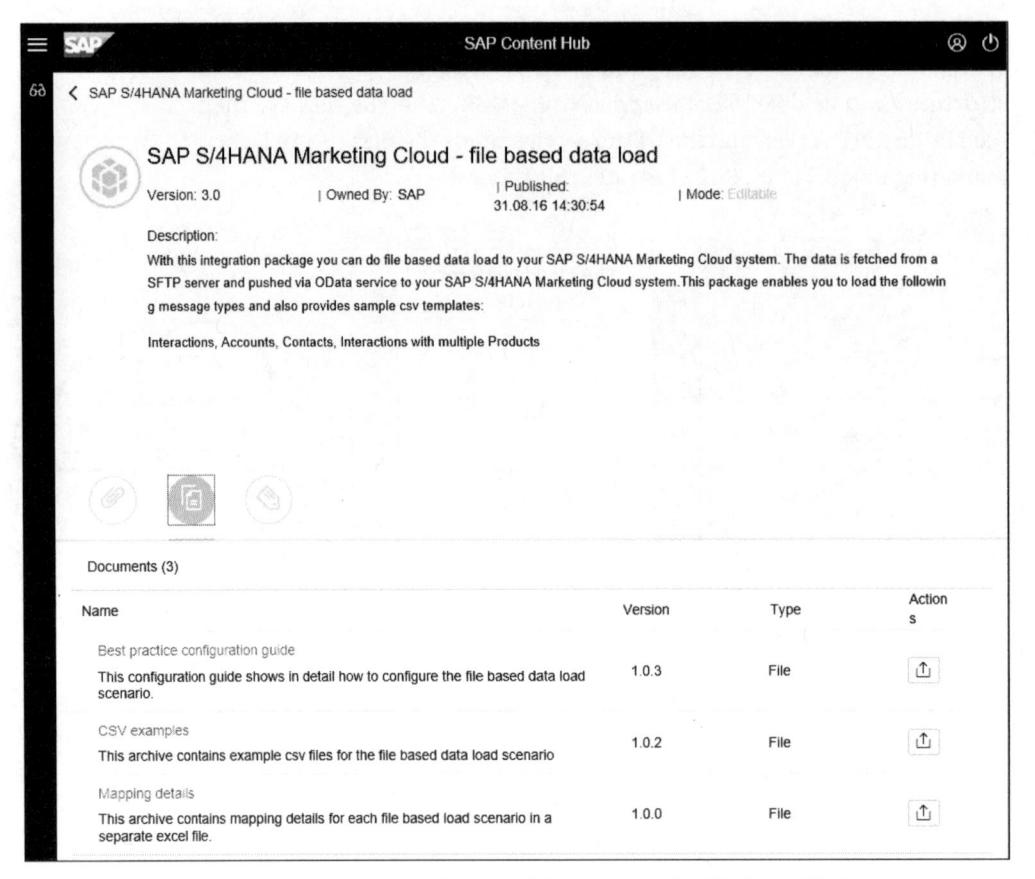

Figure 8.43 SAP API Business Hub Documents for File-Based Data Import

8.3.4 Importing Data from Social Media

Public APIs and big data platforms
Twitter and Facebook provide public HTTPS Application Programming Interfaces (*public APIs*) that allow you to search the platforms for messages (tweets/posts) that are marked as public and download them to evaluate them in detail.

However, these public interfaces are rather restricted in terms of data volume and timeframe of the data that can be evaluated. Both enterprises provide this data directly via subsidiaries or indirectly via big data platforms, such as *Gigya* or *DataSift*. These platforms enable you to find and evaluate data from numerous social media (not only those mentioned above) for a fee.

> **Information on Rate Limits**
>
> All social networks limit the data volumes that you can evaluate with their public APIs. You can find more information on the individual platforms on the following websites:
>
> - Twitter: *https://dev.twitter.com/rest/public/rate-limiting*
> - Facebook: *https://developers.facebook.com/docs/graph-api/advanced/rate-limiting*
>
> Because the platform websites often change, the links might not navigate to the desired page. If necessary, enter the name of the network and "rate limit" in a search engine.

The data of users of these social networks and the content they publish are subject to the data protection laws of the country in which the data is downloaded and analyzed. However, these laws differ from country to country. Therefore, you should always obtain approval from users to store and evaluate the data. This approval can be imported as a *marketing permission* to SAP Hybris Marketing Cloud using one of the methods described in Section 8.3.3.

Data protection

The *posts* and *tweets* from social networks are imported via HTTPS interfaces. SAP Cloud Platform Integration offers integration packages that convert this data into contacts and interactions, which are then imported to SAP Hybris Marketing Cloud using the OData service CUAN_IMPORT_SRV. Figure 8.44 illustrates this integration.

Processing posts and tweets

Integration with Twitter

The social platform Twitter enables you to publish and share short messages, so-called *tweets*. You can use the public Twitter APIs to browse tweets for tags and select them for download for evaluation purposes.

Analyzing tweets

SAP Cloud Platform provides two integration packages:

- **SAP Hybris Marketing Cloud—Twitter Integration Admin**
  With this package, you can manage and technically configure the main package, *SAP Hybris Marketing Cloud – Twitter Integration*.

- **SAP Hybris Marketing Cloud—Twitter Integration**
  The main package for the Twitter integration serves to download messages from Twitter. The messages are stored as interactions (type: SOCIAL_POSTING), and user information is stored as contacts.

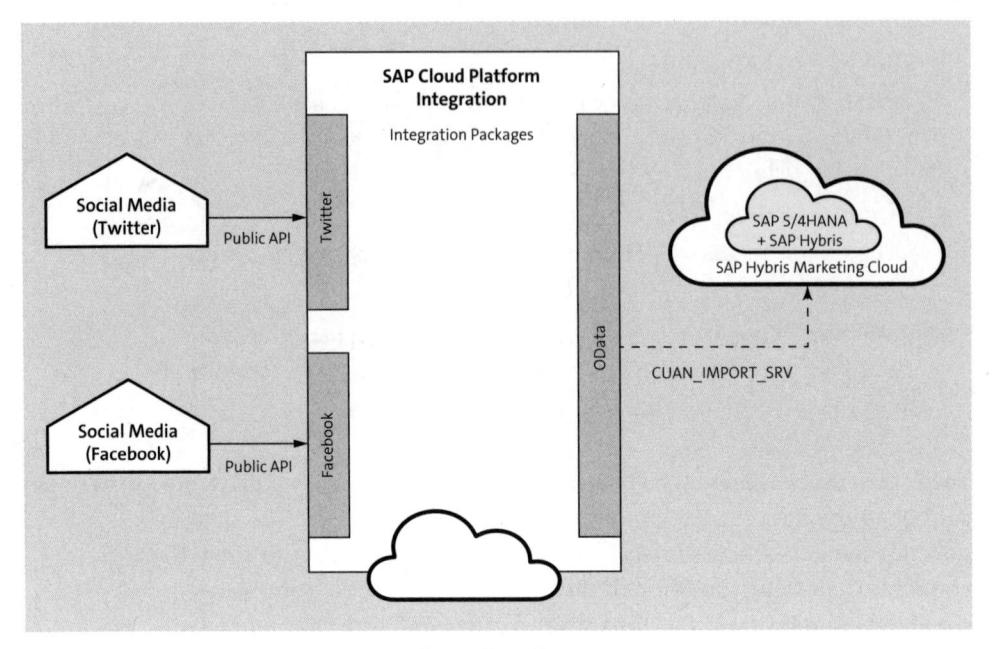

8   Integrating SAP S/4HANA Cloud into the System Landscape

Figure 8.44 Integration of Social Media

You can then evaluate the imported tweets as interactions in SAP Hybris Marketing Cloud using the **Sentiment Engagement** tile. Figure 8.45 shows an example of such an analysis.

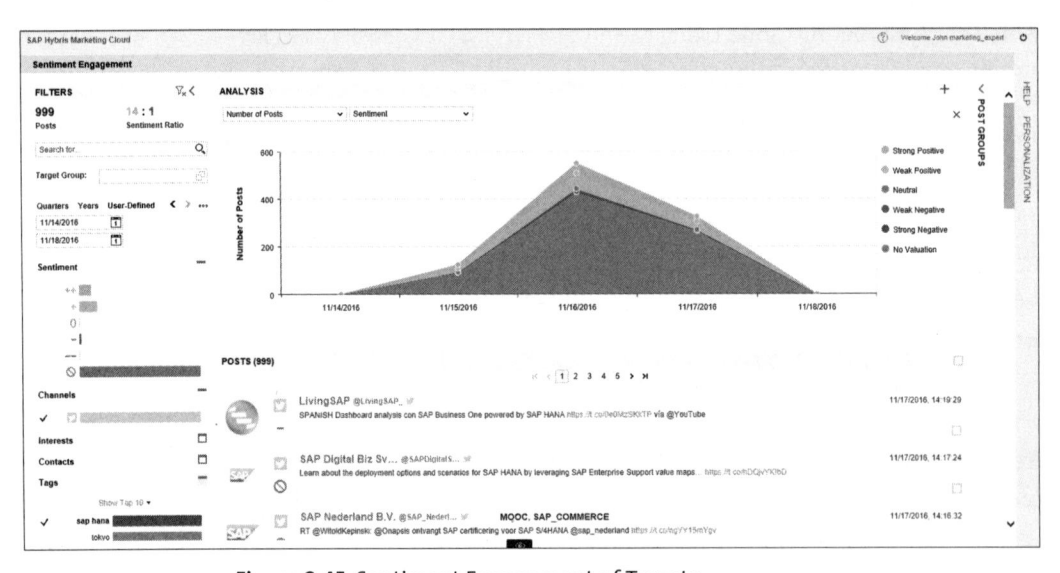

Figure 8.45 Sentiment Engagement of Tweets

Integration with Facebook

Facebook, instead, allows you to evaluate only comments (*posts*) that users of the platform enter on so-called *fan pages*. You cannot use tags to find public messages in the entire social network. You also can not browse normal user pages for messages.

Analyzing posts

> **Facebook Fan Pages**
>
> Fan pages are specific Facebook pages that represent products, enterprises, or any other venture. Many organizations—large enterprises as well as the local ice cream parlor around the corner—maintain these fan pages to market their products or enterprises.
>
> You can find more information on Facebook fan pages at the following URL:
>
> - *https://www.facebook.com/business/products/pages*
>
> This link describes how to create a fan page:
>
> - *https://www.facebook.com/pages/create*

There are two integration packages provived via SAP Cloud Platform:

- **SAP Hybris Marketing Cloud – Facebook Integration Admin**
  With this package, you can manage and technically configure the main package, *SAP Hybris Marketing Cloud – Facebook Integration*.

- **SAP Hybris Marketing Cloud – Facebook Integration**
  The Facebook integration main package lets you download messages that Facebook users have written on fan pages. The messages are stored as interactions, and the available user information is stored as contacts. The user information is very secure.

Integration packages

Figure 8.46 shows Facebook fan page messages that you can evaluate as interactions using the **Sentiment Engagement** tile.

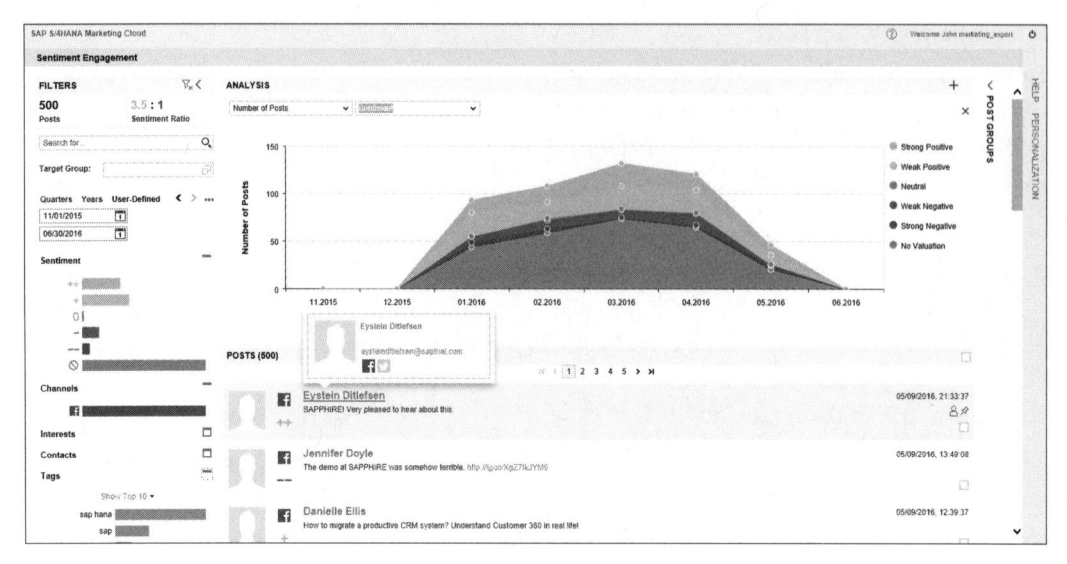

Figure 8.46 Sentiment Engagement of Posts on Facebook Fan Pages

8.3.5 Integration of SAP Hybris Cloud for Customer Systems

Integration scenarios

An additional integration package for integrating the business processes between SAP Hybris Marketing Cloud and SAP Hybris Cloud for Customer (C4C) is available. The integration package covers the following aspects:

- Automatic creation of marketing leads, tasks, appointments, or telephone calls in SAP Hybris Cloud for Customers by activating a campaign in SAP Hybris Marketing Cloud
- Replication of accounts, contacts, or individual customers and their relationships from SAP Hybris Cloud for Customer to SAP Hybris Marketing Cloud
- Replication of business documents from SAP Hybris Cloud for Customer to SAP Hybris Marketing Cloud (leads, opportunities, activities, visits, appointments, calls)
- Replication of product items from lead and opportunity documents from SAP Hybris Cloud for Customer to SAP Hybris Marketing Cloud

Figure 8.47 illustrates the different integration processes available in the integration package in the SAP API Business Hub.

8.3 Integration with SAP Hybris Marketing Cloud

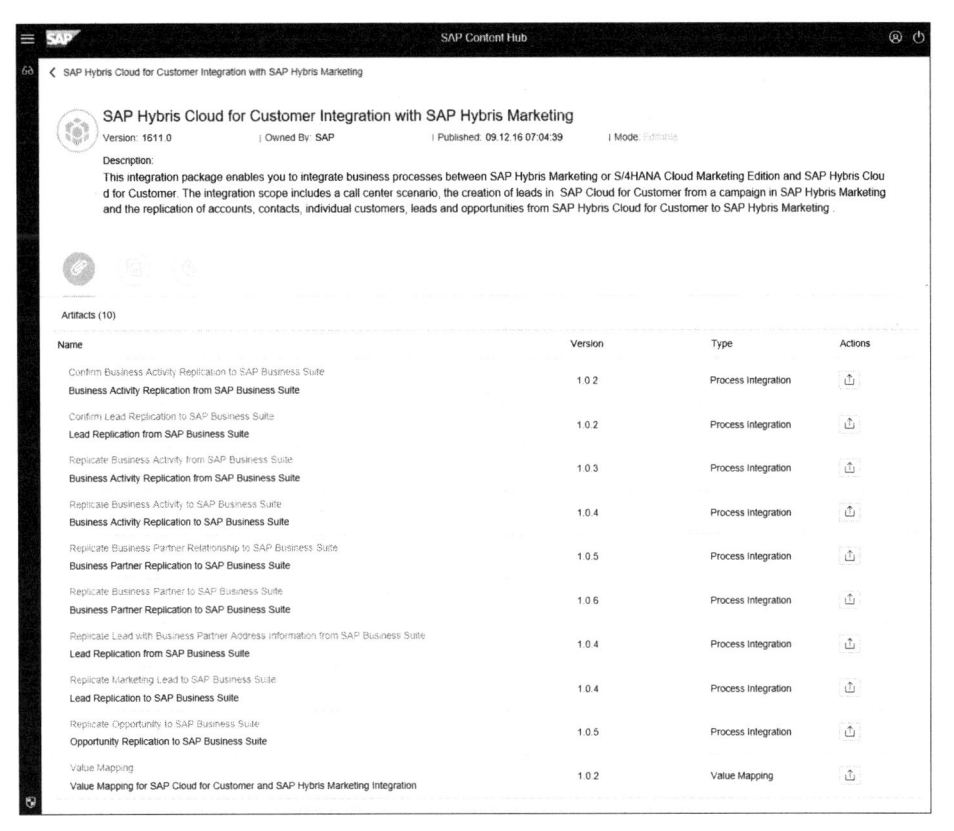

Figure 8.47 Integration Processes for SAP Hybris Cloud for Customer in the SAP API Business Hub

To integrate the business partner data and documents, you'll use the following OData services:

- CUAN_BUSINESS_PARTNER_IMPORT_SRV (business partners)
- CUAN_BUSINESS_DOCUMENT_IMP_SRV (documents)

> **SAP Best Practices for Integration with SAP Hybris Cloud for Customer**
>
> For more information on SAP Best Practices for this integration, go to *https://rapid.sap.com/bp/BP_CLD_MKT*. In **Solution Scope**, navigate to **Scope Item Group** for **Integration**. The **SAP Hybris Marketing Cloud Integration with SAP Hybris Cloud for Customer** scope item contains further information.

307

PART III
Migrating to SAP S/4HANA On-Premise

Chapter 9
Installing and Configuring SAP S/4HANA On-Premise or in the Private Cloud

When migrating to SAP S/4HANA, on-premise, you can either install a new SAP S/4HANA system or transform an existing SAP system. This chapter describes the necessary steps for installing the backend and frontend servers and for configuring the system.

In Part II, we introduced the SAP S/4HANA SaaS (*software as a service*) public cloud solution. So why does this chapter also refer to a cloud solution? This chapter discusses SAP S/4HANA in the *private cloud*, meaning we'll discuss implementing an SAP S/4HANA, on-premise, system operated by a hosting provider (i.e., an IaaS system—*infrastructure as a service*), like Amazon AWS or Microsoft Azure.

Let's make sure we understand the difference. In Part II, we described SAP S/4HANA Cloud, a standard cloud system with quarterly updates and restricted enhancement options that only allows you to access the backend system via the Cloud Service Center. In contrast, you can define the customizing and update cycles yourself with your own on-premise system. With SAP S/4HANA, on-premise, the system can be implemented either in your data center or at a hosting partner. You can also have SAP implement a private cloud for you in SAP HANA Enterprise Cloud (HEC).

With SAP S/4HANA, on-premise, you can better control the implementation of the system. Moreover, you can freely choose your target release, a crucial capability. Choosing the target release means you can migrate to SAP S/4HANA 1511, SAP S/4HANA 1605 (SAP S/4HANA Finance), or SAP S/4HANA 1610. The latter was the latest release at the time of this writing.

9 Installing and Configuring SAP S/4HANA On-Premise or in the Private Cloud

Prerequisites for migration scenarios

Before starting the migration to SAP S/4HANA, on-premise, you might have to set up the SAP S/4HANA system first. We introduced three basic SAP S/4HANA migration cases in Chapter 4, Section 4.2:

- New implementation of SAP S/4HANA
- System conversion to SAP S/4HANA
- Landscape transformation with SAP S/4HANA

Except for the system conversion scenario, migrating to SAP S/4HANA is always a new installation from the technical perspective. In addition, regardless of the migration scenario, the SAP S/4HANA system requires a frontend server to enable using SAP Fiori as the user interface. In this chapter, we'll discuss the installation of the different components.

> **Frontend Server for System Conversion**
>
> A separate SAP Fiori frontend server must be installed or SAP Fiori Cloud is required for the system conversion scenario if you want to use SAP Fiori applications.

Steps for a new installation

In case you're not using the SAP S/4HANA Fully-Activated Appliance, which we introduced in Chapter 6, you'll have to perform sizing to determine the hardware requirements as we'll introduce later.

After determining your requirements, use the *Software Provisioning Manager* (SWPM) to set up an SAP S/4HANA system with the available SAP installation media (see Section 9.1). The new system is provided with the default Customizing delivered by SAP. You then have to adapt the configuration of the new system in such a way that it meets the requirements of the business processes you want to implement (see Section 9.2).

In addition to this SAP S/4HANA instance, a frontend server also has to be installed. This frontend server (*FES*) is the central hub for the SAP Fiori user interface (see Section 9.3).

As an alternative to a new custom installation (which is mandatory for production systems), you can also use the SAP S/4HANA reference system as the SAP S/4HANA Fully-Activated Appliance, which was introduced in Chapter 6. The SAP S/4HANA Fully-Activated Appliance can be used as the starting point for the installation.

9.1 Installation

If you don't want to use the SAP S/4HANA Fully-Activated Appliance, you'll need to first perform the sizing for your specific case. The sizing process determines the hardware requirements of the SAP S/4HANA system and SAP HANA database as well as the disk size, the required memory, and the anticipated network throughput.

Sizing

> **Additional Information on Sizing**
>
> Depending on the target system release and scenario, the following links provide more information on the SAP S/4HANA sizing process:
>
> - Sizing starting point in SAP Service Marketplace: *http://service.sap.com/sizing*
> - SAP Quicksizer: *http://service.sap.com/quicksizing*
> - SAP Note 1793345 for SAP S/4HANA Finance
> - SAP Note 1872170 for ABAP sizing reports

This section describes how to set up an SAP S/4HANA, on-premise, system in your landscape. The steps remain the same for private cloud or hosting environments. For the sake of simplicity, this section explains how to install a sandbox system that contains an ABAP backend server and the SAP Fiori frontend server in the same system (*co-deployment*, see also Section 9.3).

Sandbox system

First, you need to download the installation files using the *SAP Download Manager* and the *Download Basket*. A new cloud-based tool, which will be introduced later on, helps you find the appropriate files for your installation.

Downloading the installation files

> **SAP Download Manager Download Basket**
>
> Empty the SAP Download Manager Download Basket by deleting obsolete download requests before selecting the individual components for SAP S/4HANA. As a result, you'll be able to track more effectively the files you still need to install.

To easily download the necessary files, log on to the *Maintenance Planner*—a new tool that replaces the Maintenance Optimizer (see Figure 9.1). The

Maintenance Planner

9 Installing and Configuring SAP S/4HANA On-Premise or in the Private Cloud

Maintenance Planner lets you plan new system installations, perform updates, and implement new or additional SAP products (for example, the frontend server for SAP Fiori).

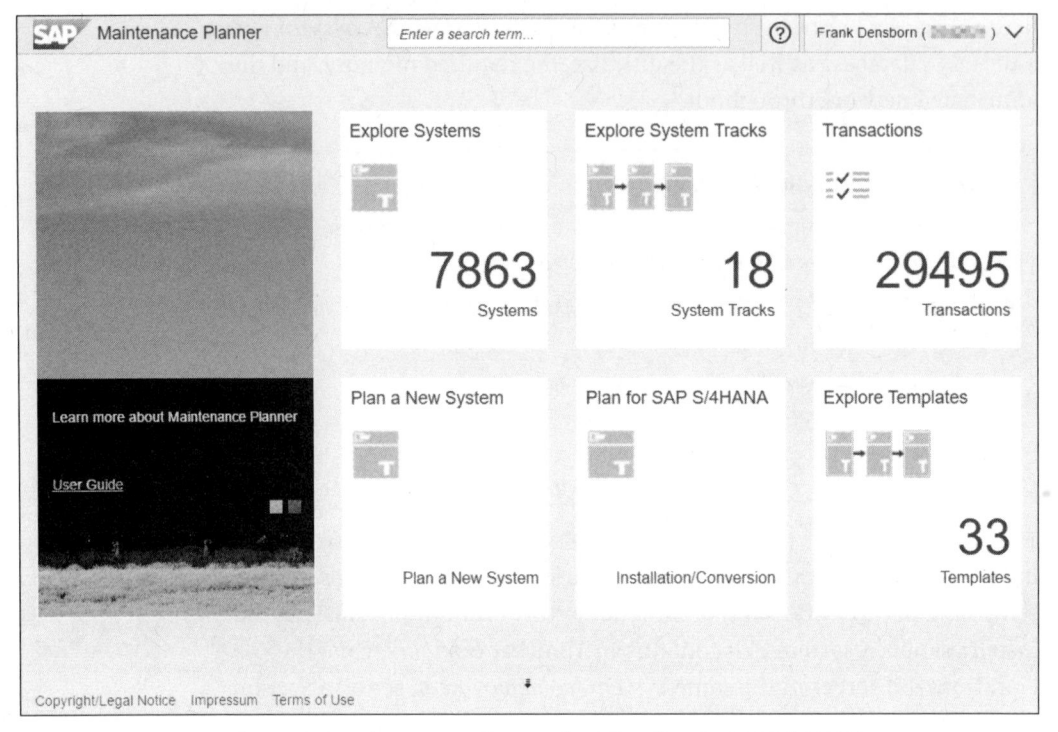

Figure 9.1 Maintenance Planner for Migrating to SAP S/4HANA

> **[»]** **Additional Information on the Maintenance Planner**
> The following link provides more information on the Maintenance Planner: *http://help.sap.com/maintenanceplanner*.

Starting the Maintenance Planner To start the Maintenance Planner, enter the following link into your web browser:

https://apps.support.sap.com/sap/support/mp

An SAP Fiori-based website opens, which you can access with your S-user credentials. For SAP partners, the partner user must be linked to the customer user to be able to view the customer's systems. The Maintenance

Planner helps you find and download the required installation files and provides the necessary documentation.

Not only can you use the Maintenance Planner to install new systems, but you can also use the Maintenance Planner for system conversions (see Figure 9.2). The tool helps you search for add-ons, business functions, and industry solutions on the existing system and also lets you determine whether your system can be converted at all (see Chapter 10).

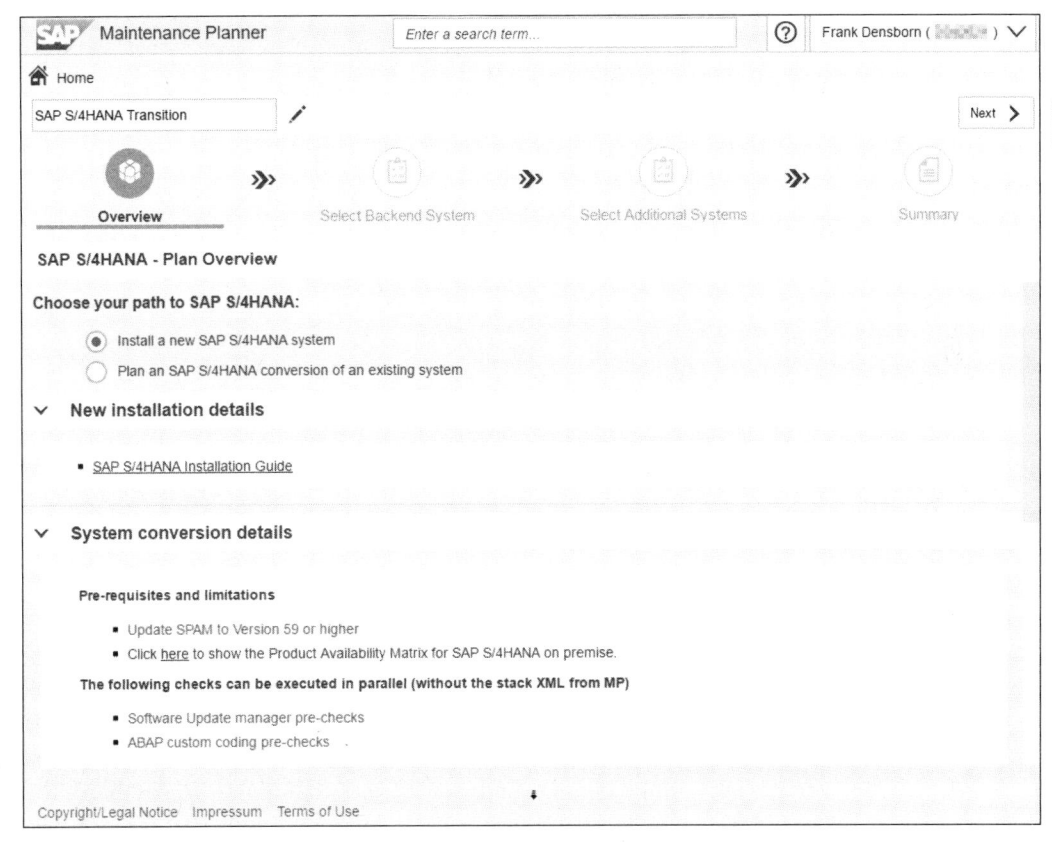

Figure 9.2 Maintenance Planner for Installing New SAP S/4HANA Systems or Converting Existing Systems

Go to the link shown in Figure 9.2 to download the *SAP S/4HANA Installation Guide* (menu item **New installation details**), which will guide you through the individual installation steps. After you have completed the

SAP S/4HANA Installation Guide

9   Installing and Configuring SAP S/4HANA On-Premise or in the Private Cloud

process, you can use the **Push to Download Basket** function (see Figure 9.3) to move the installation files to the Download Manager and directly download the files with this tool.

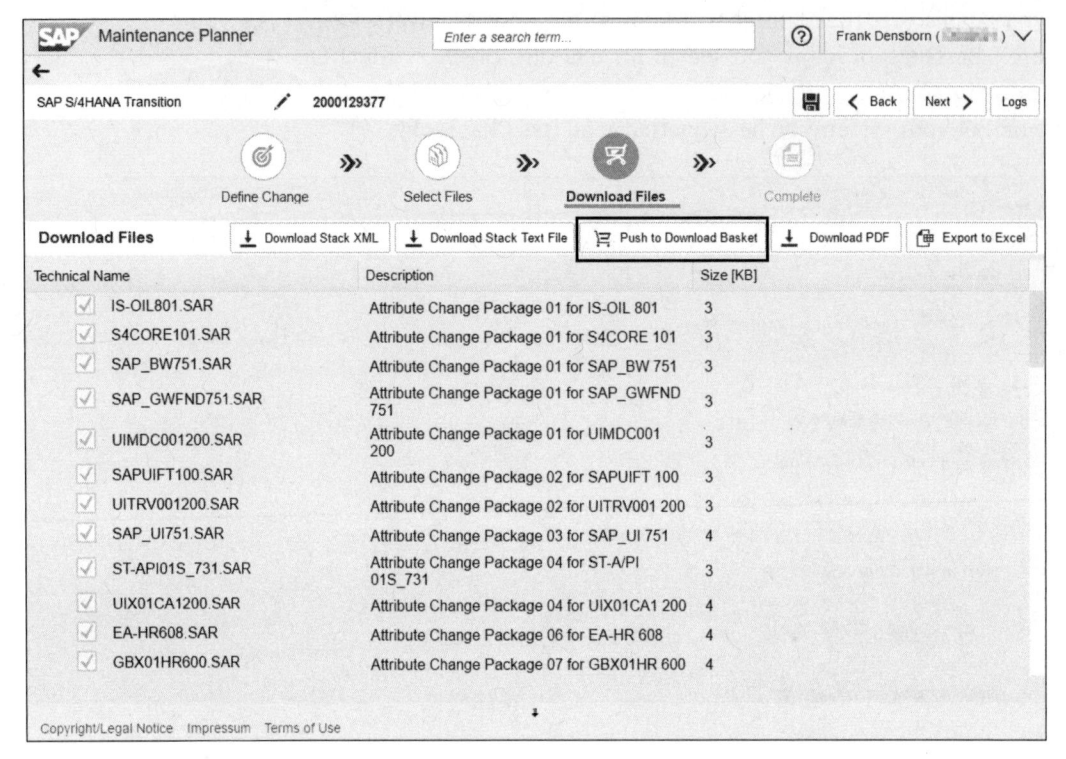

Technical Name	Description	Size [KB]
IS-OIL801.SAR	Attribute Change Package 01 for IS-OIL 801	3
S4CORE101.SAR	Attribute Change Package 01 for S4CORE 101	3
SAP_BW751.SAR	Attribute Change Package 01 for SAP_BW 751	3
SAP_GWFND751.SAR	Attribute Change Package 01 for SAP_GWFND 751	3
UIMDC001200.SAR	Attribute Change Package 01 for UIMDC001 200	3
SAPUIFT100.SAR	Attribute Change Package 02 for SAPUIFT 100	3
UITRV001200.SAR	Attribute Change Package 02 for UITRV001 200	3
SAP_UI751.SAR	Attribute Change Package 03 for SAP_UI 751	4
ST-API01S_731.SAR	Attribute Change Package 04 for ST-A/PI 01S_731	3
UIX01CA1200.SAR	Attribute Change Package 04 for UIX01CA1 200	4
EA-HR608.SAR	Attribute Change Package 06 for EA-HR 608	4
GBX01HR600.SAR	Attribute Change Package 07 for GBX01HR 600	4

Figure 9.3 Downloading the Files via the Maintenance Planner

Required tools The PDF that you can download using **Download PDF** (see Figure 9.3) also contains a link to the *SAP Software Download Center* in the SAP Support Portal. In addition, you'll need the latest *Support Package Manager* (SPAM) version and—if it has not been installed yet—an SAP HANA database. The latest *Software Update Manager* (SUM) version should also be installed. Although mostly used for system conversion, you also use the SUM for initial patches during the new installation.

Necessary information For the installation, you'll need the operating system version specified in the Maintenance Planner (in our example, *SUSE Linux*) and the SAP HANA database version. (The specifications in the Maintenance Planner also contain information on the database version.) If SAP HANA is already

9.1 Installation

implemented, you'll need to patch the database to the version that you need for your SAP S/4HANA version, and you'll have to create a new database container.

The *Software Provisioning Manager* (SWPM) then performs the actual SAP S/4HANA installation using the files you downloaded with the Maintenance Planner. This process follows the steps described in the installation guide (see Figure 9.4) and may take several hours.

Installation with the SWPM

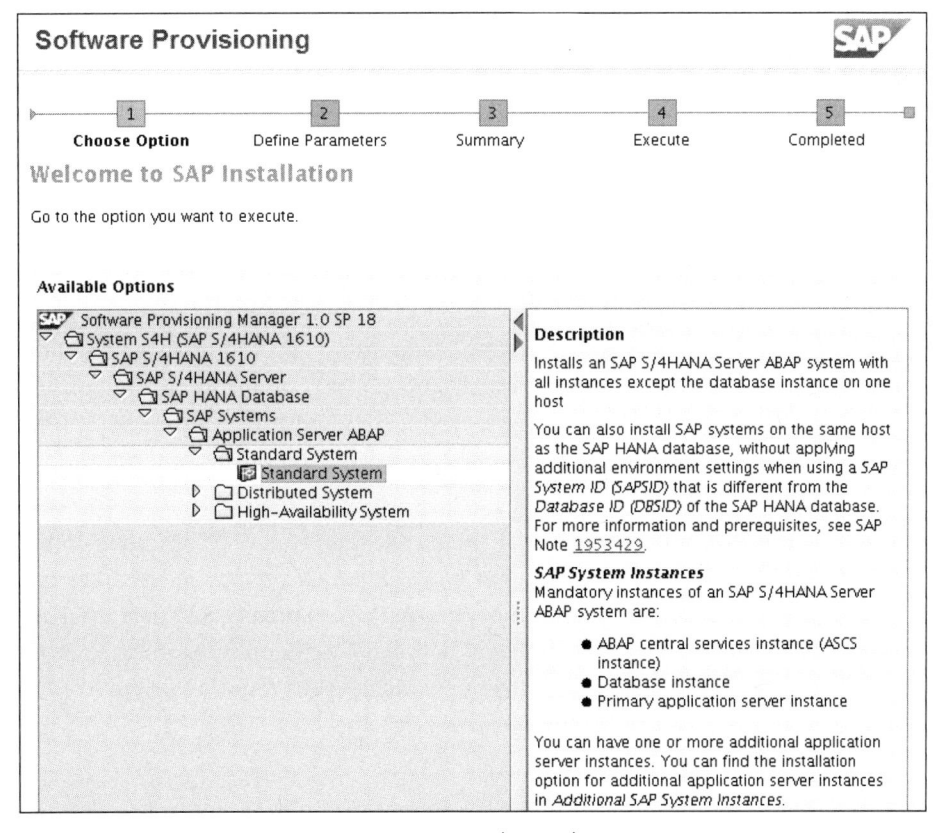

![Software Provisioning Manager screenshot showing the Welcome to SAP Installation screen with available options tree including SAP S/4HANA 1610, SAP S/4HANA Server, SAP HANA Database, SAP Systems, Application Server ABAP, Standard System (selected), Distributed System, and High-Availability System. Description panel shows details about installing an SAP S/4HANA Server ABAP system.]

Figure 9.4 The Software Provisioning Manager (SWPM)

After successfully installing a "naked" SAP S/4HANA system, you can use SUM to install the support packages you may need. (Please ensure that you're using the latest version of the Software Update Manager.)

SUM

Before starting SUM, you can archive and backup your data. The SUM process can also take several hours. You can install add-ons with the *SAP Add-on*

317

Installation Tool (Transaction SAINT) together with the Support Package Manager (Transaction SPAM).

Postprocessing — Finally, you should perform some cleanup and use Transaction SPAU to make adjustments. Then, install the SAP Notes for your SAP S/4HANA version from SAP S/4HANA Release Notes using Transaction SNOTE and install the transports. Now, your SAP S/4HANA installation is complete.

> **Additional Information on the Installation**
> You can find more information in the SAP S/4HANA Community (*https://www.sap.com/community/topic/s4hana.html*) and SAP S/4HANA Cookbook (*https://wiki.scn.sap.com/wiki/display/ATopics/SAP+S4HANA+Cookbook+-+What+is+SAP+S4HANA*).

9.2 System Configuration

SAP Best Practices — This section describes the system configuration procedure using SAP Best Practices, which is an appropriate approach for configuring all sandbox and proof of concept systems. For a production landscape, this option is only available if SAP Best Practices meets your customer requirements (see the section on fit-to-gap analysis in Chapter 5, Section 5.2).

Master client — In SAP ERP and the traditional SAP Business Suite, SAP recommends copying the major part of the content from Client 000 (*master client*) to set up a customer-specific client for the implementation project. SAP Best Practices drastically reduces the number of necessary configuration tables (by more than tenfold). SAP Best Practices only includes the required system configuration settings and the necessary basic tables to set up SAP S/4HANA, on-premise.

These clients in SAP Best Practices are referred to as *best practices clients* in the following sections, while the other clients with full master client configuration are referred to as *traditional clients*. You can run best practices clients and traditional clients in the same SAP S/4HANA system (see also Chapter 6, Section 6.3).

Client copy profiles — SAP S/4HANA provides two new profiles for client copies:

- SAP_UCUS: Customizing and user master data
- SAP_CUST: Customizing

With one of these profiles, you can set up a best practices client based on the master client. For this best practices copy, only the required tables of delivery classes C and G are copied to the target client; all other tables are not copied (for example, system tables with delivery class S). A best practices client only works when copied from the master client but can facilitate future maintenance tasks if you keep standard SAP Best Practices for the remaining configuration. Future SAP S/4HANA upgrades not only affect the software but also affect SAP Best Practices content, which is also enhanced with additional functionality.

To configure the installed SAP S/4HANA system and install SAP Best Practices, you'll use various tools after the master client has been initially (or partially) copied: the *SAP Solution Builder* for SAP Best Practices and *SAP Solution Manager 7.2*. You must not confuse these tools. These tools enable you to activate SAP Best Practices according to your customer-specific requirements at the scope item level for the specific functions with the so-called *Building Block Builder*. The system configuration from SAP Best Practices is activated in the development system and then transported to the system landscape.

Solution Builder

The SAP Best Practices activation might take several hours and follows the steps described in the *SAP S/4HANA Admin Guide*. If you activate SAP Best Practices for the U.S., you can also integrate the content with the Vertex tax system. After successfully activating SAP Best Practices with these tools, you'll only have to perform some minor postprocessing tasks manually.

Admin Guide

SAP S/4HANA Admin Guide

We recommend downloading a PDF version of the SAP S/4HANA Admin Guide to view it offline. The following link takes you to the Admin Guide for SAP S/4HANA 1610; however, you can also navigate to other on-premise versions from here: *http://bit.ly/v1448093*. To download the PDF document, use the **Download as PDF** function at the top right in the hypertext version of the Admin Guide.

The configuration process in the development system involves the following steps:

Configuring systems in the development system

1. Import the reference client:
   – Download the latest solution scope file and the installation files.
   – Upload the files to the SAP S/4HANA system to make the relevant settings and create the master data.
   – Import the settings to the Solution Builder using the solution scope file.
2. Use the scope items so select the solution scope you want to activate.
3. Activate the system.

Building blocks When activating the system, you'll implement the relevant building blocks in a predefined order using the Solution Builder as an implementation wizard. Building blocks also include test data (master data) that is created with *eCATT* and settings that are installed via *Business Configuration sets* (BC sets).

Customizing transports SAP recommends not activating content in quality assurance and production systems. Instead, you can transport the system configuration across the system landscape using the transport system. For this purpose, copy the master client using the SAP_CUST profile in the quality assurance system and the production system to create best practices clients. Then, the customizing settings are transported from the best practices client in the development system via customizing and workbench requests in the following order:

1. SAP Best Practices with the customizing from the initial activation
2. Additional customer-specific IMG customizing (that is, customizing implemented using the Implementation Guide)
3. Further master client settings according to SAP Note 2272406

The transport requests for SAP Best Practices (Step 1) and the requests with customer-specific customizing (Step 2) are therefore managed separately to allow for a successful installation of future SAP Best Practices updates. This separation ensures the future viability of your SAP S/4HANA system and simplifies maintenance.

Transport route The transport route in the SAP S/4HANA landscape goes from the development system to the quality assurance system to the production system. As already mentioned, SAP Best Practices content is not activated within the quality assurance system or the production system. However, manual postprocessing (as described in the Admin Guide) might be necessary in the individual systems.

You can decide whether or not to use SAP Best Practices for the system configuration. Table 9.1 compares the advantages and disadvantages of a full implementation versus an alternative partial implementation.

Alternative system configurations

System Configuration Option	Advantages	Disadvantages
Traditional Client: Traditional full copy of the master client (with all configuration tables) without using the SAP Best Practices system configuration	■ Comprehensive configuration of the most functional areas ■ The procedure is the same as for SAP ERP and the traditional SAP Business Suite	■ Unused configuration makes future maintenance tasks more complicated ■ No documentation ■ No consistent and connected processes
Alternative: Traditional full copy of the master client (with all configuration tables) and additionally enabled SAP Best Practices	■ Comprehensive configuration of the most functional areas ■ Partially consistent and connected processes (SAP Best Practices) ■ Partial documentation (SAP Best Practices)	■ Unused configuration makes future maintenance tasks more complicated ■ Partially redundant or inconsistent configuration, because two different configurations are used as the basis
Best Practices Client: Custom, newly created best practices client (with reduced configuration tables) and SAP Best Practices	■ Consistent and connected processes ■ Well documented ■ Only the necessary configuration is used, which facilitates maintenance tasks	■ The SAP Best Practices package is not yet available for the entire SAP S/4HANA, on-premise, solution scope

Table 9.1 Comparing Different SAP S/4HANA System Configurations

---

Free Choice of the Configuration Method

You can manually also set up and configure the on-premise system without SAP Best Practices.

For SAP S/4HANA, on-premise, the preconfigured SAP Best Practices content described in this section accelerates the implementation, but—in

Comparison to SAP S/4HANA Cloud

contrast to SAP S/4HANA Cloud—you don't necessarily have to use SAP Best Practices.

While the SAP Best Practices package in SAP S/4HANA Cloud covers various processes, SAP S/4HANA, on-premise, provides customers with a high degree of flexibility in configuration. Therefore, a fit-to-gap workshop (see Chapter 5, Section 5.2) is crucial factor successfully implementing SAP S/4HANA, on premise.

> **Additional Information and Click Demos for Configuring SAP S/4HANA, On-Premise**
>
> You can find a click demo for the SAP S/4HANA 1610, on-premise, configuration at *http://bit.ly/v1448091*.
>
> You can find a click demo for the SAP S/4HANA 1610 user administration at *http://bit.ly/v1448092*.

9.3 Setting Up the Frontend Server for SAP Fiori User Interfaces

SAP Fiori launchpad, which runs in web browsers is the sole central access point to SAP S/4HANA Cloud systems but also delivers additional features and capabilities for end users SAP S/4HANA, on-premise systems (see Chapter 2, Section 2.4).

SAP S/4HANA needs a *frontend server* (*FES*) for SAP Fiori user interfaces because SAP Fiori launchpad cannot communicate directly with the backend server. From the technical perspective, the frontend server is an *SAP Gateway*. If you already use an SAP Gateway system, you can also use it as a frontend server for SAP S/4HANA.

Because SAP Fiori launchpad leverages the frontend server for communication, users do not log on to the SAP S/4HANA backend but to the frontend server. You can also use SAP GUI, but then the user would have to toggle between SAP GUI and SAP Fiori with two different logon methods when accessing SAP GUI interfaces directly. SAP therefore recommends using the SAP Fiori launchpad as the entry point to SAP S/4HANA and as the new standardized SAP system user interface. Using the SAP Fiori launchpad makes switching between various programs unnecessary, which was the

9.3 Setting Up the Frontend Server for SAP Fiori User Interfaces

case in the traditional SAP Business Suite where content from SAP GUI was opened in web browsers sometimes.

Let's describe how to set up the frontend server. If you want to use an existing SAP Gateway system, you'll need to consider the SAP NetWeaver version and patch version required for your SAP S/4HANA version. If SAP S/4HANA 1511 and higher is installed, SAP NetWeaver 7.50 (or newer) is needed for custom frontend server installations or existing frontend servers. Here, only the SAP HANA, SAP MaxDB, and SAP ASE databases are supported (see SAP Note 2214245).

SAP Gateway version

The following frontend server components are used for the SAP S/4HANA user interface:

Components

- The *web server* transfers the data to the web browser on your computer or on mobile devices using SAPUI5 technology.
- SAP Gateway uses *OData services* to communicate with the SAP S/4HANA backend.
- The *SAP Fiori Launchpad Provider* provides the data model and services for SAP Fiori launchpad.

For analytical SAP Fiori apps, you'll additionally need *SAP Web Dispatcher* (reverse proxy).

If you don't want to set up a separate landscape for the frontend server, you can use *SAP Fiori Cloud* on demand. In this case, the frontend server in the cloud uses *SAP HANA Cloud Connector* and SAP Cloud Platform (previously SAP HANA Cloud Platform, HCP) to directly communicate with your on-premise landscape (see Section 9.3.2).

SAP Fiori Cloud

Various options are available for integrating the frontend server to your system landscape. These options refer to the type of the usage (on-premise or in the cloud) and, in the on-premise case, the type of the installation (central hub or add-on deployment):

Deployment options

- *Central hub deployment* of the frontend server for SAP Fiori
- *Add-on deployment* of the frontend server for SAP Fiori (also *embedded* or *co-deployment*)
- *SAP Fiori Cloud* using your own on-premise SAP Gateway system
- SAP Fiori Cloud without your own SAP Gateway system (*Full Fiori Cloud*)

Each option has advantages and disadvantages, which we'll describe in detail next. We hope the explanations in the following sections help you to identify the best option for your landscape and your technical and business requirements.

> **Online Support for Selecting the Deployment Option**
>
> These two links to the *SAP Enterprise Architecture Explorer* contain recommendations for the frontend server landscape:
>
> - *https://eaexplorer.hana.ondemand.com/_item.html?id=11166#!/overview*
> - *https://eaexplorer.hana.ondemand.com/_item.html?id=11115#!/overview*

9.3.1 On-Premise Installation of the Frontend Server

Central hub — This section describes implementing and using an on-premise frontend server. Although this scenario results in an additional SAP NetWeaver system in your system landscape, installing a frontend server as a central hub has the following advantages when compared to an embedded or add-on implementation in the same system:

- Software updates for SAP Fiori are decoupled from the SAP S/4HANA backend system.
- User interface (UI) innovations for SAP Fiori and other UI content can be consumed faster.
- You can also leverage the SAP S/4HANA frontend server as the frontend server for other systems in the same SAP system landscape.
- Scalability is better because you can accommodate an increasing number of users independently of the backend.
- Because the display server and data retention server are separated, data security is improved.

Add-on — For these reasons, implementing a frontend server as an embedded or add-on deployment on the system on which the SAP S/4HANA backend is installed is possible but not recommended for production landscapes. This type of implementation is rather suited for trial systems (for example, for the SAP S/4HANA Fully-Activated Appliance, which includes an embedded frontend server, see Section 6.2).

As before when we actually installed the SAP S/4HANA system (see Section 9.1), you'll have to perform sizing before installing the frontend server. Then, you'll perform the actual installation using the Software Provisioning Manager (SWPM) and implement the SAP S/4HANA add-ons for the frontend server.

Installation

Finally, you'll have to carry out manual postprocessing tasks that mainly refer to the configuration. You can obtain the required installation files through the Maintenance Planner as described in Section 9.1 for SAP S/4HANA.

The name of the appropriate SAP Fiori version is "SAP FIORI FOR SAP S/4HANA," followed by the SAP S/4HANA version number, e.g., "SAP FIORI FOR SAP S/4HANA 1610" for SAP S/4HANA 1610.

> **Additional Implementation Information**
>
> The following link contains more and up-to-date information on the implementation of the frontend server:
>
> - *https://eaexplorer.hana.ondemand.com/_item.html?id=11167#!/overview*

[«]

9.3.2 SAP Fiori Cloud

SAP Fiori Cloud is a new, simple cloud deployment variant of the frontend server for SAP systems (previously referred to as *Fiori-as-a-Service*). SAP Fiori Cloud runs on SAP Cloud Platform and consumes data from your SAP S/4HANA, on-premise, system. Technically, your SAP S/4HANA landscape thus becomes a hybrid landscape because part of it—the frontend server— is implemented in the cloud. Nevertheless, your data is still kept on-premise in your data center and is not affected. SAP Fiori Cloud allows you to reduce the costs for implementing SAP S/4HANA and addresses security concerns regarding the cloud implementation.

SAP Cloud Platform

SAP Fiori Cloud comes in two editions:

Editions

- *SAP Fiori Cloud Demo* enables you to explore SAP Fiori in your SAP landscape with various selected SAP Fiori apps.

- *SAP Fiori Cloud* allows you to use SAP Fiori in production without a separate frontend server. This edition also provides various selected SAP Fiori apps.

Similar to the central hub deployment of a single frontend server (see Section 9.3.1), SAP Fiori Cloud lets you connect several SAP systems. As a result, you'll be able to use SAP Fiori technology in your existing SAP landscape. Furthermore, you can enhance and adapt SAP Fiori apps as well as create new custom apps via the *SAP Web IDE*. In this scenario, data is retrieved from your on-premise systems through *SAP Cloud Platform OData Provisioning*—a proxy type on SAP Cloud Platform that provides OData for external systems.

With or without separate SAP Gateway server

You can use SAP Fiori Cloud with a separate (on-premise) SAP Gateway server or in the cloud without a separate SAP Gateway server. Table 9.2 lists the advantages and disadvantages of these two options.

Deployment Option	Advantages	Disadvantages
SAP Fiori Cloud with SAP Gateway, on-premise	Full functionality of SAP Gateway	You have to maintain and update SAP Gateway yourself
SAP Fiori Cloud (full cloud)—without a separate SAP Gateway installation	Minimum installation and maintenance costs for the entire SAP Fiori infrastructure	The SAP Gateway functionality is restricted (see SAP Note 1830712)

Table 9.2 Comparing Deployment Options for SAP Fiori Cloud

The full SAP Fiori Cloud option does not support all SAP Gateway functions due to the restrictions in SAP Cloud Platform OData Provisioning.

Prerequisites

Finally, we must mention that, if you use SAP Fiori Cloud, the SAP Gateway connection and the SAP Fiori backend components in SAP S/4HANA must also be configured in addition to SAP HANA Cloud Connector for the connection to the backend system. If you have multiple SAP backend systems (including non-SAP S/4HANA systems), these systems must also have the same SAP Cloud Platform OData Provisioning version.

SAP Fiori apps reference library

The SAP Fiori apps reference library (see Chapter 2, Section 2.4) lets you search for SAP Fiori apps that are available in SAP Fiori Cloud for an overview of the limitations in this case.

9.3 Setting Up the Frontend Server for SAP Fiori User Interfaces

> **Additional Information on SAP Fiori Cloud**
>
> The following links contain more and up-to-date information on using SAP Fiori Cloud:
>
> - Additional information: *https://uxexplorer.hana.ondemand.com/_item.html?id=10698#!/overview*
> - SAP Help Portal: *https://help.sap.com/viewer/product/SAP_FIORI_CLOUD_S4H/latest/en-US*
> - Product overview: *https://www.sap.com/products/fiori.html*
> - SAP Fiori Cloud Trial: *https://www.sapfioritrial.com*

Chapter 10
System Conversion

System conversion means converting an existing SAP ERP system into an SAP S/4HANA system. SAP offers many useful methods and functions to help you determine and implement the required adaptation tasks.

System conversion refers to a transition scenario in which you convert a single SAP ERP system into an SAP S/4HANA, on-premise, system. According to the vocabulary used in IT transformation projects, this scenario follows the so-called *brownfield approach*. In contrast to a new implementation of an SAP S/4HANA system (*greenfield approach*), your application data, configuration data, and custom developments are still available after the system conversion. The system conversion procedure is only available for the on-premise variant of SAP S/4HANA.

When you convert an SAP ERP system into an SAP S/4HANA system, you're migrating to the SAP S/4HANA product family. You'll change to the SAP HANA in-memory database (if you hadn't already), and the simplifications of SAP S/4HANA are implemented (see Section 10.2). This chapter introduces the procedures and tools used for system conversions.

> **The "System Conversion" Concept**
> Because converting an existing SAP ERP system into an SAP S/4HANA system also involves a product change, this transition scenario is also referred to as a *system conversion*. We would not call it an "upgrade" because an upgrade would entail installing a new version of the same product.

10.1 Overview of the System Conversion Project

You'll have to consider two aspects when converting your system: the technical procedure with which you will install the SAP S/4HANA software and

More than a technical procedure

the process of migrating to the new product, which involves changes to the functions and processes you know from SAP ERP already.

As shown in Figure 10.1, in addition to performing technical conversion steps, you'll also have to adapt the functional scope of your data structure when migrating to SAP S/4HANA.

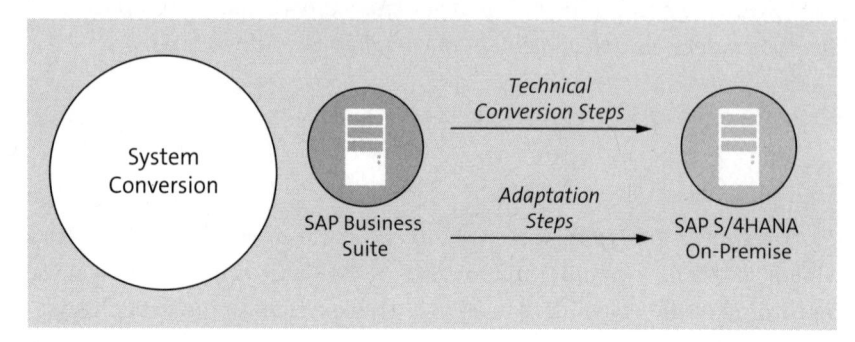

Figure 10.1 System Conversion to SAP S/4HANA: Technical Conversion and Adaptation Requirements

Example: credit management

An example of a possible adaptation requirement is the credit management function, which we introduced in Chapter 1, Section 1.2.1. According to the principle of one, SAP S/4HANA supports only one credit management solution, which might require adaptation in some cases. Customers who use Credit and Risk Management (SD-BF-CM) in SAP ERP need to change to the new credit management function, SAP Credit Management (FIN-FSCM-CR), when migrating to SAP S/4HANA. However, SAP Credit Management is already available in SAP ERP so you can change to this solution *before* you convert your system. In addition to functional adaptations due to the different solution scope of SAP S/4HANA, the simplification of the data structures can also affect your custom developments.

Determining the required adaptation work

Various methods and tools are available in the individual conversion project phases to help you determine what adaptation work you need to migrate to SAP S/4HANA:

- **Simplification list**
  The simplification list describes the potential adaptation work for functions that is required when converting your SAP ERP system to SAP S/4HANA. For more information on the simplification list, refer to Section 10.2.2.

- **Maintenance Planner**
  The Maintenance Planner helps you simulate and plan the system conversion. The Maintenance Planner informs you about add-ons (both SAP and partner add-ons) and business functions that SAP S/4HANA supports or does not support. You can find more information on the Maintenance Planner in Section 10.2.3.

- **Prechecks**
  Prechecks enable you to determine which functions need to be adjusted to migrate to SAP S/4HANA. Prechecks are provided as SAP Notes and can be implemented and executed on your SAP Business Suite source system (see Section 10.2.4).

- **Custom code migration worklist**
  You can use the custom code migration worklist to identify the required adaptation work for custom programs when migrating to SAP S/4HANA. The custom code migration worklist supplements existing analysis tools for custom programs (for example, the Code Inspector). The worklist analyzes custom code by considering the modified data structures in and the new functional scope of SAP S/4HANA. For more information, refer to Section 10.2.5.

You can use the *Software Update Manager* (SUM) to install SAP S/4HANA software during the system conversion and to install subsequent updates and upgrades. SUM provides options for reducing downtime during the migration project and is regularly updated via Software Logistics Toolsets (SL Toolsets). Section 10.2.7 explains how to use SUM.

Software Update Manager

> **Additional Information**
>
> Since June 2017, the *SAP Readiness Check for SAP S/4HANA* has been available. This cloud-based tool is available for free to anyone with a current SAP maintenance agreement. The readiness check reviews both your production (PRD) systems (or copies thereof) and your development (DEV) systems, determines their compatibility for SAP S/4HANA conversion, and provides the necessary conversion preparation steps. Among other results, the SAP Readiness Check for SAP S/4HANA displays the simplification items relevant to your specific SAP ERP 6.x system. Simplification items are identified according to factors such as transactions used and table contents.

More information (including the user guide and required configuration settings) can be found at *https://help.sap.com/viewer/p/SAP_READINESS_CHECK*.

10.1.1 System Conversion Process

Project phases and tools
Figure 10.2 illustrates the basic steps, as well as the relevant tools, you'll need to perform to convert your system into an SAP S/4HANA system.

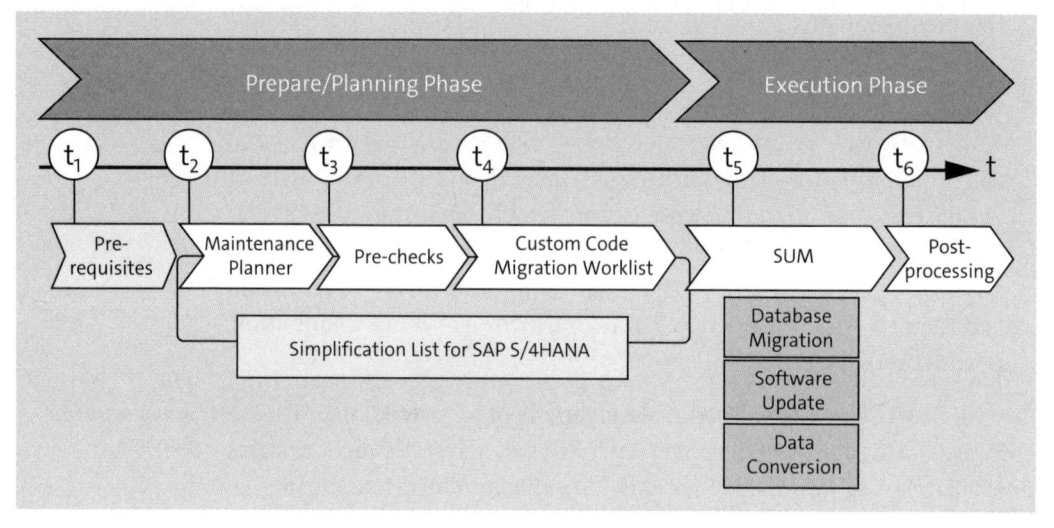

Figure 10.2 Tools Used for the System Conversion

Prepare and planning phase
During the prepare and planning phase of the system conversion project, you'll have to verify the system requirements. For example, SAP does not provide one-step system conversions for older SAP releases (for example, SAP R/3 Enterprise Edition 4.6C). You'll also use the simplification list, the Maintenance Planner, prechecks, and the custom code migration worklist to obtain an overview of the required adaptation tasks during this phase. For example, you'll have to determine the timeframe for implementing the new simplified processes and determine when you want to use the new SAP Fiori-based user interfaces and which SAP GUI transactions you want to continue to use after the system conversion.

Preparations in the source system
The tools and functions for the prepare and planning phase are already available in your existing SAP ERP source system. Because you can

implement numerous adaptations in this system (and some may need to be implemented before the conversion), you should perform the prepare and planning steps early in the conversion project.

In the adaptation and test phase (see Figure 10.3), you'll convert your development system (see Section 10.1.2) and perform the planned adaptations. Tests (usually, several test runs are required) and end-user training are preparatory steps for the go-live.

Adaptation and test phase

In the execution phase, you'll perform the technical SAP S/4HANA conversion using SUM. SUM combines three steps in one integrated process. In a one-step procedure, you'll convert to the SAP HANA database, change the software, and convert the application data from your legacy data structure to the new data structure. When the SAP S/4HANA production system goes live, you can scale back the existing SAP Business Suite system landscape.

Execution phase

Figure 10.3 provides an overview of the individual tasks for the SAP S/4HANA conversion project phases.

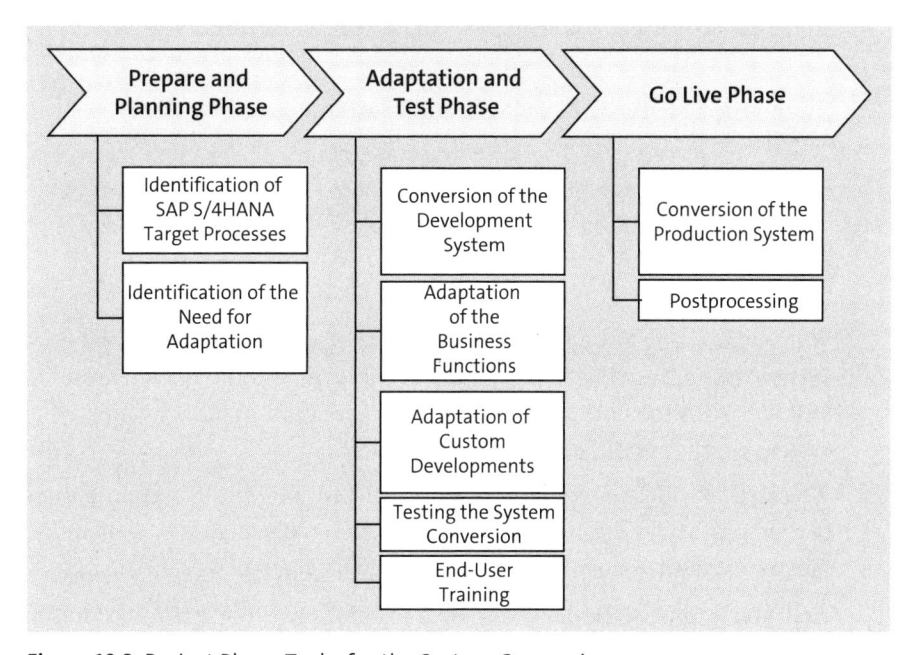

Figure 10.3 Project Phase Tasks for the System Conversion

Section 10.2 describes the individual conversion steps in detail.

10 System Conversion

> **Additional Information**
>
> The "Conversion Guide for SAP S/4HANA" provides basic information on the SAP S/4HANA system conversion process. Select your SAP S/4HANA version at *https://help.sap.com/s4hana*.
>
> SAP Note 2332030 contains additional information on specific preparatory and follow-up steps for accounting.

10.1.2 System Group Conversion

Multisystem landscape

The customer system landscape is a determining factor for the SAP S/4HANA system conversion. Usually, a system landscape consists of a group of several SAP ERP systems that are connected via transport routes. You should therefore never carry out the development and test tasks in the production system. To test and verify the developments, you should add a consolidation system to the system group. You'll then have a three-system landscape, which is used by the majority of SAP ERP customers.

> **Landscapes with Multiple Production Systems**
>
> Some customers use several production systems, for example, to map regional structures with subsidiaries in various countries. However, in this section, we'll focus on a three-system landscape with one production system.

When converting a single-system landscape, you must consider the entire system group. You'll have to migrate every system in the system group to SAP S/4HANA to continue the necessary separation of tasks by individual systems in the system group in SAP S/4HANA.

Conversion process in the system group

We can't provide general recommendations for migrating system groups because customer requirements differ considerably. Figure 10.4 therefore illustrates how to convert a system group in an abstract way.

First, you'll convert the development and quality assurance (QA) systems to SAP S/4HANA. The SAP S/4HANA development system is usually a system copy of your existing development system in the SAP Business Suite landscape, converted to SAP S/4HANA.

10.1 Overview of the System Conversion Project

During the development system conversion, you'll adapt your business functionalities (for example, the credit management function if required) and custom developments as determined in the planning phase. These adaptations are recorded by transport requests and tested in the quality assurance system.

Development system conversion

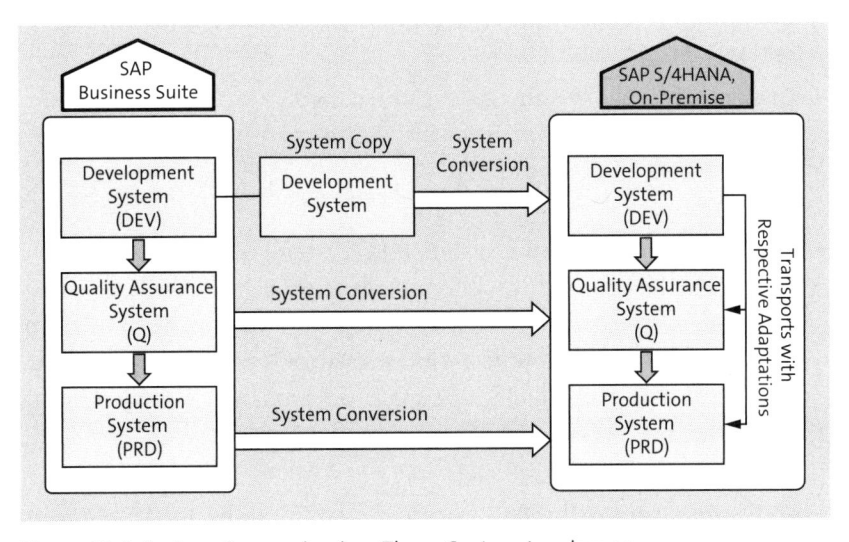

Figure 10.4 System Conversion in a Three-System Landscape

During the production system conversion, these transports are installed in the corresponding SUM phases to provide the necessary adaptations in the production system. You should carry out several test runs before you convert the production system so that you can test the entire procedure and specify measures to minimize production system *downtime*.

Production system conversion

Figure 10.5 provides an overview of the various conversion runs for common system conversions:

Several runs

1. **Initial test system conversion**
   Usually, the first step of a system conversion project is to carry out tests in the sandbox system (for example, a copy of the PRD system). You'll gain technical know-how about the conversion procedure in these tests, which you can use for subsequent conversions. End users can also make themselves familiar with SAP S/4HANA business functions in this system. In addition, you'll analyze and test your custom developments based on the new software.

2. **Development system (DEV system) conversion**
   In the SAP S/4HANA development system, you'll adapt your custom developments to the SAP S/4HANA solution scope and data structures. You'll also implement the mandatory adaptations in SAP S/4HANA if you have not already implemented them in the source system. To benefit most from the SAP S/4HANA conversion, you can implement further optional adaptations.

3. **Quality assurance system (QA system) conversion**
   You'll import adaptations from the DEV system (process adjustments and adaptations of the custom developments) and test the adapted business processes.

4. **Test run of the production system (PRD system) conversion**
   You'll test the production system conversion in the sandbox system under the same conditions that apply to your PRD system. In this context, you can prepare optimization measures for reducing downtime and can also develop and finalize the cut-over plan. You might have to repeat the tests several times.

5. **Production system conversion**
   You'll then convert the PRD system according to the specifications of your cut-over plan.

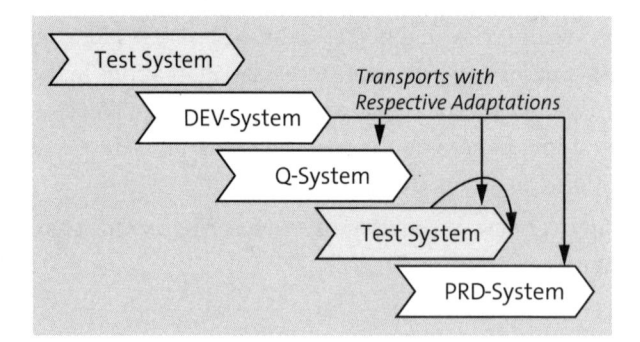

Figure 10.5 Conversion Cycles in the System Group

Transition phase

Before you convert the production system to SAP S/4HANA, you'll have to keep the initial state of the SAP Business Suite system landscape, for example, to provide necessary corrections there. Consequently, you'll maintain two development systems from the start of the SAP S/4HANA conversion project (development system conversion) up to the production system conversion. You can scale back the development system in the SAP Business Suite landscape when the production system conversion to SAP S/4HANA is complete. During this transition phase with two development systems, you'll have to develop a strategy addressing how changes made in the SAP ERP system group during this time will affect SAP S/4HANA system group in the future.

Ultimately, the SAP S/4HANA system conversion does not pose new requirements to the software lifecycle management processes in a system group or to the definition of the transport routes between the systems.

10.2 Converting Single Systems

This section explains the steps that you'll have to perform in every system you are converting to SAP S/4HANA. Note that these steps are performed in different phases and probably in different systems of the system group and at different times. For example, you can adapt your custom developments in the SAP S/4HANA development system. Also in the development system, you'll collect the adaptations in transports, which are then directly installed when you convert the production system.

You can also implement many of the mandatory or optional business process modifications or adjust your custom developments immediately on the SAP ERP start release. In this case, these conversion project steps are carried out in upstream systems. You'll have to decide for your specific conversion project whether you implement these adaptations beforehand or during the system conversion on the SAP S/4HANA development system.

In addition to the specific SAP S/4HANA conversion project steps, you'll also have to carry out standard tasks that you already know from other transformation projects, for example:

Standard tasks

- **End-user training**
  If you modify business processes or migrate to SAP Fiori-based user interfaces, you'll have to schedule specific end-user training sessions and carry them out in a timely manner.
- **IT employee training focusing on new technologies**
  SAP S/4HANA introduces new technologies, such as Core Data Services (CDS) and the new HTML5-based SAP Fiori user interfaces. You'll have to train your experts accordingly.

- **Business process tests**
  Don't forget to include application tests.

These standard tasks of transformation projects are not described in detail in this book. Nevertheless, these tasks are also critical for the success of your SAP S/4HANA conversion project and need to be performed.

10.2.1 System Requirements

Basically, you can convert any SAP ERP system to SAP S/4HANA. However, the effort and procedure required depend on the initial release.

One-step procedure

Migrating to SAP S/4HANA (or changes to a new release within SAP ERP) is a one-step procedure if you upgrade the software and migrate the database in the same technical step. You can convert your SAP ERP systems into an SAP S/4HANA system using the one-step procedure if the following requirements are met:

- **Start release**
  SAP ERP 6.0, Enhancement Packages (EHP) 0 through 8, must be installed on the source system. You might already be using an SAP HANA database, but you can also convert SAP ERP systems with other databases in one step.

- **Unicode**
  The source system must be a Unicode system.

- **Only SAP NetWeaver Application Server (AS) ABAP**
  The SAP ERP source system must be a pure ABAP system. Converting dual-stack systems (combination of AS ABAP and AS Java in one system) is not supported.

Systems on which older releases are installed or for which no Unicode conversion has been performed must be converted to SAP S/4HANA in multiple steps.

[»] **Unicode Conversion**

In mid-2014, SAP announced that all new SAP NetWeaver releases after 7.40 and all products based on higher releases would only be compatible with Unicode. Technically, non-Unicode systems based on SAP NetWeaver releases up to 7.40 cannot be converted into a product with an SAP

NetWeaver release that is higher than 7.40. You'll have to perform a Unicode conversion first.

In general, the following conversion paths to SAP S/4HANA, on-premise, are supported:

Supported conversion paths

1. From SAP ERP 6.0 to SAP S/4HANA
2. From SAP ERP 6.0 to SAP S/4HANA Finance
3. From SAP S/4HANA Finance to SAP S/4HANA

Figure 10.6 illustrates these conversion paths.

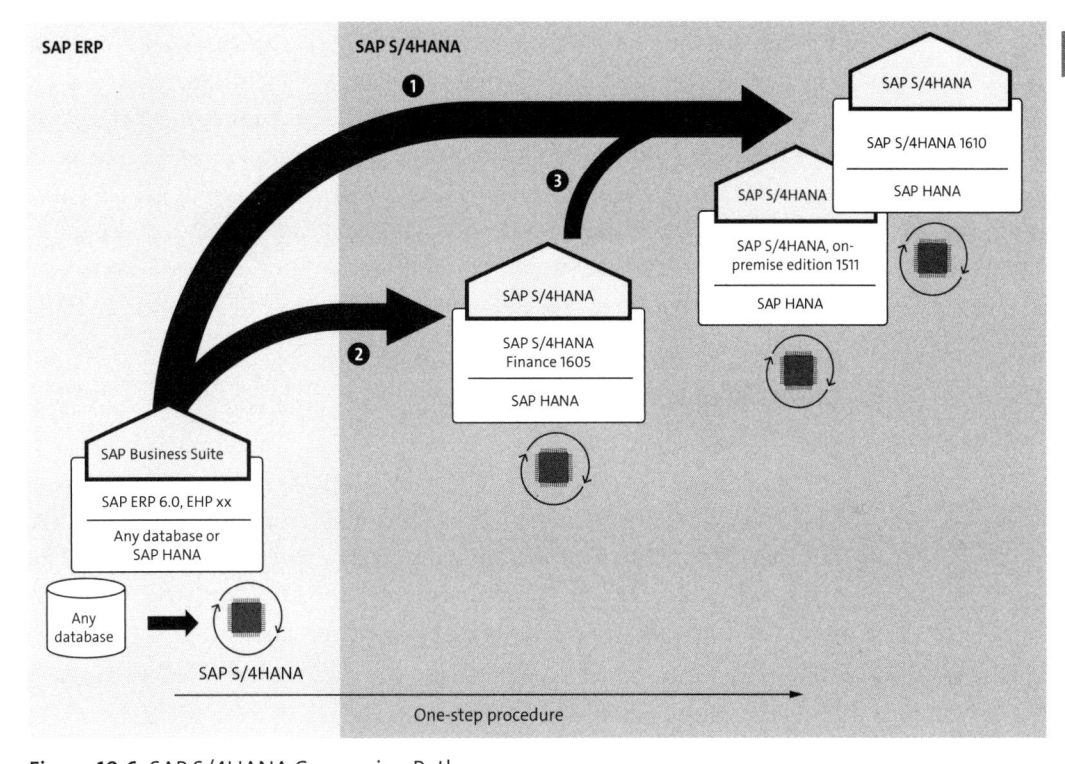

Figure 10.6 SAP S/4HANA Conversion Paths

As we described in Chapter 3, Section 3.2, SAP S/4HANA has two on-premise variants. For example, SAP S/4HANA Finance with the new functions is available in accounting, while SAP S/4HANA contains new functions for accounting and for logistics. In system conversions, the two on-premise variants differ in the following ways:

Differences between the on-premise variants

- **Adaptation requirements**

  Due to the different innovation scope of the two variants, their adaptation requirements also differ. Depending on your requirements and needs, you'll follow a step-by-step approach for the conversion. If you only want to use SAP S/4HANA's innovations for accounting, you can use SAP S/4HANA Finance to defer the logistics process adaptations until later in the project. However, as a result, the new logistics functions will not be available until your logistics processes are adapted. These adaptation requirements need to be considered individually during the planning phase.

- **Conversion procedures**

  The two variants differ in terms of technical structures and technical conversion procedures. Technically, SAP S/4HANA Finance is an exchange add-on that is based on SAP ERP 6.0 and requires the corresponding EHP (for SAP S/4HANA Finance 1605, the system must be updated to EHP 8). For system conversions to SAP S/4HANA, in contrast, the entire software core is exchanged. However, for customers, this detail in the technical procedure is unimportant because they can use SUM to execute the one-step approach for both variants.

10.2.2 Simplification List

Simplification list items

The simplification list describes the potential adaptation work that is required to convert your SAP ERP system to SAP S/4HANA at the functional level. *Simplification list items* (for short, *simplification items*) illustrate the business adaptation requirements and effects to custom developments for each function described. For more complex modifications, the simplification items provide the relevant guides to support you.

Planning tool

The simplification list is an important tool for planning the conversion project and should be used at an early stage. You can implement many of the necessary adaptations on your existing SAP ERP source system. As a result, you'll be able to start the conversion project before actually installing any SAP S/4HANA software. Consequently, the simplification list is an important source of information to schedule necessary conversion project tasks and assign the required resources.

The simplification list is supplemented by program-based analysis tools to help you identify relevant adaptation tasks, such as the Maintenance Planner, prechecks, and the custom code migration worklist, which we'll describe in detail in the following sections.

Analysis tools

The SAP Help for each SAP S/4HANA release includes the simplification list as a comprehensive document. In addition, the individual simplification items are available as separate SAP Notes.

In general, the functions listed in the simplification list can be divided into three categories:

Simplification list categories

- **Functions that are modified in SAP S/4HANA**
  Simplification items in this category refer to functions that are generally available in the same form in SAP S/4HANA but have been adapted in such a way that might affect existing processes and custom programs.

Change of the Material Number Field Length

An example of a simplification item in this category is the extension of the material number field. In an SAP S/4HANA system, the MATNR domain has a field length of 40 characters. The field length of the MATNR domain in an SAP ERP system is 18 characters. Although the function of the MATNR domain in the material master of each system remains essentially the same, this difference in field length may affect your custom code. Usually, this change in the length of the field doesn't affect your business processes because, after the system conversion, you can choose to use the longer material number field. If you want to use with 40 characters, you'll have to take into account how this choice may affect other integrated systems. For more information on potentially necessary modifications regarding the 40-character material number, see SAP Note 2267140.

- **Functions that are no longer available in SAP S/4HANA in this form**
  Simplification items in this category refer to functions that are not available in SAP S/4HANA. In these cases, you can usually change to an alternative function already available in SAP ERP.

  An example of this category is the credit management function as described in Section 10.2.1. For system conversions to SAP S/4HANA, you'll have to consider changing to an alternative function and then implementing this function (for example, the advanced credit management

341

function, SAP Credit Management). For more information on potentially necessary credit management adaptations, see SAP Note 2270544.

- **Functions that do not map to the SAP S/4HANA target architecture**
  Simplification items in this category provide information on changes that are planned for SAP S/4HANA. This category includes functions from SAP ERP that are the same in the current SAP S/4HANA version but do not map to the target architecture. Usually, alternative functions are already available.

  An example in this category is the warehouse management function of SAP Warehouse Management (SAP WM, see Chapter 1, Section 1.3.2). You can continue to use this function after the SAP S/4HANA system conversion, but SAP WM is not part of the target architecture. The target warehouse management architecture is SAP Extended Warehouse Management (SAP EWM).

Distributed across the various categories, the simplification list for SAP S/4HANA 1610 contains about 400 simplification items. Figure 10.7 shows how simplification items are distributed among these categories.

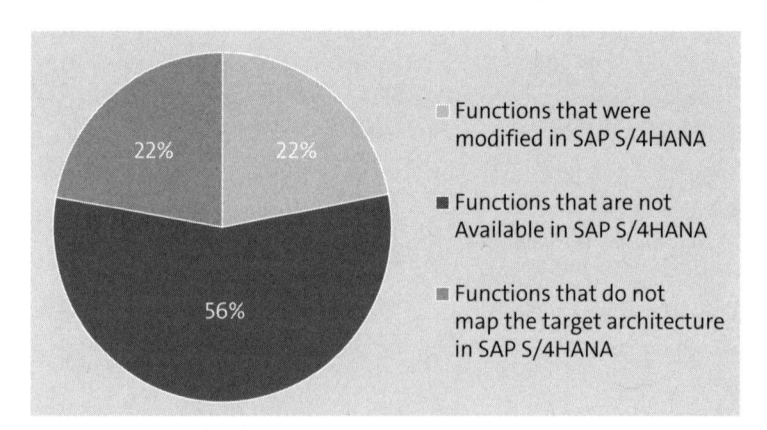

Figure 10.7 Simplification List Categories

Figure 10.8 shows how simplification items are distributed among functional areas.

Bar Chart: Simplification Items by Application Area

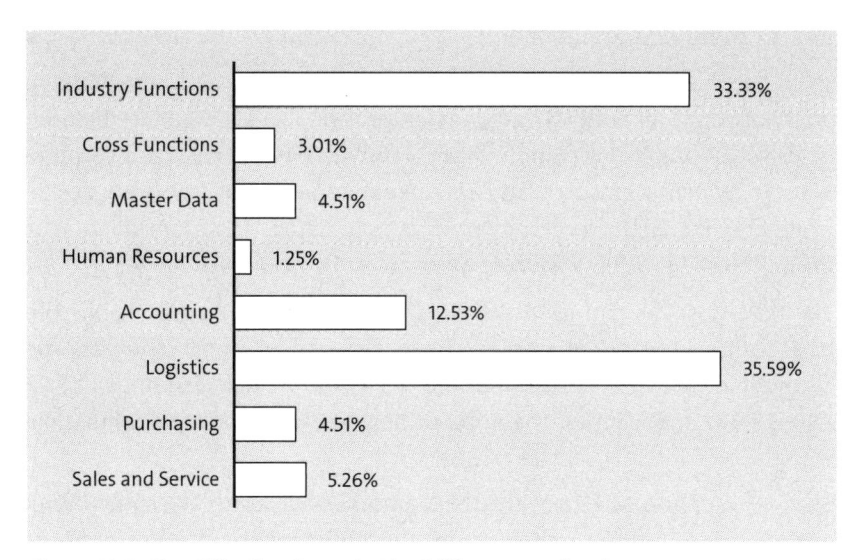

- Industry Functions: 33.33%
- Cross Functions: 3.01%
- Master Data: 4.51%
- Human Resources: 1.25%
- Accounting: 12.53%
- Logistics: 35.59%
- Purchasing: 4.51%
- Sales and Service: 5.26%

Figure 10.8 Simplification Items in the Different Application Areas

Our experience from previous SAP S/4HANA conversion projects has shown that the average number of simplification items that customers may need to adapt is between 30 and 50.

> **Additional Information**
>
> The SAP S/4HANA documentation for each release includes the simplification list as a comprehensive PDF document: *https://help.sap.com/s4hana*. In addition, the simplification list is also available in XLS format (including the corresponding application components) in SAP Note 2313884.
>
> Each simplification item has a corresponding SAP Note (so-called *business impact notes*) that provides basic information and sometimes additional information and how-to guides. You can find the appropriate SAP Notes in the XLS document. Examples of individual business impact notes for simplification items include the following:
>
> - SAP Note 2265093 (S4TWL – Business Partner Approach)
> - SAP Note 2270544 (S4TWL – Credit Management

10.2.3 Maintenance Planner

Planning and simulation
Using the Maintenance Planner is the first step in the prepare and planning phase of your SAP S/4HANA conversion project. The Maintenance Planner helps you simulate and plan the system conversion. The result is a comprehensive system landscape and maintenance plan. You can also decide whether to install the frontend server as a separate SAP Fiori installation or in combination with the backend server (see Chapter 9, Section 9.3).

The maintenance plan generated in the Maintenance Planner forms the basis for the subsequent steps in the system conversion. In addition, the Maintenance Planners checks the add-ons currently installed on your SAP ERP system and whether the enabled business functions are compatible with the SAP S/4HANA target release.

Customer landscape access
The SAP Support Portal provides the Maintenance Planner as a cloud-based application. Figure 10.9 shows how the Maintenance Planner accesses information about the customer landscape.

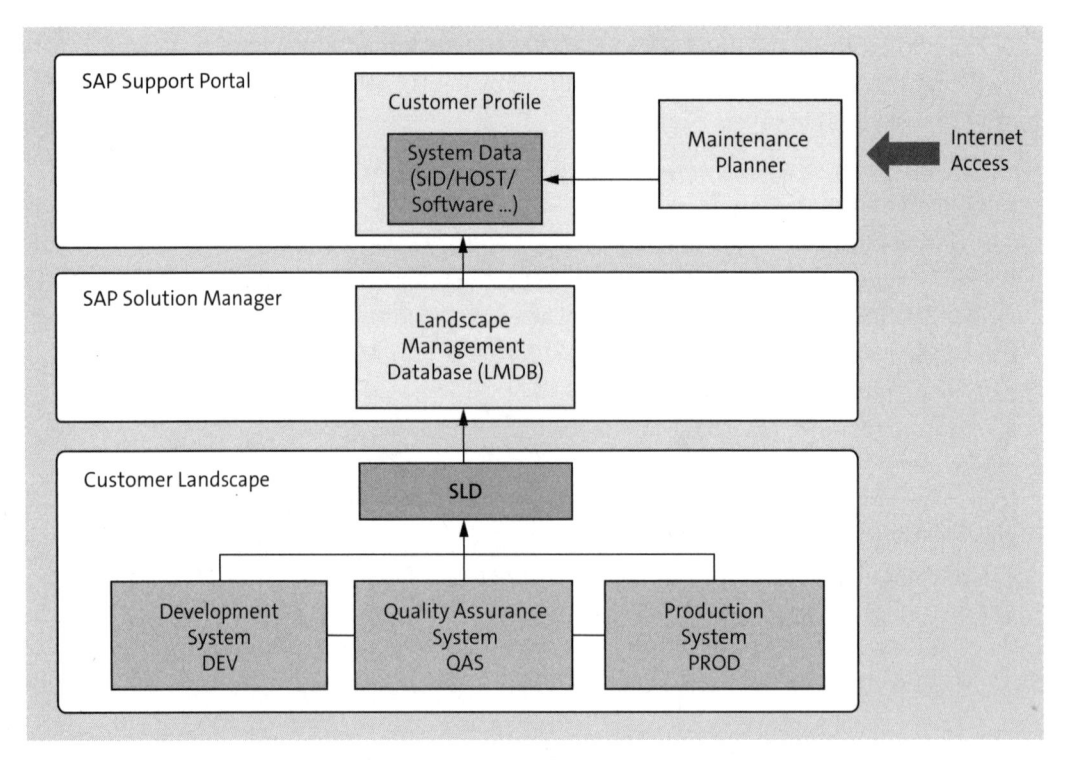

Figure 10.9 System Landscape with Maintenance Planner

The Maintenance Planner accesses the landscape data stored in your customer profile in the SAP Support Portal. The system landscape data in your customer profile is regularly updated via the *Landscape Management Database* (LMDB) of SAP Solution Manager and the *System Landscape Directory* (SLD) of your landscape. To access your individual customer data, you'll require an S-User for the SAP Support Portal (or its predecessor, SAP Service Marketplace). The SAP Solution Manager user must be assigned to the S-User.

Call the Maintenance Planner as described in Chapter 9, Section 9.1, and select the **Plan an SAP S/4HANA conversion of an existing system** option to plan a single system conversion. In the guided steps, enter the SAP ERP system you want to convert, select the SAP S/4HANA target release, and specify the frontend server for the SAP Fiori user interface. After entering this information in the Maintenance Planner, you'll receive the maintenance plan and a so-called *stack XML*, which contains information on the calculated start and target combinations. The maintenance plan is also available as a PDF document that includes a link to the SAP S/4HANA software that you want to install. You'll need the stack XML that was generated in the Maintenance Planner during the system conversion. You can use the stack XML for the prechecks (which we recommend) and will use the stack XML in SUM to ensure that only compatible maintenance operations can be executed.

Maintenance plan

Not only can you use the Maintenance Planner to plan your future system landscape, you can use its guided procedure to check the add-ons currently installed on your SAP ERP system (SAP add-ons or partner add-ons) and whether the enabled business functions are compatible with the SAP S/4HANA target release. If add-ons or business functions in your SAP ERP source system are not (yet) supported by SAP S/4HANA, the Maintenance Planner will output an error message. However, future support for currently unsupported add-ons and business functions may be expected, so you should contact SAP or your partner provider. In some cases, you can also uninstall add-ons that are installed but no longer used to proceed with the system conversion.

Supported add-ons and business functions

If you have business functions active on your SAP ERP source system with the ALWAYS_OFF status in the SAP S/4HANA target release, you will not be able to convert the system to SAP S/4HANA. With SAP S/4HANA 1610, however, you'll rarely encounter this problem.

10 System Conversion

> [»] **Additional Information**
>
> You can find additional information, links to blogs in the SAP Community Hub, and best practice guides in the SAP documentation for the Maintenance Planner at: *http://help.sap.com/maintenanceplanner*.
>
> SAP Note 2214409 provides more information on supported SAP add-ons, and SAP Note 2392527 contains details on supported partner add-ons. Note that SAP cannot make any compatibility statements for uncertified partner add-ons. Consequently, the Maintenance Planner outputs a warning message for this category of partner add-ons. SAP Note 2240359 provides further information on this procedure.

10.2.4 Prechecks

SAP S/4HANA Pre-Transition Checks (prechecks) let you evaluate the adaptation requirements for your business processes when migrating to SAP S/4HANA. The prechecks are SAP programs (delivered in SAP Notes) installed and executed on the SAP ERP source system release, which will output a results log. These results correspond to simplification items, which we discussed in Section 10.2.2.

Tasks of prechecks   Prechecks are responsible for two tasks: identifying the relevant simplification items for the system conversion and ensuring that tasks that need to be executed before the system conversion are actually performed.

An example of a task that needs to be executed before the system conversion is included in the simplification item for the customer/vendor integration for business partners (see SAP Note 2265093). In SAP S/4HANA, SAP business partners must be used to benefit from IT-related advantages such as nonredundancy and data integrity. The corresponding precheck (provided in SAP Note 2210486) verifies whether a business partner exists for each customer and vendor. This precheck results in a list of customer and vendor masters that have not been implemented yet.

Time of the execution   You'll execute prechecks in the conversion project twice. You can (and should) first execute them in the prepare phase of the project ❶. Additionally, further prechecks are automatically executed in the execution phase ❷, called automatically by SUM when checking the prerequisites. If the mandatory activities have not been performed or if the prechecks have

10.2 Converting Single Systems

not been installed in the target system, the conversion procedures will pause, and an error log will be output.

For example, implementing customer/vendor master records for SAP business partners is a mandatory activity. Implementing this master data is a prerequisite for converting existing application data to the new data structure. Figure 10.10 shows when the prechecks are executed for the system conversion.

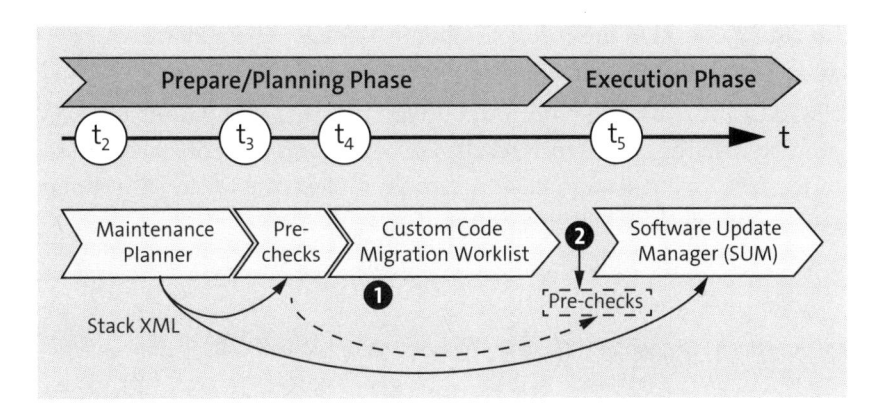

Figure 10.10 Execution of Prechecks

When executing the prechecks in the prepare phase (which we recommend), you can provide the conversion path if you include the stack XML that was generated in the Maintenance Planner. Based on the stack XML file, the SAP S/4HANA target release is taken into account when prechecks are executed, which can have an impact on the results log.

Stack XML for the target release

Executing Prechecks in the Prepare and Planning Phase

SAP Note 2182725 provides the central check report, R_S4_PRE_TRANSITION_CHECKS. Follow these steps to execute the prechecks:

Procedure

1. Implement SAP Note 2182725 (and all detailed notes listed therein) in Client 000 of all systems (i.e., DEV, QA, and PRD) of the system landscape you want to convert to SAP S/4HANA.

2. Execute the R_S4_PRE_TRANSITION_CHECKS program in the client of all systems (using Transaction SE38 or Transaction SA38). Ensure that you are using the latest version of SAP Note 2182725.

347

To use information from the maintenance plan (for example, the target release), you should also use the stack XML that was generated in the Maintenance Planner to execute the prechecks in the planning phase. In general, the checks in accounting are also executed using the R_S4_PRE_TRANSITION_CHECKS report. Note, however, that the check for Asset Accounting (FI-AA) needs to be implemented and executed separately. For this purpose, implement the report provided in SAP Note 2333236.

Executing Checks in the Software Update Manager Check Phase

As described in the previous section, SUM will call and execute the prechecks again. Only if the prechecks do not have negative results will SUM proceed with the next step. If results are negative or if the precheck classes in the conversion system have not been implemented using SAP Notes, postprocessing work will be required.

> **Additional Information**
>
> The check logic we described in this section is relevant for system conversions to SAP S/4HANA 1511, 1610, and higher releases. You can find more information on the check logic for converting SAP S/4HANA Finance 1605 in the documentation at *https://help.sap.com/sfin*.
>
> The SAP S/4HANA Community blog at *https://blogs.sap.com/2016/12/10/pre-checks-in-system-conversion/* also provides detailed information and instructions.

10.2.5 Adapting Custom Developments

Enterprises run business processes that differ from customer to customer and have had to adjust their SAP ERP system to these processes in the best possible way. In the past, enterprises frequently developed custom programs if the SAP Standard could not map these specific requirements.

The majority of SAP ERP systems probably contain additional custom program logic. SAP ERP provides various custom enhancement options from user and customer exits to Business Add-Ins (BAdIs) to modification of SAP Standard objects.

Custom code migration worklist

However, these enhancement options affect the release compatibility and the work required when changes are released. As with business functions, you'll also have to check whether your customer-specific ABAP developments are still compatible with SAP S/4HANA's data structure and functional scope when migrating to SAP S/4HANA. To check this compatibility, SAP provides the *custom code migration worklist*, a basic tool that enables you to check your enhancements, modifications, or custom developments for compatibility before the system conversion.

However, you should also leverage the migration to SAP S/4HANA to analyze your customer-specific ABAP developments in general. For example, modifying custom programs without checking whether they are used does not make sense. As a result, you should always carefully check automated inspection programs and service offers that some consulting firms provide for SAP S/4HANA conversions.

Basic usage check

We recommend performing these steps for analyzing and adapting your customer-specific ABAP developments for the system conversion in the following order:

Procedure

1. Analyzing and adapting custom developments in general:
   - Transparency for custom developments (not used/hardly used, standard custom development)
   - Optimization of custom developments (scale back, proven methods, performance optimizations)
2. Analyzing and adapting custom developments for the database migration to SAP HANA:
   - Adaptation of custom developments that use specific characteristics of the predecessor database
   - Performance optimizations on the basis of SAP HANA
3. Analyzing and adapting custom developments for the migration to SAP S/4HANA:
   - Adaptation of custom developments that are no longer mapped in the solution scope and data structure of SAP S/4HANA
   - Optional adaptation of custom developments with regard to functions that are not included in the target architecture of SAP S/4HANA
   - Analysis and implementation of possible performance optimizations

---

Additional Information

The following link provides information about the custom code adaptation process with links to related information: *https://blogs.sap.com/2017/02/15/sap-s4hana-system-conversion-custom-code-adaptation-process/*.

10 System Conversion

Analyzing and Adapting Custom Developments in General

Disadvantages of custom developments

Depending optimization needs, SAP customers have enhanced, modified, or added custom logic to standard business processes. This individual business process optimization can lead to increased costs for operating SAP software. For example, additional effort might be required for custom developments when releases are upgraded and support packages need to be installed. In general, system complexity increases with the number of custom developments. Considering the costs of custom developments, be sure to check them at regular intervals. As our experience from various customer projects have shown, 30% to 50% of custom programs are not used at all after a few years.

Transparency for custom developments

Consequently, you should first obtain an overview of your custom developments. You should always perform this basic task when migrating to SAP S/4HANA. To create this overview, use the *SAP Custom Code Lifecycle Management tool set* (CCLM) to analyze and manage the lifecycle of custom developments. *Usage Procedure Logging* (UPL) allows you to gain detailed usage information on custom objects.

Optimization of custom developments

Based on these analyses, you can now optimize your custom developments. The *Decommissioning Cockpit* lets you identify redundant or obsolete development objects and remove them from the customer system. You should also check whether your custom developments still in use correspond to the recommended programming and performance guidelines (best practices). Furthermore, you should determine whether your customer-specific enhancements can now be mapped by SAP Standard processes.

Begin in the prepare phase

Of course, you can also perform these optimization tasks prior to the actual SAP S/4HANA conversion project. When migrating to SAP S/4HANA, you should also make yourself familiar with the new enhancement options in SAP S/4HANA, which were introduced in Chapter 3, Section 3.4.

> [»] **Additional Information**
>
> You can find blogs on enhancements and exchange information in the ABAP Development Community at:
>
> - https://www.sap.com/community/topic/abap.html
>
> You can find information about Usage Procedure Logging (UPL) at the following link:

- http://bit.ly/v1448101

For SAP Best Practices for the Decommissioning Cockpit, go to:

- https://archive.sap.com/documents/docs/DOC-60525

Analyzing and Adapting Custom Developments for the Database Migration to SAP HANA

Migrating to the SAP HANA database and the related database architecture changes (i.e., from a row-based to a column-based database) can affect custom developments. Although ABAP code continues to run on SAP HANA, you'll have to adapt the custom developments that use specific characteristics of the predecessor database. Examples include:

Adjusting native database functions

- **Usage of native SQL**
  You'll have to replace native SQL statements.

- **Implicit sorting of results lists**
  You should insert explicit ORDER BY statements instead.

- **Direct access to pool and cluster tables**
  You'll have to modify code from pool and cluster tables.

In addition, you should analyze the performance optimization options in the SAP HANA database. Examples include:

Performance optimizations

- **Optimization of SELECT statements**
  You should replace general SELECT* FROM statements with SELECT statements with a restriction to the mandatory fields.

- **Use the code pushdown option**
  You should analyze whether so-called *code pushdown methods* can be leveraged, that is, whether the data calculation logic can be moved to the SAP HANA database. Code pushdown methods use CDS technology (Core Data Services) and SQLScript.

To identify conversions that are mandatory or recommended for the database migration to SAP HANA, SAP Note 1935918 provides three check variants (FUNCTIONAL_DB, FUNCTIONAL_DB_ADDITION, PERFORMANCE_DB) for the *Code Inspector*.

Code Inspector

The Code Inspector (which you can call using Transaction SCI, for example) is a generic tool to check repository objects for various aspects of static code. The *SQL Monitor*, which is available in SAP NetWeaver 7.40 (see SAP

10 System Conversion

Note 1885926 for earlier releases), enables you to analyze the SQL statements in your customer systems.

> **[o] Optimizing Custom Code Using SAP Standard Tools**
>
> You can analyze your custom developments and prepare for migration before you start the actual SAP S/4HANA conversion project. The corresponding tools are available in SAP NetWeaver.

> **[»] Additional Information**
>
> To adapt custom developments for the migration to SAP HANA, see SAP Note 1912445. You can access a sample scenario at the following link:
>
> - https://blogs.sap.com/2013/01/28/abap-for-sap-hana-reference-scenario/
>
> For more information on code pushdown, go to:
>
> - https://blogs.sap.com/2014/02/03/abap-for-hana-code-push-down/
>
> For more on optimizing ABAP applications for SAP HANA, read *ABAP Development for SAP HANA* by Gahm, Schneider, Westenberger, and Swanepoel (2nd edition, SAP PRESS, 2016, *www.sap-press.com/3973*).
>
> For more information on SAP HANA database migrations, go to:
>
> - https://archive.sap.com/documents/docs/DOC-47444
>
> For more information on the Code Inspector, go to
>
> - https://wiki.scn.sap.com/wiki/display/ABAP/Code%2BInspector

Analyzing and Adapting Custom Developments for the Migration to SAP S/4HANA

Custom code migration worklist

Due to SAP S/4HANA's new data structures and functional simplifications, you might have to adapt your existing custom developments when migrating to SAP S/4HANA. The *custom code migration worklist* identifies which custom developments you'll need to adjust for migrating to SAP S/4HANA. Separate SAP Notes with instructions for the code adaptations are available for each adaptation result in the custom code migration worklist.

The custom code migration worklist contains migration tasks for custom developments. Based on Code Inspector technology, customer-specific

10.2 Converting Single Systems

repository objects are checked to determine if they use SAP entities that will change after migrating to SAP S/4HANA. Figure 10.11 provides an overview of how customer-specific ABAP developments are checked.

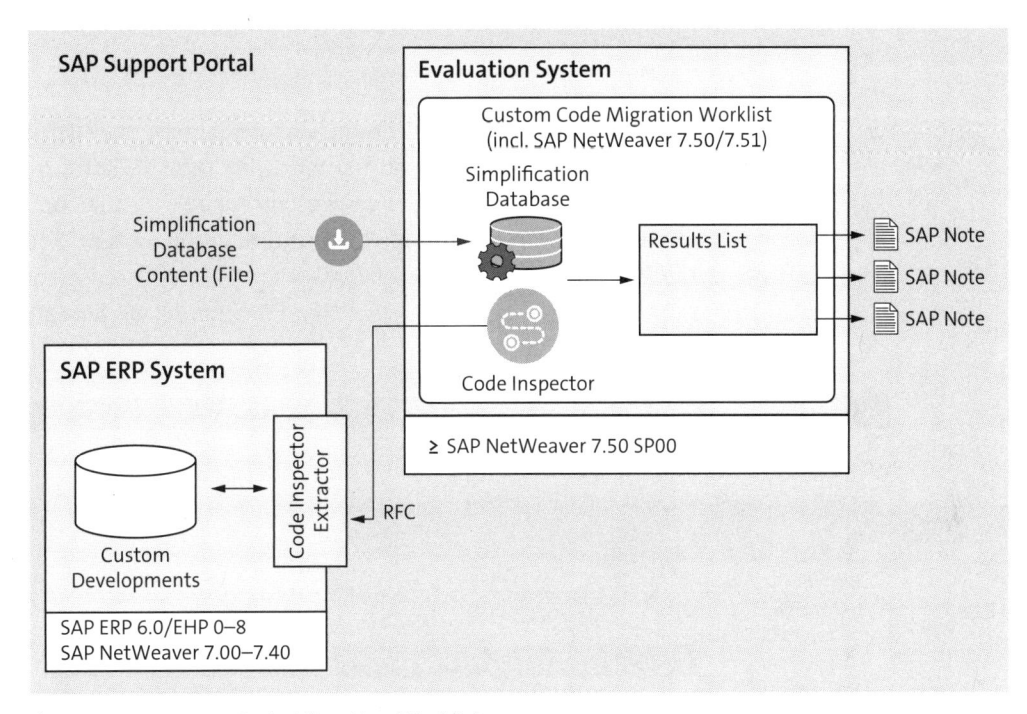

Figure 10.11 Custom Code Migration Worklist

1. SAP entities that change with the migration to SAP S/4HANA are available as files in the SAP Support Portal (for more information, see SAP Note 2241080) and are imported to the so-called *simplification database* of the custom code migration worklist.

2. The Code Inspector accesses the update information in an evaluation system (a customer system based on SAP NetWeaver 7.50 or higher) with the relevant SAP S/4HANA check variants (S4HANA_READINESS). Customer objects in the connected SAP ERP system are accessed via a remote connection.

3. After the Code Inspector check has been executed, you'll receive a results list containing the required adaptation items. References to the corresponding SAP Notes describe the relevant adaptation requirements for your custom developments.

10 System Conversion

> **Additional Information on the Custom Code Check**
>
> You can find up-to-date custom code check content (i.e., simplification database content) in the SAP Support Portal. SAP Note 2241080 provides information on how and where you can download the content.

Simplification database

SAP provides the SAP S/4HANA simplification database content as a ZIP file on the SAP Support Portal. To download the file, open the SAP Software Download Center (*https://support.sap.com/swdc*) and search for the component "CCMSIDB." Then, upload the file to your evaluation system. You can import the ZIP file using the `SYCM_UPLOAD_SIMPLIFIC_INFO` report or Transaction SYCM. In the transaction, choose **Simplification DB • Import ZIP File** (see Figure 10.12).

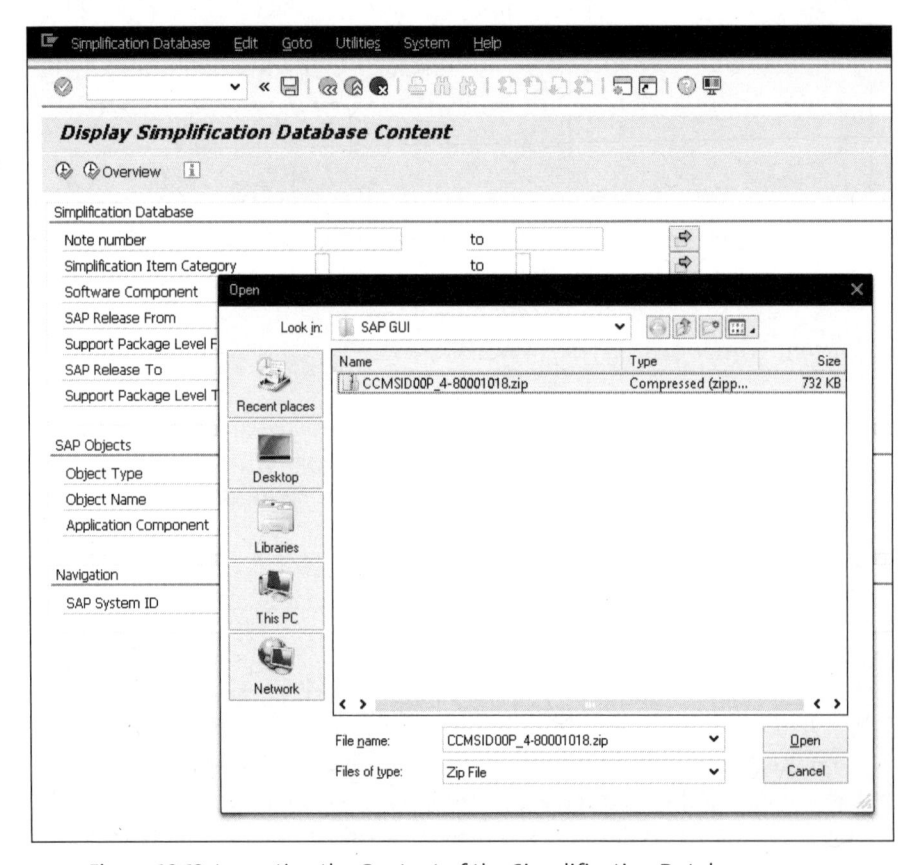

Figure 10.12 Importing the Content of the Simplification Database

10.2 Converting Single Systems

Because SAP allows you to download the update information in a ZIP file, you can access this information anytime whether you use SAP S/4HANA already or not. SAP updates the ZIP file with every SAP S/4HANA release, feature package, and support package. You should therefore always use the most current version of the ZIP file.

You can analyze your custom developments using the Code Inspector (Transaction SCI). Based on the check variants provided for SAP S/4HANA, you can determine the set of objects to analyze and start the inspection run. The inspection run takes place in the evaluation system, which is based on SAP NetWeaver 7.50 or 7.51. From the evaluation system, the Code Inspector accesses objects in your SAP Business Suite system via a remote connection. Figure 10.13 shows the entry screen of the SAP Code Inspector with a check variant, the set of objects, and the inspection run.

Analysis in the Code Inspector

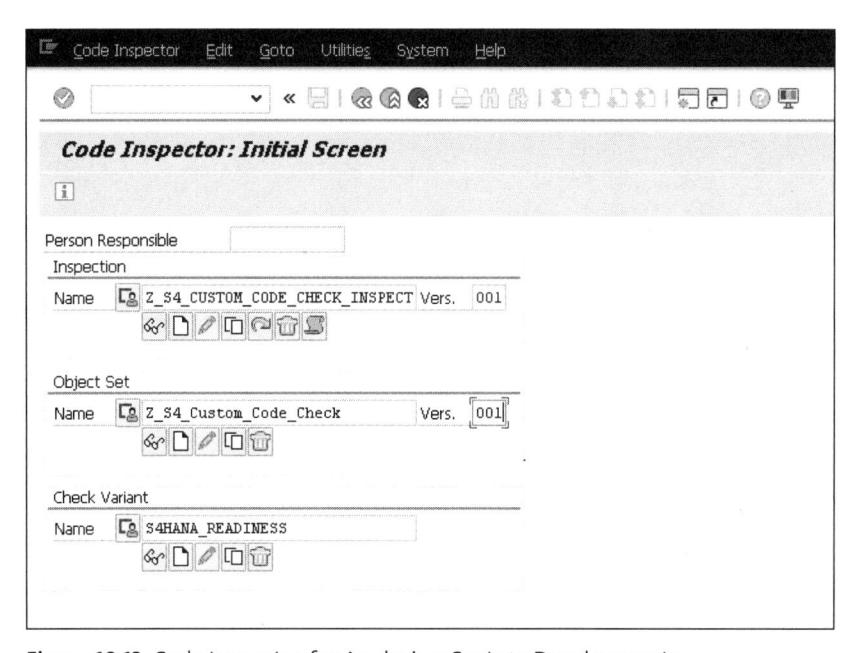

Figure 10.13 Code Inspector for Analyzing Custom Developments

The S4HANA_READINESS check variant (see Figure 10.14), which is provided in SAP NetWeaver 7.51, allows you to compare custom objects to updated information for SAP S/4HANA. The included test variant, **S/4HANA: Search**

Check variant S4HANA_READINESS

355

10 System Conversion

for usages of simplified objects, checks custom developments by comparing them to the content of the simplification database.

S/4HANA: Field length extensions is an additional test variant that specifically checks for places in custom code that refer to the material number with 40 characters in SAP S/4HANA (see the example in Section 10.2.2).

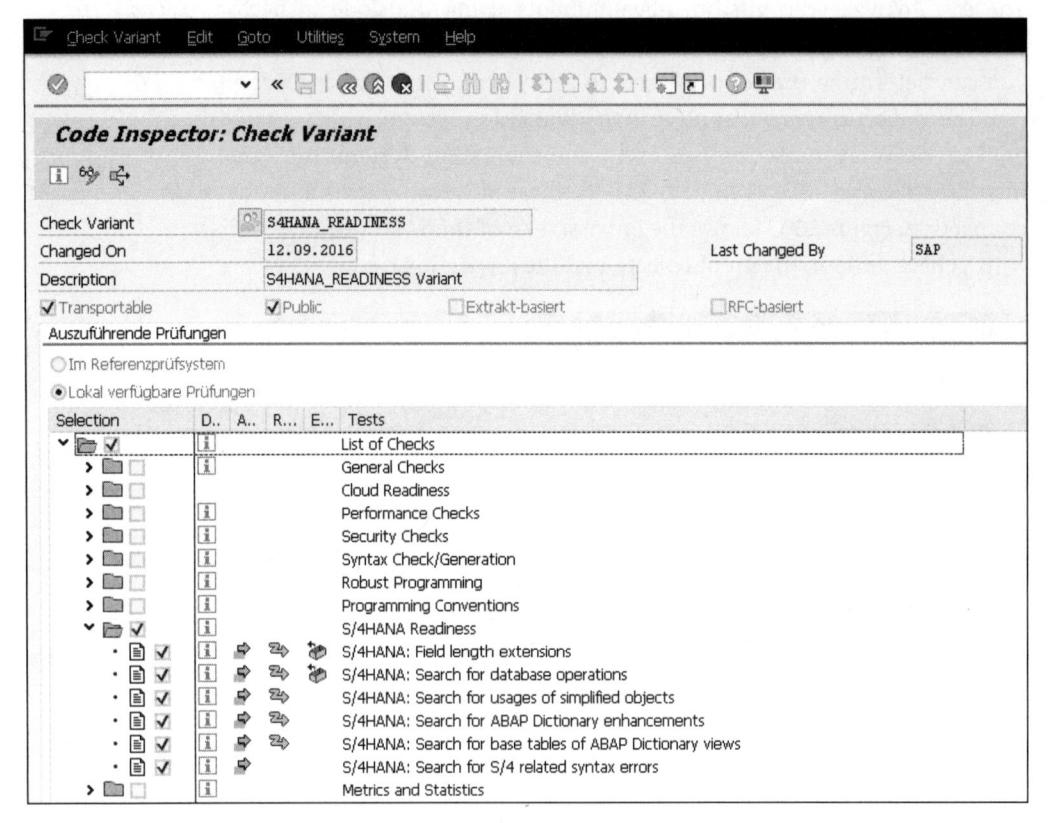

Figure 10.14 Check Variant S4HANA_READINESS

To analyze your custom developments, you should restrict the set of objects to be evaluated, for example, to packages in the Z namespace, as shown in Figure 10.15.

The check variant and the set of objects to be analyzed are merged in an inspection run, as shown in Figure 10.16.

10.2 Converting Single Systems

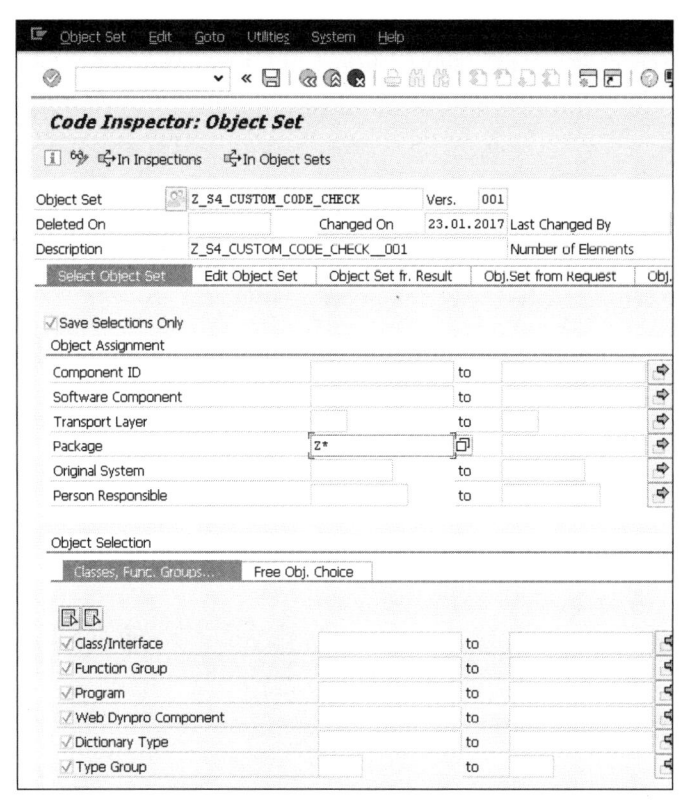

Figure 10.15 Restricting the Set of Objects

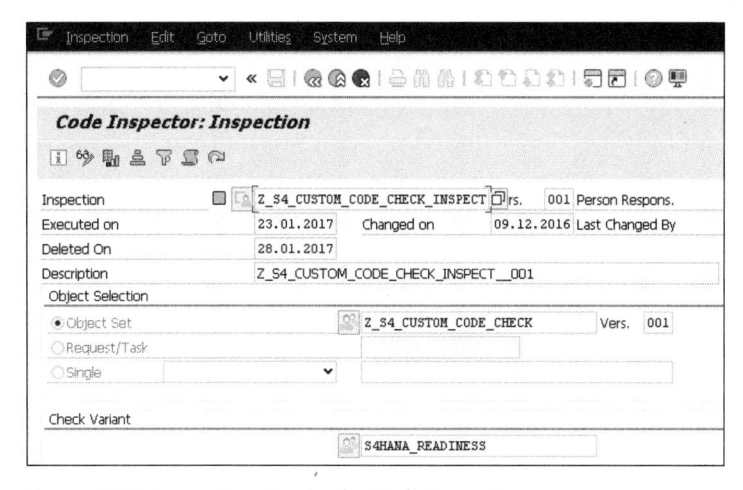

Figure 10.16 Inspection Run in the Code Inspector

10 System Conversion

Results list   As a result, the inspection run outputs a list of the custom developments that need to be checked and probably adapted (see Figure 10.17). The results list does not include customer objects that are not affected by changes in SAP S/4HANA.

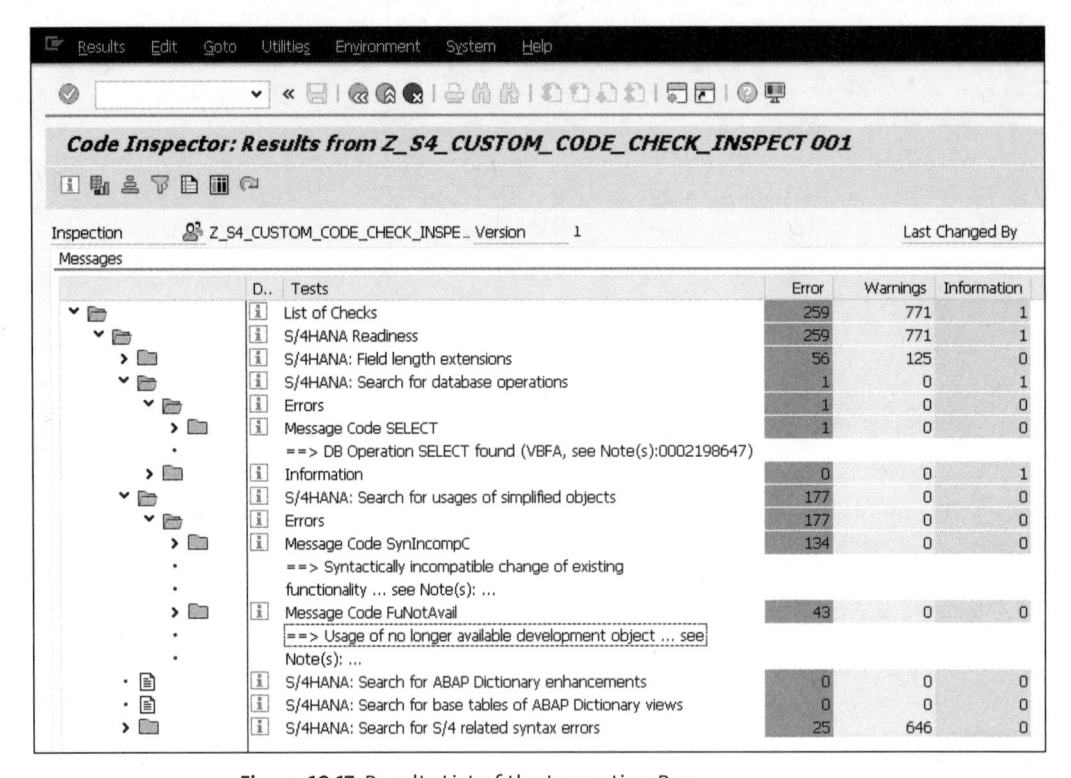

Figure 10.17 Results List of the Inspection Run

Adaptation recommendations   In our example, the Code Inspector statistics indicate that about 25,000 objects in the Z namespace were analyzed in 13 minutes. The Code Inspector found that 259 objects of the 1,000 objects probably needed to be adapted. The results list breakdown shows details about the objects. In our example, 43 recommendations refer to SAP development objects that are no longer available in SAP S/4HANA. For each object in the results list, an SAP Note is provided that explains in detail which adaptations you'll have to make for this type of object. Adaptations notes can include the following information, for example:

- Adaptations resulting from the extension of the material number to 40 characters:
  - SAP Note 2215424 (Field Length Extension for Material Number—General Information)
  - SAP Note 2215852 (Field Length Extension for Material Number—Source Text Adjustments)
- Adaptations resulting from data model changes in Sales and Distribution (SD):
  - SAP Note (SAP S/4 HANA—Changing the Data Model in Sales and Distribution)
- Adaptations resulting from data model changes in inventory management:
  - SAP Note 2206980 (Stock Management: Changing the Data Model in SAP S/4HANA)

A list of modified SAP objects is maintained, and a corresponding adaptation note is provided, for each change that affects your custom developments described in a simplification item.

You can view the total list of modified SAP objects for SAP S/4HANA using Transaction SYCM. However, to do so, the ZIP file with the simplification database content must be imported. The list provides the type of modification (has the function or data structure changed, or is the function no longer available?) and the corresponding adaptation note for each SAP object. Table 10.1 illustrates this concept with some example SAP objects.

Total list of changed SAP objects

SAP Object	SAP Object Name	Change Category	Adaptation SAP Note	Note Name
FUNC	FT_BASIC_OBJECTS_READ_DB	Function not available	2223144	SD Foreign Trade
PROG	MV52AF01 total	Function not available	2223144	SD Foreign Trade
TABL	MAZO	Function not available	2223144	SD Foreign Trade
...	...	Function not available	2223144	SD Foreign Trade

Table 10.1 Sample Information in the Object List of the Change Database

10   System Conversion

SAP Object	SAP Object Name	Change Category	Adaptation SAP Note	Note Name
FUNC	/BEV1/RP_MIGERP01	Function not available	2224144	Beverage solution
PROG	/DSD/ME_CPT	Function not available	2224144	Beverage solution
TABL	/BEV1/CAMF	Function not available	2224144	Beverage solution
…	…	Function not available	2224144	Beverage solution
TABL	FDSB	Modified function	2270400	Cash Management
PROG	RFLQ_ASSIGN_FI	Modified function	2270400	Cash Management
…	…	Modified function	2270400	Cash Management
TABL	BSAD	Modified function	1976487	FIN data model
TABL	BSAK	Modified function	1976487	FIN data model
…	…	Modified function	1976487	FIN data model

Table 10.1 Sample Information in the Object List of the Change Database (Cont.)

Making necessary changes   Depending on the change category, the adaptation required varies. For customer projects that include functions that will be unavailable in SAP S/4HANA, you can assume that specific custom developments will become obsolete. As a result, you'll have to check during the conversion project whether the successor function provided by SAP S/4HANA covers the business process, and you'll have to consider alternative business process extensions. If the data structure has changed (for example, the material number extended to 40 characters), you'll have to adjust the custom code according to the specifications in the SAP Notes.

360

The update information for SAP objects in the ZIP file from the SAP Support Portal always contains information on the latest SAP S/4HANA release so that you can analyze your custom developments regardless of the desired SAP S/4HANA target release, for example, if you have not chosen an SAP S/4HANA target release yet but want to analyze your custom developments. In addition, you should also analyze your custom developments based on the latest update information early on in an SAP S/4HANA release upgrade project (for example, upgrading from SAP S/4HANA 1511 to SAP S/4HANA 1610).

Distribution of the Adaptation Tasks in the System Group

The following lists the individual adaptation tasks in the SAP ERP and SAP S/4HANA system groups.

You can carry out the activities from Table 10.2 as preparatory steps in your existing SAP ERP system group.

SAP ERP system group

System Role	Activity
PRD system	Activating analysis tools such as SQL Monitor (SQLM), Usage & Procedure Logging (UPL), and Workload Monitor (Transaction ST03)
DEV system	Analyzing custom developments considering three adaptation categories: - General analysis - Analyses with regard to the SAP HANA database - Analyses with regard to SAP S/4HANA Implementing the adaptations that can be made in your existing SAP ERP system group: - Deleting obsolete custom developments (using the Decommissioning Cockpit, for example) - Developing adaptations with regard to the SAP HANA database (based on the Code Inspector checks in Transaction SCI) - Developing adaptations with regard to SAP S/4HANA (based on the custom code migration worklist or Code Inspector checks)

Table 10.2 Preparatory Measures in the SAP ERP System Group

SAP S/4HANA system group The activities from Table 10.3 are then carried out in the SAP S/4HANA system group.

System Role	Activity		
	Before the Conversion	During the Conversion	After the Conversion
DEV system	Analyzing custom developments considering three adaptation categories: • General analysis and transparency • Analyses with regard to the SAP HANA database • Analyses with regard to SAP S/4HANA	• Adapting modified ABAP Dictionary objects (in Transaction SPDD) • Adapting custom developments to modified SAP S/4HANA data structures	• Adapting modified non-ABAP Dictionary objects (in Transaction SPAU) • Adapting custom developments to modified SAP S/4HANA data structures
QA system		• Installing transport requests with adaptations in Transactions SPDD and SPAU • Installing transport requests with SAP HANA or SAP S/4HANA adaptations	Functional tests and performance tests
PRD system		• Installing transport requests with adaptations in Transactions SPDD and SPAU • Installing transport requests with SAP HANA and SAP S/4HANA adaptations	

Table 10.3 Activities in the SAP S/4HANA System Group

10.2.6 Database Sizing for SAP S/4HANA

When migrating to SAP S/4HANA, you'll also have to migrate the SAP HANA database if you do not already operate your SAP ERP system with

SAP HANA. You'll have to procure the required hardware and perform appropriate sizing for the database server before migrating to SAP S/4HANA and consider these steps in your planning.

Various options are available for sizing the SAP HANA database. One option is the *Quick Sizer*—a web-based tool designed for sizing new implementations of SAP HANA-based systems. For more information on the Quick Sizer, go to *http://service.sap.com/quicksizer*.

Quick Sizer

For system conversions, choose the /SDF/HDB_SIZING ABAP sizing report, which is provided with SAP Note 1872170. This sizing report analyzes the SAP ERP source system's current memory and processing needs and outputs a report providing information on the requirements for the SAP HANA database.

Sizing report

Additional Information on Sizing

You can find more information on sizing for SAP HANA at *https://service.sap.com/sizing*.

In addition, read SAP Note 2303847 for more information on the /SDF/HDB_SIZING sizing report including guidelines and FAQs.

10.2.7 Using Software Update Manager

The *Software Update Manager* (SUM) performs the technical steps for converting a single system. SAP Basis administrators have known about SUM since 2011. SUM is designed to reduce downtimes during software installation. The steps that SUM performs for SAP S/4HANA system conversions do not differ from the steps that SUM performs for SAP Business Suite upgrades. This section therefore focuses on steps specific to SAP S/4HANA or that are new.

SAP S/4HANA System Conversion Steps in Software Update Manager (SUM)

In general, SUM carries out three core tasks of various system conversion phases in one step:

Three core tasks of SUM

1. **Converting the software to SAP S/4HANA**
   SUM installs the new SAP S/4HANA software on the SAP ERP source

system. For example, SUM replaces the SAP_APPL software component with the S4CORE SAP S/4HANA Basis component.

2. **Migration to the SAP HANA database**
If your SAP ERP system is based on a different database, SUM migrates the database to SAP HANA using the Software Update Manager *Database Migration Option* (DMO).

3. **Converting the application data to the new SAP S/4HANA data structure**
Because some data structures in SAP S/4HANA change (for example, data structure changes for stock management—table MATDOC), SUM converts the application data from the old data structure to the new data structure.

Figure 10.18 provides an overview of the different SUM phases.

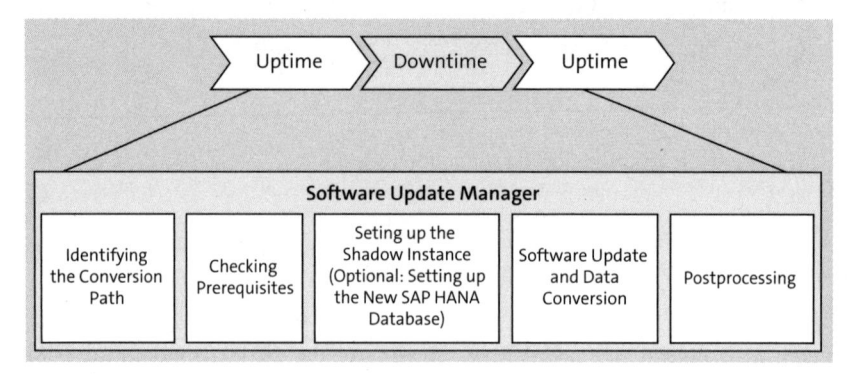

Figure 10.18 System Conversion Phases in SUM

Stack XML Based on the stack XML file generated in the Maintenance Planner, which contains the maintenance information, the system determines the best path to converting to SAP S/4HANA. Note that the conversion procedure cannot continue without the stack XML for the conversion system. Figure 10.19 shows the screen where you specify the location of the stack XML file.

In the first execution step, SUM analyzes prerequisites for the SAP S/4HANA system conversion. In addition to technical version checks for the operating system and the database version, SUM also analyzes the business requirements. The prechecks (see Section 10.2.4) are performed again. This check phase verifies, for example, whether the business partners have been assigned to customers and vendors. If not, the SUM procedure stops

10.2 Converting Single Systems

because this is a prerequisite for the next step: converting your application data from your old data structure to the new data structure in SAP S/4HANA.

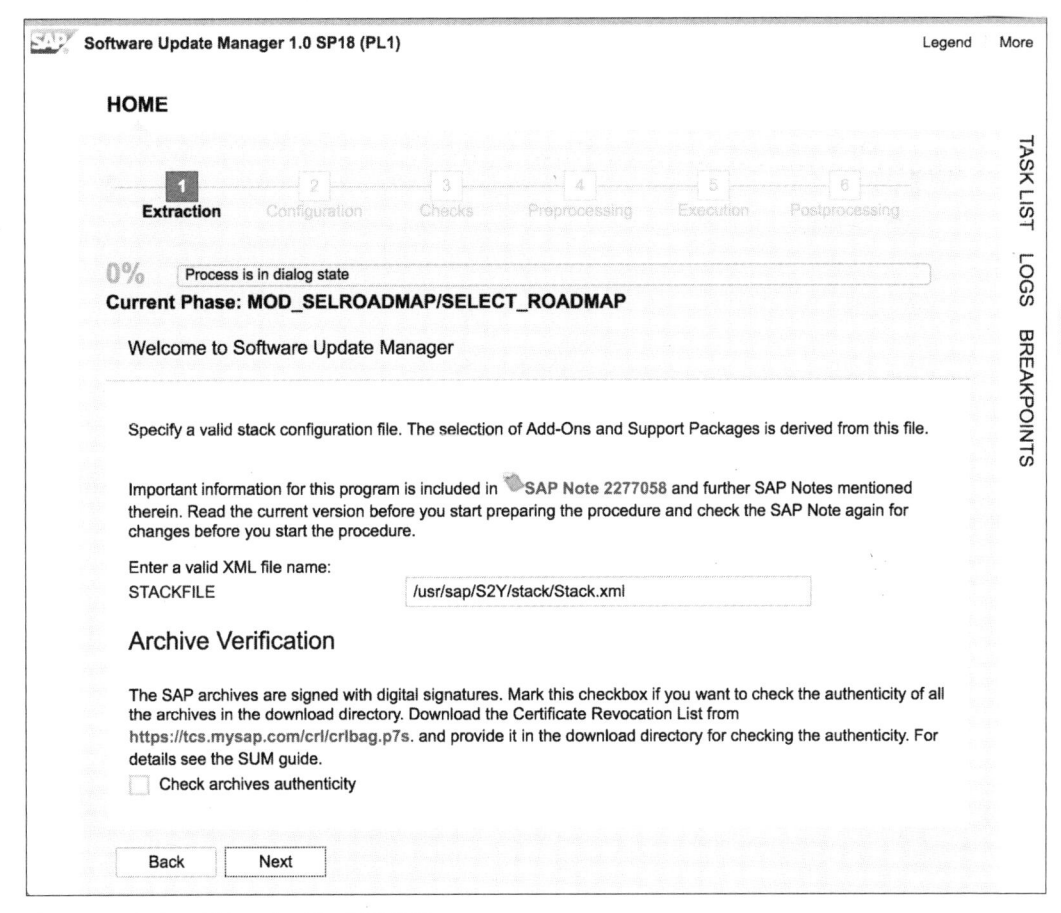

Figure 10.19 Specifying the Stack XML file

In general, the *system switch upgrade procedure* is used for the SAP S/4HANA system conversion. With this procedure, an additional instance of the target release (*shadow instance*) is generated parallel to the live system. On this shadow instance, various SAP S/4HANA system conversion steps are then performed. During these steps in SUM, the administrator will be asked to specify the relevant target information for the new database. Figure 10.20 shows the screen for entering the SAP system ID (SID) and instance number.

Analyzing the prerequisites
System switch upgrade procedure

365

10   System Conversion

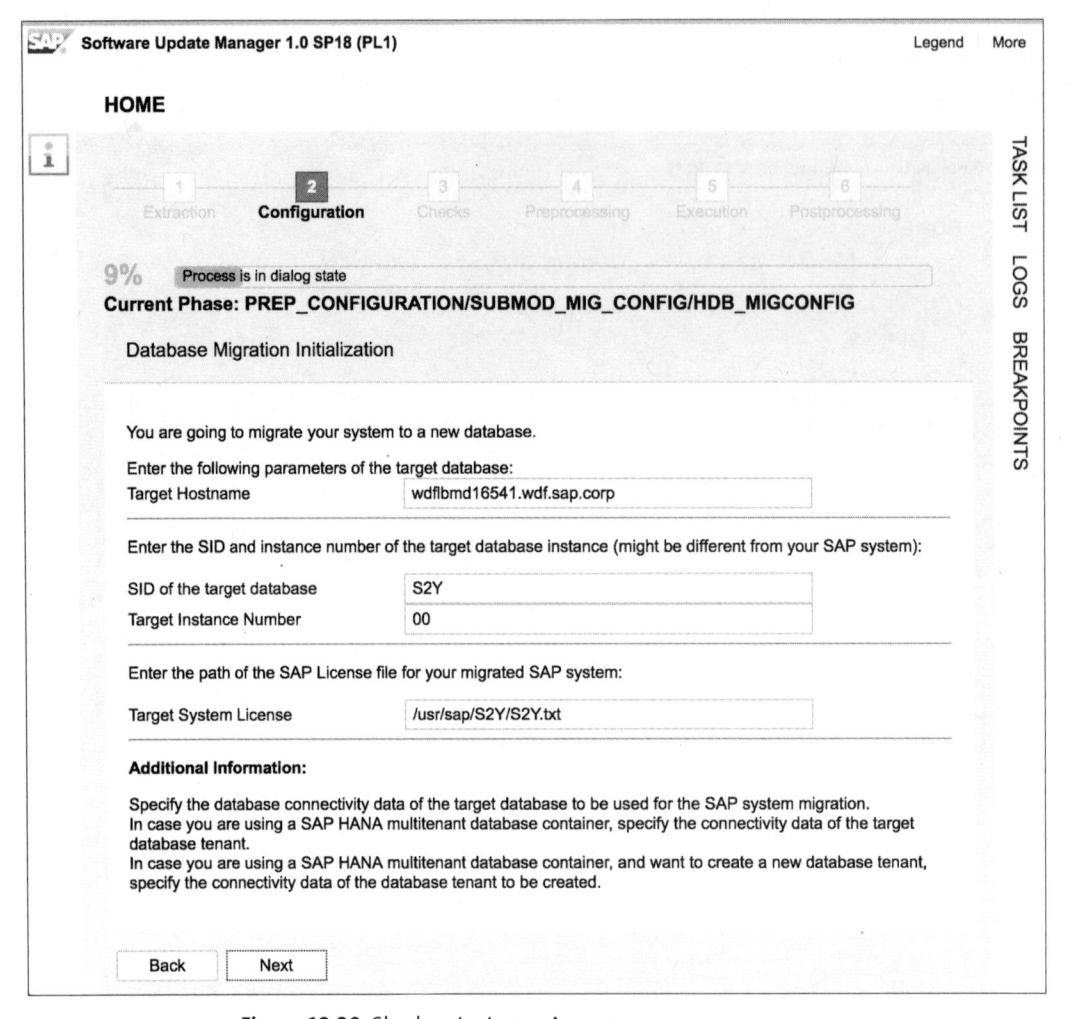

Figure 10.20 Shadow Instance Access

Downtime phase The SAP Basis tables from the target release are then installed on the shadow instance. In parallel to the activities performed by SUM on the shadow system, normal operations can continue in your SAP ERP production system. When the production system is shut down, the downtime phase of the system conversion starts. In this SUM phase, the application data is converted from the old data structure to the new data structure, for example. Ideally, you only see that the SUM execution process is running, as shown in Figure 10.21.

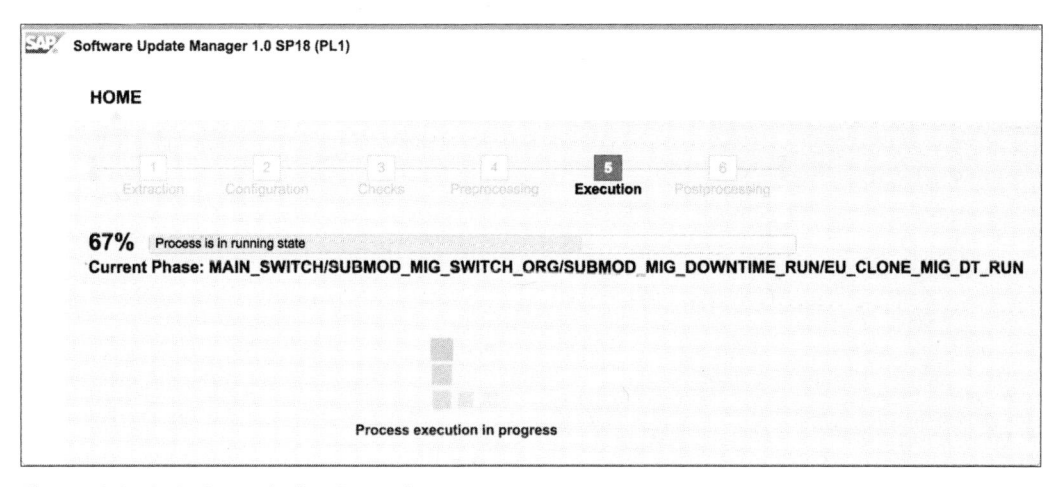

Figure 10.21 SUM Steps during Downtime

The length of downtime depends on various customer-specific factors and optimization measures implemented in the conversion system. For example, the system resources used, the database size, the number of application data to be converted, and basic factors such as the customer network play important roles in downtime. Of course, downtime also depends on the system category. For example, you could accept other downtimes and might reserve less system resources for converting a test system.

After all conversion steps have been performed successfully, the SUM execution phase is completed, and the system will display the final screen shown in Figure 10.22.

The end of the execution phase sets the stage for the postprocessing phase during downtime. One postprocessing task is to convert accounting and controlling data and their corresponding Customizing data. For more information on converting financial data, see SAP Note 2332030, which includes reference to a conversion guide for accounting.

Postprocessing

You can trace the execution of all steps in the SUM analysis file (*UPGANA.XML*), which provides detailed information on the system, the database size, and the runtimes of the individual SUM phases.

SUM analysis file

10 System Conversion

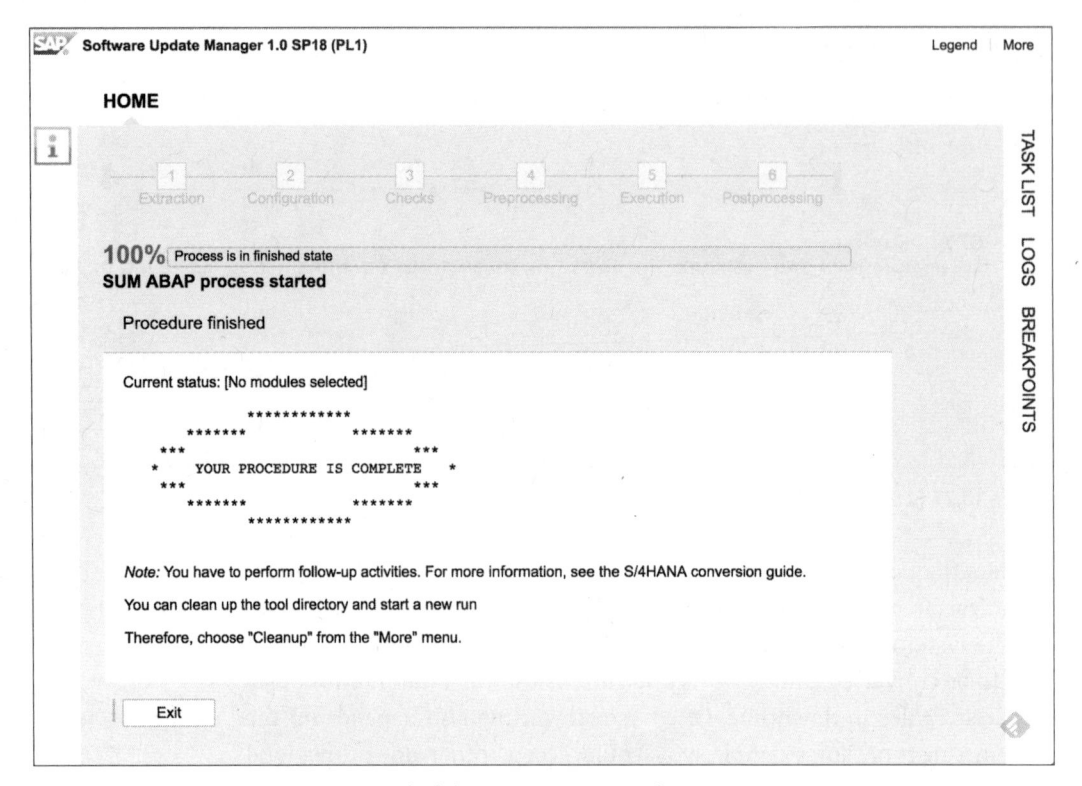

Figure 10.22 End of the SUM Execution Phase

The Different Procedures in Software Update Manager

SUM differentiates between three procedures and options for SAP S/4HANA system conversions:

- Default procedure
- Database Migration Option (DMO)
- Downtime-optimized procedure

Default procedure — The default procedure in SUM is when an additional shadow instance is generated on the same hardware to perform the conversion in parallel to running operations. You can use this default procedure (also referred to as *in-place migration*) for SAP S/4HANA if customers already use an SAP HANA database on their SAP ERP source system.

Database Migration Option (DMO) — If the SAP ERP system is based on a different database, SUM migrates the database to SAP HANA. For this purpose, the Database Migration Option

(DMO) is used. This SUM procedure is the same as the combined software update and database conversion within SAP Business Suite and is now also available for system conversions to SAP S/4HANA. In the first step, you'll generate a shadow instance on the database of the source system in parallel to running operations. Next, the new SAP HANA database is built in parallel and filled with data from the shadow instance. During downtime, you'll migrate your data to the new database. In SAP S/4HANA system conversions, you would then convert the application data to the new data structures. After these steps are completed and the postprocessing work done, you'll use the system as an SAP S/4HANA system on an SAP HANA database. The source database remains unchanged with this procedure and is available as a fallback solution.

To optimize downtimes, you should monitor system loads in test runs and optimize if required. The *DMO Migration Control Center* (see Figure 10.23) lets you monitor running `R3load` processes.

DMO Migration Control Center

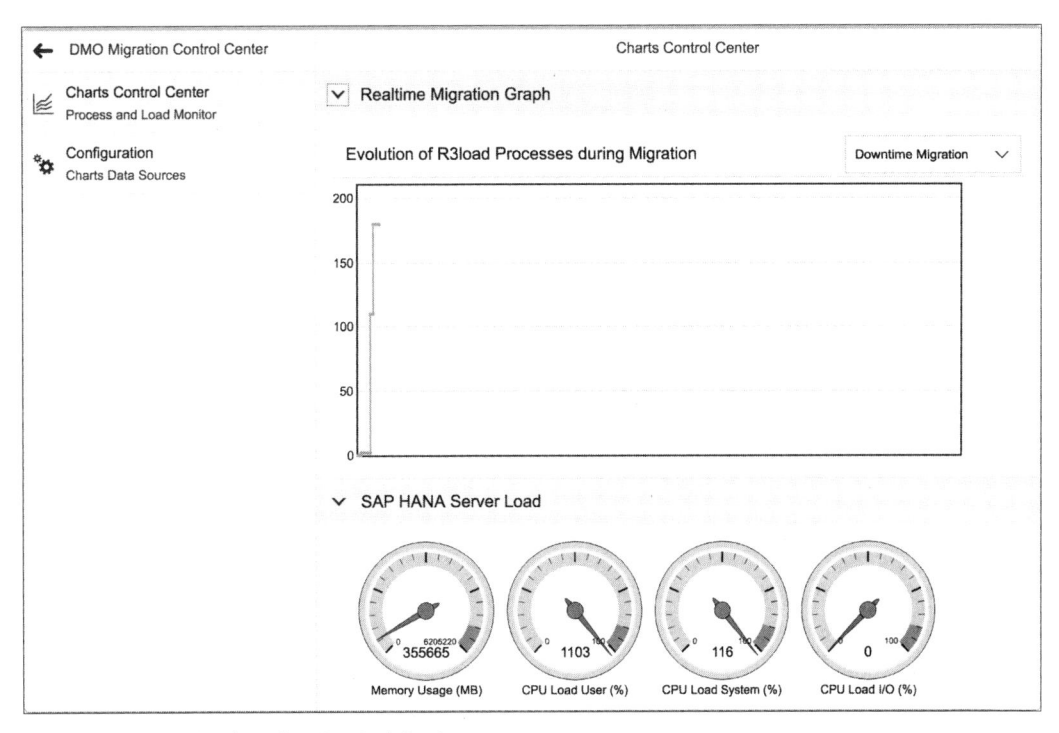

Figure 10.23 DMO Migration Control Center

10 System Conversion

Downtime-optimized procedure

The downtime-optimized procedure allows you to implement further optimizations and is currently provided as a pilot procedure but poses higher requirements on system resources. For selected applications, the application data is converted from the old data structure to the SAP S/4HANA data structure during uptime, that is, in parallel to running operations. With this procedure, you'll then only have to convert the new application data that accumulated during uptime and was recorded using a delta mechanism.

> [»] **Additional Information on Software Update Manager**
>
> You can find more information on the Software Update Manager (SUM) at:
>
> - *http://support.sap.com/sltoolset*
>
> The SAP Community Hub for SAP S/4HANA provides a SUM-specific blog at:
>
> - *https://blogs.sap.com/2015/11/24/system-conversion-to-sap-s4hana-sum-is-the-tool/*
>
> Also, you can read application-specific SAP Notes for system conversions. The following blog contains a collection of these SAP Notes:
>
> - *https://blogs.sap.com/2016/12/13/sap-s4hana-system-conversion-collective-notes/*

10.2.8 Migrating to SAP Fiori User Interfaces

SAP Fiori 2.0

The simplification resulting from migrating to SAP S/4HANA is also directly connected to the new user experience provided by SAP Fiori. In the fourth quarter of 2016, SAP published its second-generation user interface with SAP Fiori 2.0. The new interface schema, *Belize*, generates an even more attractive user experience.

Chapter 2, Section 2.4, discussed the basic characteristics of these user interfaces, while this section explains how to switch from traditional, SAP GUI-based user interfaces to the new SAP Fiori interfaces. First, you'll have to perform basic installation steps for SAP Fiori. A relevance analysis helps you determine which SAP Fiori apps are relevant for you. This relevance analysis is based on your transaction usage statistics. When implementing the SAP Fiori apps, you can migrate the applications gradually depending on the requirements of your users.

10.2 Converting Single Systems

Installing SAP Fiori during the SAP S/4HANA Conversion

To use SAP Fiori, you'll have to install it when converting to SAP S/4HANA. As described in Chapter 9, Section 9.3, you'll need to install a frontend server.

After installing SAP Fiori components, you can configure the infrastructure including SAP Fiori launchpad. Analogous to installing SAP S/4HANA, the installation is integrated into the software logistics tools of the Maintenance Planner and Software Update Manager. Figure 10.24 illustrates selecting an installation variant in the Maintenance Planner.

Installation in the Maintenance Planner

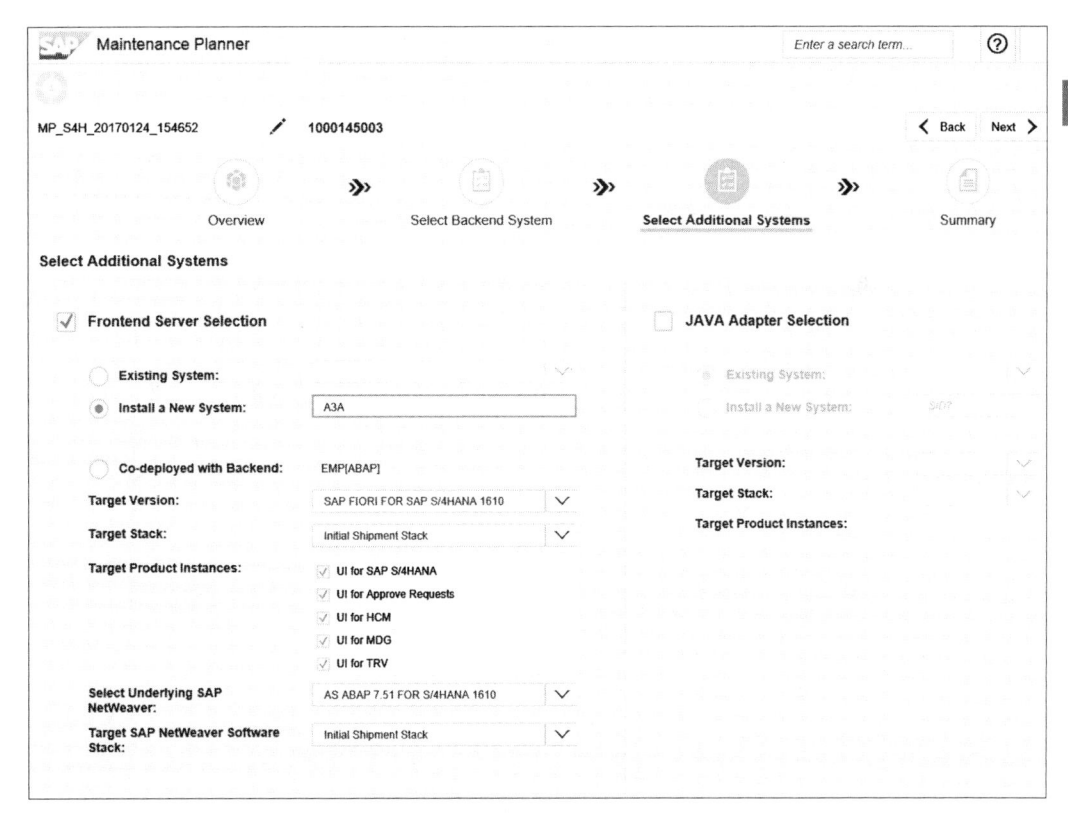

Figure 10.24 Selecting SAP Fiori for Installation in the Maintenance Planner

You can use SAP Fiori 2.0 in combination with SAP S/4HANA 1610. However, this release is not yet available for SAP S/4HANA 1511. Technically, SAP Fiori 2.0 is based on SAP Fiori Frontend Server 3.0. To use SAP Fiori Cloud

10   System Conversion

(see Chapter 9, Section 9.3.2) for SAP S/4HANA, SAP S/4HANA 1610 needs to be installed with a separate license.

Relevance Analysis for SAP Fiori Apps

Relevance and Readiness Analysis

The *Relevance and Readiness Analysis* in the SAP Fiori apps reference library is an analysis tool that helps you identify the SAP Fiori apps that are relevant for you. The tool analyzes which transactions you use in your source system and generates a list of recommended apps. Figure 10.25 shows a common results list of the relevance analysis.

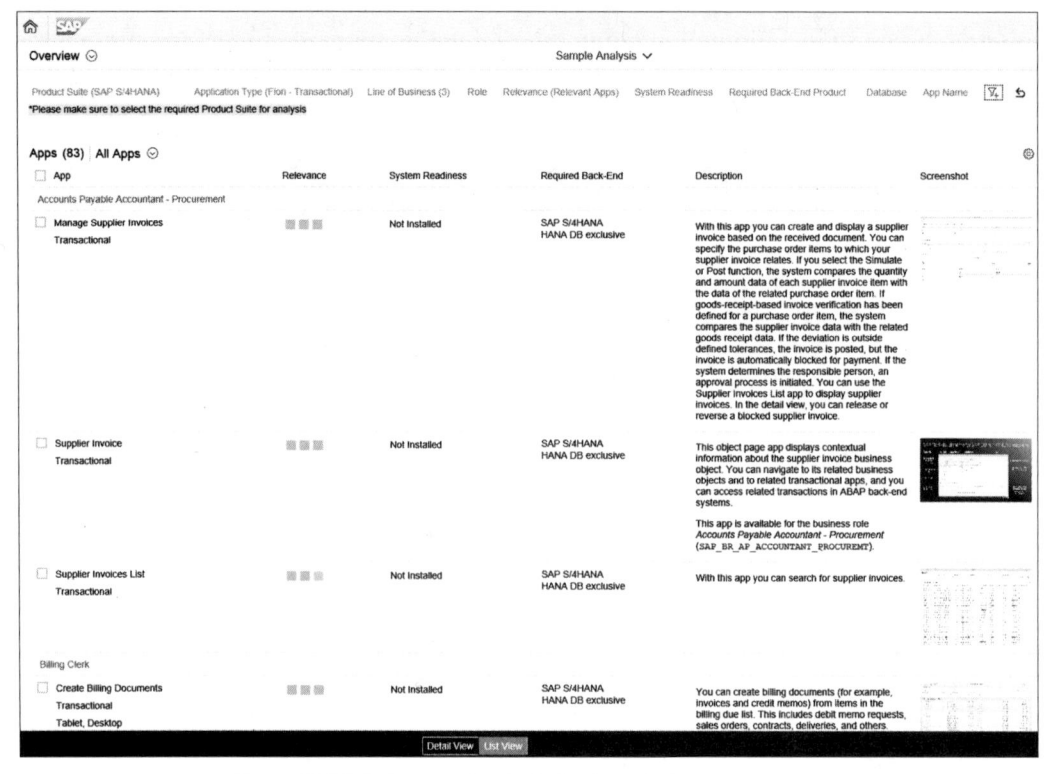

Figure 10.25 Relevance Analysis for SAP Fiori Apps

Usage analysis

You can use the Workload Monitor (Transaction ST03) to perform the usage analysis of the transaction data, for example. This usage data is then uploaded into the tool as a CSV file, and the tool analyzes the relevance of individual transactions and determines which SAP Fiori apps correspond to your most-used SAP GUI transactions.

Customizing the Conversion

The options provided by SAP S/4HANA's new, attractive, intuitive, and efficient user interfaces are just one dimension of a conversion project. Another dimension is how to migrate to the new user interfaces and their new way of working.

In this section, we'll address migrating from traditional user interfaces to the new SAP Fiori-based user interfaces, which will be available after the conversion project is completed. However, you can continue to use SAP GUI transactions after converting your system to SAP S/4HANA. In general, all of your users' transactions and favorites before the upgrade will still be available in the ABAP backend after the system conversion. Exceptions include transactions that are omitted in SAP S/4HANA for simplification reasons and for which the simplification list communicated modifications.

Note that SAP S/4HANA's new functions are usually only provided with SAP Fiori-based user interfaces. Thus, the question is not *whether* you migrate to the new user interfaces but *how* you perform the migration and which steps you carry out.

Figure 10.26 illustrates a possible gradual migration from traditional SAP ERP user interfaces to a target architecture based on SAP Fiori.

Gradual migration

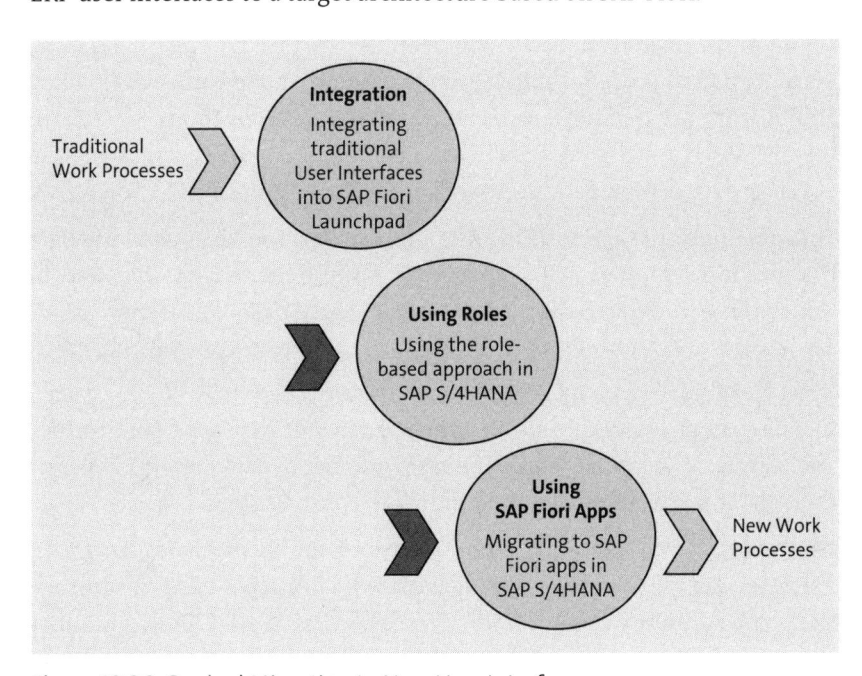

Figure 10.26 Gradual Migration to New User Interfaces

Integrating various applications

Following this model, you would first introduce SAP Fiori launchpad, which will serve as the central, web-based entry point for all users that will use the SAP S/4HANA system. In SAP Fiori launchpad, you can consolidate applications from various user interface technologies (for example, SAP GUI, portals) on multiple devices (desktop PC, tablet, or smartphone).

You can integrate traditional user interfaces and continue to use your functions and business processes in the same way as before the system conversion.

For example, you can integrate a selection of Web Dynpro-based and SAP GUI-based applications from your ABAP backend or integrate entries from the SAP Easy Access menu with SAP Fiori launchpad. As of SAP S/4HANA 1610, on-premise, the design of traditional interfaces has also been adjusted to match the design of SAPUI5-based SAP Fiori apps to support a uniform user experience.

Role-based access

Immediately after you have converted your system, you should grant end users role-based access to the SAP Fiori launchpad. In role-based access, you'll break down complex applications into useful task-based subunits. End users will only access the user interfaces they require for carrying out the steps for which they are responsible and authorized to perform.

For example, managers need different information than administrators. Managers often process approval steps on their mobile end devices, while administrators often need access to detailed interfaces to process exceptional cases. If you use predefined roles and authorizations, you can define which apps, and what data, users are authorized to access.

The *App Finder* (the app store in SAP Fiori launchpad) enables users to select the apps for their roles that support their tasks in the best possible way. In this context, whether the app is an SAP Fiori, SAP GUI, or Web Dynpro ABAP application does not matter. You can also integrate custom SAP Fiori apps into the App Finder.

Replacing obsolete applications

In a next step, you can decide whether to use SAP Fiori apps even further and replace all of your traditional user interfaces. Many enterprises start this migration by modifying their individual process steps.

For example, you can adapt approval processes or processes for travel expenses mainly for mobile end devices, which may be used most often. Next, you can adjust core business processes that affect a limited number of users. Then, you can modify business processes that affect the majority of your end users.

Ultimately, you'll have to decide yourself how and how quickly you want to migrate to the new SAP Fiori user interfaces.

> **Additional Information**
>
> You can find additional information about the SAP Fiori's Relevance and Readiness Analysis in the SAP Fiori apps reference library or via the following link: *https://fioriappslibrary.hana.ondemand.com/sap/fix/external Viewer/docu/Relevance_and_Readiness_Document.pdf*.
>
> The "SAP Fiori 2.0 Administration and Developer Guide" (*https://experience.sap.com/documents/sap-fiori-2-0-administration-and-developer-guide.pdf*) explains how to integrate Web Dynpro-based applications and SAP GUI-based applications into the SAP Fiori launchpad.
>
> For more information on the new interface schema *Belize* and its availability in SAP GUI for HTML, SAP GUI for Java, and SAP GUI for Windows, read SAP Note 2365556.
>
> For more information on the App Finder, go to *https://experience.sap.com/fiori-design-web/app-finder/*.

Chapter 11
New Implementation of Single Systems

This chapter describes the data migration process for new SAP S/4HANA implementations as well as the tools, methods, and approaches used.

While Chapter 10 described converting an existing system to SAP S/4HANA, on-premise, this chapter explains how to perform a migration for a new implementation. This approach, also referred to as a greenfield implementation, allows long-term SAP customers to get rid of any legacy systems (for example, if the SAP ERP system has been used for a long time) and start from scratch. This scenario is also ideal if you have not used SAP ERP yet.

With a new implementation, you'll benefit the most from SAP S/4HANA's simplifications and from SAP Best Practices. If your system contains numerous custom modifications, you can return to the standard and start from scratch.

Back to standard

To migrate data after the initial implementation (see Chapter 9), you'll use migration tools similar to the ones introduced in Chapter 7, Section 7.3, for SAP S/4HANA Cloud editions. These tools may differ from those you've used so far in SAP Business Suite and other SAP systems.

Section 11.1 describes the data migration procedure in the overall implementation project and introduces the individual data migration phases. Section 11.2 discusses the migration objects supported by SAP Best Practices. Which migration objects are available depends on the migration tool you use. The different migration tools are introduced in Sections 11.3 and 11.4:

- Rapid Data Migration for SAP Data Services
- The SAP S/4HANA migration cockpit, which we discussed as a migration tool for SAP S/4HANA Cloud in Chapter 7, Section 7.3

To address the extended solution scope and enhancement options of SAP S/4HANA, on-premise, Section 11.5 introduces the *SAP S/4HANA migration*

11 New Implementation of Single Systems

object modeler, which you can use to add additional fields to migration objects.

Finally, Section 11.6 discusses various ways to use the migration tools and summarizes their relative advantages and disadvantages. Finally, we'll also describe the limitations of and the usage options in the *Legacy System Migration Workbench* (LSMW) for SAP S/4HANA, which is often used for SAP Business Suite, to complement this overview of migration tools.

11.1 Data Migration Phases

In general, the data migration phases in SAP S/4HANA correspond to the phases common in data migrations for SAP Business Suite systems. We'll differentiate between seven phases:

1. Data analysis
2. Mapping
3. Implementation
4. Data migration test
   – Functional testing
   – Productive Data Load Test (PLT)
5. Data validation
6. Data cleansing
7. Productive load and support

Phases according to ASAP For SAP Business Suite implementation projects in the SAP Standard implementation model, *AcceleratedSAP* (ASAP), these phases are implemented, as shown in Figure 11.1.

SAP Activate As we described in Chapter 5, the most recent version of the ASAP implementation method, ASAP 8, was further developed to become *SAP Activate*. Figure 11.2 illustrates how the data migration phases are integrated into the SAP Activate phases.

You can find further information on SAP Activate in Chapter 5. The following sections describe the individual data migration phases and how these phases are integrated into the SAP Activate phases.

11.1 Data Migration Phases

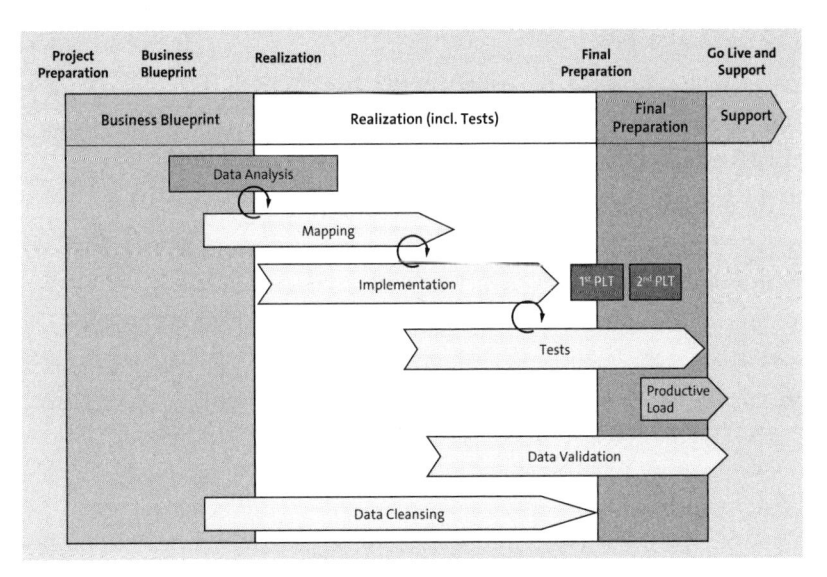

Figure 11.1 Data Migration Phases in ASAP Methodology

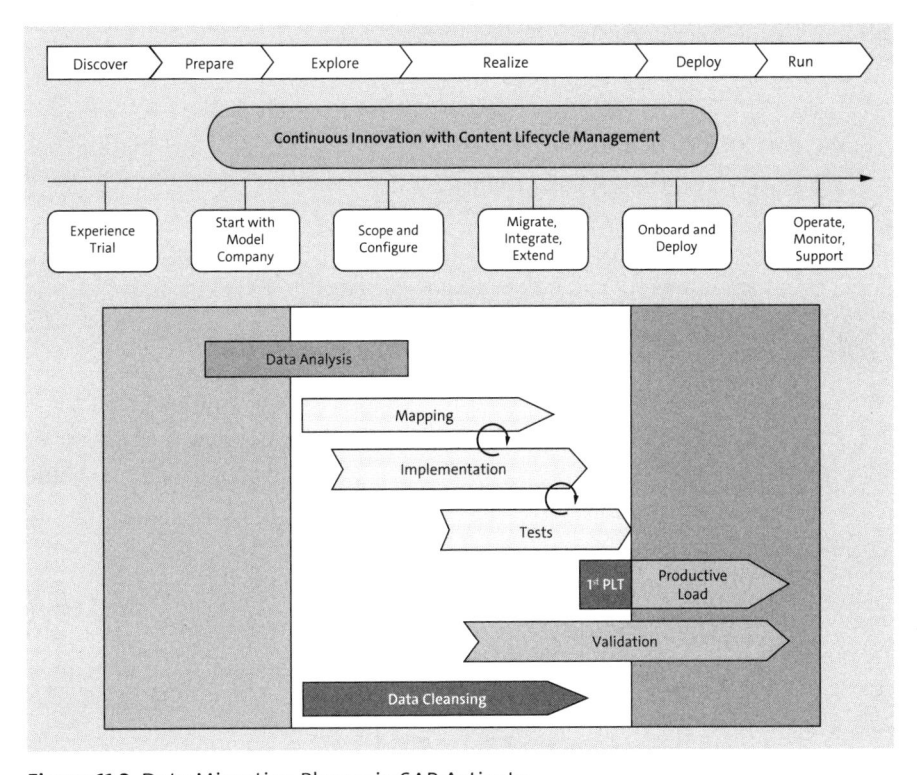

Figure 11.2 Data Migration Phases in SAP Activate

379

11.1.1 Data Analysis

Prepare and explore phase

You'll usually start the data analysis in the *prepare* and *explore* (*blueprint* in ASAP) phases. When you model your individual business processes, you'll specify the required business objects, the master data, and the transaction data used.

> **Business Object versus Migration Object**
>
> A *business object* is an individual data object that is needed to model a business process, for example, a material, customer, or purchase order.
>
> A *migration object* is part of the business object that is used to migrate the business object. Business objects sometimes have to be divided into smaller units for technical reasons. For example, certain parts of a business object could be installed via different Application Programming Interfaces (APIs) or their data sources could differ. As a result, one business object may require more than one migration object.

> **Master Data versus Transaction Data**
>
> *Master data* is data that is stable and used as the basis for business objects. Master data changes only slightly or not at all over a specific period of time. Common master data objects include, for example, customers, suppliers, materials, banks, and bills of material.
>
> *Transaction data* is data that is volatile and subject to continuous change. Common transaction data objects include stock levels, all types of orders, account data, or contracts.

Preparing data

In the data analysis phase, you'll analyze the origin of your data and check whether manual or automatic data migrations are necessary. Many enterprises use various data retention systems for migrating data. You should always use the most current data sources with the highest data quality for the data migration.

Frequently, you'll have to consolidate data from different data sources into one data migration source. Depending on the number and origin of the data objects, manually transferring the data to the new system may make sense: For example, the amount of time and money for converting the data to a new format automatically could be too high. Transferring the data manually would make the most sense.

> **300,000 Data Records Become 5,000 Data Records** [Ex]
>
> An SAP customer from the automotive industry wanted to import 300,000 suppliers from an external system to a new SAP S/4HANA system. A detailed data analysis showed that only about 5,000 suppliers were relevant. The other 295,000 suppliers were mainly inactive members whose records had accumulated over time but who had not been contacted for decades.
>
> The records of some inactive suppliers, for example, included obsolete country names such as "Yugoslavia." Ultimately, importing 5,000 suppliers was by far less time-consuming than importing 60 times that number.
>
> Thus, finding ways to reduce the volume of the data to be migrated always makes sense: The fewer data records to migrate, the faster the import to the relevant migration tools and the shorter the total import time.

When determining migration objects, you should record the following information for each object:

- The SAP target system (if multiple target systems exist)
- The migration object and a description of the object
- The object type (master data, transaction data, Customizing data, other data)
- The estimated complexity of the migration object (1 = less complex to 10 = very complex)
- The object's relationships to other migration data objects
- The number of data records to be imported
- The source system(s)
- Important contact persons
- The planned data transfer method
- Related planning documents or business processes

Determining migration objects

The best way to store this information is in a table, for example, in Microsoft Excel. You can then add necessary object and status information to this table. Figure 11.3 shows a section from a sample table.

Migration object overview

										Source systems					Objec				
																Region 1	Region 2	Region 3	
No.	Area	Object number	Object name	Object Sub number	Description	Comments	MD= master data CU=Customizing TD=Transactional data	Data migration needed Y or N or M = manually	Upload Volume (number of records)	System 1	System 2	System 3	System 4	System 5	Business lead (SAP) e.g. Mapping, Validation	Business lead (Customer) e.g. Mapping, Validation			SAP Technical responsible e.g. Upload
1	SD	001	**Customer Master**	001	**Load Additional Customers (Create new)**	09/27/07 Mr SAP1: ask Ms Gamma for further informations	MD	Y		X		X			Mr SAP1	Mr Beta	Ms Gamma	n/a	
2	SD	001	**Customer Master**	002	**Additions to existing Customers (Change existing)**	02/21/08 eMail by Mr Alpha Shipping conditions "E.	MD	Y		X		X			Ms SAP2	Mr Alpha Ms Fox	n/a	n/a	
3	MM	002	**Vendor Master**	001	**Local Purchase Vendors**	09/27/07 Mr Beta: no migration except for some bolt-on's. Ms Fox to cleanse and further informations Spreadsheets exists for	MD	Y				X			Mr SAP1	Mr Beta	n/a	n/a	
4	MM / SD	003	**Material Master**	001	**New materials to create & existing to extend (org struct)**	09/27/07 Ms SAP2 and Mr SAP1 * Only new materials, * no field changes in for existing materials (to verify) ,	MD	Y		X					Ms SAP2 Mr SAP1	Mr Alpha Ms Fox	n/a	n/a	
5	MM / WM / SD / PP	003	**Material Master**	002	**Plant extensions of existing materials MRP + Work scheduling + Storage location**	10/04/07 Mr Beta: - MRP1 to MRP4 (MRP1 no dispo areas MRP4 sloc MRP indicator MARD-DISKZ) - Work scheduling (Serial number may be needed)	MD	N		X	X				Mr SAP1	Mr Alpha Mr Beta	n/a	n/a	

Figure 11.3 Sample Table for Documenting Migration Objects

[»]

Downloading Sample Tables

You can download this table to use as an example of migration object documentations at *www.sap-press.com/4247*, where you'll also find other materials for this book. You can change and modify the table as required.

11.1.2 Mapping

Field mapping

After you have specified which data objects you want to migrate, you should immediately start to map the structures and fields of your source data to the structures and fields of the target system. You'll usually do this in parallel to determining the business processes during the *fit gap workshop* in the SAP Activate explore phase. Because some of the master and transaction data is used in various business processes, the mapping of these objects should be completed when the data analysis phase is complete. (This corresponds to the end of the explore phase in the SAP Activate methodology.)

SAP provides predefined mappings via the SAP Best Practices Rapid Data Migration solution and the SAP S/4HANA migration cockpit. If you use the SAP S/4HANA migration cockpit, you'll only have to enter your data into the existing migration template and convert your source system values in the migration cockpit accordingly. However, using these predefined mappings also restricts your implementation options for using alternative mapping rules. The SAP Data Services-based Rapid Data Migration solution instead provides the flexibility of SAP Data Services for modifying the predefined mapping rules.

Predefined mappings

Frequently, initial tests of original data result in analysis and configuration errors that will require adjusting the target configuration and thus also the corresponding mapping and conversion rules. The mapping can consequently often not be completed until the last third of the implementation phase has been reached.

Analysis and configuration errors

Alternative Units of Measure Suddenly Emerging

When the first test data was imported, an analysis of the source data showed that some international subsidiaries maintained material masters with different units of measures than in the leading system.

In the fit gap workshop, alternative units of measure were not considered necessary. The data of the leading system is usually loaded first, which consequently determines the basic unit of measure. However, because stock levels in SAP S/4HANA systems are posted in the base unit of measure, this new information required an adaptation of the configuration and the introduction of alternative units of measure. Otherwise, 400m of fabric in one subsidiary would be posted as 400 bolts of fabric (the basic unit of measure in the leading system). One role is about 100m long; so that posting would have led to an incorrect increase in stock levels.

11.1.3 Implementation

In the implementation phase of an SAP Business Suite implementation, you would normally run extraction programs on the source systems and run transfer routines on the target system.

SAP Best Practices

You should use the data transfer tools and solutions recommended by SAP in SAP S/4HANA systems set up with SAP Best Practices.

For the Rapid Data Migration solution (see Section 11.3) and the SAP S/4HANA migration cockpit (see Section 11.4), predefined migration content is available for the migration objects listed in Section 11.2. This content is based on SAP Best Practices. Here, you'll usually have to enter the source data into the provided migration templates and maintain the source/target value conversions. When you use SAP Best Practices, costs are more transparent and can be better calculated than when implementing completely new business processes.

Using released interfaces

For migration objects not offered in SAP Best Practices, in SAP S/4HANA, on-premise, you'll have to implement transfer routines in the target system, including mapping and conversion rules, as well as implement extraction routines in the source system.

In contrast to SAP Business Suite systems, for SAP S/4HANA, you must ensure that the interfaces and technologies (BAPIs, IDocs, batch input, etc.) you want to use have been released. (For more information, see Section 11.6.)

The implementation phase runs in parallel to mapping in the realize phase (also called the realize phase in the ASAP methodology).

11.1.4 Testing

Tests reduce operating costs

Tests can be decisive factors in the success of an implementation, but experience has shown that they are usually not planned sufficiently. In most cases, too little attention is paid to tests and postprocessing tasks.

The more data sources and conversion rules you have, and thus the more complex the data migration is, the more rigorously you'll have to test your migration. The more tests you can conduct with original data, the more errors you can eliminate and the higher the final data quality of the imported data.

The quality of the imported data is essential for your business processes and can considerably impact costs during live operations. You should schedule at least one *Productive Load Test* (PLT) as a dress rehearsal.

11.1.5 Data Validation

Two approaches are available for validating your data during a data migration:

- Before the data transfer
- After the data transfer

You can also combine the two approaches to be on the safe side. The important thing is that you check whether the data is correct with regard to its syntax and semantics.

The *syntax* of a data value is correct if the value contains the data type, is the length of the target field, and lies within the value range of an underlying value table. Usually, the relevant migration APIs verify the correctness of the syntax.

Correctness of syntax and semantics

The migration cockpit uses mainly released BAPIs and function modules as migration APIs. The Rapid Data Migration solution uses IDoc interfaces. Nearly all APIs used will check the correctness of your data's syntax and semantics.

However, in some APIs, these checks are only roughly implemented. If so, you should check data values before transferring the data to avoid loading defective data. Chapter 7, Section 7.3.1, Table 7.2, provides an overview of the APIs of the migration objects in the SAP S/4HANA migration cockpit.

The *semantics* of a data value is correct if the data value makes sense in combination with other field values of the data record.

> **Semantic Errors** [Ex]
>
> An administrator for a customer from Northern Ireland maintained NI as the country key in the source system. For all other customers, the administrator used the common ISO country keys, as used in SAP S/4HANA. Because nobody noticed this mistake, all values were converted on a 1:1 basis. Consequently, after the conversion, customers from Northern Ireland were displayed as Nicaraguan customers because NI is the valid SAP S/4HANA country key for Nicaragua.

Don't assume the correctness of your source data and always validate your data. Various tools are available for data validation. However, you should always define validation rules on the basis of expected conversion rules.

Defining rules

Depending on your specific situation, you'll validate your data before or after the data migration: The more complex to cleanse imported data or restore systems from a backup to a defined state and the less the data migration APIs provide for simulations, the more important it is to validate the data before you migrate the data.

Numerous data validation tools, such as SAP Query, SAP Data Services, etc., are available. The Rapid Data Migration solution contains predefined validation rules, which you can use to validate your data before and after the import.

11.1.6 Data Cleansing

Garbage in, garbage out

If you find errors during the data analysis and tests, you should eliminate these errors immediately in your source system. The better the quality of the original data, the fewer errors will arise during the data migration and the better the quality of the imported data.

Cleanse your data as early as possible and use existing data cleansing processes and teams, which are required in many enterprises to satisfy quality audits and certifications.

The results of your first data migration tests are vitally important for future data cleansing processes in the source system. You should therefore integrate your existing data cleansing teams into the SAP S/4HANA migration team. If possible, the data cleansing process should be complete before you perform the initial load of the productive load test.

11.1.7 Productive Load and Support

The productive load process, also referred to as the *initial load*, is the final and most critical data migration phase. The productive load process shows whether you have done everything correctly in previous phases and in the test phase. The higher the data quality and the more tests you run in advance, the more relaxed you will be during the go-live.

In the productive load process, we strongly recommend you carry out the data migration, scheduled and as real as possible, in a dress rehearsal. Often, small details, for example, enabled source system backups or unscheduled maintenance work, can jeopardize data migrations.

Regional regulations

You'll have to take into account many considerations that you may not have anticipated before. The following list includes a few examples:

- *Nightwork, weekend work, or extra hours* often needs to be approved in many European countries, and also other countries worldwide, by notifying the relevant workers' council, union, or supervisory authority. These processes require lead times and cannot be rushed. Otherwise, for example, you may find that only 2 of your 50 warehouse employees might be available for the final physical inventory on the weekend. If these processes are scheduled too late, your entire cut-over plan can be jeopardized.

- *Different time zones and public holidays* are often incorrectly considered or not considered at all. For example, if you scheduled a data transfer for 9am (CET), you should ensure that a contact person is available in the data center in San Francisco to provide you with the source data.

- You should also plan for *IT downtimes* in detail, for example, to avoid having numerous trucks waiting at your loading ramp to be loaded when they cannot be loaded. In addition, all interfaces to and from existing source systems should be disabled during the data migration. Disabling these interfaces helps you avoid falsified data and ensures that the data in your source file corresponds to the data in the source system at the time of your productive load.

These are only a few considerations (based on real-life examples) that you should consider to avoid the mistakes other people have made.

> **Additional Information on Planning Data Migration Objects**
>
> You can find more information on the data migration process in the SAP environment and on the general planning and structuring of data migration projects in *Data Migration with SAP* by Frank Densborn, Frank Finkbohner, Johann Gradl, Michael Roth, and Michael Willinger (3rd edition, SAP PRESS, 2016, *www.sap-press.com/4019*).

11.2 Supported Migration Objects

SAP delivers and recommends two solutions for migrating data to SAP S/4HANA, on-premise. The following sections describe these tools and migration approaches in detail:

11 New Implementation of Single Systems

- Rapid Data Migration ("RDM" in Table 11.1)
- SAP S/4HANA migration cockpit ("MC" in Table 11.1)

Migration objects for each tool These two solutions support the loading of master and transaction data to SAP S/4HANA. Table 11.1 provides an overview of the migration objects available for each solution.

Object Name in MC or RDM (If Not Included in MC)	Area	RDM	MC
Activity type	CO	X	X
Cost center	CO	X	X
Activity price	CO	X	X
Internal order	CO	X	X
Profit center	FI	X	X
Bank	FI	X	X
Customer	FI, SD	X*	X
Supplier	FI, MM-PUR	X*	X
Accounts receivable (Customer) open item	FI	X	X
Accounts payable (Vendor) open item	FI	X	X
Fixed assets incl. Balances	FI-AA	X	X
G/L account balance	FI	X	X
G/L account open item	FI	X	X
Exchange rate	FI	X	X
Inventory balances	MM-IM	X	X
Material	LO-MD	X	X
Material – Long text	LO-MD	X	X
Material consumption	LO-MD	X	X
Purchasing info record	MM-PUR	X	X

Table 11.1 Migration Objects Supported in the Migration Solutions (SAP S/4HANA, On-Premise, 1610)

11.2 Supported Migration Objects

Object Name in MC or RDM (If Not Included in MC)	Area	RDM	MC
Purchase order	MM-PUR	X	X
Contracts (Purchasing)	MM-PUR	X	X
Source list	MM-PUR	X	X
Sales order	SD	X	X
Batch	QM, SD, PP-PI	X	X
Bill of material (BOM)	PP	X	X
Work center	PP, QM	X	X
Routing	PP	X	X
Equipment	PM	X	X
Maintenance task list	PM		X
Functional location	PM	X	X
Characteristic	CA	X	X
Class	CA	X	X
Secondary Cost Element	CO	X	
Configuration Profiles for Material	LO-VC	X	
Activity Type Group	CO	X	
Profit Center Group	EC-PCA	X	
Inspection Type	QM	X	
Inspection Plans	QM	X	
Service Master	MM-SRV	X	
Object Dependencies	LO-VC	X	
Reference Operation Set	PP-BD	X	

Table 11.1 Migration Objects Supported in the Migration Solutions (SAP S/4HANA, On-Premise, 1610) (Cont.)

11   New Implementation of Single Systems

Object Name in MC or RDM (If Not Included in MC)	Area	RDM	MC
Cost Center Group	CO	X	
Planned Independents Requirements		X	
Order Reservation	PP-MRP	X	
Purchase Requisition	MM-PUR	X	
Open Delivery	IS-R	X	

Table 11.1 Migration Objects Supported in the Migration Solutions (SAP S/4HANA, On-Premise, 1610) (Cont.)

The objects marked with an asterisk (*), *Customer* and *Supplier*, are covered by a single object called *Business Partner* in the Rapid Data Migration content. Section 11.3 discusses this innovation, which is based on *Customer Vendor Integration* (CVI), in more detail.

As shown in Table 11.1, the Rapid Data Migration solution in SAP S/4HANA 1610 covers more objects than the SAP S/4HANA migration cockpit. Furthermore, using Rapid Data Migration provides benefits due to additional data cleansing objects and unrestricted extensibility. Therefore, the following section takes a closer look at this comprehensive data migration solution.

11.3   Rapid Data Migration

This section introduces the Rapid Data Migration solution, which serves to migrate data to SAP S/4HANA, on-premise. Rapid Data Migration is an SAP Best Practices package that provides migration content for the *SAP Data Services* tool. The data migration approach with SAP Data Services and Rapid Data Migration focuses on the data quality and data validation for SAP S/4HANA.

11.3.1   Tools

ETL tool   The SAP Data Services tool is a product from the *SAP Enterprise Information Management (EIM)* portfolio, which provides functions for integrating data (*Data Integrator*) and ensuring data quality (*Data Quality*).

SAP Data Services is a proven and tested ETL (Extract, Transform, and Load) tool, which has a graphical user interface (designer) and can be connected to numerous source systems (extract) and target systems (load) through various interfaces. You'll map (transform) the data on the tool's drag-and-drop user interface.

SAP Data Services also enables you to continuously improve the quality of your imported data both before and during the data migration. Unlike traditional migration scenarios, you'll avoid migrating incorrect, redundant, and unnecessary data records.

Data quality

In addition, Rapid Data Migration uses the *SAP BusinessObjects BI* platform for advanced, but optional, data migration monitoring. The platform provides predefined reports as SAP Best Practices to support data migration projects for analytics and troubleshooting. The reports are created as *SAP BusinessObjects Web Intelligence* reports, which allows you to support your migration projects by determining data quality and mapping issues at an early stage.

Web Intelligence

In addition to SAP Data Services, which is a standalone software to connect source and target systems, SAP also delivers further helpful tools in the EIM portfolio that you can use for data migrations. Of particular interest is the *SAP Information Steward* tool. Both tools provide the *profiling* function (to identify similarities and structures in data) and *deduplication* function for data (to find duplicates) and *data lineage* (to reconcile data between source and target systems).

SAP Information Steward

> **Rapid Data Migration Not Only for SAP S/4HANA**
>
> In addition to the data migration content for SAP S/4HANA, SAP provides several Rapid Data Migration packages for target systems, such as SAP ERP, SAP Customer Relationship Management (CRM), SAP Business Suite on SAP HANA, SAP SuccessFactors (for example, SAP SuccessFactors Employee Central), and SAP Hybris Cloud for Customer (C4C). You can find an overview of these packages at the following link: *http://service.sap.com/public/rds-datamigration*.

Because you'll use a standardized ETL tool, you won't have to use custom one-off programs for migrating to SAP S/4HANA but will use standard interfaces, such as *IDocs* (Intermediate Documents), *BAPIs* (Business Application

Benefits

Programming Interfaces), and SAP function modules. Using SAP Data Services for data migrations provides further advantages, for example:

- Direct connection to one or more source systems via database interfaces (both SAP ERP and non-SAP systems)
- Additional integration of data from CSV files, flat files, and Microsoft Excel files
- Standardization of source data from various legacy systems and files into a unified format
- Data record cleansing on the source system
- Deduplication of data and determination of the entire data record that merges and replaces duplicates (referred to as the *golden record*)
- Start of the mapping and validation process before you've completed the Customizing of SAP S/4HANA
- Simple and reusable mapping via drag and drop
- Visualization of the entire data flow from the source system to the target system
- Reusable check routines to minimize custom code
- Validation of external data against SAP S/4HANA check routines without having to load data records into SAP S/4HANA
- Test runs without updating data
- Usage of SAP S/4HANA standard interfaces

11.3.2 Architecture

Components The Rapid Data Migration solution combines SAP Data Services with migration content specifically developed for data migrations. Technically, the SAP data migration solution consists of three components:

- The actual software
- A database server
- A web server

The database server is used to manage *repositories* in several separate database instances. For example, one repository contains the entire SAP Data Services content and metadata about interfaces, which describes the interface structure as "data about data."

The web server permits access to the software through a web browser, for example, via the *Central Management Console* (CMC) for reporting with SAP BusinessObjects BI platform.

In addition to the software components, the SAP S/4HANA data migration solution package contains the following components:

Package content

- Data migration templates (*content*) including mappings for SAP Data Services (see Section 11.3.3)
- *Migration Services* tool for value mapping (see Section 11.3.7)
- Reports from SAP BusinessObjects Web Intelligence for monitoring and reporting (see Section 11.3.10)
- Content for the reconciliation between SAP target system and source system(s) (see Section 11.3.10)

SAP provides these components as a SAP Best Practices package for SAP S/4HANA, *Rapid Data Migration*. In addition to predefined business best practices content and implementation best practices for configuration, Rapid Data Migration packages contain services for data migration projects, provided by SAP Consulting or SAP partners. However, you can use this SAP Best Practices content yourself without being supported by SAP or an SAP partner by downloading the package from the SAP Best Practices Explorer free of charge (see Section 11.3.3).

SAP Best Practices

The predefined migration content for SAP Data Services contains the metadata of the SAP S/4HANA target interface as well as validations for simplifying the source mapping. More than 50 business objects are supported. Theoretically, every IDoc, every asynchronous BAPI, and every web service can be used. Even RFC-enabled function modules, which are used in the standard content for the business partner object, are possible. (See Chapter 7, Table 7.2, for a list of available migration objects.)

IDocs and BAPIs

[Ex]

Sample Migration Content

Examples of predefined templates include the following:

- For business partners with customer and supplier masters
- For logistics data such as material masters, bills of materials (BOMs), and sales documents
- For SAP Financials (FI) data, such as receivables and payables

393

11   New Implementation of Single Systems

For BAPIs without a provided IDoc interface, you can use Transaction BDBG to easily create a BAPI/ALE interface in the customer namespace. You can then also enhance SAP Data Services content without any restrictions. The SAP Best Practices package includes an *enhancement guide* for more information.

Data migration platform   With Rapid Data Migration content, the ETL tool, SAP Data Services, becomes a data migration platform perfectly attuned to SAP S/4HANA, on-premise. Figure 11.4 illustrates the corresponding architecture with SAP Data Services in the center.

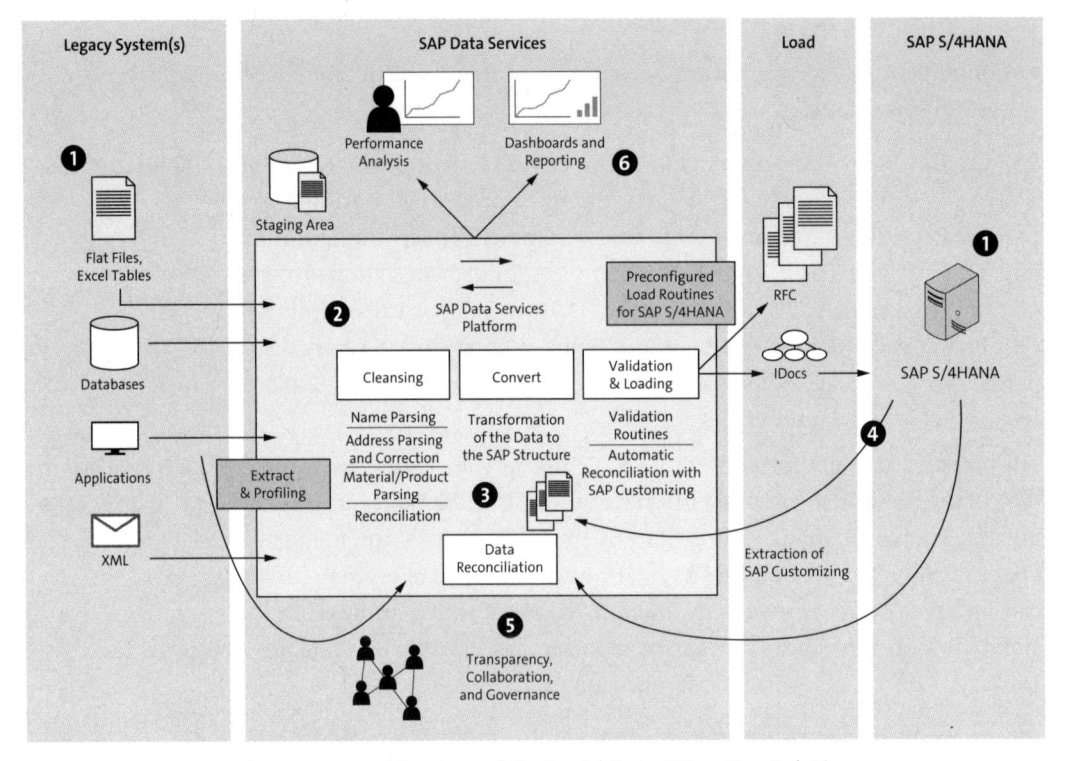

Figure 11.4 Architecture of the Rapid Data Migration Solution

The platform itself runs on a relational database that is also used as a *staging area*. SAP Data Services can connect to any source systems via adapter frameworks, such as Open Database Connectivity (ODBC), file interfaces, Mainframe, XML files, and Microsoft Excel files:

1. **Source and target system**
   On the left side of Figure 11.4, the system is integrated with one or more legacy systems via various interfaces; on the right side, the system is integrated with an SAP S/4HANA system. For new implementations of SAP S/4HANA, the legacy system can be an SAP ERP system or any other non-SAP system. However, legacy systems can also be mixed systems (for example, an SAP Business Suite system with multiple external add-on systems that all will be consolidated into one SAP S/4HANA system).

2. **Extraction and profiling**
   The staging area between the source and target systems is provided by the database on which SAP Data Services runs, which may be, but not always is, the SAP HANA database. Depending on the size of the repository, we recommend maintaining a smaller landscape, for example, on the basis of an *SAP Adaptive Server Enterprise* (ASE) database, which can also be used with an SAP HANA database license.

   In this step, you'll extract and analyze data from the source system. This analysis (*profiling*) is a critical step that provides detailed insights into the legacy system. These insights enable you to determine data patterns and check important details: For example, do all ZIP codes for the US have five digits (plus possible 4 digit extensions) and are only numbers used? What notations are used to designate the United States in your legacy system (e.g., "United States of America," "U.S.," and/or "USA")?

3. **Cleansing, conversion, validation, and loading**
   This step includes the cleansing of data records so that they follow a specific pattern, the conversion of certain rules, and, finally, the reconciliation with the Customizing for SAP S/4HANA. These processes can entail, for example, merging two fields into one field, dividing fields, converting values to a specific format (for example, converting telephone numbers into the international format with "+1" for the U.S., for example), and validating mandatory fields and check tables. The cleansed and verified data is then imported to the SAP S/4HANA system.

4. **Customizing extraction from SAP S/4HANA**
   Because you can configure SAP S/4HANA, you'll need to transfer the Customizing (for example, for company codes, plants, material types, and material groups) to the intermediate layer of SAP Data Services by replicating the Customizing in SAP Data Services using predefined content. This process enables you to ensure, in SAP Data Services, that the data

records you want to import are compatible with the SAP S/4HANA system. You can repeat the delta reconciliation several times if required, for example, if you need to make changes to the Customizing in the SAP S/4HANA system.

5. **Data reconciliation**
After the data has been loaded, the data that is actually imported to the SAP S/4HANA system is reconciled with the expected data for the SAP Data Services migration.

6. **Dashboards and reporting**
The technical and functional resources involved in the data migration can trace the entire process anytime using dashboards and reports. As a result, the status of the data transfer is always transparent.

You can continue to use SAP Data Services as a fully functional connection and orchestration platform for the master data integration from several systems or for processes to ensure data quality (*data governance*) after the data has been transferred successfully.

11.3.3 Migration Content

Jobs The data migration content, which is available in packages, contains *jobs* for SAP Data Services. One job is delivered for each business object, and this job usually corresponds to one IDoc type. (IDocs can also call BAPIs; see below.)

> **Customer Vendor Integration**
>
> SAP S/4HANA introduced innovation into the traditional customer master migration object. Customers and vendors are merged by *Customer Vendor Integration* (CVI) via the business partner interface for which no IDoc or BAPI is available. A new and specially developed interface in SAP S/4HANA can be addressed using a remote function module (via Remote Function Call, RFC) and is used by the Rapid Data Migration content in SAP Data Services.

All provided and modeled jobs are used as templates for the SAP Data Services platform and are available in a proprietary file format (*.atl*), which is a file format specific to SAP Data Services. Moreover, these packages also contain documentation as installation guides specific to the business content. These guides also include mapping templates for all business objects (tables for mapping on paper), enhancement guides (to add custom interfaces or customer-specific fields), and business process descriptions (for each business object) to enable you to understand the IDoc structure in detail.

> **SAP Best Practices Migration Content beyond SAP S/4HANA**
>
> SAP not only provides free migration content for SAP S/4HANA but also for the SAP solutions listed below. You can download these packages for free (you'll only need your SAP login, such as an S user) in the SAP Best Practices Explorer at the following links:
>
> - SAP Business Suite on SAP HANA:
>   http://rapid.sap.com/bp/RDM_ERP_CRM
> - SAP ERP (including SAP Retail and SAP HCM):
>   http://rapid.sap.com/bp/RDM_ERP_CRM
> - SAP CRM:
>   http://rapid.sap.com/bp/RDM_ERP_CRM
> - SAP Billing for Utilities:
>   http://rapid.sap.com/bp/RDM_CRM_UTIL
> - SAP SuccessFactors Employee Central:
>   http://rapid.sap.com/bp/RDM_SOD_SFSF
> - SAP Hybris Cloud for Customer (C4C):
>   http://rapid.sap.com/bp/RDM_SOD_SFSF
>
> For more information, access the SAP Service Marketplace at:
>
> - http://service.sap.com/public/rds-datamigration
>
> or
>
> - http://service.sap.com/bp-datamigration.
>
> (You might have to log on with your user credentials.)

Note that the predefined content can be localized for various countries, but technical content is provided in the English language only.

Localization

The import function in SAP Data Services lets you easily upload all available objects from the .atl files provided. Similarly, you can also use this function to save your mapping specifications or validations for reuse in other projects. We recommend using the export function for regular backups.

Importing the content

397

11 New Implementation of Single Systems

Now, let's turn to migrating data to SAP S/4HANA. The individual ETL functions of the SAP Data Services platform are beyond the scope of this book and not discussed in detail here.

> **[»] No Separate License Required**
>
> The product license for SAP Data Services covers both the ETL part (*Data Integrator*) and data cleansing part (*Data Quality*). If you do not have a separate software license for SAP Data Services and do not have to cleanse your data, you can request a free Data Integrator key code anytime by using your SAP HANA database license.
>
> You can then use this key code with a valid SAP HANA REAB (*Runtime Edition for Applications and SAP BW*) database license, or with the full SAP HANA Enterprise database license, to load data to SAP S/4HANA or to the SAP HANA database without having to pay for additional licenses. As SAP HANA database licenses, either license (SAP HANA REAB or SAP HANA Enterprise) is included in the SAP S/4HANA license package.
>
> For more information, go to *https://blogs.sap.com/2016/06/21/how-to-migrate-to-sap-s4hana/*.
>
> The following link navigates you to a guide describing how to request the required key code: *https://blogs.sap.com/2016/06/20/request-an-sap-data-integrator-key-code-for-rapid-data-migration-to-sap-s4hana/*.

Interfaces as Part of the Migration Content

Using IDocs

For migrating data to SAP S/4HANA, as mentioned earlier, the Rapid Data Migration solution uses IDocs, which is the SAP standard interface technology, for all objects (because all BAPIs are called via their IDoc interfaces) except for business partners to send data to SAP S/4HANA. As part of the content, the structure of the IDocs as well as their fields have been replicated as metadata in SAP Data Services. As a result, you can map the source system (your legacy system) to the SAP S/4HANA target structure in the *SAP Data Services Designer*.

An IDoc is a hierarchically nested structure. Individual data records in IDocs are called *segments*. IDocs are updated via function modules. Unlike direct updates, the *ALE layer* is used here. Consequently, the IDocs are always addressed via the same function module in the SAP S/4HANA target system: the RFC-enabled `IDOC_INBOUND_ASYNCHRONOUS` module. SAP Data

Services is responsible for the entire process, and you won't have to do anything. The business partner object is an exception (see Chapter 7, Section 7.3.1, Table 7.2) because it is directly and remotely addressed by a wrapper function module (via RFC).

IDocs always have defined statuses in the SAP system. The most important status values for the data transfer in inbound IDocs are the following:

IDoc status values

- **Status 64 (waiting)**
  You can transfer the IDoc to the application.

- **Status 53 (IDoc successfully updated)**
  The application document was updated.

- **Status 51 (error in IDoc)**
  The application document was not updated.

You can differentiate between *IDoc message types*, which indicate the semantics of IDocs, and *IDoc basic types*, which define their syntax. For example, the IDoc message type ORDERS is responsible for order data, while the different versions of the basic types, ORDERS04 or ORDERS05, specify the exact syntax of the segments and all fields contained therein. The version concept specifies that fields and segments can always be added but never deleted. Consequently, ORDERS05 covers all functions of ORDERS04 plus additional new fields. This version control ensures that new systems can handle obsolete IDocs (*upward compatibility*) and that new systems with a higher version can send IDocs to older systems (*downward compatibility*).

Message type and basic type

The relationship between a message type and a basic type, however, is not always *1:n*, as may seem at first, but *n:m* because the IDoc basic type ORDERS05 transfers two logical message types: In addition to purchase orders in the ORDERS IDoc message type, the ORDRSP message type for purchase order confirmations is also available, resulting in different meanings for the IDoc messages.

An enhancement concept is available for IDocs, which allows for IDoc extensions, such as ZORDERS05, which combines additional customer-specific fields or customer segments in the so-called *IDoc type*.

IDoc type

Although IDocs are a broad topic, this level of detail on IDoc technology is sufficient in this context. SAP Data Services will perform the tasks for you using the Rapid Data Migration content and will ensure that the IDocs are set up with the correct IDoc control records and syntax.

11   New Implementation of Single Systems

Transaction BDBG Over time, IDocs have proven to be solid and consistent interfaces with a smart version concept. Moreover, updates of IDocs are secure because the IDocs are completely rolled back and available for processing again when the update is canceled. For these reasons, SAP provides Transaction BDBG as a tool to generate IDoc interfaces based on asynchronous BAPIs at the touch of a button. Asynchronous BAPIs are BAPIs that can load data independently to a system instead of having to carry out an operation and providing a response. The only information returned is a success or failure indicator, similar to traditional IDocs. Transaction BDBG allows you to extend the IDoc world considerably.

BAPI/ALE interface Most of the BAPIs already include the *BAPI ALE interface*, which you can use to generate the IDoc structure and IDoc type from the BAPI. The IDoc will serve as a wrapper around the BAPI, and data will be sent as IDoc instead of directly calling a BAPI in a remote system. The inbound IDoc is then "unwrapped," and the BAPI is called locally in the target system. In general, a BAPI is an SAP function module with a defined interface and documentation. The advantage of using BAPIs is that the send process is decoupled from processing, as is the case for Application Link Enabling (ALE). Otherwise, the connection between the systems must be open during the entire BAPI processing time.

Example: Migrating Bank Master Data

Bank master The following sections focus on a simple example: transferring bank master data to an SAP S/4HANA system.

The object is updated in the SAP S/4HANA system using the BAPI BAPI_BANK_CREATE. However, the BAPI is called via the BAPI ALE interface and, thus, via an IDoc. As a result, in this case, SAP Data Services first sends an IDoc to the SAP S/4HANA system, while the BAPI is directly called in the SAP S/4HANA system if the SAP S/4HANA migration cockpit is used (see Section 11.4). The SAP S/4HANA migration cockpit will run as an application in SAP S/4HANA, while you'll be able to use SAP Data Services for mapping as a standalone tool at an early stage without having to connect your source and target systems.

Our example is restricted to the required bank master data only and uses two IDoc segments of the generated IDoc type, BANK_CREATE01 (message type BANK_CREATE). The technical SAP names of the segments are E1BANK_CREATE and E1BP1011_ADDRESS.

In the SAP Data Services content, these segments are BANKHeader_E1BANK_CREATE_Required and BANKBankAddress_E1BP1011_ADDRESS_Required. These names indicate, respectively, a header record and an address record. In contrast to most objects, our brief example won't include further IDoc segments at lower levels. Depending on the IDoc type definition, these deeper nested structures can be repeated several times but are not always mandatory.

Due to the default IDoc structure used, the content from SAP Data Services has the same structure for every business object and includes mapping (*_Map), validation (*_Validate), and data enrichment (*_Enrich).

The default structure of the user interface in the SAP Data Services Designer (see Figure 11.5) comprises *Project Area* ❶ and *Local Object Library* ❷ on the left. The entire section on the right ❸ next to the *Start Page* provides graphical illustrations of process flows. These illustrations map the flow of data records from the top left to the bottom right.

Workspace

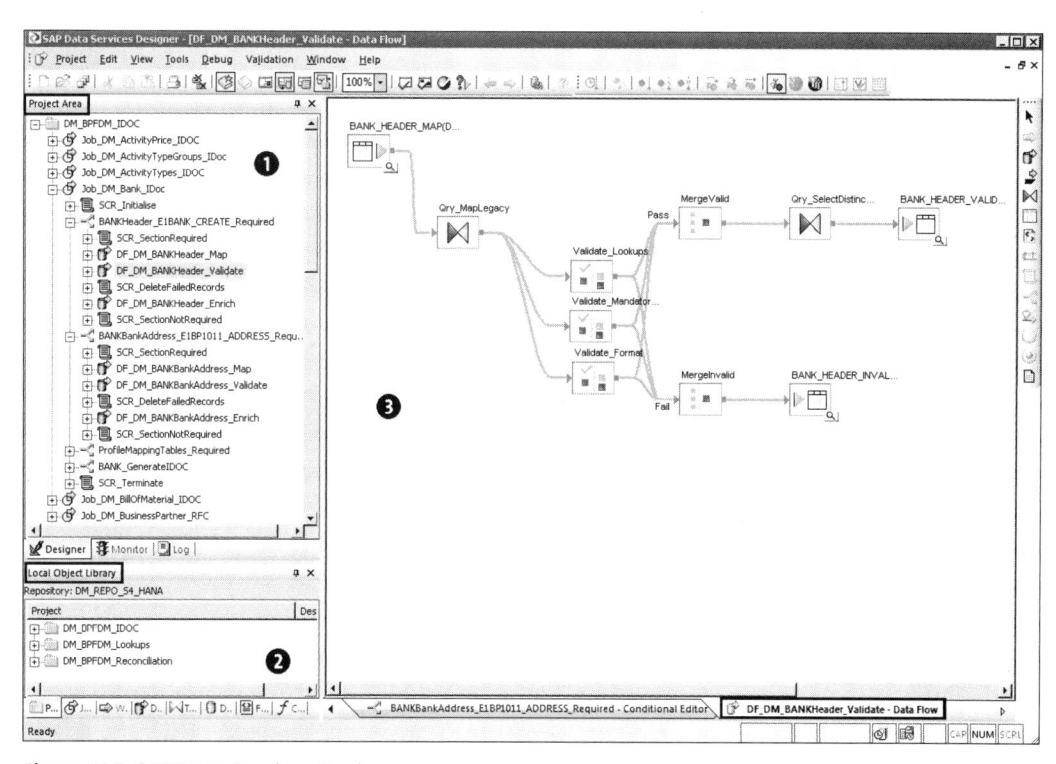

Figure 11.5 SAP Data Services Designer

11 New Implementation of Single Systems

The example in Figure 11.5 shows the Job_DM_Bank_IDoc customer job with the DF_DM_BANKHeader_Validate data flow for the bank header data. The system always displays new windows as tabs on the right-hand side.

Projects The imported content for SAP S/4HANA has the structure shown in Figure 11.6. Jobs in SAP Data Services are organized in projects; one job can be assigned to several projects. If you modify a specific job, these modifications affect all projects. So the project name is basically only a collection of references to jobs in SAP Data Services. The same applies to all subordinate objects, such as data flows. They can be reused; modifications always affect all instances. To avoid unintentional changes, you should replicate each object and use the copy for your specific purposes.

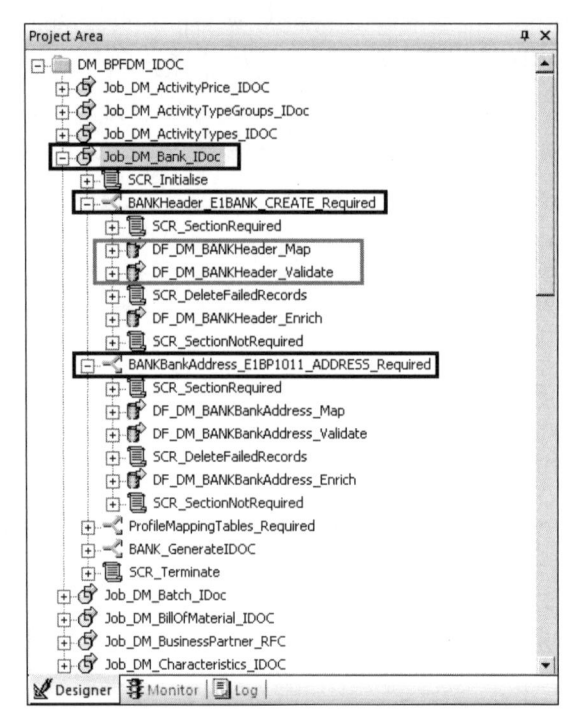

Figure 11.6 Project Structure with Job and IDoc Segments

We'll use the project DM_BPFDM_IDOC in our example. The project contains one job for each business object because data migration with Rapid Data Migration—as is the case for all other methods—always migrates the data of an entire business object as a logical unit and not for each SAP table.

402

11.3 Rapid Data Migration

We'll use job Job_DM_Bank_IDoc to transfer the bank master. In general, two data flows are significant for all data migrations and will have to be processed for each IDoc segment (for example, our first segment, E1BANK_CRE-ATE, the header segment):

Data flows

- DF_DM_BANKHeader_Map (mapping data flow, see Section 11.3.6)
- DF_DM_BANKHeader_Validate (validation data flow, see Section 11.3.8)

During the mapping, the fields are mapped, while the validation data flow enables you to display the results of various data validations after they have been carried out. Finally, the DF_DM_BANKHeader_Enrich data flow also exists, which is discussed in detail later in this section. To migrate your data, this step is not that important at first because empty fields will be populated with default values regardless.

For a mapping template, we'll create a mapping on paper. These mapping templates including content, provided for each business object, to facilitate assigning fields and values in the tool. In addition, mapping templates are an appropriate means to discuss complex field relationships with the persons responsible in the various user departments. You can immediately enrich your mapping templates with test or production data to simplify the loading without having to carry out field mappings. To make handling template files easier in the Microsoft Excel format, templates are included in the Rapid Data Migration package and are already filled with test data.

Mapping template

Figure 11.7 shows the IDoc target structure as an excerpt of the mapping template for the BANK_CREATE01 IDoc.

System Required	Enrichment Rule	Look Up Required	Text Description	Field Name	SAP_Table	SAP_Technical_Field_name	Field Length	Additional Instructions and Comments	Segment Name	Lookup Table
E1BANK_CREATE-Header Segment										
*		+	Bank country key(BANK_CTRY)	BANK_CTRY	BNKA	BANKS	3		E1BANK_CREATE	T005
*			Bank Keys(BANK_KEY)	BANK_KEY	BNKA	BANKK	15		E1BANK_CREATE	
E1BP1011_ADDRESS-Transfer structure object 1011: Bank address										
*			Name of bank(BANK_NAME)	BANK_NAME	BNKA	BANKA	60		E1BP1011_ADDRESS	
*			Bank Keys(BANK_KEY)	BANK_KEY	BNKA	BANKK	15		E1BP1011_ADDRESS	
		+	Region (State, Province, County)(REGION)	REGION	BNKA	PROVZ	3		E1BP1011_ADDRESS	T005S
			House number and street(STREET)	STREET	BNKA	STRAS	35		E1BP1011_ADDRESS	
			City(CITY)	CITY	BNKA	ORT01	35		E1BP1011_ADDRESS	
			SWIFT Code for International Payments(SWIFT_CODE)	SWIFT_CODE	BNKA	SWIFT	11		E1BP1011_ADDRESS	
			Bank number(BANK_NO)	BANK_NO	BNKA	BNKLZ	15		E1BP1011_ADDRESS	
			Bank Branch(BANK_BRANCH)	BANK_BRANCH	BNKA	BRNCH	40		E1BP1011_ADDRESS	

Figure 11.7 SAP S/4HANA Target System as an Excerpt from the Mapping Template

403

11   New Implementation of Single Systems

The following sections describe the individual columns of the templates with the terms used in all mapping templates (as seen in Table 11.2). The following symbols are used as abbreviations in SAP Data Services as well as in all templates:

- The asterisk (*) for mandatory fields
- The dollar sign ($) to highlight existing default values (there are no default values for bank master data)
- The plus sign (+) for fields with check tables in the SAP system

Fields with a plus sign for which *value mapping* is required (that is, a *conversion table*), in addition to field mapping generally, are discussed in detail in Section 11.3.7.

Column	Description
System Required	A mandatory field
Enrichment Rule	Populated with a default value if you have not assigned a source field
Look Up Required	A check table (lookup table) for this field (Only values from the input help F4 are permitted.)
Text Description	A unique and detailed description
Field Name	Field name in Rapid Data Migration content
SAP_Table	Technical name of the table in the ABAP Dictionary
SAP_Technical_Field_name	Technical name of the field in the ABAP Dictionary
Field Length	Field length in the SAP target system
Additional Instructions and Comments	Default value for fields with dollar signs
Segment Name	Name of the IDoc segment
Lookup Table	Check table for the field that impacts valid values when the values are mapped later on

Table 11.2 Critical Columns on the SAP S/4HANA Target Side in the Mapping Template

The data migration content for SAP Data Services uses the IDoc interface to provide the same design and functionality for all business objects in the modeled data flows and for all mapping structures. As a result, you'll be able to use new business objects without deep application expertise.

11.3.4 Connecting to Source Systems

Now that you're familiar with the basic structure of the content provided, let's take a look at the actual data migration process and the integration of the source system. First, you'll integrate the legacy system into SAP Data Services, which will make legacy structures and metadata known to the system.

Source systems

You can also integrate several source systems to SAP Data Services using different interfaces. In our example, we won't use data from external systems; instead, we'll provide our source data using the migration templates provided in the Rapid Data Migration content (see Section 11.3.6).

As an example, let's first discuss briefly customer data: Let's assume we are using a table from the legacy system database called CUSTOMERADDRESS as well as a Microsoft Excel file called *Customer_Header.xls*, which contains customer names from the legacy system. (Of course, direct integration using an application or by loading flat files is also possible.)

To integrate the table CUSTOMERADDRESS from the legacy system, first perform the following steps: Navigate to the **Datastores** tab in the **Local Object Library** and create a database connection by right-clicking in the empty area.

Integrating the database

In our example, you'll integrate the DS_LEGACY database using an ODBC interface. Each connection is provided with a subitem called **Tables**, which you can use to select all or a set of tables of the legacy system. This connection also makes metadata, such as *field names* and *field lengths*, known in SAP Data Services. This connection also enables you to view the existing data records in the table (see Figure 11.8).

11 New Implementation of Single Systems

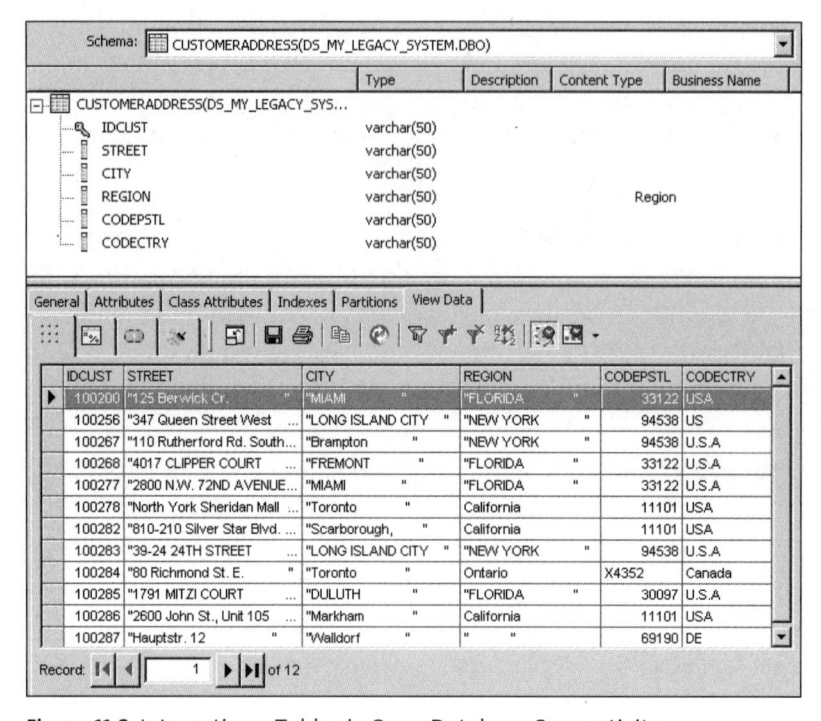

Figure 11.8 Integrating a Table via Open Database Connectivity

File interface Next, you'll integrate the Microsoft Excel files by right-clicking on the **Formats** tab and selecting the **New** menu item. Next, select a specific spreadsheet and an area within the table. If the table contains column names in the first row, you can copy the metadata directly from the Microsoft Excel file by selecting the corresponding function, as shown in Figure 11.9, and confirming your selection by clicking the **Import Schema** button.

You can adjust the default data formats, such as `varchar 255` manually if required. Be sure to use the character data type for all purely numerical values that should not be used in mathematical operations.

For integrated Microsoft Excel files, you can preview data in the same way as displaying table data records if SAP Data Services can access the file. After importing your data to SAP Data Services, you won't see any major difference, and you can use the two objects in the same way. However, one restriction applies: In SAP Data Services, database tables and flat files can be the sources as well as the targets of the data, Microsoft Excel files can only be used as a source, i.e., you cannot write to the Microsoft Excel file directly.

11.3 Rapid Data Migration

Figure 11.9 illustrates the integration of the Microsoft Excel file, which was assigned a name based on Customer_Header, namely, Customer_Header.xls.

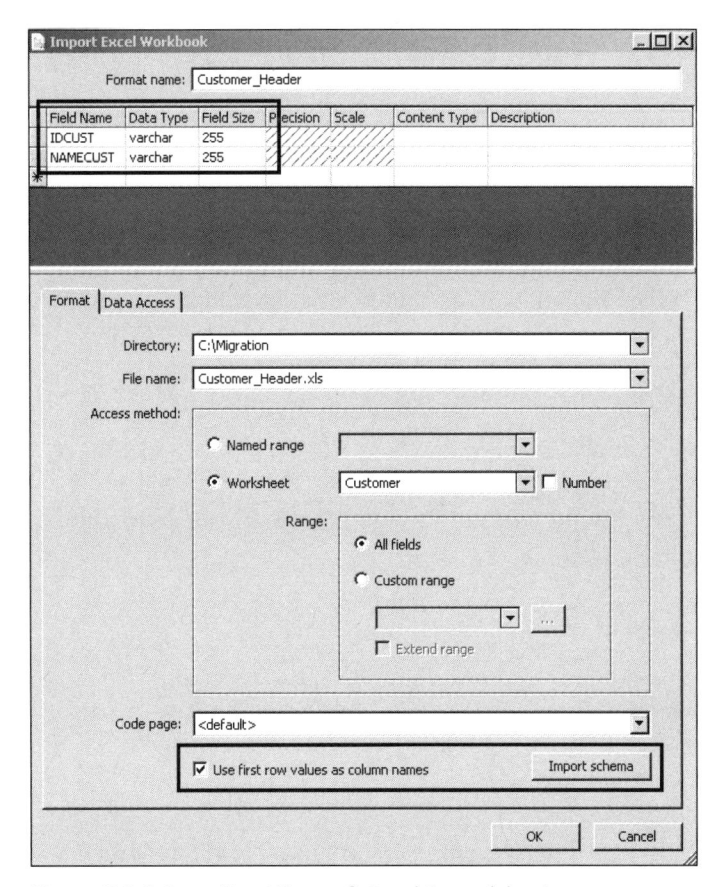

Figure 11.9 Integrating Microsoft Excel Spreadsheets

> **Formatting in Microsoft Excel**
>
> Because Microsoft Excel is a spreadsheet program and not a word processor, cells with numeric content are automatically formatted as numbers, which might result in undesired exponential notations and the loss of leading zeros. This issue occurs frequently for US ZIP codes, which sometimes start with a zero. You should therefore format the corresponding columns as text columns.

407

11.3.5 Data Profiling

Profiler At this point, you have integrated the metadata of two different legacy systems (table and Excel) into SAP Data Services. You can now use the *Profiler*, which is embedded in SAP Data Services, to find patterns in and check the quality of the data in the legacy system prior to the mapping. For data profiling, the data must be stored either in tables or in flat files.

Column profiling To profile your data, in **Local Object Library** select the table CUSTOMERADDRESS and right-click on the table name. In the context menu that opens, select the **Submit Column Profile Request** function. In the example shown in Figure 11.10, the system will submits a detailed profiling request for each column when you click **Submit**. You can submit a new profiling request in the **View Data** section anytime.

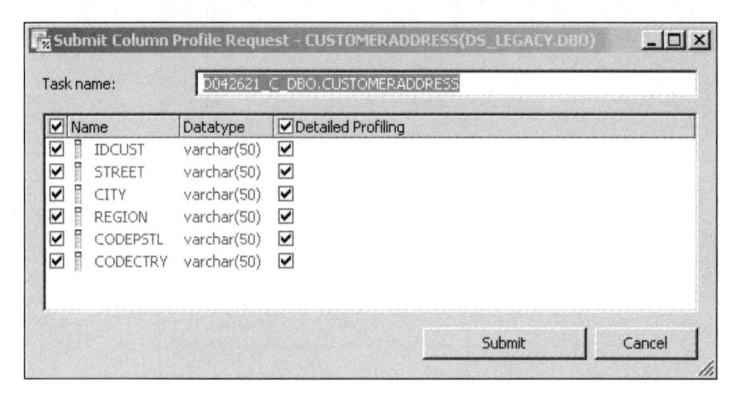

Figure 11.10 Column Profiling

The results are displayed in Figure 11.11. The column profiling shows that a ZIP code may be incorrect. Of the twelve data records from the various countries, only one ZIP code contains letters instead of just numerals. This ZIP code with the value "X4352" is from a customer from Canada and would be identified even if a larger dataset was profiled.

Thus, the question now is whether a postal code in Canada is allowed to have the format X9999, that is, a letter followed by four numbers. We can answer this question by evaluating the validations embedded in SAP Data Services (see Section 11.3.8).

11.3 Rapid Data Migration

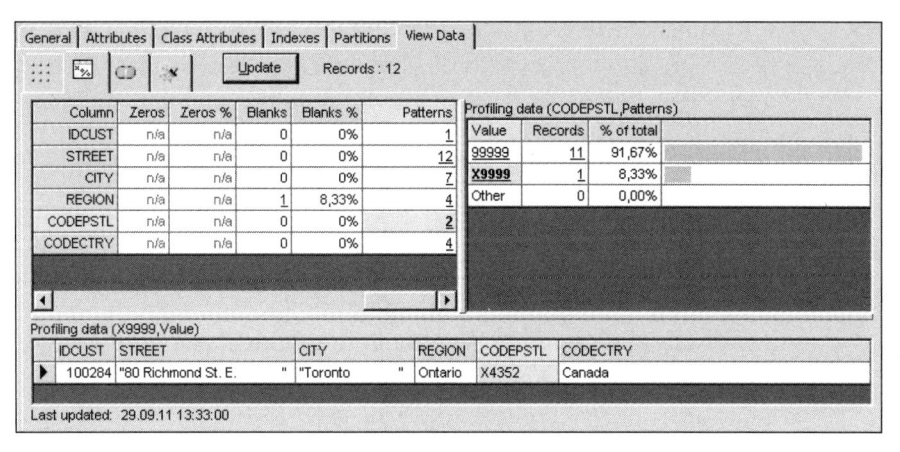

Figure 11.11 Column Profiling Result

In addition to the *patterns* of the data records used in this example, further column profiling analyses are available, for example:

- **Min**
  Minimum value according to lexicographical order
- **Max**
  Maximum value according to lexicographical order
- **Median**
  Median value
- **Min string length**
  Shortest value
- **Max string length**
  Longest value
- **Average string length**
  Value with an average length
- **Distincts**
  Number of disjoint values
- **Nulls**
  Missing values

This analysis allows you to identify incorrect values, and experienced users can use the **Max string length** function to determine which values are too long.

11   New Implementation of Single Systems

Relationship profiling

You can also start more complex profiling requests to compare database tables with one another and find incomplete data records (data records without headers, headers without items, and so on) by analyzing their relationships.

To compare database tables, start the data profiling from the first table by right-clicking on the table name and selecting **Submit Relationship Profile Request With…** in the context menu. The cursor will become a crosshair, which you'll use to select the second table (or alternatively a flat file).

In the next dialog box, you'll click **Submit** to submit a *relationship profile request* after having confirmed or adapted the key relationship between the two tables accordingly. In our example, table CUSTOMERHEADER is integrated directly from the legacy system instead of using a Microsoft Excel file. The key is the customer number in the legacy system, IDCUST (see Figure 11.12).

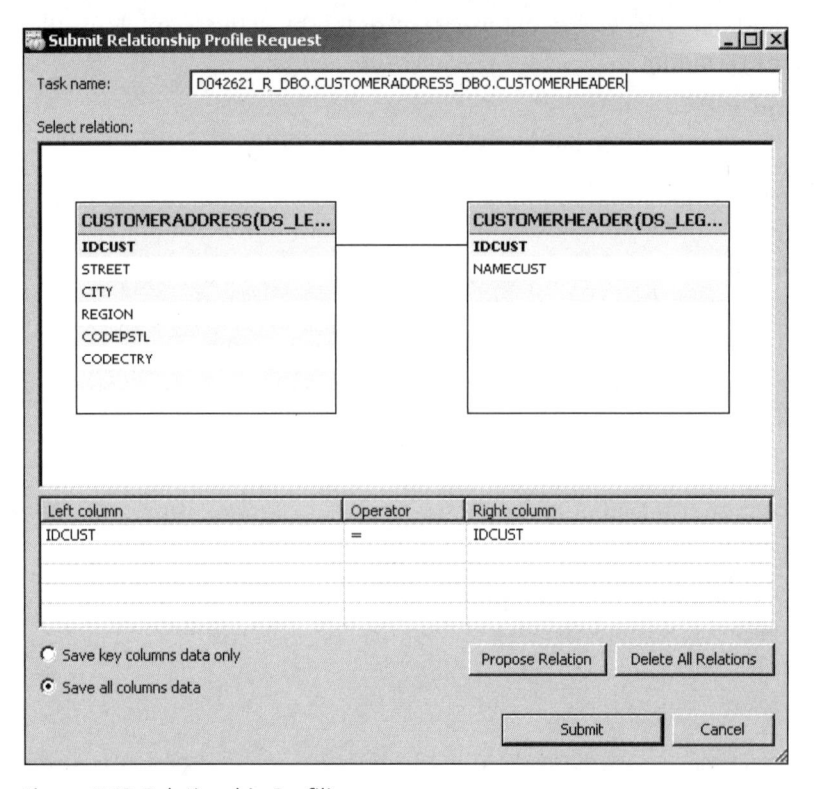

Figure 11.12 Relationship Profiling

11.3 Rapid Data Migration

The result of the relationship profiling, as shown in Figure 11.13, indicates that 8.33% of all addresses lack a header record and 15.38% of all header data records lack an address. In our limited example of only twelve data records, one address has not been used for a long time. This address is not assigned to any customer and is stored in the legacy system as an address without any reference. Also, two customer records lack address data in the legacy system. We know that these two data records will definitively not be transferred to SAP S/4HANA because mandatory address data is missing.

SAP Data Services additionally enables you to display problematic data records. In our example, as shown in Figure 11.13, the data record for legacy customer number **100289** is problematic. You can also have the system display the missing address that the application could not find in a relational database without any problems because the header data is missing.

Displaying problematic data records

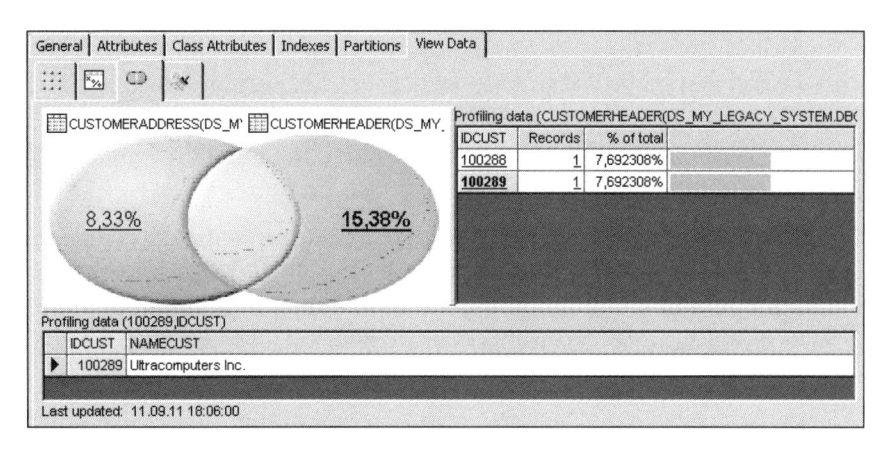

Figure 11.13 Relationship Profiling Result

The next steps depend on your specific case. However, experience has shown that deciding, in the legacy system, whether an address will be transferred or not and, if required, whether the data will be corrected will pay off. If the data in the legacy system is no longer up-to-date or inconsistent, *not* transferring the data will save you unnecessary time and effort.

11.3.6 Field Mapping

Now let's return to bank data. So that you can compare our example to the file upload using the SAP S/4HANA migration cockpit, which we'll describe

Using data migration templates

411

in Section 11.4, we assume that the source data has already been cleansed. For simplification, we'll only use two data records in our example of migrating bank data.

In contrast to direct integrations (see Section 11.3.4), we'll use the data migration templates specifically provided for SAP S/4HANA. These Microsoft Excel files are included in the Rapid Data Migration content, which has a separate Excel sheet for every segment to be migrated and contains mapping notes, rules, and descriptions of mandatory fields.

If you use these migration templates, the entire field mapping is already implemented in SAP Data Services, provided with the test data used by SAP. If you want to integrate custom formats (tables or files), however, you'll have to assign the SAP fields first.

In general, mapping fields is the central step in any data migration: The available fields of the source system are assigned to the predefined fields of the target system (SAP S/4HANA). In our case, analogous to mapping templates, the target system is already defined by the IDoc segments. The source system, instead, is defined by its source structures, in our example by an Excel migration template.

Mapping on paper Let's first take a look at mapping on paper for our two source structures, as shown in Figure 11.7 in Section 11.3.3. The left side of the table features a free area for the legacy system, not displayed in the figure, and the structure of the SAP S/4HANA system is on the right. The same concept applies to the source data in the Excel migration template. In our example, the template has already been populated with test data, as shown in Figure 11.14, which includes all four Excel sheets:

- **Introduction** with descriptions
- **Field List** with notes on mandatory fields and check tables
- **Header** filled with two table data records
- **BankAddress** for address data records (in our example, filled with two test records in relation to header records)

At first glance, you can see that all mandatory fields (*) have been populated and that no fields contain default values ($). Despite being mandatory fields, fields with default values don't have to be mapped if you provide a constant as a global variable in SAP Data Services.

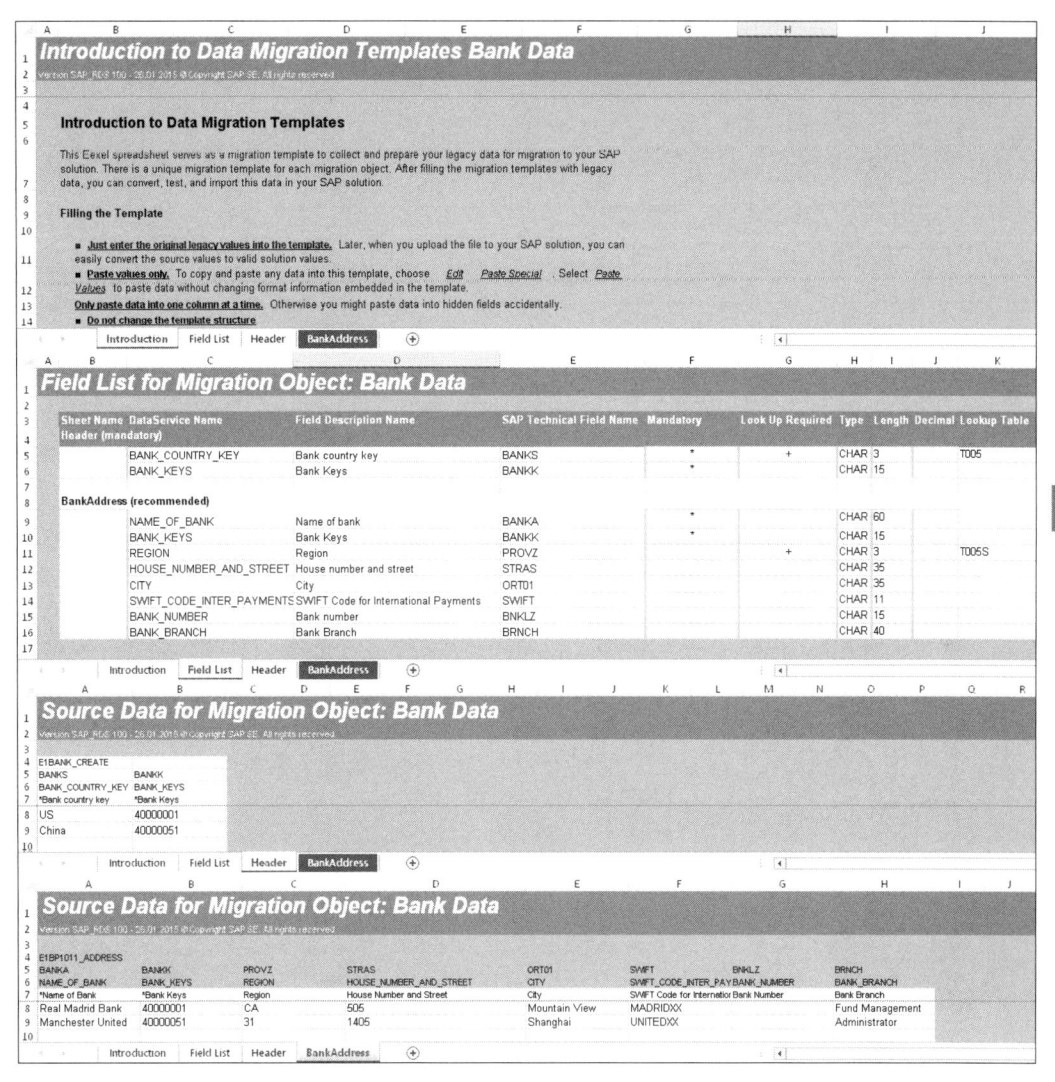

Figure 11.14 SAP S/4HANA Data Migration Template for Source Data

Usually, you'd now have to implement the mapping on paper in SAP Data Services Designer. Call the mapping view by clicking on the name of the DF_DM_BANKBankAddress_Map data flow in **Project Area** or by double-clicking on the icon in the parent data flow (shown in Figure 11.15). Because we are using a migration template, we can copy the entire mapping on a 1:1 basis.

Mapping in the designer

11 New Implementation of Single Systems

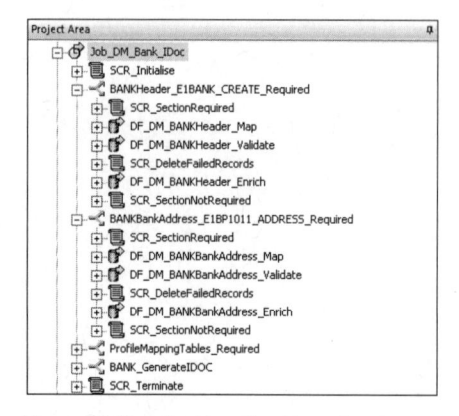

Figure 11.15 Selecting the Mapping Step

Integrating the legacy system If you now want to modify the mapping or insert specific sources, select and remove the placeholder for the source file and drag and drop the desired source (file or table) to the data flow workspace. By connecting the source with the `Qry_BestPractices` query, the source fields in the workspace are available for simplified mapping. Figure 11.16 shows the correct data flow.

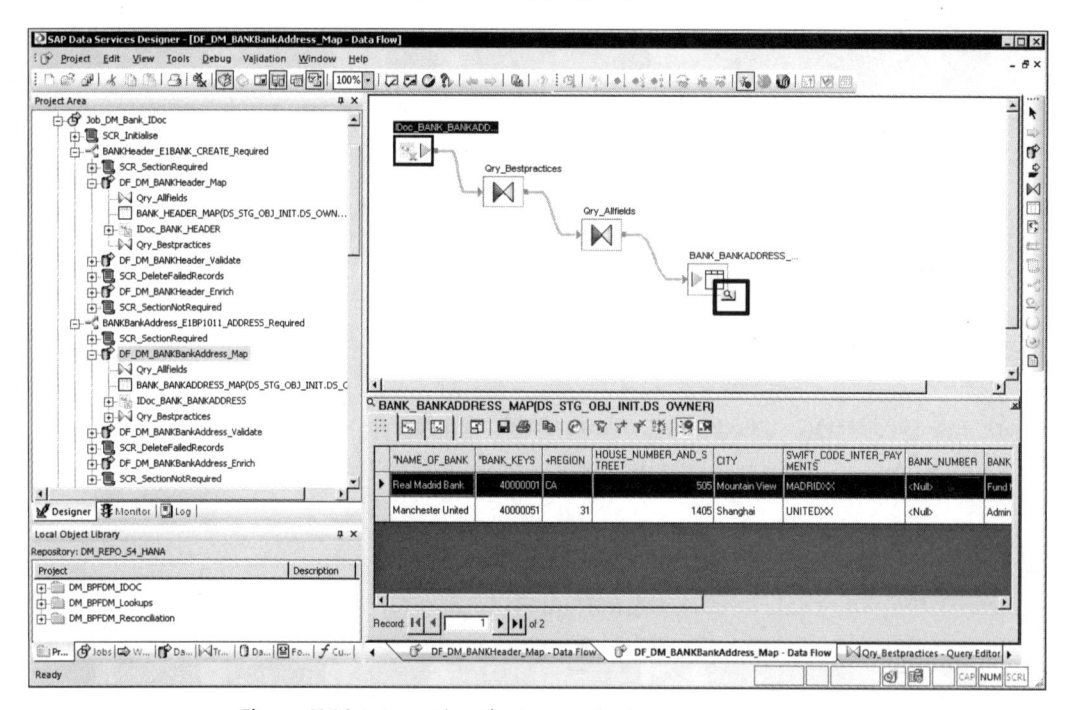

Figure 11.16 Integrating the Legacy System

414

> **Displaying Object Content**
>
> You can use the small magnifying glass [Q] next to the objects in the data flow to have the system display the content. Now, you can always keep an eye on individual or typical data records (via profiling, which is also possible in this display). Troubleshooting is thus much easier.

If you need more fields than what is available in the Baseline scope of SAP Best Practices, you can find them in the second query, `Qry_AllFields`. However, in our example, we'll only use the simplified version that contains the fields set up using SAP Best Practices for a new SAP S/4HANA system.

Carrying out internal validations in SAP Data Services when working in the data flows or in the queries makes sense. You can then quickly identify mapping errors or inconsistent settings. Use the **Validate Current** button to validate the local object or **Validate All** to check the syntax across all objects. Alternatively, you can select **Validation • Validate** from the main menu.

Internal validations

The section under the mapping in the mapping view displays the code for assigning the script language for SAP Data Services. (This script language does not have a name.) The code is generated here for all default functions. However, you can always modify the system-generated script or insert your own custom code.

Generating the assignment script

> **Using the Functions Provided**
>
> Use one of the numerous predefined functions and adapt the script code to meet your requirements. With predefined functions, you'll be able to create your own conversion rules easily, without having to start from scratch every time.

If you have more than one source structure, you'll have to define a unique key relationship between the sources. You can freely define this key relationship in the script editor or use the **Propose Join** function to generate the code in the `WHERE` condition automatically. The proposed join is based on the key relationships or on appearances of the same name in different sources, as shown in Figure 11.17.

Unique key relationship

11　New Implementation of Single Systems

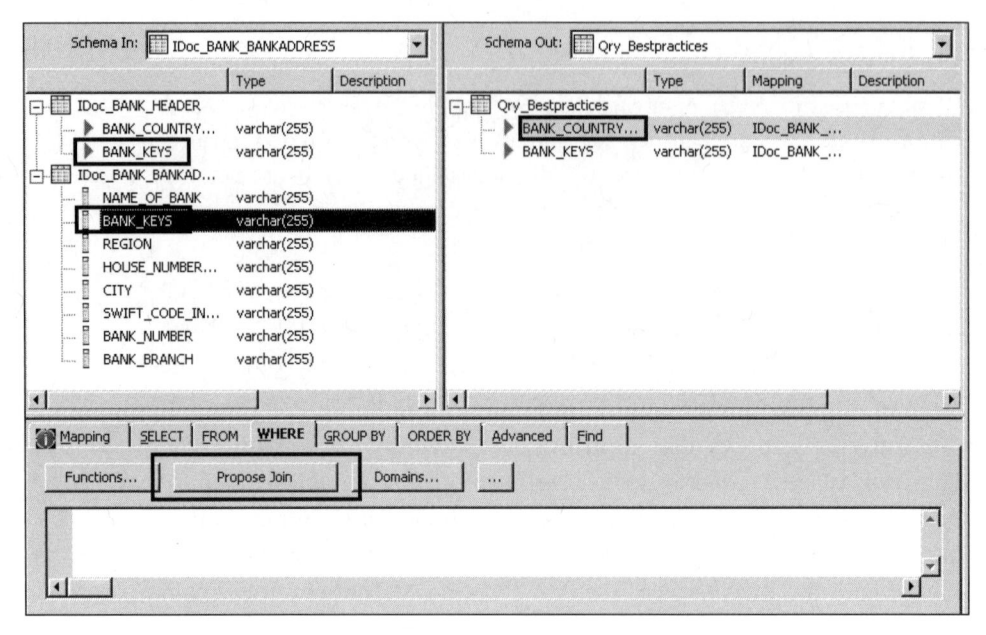

Figure 11.17 Key Relationship in Multiple Source Structures

Copying the mapping

In our case, we'll rely on the SAP S/4HANA migration template and simply copy the mapping. If you want to adapt the mapping, select the required fields on the left, then drag and drop them on the relevant target field to the right. Figure 11.18 shows the results. The actual mapping is now performed according to the mapping template if you don't have to make any adaptations.

If a field has already been assigned (or has a NULL initial value), you'll be asked during the mapping process whether you want to remap the field. To remap a field, right-click on the relevant field and select **Remap Column** in the context menu.

Type conversion

After you've completed the mapping and perhaps added custom code, select the validation using the **Validate Current** button or the **Validate All** button. Alternatively, you can navigate to the **Validation • Validate** option in the main menu to validate the mapping. If no error message appears, you can proceed with the remaining steps. Often, however, the system will output a warning for all fields have different data types in the source system and target system. You can ignore this warning for now

416

because the types will be automatically converted during runtime. If this conversion works for all data records (for example, converting number fields to text fields of the **Character** type), further phases of the process will not be affected.

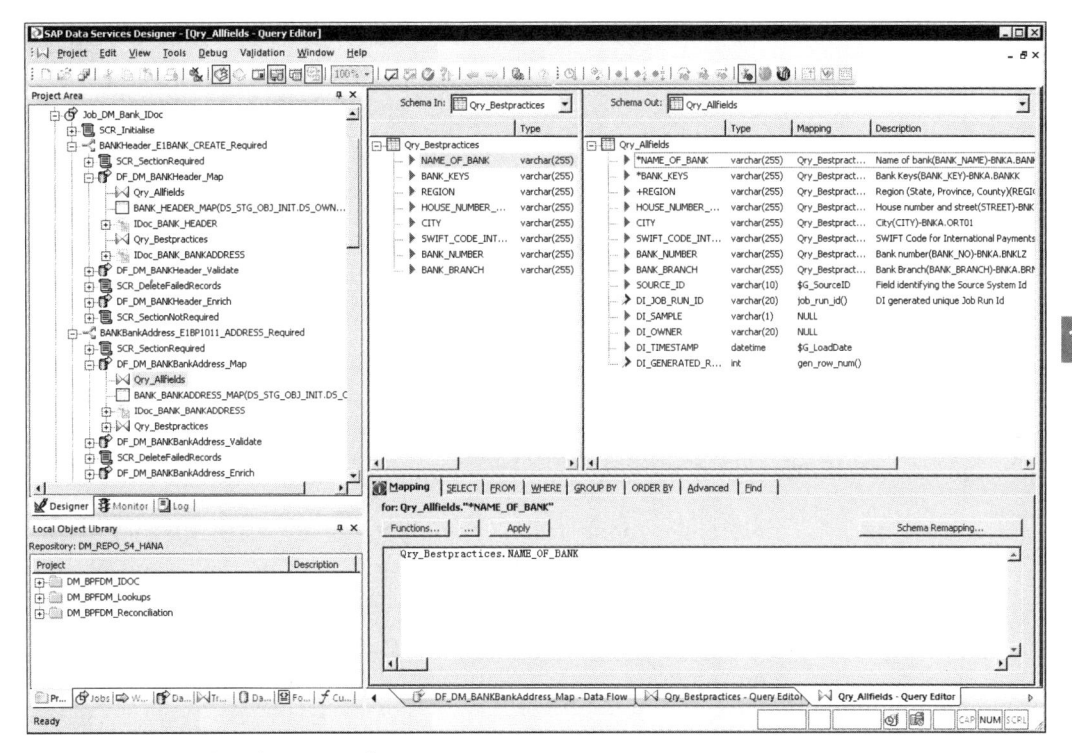

Figure 11.18 Mapping via Drag and Drop

Let's now take a closer look at the mapping and explain the individual assignments in the ETL process. Up to this point, we used a direct mapping process where fields were mapped to fields without transformations or complex rules. Compare the mapping in Figure 11.19 with the migration template from Figure 11.14; this comparison illustrates how SAP Data Services has implemented the mapping. Because the migration template uses the same names on the source and target side, the mapping is pretty straightforward.

Checking the mapping

11 New Implementation of Single Systems

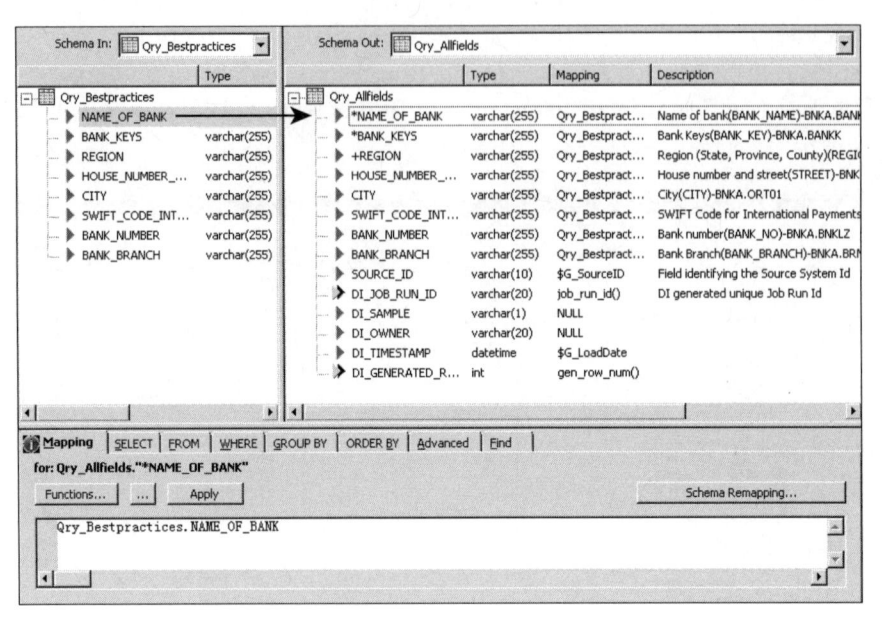

Figure 11.19 Detailed Field Mapping

Assigning the global variable

As an alternative to the field mapping, you can also assign global variables or constants in SAP Data Services. Figure 11.20 shows a constant, the ISO code for Germany (`'DE'`), assigned to the country field.

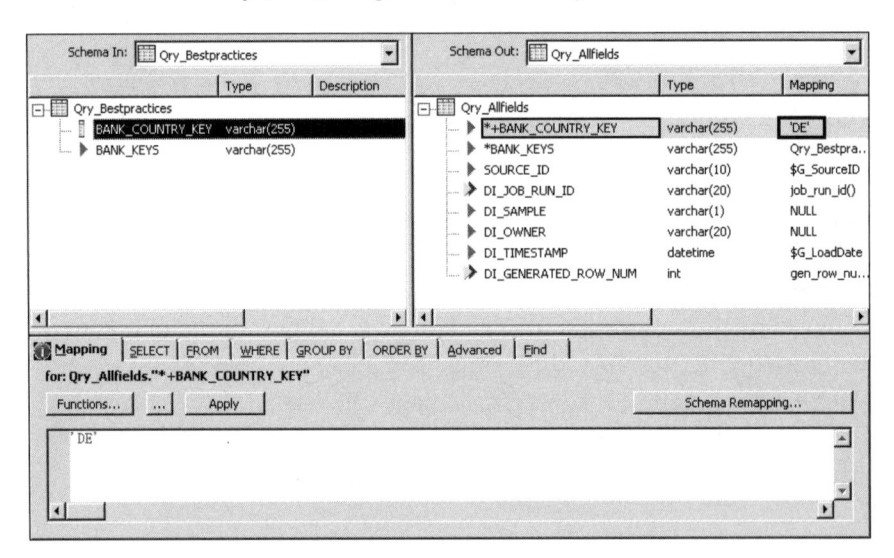

Figure 11.20 Mapping a Constant

> **Resetting the Mapping**
>
> If you want to reset a field mapping that you have performed manually or via drag and drop, deleting the generated or custom code is not sufficient. When validating the data, you'll see that empty mappings are not permitted. Instead, you'll have to reset the code by replacing the code in the input field with NULL.

11.3.7 Value Mapping and Conversion Tables

After completing a basic mapping in the central SAP Data Services Designer step, you can convert the remaining values, that is, perform a *value mapping*, for country (BANK_COUNTRY_KEY) and region (REGION). The region involves a multilevel conversion because this field also depends on the country and becomes unique when both region *and* the country are converted.

For value conversions, you'll use the *Migration Services* tool, which is provided in the Rapid Data Migration content. This tool can access the staging area where all SAP check tables have been replicated from your connected SAP S/4HANA system (see Figure 11.21). The Migration Services tool enables you to assign the correct values from the legacy system to the SAP-generated values, such as the ISO code for a country.

Migration Services

You can only change the column for legacy data in the Migration Services tool. The side for the SAP S/4HANA system corresponds to the Customizing in SAP S/4HANA and cannot be changed. Thus, the tool is a conversion table, similar to the table from Chapter 7, Section 7.3, in the SAP S/4HANA migration cockpit.

You should perform an initial job run before you start mapping the values, even before the actual mapping is complete. In this initial run, the internal number ranges and required buffer tables are initialized. In addition, the specifications for various values are collected in the legacy system for all fields whose values will be converted (*lookup fields*). This process easily identifies values that still lack data. The reason for the initial job run is that—despite the previous profiling process—you still don't know all the specifications of the values from the legacy system and thus cannot provide data for your existing specifications in the mapping process.

Lookup table

11   New Implementation of Single Systems

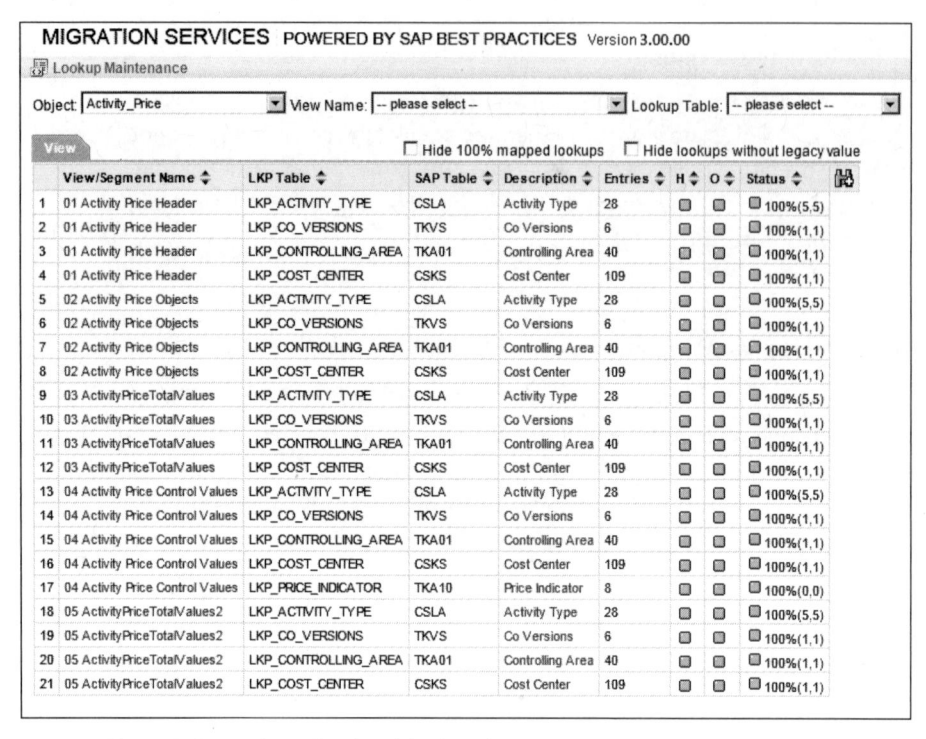

Figure 11.21 Lookup Check Tables in Migration Services

Starting the test job

To start a data migration job, right-click on the relevant node in **Project Area** (in our example shown in Figure 11.22, `Job_DM_Bank_IDoc`). Next, press **Execute**....

Determining job parameters

In a popup, SAP Data Services will let you specify parameters for the job run. Navigate to the **Global Variable** tab. For this run, be sure to set the value of the global variable `$G_ProfileMapTables` to `'Y'` for "Yes." With this selection, during the run, values from the legacy systems will be collected. This tab also provides an overview of the global variables that will be used to prepopulate the $ fields later on (as shown in Figure 11.23). You can change these values in the job run or define and store these values as a characteristic for all runs of a job by right-clicking on the context menu and selecting **Properties**.... Besides prepopulating data, you can also determine the IDoc message type and the so-called *SAP partner system* (the technical name of SAP Data Services as the sending system and of SAP S/4HANA as the receiving system). Later, SAP Data Services will write these values to the control record of the IDoc before sending the control record to SAP S/4HANA.

11.3 Rapid Data Migration

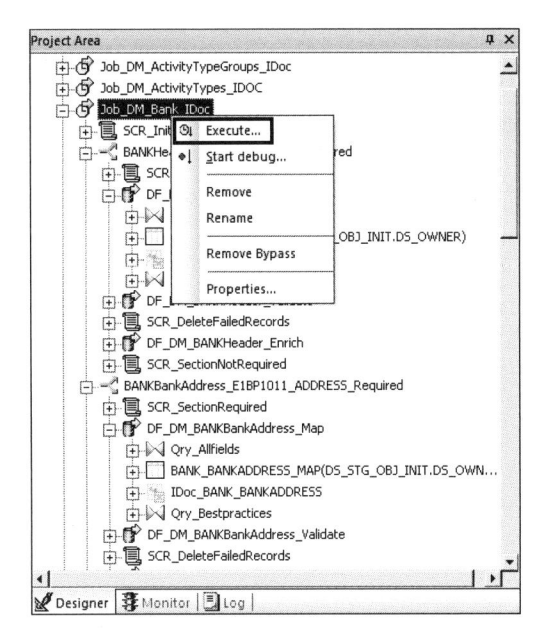

Figure 11.22 Executing a Job in SAP Data Services

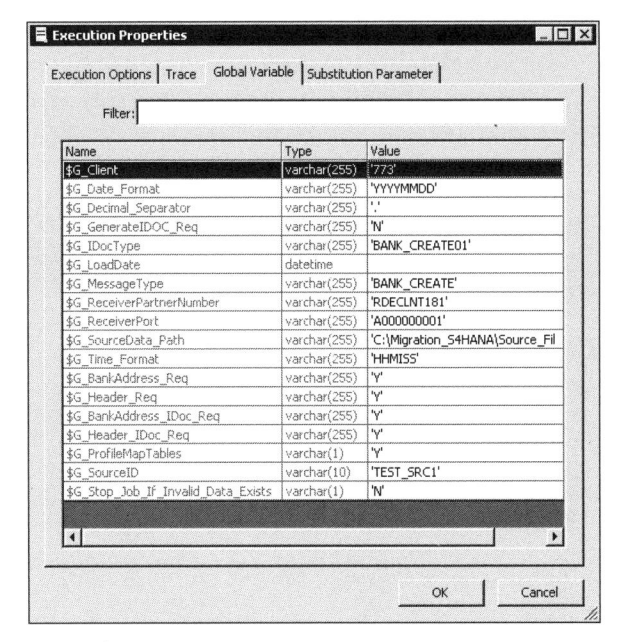

Figure 11.23 Global Variables for the Job Run

11 New Implementation of Single Systems

Job log The result of this job run is a log that, ideally, display no errors (as shown in Figure 11.24).

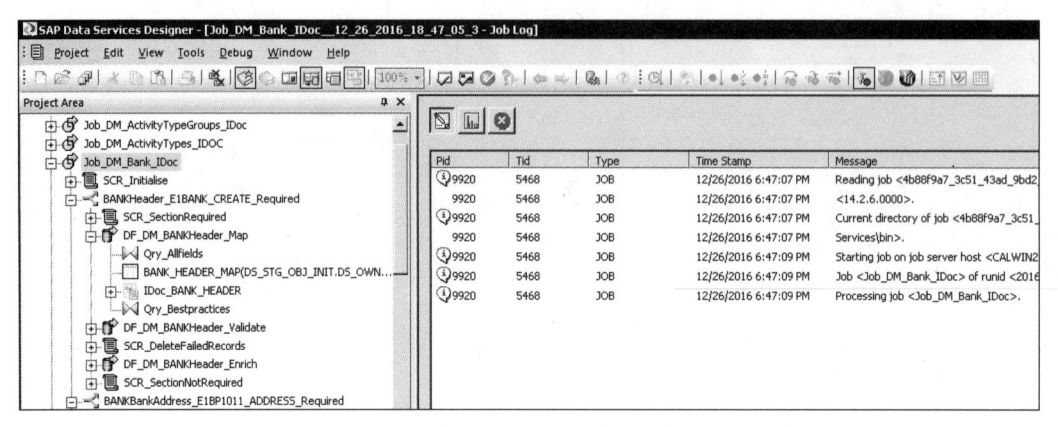

Figure 11.24 Information Messages during the Job Run in the Log

In the **Monitor** tab, you can monitor and stop the job runs (see Figure 11.25). The green traffic light symbol indicates that the job is still running; the red traffic light symbol indicates that the job has been completed. However, this indicator is independent of the actual status of the job, that is, the indicator does not tell you if the job has been completed successfully or terminated prematurely. If the job has been terminated, the log will display a red button, as shown in Figure 11.26. Click this button to display details about the error.

Example: value mapping for the country field During this initial job run, SAP Data Services will "learn" which field values exist in the legacy data. You can perform this test run with a subset of the data that you want to convert or with all the data you have available.

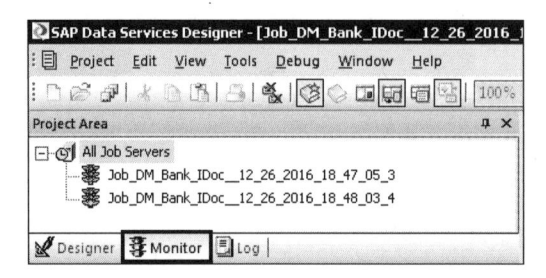

Figure 11.25 Job Monitor in the Project Area

11.3 Rapid Data Migration

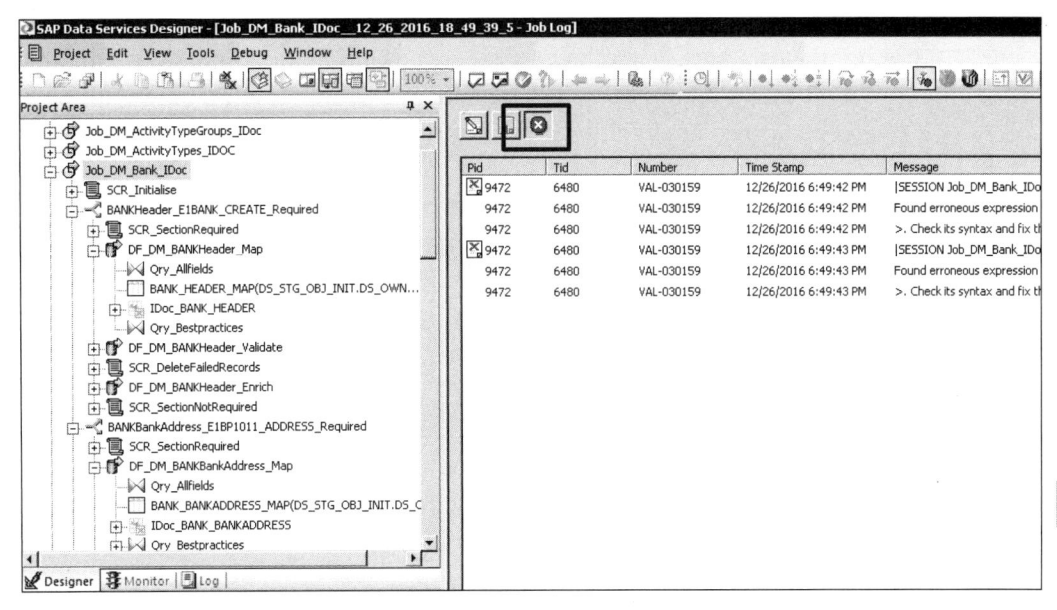

Figure 11.26 Cancelation and Error Messages in the Log

Let's return to our example with the country codes: If your legacy system includes the countries in plain text notations and does not use standard codes, you still might need different specifications for the same country to correct inconsistencies or typos. In the SAP system, with value mapping, all these fields will be merged into one value, i.e., the correct ISO code for the country, as shown in Table 11.3.

Value in the Legacy System	ISO Code in the SAP System
Deutschland	DE
Deutschlnd	DE
BRD	DE
USA	US
U.S.A	US

Table 11.3 Sample Value Mapping for the Country Field

423

11 New Implementation of Single Systems

Maintaining field values manually In our example, we'll use the migration template from Figure 11.14 to obtain the necessary field values for existing countries and regions. You can then maintain these field values manually in Migration Services. Because you performed an initial job run after mapping out these fields, they will be available in the tool. Thus, value mappings are as simple as field mappings. In Migration Services, you'll now assign the collected values to the relevant SAP values via drag and drop (as shown in Figure 11.27) or by selecting from a dropdown list (as shown in Figure 11.28). A a searchable help function is also available (see Figure 11.30).

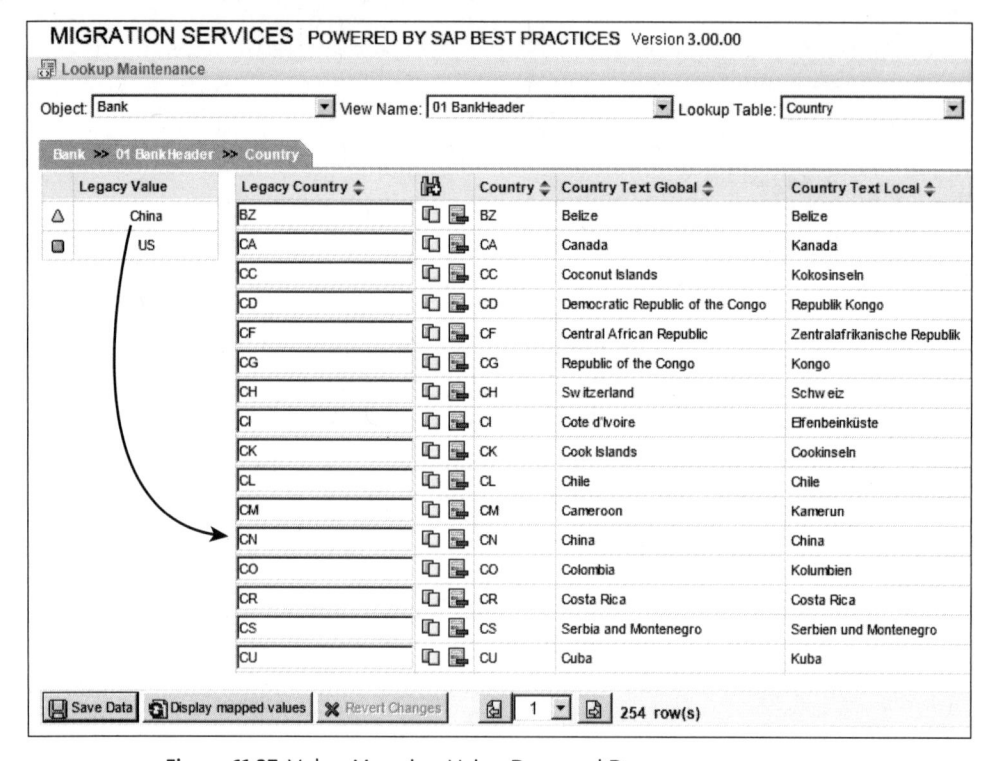

Legacy Value	Legacy Country		Country	Country Text Global	Country Text Local
⚠ China	BZ		BZ	Belize	Belize
▢ US	CA		CA	Canada	Kanada
	CC		CC	Coconut Islands	Kokosinseln
	CD		CD	Democratic Republic of the Congo	Republik Kongo
	CF		CF	Central African Republic	Zentralafrikanische Republik
	CG		CG	Republic of the Congo	Kongo
	CH		CH	Switzerland	Schweiz
	CI		CI	Cote d'Ivoire	Elfenbeinküste
	CK		CK	Cook Islands	Cookinseln
	CL		CL	Chile	Chile
	CM		CM	Cameroon	Kamerun
	CN		CN	China	China
	CO		CO	Colombia	Kolumbien
	CR		CR	Costa Rica	Costa Rica
	CS		CS	Serbia and Montenegro	Serbien und Montenegro
	CU		CU	Cuba	Kuba

Figure 11.27 Value Mapping Using Drag and Drop

The value mapping status is indicated by traffic light symbols in Migration Services:

- Green square: mapped
- Yellow triangle: not mapped yet
- Red circle: mapped twice/not mapped uniquely

11.3 Rapid Data Migration

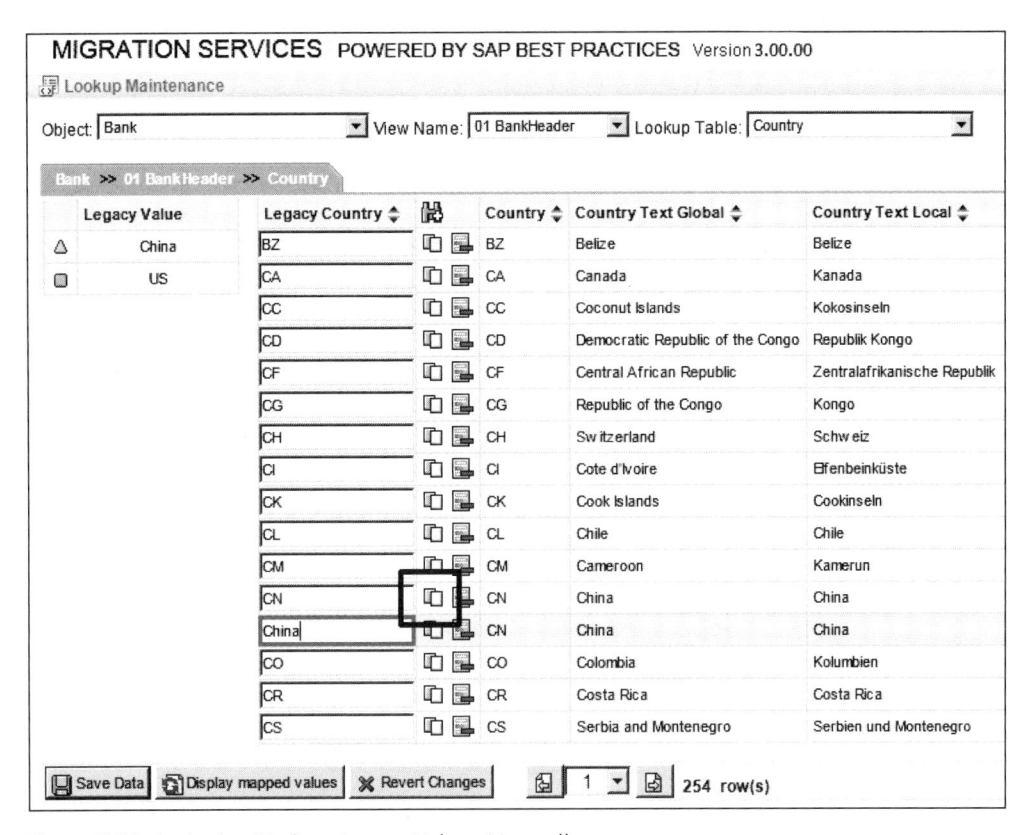

Figure 11.28 Assigning Various Legacy Values Manually

Figure 11.27 and Figure 11.29 show some examples of value mapping statuses. With these symbols, you'll be able to easily track progress during the value conversion. Now the data is ready for validation.

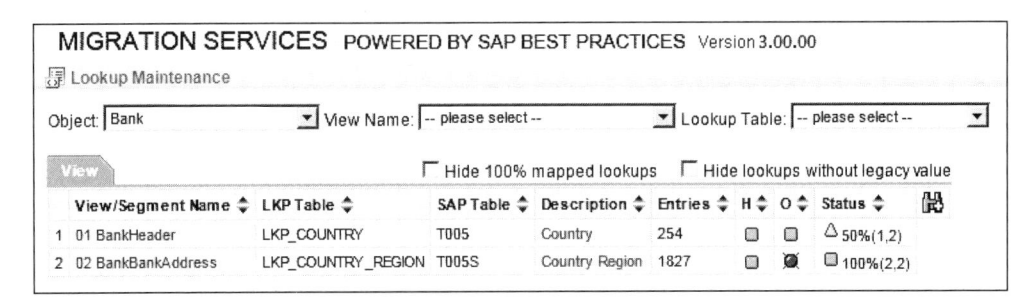

Figure 11.29 Status of Value Mapping in Migration Services

11   New Implementation of Single Systems

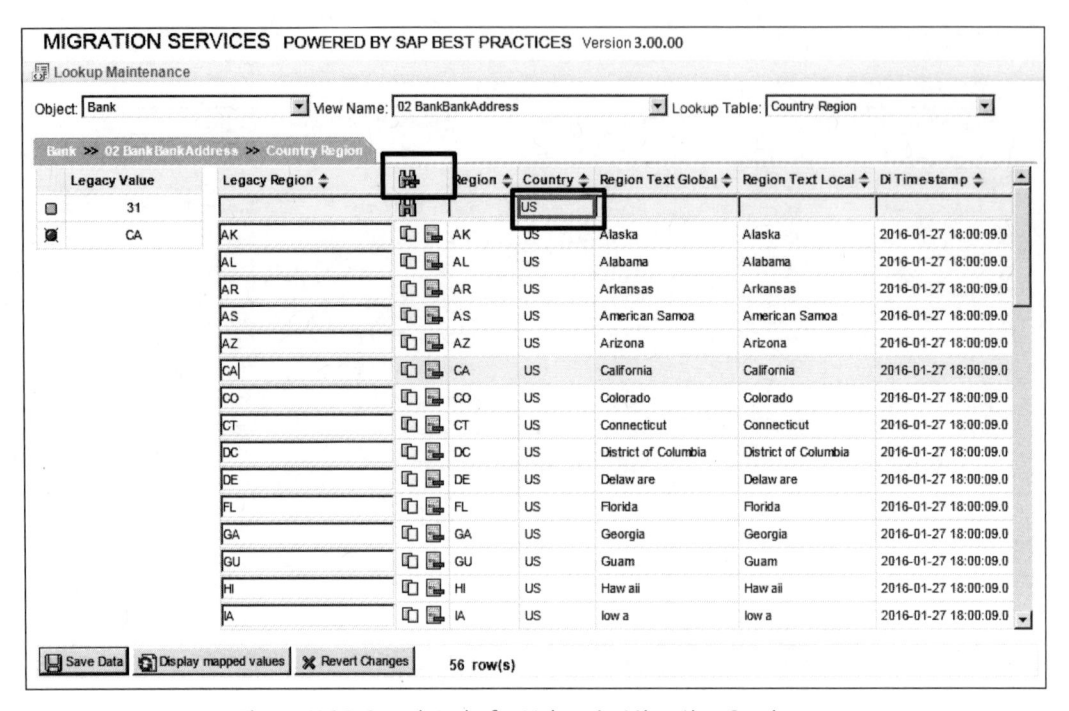

Figure 11.30 Search Help for Values in Migration Services

11.3.8   Data Validation

After successfully mapping values using Migration Services, let's now turn to data validations in the SAP Data Services Designer.

Validations

SAP Data Services does not import data records to SAP S/4HANA that have not passed all of the three following validations (see Figure 11.31):

- **Validation using check tables** (Validate_Lookups)
  For all fields marked with a plus sign (+), the values are compared to the values in the SAP check tables. Only legacy values that were previously converted to a lookup value in Migration Services will pass this test.

- **Validation of mandatory fields** (Validate_Mandatory_Columns)
  For all fields marked with an asterisk (*), values must exist (NOT NULL).

- **Validation of the format** (Validate_Format)
  This validation is carried out for all fields subject to format checks in SAP S/4HANA if the data migration content provides for these format checks. The system will check, for example, for correct field lengths in SAP

S/4HANA (see our earlier example regarding the length of the material number field in Chapter 10, Section 10.2.2) or check that ZIP codes follow the correct syntax.

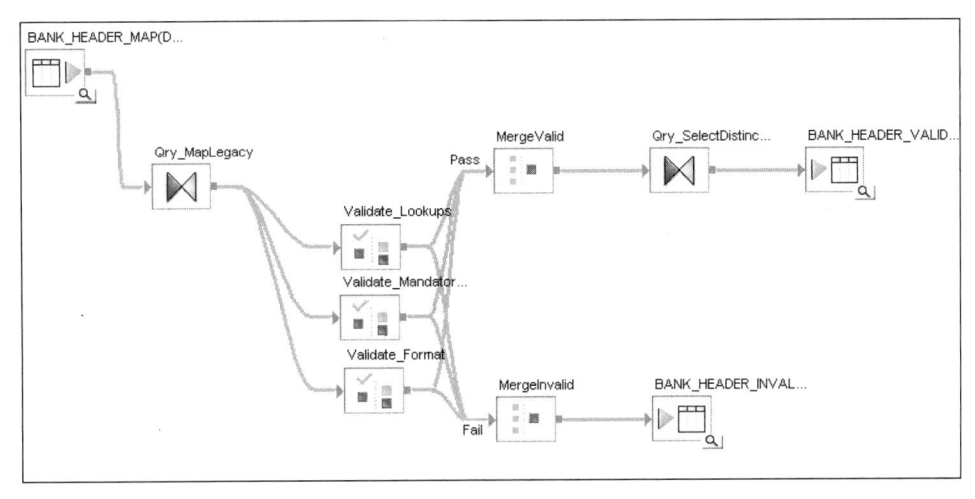

Figure 11.31 Data Flow for Validations in SAP Data Services

To execute the check routines, you'll run the `Job_DM_Bank_IDoc` job again. However, this run will not send any IDocs to the SAP S/4HANA system—a dry run that you can carry out as many times as required until satisfied with validation results.

Job run

Validations are not carried out successively but in parallel, which means that all fields will undergo all validations and that the validations do not terminate when an error occurs, as is the case with many other methods. Also, data records can fail several validations at once. For example, if the country of a bank (*+BANK_COUNTRY_KEY, a mandatory field) is not populated, the field will fail validation twice. First, this mandatory field is not populated (Validate_Mandatory_Columns), and second, the requirement that the value be converted (Validate_Lookups) has not been met. According to the data flow shown in Figure 11.31, the value will receive a `Fail` status and will end up in the **Invalid** area twice.

Validation process

You can use the small magnifying glass at the end point (see Figure 11.32) to display failed records in SAP Data Services Designer and identify the cause. So that values that received a `Pass` are not displayed twice in the **Valid** area, you can use the SELECT DISTINCT statement for data records that

11 New Implementation of Single Systems

have passed the validation. Only valid data can be further processed and populated with default values or imported via IDocs.

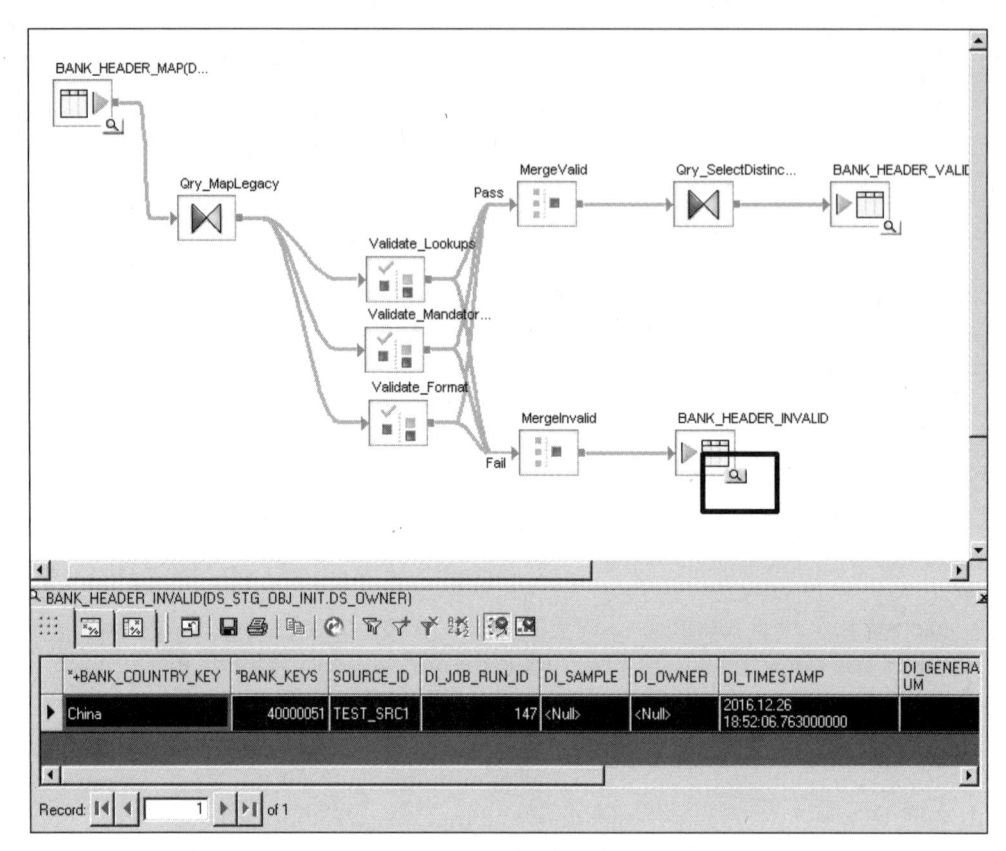

Figure 11.32 Incorrect Data Records after the Test Run

> [»] **Embedded Validation Functions**
>
> The Rapid Data Migration content not only provides data flows and mappings, it also contains validation functions, such as a function for ZIP code validations.
>
> In Section 11.3.5, we noticed a data record with a Canadian postal code, which would not pass the format validation: X4352 is not a valid postal code for Canada. Actually, Canadian postal codes have a much more complex structure. Instead of the format X9999 (1 letter—followed by 4 numbers), the syntax is X9X 9X9, which also implies that the postal code has 6 digits

11.3 Rapid Data Migration

instead of 5. This validation function is an ideal example of a function available with SAP Best Practices and embedded into SAP Data Services.

The code for the ZIP code validation function is written in the specific SAP Data Services script language, which can be extended to any country. The code is based on the *Backus-Naur Form* (BNF)—a metalanguage for grammar. Figure 11.33 shows the editor and the provided code for ZIP code validations.

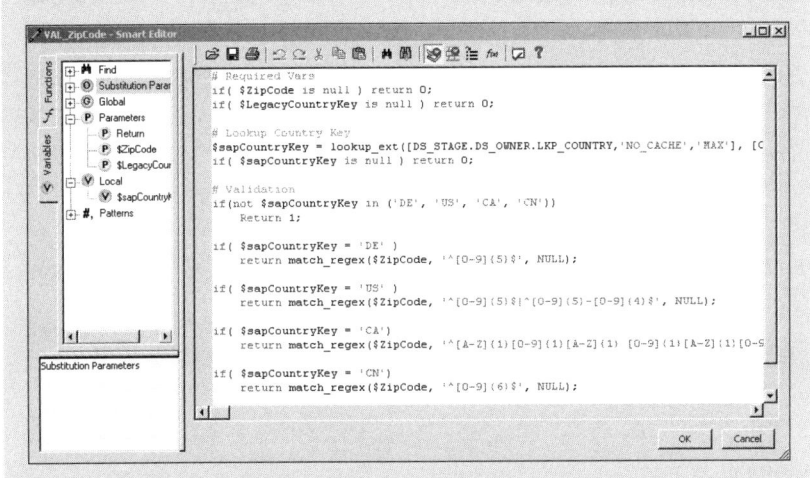

Figure 11.33 Function Editor in SAP Data Services

Note, however, that this validation only checks the syntax and does not include a plausibility check for the ZIP code. While validating a concrete ZIP code with the corresponding city and street can technically be implemented easily in SAP Data Services using the Data Quality function, for plausibility checks, you'll have integrate fee-based databases provided by local postal operators that must be updated continuously.

When errors exist, how do you proceed? In general, you can discard and exclude from the migration all data that was filtered by SAP Data Services. In this case, you won't have to do anything. However, correcting all identified inconsistencies in the legacy system makes more sense because doing so additionally improves your data quality. After you have cleansed your data records, they are loaded again for the next run and pass the validations. This procedure is iterative: You can repeat the process until only discarded data records are caught in SAP Data Services. These data records won't be migrated to SAP S/4HANA.

Troubleshooting

429

11.3.9 Importing Data

After successfully importing, converting, transforming, and validating your data records, you can perform the next step: loading the IDocs to the SAP S/4HANA system. In this context, be aware that the source data is always extracted from the data sources for each job run, which means that you won't work with data temporarily stored in SAP Data Services but instead with current values from the migration template or other source files or databases you use.

Connection to SAP S/4HANA

Before you can import IDocs into the SAP S/4HANA system, you'll have to modify the connection to your SAP S/4HANA system in SAP Data Services. The DS_SAP SAP datastore (**Local Object Library • Datastores**) is provided with a dummy connection only. To integrate your SAP S/4HANA system, you'll need to gather various system information.

Table 11.4 compares the terms used in the SAP S/4HANA world to the names used in SAP Data Services for configuring connections.

SAP S/4HANA	SAP Data Services	Example
Application server	Application server	myserver01.me.com total
Instance number	System number	00
System ID	–	PRD
Client	Client number	100
User	User name	–
Password	Password	–

Table 11.4 Differences in the Names for the Configuration

Figure 11.34 shows the window for entering the SAP S/4HANA system parameters. You can also find information on the configuration in the Configuration Guide of the Rapid Data Migration package.

IDoc transfer via RFC

To actually load IDocs in the next run, you'll have to change the default value of a critical global variable, $G_GenerateIDOC_Req. If you change this value to 'Y', the system will not only carry out the test run but also will also set up the IDocs in SAP Data Services and transfer them to the SAP S/4HANA system via *Remote Function Calls* (RFCs).

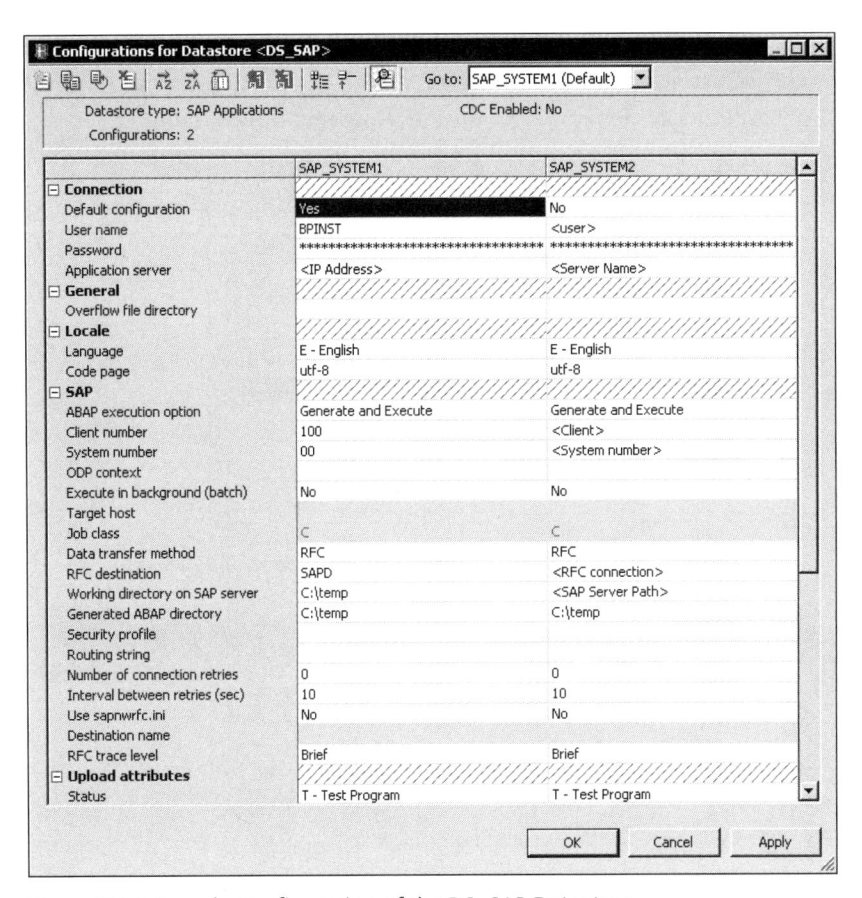

Figure 11.34 Sample Configuration of the DS_SAP Datastore

Alternatively, you can also store IDocs in local files, which may be necessary, for example, if you cannot integrate the SAP S/4HANA system or if the system is not yet available. In this case, you'll need to transfer the files to the SAP application server in a separate FTP process.

Figure 11.35 shows the popup dialog for confirming the update run. The BANK_CREATE IDocs of the BANK_CREATE01 basic type are sent to the SAP S/4HANA system with the RDE ID and Client 181. The global variables maintained here will be written to the IDoc control record, which serves as an "envelope" for the IDoc.

Confirming update runs

If the job has successfully completed, the IDocs were sent to the SAP S/4HANA system and updated there—provided the *inbound IDoc* is set correctly. The

Rapid Data Migration Configuration Guide describes in detail the settings for IDoc Customizing in your system. You can download the guide from the SAP Best Practices Explorer and the SAP Note mentioned there.

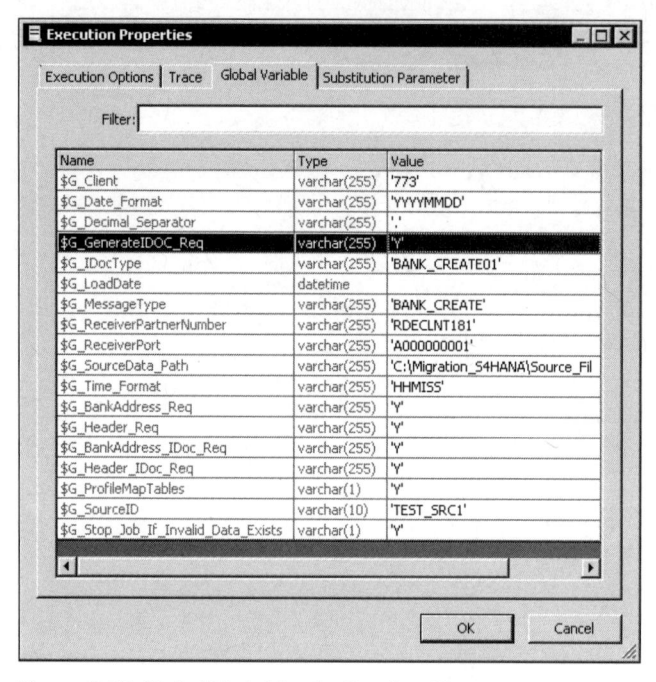

Figure 11.35 Global Variables for Sending IDocs

You can now log on to the SAP S/4HANA system, use the IDoc monitor there, or have the system display our newly created banks in a corresponding application. The following section explains how you can implement this much more elegantly, without leaving SAP Data Services.

11.3.10 Monitoring

SAP BusinessObjects Web Intelligence reports

Integrating SAP Data Services with SAP BusinessObjects Business Intelligence (BI) allows for integrating Business Analytics reports in an easy way. The data migration content provided contains predefined Web Intelligence reports for monitoring data migration projects (see Figure 11.36).

You can either use these reports as templates and adapt them or use them without any modifications.

11.3 Rapid Data Migration

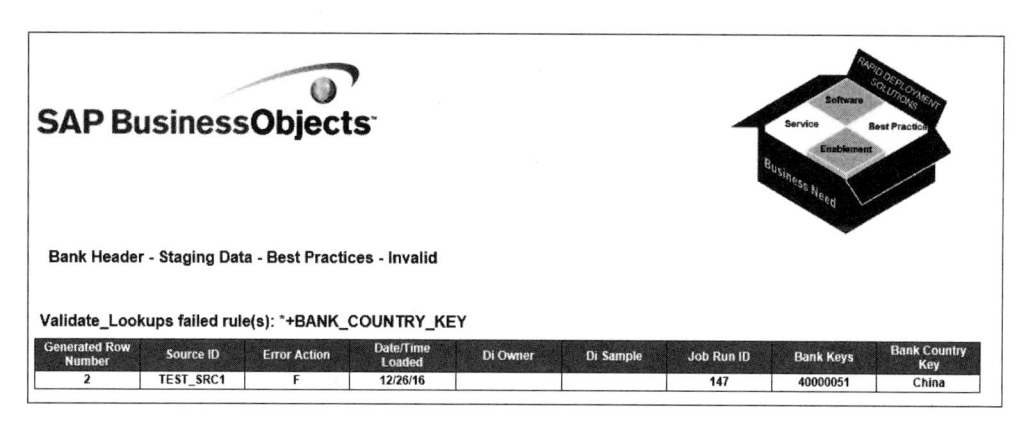

Bank Header - Staging Data - Best Practices - Invalid

Validate_Lookups failed rule(s): *+BANK_COUNTRY_KEY

Generated Row Number	Source ID	Error Action	Date/Time Loaded	Di Owner	Di Sample	Job Run ID	Bank Keys	Bank Country Key
2	TEST_SRC1	F	12/26/16			147	40000051	China

Figure 11.36 Web Intelligence Reports to Indicate Missing Data Records

Similar to the Migration Services tool, you'll access these reports using a web browser. The *BI Launchpad* (see Figure 11.37) even enables functional users that were not involved in the data migration or system setup to access and create these reports.

BI Launchpad

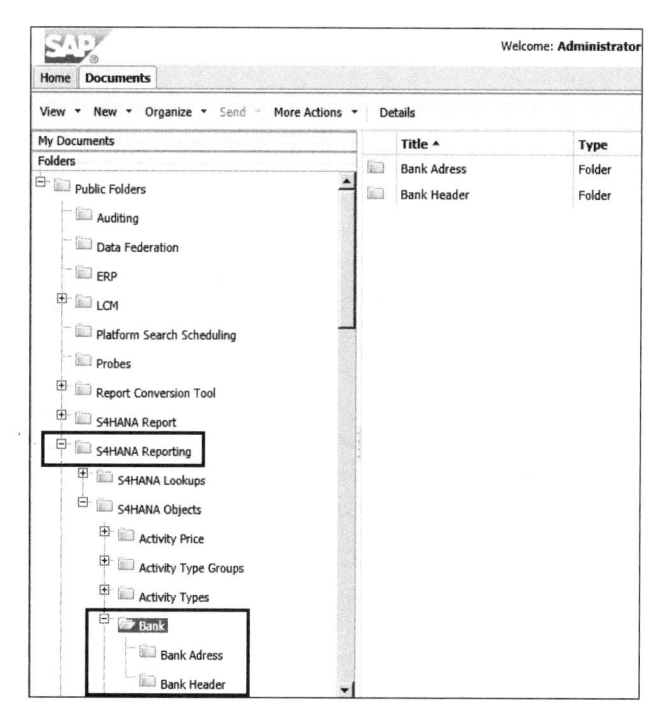

Figure 11.37 BI Launchpad in SAP BusinessObjects BI Platform

Usually, involving functional user departments makes sense because legacy system users will often have the required know-how to use the data records and to troubleshoot. You can analyze, update, change (without additional software), and print Web Intelligence reports. You should update the data of the report after every job run.

In addition to reports for validating business objects and IDoc segments, numerous predefined evaluations are available for mass data uploads. In our example with two banks, reporting may not play a major role, and the magnifying glass 🔍 in the data flows in the SAP Data Services Designer to view data records may be sufficient. However, if you have large data volumes, you'll appreciate these reports.

IDoc status In the `DM_BPFDM_Reconciliation` Rapid Data Migration project, which is included in the SAP Best Practices package, you can execute the `Job_DM_CheckIDocStatus` job in SAP Data Services to get an IDoc monitoring tool for the migration. This monitor lets you view the status of the IDocs without having to log on to the SAP S/4HANA system. The evaluation contains information similar to the information provided by the IDoc monitors found in Transactions WE02/WE05 or BD87. You can monitor the correct update of IDocs in SAP Data Services or with an available Web Intelligence report.

Data comparison If the IDoc monitor indicates that the legacy data was successfully validated with regard to the Customizing replicated from the SAP S/4HANA system and the IDocs were loaded without any errors, the data migration project for the bank master is nearly complete. However, after the successful load process, whether the data was actually imported to the SAP S/4HANA system as expected should be examined.

You can usually only answer this question by performing extensive tests. However, using the content provided in the `DM_BPFDM_Reconciliation` project, you can compare the expected data to the current data existing in the SAP S/4HANA system with `Job_DM_Reconcile`. This assessment is quite helpful because relationships to data that had not been included previously could lead to unexpected results when the data is updated in the SAP S/4HANA system. You can also call the result of this job run using BI Launchpad.

11.3.11 Optimizing IDoc Performance

This section provides information on how to use IDoc technology efficiently.

11.3 Rapid Data Migration

The default setting in the ALE partner agreements in SAP S/4HANA (Transaction WE20) is **Trigger Immediately**, which results in the nearly synchronous processing of the IDoc after receipt. However, because this processing constitutes a separate work process for each IDoc, this procedure is not always ideal, for example, for large data volumes where resources would quickly bottleneck. An alternative is to use background processing, which is triggered by the RBDAPP01 background program.

Background processing

To achieve high performance when mass uploading IDocs for data migrations, background processing is mandatory. Only in this way can you transfer several IDocs as packages to a work process for processing in parallel. Ideally, you'll directly use multiple SAP work processes that each process a package of IDocs, which will decouple the receiving process from the processing of the IDoc. In direct processing, a single IDoc is received via an RFC and processed. However, if you collect inbound IDocs using the **Trigger by Background Program** setting in Transaction WE20, you can improve the update performance for IDocs. Basically, triggering background processing means that the IDocs first wait in Status 64 (see IDoc status values in Section 11.3.3) for processing. Background processing is not the only available option; you can also start the processing in a dialog. The best way to process IDocs is to schedule the RBDAPP01 report as an ABAP job in the background using Transaction SM36 or start the report immediately using Transaction SE38 (see Figure 11.38).

Report RBDAPP01

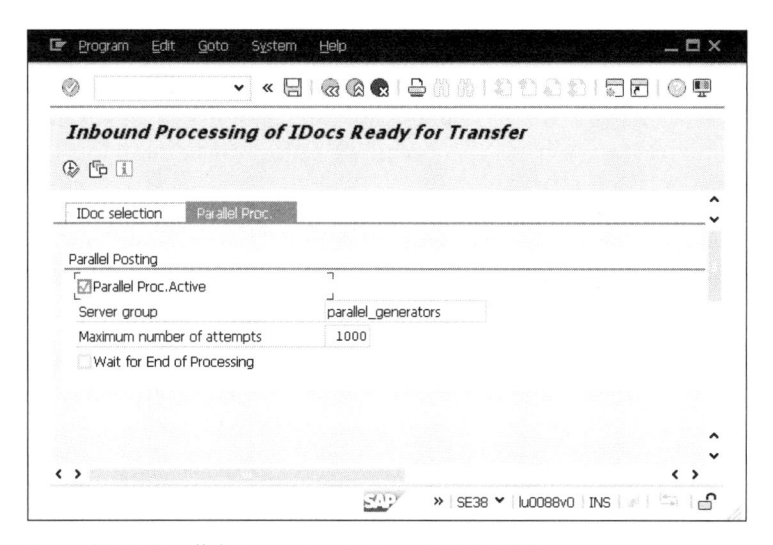

Figure 11.38 Parallel Processing in Report RBDAPP01

The following settings in the selection screen of program RBDAPP01 are critical:

Configuring background programs

- **Doc Selection** tab
  - **Package Size**: The package size controls the maximum number of IDocs to be processed in a logical unit of work (LUW) in a dialog work process. A large package reduces the number of required processes to a minimum but also requires a large roll area. Either the database commit is performed for the entire package, or the database is rolled back and no package data is stored.
- **Parallel Processing** tab
  - **Parallel Proc. Enabled**: This switch activates parallel processing. If you select this checkbox, the application server uses a free dialog process for each IDoc package for inbound processing; the packages are thus processed in parallel. If you select too many packages, all dialog processes of the server will be occupied. You should therefore specify a server group that controls how work processes are assigned (for example, parallel_generators) to avoid overloading the system. If the indicator is not selected, IDocs will not be processed in parallel. Instead, each package will be transferred to the application sequentially. In total, only one work process will be occupied on the application server.
  - **Server Group**: The server group determines how resources are distributed across the existing work processes of the application server(s), that is, how many work processes are provided in each application server. You can make the corresponding settings in Transaction RZ12 (shown in Figure 11.39).

Testing the package size and number of work processes

We can't make general recommendations about package size and number of work processes in a server group for parallel processing. You should always use test data to determine the best values for you. This value depends on the IDoc types and IDoc sizes (number of the segments) as well as database performance and server performance. For large IDoc segments, 50 IDocs per package and, for smaller segments, 100 IDocs per package are good starting values.

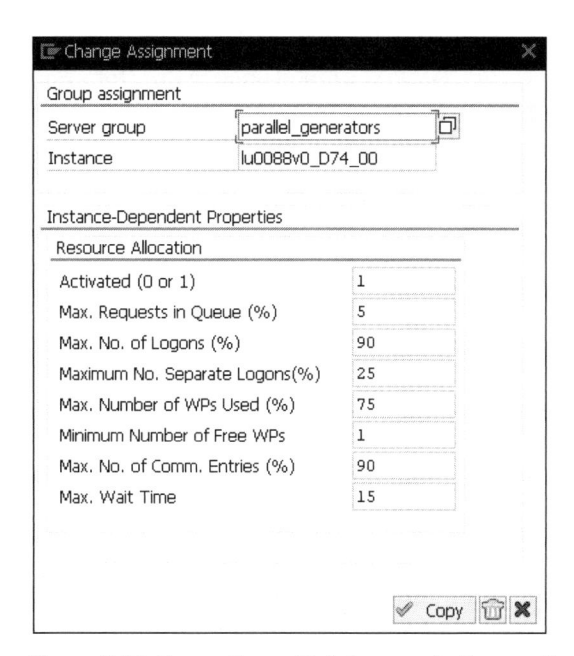

Figure 11.39 Server Group Maintenance in Transaction RZ12

> **Rapid Data Migration Demo Video**
>
> You can find a demo of a data migration to SAP S/4HANA, on-premise, using Rapid Data Migration, as well as further information, on the SAP YouTube channel, *SAP Digital Business Services*, at the following links:
>
> - http://bit.ly/v1448111
> - https://bit.ly/v1448112

11.4 SAP S/4HANA Migration Cockpit

The SAP S/4HANA migration cockpit provides the only option for migrating data to SAP S/4HANA Cloud, as described in Chapter 7, Section 7.3. For SAP S/4HANA, on-premise, editions, the migration cockpit is an alternative to other options such as the Rapid Data Migration solution, which we discussed in the previous section.

11   New Implementation of Single Systems

Transaction LTMC As of SAP S/4HANA 1610, the migration cockpit is also available for on-premise editions (via Transaction LTMC). As we explained in Chapter 7, Section 7.3, the migration cockpit is technically based on the Migration Workbench (MWB), and the available migration objects, mappings, and conversion rules are modeled from MWB. However, you can only use these migration objects with the migration cockpit. Refer to Chapter 7, Section 7.3.1, Table 7.2, for a list of the migration objects supported by the migration cockpit.

The same functions as in the cloud The functionality and handling of the migration cockpit for on-premise editions mainly correspond to the functions described in Chapter 7, Section 7.3, for cloud editions.

Chapter 7, Section 7.3.2 also provides information on how to access the help pages for the migration cockpit and refers to the migration cockpit demo video we mentioned earlier.

Viewing source data In contrast to migrating data to SAP S/4HANA Cloud, when migrating data to an SAP S/4HANA, on-premise, edition, you can still edit the data after the data is uploaded to the migration cockpit. To edit this data, select the XML file that contains your source data and click on the **Open** button or on the file name, as shown in Figure 11.40.

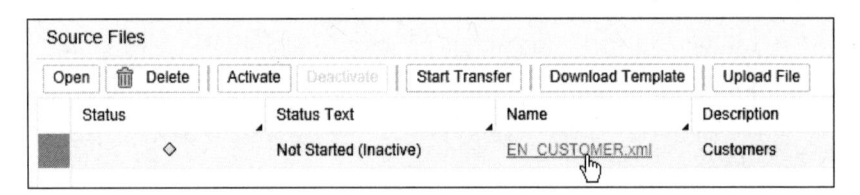

Figure 11.40 Opening Source Data in the SAP S/4HANA Migration Cockpit

The system then displays the data uploaded from the file in the staging area. Figure 11.41 shows an example staging area using a sample file with customer data.

You can now press the **Edit** button to modify the data. As shown in Figure 11.42, we entered a title that was missing.

Next, click **Save** to save your changes. By clicking **Cancel**, you can reset your entries. The **<Back** button navigates you to the source data overview.

11.4 SAP S/4HANA Migration Cockpit

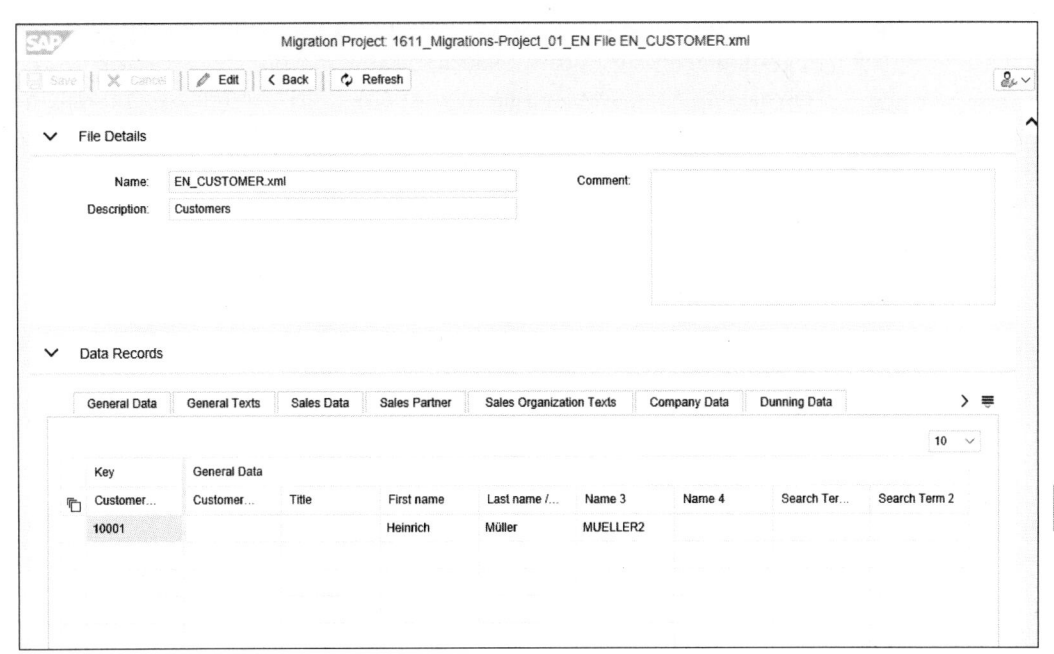

Figure 11.41 Staging Area in the SAP S/4HANA Migration Cockpit

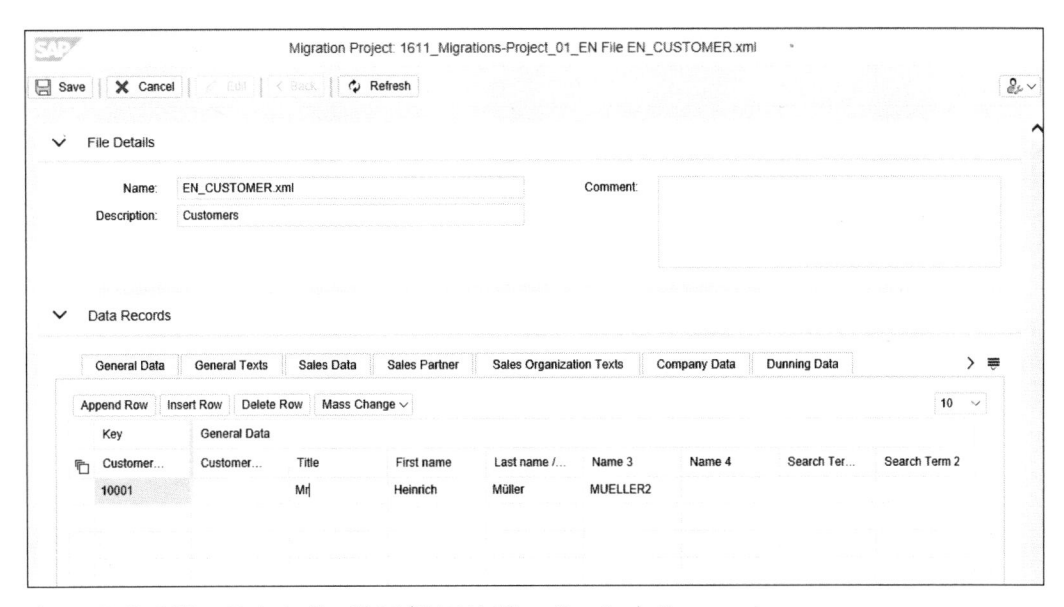

Figure 11.42 Editing Data in the SAP S/4HANA Migration Cockpit

11 New Implementation of Single Systems

Downloading edited data In the source data overview, you can download the modified data in the migration template format. Select the row of your file and click on the **Download** button. Depending on your SAP S/4HANA release, you may be asked to select the specific view for the migration template (see also the "Downloading Migration Templates" section in Chapter 7, Section 7.3.2). By default, SAP only provides the **BP On Premise Enterprise Management** view in the on-premise version. Figure 11.43 shows an example of a selection.

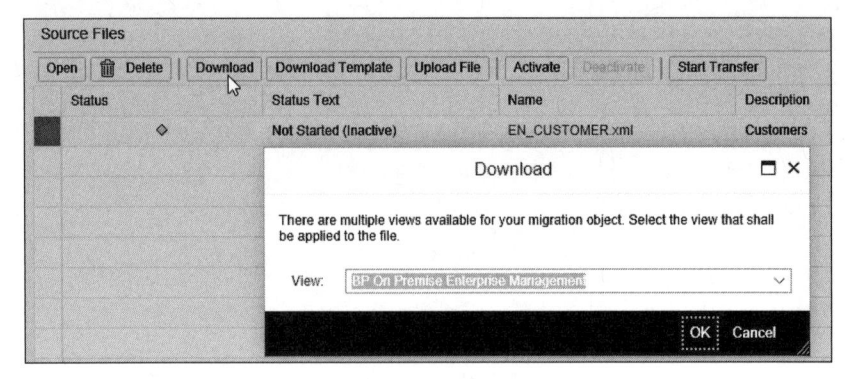

Figure 11.43 Downloading Edited Data in a Migration Template File

The downloaded file contains the changed data, in our case, the entire data record including the title (see Figure 11.44).

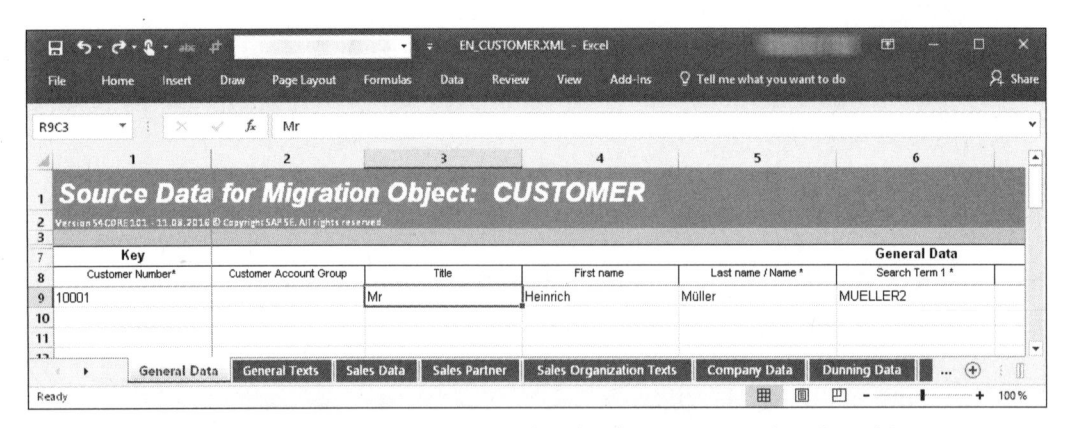

Figure 11.44 Migration Template for the Customer Migration Object

You can now edit the migration template offline. We always recommend, and sometimes you may be required, you store a backup copy of the imported data records for validation or as a copy of a certification outside of the target system.

11.5 SAP S/4HANA Migration Object Modeler

In SAP S/4HANA, on-premise, editions, you can customize business processes according to your specific requirements better than in SAP S/4HANA Cloud. If the predefined migration objects in the SAP S/4HANA migration cockpit do not meet your technical requirements, you can use the *SAP S/4HANA migration object modeler* to adjust them. This tool is only available in SAP S/4HANA, on-premise. Fields that are missing in the target structure of the provided template, but still exist in the used default import interface, can be displayed using the *migration object modeler*.

Modifying migration objects

Default APIs (BAPIs or function modules), released by SAP for SAP S/4HANA, are used to transfer data via the migration cockpit.

Some of these APIs, in particular BAPIs, include so-called *function module documentation*. You can access this documentation, which provides useful information on import structures and their fields, via the Function Builder (Transaction SE37).

Function module documentation

Table 11.5 provides an overview of the APIs the migration cockpit uses for each migration object. To update data, some of these APIs require a chain of function module calls and are thus called using so-called wrapper function modules. In the "Wrapper" column in Table 11.5, the APIs that require being called via these wrapper function modules are indicated. In the "APIs Used" column, this wrapper function module is specified if using a complex call of multiple function modules is necessary.

Standard interfaces

Migration Object	APIs Used (BAPI or Function Module)	Wrapper
Activity type	BAPI_ACTTYPE_CREATEMULTIPLE	
Cost center	BAPI_COSTCENTER_CREATEMULTIPLE	
Activity price	BAPI_ACT_PRICE_CHECK_AND_POST	
Internal order	BAPI_INTERNALORDER_CREATE	X
Profit center	BAPI_PROFITCENTER_CREATE	X

Table 11.5 APIs Used in the SAP S/4HANA Migration Cockpit for the Migration

11　New Implementation of Single Systems

Migration Object	APIs Used (BAPI or Function Module)	Wrapper
Bank	BAPI_BANK_CREATE	X
Customer	RFC_CVI_EI_INBOUND_MAIN	
Supplier	RFC_CVI_EI_INBOUND_MAIN	
Accounts receivable (Customer) open item	BAPI_ACC_DOCUMENT_POST	X
Accounts payable (Vendor) open item	BAPI_ACC_DOCUMENT_POST	X
Fixed asset incl. Balances	BAPI_FIXEDASSET_OVRTAKE_CREATE	
G/L account balance	BAPI_ACC_DOCUMENT_POST	X
G/L account open item	BAPI_ACC_DOCUMENT_POST	X
Exchange rate	BAPI_EXCHRATE_CREATEMULTIPLE	X
Inventory balances	BAPI_GOODSMVT_CREATE	
Material	BAPI_MATERIAL_SAVEREPLICA	
Material – Long text	BAPI_MATERIAL_SAVEREPLICA	
Material consumption	BAPI_MATERIAL_SAVEREPLICA	
Purchasing info record	DMC_MIG_PURCH_INFO_RECORD	X
Purchase order	BAPI_PO_CREATE1	
Contracts (Purchasing)	BAPI_CONTRACT_CREATE	
Source list	DMC_MIG_SOURCE_LIST	X
Sales order	BAPI_SALESORDER_CREATEFROMDAT2 total	
Batch	BAPI_BATCH_SAVE_REPLICA	X
Bill of material (BOM)	CSAP_MAT_BOM_MAINTAIN	X
Work center	CRAP_WORKCENTER_CREATE	X
Routing	BAPI_ROUTING_CREATE	
Equipment	BAPI_EQUI_CREATE	X

Table 11.5 APIs Used in the SAP S/4HANA Migration Cockpit for the Migration (Cont.)

11.5 SAP S/4HANA Migration Object Modeler

Migration Object	APIs Used (BAPI or Function Module)	Wrapper
Maintenance task list	DMC_MIG_EAM_TASKLIST	X
Functional location	BAPI_FUNCLOC_CREATE	X
Characteristic	BAPI_CHARACT_CREATE	X
Class	BAPI_CLASS_CREATE	X

Table 11.5 APIs Used in the SAP S/4HANA Migration Cockpit for the Migration (Cont.)

You can call the SAP S/4HANA migration object modeler using Transaction LTMOM in SAP S/4HANA, on-premise. Because the modeler changes migration objects, you'll first have to select the project containing the migration object that you want to modify, as shown in Figure 11.45.

Transaction LTMOM

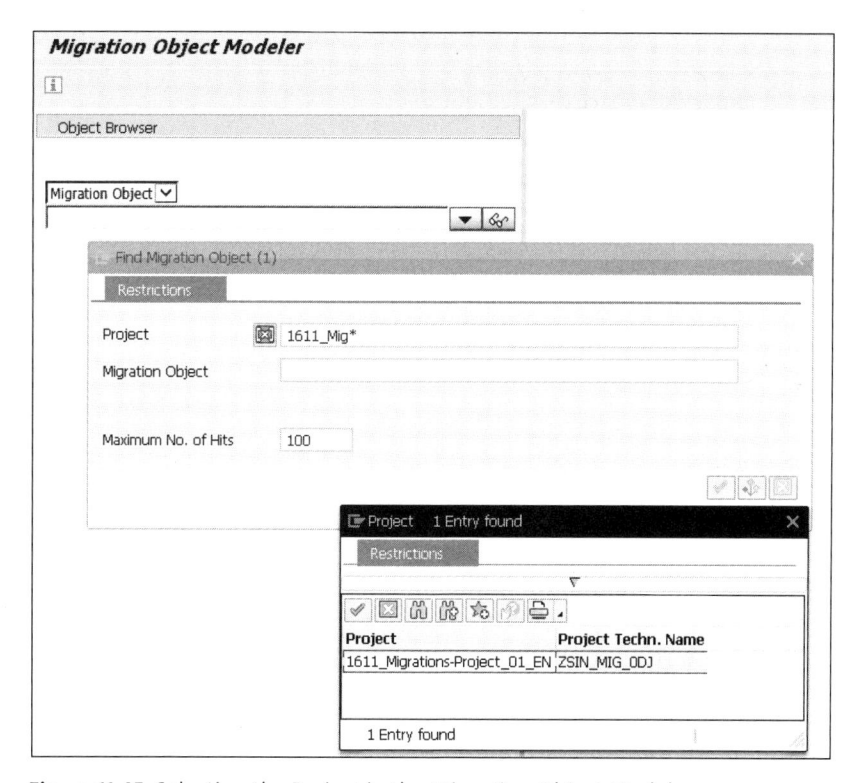

Figure 11.45 Selecting the Project in the Migration Object Modeler

11 New Implementation of Single Systems

Selecting the migration object
Then, you'll select the migration object that you want to modify (as shown in Figure 11.46).

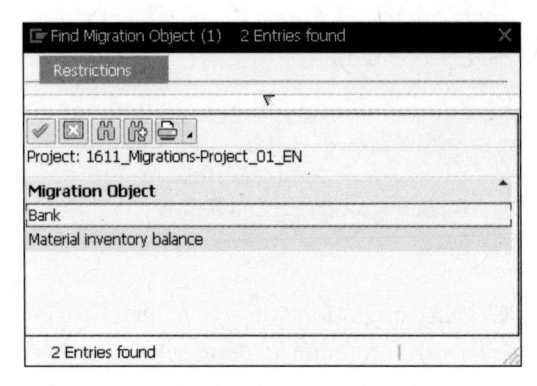

Figure 11.46 Selecting the Migration Object

The full range of modeler functions for this migration object is now available. As shown in Figure 11.47, the modeler consists of a selection area on the left and a workspace on the right.

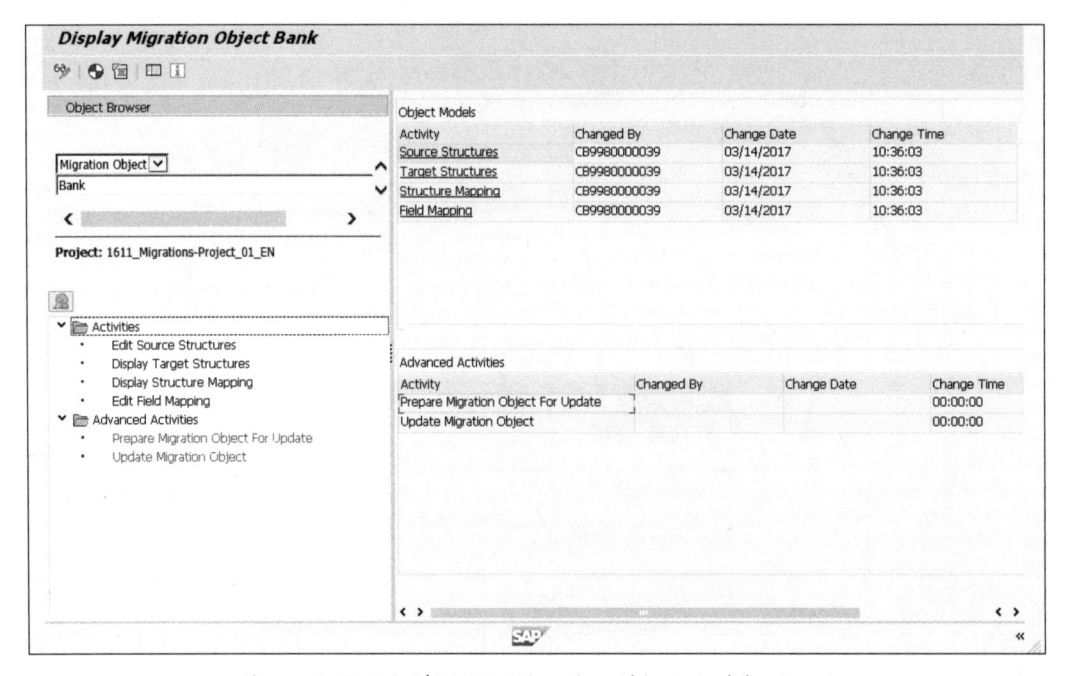

Figure 11.47 SAP S/4HANA Migration Object Modeler Structure

11.5 SAP S/4HANA Migration Object Modeler

The modeler has the following functions, which are divided into **Activities** and **Advanced Activities**. These functions can be selected in the left-hand selection area:

- The following functions are listed in **Activities**:
  - Edit Source Structures
  - Display Target Structures
  - Display Structure Mapping
  - Edit Field Mapping
- The migration objects provided by SAP can be, if required, adapted to your modified business processes in every release. If an object that you created and modified in an earlier release needs to be adapted after a release change, the system will prompt you to perform one of the following **Advanced Activities**:
  - Prepare Migration Object For Update
  - Update Migration Object

Modeler functions

In addition, the **Migration Object** menu item and the functions in the application bar provide the following technical functions:

Technical functions

- **Generate Runtime Object**
- **Display Generated Function Group** (You cannot select this function until a new function group has been generated.)

The following sections describe these functions in detail.

11.5.1 Edit Source Structures

The interface for transferring a migration object usually contains more structures and fields than SAP Best Practices covers. You can use the **Edit Source Structures** function to add missing fields to the migration template of an object. First, switch to the change mode by clicking the **Display<->Change** button in the application bar. Then, select the **Edit Source Structures** activity, which will take you to the view shown in Figure 11.48.

Adding fields to the migration template

11　New Implementation of Single Systems

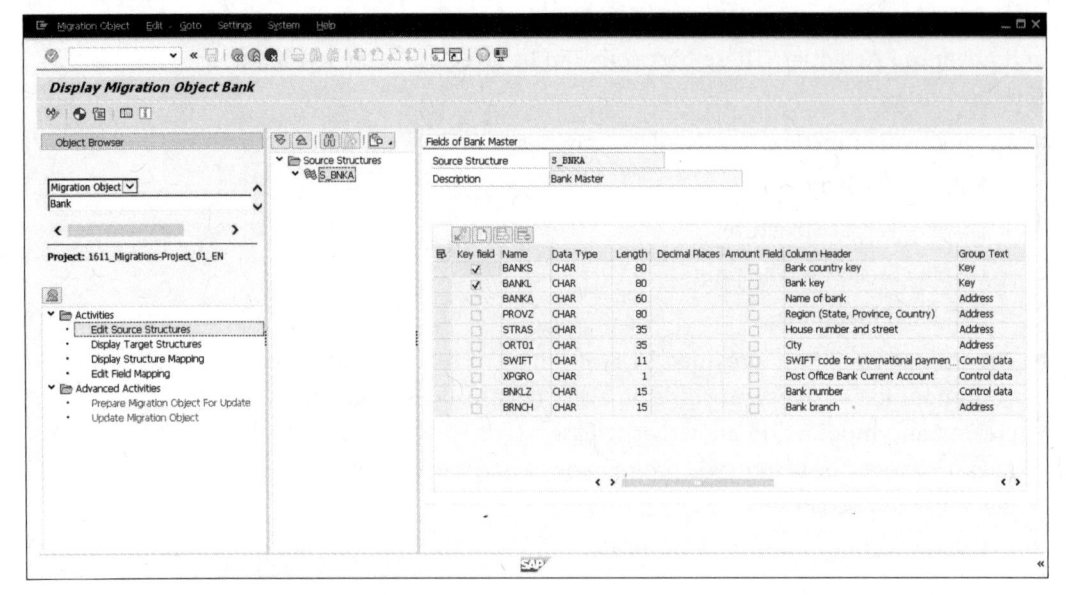

Figure 11.48　Edit Source Structures

You can edit the fields of a structure by double-clicking on the field in the structure tree in the central pane of the modeler. By navigating to **Settings • Technical Names on/off**, you can show or hide the technical names of the fields in the structure tree.

Above the field list, in the right-hand pane of the modeler, you can find the following three functions:

- Add Field
- Insert Field
- Delete Field(s)

Add Field　In our example, we added a new field, PSTKO (Post office bank current account number), to the source structure of the bank data that we previously used as sample data in Section 11.3. To add a new field, select the **Add Field** function and enter the desired values for field name, data type, field length, etc., into the new line, as shown in Figure 11.49.

11.5 SAP S/4HANA Migration Object Modeler

Key field	Name	Data Type	Length	Decimal Places	Amount Field	Column Header	Group Text
✓	BANKS	CHAR	80		☐	Bank country key	Key
✓	BANKL	CHAR	80		☐	Bank key	Key
☐	BANKA	CHAR	60		☐	Name of bank	Address
☐	PROVZ	CHAR	80		☐	Region (State, Province, Country)	Address
☐	STRAS	CHAR	35		☐	House number and street	Address
☐	ORT01	CHAR	35		☐	City	Address
☐	SWIFT	CHAR	11		☐	SWIFT code for international payments	Control data
☐	XPGRO	CHAR	1		☐	Post Office Bank Current Account	Control data
☐	BNKLZ	CHAR	15		☐	Bank number	Control data
☐	BRNCH	CHAR	15		☐	Bank branch	Address
☐	PSTKO	CHAR	16		☐	Post office bank current account number	

Figure 11.49 Adding a Field to the Source Structure

Now, click on **Save** 💾 to save your changes. Your source structure now includes the new field.

You can use the **Edit Source Structures** function to modify the migration template view of any SAP S/4HANA, on-premise, edition. First, select the **Display View** function in the context menu of the source structure. You can now change the visibility of structures and fields of the already assigned views. The example shown in Figure 11.50 shows the source structure view **Bank Master** (S_BNKA) of the migration object for the bank master.

Modifying the migration template view

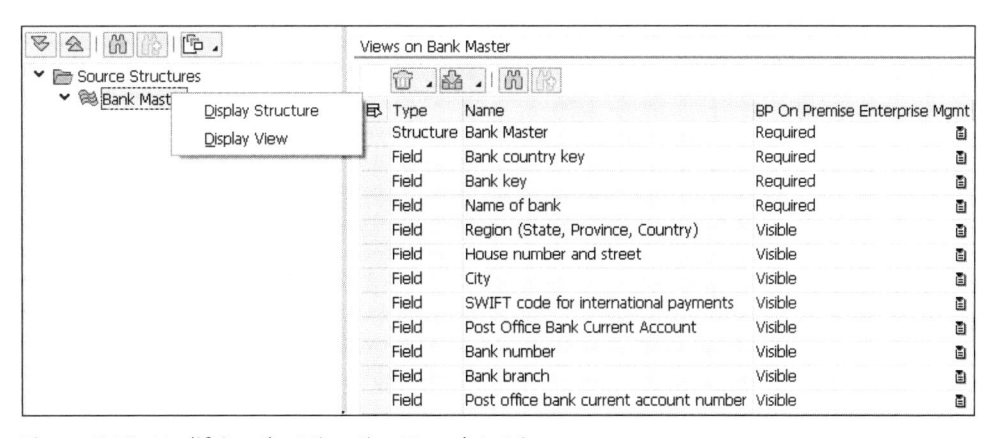

	Views on Bank Master		
▼ 📁 Source Structures			
▼ 🏦 Bank Mast	Type	Name	BP On Premise Enterprise Mgmt
Display Structure	Structure	Bank Master	Required
Display View	Field	Bank country key	Required
	Field	Bank key	Required
	Field	Name of bank	Required
	Field	Region (State, Province, Country)	Visible
	Field	House number and street	Visible
	Field	City	Visible
	Field	SWIFT code for international payments	Visible
	Field	Post Office Bank Current Account	Visible
	Field	Bank number	Visible
	Field	Bank branch	Visible
	Field	Post office bank current account number	Visible

Figure 11.50 Modifying the Migration Template View

To assign a new view, select the view that you want to assign using the **Assign View** function 🏦, as shown in Figure 11.51.

11 New Implementation of Single Systems

You can change the visibility of structures and fields with the following values:

- **Not Visible:** The field or structure will not be visible in the migration template. However, hidden structures and fields may cause the data import to be terminated with an error.
- **Visible:** The field or structure is visible in the migration template and can be populated.
- **Required:** The structure or field is mandatory and needs to be populated.

Type		BP On Premise Enterprise Mgmt
Structure	Bank Master (Customer View 1)	Required
Field	Bank country key	Required
Field	Bank key	Required
Field	Name of bank	Required
Field	Region (State, Province, Country)	Visible
Field	House number and street	Visible
Field	City	Visible
Field	SWIFT code for international payments	Visible
Field	Post Office Bank Current Account	Visible
Field	Bank number	Visible
Field	Bank branch	Visible
Field	Post office bank current account number	Visible

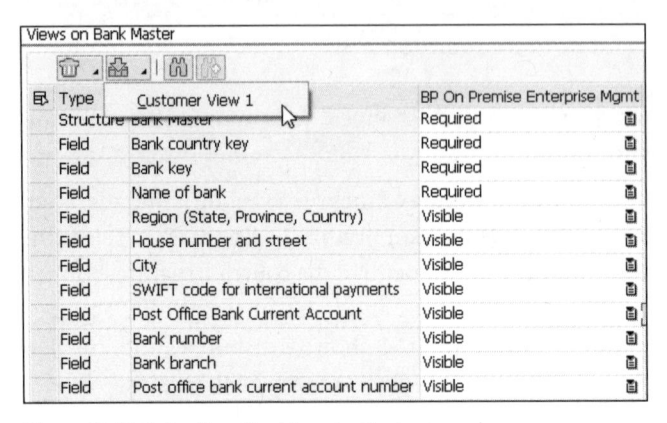

Figure 11.51 Selecting the View to Be Assigned

Then, press [Enter] to activate the **Save** button in the system function bar. Click on the **Save** button to save your changes.

11.5.2 Display Target Structures

Field and structure of the function module — The **Display Target Structures** function displays all fields and structures of the function module used to transfer the data of the migration object. On the right (as shown in Figure 11.52), you can have the system display the fields of the target structure by double-clicking on the desired structure or field. Alternatively, you can use the **Display Structure** entry in the context menu.

The root node includes the name of the function module used for the data transfer. As shown in Figure 11.52, we are using the DMC_MIG_BANK function module, which is a wrapper function module that wraps and calls the BAPI_BANK_CREATE function module, as mentioned in Table 11.5.

11.5 SAP S/4HANA Migration Object Modeler

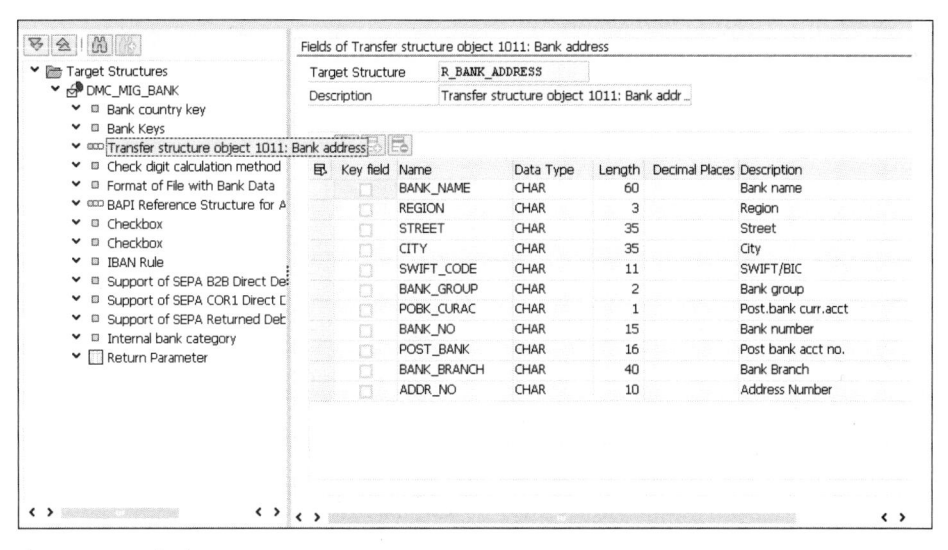

Figure 11.52 Display Target Structure

11.5.3 Display Structure Mapping

The **Display Structure Mapping** activity displays the mapping of the source structures (right area of the screen) to the target structures (left area of the screen). You can view the assigned source structures in the left area next to the target structures. After the name of the target structure, separated by <<, the system displays all source structures assigned to this structure. Figure 11.53 shows an example of a bank master migration object (**Bank Master**).

Mapping source structures to target structures

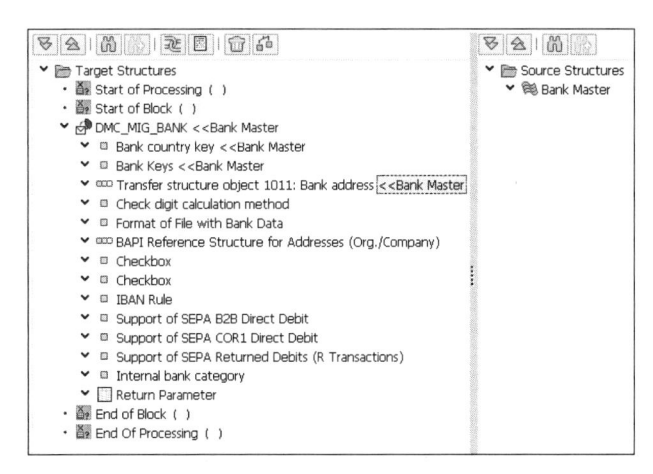

Figure 11.53 Display Structure Mapping

449

11 New Implementation of Single Systems

11.5.4 Edit Field Mapping

Assign customer fields only

In **Edit Field Mapping**, you can drag and drop so-called *customer fields*, which you assigned to the source structure previously in Section 11.5.1, to an unassigned field in the target structure on the right. (The unassigned field is marked by a red circle with a white cross .) See Figure 11.54.

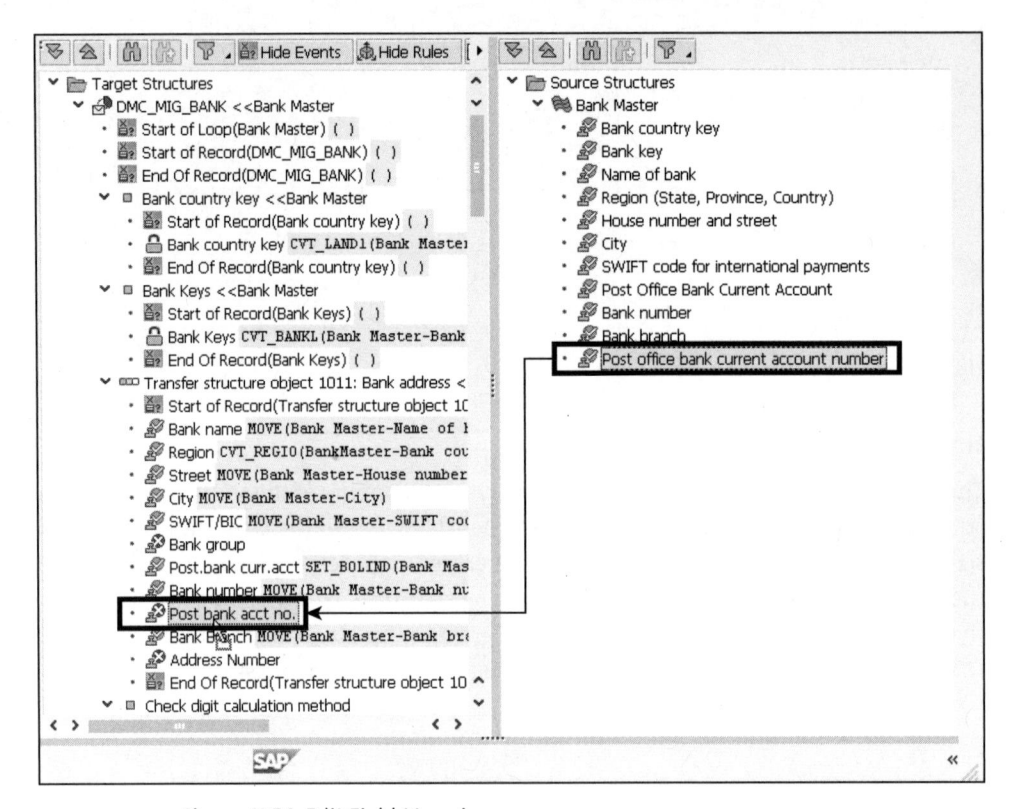

Figure 11.54 Edit Field Mapping

Type conflict

If the field definitions of the customer fields and the target structure differ, the system shows a dialog box indicating this conflict and asks whether you really want to implement this field assignment. A MOVE rule that specifies a 1:1 mapping is defined for the assignment. Thus, the values to be migrated to this new field must be written in the migration template file in the appropriate target format and cannot be converted in the migration cockpit using validation rules. The result of such an assignment is shown in Figure 11.55.

11.5 SAP S/4HANA Migration Object Modeler

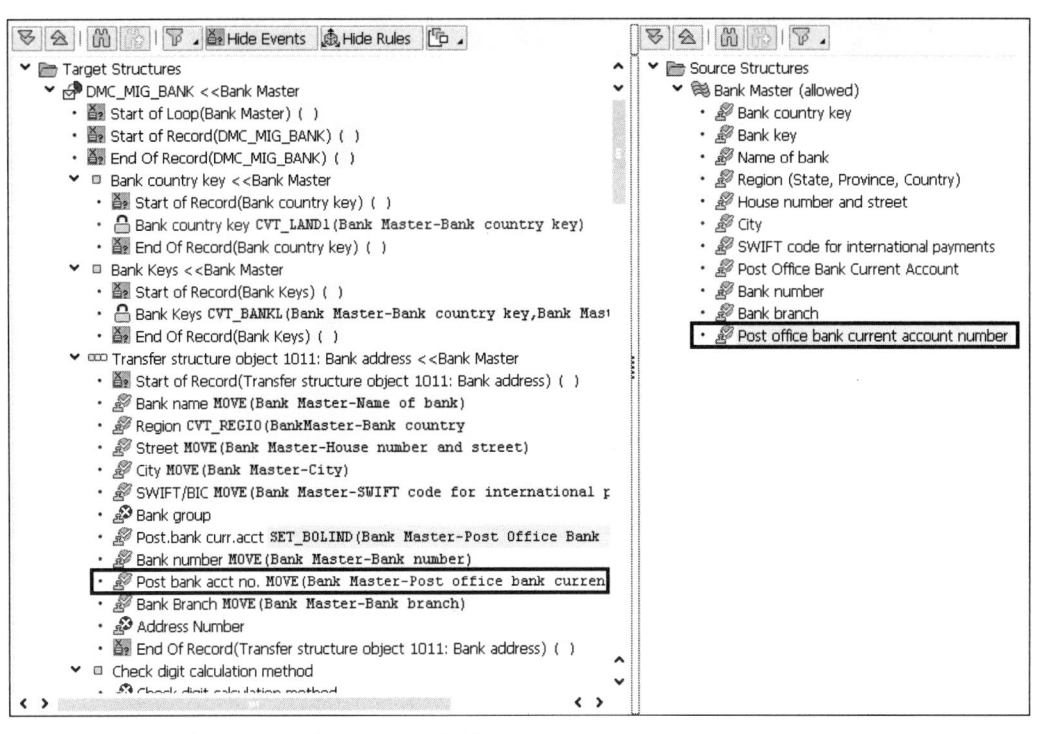

```
Target Structures
  DMC_MIG_BANK <<Bank Master
    Start of Loop(Bank Master) ( )
    Start of Record(DMC_MIG_BANK) ( )
    End Of Record(DMC_MIG_BANK) ( )
    Bank country key <<Bank Master
      Start of Record(Bank country key) ( )
      Bank country key CVT_LAND1(Bank Master-Bank country key)
      End Of Record(Bank country key) ( )
    Bank Keys <<Bank Master
      Start of Record(Bank Keys) ( )
      Bank Keys CVT_BANKL(Bank Master-Bank country key,Bank Mast
      End Of Record(Bank Keys) ( )
    Transfer structure object 1011: Bank address <<Bank Master
      Start of Record(Transfer structure object 1011: Bank address) ( )
      Bank name MOVE(Bank Master-Name of bank)
      Region CVT_REGIO(BankMaster-Bank country
      Street MOVE(Bank Master-House number and street)
      City MOVE(Bank Master-City)
      SWIFT/BIC MOVE(Bank Master-SWIFT code for international p
      Bank group
      Post.bank curr.acct SET_BOLIND(Bank Master-Post Office Bank
      Bank number MOVE(Bank Master-Bank number)
      Post bank acct no. MOVE(Bank Master-Post office bank curren
      Bank Branch MOVE(Bank Master-Bank branch)
      Address Number
      End Of Record(Transfer structure object 1011: Bank address) ( )
    Check digit calculation method
```

```
Source Structures
  Bank Master (allowed)
    Bank country key
    Bank key
    Name of bank
    Region (State, Province, Country)
    House number and street
    City
    SWIFT code for international payments
    Post Office Bank Current Account
    Bank number
    Bank branch
    Post office bank current account number
```

Figure 11.55 Modeler: Assigned Customer Field

Save your changes by clicking the **Save** button in the system function bar.

11.5.5 Technical Functions

You can use the technical function **Generate Runtime Object** in the application bar to generate a local function module for the Migration Workbench (MWB) to use in the background for the migration cockpit. This newly generated function module is required after the source structures or fields have been mapped because the fields will not be processed otherwise.

Generate Runtime Object

You can use the **Display Generated Function Group** function to view the entire function group of the newly generated function module in the application bar. The ABAP Editor then displays the function group, as shown in Figure 11.56.

Display Generated Function Group

451

11 New Implementation of Single Systems

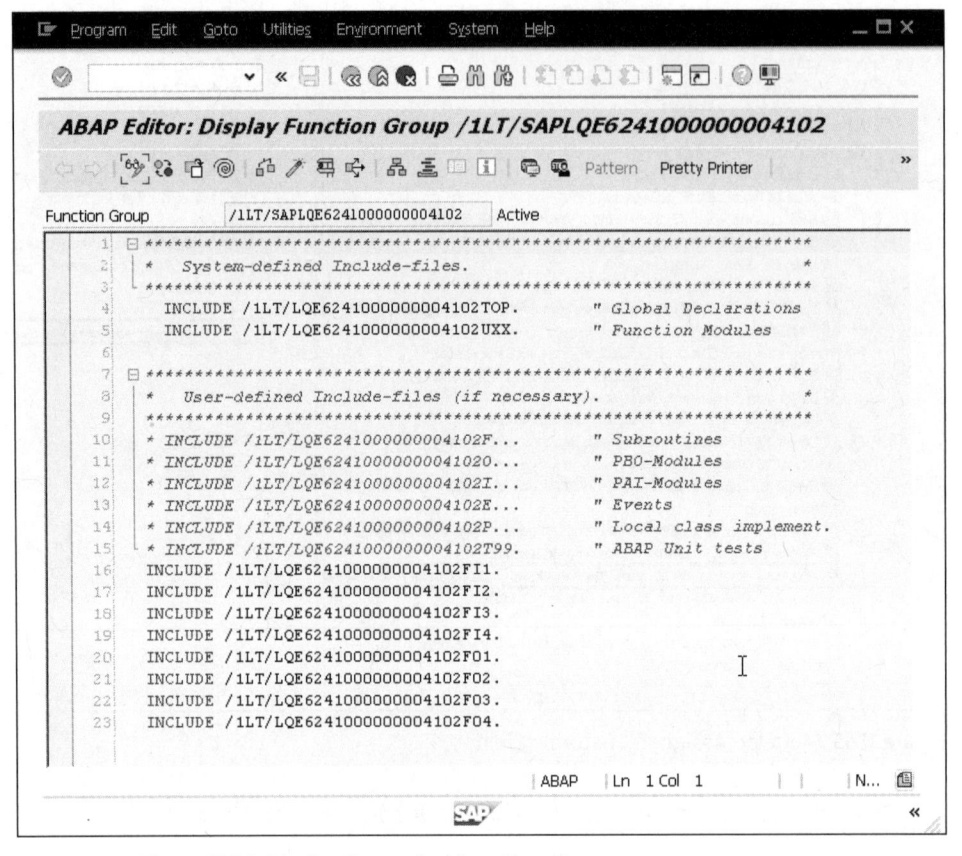

Figure 11.56 Display Generated Function Group

11.5.6 Advanced Activities

Field mapping modifications

You can only perform the **Prepare Migration Object for Update** step if an update from SAP affects your modified customer migration objects. If you try to start such a migration object using the migration cockpit, the system will display a message indicating that the migration object contains modifications, and you'll have to perform the **Prepare Migration Object for Update** activity to validate this object before the object can be updated with the new migration object content provided by SAP.

The system will only display this activity if you have changed the field mapping. These changes or modifications will be deleted after you've carried out the **Prepare Migration Object for Update** activity. You should therefore save all modifications that you want to continue to use.

If you have not modified the field mapping, you can simply carry out the **Update Migration Object** activity, which copies all changes to the migration content provided by SAP.

Update the Migration Object

> **SAP S/4HANA Migration Object Modeler Help**
>
> You can access the SAP S/4HANA migration object modeler help if you choose the Info function in the application bar.

11.6 Comparison of Migration Tools

You now have an overview of existing and SAP S/4HANA-specific migration tools. However, the differences among the tools also raise the question of which approach you should follow in your situation.

Which tool for which purpose?

We cannot give general recommendations on this choice because multiple solutions can also be used in parallel; however, in this section, we'll provide you with an overview of how to choose a tool for your situation.

Table 11.6 compares the different migration tools we introduced in this chapter.

Criterion for Comparison	SAP S/4HANA Migration Cockpit	SAP S/4HANA Migration Object Modeler	Rapid Data Migration Using SAP Data Services
Availability	In any SAP S/4HANA system, cloud-based or on-premise	In any SAP S/4HANA, on-premise, system as of Version 1610	ETL tool to be installed separately; not available for SAP S/4HANA in the public cloud (software as a service, SaaS)

Table 11.6 Comparison of Migration Tools

Criterion for Comparison	SAP S/4HANA Migration Cockpit	SAP S/4HANA Migration Object Modeler	Rapid Data Migration Using SAP Data Services
Coverage	Only tool for SAP S/4HANA Cloud (SaaS) with a holistic SAP Best Practices scope; only basic tool with file upload; compared to SAP Data Services, restricted extensibility for on-premise editions	Add-on for the migration cockpit in SAP S/4HANA on-premise, systems for extending fields beyond the SAP Best Practices content	Can only be used for SAP S/4HANA, on-premise; best object coverage and unrestricted extensibility
Advantages	Covers the exact solution scope of SAP Best Practices; easy to use	Extends fields not covered by SAP Best Practices	Direct connection with source systems; data cleansing
Disadvantages	No data extraction; defined migration templates; no data cleansing	Not available for SAP S/4HANA Cloud; structure extension not possible yet	Separate hardware; data cleansing requires additional license

Table 11.6 Comparison of Migration Tools (Cont.)

LSMW You may also know other SAP migration tools because, like SAP Business Suite, SAP S/4HANA is based on ABAP and also contains SAP NetWeaver as a basic component. The *Legacy System Migration Workbench* (LSMW) is a component of SAP NetWeaver and is a data migration tool for the traditional SAP Business Suite.

Simplification list recommendation Although this tool is still available via Transaction LSMW in your SAP S/4HANA, on-premise, system (but not in SAP S/4HANA Cloud), you should only use LSMW as a supporting tool, if at all, in addition to the migration tools specifically designed for SAP S/4HANA that we described in this chapter. LSMW is listed in the *simplification list* (see Chapter 10, Section 10.2.2), meaning it should no longer be used. Instead, refer to SAP Note 2287723, which discusses the approaches described in this book as alternatives.

If you still want to use LSMW additionally, you should always carefully check your LSMW projects because, due to modifications and simplifications from SAP S/4HANA, proper implementation of LSMW projects can no longer be ensured.

If your LSMW migration projects test successfully, you can (at your own risk) still use LSMW for migrating to your SAP S/4HANA production system—in addition to the SAP S/4HANA standard migration solutions mentioned throughout this book.

> **Additional Information on SAP S/4HANA and SAP Best Practices**
>
> You can find more details on SAP S/4HANA Best Practices, including migration content in the SAP S/4HANA Community and the SAP Best Practices Explorer, at the following links:
>
> - SAP S/4HANA Community:
>   *http://www.sap.com/community/topic/s4hana.html*
> - SAP Best Practices for SAP S/4HANA, on-premise:
>   *http://rapid.sap.com/bp/BP_OP_ENTPR*
> - SAP Best Practices for SAP S/4HANA Professional Services Cloud:
>   *http://rapid.sap.com/bp/BP_CLD_PROJ_SERV*
> - SAP Best Practices for SAP S/4HANA Enterprise Management Cloud:
>   *http://rapid.sap.com/bp/BP_CLD_ENTPR*
> - SAP Best Practices for SAP S/4HANA Finance Cloud:
>   *http://rapid.sap.com/bp/BP_CLD_FIN*

Chapter 12
Landscape Transformation

In this chapter, we'll describe landscape transformations, which actually refer to several different scenarios that we'll discuss in detail.

This chapter explains the third and last transition scenario, a landscape transformation. This scenario is the only one of the three transition scenarios with several alternative forms: You can perform a system consolidation, transfer an organizational unit, or transfer a specific application area (such as the financial data).

Before we explain the technical details, this chapter first addresses the question why SAP customers choose one landscape transformation scenario over the others. Compared to a system conversion, whereby the entire system is converted, and a new implementation, whereby the customer begins with a completely new system (greenfield approach), a landscape transformation falls between these two scenarios. Depending on your requirements, only certain parts of your existing SAP system are transferred to SAP S/4HANA. How long each system transformation project can take is estimated in advance using the *runtime estimate*. The actual conversion is carried out during a period of system downtime (usually over a weekend).

All of these scenarios are supported by *SAP Landscape Transformation* (SAP LT). This software has a large number of quality-approved and globally certified tools for the safe adaptation and conversion of running SAP systems to meet the changing requirements of an enterprise. Appropriate transition scenarios are supported specifically for SAP S/4HANA. SAP LT enables fast and efficient business and IT transformations by providing a standardized set of preconfigured transformation solutions and by providing all the tools to plan, analyze, and carry out the required transformation projects. As a result, all scenarios follow a clearly defined structure and are fully documented in a continuous process journal.

SAP Landscape Transformation

12 Landscape Transformation

12.1 The Three Transformation Scenarios

System consolidation

The first of the three landscape transformation scenarios that SAP LT specifically supports for SAP S/4HANA involves the consolidation of two or more systems into a central SAP S/4HANA system. The principle behind this scenario is shown in Figure 12.1.

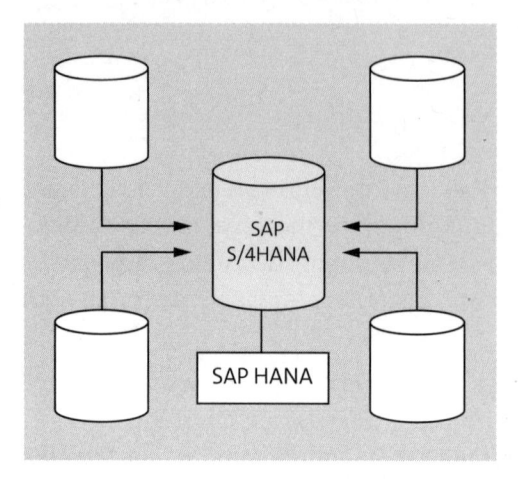

Figure 12.1 Consolidating Multiple Systems in an SAP S/4HANA System

Company code transfer

The second supported scenario allows you to transfer a single company code to SAP S/4HANA. In this scenario, SAP LT consistently separates all data of relevance to this company code from one source system and transfers them to SAP S/4HANA, as shown in Figure 12.2.

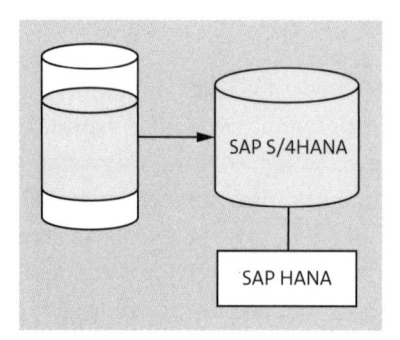

Figure 12.2 Migrating a Company Code to SAP S/4HANA

The last landscape transformation scenario allows selected applications to be converted. When moving to SAP S/4HANA, converting applications can mean simply transferring financial data from your old system to a newly implemented SAP S/4HANA Central Finance system (see Figure 12.3).

Conversion of selected applications

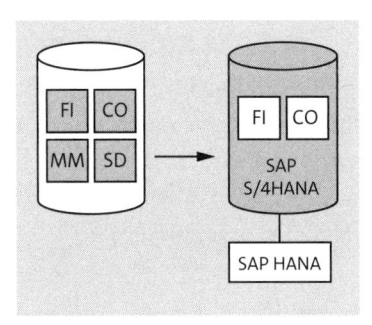

Figure 12.3 Migrating Selected Applications to SAP S/4HANA

Technically, SAP LT consists of two add-ons that are installed on the SAP systems involved (the source and target systems) and SAP Solution Manager (as a central system). On the one hand, the add-on contains the collective knowledge and know-how that was available using the SAP Consulting Service *System Landscape Optimization* (SLO) (best practices, roadmaps) and, on the other hand, the software to analyze and transform your systems.

> **Additional Information on SAP Landscape Transformation** [«]
> Further information on SAP LT is available from the SAP Help Portal at *http://help.sap.com/viewer/p/SAP_LANDSCAPE_TRANSFORMATION* or in the SAP LT brochure at *http://bit.ly/v1448121*.

12.2 Carrying Out a Transformation Project

As we discussed earlier in Chapter 5, each SAP S/4HANA project can be divided into various project phases. These phases also apply to system landscape transformations, and deviations may occur within the various transformation scenarios. The following phases are usually carried out in landscape transformation scenarios:

Project phases

1. Preanalysis and planning
2. Blueprint document and project team finding
3. Test runs
4. Production conversion
5. Support after go-live

Runtimes of the phases The runtimes of the individual phases can differ significantly and can also depend on the complexity of the individual projects. A rough guide is shown in Figure 12.4. In general, you can assume that, above all, several test runs of the system transition will take up the largest share of the time required for the overall project, followed by detailed preanalysis.

Duration	Phase
A few months	Pre-analysis and Planning
A few weeks	Blueprint and Project Team
Multiple months	Test Runs
Weekend	Go Live
Multiple days	Support after Go Live

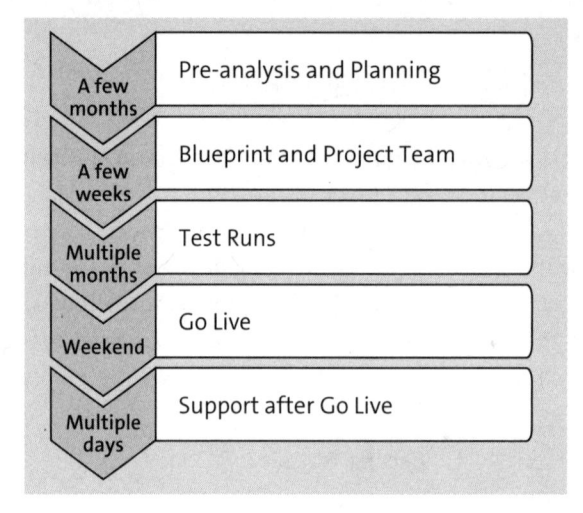

Figure 12.4 Duration of the Individual Project Phases

Overview of activities The following overview lists typical activities within the individual project phases:

- Preanalysis and planning:
  - Analysis of the current situation and design of the target situation with a clear definition of the desired transformation
  - Technical analysis of the systems, e.g., delta Customizing, in the case of a system consolidation
  - Definition of the required roles in the project and of their responsibilities

- Creation of a business case
- Decision on a realization path
- Provision of a project budget
- If necessary, procurement of professional consultation
- Blueprint and project team
  - Concept creation using a blueprint
  - Structure of the project team and the initial kick-off
  - Provision of the necessary infrastructure, e.g., the test systems
  - Planning of the test cycles and test cases
  - Installation of the required tools
- Test runs
  - Multiple test conversions of the system to be transformed. A distinction can be made between purely technical tests, which are usually carried out at the beginning of a project, and at least one complete run in order to simulate the production conversion.
  - Dynamic adjustment of the conversion based on the results from the test runs
- Production conversion
  - Preparing the existing system landscape for the conversion to the new systems
  - Locking the systems involved for the actual conversion
  - The actual production conversion (typically taking place over a weekend operating 24 hours per day)
  - Final acceptance of the converted system by the end users
- Support after go-live
  - Support from the project team for end users working with the new system landscape after the production conversion
  - Integration of SAP Support for the newly introduced SAP S/4HANA standard components

The following sections discuss the activities during the individual phases in more detail.

12.2.1 Preanalysis and Planning

Preanalysis The aim of preanalysis is to evaluate the upcoming tasks and to find and discuss possible solutions. In addition to technically driven questions (such as the question of providing the infrastructure for the transformation, for example), preanalysis also includes a cost-benefit analysis. The result of the process should be a clear recommendation for action that provides direction for the subsequent phases of the project.

SAP LT offers numerous options to technically support such preanalysis. The results can be relevant depending on the scenario so you can estimate the cost of the necessary conversions. Only on this basis can a comprehensive business case be prepared and thus the feasibility of a project be examined.

Not day-to-day business Particularly when new products are introduced to the market, such as SAP S/4HANA, detailed knowledge is essential for successful project completion. System landscape transformation projects in particular are not part of the traditional day-to-day business of IT departments, which is why the expertise of external consultants is often sought. Based on the preanalysis, the requirements for these specialized roles can be defined by the project's participants, and the right experts and consultants can be contracted.

Project plan Preparing a project plan is also recommended at this point. The initial milestones can be set so you can better estimate the total duration of the project. Ideally, time planning uses backward scheduling from the go-live date. Particularly for international organizations, only limited maintenance windows are available for a transformation scenario during the course of a calendar year. Based on the project plan, you can determine early on whether the planned schedule is realistic and when you should have an alternative go-live date for possible delays in the project.

12.2.2 Blueprint and Project Team

The central document for any project is a blueprint. A blueprint accurately describes the transformation you want to carry out as well as its impact on the system landscape and business processes. Depending on the transformation scenario, a blueprint can also be used as one of the documents of relevance to the auditor. As you can see, this document is quite important, and you should prepare blueprints with great care.

Blueprints should completely document the whole conversion in order to anticipate any effects on the IT landscape. A blueprint can be structured in various ways depending on the scenario. In general, however, the following aspects should be included:

- **All modifications and the objects and processes affected**
  All business objects affected by an implementation must be listed, and you must provide information on the form of implementation you want. (You can read more on this in the following sections, for example, in Section 12.3.)

  This list also contains all process changes and technical adjustments, such adjusting number ranges, and as describes rules about how you want to carry out these adjustments.

- **Overall project plan**
  The overall project plan includes all phases of the project as well as the schedule for each step and for the production conversion.

- **Impact on the overall landscape**
  You have to check all effects, not only those that impact the landscape you are transferring, but also any satellite systems that may exist (for example, through existing interfaces), including programs and solutions developed by your customers.

- **Test concept**
  The test concept is also central, along with an overview of all scheduled test cycles including the test cases to be implemented. This applies both to the regular test conversions as well as to the acceptance test after the production conversion.

- **Project team**
  Finally, you'll need an overview of all teams and team members so you can contact the parties responsible for specific topics at any time. This team overview should also include an escalation path for potential issues through all levels of the team hierarchy.

Contents of the blueprint

To prepare such a blueprint, a large number of employees from all affected areas of the company must work together closely. As already mentioned, external experts involved in transformation projects on a regular basis have the required project know-how and are often brought in for this purpose. After the blueprint is prepared, the document is accepted by all

Project team

463

12   Landscape Transformation

parties involved for several reasons. First, this buy-in ensures that all parties involved are comprehensively informed of any planned changes and, second, that individual parts of the blueprint do not contain any gaps that could lead to problems at later stages in the project.

During this phase, the infrastructure is also provided, and the tools are installed. The number of required test systems varies from scenario to scenario and depends on the number of affected systems in the IT landscape. As SAP LT is delivered as an SAP add-on, the installation is relatively easy. Additional tools required should also be integrated into the landscape at an early stage, so that they are immediately available on the test systems set up later on, thus reducing the cost of basic activities.

Providing the infrastructure

12.2.3   Test Runs

In this phase, all transformation tests are carried out. Even if the various test runs have different requirements depending on the progress of the project, their conditions should always correspond as precisely as possible to the conditions of the planned production conversion. These test runs are the only way to identify problems at an early stage and provide reliable estimates for the cut-over. The number of test runs also varies from scenario to scenario. However, at least two complete tests are recommended at minimum. In complex consolidations, four or more test conversions may be necessary.

These tests are primarily about ensuring quality and consistency. The implementation rules are set and validated by the following end-user tests. Depending on the scope of the adjustments, for example, between 1 and 3 weeks per cycle may be scheduled.

Quality and consistency

The requirements of the individual test runs can differ as follows to cover all factors:

Individual test runs

- **Technical validation**
  The first test primarily serves as a technical validation: Are all tools available? Are users and authorizations set up correctly? Do the connections within the network work? Is the performance of the test systems sufficient?

- **Testing the transformation**
  Further tests then serve to test the transformation: Were all implemen-

tation rules defined? Can all business processes be executed without restriction? Can all end users find their bearings? It is particularly important for this user group to test all test cases thoroughly.

- **General test**
  The last test run before the cut-over is a general test that simulates the production conversion. Ideally, all steps of the production conversion are also carried out in sequence, even if this test requires 24-hour shifts over several days. You should be aware that test systems are usually set up on hardware with poorer performance than the target system. If hardware that approaches the performance of the production system is not available for a general test, you will need to account for this difference when discussing system downtime.

The actual goal of the many tests is the gradual adaptation and improvement of the transformation. During the tests, you may discover, for example, that conversion tables and rules still need to be fine-tuned. Some changes (for example, changes within the context of Customizing) only show their overall effects when merged for the first time in the tests. Further changes may subsequently be required.

Test steps

The same applies to the impact of custom developments on the new system. Therefore, we strongly recommend repeatedly providing the test systems with current data from the existing production system in the case of longer test phases.

Be sure to plan the time and effort needed for the tests so that the employees required for the tests are also available at the right time. Changes to implementation rules or found errors often have to be discussed with the user departments, which can be a time-consuming process during the test phase. How time consuming depends on the complexity of the transition scenario and your company's organization.

Scheduling staff and time

Similarly, your employees involved in basic administration tasks must be included, so that the test systems are always provided in a timely manner and can be set up again after each test run. Depending on the technology used to deploy your test systems, this process can take several days. Especially when large and/or highly integrated systems are part of the transformation, rather time-consuming tasks must absolutely be taken into account during planning.

12.2.4 Production Conversion

Informing all parties affected

Once all the tests, including the general test, have been successfully completed, the next step is to convert the production system. Even if technically carried out over the weekend, the preparation for converting the production system often begins weeks earlier. Generally, all users of an affected system need to be informed of the potential downtime. Even if some employees were involved in the transformation planning, they never represent the entire user group for a system. Even for highly available systems or systems accessed from multiple time zones, overlaps exist, and every affected party must be aware that the transition will occur on the weekend scheduled.

Final preparations

A few days before the cut-over, final preparations are made, for example, last-minute adjustments to the transformation rules and the technical preparation of the production system. At this point, no more changes to the Customizing or to the program or ABAP changes can be made to the system.

Conversion weekend

The actual conversion on the weekend starts with blocking the system to all users except for users in the project team and the persons involved in maintaining the technical operation. Jobs in the SAP system are now deallocated, background programs are stopped, and interfaces are brought to a standstill. After the system has been isolated, a full backup is created so that, in the event of an emergency, the status before the transformation can be restored.

Next, you can optimize the system so that performance resources are fully available for the transformation. For many databases, you can, for example, deactivate database logging, thus achieving a significant increase in performance. While deactivating database logging does prevent a database recovery, an extra full backup should be prepared before the conversion. After completing the transformation, these settings should be reset for normal operations.

Monitoring

The main tasks at this stage are monitoring and the personnel process. On the one hand, current progress is monitored to continuously estimate the remaining downtime and identify problems at an early stage. On the other hand, a smooth process between the parties involved must be ensured. A clean handover between the project teams and their tasks without any loss of time is essential to meeting the cut-over schedule.

After the transformation has been successfully concluded, the validation and final acceptance test needs to be carried out by the end user. For this test, transactions are started and business processes are simulated in the system, system contents are checked based on lists, and test postings are carried out on the converted system. If no errors are found, the system can be released to all users. You should create a full backup at this point again so you have a starting point that captures the system immediately after the conversion.

Between transformation and go-live

12.2.5 Support after Go-Live

During this phase, the production system is still monitored closely for a few days after the conversion to uncover any sources of errors and to address these errors immediately if necessary. Furthermore, the development and quality assurance systems can now be converted. Depending on your requirements, transforming the test system can be carried out in parallel to the production system. Alternatively, you can also set up the test system using a copy of the production system. This decision depends on your individual conditions and the transition scenario.

Transformation of the system network

Like the production system, the development system is converted through transformation. The amount of data is normally much lower, which significantly reduces runtime for the transformation. However, particularly for adjustments in Customizing, exact planning is required so that no obsolete settings are transported into the new production system later on.

12.3 System Consolidation

Many reasons exist to undertake a system consolidation. In general, these advantages can be summarized under the rubric of reducing IT operating costs (*Total Cost of Ownership*, TCO) and implementing business objectives on the basis of a corporate strategy. In particular, regarding SAP S/4HANA as the central system of the future, consolidation can bring many advantages.

Reasons to consolidate

The following list describes some areas that may benefit from cost reduction through system consolidation:

- **Hardware**
  After a consolidation, a single system imposes lower requirements on the hardware than the combined source systems. Newly certified hardware for SAP HANA, in particular, results in savings.

- **Maintenance, patches, and backups**
  After consolidation, the costs of maintenance activities, implementing patches, and executing regular backups are drastically reduced depending on the number of systems replaced.

- **Updates**
  On the one hand, the costs for projects to update multiple systems are reduced, such as the costs for testing, for example. On the other hand, all end users benefit from the updated version of the central system at the same time.

- **Transports**
  A unified transport landscape simplifies transport logistics and reduces the total number of transports required.

- **Custom developments**
  Custom developments for the new system must only be created and tested once. After testing, your custom developments are immediately available to all users.

- **Support**
  Because all users work with a system with the same release status for all users, support for the users is greatly simplified.

- **Reporting**
  After a consolidation, reports and evaluations can be prepared on the basis of a uniform and central dataset.

- **Interfaces**
  The number of interfaces can be significantly reduced because, instead of distributed systems, a central system is now available. On the one hand, this centralization reduces the maintenance costs for the interfaces and, on the other hand, simplifies the development of new interfaces.

Standardizing business processes
In parallel to the more technical savings, the process and data harmonization that SAP S/4HANA strives to achieve provides the opportunity to standardize, simplify, and therefore accelerate existing business processes.

Among other things, harmonization provides benefits in the following areas:

- **Users and authorizations**
  Especially for users who log on to various systems for their work in a distributed system landscape, a central system significantly reduces the time required for administrative activities. Authorizations can also be unified now, thus simplifying monitoring.

- **Finance**
  Various approaches are available for consolidating financial activities. One example is harmonization towards a uniform chart of accounts, which could establish a basis for group-wide reporting.

- **Organizational units**
  In distributed landscapes, some technical identifiers may be used in preference, for example, "Company Code 1000." These identifiers must correspond in the various systems but not to the same business organizational unit. A system consolidation gives you the option of separating legal entities and, in this way, of generating clear reporting.

- **Master data**
  One major advantage of system consolidation is the harmonization of master data. For example, a single representation of a vendor makes clear reporting and controlling possible and thus helps you analyze business relations clearly, in turn resulting in improvements in purchasing conditions.

We've mentioned just some of the potential benefits of a complete system consolidation. However, the individual benefits for customers must be determined in detail.

This section looks at the technical aspects of a system consolidation. Consolidating several systems can be carried out in two different ways: by transferring clients or by merging clients. A client transfer is technically easy to implement and results in the creation of a multiclient system, as shown in Figure 12.5.

Client transfer or merge

In contrast, a client merge also consolidates the individual clients as a single-client system, as shown in Figure 12.6.

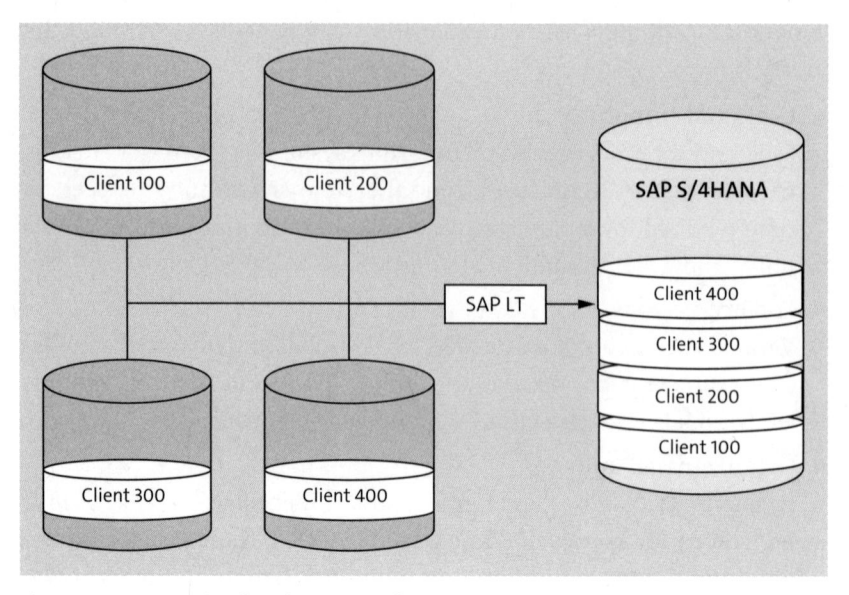

Figure 12.5 Example of a Client Transfer

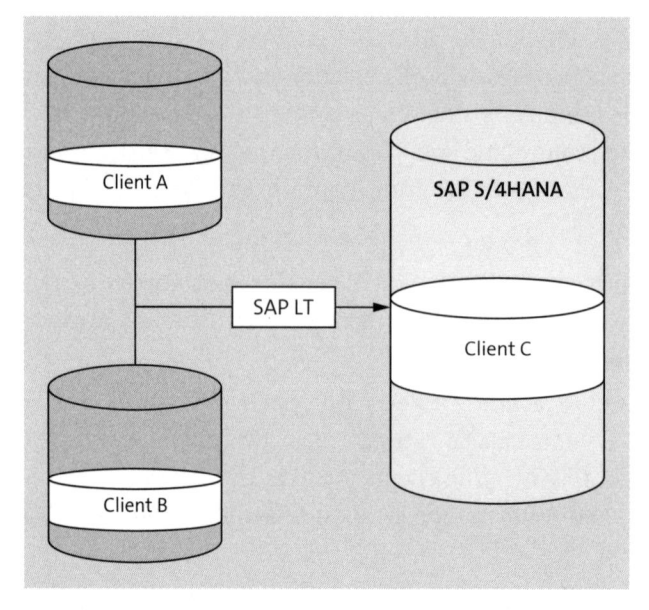

Figure 12.6 Example of a Client Merge

From the project perspective, a system consolidation involves three steps:

1. First, you'll have to define the overall objective, meaning you'll define whether a client transfer or a client merge will be carried out. How many systems and clients you want to consolidate is also important.
2. Second, you'll conduct a thorough analysis of all the systems involved to determine the differences between the project requirements in terms of volume and duration.
3. Finally, the actual consolidation is carried out, which consists of several test cycles and is completed with the actual production conversion. During the test phase, the data from the different systems must be harmonized.

System consolidation steps

To decide between a single-client or a multiclient system, a basic understanding of the client concept within an SAP system is of central importance. Users log in to the system at the client level. One client usually corresponds to one enterprise. Users are isolated within a client and therefore cannot view or change any data from another client. As a result, several enterprises that are logically separated can be technically run within one system.

Client concept

As a result, a multiclient system is much easier to construct than merging clients. For transferring clients in a multiclient system, only the general settings and Customizing have to be adapted and, if conflicts exist, harmonized. A simple example of such a conflict would be an identical client number used in different systems for different clients.

Client transfer

For a complete merge, on the other hand, all client-dependent data must also be adjusted and, if conflicts exist, harmonized. The merge is easier the more similar the systems and clients to be consolidated are.

Client merge

However, central areas (for example, various number ranges) have to be adjusted in almost every project. As with our earlier example of client numbers, in this case, the same numbering for organizational units, such as company codes for example, must be harmonized if necessary.

When combining individual systems and clients, other areas are also affected, for example, users and their authorizations.

Because this transformation scenario is complex, a thorough analysis of the systems involved is required to identify conflicts between settings, data, and programs. Table 12.1 provides an overview of the relevant areas you'll need to analyze for a client transfer or a client merge.

Analysis of the source systems

Area to Be Analyzed	Client Transfer	Client Merge
ABAP Dictionary (data type and tables)	X	X
Customer-specific programs (such as programs in the Z namespace)	X	X
Modifications (to the SAP Standard) and user exits	X	X
Client-independent Customizing	X	X
Client-dependent Customizing		X
Application data (master and transaction data)		X
Number ranges		X
Users and authorizations		X
Program variants		X
Archives (created using Transaction SARA)		X

Table 12.1 Analyses Required for Client Transfer and Client Merge

This comparison once again shows the difference in complexity between the two system consolidation options.

Harmonizing these different areas requires various approaches. As shown in Table 12.1, the following areas are relevant for both client transfers and client merges:

- **ABAP Dictionary**
  The ABAP repository must be mentioned as an object to be consolidated, in addition to the SAP standard programs and data types. The ABAP Dictionary contains all structure information for SAP tables. Possible conflicts must also be identified in the ABAP Dictionary beforehand. By using the simplification list, conflicts are identified regarding the difference between a classic SAP ERP system and SAP S/4HANA. These conflicts are technically addressed by the conversion programs, which are also used for system conversions (see Chapter 10). These conversion programs are currently not integrated into SAP LT and must, for example, be carried out separately after consolidation.

- **Custom programs**

  If technical conflicts exist, custom programs must also be harmonized during consolidation. Conflicts may exist both in individual customer namespaces as well as in the traditional Z namespace. A simple example of the need to harmonize would be programs with the same name but with different structures or content. If the source texts of these programs differ, harmonization can be implemented quite simply by renaming one of the two programs. However, renaming is only one option. A detailed analysis of custom developments and related harmonization tasks must be scheduled along with the appropriate effort. In its analysis, SAP LT helps you use the appropriate functions, or you can use internal SAP tools such as custom code analysis via Transaction /SDF/CD_CCA.

- **Modifications and user exits**

  User exits constitute a special case because they are no longer created in current SAP solutions. Where possible, user exits have been replaced by Business Add-Ins (BAdIs). However, user exits continue to be used by many SAP customers and must also be considered before consolidation. The ABAP code of a user exit itself is client-independent. During harmonization, therefore, you must ensure that the extensions are assigned to their correct clients, which also applies for modifications previously made to the SAP standard.

- **Client-independent Customizing**

  Client-independent Customizing consists mainly of technical settings and thus usually does not require much effort to harmonize. A common example of Customizing settings that may need harmonizing is when your company has several factory calendars, with different validity periods in different systems, that need to be consolidated.. To resolve these conflicts, a uniform period of validity must be determined for the calendar. Technically, such an implementation involves little effort.

On the other hand, the following areas are of relevance, particularly if clients are merged into a single-client system. Harmonization needs can be extensive and complex in the following areas:

Harmonization areas

- **Client-dependent Customizing**

  Compared to harmonizing client-independent Customizing, harmonizing client-dependent Customizing is much more complex and costly.

Comparing these Customizing settings already presents a challenge due to their high number. Therefore, an early analysis is essential to estimate the necessary steps. We recommend transferring the delta Customizing from the source system(s) to the target system. The target system should ideally be a copy of the existing development system. Thus, differences can be analyzed without restriction, and harmonization can be implemented.

The effort required for manually processing conflicts also depends on coordinating changes within the company because central Customizing settings are affected, for example:

- Organizational units
- Units of measure
- Currencies
- Document types
- Material types
- Material groups
- Account groups

Mapping rules are a simple method for harmonization, for example, if organizational units have the same name. You can assign new values that are not yet used in the target system to various source values. If a simple renaming is not possible, you'll have to decide how to handle a more complex conversion process.

- **Application data and number ranges**
  Application data concerns the actual data in a system or a client in the form of master and transaction data. Harmonization thus primarily concerns classic master data, such as materials, accounts receivable, and accounts payable. For numbers previously assigned internally within clients, overlaps in the number ranges may exist or numbers were assigned externally that occur in all systems but not for the same master data.

  Even in these cases, you can execute conversions. However, each data record would need to be converted individually. With high data volumes, however, this individual approach is impractical. Instead, you could use a *prefix* or an *offset*.

> **Prefix and Offset**
>
> In the simplest case of prefixing, an entire number range in master data is prefixed by a letter or a letter combination, thus creating a completely new number range.
>
> In an offset, a fixed number value is added to an existing number. As a result, the whole number range is moved, thus retaining its original intervals and conditions.

These three methods, put simply, again involve renaming and adding the entire dataset from the source system to the target system. Particularly for accounts receivable and accounts payable, *data quality* is often critical for merging the content of data records that are numbered differently between the systems but that are perhaps identical in terms of content. Content-related cleansing can provide considerable added value to the organization, but you should not lose sight of the considerable additional costs for such data cleansing within a system consolidation.

- **Users and authorizations**
  Users and their authorizations are client specific and, depending on the objective, may require a comprehensive or simple harmonization. Often, within the different systems of a company, you may find similarly designed authorization concepts. If role types and authorizations differ significantly, creating new users may make more sense than a complex harmonization. If authorizations need to be adapted, you must ensure that fixed values can be stored within these authorizations that, for example, check the rights for a specific company code. These values must then be adjusted accordingly.

- **Program variants**
  For harmonizing program variants, the variants themselves are not necessarily the problem; rather, the data that was changed in the course of consolidation needs to be harmonized. Thus, the program variant might no longer work properly or may access incorrect values. If, for example, selection fields were preset with values that have changed or wildcards were used that now access a larger dataset, problems may arise. Although you can use analysis tools (for example, in the ABAP Workbench) to examine variants for this purpose, in most cases, manual work will be required if problems are identified.

- **Archives**

  Archived data from your SAP ERP system is still relevant for harmonization because these archives contain data relating to information that may be present in another form after a consolidation. Two options are available for adapting archive data in the course of the harmonization:

  - On the one hand, the archives can be uploaded back into the system's database and thus be converted like other data during the consolidation.
  - Alternatively, you can convert the archives, which requires the archives are read first. The data is then converted as required for the harmonization and written into a new archive file. Different procedures may be used, depending on the storage system that you use for your archives.

Defining transformation rules

If all necessary changes, as identified according to the analysis based on SAP LT or SAP Standard tools, have been addressed, you can define the transformation rules in SAP LT. You can determine, based on the nature of the conflict between the systems involved, how you want to resolve these conflicts, including all areas, for example, in which master data is received or overwritten, if identical numbers exist in the systems, or which Customizing settings are now the leading settings. Based on these rules, SAP LT transforms the individual data records and transfers them from the source system (or from multiple source systems) to the dedicated target system.

[!] **SAP Consulting Required**

SAP LT supports system consolidation scenarios, but system consolidations cannot be implemented using SAP LT exclusively. Due to the complexity of system consolidation projects, the necessary expert functions are currently only available through SAP Consulting (from SAP or a third-party provider).

12.4 Company Code Transfer

The second landscape transformation scenario involves transferring an organizational unit, more precisely a company code, according to SAP S/4HANA. Gradually introducing SAP S/4HANA to your enterprise may well begin with a single business area. Often, individual subsidiaries are mapped in company codes. Therefore, you can, for example, only transfer one subsidiary (for example, Germany) to SAP S/4HANA from a European system in which multiple countries are mapped as one company code.

The simplest approach to implementing a company code migration is the Company Code Deletion function. This standard scenario within SAP LT can be carried out by any IT organization without incurring additional consulting costs. Figure 12.7 shows an overview of the package and its implementation phases.

Deleting company codes

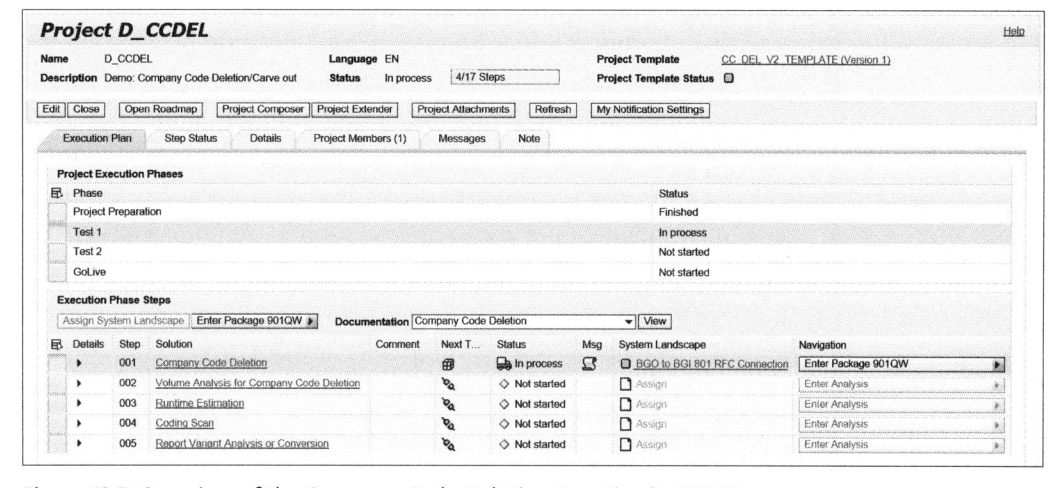

Figure 12.7 Overview of the Company Code Deletion Function in SAP LT

After deleting the company code, a system conversion of the newly set-up system is carried out.

SAP LT consistently deletes all relevant data from one or more selected company codes from the system. If all company codes for an associated controlling area are selected, the entire controlling area is deleted. Such a project is usually carried out in two phases and involves several steps. The first phase is known as the *deletion*, while the second phase is called the *counter-deletion*. The organizational structure of your enterprise is therefore cleanly separated after both phases.

Project phases

In the first phase, the following steps are carried out:

Deletion phase

1. You'll create a full system copy of the system from which the company code will be deleted.

2. Select the delete function in SAP LT and prepare for this technically, as described further in this section.

3. The deletion is carried out.

4. A test cycle is carried out in which the newly created system is tested after the deletion.

5. Depending on the results of the tests, steps 1 to 4 are repeated in order to make adjustments if necessary.

Counter-deletion phase

Finally, the counter-deletion is carried out:

1. You'll prepare the counter-deletion in the production source system from which the company code has been deleted. Because this process takes place in your SAP ERP production system, you must allow for a corresponding downtime and inform your end users.

2. A final system copy is created. The relevant real data is deleted from the copy and from the source system. The result is an additional production system that only contains the selected company code.

3. Now, you'll set up the development and quality assurance systems for the newly established production system.

The whole procedure is usually fully executed in at least two cycles with a current copy of the existing production system. The deletion is executed on this system copy, which has no impact on the existing system landscape. Key findings from this test run include the total runtime of the deletion as well as the identification of potential errors.

Organization derivation

The *organization derivation* in SAP LT is used to determine what data should be deleted for all SAP applications. Technically, the SAP organizational structure is analyzed via the Customizing, and all of the company code-dependent organizational units are identified. Figure 12.8 shows a detailed view of the individual phase steps.

SAP LT creates a worklist from this containing the master data, transaction data, and documents that are to be deleted. These items are then removed from SAP application tables during the actual deletion. Data in Controlling (CO) and Profitability Analysis (CO-PA) can be deleted consistently using this method even if you start with one company code first. Figure 12.9 shows a complete organization with company codes selected for transfer.

12.4 Company Code Transfer

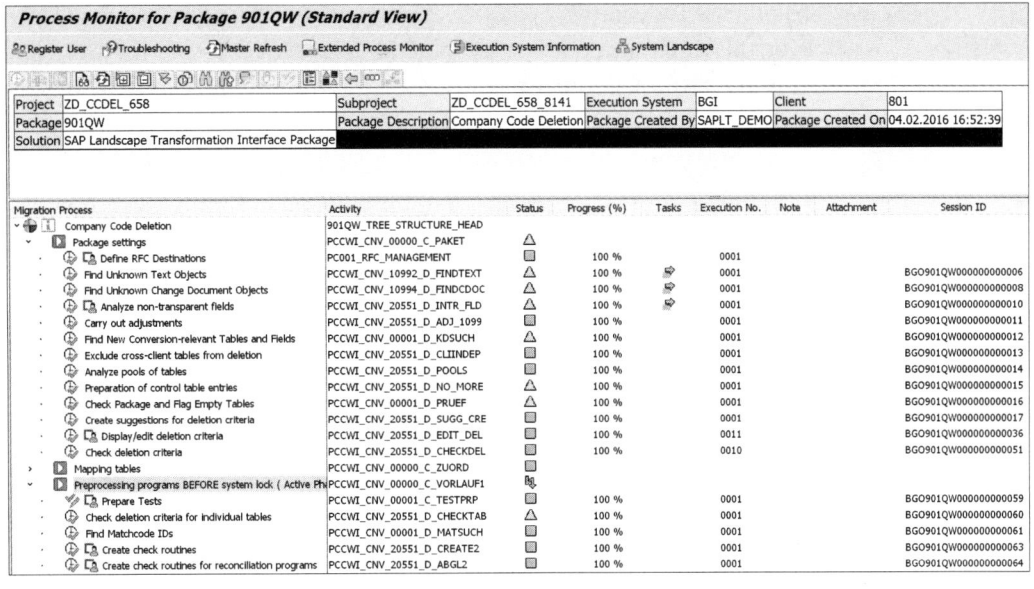

Figure 12.8 Individual Steps in the Company Code Deletion Procedure

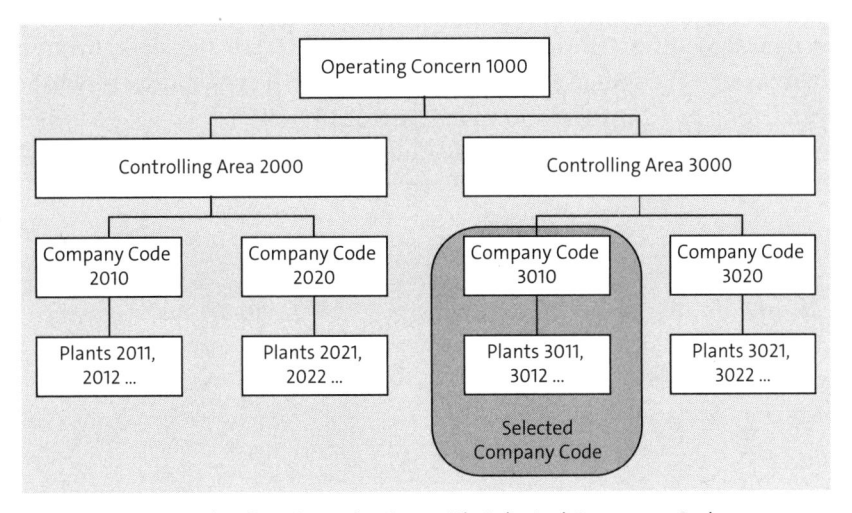

Figure 12.9 Example of an Organization with Selected Company Code

In test cycles, the primary objective is to troubleshoot and determine if too much or too little data was deleted. If some processes are managed across company codes, either situation could be the case. Possible examples include processes that are used both by sales and procurement.

Test cycles after the deletion

479

Test cases To prepare for company code deletion, 1 week is usually scheduled. However, this timeframe does not account for a subsequent system conversion, only the SAP LT Company Code Deletion function. In this first week of preparation, SAP LT is configured and test cases are prepared. Depending on requirements, these test cases include two areas:

- Simple lists of the dataset prior to the deletion to compare volume
- Separate postings that identify whether all business processes still function fully after the deletion

Systems for counter-deletion Because the source system is still used in production, the counter-deletion is usually carried out on a weekend. Copies set up for test purposes usually have no time limit, which is also technically justified because the hardware used for testing is usually cheaper (but has a lower performance). Therefore, test processes simply take longer by comparison. However, the test system must be available exclusively for testing purposes, and no other projects should be run on the test system in parallel. Further, the copy must be complete in order to work on the entire database and not be a significantly reduced system. As a result, the deletions of the complementary company codes can be executed properly. If, for example, company code 1000 is migrated to SAP S/4HANA, only this company code will remain in the new system after the system copy and deletion. All other company codes will be removed using SAP LT, as shown in Figure 12.10.

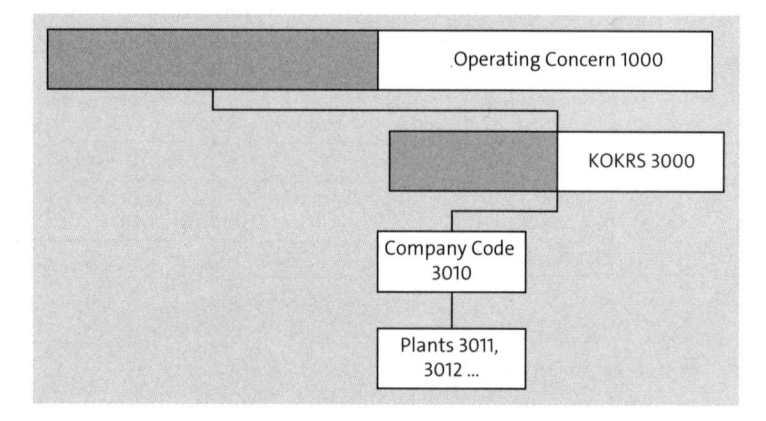

Figure 12.10 A New System with an Isolated Company Code

The new production system If the new production system has been fully set up, usually simple system copy procedures are carried out to create new development and quality assurance systems. You'll again have a three-tier system landscape but only with the relevant data for the individual company code. What is important here is when and how the system conversion is performed. Depending on your requirements, you can initially set the new system to live in the current release and operate it for a while before you then carry out a system conversion. Due to the high level of standardization of the deletion procedure and the relatively short runtime, you can also combine the two processes into a single project, of course.

When the company code has been copied to the new system, this particular company code is deleted from the previous source system in the second phase. You could also simply lock this company code from postings. However, often reasons exist in favor of deleting company codes: For instance, lower data volumes will result in less strain on the system. Deletion may also provide a clean break from the old system. Figure 12.11 shows the structure of a legacy system after the counter-deletion.

Counter-deletion in the source system

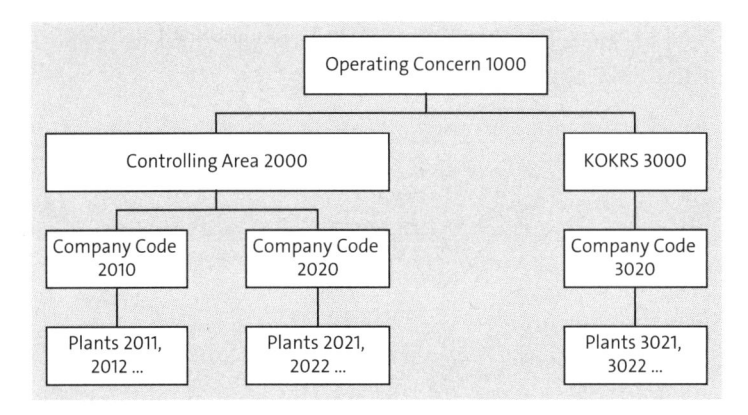

Figure 12.11 Legacy System after Cleansing via Counter-Deletion

In this second phase, two test cycles are also usually carried out. After the production counter-deletion has been performed over a weekend, the remaining system landscape, such as your test and quality assurance systems, is cleansed. This cleansing is not time-critical and can also be carried out during normal business hours. You can also consider rebuilding your quality assurance systems using a full system copy, similar to the procedure in the case of the new system.

Test cycles after the counter-deletion

Next, a deletion is usually also carried out because the delete procedure is so simple and because parallel projects may be running in the old system landscape. A further reason for the deletion may be that you are unsure whether the dataset in your nonproduction systems is complete. If all delete procedures are complete, you can begin to convert the system on the newly created system with the isolated company code, thus giving you a separate but fully functional company code on SAP S/4HANA.

12.5　Transformation to Central Finance

Architecture of the Central Finance transformation

While Chapter 3, Section 3.2.1, only introduced Central Finance, this section focuses on the technical components and other important aspects of introducing the solution. Introducing Central Finance is a variant of a landscape transformation. Therefore, SAP LT plays a central role as a tool for setting up Central Finance as well. Figure 12.12 shows a more comprehensive overview of this scenario.

To operate Central Finance, you must, in simple terms, carry out two steps:

- Set up the SAP Landscape Transformation (SAP LT) Replication Server
- Set up the Central Finance system

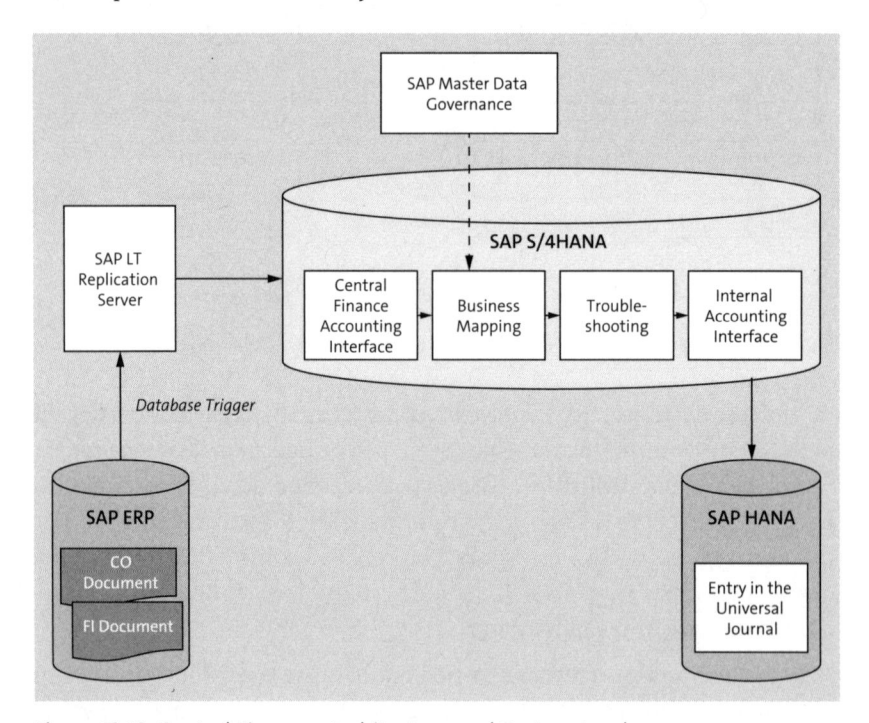

Figure 12.12 Central Finance: Architecture and System Landscape

The SAP LT Server establishes the connection between the local systems. Because the SAP LT Replication Server works at the database level, you can also integrate non-SAP systems. Using database access, no adaptations are necessary at the application server level. The SAP LT Replication Server itself can either be set up as a separate standalone system or can be installed on one of your source systems or on the Central Finance system.

SAP Landscape Transformation Replication Server

Where you set up SAP LT Replication Server depends mainly on the utilization of the relevant systems to date and on the expected data throughput. The more complex the landscape, the more likely a separate instance for the SAP LT Replication Server should be set up.

The Central Finance system is operated on the basis of SAP S/4HANA as a central financial system. Data from the connected systems is loaded into Central Finance, and among other things, the master data is harmonized to ensure a uniform view. This harmonization can either be carried out manually or, if SAP Master Data Governance (SAP MDG) is available in the landscape, called from the SAP MDG tool. Using SAP MDG is optional.

SAP Master Data Governance

You can also install the new Central Finance instance and the necessary SAP LT Replication Server in SAP HANA Enterprise Cloud (SAP HEC), which is a good alternative if you do not want to integrate a new instance of Central Finance into your existing landscape.

SAP HANA Enterprise Cloud

12.5.1 Implementing SAP S/4HANA Central Finance

In this section, we'll look at the most important steps to implement Central Finance. First, we'll look at the technical settings required to set up the various system connections and also examine the business logic with which you can convert general ledger entries. Converting these entries is an important step towards setting up Central Finance because you'll need to know how to assign these postings to the proper general ledger account and the account assignments (cost center, order, etc.) and how to derive other report dimensions, such as profit center, function area, etc., using these account assignments. These settings and the settings for the initial data load using the SAP LT Replication Server are covered centrally by a Central Finance-specific Implementation Guide (IMG).

The IMG shown in Figure 12.13 comes from a current development system and, therefore, may appear differently depending on the release version you use.

12 Landscape Transformation

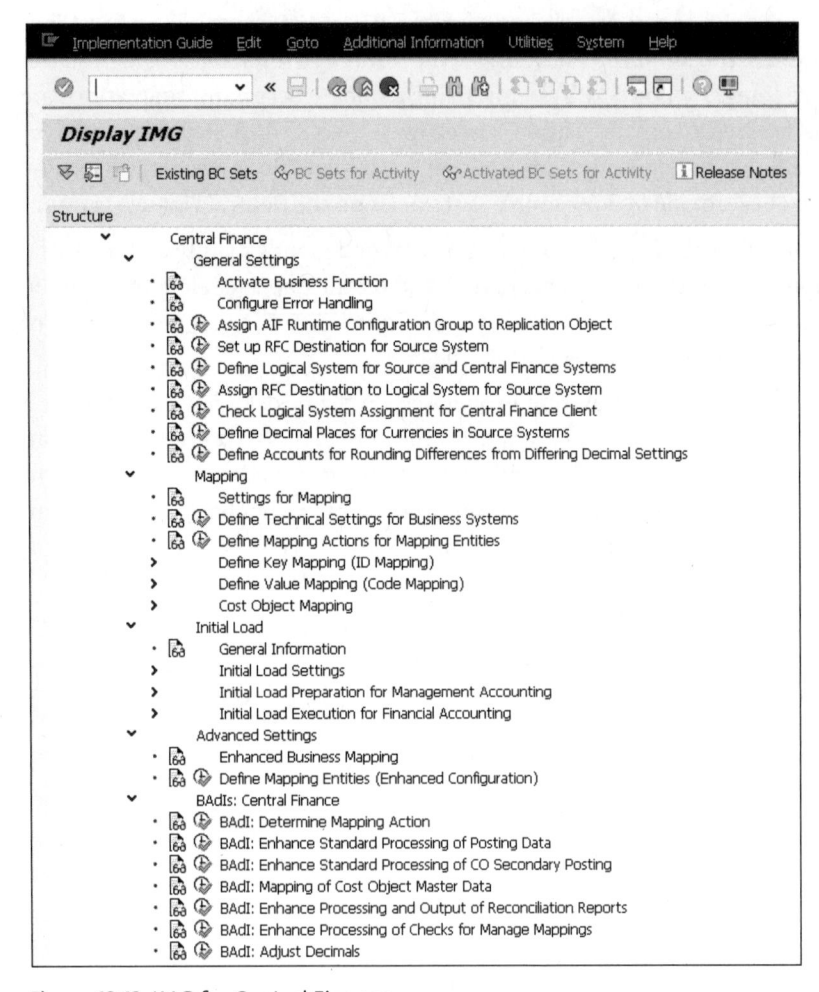

Figure 12.13 IMG for Central Finance

System connections
A major step is configuring the system connections between all of the systems involved. Although these connections are created for an entire system, you can begin with a few selected company codes. You'll thus get a feel for the potential of the new system without having to worry about your entire, complex enterprise landscape.

Activating Central Finance
The first step in implementing Central Finance is to activate the `FINS_CFIN` (Central Finance) business function. In parallel, you'll also activate two further business functions, `FIN_GL_ERR_CORR` and `FIN_GL_ERR_CORR_SUSP`, so you can perform preliminary postings and error corrections later on. These two

12.5 Transformation to Central Finance

functions ensure that all general ledger entries that originate from the local systems, including general ledger accounts and account assignments not yet created in the central system, are parked as work items on an error list.

You'll begin the technical definition of the system landscape by creating an RFC (Remote Function Call) connection. Entries in the Universal Journal in Central Finance are technically linked to documents in your local systems. You'll also need the RFC connections to select data from your local systems during the first data migration and to create the master data mappings to Central Finance.

RFC connections

Because these two tasks will probably be carried out by different users (the initial and more technical data migration is often in the hands of a system administrator, whereas an accountant or analyst is responsible for the functional document links), you may want to establish different RFC connections to differentiate between the two tasks according to user type.

You'll also have to define all connected systems as *logical systems*. The idea behind a logical system is to clearly define every system-client combination within your system landscape; so if we look at a document's header, we can clearly see which combination of system and client was the source of the document.

Logical system names

Finally, you'll assign the logical system to the Central Finance client and the RFC destination of your logical system. To make these assignments, select the **RFC Destination for Source System** IMG entry and maintain the logical connections, as shown in Figure 12.14.

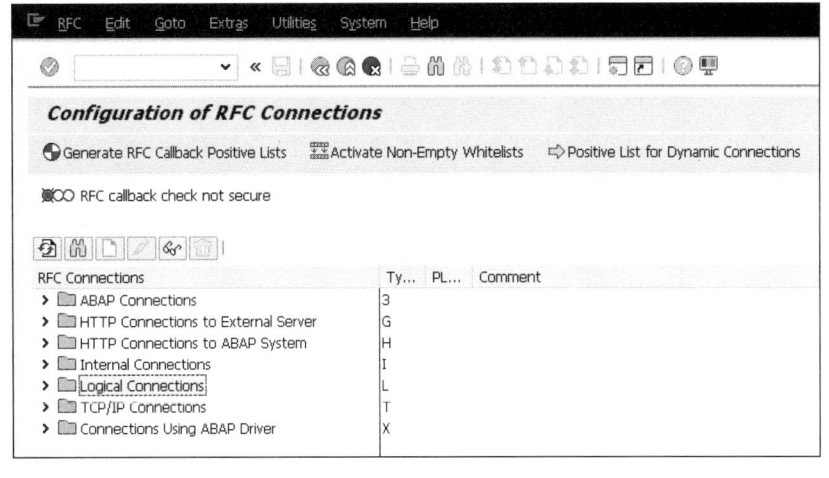

Figure 12.14 Configuration of RFC Connections

12 Landscape Transformation

Local systems   Preparations must also be made on the local system. Verify that the *Data Migration Server* (DMIS) add-on (Release 2011_1_700 or higher) is installed on each source and target system (Support Package (SP) 8 is recommended) and that you have implemented SAP Note 2124481 (SAP LT SP08, Correction 3) on the add-on.

If your organization does not yet implement SP 8 or higher, you'll have to implement some code changes in your local systems to ensure that you can prepare the general ledger entries for the transfer to Central Finance.

> [»] **Additional Information and Collective Note**
>
> As these systems are continuously being further developed, SAP Collective Note 2148893 provides a good starting point for current information. This Note is updated on a regular basis, so that you are informed if further improvements are added.

SAP LT Replication Server   As mentioned earlier, the SAP LT Replication Server is a central component of this Central Finance scenario, which connects the various systems. SAP LT Replication Server is basically a server that collects the messages from the local system and sends them to the central system. Setting up the complete SAP LT Replication Server for other scenarios can be a large undertaking.

> [»] **Additional Information on the SAP LT Replication Server**
>
> You can find further information on the SAP LT Replication Server in the SAP Help Portal at *http://help.sap.com/viewer/p/SAP_LANDSCAPE_TRANSFORMATION*. We also recommend SAP Note 2154420 for further information on Central Finance systems.

The SAP LT Replication Server uses tables and an initial load object and a replication object for each table to be transferred. Therefore, automatic triggers are set for the relevant tables in the source systems to transfer documents from the SAP ERP Financial Accounting system (FI). However, you do not have to set up these triggers manually because they are predelivered with the latest version of the SAP LT Replication Server.

However, before the actual data transfer can begin, you must think about your individual organizational units and their master data during the course of the transformation of business processes. The next section starts with organizational units.

12.5 Transformation to Central Finance

> **Additional Information on the Implementation of Central Finance**
>
> For a complete description of all steps, both on the technical and the application sides, refer to the documents at *http://help.sap.com/sfin200*.

12.5.2 Global Parameters

Global parameters (such as country and company codes) will seem familiar to you, as you already use these in your existing systems. In most cases, you'll carry out a one-to-one transfer of these parameters to Central Finance, and in other cases, you will have to transform them. As these parameters are essentially stable, you can also map their values using SAP MDG. This approach also covers Customizing settings, for example, settings for reminders and payment terms that can be assigned to customers. The following settings are therefore applied to the Central Finance side.

Let's start with the countries that you want to map in Central Finance. In order to maintain countries, select **SAP NetWeaver • General Settings • Countries • Define Countries in mySAP Systems** in the IMG (see Figure 12.15).

Participating countries

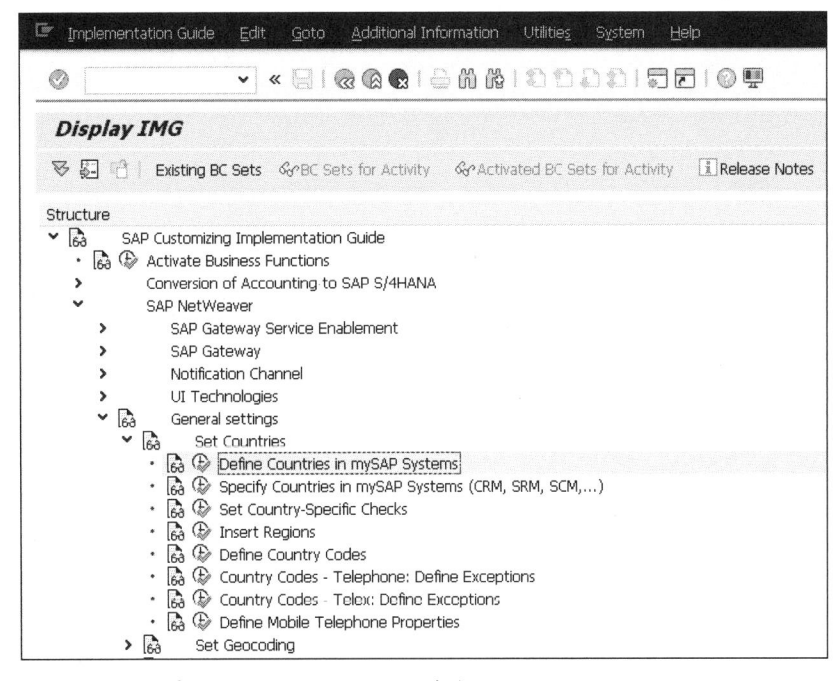

Figure 12.15 Defining Countries in Central Finance

12 Landscape Transformation

You can copy these settings from your local systems unless you want to create additional countries in Central Finance for evaluation purposes—if, for example, data has been added from non-SAP sources. Make sure that you are informed of the specific legal requirements for these countries to avoid losing any country-specific information in centralized reporting. Such information should instead be mapped in local reporting.

Participating companies

Next, you'll specify which of your companies should be mapped out in Central Finance. This step is particularly important if business transactions occur between these companies, for example, if a company within your group supplies goods to another.

These business relationships are mapped in Central Finance and must be maintained. However, if you do not create a company that is involved in general transactions, data from the source will not be transferred, and the process will be fully presented.

You can define companies by following the IMG menu path **Company Structure • Definition • Financial Accounting • Define Company**. You will also need to provide the companies with the appropriate company codes using **Company Structure • Map • Financial Accounting • Company Code—Assign Company**, as shown in Figure 12.16.

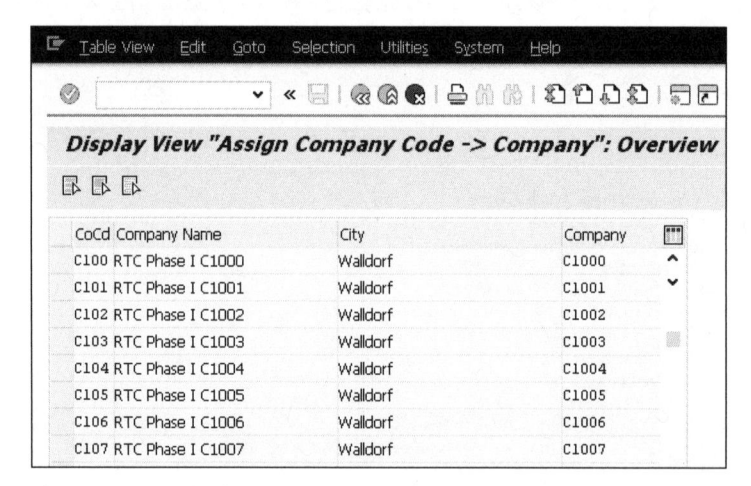

CoCd	Company Name	City	Company
C100	RTC Phase I C1000	Walldorf	C1000
C101	RTC Phase I C1001	Walldorf	C1001
C102	RTC Phase I C1002	Walldorf	C1002
C103	RTC Phase I C1003	Walldorf	C1003
C104	RTC Phase I C1004	Walldorf	C1004
C105	RTC Phase I C1005	Walldorf	C1005
C106	RTC Phase I C1006	Walldorf	C1006
C107	RTC Phase I C1007	Walldorf	C1007

Figure 12.16 Assigning a Company Code to a Company

Participating company codes

Now looking at the company codes, you'll not only accept the type of attributes required by reporting solutions but also the settings that affect how entries are updated in the Universal Journal. You'll have to consider the following settings in Central Finance:

- **Chart of Accounts**: If you want to use a central chart of accounts, you should enter the chart of accounts in this field. You should ask whether you need also need a local chart of accounts for local reporting purposes and whether these local requirements should report to the central chart of accounts.

- **Fiscal Year Variant**: The fiscal year variant determines the number of fiscal year periods and the special periods you want to work with. Remember that, if you are consolidating into a single controlling area, you'll also have to settle a fiscal year variant for all entities that will be part of this controlling area. If you have countries with different fiscal year structures, you'll also have to create a separate ledger with the corresponding fiscal year variants for these countries.

These global parameters for the relevant company code can be found by following the IMG menu path **Financial Accounting (new) • Basic Settings Financial Accounting (new) • Global Parameters for the Company Code • Check and Add Global Parameters**. The example shown in Figure 12.17 illustrates how the chart of accounts **INT** provides the option of specifying a country chart of accounts and the fiscal year variant **K4**.

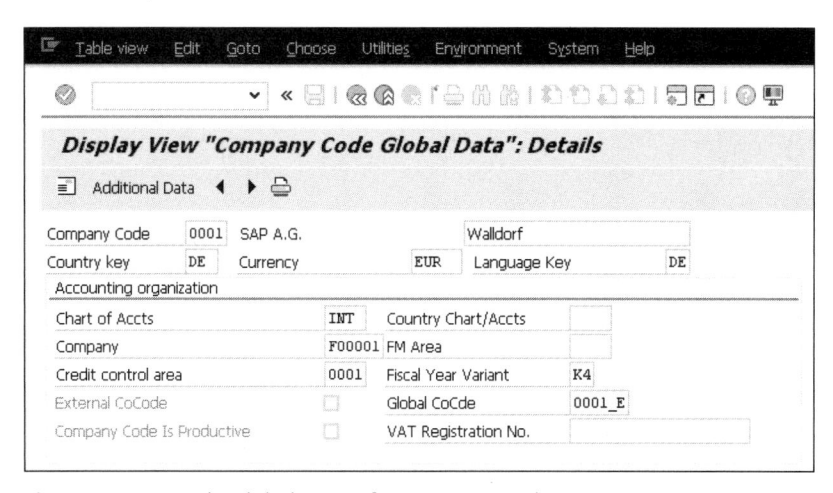

Figure 12.17 Sample Global Data of a Company Code

Defining ledgers Within individual company codes, you can define *ledgers*. If you are already using the new general ledger, you should be familiar with the ledger concept to separate postings based on different accounting standards, such as IFRS (International Financial Reporting Standards) and US-GAAP (United States Generally Accepted Accounting Principles). In this context, notice that no settings are available to update profit centers, segments, business partners, functional areas, etc. in the general ledger settings. These settings are outdated in Central Finance because the Universal Journal contains all of these fields by default. Figure 12.18 provides an overview of the maintenance of the ledgers.

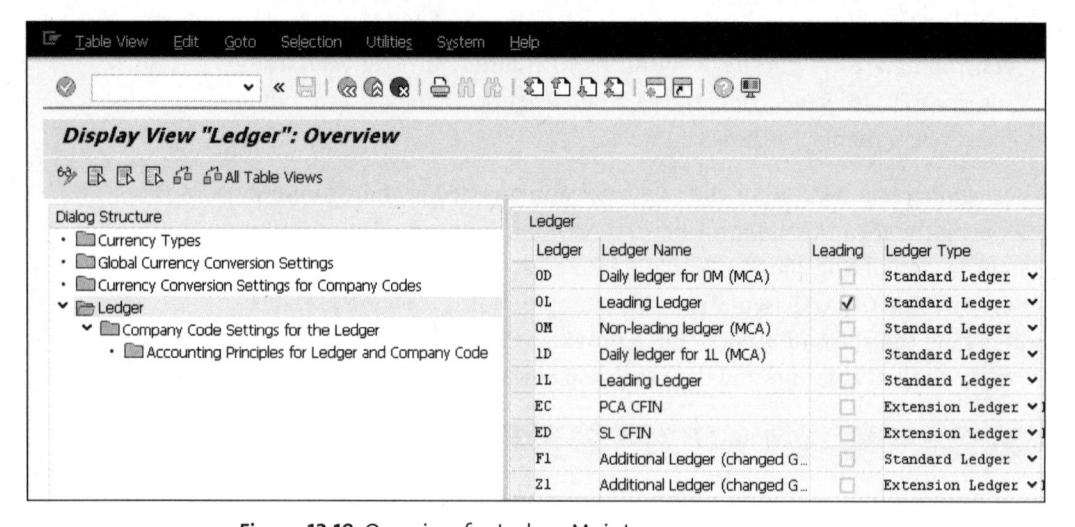

Figure 12.18 Overview for Ledger Maintenance

Currencies When you define a ledger, you should consider the relevant currencies you use. The local currency for your company code is probably the one you are already using in your local system for this company code. But you should consider introducing a global currency or group currency if you have not already done so.

You can also make some changes to your nonlocal currencies, if you operate internationally. You can set up currencies in ledgers by following the IMG menu path **Financial Accounting (new)** • **Basic Settings Financial Accounting (new)** • **Ledger** • **Define Settings for Ledger and Currency Types**. By default, a company code currency and a group currency are used for controlling purposes. Figure 12.19 shows some possible currency types.

12.5 Transformation to Central Finance

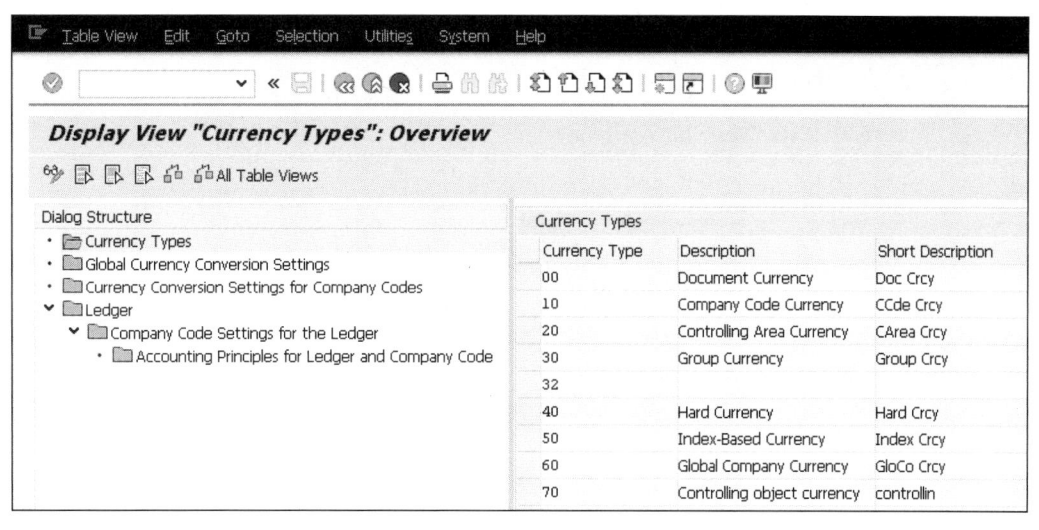

Figure 12.19 Overview of Possible Currency Types

Next, you'll define your controlling area. We have deliberately written "controlling area" in the singular because your life will be much easier if you can consolidate all of your data into one controlling area in Central Finance. As with the company code, these are the critical settings:

- **Currency** (please note that the currency type for the group currency is now part of the settings)
- **Chart of accounts** (again including accounts and cost elements)
- **Fiscal year variant**

You must select the cross-company code cost accounting option because your controlling area normally comprises several company codes. To define your controlling area, follow the IMG menu path **Company Structure • Definition • Controlling • Maintain Controlling Area**. Figure 12.20 shows sample data for maintaining a controlling area.

In addition to these basic financial settings, the controlling area determines which entities you can use for reports in Central Finance. Here you'll define which *account assignments* are active in your Universal Journal (cost center, order, etc.). The cost center, order management, process-based cost accounting, and cost-effectiveness analysis components are often selected. Profit center accounting is not activated as a separate account assignment because it is covered in the Universal Journal.

Defining the controlling area

Account assignments

491

12 Landscape Transformation

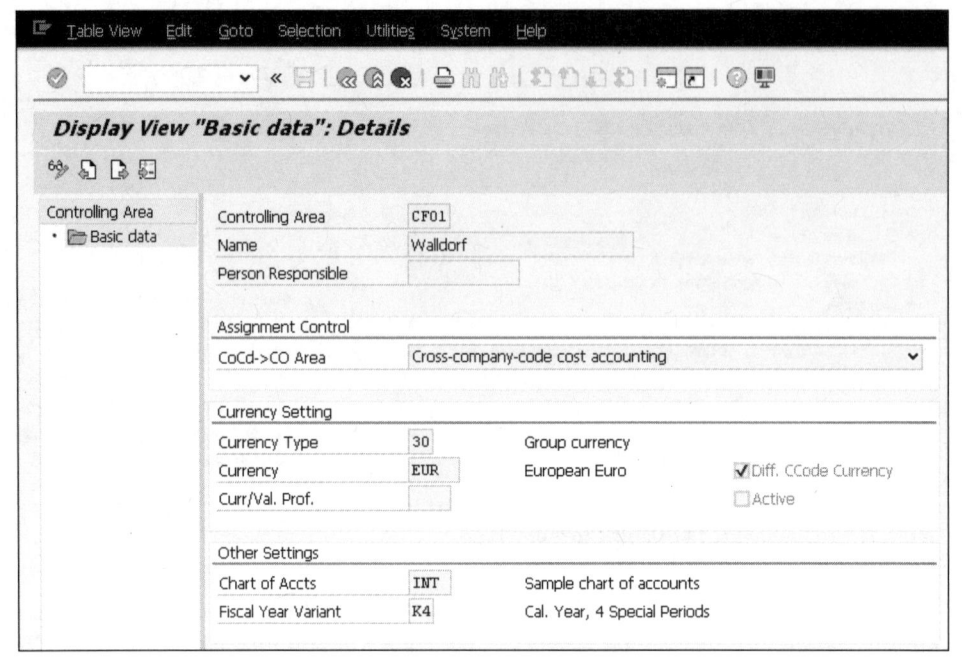

Figure 12.20 Sample Data for Maintaining a Controlling Area

Defining the operating concern

Next, you'll define your operating concern. To use the full potential of the Universal Journal, you'll have to activate *account-based profitability analysis*. For primary cost and revenues, account-based profitability analysis ensures that all of the sales postings, revenue reductions, and costs of goods sold included in accounting documents can be automatically posted to a combination of CO-PA characteristics, such as product, customer, and region. These settings for maintaining the operating concern and the characteristics are found under the familiar controlling menu items, not under **Financial Accounting (New)**.

Mapping organizational units

Finally, you'll have to map your organizational units. The global parameters for country companies, company codes, etc., introduced previously are usually managed using the value mappings that you created as described earlier in this section. If you are working in the SAP Standard, you normally won't have to adjust these settings for assignment entities, as shown in Figure 12.21. However, you'll have to add entities if you want to map your own fields or fields from an external system in Central Finance. When you've

492

completed these settings, the main organizational structures for Central Finance are available.

Display View "Mapping Entity": Overview

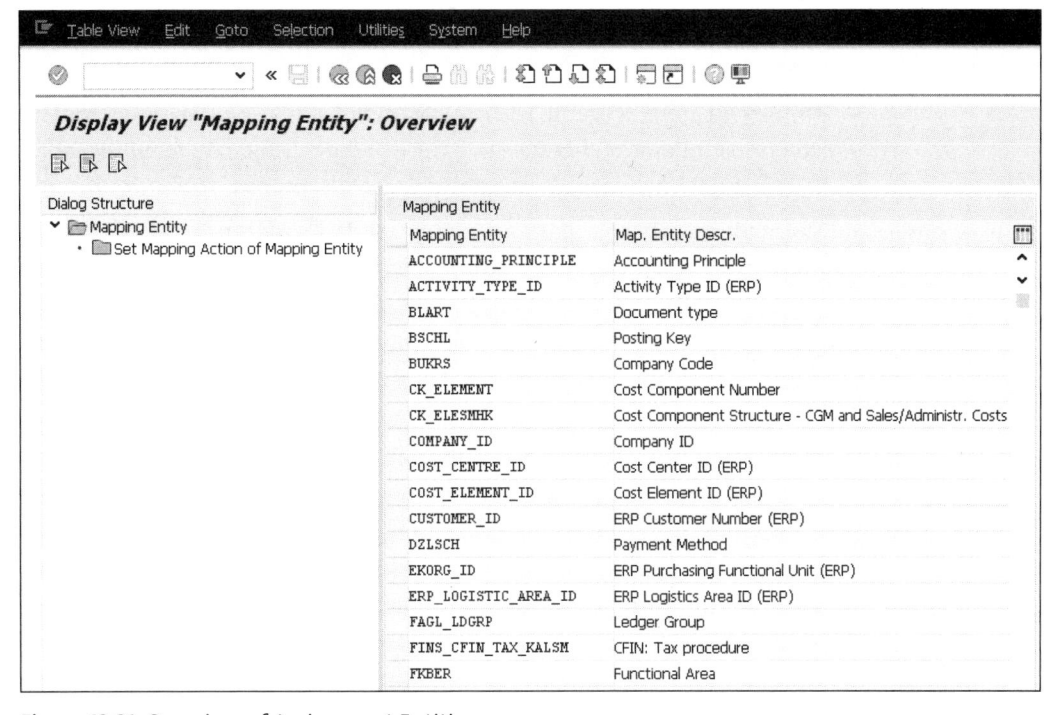

Mapping Entity	Map. Entity Descr.
ACCOUNTING_PRINCIPLE	Accounting Principle
ACTIVITY_TYPE_ID	Activity Type ID (ERP)
BLART	Document type
BSCHL	Posting Key
BUKRS	Company Code
CK_ELEMENT	Cost Component Number
CK_ELESMHK	Cost Component Structure - CGM and Sales/Administr. Costs
COMPANY_ID	Company ID
COST_CENTRE_ID	Cost Center ID (ERP)
COST_ELEMENT_ID	Cost Element ID (ERP)
CUSTOMER_ID	ERP Customer Number (ERP)
DZLSCH	Payment Method
EKORG_ID	ERP Purchasing Functional Unit (ERP)
ERP_LOGISTIC_AREA_ID	ERP Logistics Area ID (ERP)
FAGL_LDGRP	Ledger Group
FINS_CFIN_TAX_KALSM	CFIN: Tax procedure
FKBER	Functional Area

Figure 12.21 Overview of Assignment Entities

The next section looks at how to maintain the master data used in financial documents.

12.5.3 Master Data

This section looks at the required master data. In Central Finance, you'll have to differentiate between long-term master data (such as accounts and profit centers for which an established master data governance process is usually available) and dynamic master data (for example, orders and projects that are created on demand). For master data uploaded to or updated in Central Finance at regular intervals, such as customers, suppliers, materials, and accounts, you'll carry out a mapping based on the key fields.

Cleansing master data
Introducing Central Finance can also trigger a cleansing of your master data. If you already use SAP Master Data Governance (SAP MDG), you've already cleansed your data and are thus at an advantage because Central Finance can read these assignments. Central Finance uses some mapping tables from SAP MDG.

Even if you aren't working with SAP MDG yet, you can prepare the way for later implementation because you can use the master data mapping tables in Central Finance without a separate SAP MDG license.

Data warehouse
Alternatively, when preparing your master data, you can also use your data warehouse. Your organization probably harmonized your master data in the data warehouse, and now, you have predefined transformations from when you transferred data to the data warehouse. The entities listed in this section represent the focus of reporting here. You must ensure that all the field content used in reporting is also available in Central Finance as master data, including master data for control procedures, payment terms, etc.

Accounts in the general ledger
Let's start with creating accounts in the general ledger. This section does not get into the specific functions of the general ledger and does not look at all accounts types in detail. What is essential, however, is that all locally used accounts also exist in Central Finance. If these accounts do not exist, the relevant data records are parked in an error list.

Primary cost elements
One special consideration is the primary cost elements. In Central Finance, the two master data types—*accounts* and *cost elements*—are merged into one. As a result, a separate data record exists—not for the cost element, but for the account only. The following lists the most important types of cost elements (see also Figure 12.22) for which you'll require accounts in Central Finance. We'll also explain how to determine the relevant data for each cost element:

- **01: Primary costs/Cost-Reducing Revenues**
  Check your balance of accounts and the settings for the controlling area to identify all accounts/cost elements for wages and salaries, depreciation of plant and equipment, material movements, etc.

- **11: Revenues**
  Look at the balance of accounts again to identify all accounts/cost elements for sales both to external customers as well as to internal business partners.

- **12: Sales Deduction**

    Compare your balance of accounts to the conditions of sale applied when you issue bills to your customers.

- **22: External Settlement**

    Determine where you have investment costs that can be billed with plant and equipment in construction or where production orders are billed to the finished goods warehouse.

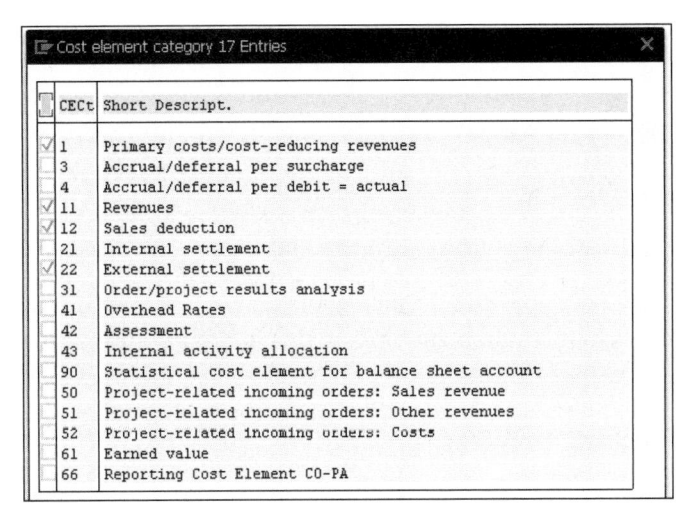

```
Cost element category 17 Entries

CECt  Short Descript.
✓ 1    Primary costs/cost-reducing revenues
  3    Accrual/deferral per surcharge
  4    Accrual/deferral per debit = actual
✓ 11   Revenues
✓ 12   Sales deduction
  21   Internal settlement
✓ 22   External settlement
  31   Order/project results analysis
  41   Overhead Rates
  42   Assessment
  43   Internal activity allocation
  90   Statistical cost element for balance sheet account
  50   Project-related incoming orders: Sales revenue
  51   Project-related incoming orders: Other revenues
  52   Project-related incoming orders: Costs
  61   Earned value
  66   Reporting Cost Element CO-PA
```

Figure 12.22 Relevant Primary Cost Elements for Central Finance

Secondary cost elements are also created as accounts. Experienced SAP users may find it strange to create accounts for secondary cost elements, but let's look at the various types of cost elements you'll need in Central Finance more closely. Start by providing a list of cost elements that you currently use (using Transaction KA23, Cost Elements: Master Data Report). After gaining an understanding of the process in which every cost element is updated, you can then decide whether you want to keep the same granularity of the cost elements for the process in Central Finance or whether you would prefer a different mapping.

Secondary cost elements

Postings for the following types of cost elements (as shown in Figure 12.22) can currently be transferred to Central Finance:

- **21: Internal Settlement**

    Check the settlement structures in your local system to determine which cost elements are used to send the costs of orders and projects to other recipients in Controlling.

- **41: Overhead Rates**
  Check the costing sheets in your local system to determine which cost elements are used to send the costs of cost centers to orders and projects in Controlling.

- **42: Assessment**
  Check the assessment cycles in your local system to determine which cost elements are used to send the costs of cost centers to other cost centers in Controlling.

- **43: Internal Activity Allocation**
  Prepare a list of activity types and business processes from your local system to determine which cost elements are used to send the costs of cost centers to orders and projects in Controlling.

Profit centers and cost centers

Furthermore, you'll have to define profit centers and cost centers. Profit centers don't have major requirements, except that in Central Finance the profit center exists with segments before profit center billing can be carried out. The cost center, in turn, is, in addition to an account, the one master data that is almost certainly accepted to Central Finance.

If you want to change to a single controlling area to simplify reporting, identifying which cost centers belong to which company code can be a challenge. Therefore, you should use appropriate and unique numbering conventions and identify whether the same cost center key can exist in multiple systems to avoid conflicts if various local systems are connected. Because the attributes of the cost center also determine how cost centers are allocated to the functional areas, profit centers, and business areas, cost centers should be carefully assessed.

> **[!] Cost Centers Attributes**
>
> Pay attention to how cost center attributes are maintained. The profit center or the functional area derived, for example, from the cost center overrides any assignment maintained in the mapping tables (see also Figure 12.21).

The idea of centralizing and harmonizing all of the material masters in their entirety can be a complex undertaking. In Central Finance, however, you are only interested in a smaller subset. All settings that control demand planning, production, procurement, inventory management, etc., can remain in the local systems. The most important elements to consider include the following:

- **Naming/numbering conventions**
  These conventions generally do not cause problems if you use data from the first local system. However, problems can occur in each subsequent system if you have not already cleansed your material masters. Remember to prepare the way for end-to-end inventory reporting if possible and prepare a central materials ledger even if you do not use this function directly in Central Finance.

- **Assignment to product hierarchies**
  Because product hierarchies are one of the most important ways to aggregate families of similar products in CO-PA, investing some time on this topic is worthwhile. Whether you then consciously decide to use "messy" product hierarchies in the local system and use a different structure in Central Finance or indeed harmonize your product hierarchies, this complex question cannot be answered by the finance department alone.

- **Assignment to material groups**
  Concerns regarding product hierarchies apply similarly to material groups. You should also know whether you have material attributes in your material masters that are required for central reporting, such as expenditure categories, for example.

Material masters

The master data for customers and suppliers can be kept quite minimalistic because you do not initially need any settings that regulate procedures such as payments or exports. Insofar as customers are affected, you are primarily interested in attributes, such as the customer group, that you require for strategic reporting in the profit and loss account as well as in suppliers and in the settings for company-wide reconciliation. If you develop the sequence in which the data is transferred between the systems, you must be careful with data used across all customers and suppliers if a specific business area will not be included in Central Finance.

12 Landscape Transformation

12.5.4 Mapping, Error Handling, and Initial Data Load

Key mapping for master data

Now that you have identified the most important master data for Central Finance, you must consider whether a 1:1 relationship exists between the sender and receiver systems or whether a conversion must be performed. If you change nothing at all, the system will assume a 1:1 relationship, and the postings will be carried out when the corresponding master data is available. Please note that you also need to ensure that the appropriate document types, posting keys, and so on are available in Central Finance because this data is all part of a Universal Journal entry. If you want to override this for one of the entries, you must assign a corresponding action.

Mapping options

For each entity (shown in Figure 12.21), the following mapping options are available in Central Finance (shown in Figure 12.23):

- **Keep Data**: This setting is the default. Field values of this type are not converted at all, and the units that are transferred from the sender system are retained.

- **Mapping Obligatory**: The field values for all populated fields must be mapped. If no mapping data is available for the data in the FI documents, an error is issued, which can be corrected by the error correction system (Error Correction and Suspense Accounting, ECS).

- **Map if Possible**: The system attempts to map all populated fields. If no conversion is maintained, no error is issued. Instead, the original data that was transferred from the sender system is used.

- **Clear Data**: The sender system will only occasionally transfer a field for which you have no use in Central Finance. If you have fields that you do not want to transfer, you must use this setting to ensure that these fields are deleted or removed from the document.

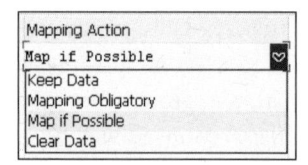

Figure 12.23 Mapping Actions

The most common mapping is *pair mapping*, in which account A from the local system is converted to account B in Central Finance. To prepare the mapping, use the Web Dynpro application MDG_BS_WD_ID_MATCH_SERVICE.

Remember also that all new documents you create will go through the normal interfaces in accounting. As a result, all common options for conversions and the implementation of user exits are available.

If you are planning the conversion of your data, you'll need to decide what to do when things go wrong. Errors may concern all incoming documents (for example, if a period in Central Finance has not been opened yet) or specific master data (for example, locked cost centers).

Error correction and suspense accounts

If you have activated the business functions for preliminary posting and error correction, you'll receive a list of the documents that could not be posted and were recorded in the worklist as an error. You can either select a single element and manually correct the master data or adjust the conversion rules and update the list. Note that, at the time of posting, only errors in the FI documents are covered by this function. If, for example, an error occurs in a CO document, because a certain type of activity does not exist in Central Finance, the system will output an error directly in the SAP LT Replication Server.

Consistency is key for the initial load of data to Central Finance. You'll want to ensure that all data from the local system is transferred and cleansed, and during the upload process, you'll want to prevent users from making new postings or scheduling new jobs. You should therefore block postings during the periods when the transfer to posts transactions to prevent accidental updates.

Initial load of data

To ensure that the data in your sender system is clean, various reports are available, which you should run before the migration:

Reports regarding the quality of the data

- To prepare for transferring your asset postings, close the periodic asset posting using the RAPERB2000 program and then execute the periodic depreciation run using the RAPOST2000 program.

- Make sure that the index tables and transaction numbers in the new general ledger match so that the RFINDEX report can run for all fiscal years. Limit the selection in the local system to the company codes you want to transfer to Central Finance.

- Using the TFC_COMPARE_VZ report or Transaction FAGLF03, make sure that the figures in the new general ledger correspond to those in the subsidiary ledgers.

12 Landscape Transformation

- If you use the new general ledger in your local system, you must ensure that the numbers in your different ledgers match. Use the RGUCOMP report or Transaction GCAC for the selected company codes.
- Also, make sure that the values in the SAP ERP Materials Management are in line with the figures in the new general ledger by executing the RM07MBST and RM07MMFI reports for the relevant company codes.
- Prepare your balances for all currencies and ledgers. Run the SAPF010 report for your accounts payable and accounts receivable and the SAPF-GLBCF report for the SAP General Ledger.
- Prepare an excerpt of your closings (program RFBILA00) that contains the totals per cost center (Transaction S_ALR_87013611), the general ledger account balances for the corresponding company codes (report RFSSLD00), and the document journal (report RFBELJ00).

You are now ready for the initial data transfer. Follow the process in the IMG (see Figure 12.24) and select the logical system from which you want to copy the data.

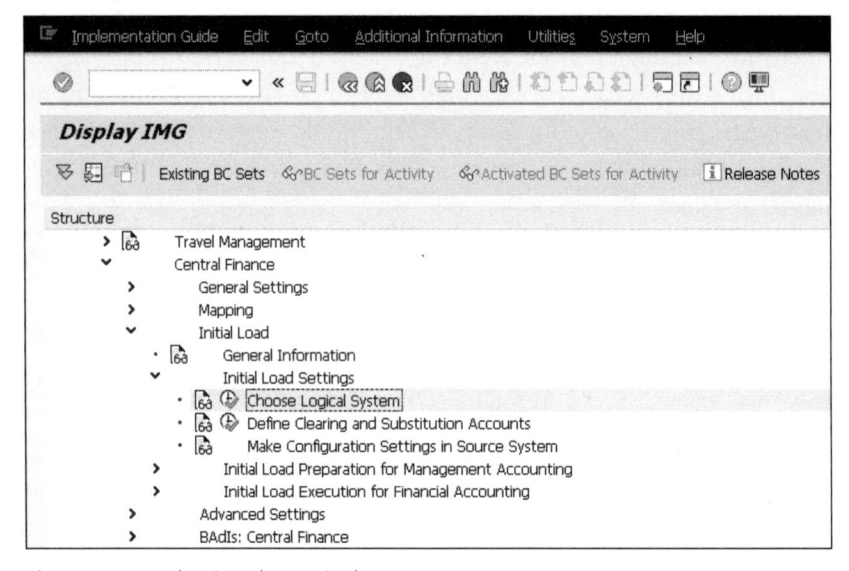

Figure 12.24 Selecting the Logical System

You'll also designate corresponding accounts for each company code, which are used during the migration for counter-postings. Once the data transfer is complete, the balances on these accounts should be zero. During the extraction, the data is initially stored in a temporary table in Central Finance. The posting is only simulated.

After reviewing the content, if you are satisfied with the results, use **Post Initial Load Data** (see Figure 12.25) to confirm, which will trigger the actual posting in Central Finance.

Posting in Central Finance

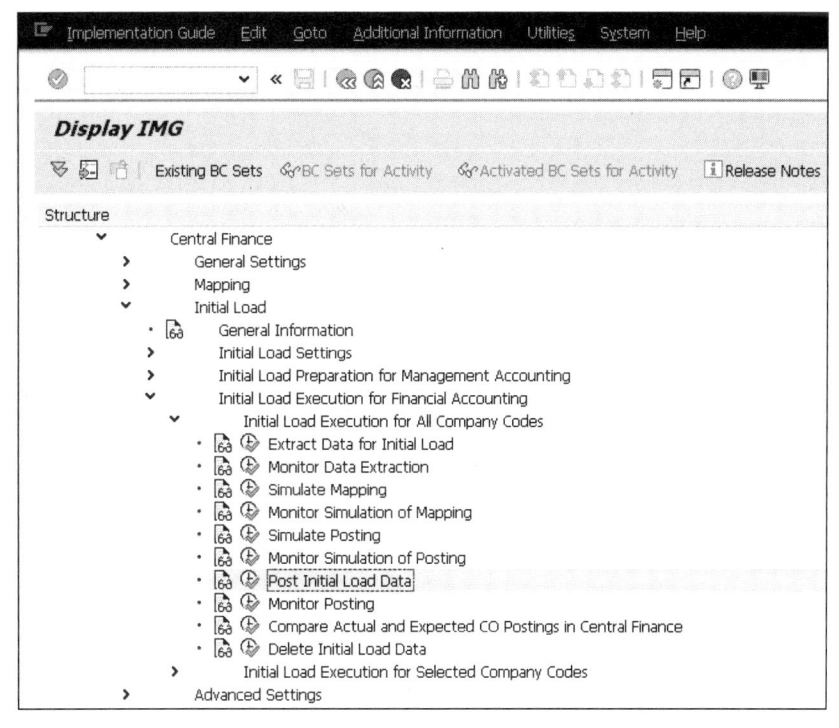

Figure 12.25 Confirming the Production Data Transfer

Once the actual postings are finished, run the `RFINS_CFIN_MATCH_FI_TO_CO` report to check the consistency of the CO postings. Furthermore, you can also carry out a final preparatory step for the closings you carried out on the local systems in Central Finance to ensure consistency.

Now, you have completed the initial technical setup of Central Finance. You have transferred all FI-relevant documents and uploaded the initial data to your Central Finance system. The first data transfer is now complete, and you can continue to use your CO documents after you upload process separately.

Of course, completely configuring a Central Finance system or the SAP S/4HANA Finance platform still involves many more steps. Further information on SAP S/4HANA Finance is available, for example, in *SAP S/4HANA Finance: An Introduction* by Jens Krüger (2nd edition, SAP PRESS, 2016, *www.sap-press.com/4122*).

Chapter 13
Integrating SAP S/4HANA, On-Premise, into the System Landscape

This chapter explains the integration of SAP S/4HANA systems with SAP Ariba, SAP SuccessFactors, and further existing SAP systems in the landscape.

Like SAP Business Suite, SAP S/4HANA is based on SAP NetWeaver. As a result, integrating SAP S/4HANA into an existing SAP Business Suite system landscape should be feasible without major issues. In this chapter, we'll discuss integrating with the Ariba Network and with SAP SuccessFactors. In the last section, we'll also provide information on integration with existing SAP systems.

13.1 Integration with SAP Ariba Solutions

SAP S/4HANA provides native, easy-to-implement direct connections to SAP Ariba solutions. Neither add-ons nor middleware is required.

Supported technologies

The following section addresses the main things you should consider when integrating SAP S/4HANA, on-premise, systems with SAP Ariba solutions.

13.1.1 Integrated Business Processes with SAP Ariba Solutions and SAP S/4HANA

In Chapter 8, Section 8.1, we discussed procurement and accounting business processes that can benefit from the digitalization and integration of SAP S/4HANA and SAP Ariba solutions as well as how to implement these business processes. In this section, we'll only describe the differences between integrating SAP S/4HANA Cloud versus integrating SAP S/4HANA, on-premise, with SAP Ariba solutions.

Differences between cloud and on-premise

Integration with SAP Ariba Solutions	Business Processes and Scope Items	Middleware	Implementation in the System
SAP S/4HANA Cloud 1611	• 1A0 SAP Ariba Sourcing • 1L2 Ariba Quote Automation • J82 Ariba Purchase Order to Invoice Automation • 19O Ariba Payment and Discount Management	Middleware not required or supported	SAP Fiori tile for the configuration
SAP S/4HANA 1610	Native SAP S/4HANA integration: • 1A0 SAP Ariba Sourcing • J82 Ariba Purchase Order to Invoice Automation • 19O Ariba Payment and Discount Management	No middleware required; SAP Process Orchestration (PO) and SAP Cloud Platform Integration supported	SAP Implementation Guide (IMG)
	Obsolete technologies based on IDoc, BAPI, RFC, and Ariba Cloud Integration (CI):	SAP Process Orchestration (PO) or SAP Cloud Platform Integration required	SAP IMG

Table 13.1 Comparing the Integration Variants of SAP S/4HANA Cloud 1611 and SAP S/4HANA 1610 with SAP Ariba Solutions

Integration with SAP Ariba Solutions	Business Processes and Scope Items	Middleware	Implementation in the System
	<ul><li>SAP Ariba Sourcing</li><li>Ariba Purchase Order to Payment</li><li>Ariba Spot Quote/Quote Automation*</li><li>SAP Ariba Contracting</li><li>SAP Ariba Buying and Invoicing (P2P/P2O)*</li><li>SAP Ariba Supply Chain Collaboration (SCC)*</li></ul>		

* Technically released for Ariba Cloud Integration CI-8 on SAP Process Orchestration 7.5 in combination with SAP S/4HANA 1511; technically released for CI-9 with SAP Process Integration (PI) 7.5 and SAP S/4HANA 1605. If technically released, customers can have SAP Ariba certify their implementations. Contact SAP Ariba for further information. SAP does not test these scenarios as standard scenarios with SAP S/4HANA.

Table 13.1 Comparing the Integration Variants of SAP S/4HANA Cloud 1611 and SAP S/4HANA 1610 with SAP Ariba Solutions (Cont.)

The scope of the supported business processes, the technical implementation scenarios, and the physical implementation in the system all differ (see Table 13.1).

If you compare SAP S/4HANA, on-premise, to SAP S/4HANA Cloud, you'll notice that, in general, the same processes are supported as long as so-called *native integration* with SAP Ariba is used, which was developed for SAP S/4HANA and is based on cXML.

Native integration and IDoc

13 Integrating SAP S/4HANA, On-Premise, into the System Landscape

13.1.2 Technical Integration of SAP S/4HANA with SAP Ariba

With or without middleware

Depending on the business processes that you selected for integration with SAP Ariba, the implementation can take place with or without middleware: The native integration, which is based on cXML, does not require any middleware. (cXML is the protocol of SAP Ariba, which is supported by SAP S/4HANA in selected scenarios without any add-on or adapters.)

If you still want to use middleware between your SAP S/4HANA, on-premise, system and the SAP Ariba instance in the cloud, you can use this middleware either on-premise (via *SAP Process Orchestration*, PO) or in the cloud (via *SAP Cloud Platform Integration*, previously *SAP HANA Cloud Integration*). If you want to use SAP PO, you'll have to implement the *Ariba Cloud Integration adapter* (CI-8 or higher) on it. Refer also to SAP Note 1991088.

> **SAP Best Practices**
>
> The SAP Best Practices package for integrating SAP S/4HANA with SAP Ariba solutions supports you with step-by-step instructions for both native and indirect integration. For more information, go to *https://rapid.sap.com/bp/RDS_S4_ARI*.

Processing the cXML protocol

For indirect integration using middleware, the data is only passed in the cXML format. In SAP PO or SAP Cloud Platform Integration, no data transformation takes place.

Older integrations based on IDocs, EDI (Electronic Data Interchange) connections, BAPIs (Business Application Programming Interfaces), or RFC (Remote Function Call) connections are deliberately not documented as an SAP S/4HANA function. For these integrations, you'll always need middleware such as SAP PO or SAP Cloud Platform Integration to transform the protocols from IDoc, EDI, BAPI, or RFC to cXML, and vice versa. Furthermore, Ariba Cloud Integration (CI) must be installed on the middleware, and the corresponding transports to the SAP S/4HANA system must be carried out. For further information, read the "Integrating Ariba Cloud Solutions with SAP" white paper at *http://bit.ly/v1448131*.

Rapid deployment solutions

The Rapid Deployment Solutions (RDS) and SAP Best Practices that SAP developed for integrating SAP Business Suite with SAP Ariba can be useful for processes that have not yet been released for SAP S/4HANA. Experienced users will recognize some roughly similar settings, for example, from integrating SAP ERP with SAP Ariba Buying or SAP Ariba Supply Chain Collaboration. You can find information on the rapid deployment solutions for these scenarios at *https://rapid.sap.com/bp/RDS_ARIBA_P2P* and *https://rapid.sap.com/bp/RDS_ARI*.

Because SAP S/4HANA is a standalone, newly defined product, despite its numerous similarities with SAP ERP, you'll have to consider their differences. You can find these differences in the simplification list, which you can find at *https://help.sap.com/s4hana*; select your product version, for example, SAP S/4HANA 1610.

You may also want to consider reviewing the *compatibility matrix* as well as possible release restrictions and SAP Notes, which you can also find at *https://help.sap.com/s4hana*.

[«] **Additional Information on SAP Best Practices and SAP Activate**

In SAP S/4HANA, the common SAP Implementation Guide (IMG) is used. In addition, SAP recommends using the SAP Solution Manager. The SAP Best Practices package for SAP Ariba integration (*https://rapid.sap.com/bp/RDS_S4_ARI*) and the SAP Best Practices package for SAP S/4HANA (*https://rapid.sap.com/bp/BP_OP_ENTPR*) provide information on the settings you'll have to make in the IMG or SAP Solution Manager. Here, navigate to **Accelerators • General Documents • Software and Delivery requirements**. The SAP Activate implementation method is also used for the integration of SAP S/4HANA.

With regard to the Ariba Network, native integration with SAP S/4HANA is managed in the same way as the integration with SAP S/4HANA Cloud (see Chapter 8, Section 8.1). Thus, the following sections discuss the specific settings in the SAP S/4HANA Implementation Guide. In our example, we'll focus on the native integration of the scope items for requests for quotations (*SAP Ariba Sourcing*, scope item 1A0), automation of the document flow from purchase order to invoice (*Purchase Order to Invoice Automation*, scope item J82), and payment and discount management (*Ariba Payment and Discount Management*, scope item 19O). We'll also address the specific settings for indirect integration with SAP PO or SAP Cloud Platform Integration when they deviate from the direct integration settings.

Technical settings

The general settings cover specifying the infrastructure (for example, a secure connection with a certificate or shared secret), message control, RFC

Network settings

and background RFC connections, and job scheduling as well as the definition and setup of services for inbound cXML messages and consumers for outbound messages.

Application-specific settings

Depending on the specific application, you'll also have to assign the Ariba Network ID to company codes and set up the output control in two variants—*Message Control* (MC) or *Business Rule Framework plus* (BRFplus)—and the *SAP Application Interface Framework* (AIF).

For indirect integration using SAP Cloud Platform Integration, you'll additionally have to set up encrypted communication and SSL as well as inbound and outbound scenarios. If you use SAP Process Orchestration, you'll have to set up the cXML adapter and configure some communication channels.

Configuration guides

You can find all these settings in the SAP Best Practices configuration guides for the various integration scenarios at the following URLs:

- RFx with SAP Ariba Sourcing (1AO): *https://rapid.sap.com/bp/#/browse/categories/sap_s%4hana/areas/integration/packageversions/RDS_S4_ARI/ARINET/ALL/XX/3/EN/scopeitemversions/7fd87108f9ae4eed898fed310fc33029*
- Ariba Purchase Order to Invoice (J82): *https://rapid.sap.com/bp/#/browse/categories/sap_s%4hana/areas/integration/packageversions/RDS_S4_ARI/ARINET/ALL/XX/3/EN/scopeitemversions/6ad5724e605445fe80a295916a98b15d*
- Ariba Payment and Discount Management (19O): *https://rapid.sap.com/bp/#/browse/categories/sap_s%4hana/areas/integration/packageversions/RDS_S4_ARI/ARINET/ALL/XX/3/EN/scopeitemversions/354a49e66ace4d3d8cbe7e27c45eca91*

BAdIs for process optimization

Currently, SAP Best Practices is restricted to technical integration and the corresponding business processes that are directly supported. Further process optimization and automation are not mapped; however, you should consider optimization and automation in your planning whenever it makes sense.

For example, let's ask what process should be triggered when purchase orders are rejected by suppliers: Is SAP S/4HANA supposed to automatically contact the next supplier? Is a sourcing process supposed to be triggered? Is the rejection supposed to affect the assessment of the corresponding supplier? In SAP S/4HANA, on-premise, Business Add-Ins (BAdIs) are available that allow for further optimization. You can find them in the IMG.

In SAP Ariba, further process optimizations are possible if you set up the configuration under **Administration**. You can find the corresponding documentation on the SAP Ariba support pages at *https://connect.ariba.com/AC*.

> **[«] Additional Information on Integrating SAP S/4HANA, On-Premise, with SAP Ariba**
>
> You can find more information on the integration of SAP S/4HANA and SAP Ariba on the following pages:
>
> - SAP S/4HANA Sourcing and Procurement Flipbook:
>   *http://bit.ly/v1448135*
> - Product documentation for the SAP S/4HANA integration in the SAP Help Portal (see also Chapter 6):
>   *https://bit.ly/v1448136*
> - White paper on the integration of SAP Ariba Cloud solutions with SAP:
>   *http://bit.ly/v1448131*
> - Automation of the business processes from purchase order to invoice:
>   *http://bit.ly/v1448138*
> - SAP S/4HANA Finance and Ariba Discount Professional (video):
>   *http://bit.ly/2w2KBEh*
> - Value of the automation in the SAP Ariba Network for suppliers:
>   *http://bit.ly/v14481310*

13.2 Integration with SAP ERP HCM and SAP SuccessFactors

To run human resources (HR) processes in combination with SAP S/4HANA in your landscape, SAP provides various options. Three main scenarios are distinguished:

- SAP S/4HANA is integrated with an SAP ERP HCM (Human Capital Management) system.
- SAP ERP HCM is operated within the SAP S/4HANA instance.
- SAP S/4HANA is integrated with SAP SuccessFactors Employee Central.

We'll discuss these three scenarios in detail in the following sections.

Integration scenarios

13.2.1 ALE Integration with SAP ERP HCM

Integration with ALE The first case does not differ much from operating a traditional SAP ERP system with an integrated SAP ERP HCM system. The process for setting up the integration via an ALE (Application Link Enabling) connection is also the same. You can find detailed information about ALE connections in the "SAP S/4HANA Installation and Administration Guide."

Setting up the ALE integration Let's look at the basic steps for configuring this integration. One prerequisite is that users must exist in the two systems (SAP S/4HANA and SAP ERP HCM) that are used for the communication. These users should have the same names in each system and need to be authorized for executing IDoc transfers.

Enabling master data distribution Afterwards, you'll have to activate the SAP ERP HCM system as the system allowed to distribute HR master data across other systems via Transaction SALE. First, navigate to **IDoc Interface/Application Link Enabling (ALE)** • **Modeling and Implementing Business Processes** • **Configure Predefined ALE Business Processes** • **Human Resources** • **Master Data Distribution** • **Distributed HR Master Data**. Next, select the **ALE: Original System for Personal Data Enabled** system switch and enter "REPPA" into the **sm. Abbreviation** column (see Figure 13.1).

Logical systems Now, you'll have to create logical systems for the two systems in Transaction SALE. First, navigate to the **Basic** settings under **IDoc Interface/Application Link Enabling (ALE)**. Follow the naming convention "system name + CLNT + client number." For example, we assigned the name SYSCL-NT100 to the system, as shown in Figure 13.1. Next, you'll assign the logical systems to the relevant clients in both systems.

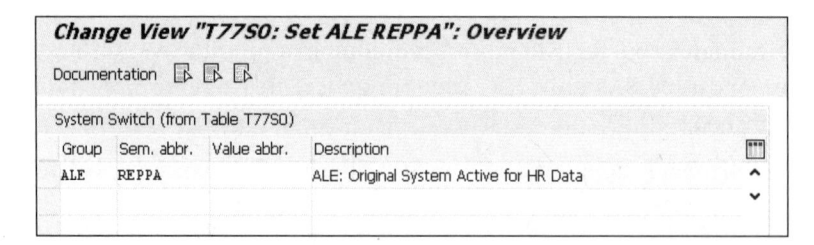

Figure 13.1 Activating the SAP ERP HCM System to Distribute Master Data

RFC connection Now, you can create the RFC connections between the systems by calling Transaction SM59 of the SAP ERP HCM system and SAP S/4HANA system. Use the user that you created in the first step.

Next, create the distribution model using Transaction BD64. Select the message type and define the SAP ERP HCM system as the sending system and the SAP S/4HANA system as the receiving system.

Distribution model

Now, back in Transaction SALE, activate the change pointer for each message type for this message type.

Finally, use Transaction WE21 to maintain the port for IDoc processing in the SAP ERP HCM system and use Transaction WE20 to maintain the partner profile.

Now, you can start the initial distribution of your employee master data. You should create a batch job to distribute changes in master data.

13.2.2 Integration of SAP ERP HCM within the SAP S/4HANA Instance

The second integration scenario for SAP ERP HCM requires a special license agreement for SAP S/4HANA that allows customers to use traditional functions from SAP ERP HCM within the SAP S/4HANA instance using SAP S/4HANA Compatibility Packages (see Chapter 3, Section 3.2.1).

Compatibility packages

In this case, specific integration scenarios with *SAP SuccessFactors Talent Management Suite* are available, thus allowing hybrid integrations. As a result, your basic personnel administration processes will run in SAP ERP HCM within SAP S/4HANA, but individual business processes use modules from SAP SuccessFactors Talent Management Suite. You can set up this integration using SAP Cloud Platform Integration or SAP Process Orchestration as the middleware.

In addition to transferring employee data, you can integrate the following data with SAP SucessFactors Talent Management Suite (see Figure 13.2):

Data exchange

- Recruitment data
- Onboarding data
- Offboarding data
- Employee data and organizational data
- Compensation data
- Data of variable payment
- Evaluation data
- Qualification data

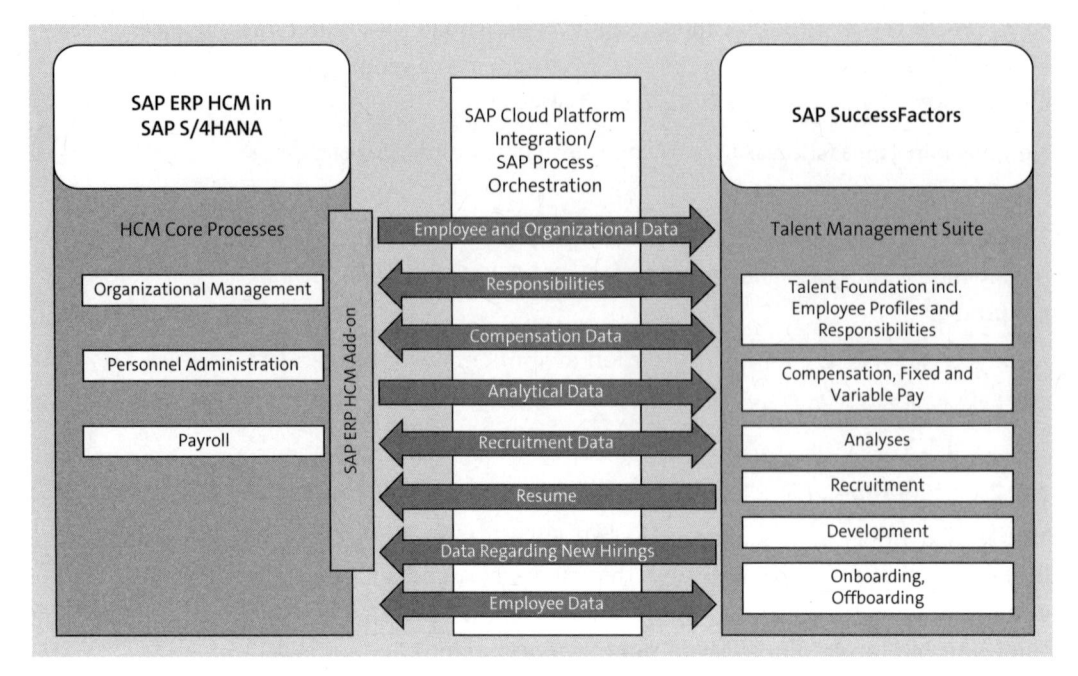

13 Integrating SAP S/4HANA, On-Premise, into the System Landscape

Figure 13.2 Scope of the Integration in SAP SuccessFactors Talent Management Suite

This data is used by the following SAP SuccessFactors Talent Management Suite modules:

- Compensation
- Recruiting
- Learning Management System
- Onboarding
- Workforce Analytics

You can carry out this integration using the SAP integration add-on for SAP ERP HCM and SAP SuccessFactors; detailed documentation is available in the SAP Help Portal at *https://help.sap.com/cloud4hr*. Implementing these specific integration scenarios does not include steps specific to SAP S/4HANA. Rather, these scenarios relate to integrating an SAP ERP HCM system with SAP SuccessFactors Talent Management Suite.

Integration content Unlike integrating with SAP SuccessFactors Employee Central, which is described later in Section 13.2.3, for this integration, predefined integration content is available for the on-premise middleware, SAP Process Orchestration. However, SAP recommends using SAP Cloud Platform Integration for integrations with SAP S/4HANA, regardless of whether your system is cloud-based or on-premise.

Side-by-Side Operation of SAP ERP HCM and SAP SuccessFactors [«]

A specific case for operating SAP ERP HCM within the SAP S/4HANA instance is a *side-by-side operation*. In this case, SAP ERP HCM and SAP SuccessFactors Employee Central operate as equal systems for personnel administration. Employee data is transferred in both directions between the systems. However, you should define one of the systems as the leading system, so you can analyze all employees.

Technically, implementing this integration is similar to the full integration of SAP S/4HANA and SAP SuccessFactors Employee Central, which we described in Section 13.2.3. You'll only have to use additional information flows (iFlows) in SAP Cloud Platform Integration.

13.2.3 Integration with SAP SuccessFactors Employee Central

The third integration scenario in the HR area involves using SAP SuccessFactors Employee Central as the central and single system for HR. As a result, all employees and employee-related data is entered in SAP SuccessFactors Employee Central and transferred to the SAP S/4HANA system from there. In SAP S/4HANA, this data is stored in the existing tables from SAP ERP HCM and is thus available for subsequent business processes.

You perform the integration with SAP Cloud Platform Integration middleware. This middleware is used to integrate cloud application scenarios. You can set up and run these integration scenarios on the *SAP Cloud Platform*, which is hosted in SAP Cloud. Integration via SAP Cloud Platform Integration is the preferred method for SAP S/4HANA.

SAP Cloud Platform Integration

Additional Information on SAP Cloud Platform Integration [«]

For more information on SAP Cloud Platform Integration, go to *https://help.sap.com/cloudintegration*.

Integration with SAP SuccessFactors Employee Central includes the following components (see Figure 13.3):

Components of the integration

13   Integrating SAP S/4HANA, On-Premise, into the System Landscape

- The replication of employee master data from SAP SuccessFactors Employee Central to SAP S/4HANA
- The replication of organizational data from SAP SuccessFactors Employee Central to SAP S/4HANA
- The replication of cost centers from SAP S/4HANA to SAP SuccessFactors Employee Central. In SAP SuccessFactors Employee Central, you'll maintain the current cost centers in the employee data.

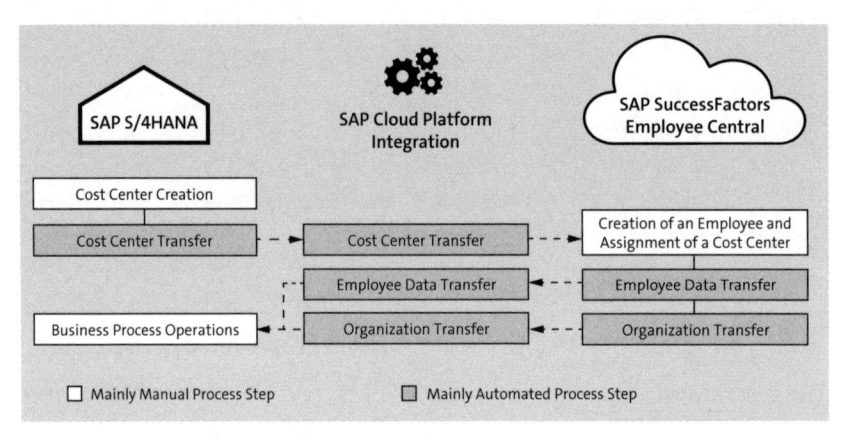

Figure 13.3 Integration with SAP SuccessFactors Employee Central

Because setting up this integration is beyond the scope of this book, we restrict the following description to replicating employee master data as an example. Three systems are involved in this integration: SAP S/4HANA, SAP SuccessFactors Employee Central, and SAP Cloud Platform Integration.

[»]   **Additional Information on the Integration of SAP SuccessFactors Employee Central**

You can find the complete documentation of the configuration steps in three guides on the SAP Help Portal at *https://help.sap.com/s4hana*. Select **Additional Information** • **Integration Information**.

Preparing the Employee Central System

SAP S/4HANA as the target system

In the first step, you'll define the SAP S/4HANA system as the target system for the employee master data replication in SAP SuccessFactors Employee

514

13.2 Integration with SAP ERP HCM and SAP SuccessFactors

Central. Go to the **Admin Center** in SAP SuccessFactors Employee Central and enter "manage data" in the tool search. In the Manage Data application, select the **Replication Target System** at the top and to the left of **Create**. In the app, maintain the relevant fields as shown in Figure 13.4. In the **External Code** field, enter the logical system name of the SAP S/4HANA system.

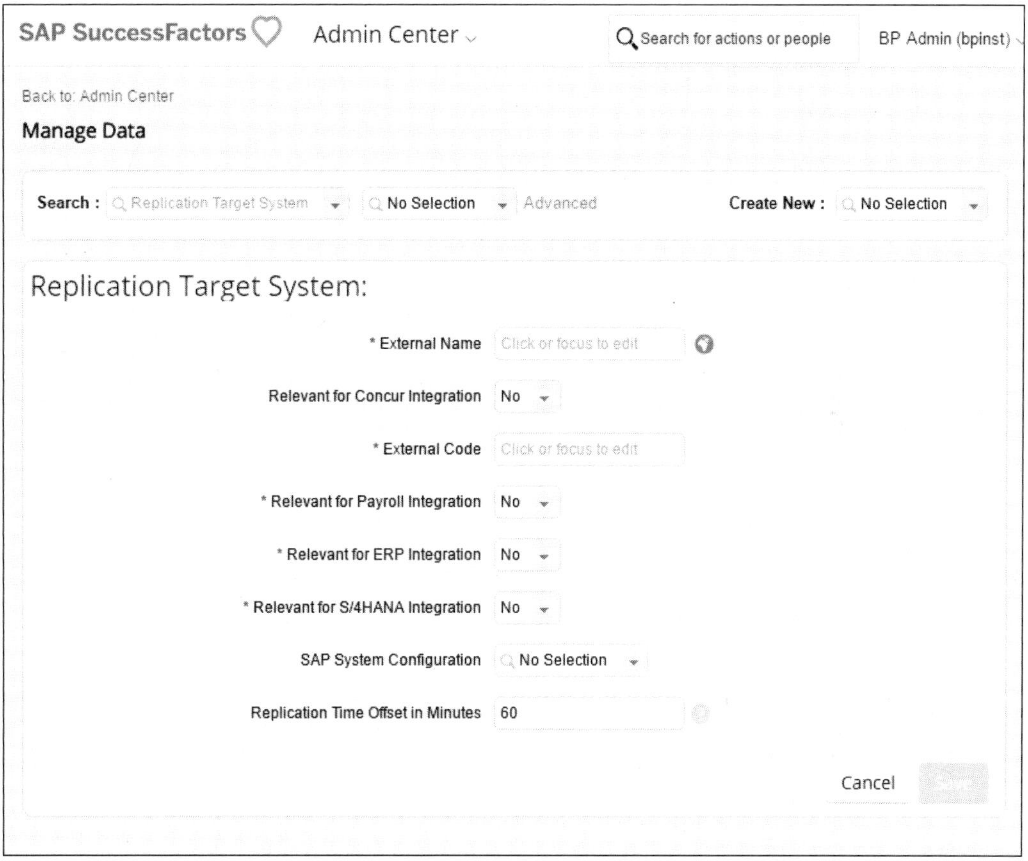

Figure 13.4 Creating the Replication Target System

If you use SAP S/4HANA as your payroll system, activate the **Payroll Information** field in the HR data. Now, you must assign the required authorizations to the technical user that will perform the replication. To authorize the user, use the tool search to find the **Manage Authorization Roles** tool in the Admin Center to maintain the SFAPI user (see Figure 13.5).

515

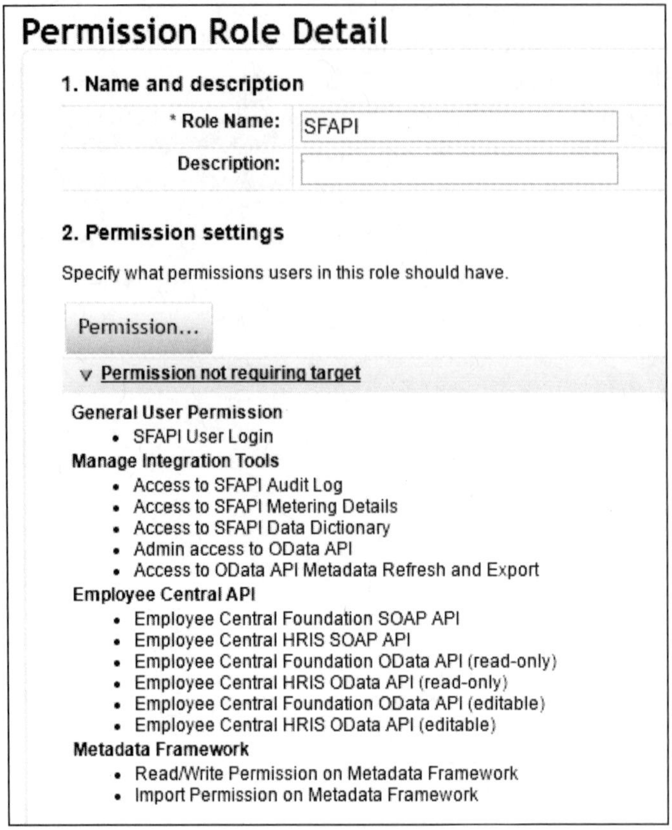

Figure 13.5 Maintaining Authorization Roles

Provisioning framework
In the *provisioning framework* of your SAP SuccessFactors Employee Central system, you now must configure and activate **ERP Integration**, which must be done by an SAP consultant or certified SAP partners.

Data replication error
If errors occur in the data replication, the system repeats the replication automatically, depending on the error type. For example, if an employee record is locked, the replication of this data record is immediately repeated. You can also trigger the replication of individual data records manually via **Data Replication Monitoring** where you can also monitor the replication of the employee master data if the integration has been completed.

You can find the data replication monitoring function in the Admin Center in Employee Central under **Admin Messages**. Double-click on **Employee Master Data**, as shown in Figure 13.6.

13.2 Integration with SAP ERP HCM and SAP SuccessFactors

Admin Center

Admin Alerts

→ STALLED WORKFLOW REQUESTS

    For more than 3 days (0)

HR DATA ISSUES

    Invalid Cost Center
    Invalid Pay Group

$ PAYROLL INTEGRATION   6

    Employee Master Data (6)

SAP ERP INTEGRATION   10

    Employee Master Data (6)
    Employee Organizational Assignments (4)

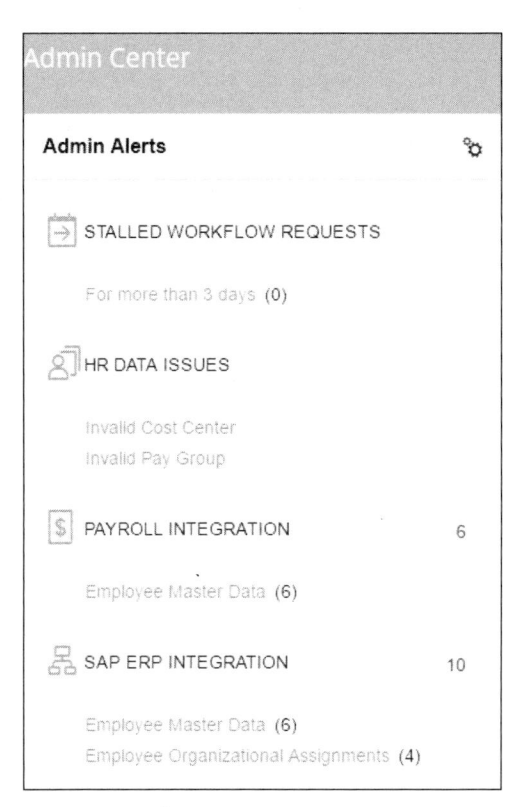

Figure 13.6 Admin Messages

Configuration in SAP S/4HANA

To receive data from SAP SuccessFactors Employee Central, a web service must be activated in SAP S/4HANA called `EmployeeMasterDataBundleReplicationRequest_In`. This web service is activated in the SOA Manager.

Receiving data

In addition, you'll have to enable the distribution of HR data from other systems by configuring Infotypes in the Implementation Guide (IMG). In the IMG, you can also define which actions are permitted for distributed data, for example, hiring employees or when employees return from leave.

You must also define, in the IMG, how your SAP S/4HANA system should behave when errors occur.

Because SAP SuccessFactors Employee Central and SAP S/4HANA use different terms in organizational management, you'll have to map them accordingly for the integration. You have to maintain these relationships, for

Value mapping

517

example, for cost center values or workspaces in the IMG. Table 13.2 lists various sample codes for the marital status in SAP SuccessFactors Employee Central and SAP S/4HANA. The same applies to many address fields or data.

Code in SAP SuccessFactors Employee Central	Technical Value in SAP S/4HANA
S = single	0 = single
M = married	1 = married
W = widowed	2 = widowed
D = divorced	3 = divorced
	4 = separated

Table 13.2 Examples of Different Value Codes

Configuration in the Middleware

Data exchange process

Data is exchanged between SAP S/4HANA and SAP SuccessFactors Employee Central in the following way:

1. The middleware, i.e., SAP Cloud Platform Integration, uses what's called the *compound employee API* to ask SAP SuccessFactors Employee Central whether modified employee data is available.
2. SAP Cloud Platform Integration then transfers this modified data to SAP S/4HANA, where it can be processed.
3. The data is stored in the relevant tables in SAP S/4HANA.
4. Afterwards, SAP S/4HANA sends a confirmation message to SAP Cloud Platform Integration.
5. An OData interface is used to move the data from SAP Cloud Platform Integration to the data replication monitoring solution in SAP SuccessFactors Employee Central where the status of the data replication is displayed.

The communication between SAP S/4HANA and SAP Cloud Platform Integration is secured by certificates and authorizations and is implemented using the HTTPS protocol. For the communications between SAP Cloud Platform Integration and Employee Central, a technical integration user is required. In SAP Cloud Platform Integration, you can copy the integration packages provided by SAP including the bundled iFlows to your custom workspace and configure and deploy the integration packages there.

> **Accessing Integration Packages** [«]
>
> You can find the integration packages for the distribution of employee data and the related configuration guide in the SAP API Business Hub at *https://cloudintegration.hana.ondemand.com*. Narrow the search, for example, with the search string "employee."
>
> To access the SAP API Business Hub, you'll need a user account for the SAP Community (*www.sap.com/community*).

13.2.4 Synchronizing Employee Data with Business Partners

Employee data is required in business partners with the **Employee** role for the new data model in SAP S/4HANA. For all the integration scenarios we described earlier, the employee data is stored in SAP ERP HCM tables. Changes will need to be synchronized with business partner data, which also allows you to use *CDS* (Core Data Services) views in SAP S/4HANA.

"Employee" role

> **CDS Views** [«]
>
> A CDS view is a database view of the ABAP Dictionary. You can access CDS views in read-only mode using Open SQL (ABAP). The system then displays the data in SAP S/4HANA.

SAP provides a report for this synchronization. The technical name of the report is /SHCM/RHSYNC_BUPA_FROM_EMPL.

Report for synchronization

To enable this report, follow the IMG menu path **Integration with Other SAP Components • Integration with SAP SuccessFactors (Employee Central) • Define Reconciliation Accounts for Employees in Role FI Supplier**. Verify that reconciliation accounts were defined in the general ledger for enterprises (**Suppliers**) that originate from the synchronization with employee data (see Figure 13.7). These reconciliation accounts must be available for all relevant company codes.

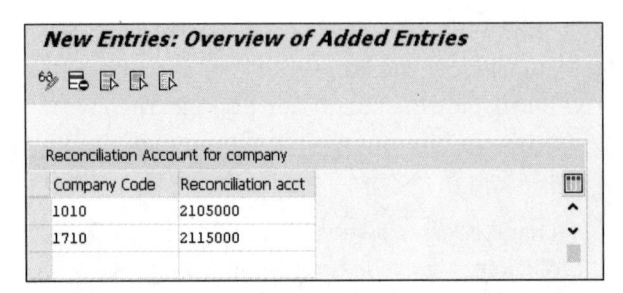

13 Integrating SAP S/4HANA, On-Premise, into the System Landscape

Figure 13.7 Creating and Maintaining Reconciliation Accounts for Enterprises Using the "Employee" Role

Another prerequisite for using the synchronization report is that the HRALX PBPON switch in table T77SO in Transaction OO_CENTRAL_PERSON must be disabled, as shown in Figure 13.8.

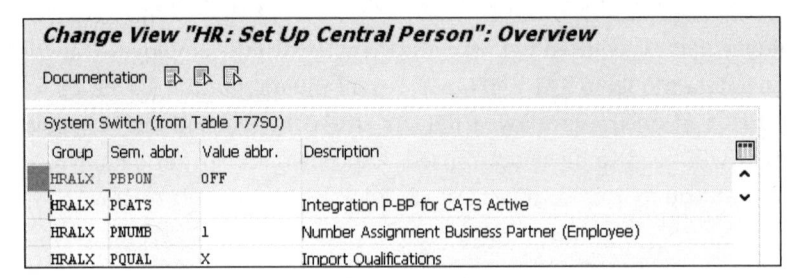

Figure 13.8 Deactivating the HRALX PBPON Switch

Triggering the synchronization

Three options are available for triggering the report:

- By creating an employee in the integrated Employee Central system. In this case, the report is triggered by the following BAdI implementations:
    - HRPAD00INFTYDB: /SHCM/TRIGGER_BUPA_SYNC
    - HRPAD00INFTY: /SHCM/TRIG_BUPA_SYNC

- By processing new employee data from a system that is integrated via ALE (see Section 13.2.1). The report is triggered by a BAdI: HRALE00INBOUND_IDOC: /SHCM/BUPA_SYNC_TRIG.

- The third case is the maintenance of employees in SAP ERP HCM transactions in SAP S/4HANA. In this case, two BAdIs are used:
    - HRPAD00INFTYDB: /SHCM/TRIGGER_BUPA_SYNC
    - HRPAD00INFTY: /SHCM/TRIG_BUPA_SYNC

> **Scheduling the Synchronization Report on a Daily Basis** [!]
>
> Some employee data is time based, and some business partner data is not. Thus, you should set up the system in such a way that the synchronization report runs daily. Daily reports are the only way to ensure that all business partner data is updated and corresponds to the employee data. If synchronization was not successful for any reason, all employee data is again synchronized during the next run.

13.3 Integration with Existing SAP Systems

Integrating an SAP S/4HANA system into an existing SAP system landscape is nearly identical to the integration of SAP Business Suite systems. You can continue to use the familiar synchronous and asynchronous interface technologies, such as *ALE/EDI business processes* (Application Link Enabling/Electronic Data Interchange), and the common integration tools, such as *SAP Process Integration (PI)* or *SAP Process Orchestration (PO)*. In addition, you can also use the following SAP NetWeaver technologies and frameworks:

Using standard tools

- **Enterprise Services**
  These web services provide business processes or business process steps with reference to an Enterprise Service definition.

- **SAP Application Interface Framework (SAP AIF)**
  SAP AIF is a framework for managing the interfaces of various SAP technologies, such as IDocs, web services, Core Interfaces (CIF), queued Remote Function Calls (qRFC), transactional Remote Function Calls (tRFC), files, batch input, etc. Development, monitoring, and troubleshooting via SAP AIF take place in the SAP backend. SAP AIF is as an add-on for SAP NetWeaver 7.0 or higher. You may need a separate license to use the framework.

You can find more information and exceptions using certain interfaces and/or technologies in the simplification list. Before you integrate an SAP S/4HANA, on-premise, system into your existing system landscape, you should refer to the simplification list for your release.

Simplification list

The simplification list includes notes on changes in SAP S/4HANA and other aspects you'll have to consider. You may have to adjust existing SAP standard interfaces and custom interfaces due to the modified data storage and adapted standard function modules.

Particularly when using function modules for posting data, you'll need to ensure that the data can still be used in SAP S/4HANA. Many previously used function modules were enhanced for usage with SAP S/4HANA or replaced by new functions. Chapter 10, Section 10.2.2, describes how to access the simplification list.

> **Additional Links and Help for the Integration**
>
> Describing SAP NetWeaver technologies and frameworks, which have been tried and tested for numerous years, would go beyond the scope of this book. You can find more information at the links and in the books listed here. Detailed information is available in the SAP Help Portal at *http://help.sap.com/s4hana*.
>
> 1. In the SAP Help Portal, select your release, for example, "SAP S/4HANA 1610."
> 2. On the next page, select **Product Assistance** and your language.
>
> In the menu tree under **Enterprise Technology**, you'll find detailed information on integration scenarios using the following technologies:
>
> - SAP Application Interface Framework (SAP AIF)
> - Enterprise Services
> - ALE/EDI business processes
>
> The following links in the *SAP Community Wiki* provide useful tips, presentations, and help for Enterprise Services:
>
> - *https://wiki.scn.sap.com/wiki/display/ESpackages/ES%2BWiki%2BHome*
> - *https://wiki.scn.sap.com/wiki/display/ESpackages/Enterprise%2BServices%2BCommunity*
> - For more information on SAP AIF, go to:
> - SAP Help Portal: *http://help.sap.com/aif*
> - SAP Community: *www.sap.com/aif*
> - The E-Bite "Serializing Interfaces in SAP AIF" by Michal Krawczyk, Krzysztof Łuka, and Michal Michalski (*www.sap-press.com/3943*)

The last part of the book looks back at the scenarios we described in the previous chapters. You must determine which scenario is relevant to you and learn the necessary steps for its implementation. You'll need an appropriate strategy, one that depends on your initial situation. The following chapter thus introduces the path to making the right decisions, using examples to provide an overview of the different procedures available as well as their relative advantages and disadvantages.

PART IV

Assessing the Transformation Scenarios

Chapter 14
Selecting Your Migration Scenario

To successfully migrate to SAP S/4HANA, the strategy you follow is a decisive factor. This chapter provides support for deciding among the individual SAP S/4HANA migration scenarios.

This final chapter summarizes and compares the advantages and disadvantages of the individual scenarios to provide decision-making support. However, we must mention that we can't decide for you which scenario you should use. Every customer situation is specific, and consequently, numerous factors play a role when making the decision. In general, the three doors to SAP S/4HANA are always open for all customers if an SAP ERP system already exists. Therefore, careful planning and analysis of your current situation are essential.

The most critical decision is the decision of whether to implement a new system or to convert your existing system. A landscape transformation is a special case because it can be combined with both scenarios. However, you should choose the most economically sensible scenario for your enterprise, and your decision should be based on technical requirements.

New implementation or conversion

The first section starts with a summary of the different options provided by SAP for migrating to SAP S/4HANA. Then, we'll go into more detail through examples and expectations about possible target landscapes.

14.1 Overview of Procedures and Input Helps

Let's start with an overall overview, as shown in Figure 14.1. An essential criterion for deciding among the scenarios is your initial situation. Does your source system run SAP ERP 6.0 (or higher), or do you have a different system?

Initial situation

14   Selecting Your Migration Scenario

If your SAP system is not supported or if you are using a non-SAP system, you will have to implement a new system. Depending on the volume and quality of your (master) data to be transferred, in a new implementation, you would use the SAP S/4HANA migration cockpit for standard cases or use SAP Data Services for complex data transfers.

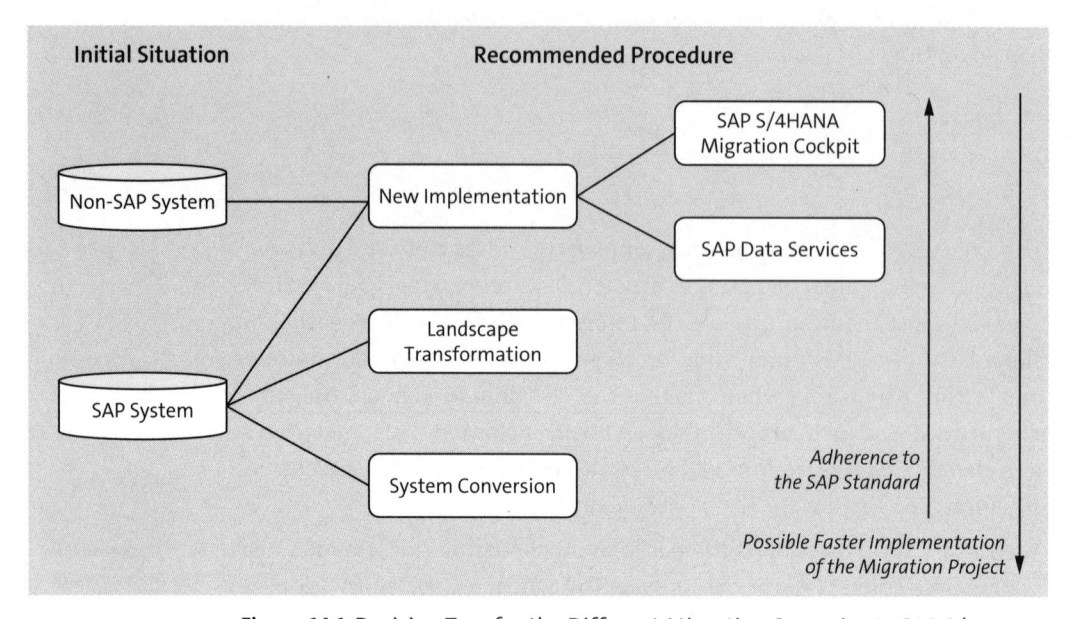

Figure 14.1 Decision Tree for the Different Migration Scenarios to SAP S/4HANA

Preliminary analyses

Only for source systems with SAP ERP 6.0 or higher are all three migration scenarios possible. However, you should always consider the following criteria when analyzing your initial situation at an early stage:

- What are the results of the prechecks provided by SAP?
- How much would adapting your custom programs cost, according to the recommendations of the custom code analysis?
- Analyze which new SAP S/4HANA functions you want to use. In this context, which makes more sense: adapting or rethinking existing business processes? Also, consider the simplification list.
- Which parts of the existing landscape do you want to migrate to SAP S/4HANA over what period of time?

With this information, you'll perform detailed analyses. In general, we recommend the scenarios at the top of Figure 14.1 if comprehensive adaptation work is necessary. The procedures listed in the bottom area are usually considered if the source system already provides a good basis for the target situation and does not need to be changed considerably. In this case, too, you should also think long term; for example, consider whether the current form of your existing business processes (their configurations and existing specific enhancements) must be kept.

By default, your planning should include a careful evaluation of the migration scenario you selected. You can make the right decision and find the procedure best suited to your needs only if you include all technical information from the prechecks, the custom code analysis, a consideration of the forms of new and existing processes, and other information.

Valuating the scenario selected

Because the final choice of migration scenario is based on numerous specific factors, SAP provides various support services. We recommend using the *Innovation Strategy & Roadmap* service to obtain a specific recommendation for your situation. Figure 14.2 provides a rough overview of the services in the different phases of the migration project.

SAP services

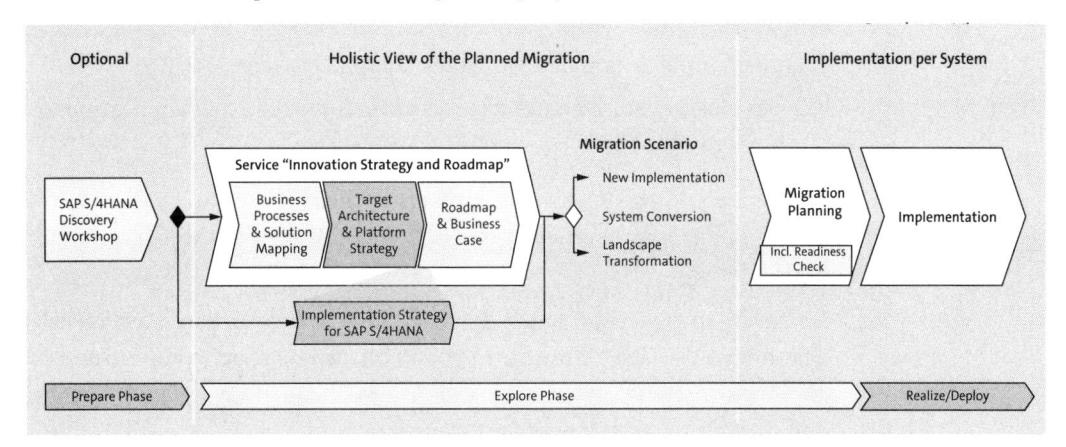

Figure 14.2 SAP Services for Migrating to SAP S/4HANA

The Roadmap Viewer provided by SAP is a detailed checklist for the concrete planning and implementation of your SAP S/4HANA transformation process. You can find the Roadmap Viewer at *https://go.support.sap.com/roadmapviewer*. Of course, you can also implement your planning without using the SAP services, which we'll discuss next.

14.2 Creating Your Own Roadmap

To help you create your own roadmap, in this section, we'll use examples to discuss different initial situations. This section describes the details you'll have to keep in mind and provides recommendations. In this context, we'll start with determining the new target landscape first and then identifying the best way to achieve this goal. Nevertheless, we cannot cover every possible customer situation. So your specific roadmap may differ significantly from the ways we describe for various reasons.

Target landscape

For new customers who have not used SAP products at all, the best way to introduce SAP S/4HANA is as a new implementation. For customers using SAP ERP, the first step is to define or analyze the current target landscape. Depending on how long ago the system landscape was established and how the existing architecture meets today's business and IT requirements, this assessment involves more or less effort. Your first analysis should answer the following questions, for example:

- Which applications can be used to meet future business requirements in the best possible way?
- How many SAP S/4HANA production systems are supposed to be used (for example, regional or global production systems)?
- Does existing architecture need to be retained for other applications, or are certain functions covered by SAP S/4HANA?

This first planning step and the answers to these questions, by themselves, cannot determine whether a new implementation or a system conversion is ideal for you.

However, in a decentralized system landscape, you can now identify whether you'll have to transform your landscape through a system consolidation. In general, migrating to SAP S/4HANA always allows you the opportunity to rethink your landscape strategy.

[»] **Additional Information on the Production System Strategy**
Criteria for defining an optimum production system strategy still apply in SAP S/4HANA. The relevant SAP white paper is available at *http://tinyurl.com/Strategy-Whitepaper*. (Access to the SAP Enterprise Support Academy required.)

14.2 Creating Your Own Roadmap

Consolidating system landscapes has been an issue for SAP customers for more than ten years. Many customers have already consolidated their SAP ERP systems and harmonized their business processes. You'll have to take into account and evaluate various criteria.

Consolidation of system landscapes

The most important criteria are the business requirements for global process harmonization and for the global management of business processes. These criteria should be the driving factors of the strategy you select. You should analyze whether a global harmonization makes sense or whether adaptations at the regional level or within business areas is feasible. These decisions also have an impact on the technical side. Globally consolidated systems require a single defined system configuration as well as efficient change and troubleshooting processes. Furthermore, a uniform release calendar with test periods and downtimes can be implemented. Another criterion is how risks regarding system performance, scalability, and operation issues are addressed. Figure 14.3 illustrates some considerations to keep in mind when developing your landscape strategy.

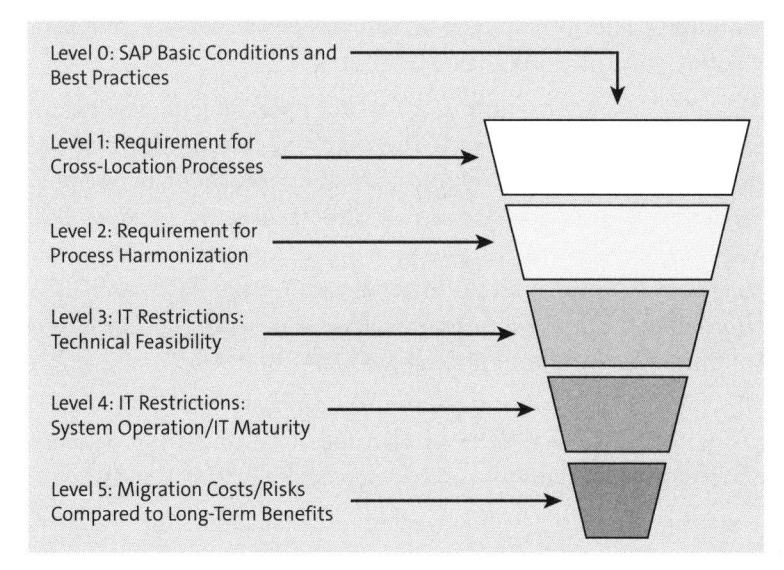

- Level 0: SAP Basic Conditions and Best Practices
- Level 1: Requirement for Cross-Location Processes
- Level 2: Requirement for Process Harmonization
- Level 3: IT Restrictions: Technical Feasibility
- Level 4: IT Restrictions: System Operation/IT Maturity
- Level 5: Migration Costs/Risks Compared to Long-Term Benefits

Figure 14.3 Decision Process for a Landscape Strategy

Let's take a traditional SAP ERP system that covers financial and logistics functions as an example. Typically, the result of a system strategy is one of the following configurations:

Production system strategies

- **A single global production system**
  This case is common among small regional enterprises or global enterprises that leverage globally harmonized processes and a global supply chain.

- **Global production systems per business area**
  This strategy is ideal for varying or organizationally independent business areas.

- **Regional production systems using a global template and uniform master data system**
  This configuration is often used in large enterprises with regional supply chains, for example, in the consumer goods industry.

Landscape strategy for SAP S/4HANA

The main difference when determining your landscape strategy for SAP S/4HANA compared to traditional SAP ERP systems is that SAP ERP can be found in the transactional system. In most enterprises, dividing the landscape into regional SAP ERP systems based on a global template would not reduce the business value more than a global SAP ERP system. SAP S/4HANA now enables you to perform comprehensive analyses and planning activities within the transactional system.

A global SAP S/4HANA system thus allows for operational reporting and financial planning at a global level in real time. In contrast, a regional SAP S/4HANA configuration would require a separate installation of SAP Business Warehouse (SAP BW). Consequently, the business value added by a global SAP S/4HANA system is higher than that of a global SAP ERP system when compared with the relevant regional architecture. Technically, system performance and scalability are no longer barriers to a global system thanks to the performance and throughput of SAP S/4HANA.

Global landscape configurations

SAP S/4HANA makes global configurations more attractive. Compared to the previous SAP ERP system, SAP S/4HANA does not change the production system strategy of most enterprises that already use a central landscape.

For enterprises that use a decentralized, nonconsolidated, and/or nonharmonized SAP ERP landscape, the following considerations are relevant:

- In the long run, you should benefit from the innovations found in SAP S/4HANA.

- Even in an entirely technical system conversion to SAP S/4HANA, you will have to make some application-specific adaptations to the existing solution.

- Instead of converting all decentralized systems separately, combining the conversion with a landscape consolidation makes sense—provided that a consolidated landscape is suitable.

- Migrating to SAP S/4HANA would create more value and reduce operating costs.

Consequently, for enterprises with decentralized landscapes, migrating to SAP S/4HANA is the ideal starting point to also consolidate their systems.

SAP S/4HANA also enables you to use functions within the system that previously belonged to separate, additional applications. Examples include production planning and detailed workflow planning, which was previously only available in SAP Advanced Planning and Optimization (SAP APO).

Merging functions

However, we must mention that all existing deployment scenarios for SAP ERP are still feasible with SAP S/4HANA. No technical requirements for changing the landscape exist, and you should always implement potential changes with a detailed business case. To help you define a target landscape for components that can be used directly in the SAP S/4HANA system, consider the following:

Single system versus codeployment

- **Global views as single systems**
  If several regional SAP S/4HANA systems are part of the planned target landscape, you'll have to set up all applications that require a global view as global single systems. Examples include SAP BW systems or SAP BusinessObjects for global reporting, planning, and consolidation. If required, you can also use SAP APO or SAP Integrated Business Planning (SAP IBP) and/or SAP Transportation Management (SAP TM) for global transport planning, which would be the same as in an SAP ERP-based landscape.

- **Mission-critical systems as single systems**
  All mission-critical systems, such as systems that automate production processes or warehouse management processes, should be defined as single systems. A common example is SAP Extended Warehouse Management (SAP EWM). If you had SAP EWM set up as a single, SAP ERP-independent system in your existing landscape, this setup would probably still be the case after migrating to SAP S/4HANA because SAP EWM plays a critical role for the enterprise.

  A separate system offers several advantages, such as independence for software modifications and the reduced risk of collateral effects.

14　Selecting Your Migration Scenario

However, if SAP EWM system covers rather uncritical processes (more like traditional SAP Warehouse Management in SAP ERP), you should think about codeploying SAP EWM in combination with SAP S/4HANA.

Considering value added and disadvantages Finally, you should check the added value from the newly integrated processes that are only available when specific functions of SAP S/4HANA are codeployed. You should compare the potential benefits and disadvantages, as well as the costs, of such a migration.

Examples include the ability to use operational reporting with SAP S/4HANA embedded analytics instead of operational reporting with SAP BW or the ability to use detailed production planning integrated in the new material requirements planning (MRP) function within SAP S/4HANA instead of a separate SAP APO system.

Some potential disadvantages you'll have to consider include standardized maintenance and release cycles, common system downtimes, and possibly longer downtimes for smaller functions because the software is updated for all components in parallel.

Scenario and sequence After defining the new target landscape, you can specify the appropriate migration scenario and the sequence of the actions required. Depending on the target situation, the following questions may arise:

- Is a system conversion the appropriate scenario for your migration to SAP S/4HANA, or should you consider a new implementation?
- What is the appropriate approach for a system conversion if multiple SAP ERP systems need to be consolidated into a few SAP S/4HANA systems?
- How can the necessary steps be sequenced appropriately, and what relationships need to be taken into account?

The following sections use examples from different customer situations to identify the possible answers to these individual questions.

14.2.1　Initial Scenario: Single System

Possible scenarios In the first scenario, your enterprise has a central single SAP ERP system. Because a system consolidation is out of scope here, you can only choose between a system conversion and a new implementation. The following options are possible:

- **Standard: system conversion**

  Assumption:
  - The existing solution mainly meets your existing business requirements.
  - Your business requirements do not need a completely new implementation.

  Advantage:
  - A one-step procedure to SAP S/4HANA without reimplementation is possible.

- **New implementation according to the greenfield approach using the model company**

  Assumption:
  - The existing solution is too complex and/or no longer meets your existing business requirements.
  - You have business requirements that need a new implementation and a return to the standard (irrespective of SAP S/4HANA).

- **New implementation reusing an existing template**

  Assumption:
  - The existing solution still meets your business requirements, but the system contains a large volume of (unused) legacy data.

For many SAP customers, at first glance, the standard method for system conversions seems to be the ideal solution to convert an existing SAP ERP system into an SAP S/4HANA system. The major advantage of this scenario is that your existing configuration and data are kept. This kind of conversion can also be implemented in one step, depending on your initial situation.

System conversion

For this recommendation, we assume that the solution used so far meets the business requirements and a complete new implementation is not necessary. You can also implement minor changes (such as returning to the standard for customer-specific adaptations in isolated areas, cleansing custom code, and implementing new functions) in system conversions.

If the solution currently used is too complex or no longer meets existing requirements and/or if you generally want to implement a new system (irrespective of SAP S/4HANA), this way is the ideal solution. If your system is 20 years old or older, starting from scratch is likely ideal because requirements have likely changed considerably over time.

New implementation

14   Selecting Your Migration Scenario

In this case, migrating to SAP S/4HANA is ideal for implementing a new system. You can use SAP Best Practices and the preconfigured model company to reduce costs and implementation project duration to a minimum (see Chapter 6). For a new implementation, you'll only transfer your master data and open items from your existing SAP ERP system. Historically completed data is not copied in general. In special cases, you can set up an SAP S/4HANA system from an existing template, which means that the configuration and custom code from the existing SAP ERP system will continue to be used.

Multiple SAP ERP systems   Even if this example refers to a customer with a single system, the procedure would be the same if multiple SAP ERP systems existed—if the landscape stays the same on SAP S/4HANA and a consolidation is not required.

One-step or multiple-step procedure   For customers who decide to convert their SAP ERP system to SAP S/4HANA, the question arises whether the system is supposed to be converted in one step or in multiple steps. As we discussed in Chapter 10, various ways to perform a conversion are available. Figure 14.4 provides an overview.

In most cases, the one-step procedure for converting from SAP ERP to SAP S/4HANA is technically feasible and makes sense. Nevertheless, customers may ask themselves whether the one-step procedure is generally the simplest way or whether two or even more projects should be planned and implemented, in particular if only migrating to the SAP HANA database is planned as an intermediate step. Table 14.1 summarizes these differences again.

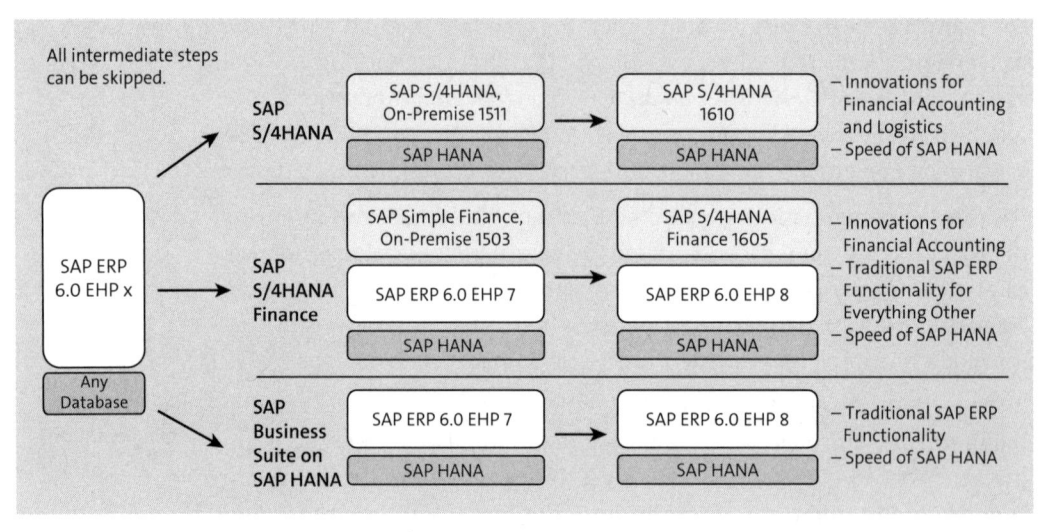

Figure 14.4 SAP S/4HANA Implementation Paths

Criterion	Option 1	Option 2
	One-Step Conversion to SAP S/4HANA	First Project: Database Migration to SAP HANA Second Project: System Conversion to SAP S/4HANA
Time to value	Faster implementation of the SAP S/4HANA target environment (analytics, new financials solution, new MRP run, SAP Fiori, etc.)	- Faster on the first level with SAP HANA (better performance, SAP HANA Live, etc.) - More time to implement the SAP S/4HANA target solution
Migration costs	In total, lower costs because you'll implement one large project with one test phase	- Higher costs due to two separate projects with two separate test phases - Overlapping tasks can lead to unnecessary costs
Risks and consequences of the migration	- Higher project complexity - Potentially longer downtime	- Lower project complexity - Two potentially long downtimes - Potentially higher risk due to reduced focus on individual test phases

Table 14.1 Comparing One-Step and Multiple-Step Procedures

When evaluating the different options, you should always consider and compare the duration of the implementation project, its overall costs, and its risks:

Duration, costs, and risks

- The *one-step procedure* provides the major advantage that only one project is required—the fastest way to SAP S/4HANA. In comparison, costs are also lower because the costs of test cycles or for project management are only incurred once.

- For *two-step procedures*, two projects are necessary; the second project may be delayed due to other priorities (for example, due to additional rollouts or functional projects). Depending on how long the first status is kept (which would be an SAP Business Suite powered by SAP HANA here), unnecessary and redundant costs may be incurred. For example, if SAP HANA Live or SAP Fiori are to be introduced after the first step, additional costs may be incurred for modifications that are necessary at a later stage because many of these functions are included in SAP S/4HANA.

On the other hand, the project complexity of a one-step procedure is higher than of pursuing two subsequent projects. Therefore, the general project risks are also higher. However, you can still minimize these risks with in-depth preliminary analyses and planning processes as well as by scheduling sufficient resources and test cycles. Unfortunately, enterprises often underestimate the test effort required for two separate projects, which would leads also to higher risks. Experience has shown that the project risks for the two approaches are nearly identical.

General considerations

In the end, your decision should be based on general considerations:

- The balance between identified business requirements with the new options available in SAP S/4HANA, taking into account the schedule for implementing these potential benefits
- System-specific migration risks and options for minimizing risk
- Other dependencies, for example, the estimated duration of the implementation project, how the project fits into the release calendar with other projects, and the availability of required resources
- The current status of the existing system, taking into account the necessary technical requirements

SAP S/4HANA Finance as an intermediate step

When making these decisions, the question often arises whether an additional intermediate step to SAP S/4HANA Finance makes sense instead of directly migrating to SAP S/4HANA.

In this case, you should consider the duration of the project, its costs, and its risks to decide whether to deploy SAP S/4HANA Finance as an intermediate step. In individual cases, business areas may expect significant benefits provided by the new financials functions in SAP S/4HANA and want to achieve this added value as fast as possible. This intermediate step is particularly relevant if the implementation to SAP S/4HANA suffer from delays due to customer-specific complexity in the logistics area or if the necessary third-party applications are not yet supported.

14.2.2 Initial Scenario: Decentralized System Landscape

As we described earlier, migrating to SAP S/4HANA offers a good opportunity for decentralized system landscapes to be consolidated. Several options exist to combine an SAP S/4HANA project with a system consolidation. In general, the following approaches are useful:

Approaches to system consolidation

- A *new implementation*, either based on an existing template or using SAP Best Practices, including preconfiguration and subsequent data migration. In this approach, your data will be copied from all your existing SAP ERP systems, which and usually includes master data and open items. Under certain conditions, you can also copy other historical data; however, this data duplication would increase costs and effort.

- A *system conversion* of your existing SAP ERP system followed by the migration of the data from all your other existing SAP ERP systems. In most cases, you'll convert one of your more central systems, the one with the most appropriate existing configuration or system size. As with the first approach, the data migration only includes master data and open items.

- A complete *consolidation* of all SAP ERP systems into a central SAP ERP system, where all historical data is kept, as described in Chapter 12. This consolidation can be performed by following a one-client or a multiple-client approach; afterwards, the resulting SAP ERP system is converted to SAP S/4HANA.

The criteria described in the previous sections can help you find the best possible way for this example. How well does the solution you currently use meet existing and future business requirements? Do you have a general requirement for a new implementation of the existing landscape, and does historical data have to be transferred? Answering these questions helps you make the right decision.

The following examples may be used for orientation:

Sample requirements and solutions

- **Consolidation if business requirements remain the same**
  Your current solution still meets all business requirements in all SAP ERP systems, but you want to consolidate the systems. You can use one of the systems as the starting point for SAP S/4HANA. Further adaptations (such as returning to the standard, code modifications, and activating additional SAP S/4HANA functions) are planned. You can create a solution based on a uniform template and then implement the solution

in several systems. Then, you can consolidate these systems into a smaller number of regional systems or into one global system.

- **Consolidation based on a leading configuration**
  Configuring one SAP ERP system is ideal because you can then use the system as a template for all other business areas or regions that are currently mapped in other systems or with other configurations. For example, a solution used in one of the larger regions is ideal for smaller, deviating implementations in satellite regions. In this case, the goal is to consolidate and harmonize all the systems on the basis of the configuration of the leading region.

- **General modifications required**
  An existing solution usually meets the requirements of at least one system, but general modifications are often necessary to stay competitive, regardless of whether you have migrated to SAP S/4HANA. In this case, a new implementation based on a template from at least one existing and largely appropriate system is feasible.

- **No SAP system as the basis**
  The existing solution no longer meets your business requirements, and no SAP ERP system is available to be used as a template or starting point for SAP S/4HANA. In this case, a new system must be implemented, ideally using SAP Best Practices.

Historical data   For historical data that needs to be transferred, the main issue is data volume. Normally, only master data, as well as transaction data in the form of open items, is transferred for new implementations. If historical data plays a role in your new system landscape for critical reasons, the complexity of the project may increase considerably, thus increasing effort and costs because of additional required data transformations. As a result, you should always discuss this kind of requirement thoroughly and consider alternatives, such as data archiving, first. Depending on your current situation, various options are available (see Figure 14.5).

Decision matrix   Depending on your answers, the matrix shown in Figure 14.5 can guide you to the preferred migration scenario. Note that these recommendations are only rough proposals and do not replace general and customer-specific analyses and evaluations. You'll always have to take into account the time to implement (based on the duration of the project) as well as costs, benefits, and risks. Factors that you don't have to consider include the current status of the system, the need for historical data, the number of systems to be consolidated if required, and consequently the differences between the systems involved. The technical feasibility of the selected scenario does not have to be analyzed in detail, in particular in the case of specific data migration requirements.

		How well does the existing solution meet the business requirements?			
		Solutions meets requirements of all systems, no changes required	Solution meets requirements of one system, minor adaptations required	Solution meets basic requirements, changes required	Solution no longer meets the requirements of the existing systems
How much historical data is supposed to be transferred?	Open items/ stock levels are sufficient	New implementation on the basis of an existing template is possible			New implementation, model company
	Selective migration of historical data			You can migrate additional data; this increases costs and effort.	You can migrate additional data; this increases costs and effort.
	Complete history for one system	System conversion of one system, followed by a data migration from the other systems			Does not make sense and questionable from the technical perspective
	Complete history for all systems	System consolidation, then system conversion	You can migrate additional data; this increases costs and effort.		

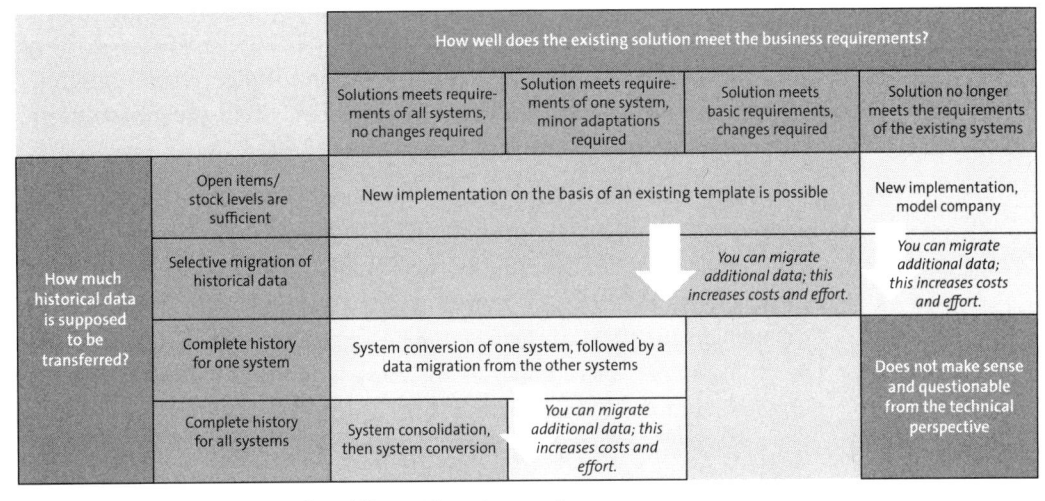

Figure 14.5 Decision Matrix for Different Requirements

Relevance of System Consolidation When Migrating to SAP S/4HANA
Consolidation activities are not a prerequisite for migrating to SAP S/4HANA and should not be considered necessary if you had not identified a need for these activities before. You can generally expect that a system conversion of a single system or a new implementation of SAP S/4HANA, followed by data migration from the other SAP ERP source systems, is always easier to implement than harmonizing all systems in advance.

SAP S/4HANA provides entirely new deployment options for your system landscape. Functions that previously required separate systems are now available as components of SAP S/4HANA. Customers often ask how these new functions impact migrating to SAP S/4HANA and defining a roadmap, including the relationships among the individual steps included in the migration.

Codeployment

We should mention that there is no technical requirement for modifying an existing landscape. You can convert existing SAP ERP systems to SAP S/4HANA and keep and continue to operate all related systems, such as

SAP BW, SAP APO, or SAP Supplier Relationship Management (SAP SRM). If you need additional single systems, you can add them to the landscape, regardless of whether you've migrated to SAP S/4HANA.

In other words, these systems run on both SAP ERP and SAP S/4HANA. For example, you can start by introducing SAP EWM, regardless of other required migration steps. However, if you use one or more of SAP S/4HANA's new codeployment options and want to replace the corresponding function from the existing single systems, you can only start the project during or after migrating your SAP ERP system to SAP S/4HANA.

Numerous examples of these projects are available, such as implementing the *Advanced Available-to-Promise* (aATP) materials management function in SAP S/4HANA, which replaces the *Global Available-to-Promise* (GATP) function from SAP APO. Another example is implementing the *Self-Service Procurement* function in the SAP S/4HANA procurement solution, which covers the same functionality as the corresponding function within SAP Supplier Relationship Management (SAP SRM).

14.2.3 Sample Roadmaps

This section provides sample roadmaps for migrating to SAP S/4HANA to better illustrate the topics discussed in previous sections. Even though the situations described in this section may not exactly map to your specific situation for your system landscape, you can still obtain useful information for creating your own roadmap.

From a Single System to an SAP S/4HANA Single System

Initial solution

The first example involves a global SAP environment with regional SAP EWM systems. The existing solution consists of the following components:

- A single global SAP ERP system
- A single global SAP APO system used for the GATP function
- A single SAP SRM system for the *Self-Service Procurement* function
- A single SAP BW system for operational and strategic reporting as well as SAP BusinessObjects Planning and Consolidation for financial planning and consolidation
- The recent introduction of SAP EWM with the aim of creating three regional systems in order to minimize risks

14.2 Creating Your Own Roadmap

A long-term target landscape with SAP S/4HANA looks as follows:

Long-term target landscape

- A single global SAP S/4HANA system will be introduced. In addition to the functions used in SAP ERP today, the plan is to map the following functions with SAP S/4HANA:
  - Real-time reporting with SAP S/4HANA embedded analytics
  - Financial planning and consolidation as a part of SAP S/4HANA
  - Advanced ATP and Self-Service Procurement
- In addition, a global SAP Integrated Business Planning (SAP IBP) system will operate in the cloud for sales and distribution, planning, and procurement.
- A global SAP BW system will be used for strategic reporting based on historical data.
- Three regional SAP EWM systems will limit the risk of failure.

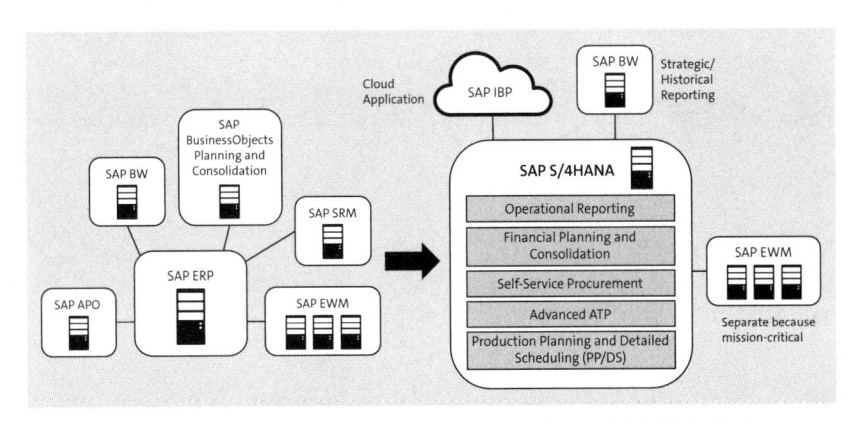

Figure 14.6 From a Single SAP ERP System to a Single SAP S/4HANA System

Figure 14.6 illustrates these changes graphically. A value-driven roadmap for migrating to this new target landscape could look as follows:

Roadmap

- You can proceed with the implementation of the SAP EWM systems as planned because no changes are necessary.
- First, SAP IBP in the cloud is used for new functions, such as *SAP IBP for Response and Supply*, which complements your existing SAP APO implementation. This cloud-based implementation is a new implementation, which you can carry out regardless of whether you're migrating to SAP S/4HANA.

543

- You can then add the planning function for demand (*SAP IBP for Demand*) to SAP IBP, which replaces the corresponding function of the SAP APO implementation. This adoption is also independent of migrating from SAP ERP to SAP S/4HANA.
- You can convert the SAP ERP system to an SAP S/4HANA system in one step because the solution currently used still meets most of your business requirements.
- When converting to SAP S/4HANA, and in subsequent projects, new functions will be added to the new system (for example, operational reporting and Advanced ATP), which replace their corresponding functions in SAP BW and SAP APO.
- After converting to SAP S/4HANA, you should migrate your financial planning and consolidation functions from the separate SAP BusinessObjects Planning and Consolidation (BPC) system to the corresponding function embedded in SAP S/4HANA. The previous Self-Service Procurement function is also migrated from the separate SAP SRM system.

Figure 14.7 graphically illustrates the entire roadmap for this example.

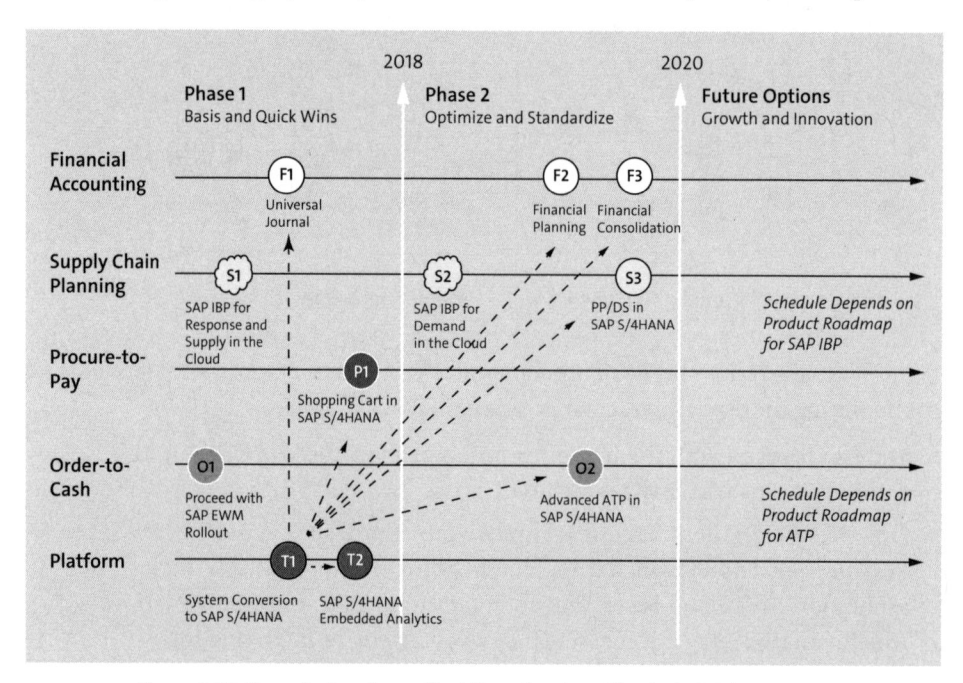

Figure 14.7 Sample Roadmap for Migrating to a Single SAP S/4HANA System with Integrated Systems

From an SAP ERP Landscape Distributed across Regions to a Global SAP S/4HANA Landscape

In our second example, we'll start with a system landscape distributed across multiple regions that will be consolidated into a global system landscape. The initial situation of our landscape distributed across multiple regions is the following:

- Three regional SAP ERP systems use a harmonized global template. One SAP ERP system, for the leading region, is much more comprehensive, while two smaller regional satellite systems also exist.
- Three regional SAP BW systems are used for regional operational and strategic reporting.
- A fourth global SAP BW system, including BPC, is used for enterprise-wide reporting as well as for financial planning and consolidation.

Initial solution

The long-term planning for this SAP S/4HANA target landscape could look as follows:

Long-term target landscape

- You introduce a single, global SAP S/4HANA system because day-to-day operations have been globalized. In addition to the SAP ERP functions used so far, the following functions will be added:
  – Real-time reporting with SAP S/4HANA embedded analytics
  – Replication-free financial planning and consolidation with the BPC function included in SAP S/4HANA
- A global SAP BW system is used for strategic reporting based on historical data.

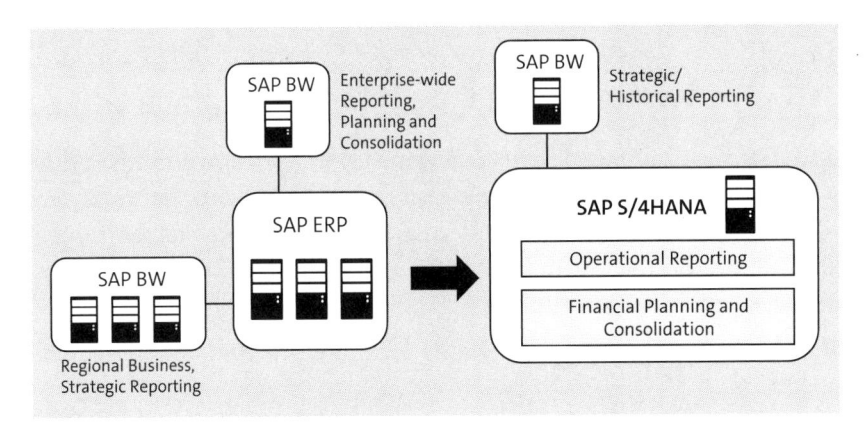

Figure 14.8 From a Regional SAP ERP Landscape to a Global SAP S/4HANA Landscape

Roadmap Figure 14.8 shows the entire landscape before and after the conversion. An appropriate roadmap for this migration to the target landscape could look as follows:

- You convert the largest SAP ERP system of the leading region into an SAP S/4HANA system in one step.
- You then migrate selected data from the regional satellite systems to the new SAP S/4HANA system. This data includes relevant master data and transaction data in the form of open items.
- You add the new real-time reporting function to the new SAP S/4HANA solution. You can add these real-time reporting functions during the system conversion or add them before or after migrating the data from your other regional systems. You can then gradually add further reports to replace the reporting from your regional SAP BW systems.
- From the separate BPC system, you can migrate the financial planning and consolidation function to the corresponding function in SAP S/4HANA. However, all regions must be integrated into the new SAP S/4HANA target landscape before you can move these functions. After integrating all the regions, the financial dataset is complete, which is required for financial planning and consolidation in SAP S/4HANA.
- The global SAP BW system remains unchanged and is populated with data that is relevant for strategic reporting and historical data from regional SAP BW systems. These systems can be removed from the landscape after this process has been completed. This step is largely independent of the actual migration to SAP S/4HANA.

14.3 The Most Important Criteria for Your Decision

Based on the examples described in this chapter, let's now summarize the most important criteria for your decision-making. The four figures in this section refer to two questions. Indicators in each figure provide recommendations, irrespective of your answer to the question. Again, these recommendations are only examples and depend on your specific situation.

Requirements The first recommendation (see Figure 14.9) refers to your system requirements.

14.3 The Most Important Criteria for Your Decision

	New Implementation	System Conversion
Are you able and do you want to use the one-step procedure to migrate to SAP S/4HANA?	No	Yes
Have you identified add-ons or functions that are not supported by SAP S/4HANA yet?	Yes	No

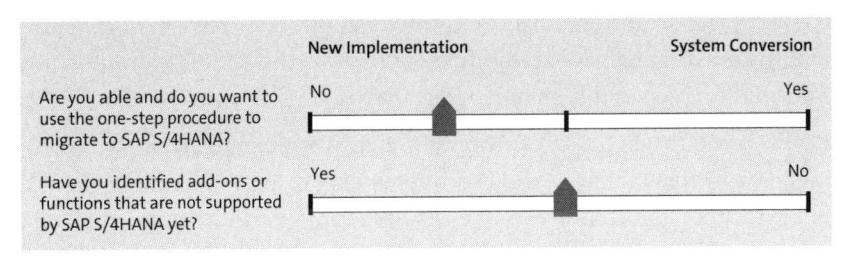

Figure 14.9 Questions and Evaluations Regarding System Requirements

If your current SAP Business Suite system is a rather old release (lower than SAP ERP 6.0), you'll have to perform multiple steps when migrating to SAP S/4HANA. First, you'll have to switch to a release that allows for a system conversion to SAP S/4HANA from a technical perspective. For old releases, a new implementation is the ideal solution, saving you the time and costs required for switching to a newer release. A new implementation would even be faster.

However, certain add-ons and business functions might not be available on the SAP S/4HANA roadmap for now, such as industry solutions. The nonavailability of these functions or add-ons that have not been released yet could delay the implementation of SAP S/4HANA. However, we cannot make specific recommendations in these cases because this limitation applies to all migration scenarios, from new implementations to system conversions.

The second block of questions shown in Figure 14.10 refers to business processes. **Business processes**

	New Implementation	System Conversion
Do your business processes basically meet your existing business requirements?	Business processes basically do not meet requirements	Business processes basically meet requirements
Do you want to redesign your business processes?	Yes	No

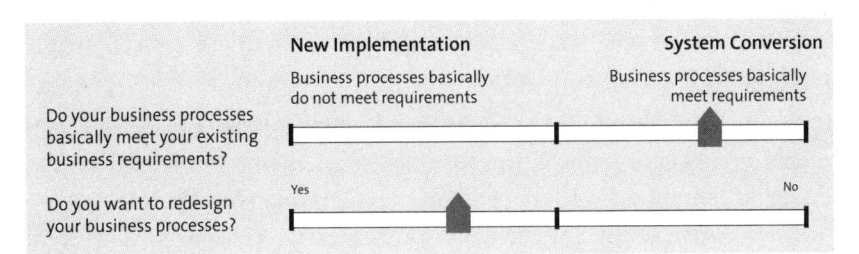

Figure 14.10 Questions and Evaluations Regarding Business Processes

If the business processes used so far and the configuration of your existing system meet current business requirements, a system conversion is probably the right solution. For system conversions, the present configuration and the existing dataset are both kept. Refer to the simplification list for information on possible changes relevant to SAP S/4HANA.

If you want to adapt your processes, a new implementation is recommended. In this scenario, you can implement business processes via SAP Best Practices and thus determine the best configuration for your system. Application data is transferred to the new system in a data migration process so that the data corresponds to these new processes.

Custom developments

The third area refers to your custom developments (as shown in Figure 14.11).

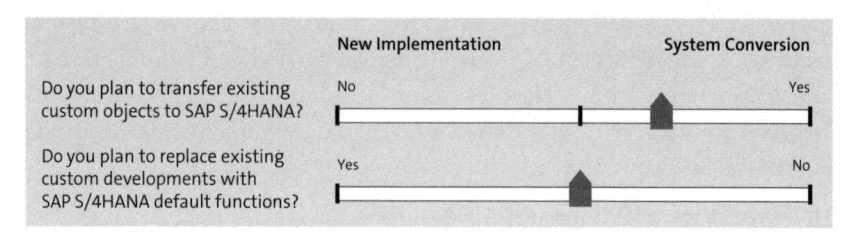

Figure 14.11 Questions and Evaluations Regarding Custom Developments

If you wanted to transfer existing code and custom developments (which makes sense if your specific requirements are not yet met by SAP S/4HANA), a system conversion would probably be the better solution. In the case of system conversions, existing custom objects are kept and can be modified, using the custom code migration worklist, for example, to consider changes to data structures in SAP S/4HANA. However, this aspect is not that critical because you can also transfer custom developments in a new implementation. Our experience has shown that these concerns only rarely apply to custom developments.

If you may want to return to the SAP Standard for existing custom developments, you should probably opt for a new implementation first. However, this requirement does not depend on the migration scenario because you can also return to the SAP Standard for custom developments via system conversions. You'll need to analyze the existing code in detail and schedule the steps for the relevant SAP S/4HANA functions.

The last block of questions (see Figure 14.12) refers to the *time to value*, that is, to the period of time before the relevant value has been achieved.

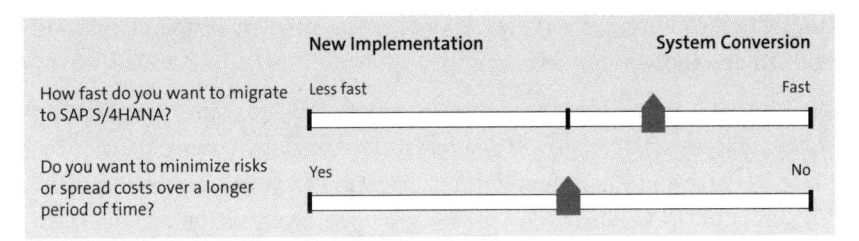

	New Implementation	System Conversion
How fast do you want to migrate to SAP S/4HANA?	Less fast	Fast
Do you want to minimize risks or spread costs over a longer period of time?	Yes	No

Figure 14.12 Questions and Evaluations Regarding Time to Value

How long the migration to SAP S/4HANA takes depends on your individual requirements. Depending on the size and complexity of your existing landscape, a system conversion is often the fastest method if the one-step procedure can be applied. Because your system settings would remain the same, a conversion is usually faster than a new implementation, which may involve a complete redesign of your business processes.

However, SAP Best Practices, in particular the best practices package for SAP S/4HANA, considerably accelerates new implementations. In particular, comprehensive, preconfigured cloud solutions can be available in a few weeks, which is especially interesting if you want to migrate subsidiaries to SAP S/4HANA. With a new implementation, whether the source system is an SAP ERP system or a non-SAP system does not matter because cloud-based systems are always implemented from scratch.

We cannot make general recommendation regarding these risks, which rather depend on the roadmap developed than on the scenario selected. You can select any adaptation speed that meets your current requirements. Whether you transfer a single company code to SAP S/4HANA first or start with SAP S/4HANA Finance is up to you. The only thing that we should mention—as described in this chapter—is that SAP S/4HANA implementations in small steps usually take longer and involve more costs.

14.4 Conclusion

This chapter concludes our journey to SAP S/4HANA. Hopefully, we've provided you with useful information to better orient you during the migration process. You are now familiar with the required tools and considerations to determine the best solution for your enterprise. Whether new implementation or system conversion, on-premise or in the cloud, now, you'll make all the right decisions.

Whether you're a member of the migration project team or a decision-maker who must determine the appropriate strategy—we hope that this book has proven to be a good guide answering all your questions and will further support you as a reference book in your migration project. Now, all that remains is for us to wish you success migrating your system to SAP S/4HANA.

The Authors

Frank Densborn joined SAP in 2004 and is now a product manager for SAP S/4HANA in Palo Alto, CA. His work focuses on data migration for new implementations and migrations to the cloud. He has worked in the Enterprise Information Management (EIM) area and has added Rapid Data Migration solutions to the SAP portfolio. Previously, he developed SAP Best Practices packages for business intelligence as a project lead and was significantly involved in developing data migration solutions with SAP Data Services. He was also responsible for the Legacy System Migration Workbench (LSMW) development and gained real world migration experiences by supporting data migration projects at customers. Frank Densborn studied mathematics, physics, and computer science at the Johannes Gutenberg University in Mainz, Germany.

Frank Finkbohner is the project manager for the development of the predefined cloud data migration content for the SAP S/4HANA Migration Cockpit at SAP. He joined SAP in 1999 and worked at SAP Consulting for 13 years, supporting customers in developing new or enhancing existing ABAP applications. His main focus was to plan and implement data migrations. In several customer projects, he used the whole spectrum of SAP's data migration tools, methods, and programs (for example, the Legacy System Migration Workbench (LSMW), Batch Input, BAPIs, IDocs, Rapid Data Migration). During his work as a project manager for data transfer projects, he developed a specific method for grouping migration projects into work packages (SEAMAP) and has used this method successfully in customer projects. Frank Finkbohner has a degree in computer science from the University of Applied Sciences in Fulda, Germany, and a degree in industrial engineering from the University of Esslingen, Germany.

The Authors

Dr. Jochen Freudenberg is the head of the Development Landscape Management—Architecture department, dealing with the definition of system landscapes for SAP software development projects. The team also prepares the technical delivery of SAP applications, focusing on SAP ERP Enhancement Packages (EHPs), SAP S/4HANA, SAP Fiori, and enhancements based on SAP Cloud Platform. He holds a doctorate degree in physics and has more than 16 years of SAP experience in the areas of ABAP development, process standards for software development, and release and maintenance strategies for SAP products.

Kim Mathäß is a product manager for SAP S/4HANA data management and for migration to SAP S/4HANA at SAP. He is responsible for the further development of tools and solutions for the transition to SAP S/4HANA. Kim Mathäß conducts lectures and sessions on SAP S/4HANA transition scenarios and migration regularly at national and international conventions. He joined SAP in 2006 and has held various roles and positions. As a senior consultant and business development manager, he has conducted numerous projects at both international enterprises and medium-sized corporations in Europe. His experience ranges from SAP new implementations to the subsequent adjustment of systems and system landscapes. These projects include system consolidations, mergers and acquisitions, and divestitures as well as traditional data migrations from SAP and non-SAP systems.

Frank Wagner is a product expert on migrating to SAP S/4HANA in the context of the SAP S/4HANA product development. Responsible for the simplification list for SAP S/4HANA, he has provided methods and tools to support customers in the transition phase. He has worked within SAP's consulting, support, and development organizations; has supported numerous customers in adopting and using SAP Retail and SAP Apparel and Footwear (SAP AFS);

and has worked as an escalation manager in the SAP back office. In the SAP development division, he was a product expert and was responsible for the implementation methodology and business configuration of SAP Business ByDesign. Frank Wagner has a degree in economics from Saarland University, Germany.

Contributors to This Book

Andreas Muno is a product manager for SAP S/4HANA Cloud. His work focuses on integration with the SAP business network. He is responsible for developing SAP Best Practices for integrating SAP Ariba solutions with SAP S/4HANA and the SAP Business Suite. Andreas Muno wrote Chapter 8, Section 8.1, and Chapter 13, Section 13.1.

Markus Trapp works in the product management area for SAP S/4HANA Cloud and is responsible for HR integration solutions, in particular for integration with SAP SuccessFactors. He conducts lectures and sessions on SAP S/4HANA integration scenarios and SAP cloud applications regularly at national and international conventions. He studied computer science at the University of Heidelberg, Germany. Markus Trapp wrote Chapter 8, Section 8.2, and Chapter 13, Section 13.2.

Index

A

ABAP Data Dictionary 126, 472
ABAP Dictionary table 86
ABAP enhancements 131
ABAP Repository 472
AcceleratedSAP 158, 378
Accelerator 173
Account, Central Finance 494
Accounting 47–48
   parallel 48
   simplification 42
Accounts payable 51
Accounts payable data 475
Accounts receivable 51
Accounts receivable data 475
Activate → SAP Activate
Actual data 50
Adaptive Server Enterprise 395
Add-on 147
   partner 345
   SAP 345
Admin Center 515
Admin guide 319
Advanced Available-to-Promise 542
Aggregate 82, 84
AIF 521
ALE → Application Link Enabling
ALWAYS_OFF 345
Amazon Web Services 181
Analysis phase 460
Analysis, simplification 45
Analytical app 89
API 126, 284
API, public 302
APO 39, 55
App
   analytical 89
   transactional 89
App Finder 374
Appliance 182

Application data, harmonization 474
Application Interface Framework 521
Application Link Enabling .. 400, 510, 521
Application management service 114
Application Programming Interface → API
Archive, consolidation 476
Archiving 146, 540
Ariba Cloud Integration Adapter 506
Ariba Collaborative Sourcing → SAP Ariba Sourcing
Ariba Payment and Discount
   Management 508
Ariba Purchase Order to Invoice 508
Ariba spot quote 246
ASAP 158, 378
ASE 395
Asset accounting 348
.atl 396
Authentication, SAP S/4HANA Cloud 200
Authorization, harmonization 475
Automation 31
Availability check, global 53
AWS 181

B

B2B 51
Backend system 90
Backup 466
BAdI, Ariba integration 508
BAiO 161
Balance of accounts 494
Bank master 400
BAPI 95, 126, 391, 400, 441
   ALE interface 400
   asynchronous 400
BC sets 320
Belize 370
Best Practices Explorer 164, 397
Best practices → SAP Best Practices

555

Index

BI Launchpad 433
Bing 71
Blueprint 462
Blueprint phase 380
BPC 49
Brownfield 99, 121, 329
Browser 90
Building block 166, 320
Building Block Builder 319
Business All-in-One 161
Business Application Programming Interface → BAPI
Business case 462
Business configuration sets 320
Business function 345
   FIN_GL_ERR_CORR 484
   FIN_GL_ERR_CORR_SUSP 484
   FINS_CFIN 484
Business impact note 343
Business model, change 29
Business object 380
   custom 130
Business partner 277, 519
Business process 547
   enhancement 125
   harmonize 531
Business process document 163
Business suite 78
BW 532

C

Campaign execution 287
Career Site Builder 61
CCLM 350
CDS 126, 351
CDS view 519
Central Finance 48, 108, 482
   companies 488
   data transfer 486, 499
   global parameters 487
   Implementation Guide 483
   master data 493
   system connections 483
Central hub 324

Central Management Console 393
Change pointer 511
Chart of accounts 489
Check data value 385
Check list, SAP S/4HANA Cloud 210
Check routine, SAP Data Services 427
Check variant 351
Client 187
   000 318
   concept 471
   copy 318
   merge 469
   profile 318
   SAP Best Practices 318
   traditional 318
   transfer 469
Cloud 99
   deployment model 102
   edition 104
   operating model 101
   security 36, 101
   service models 101
Cloud Appliance Library 180
Cloud computing 35
Cloud Connector → SAP HANA Cloud Connector
Cloud Identity 200
CMC 393
Code Inspector 351, 355
Code pushdown 86, 351
Co-deployment 313, 541
Column-based storage 83
Comma Separated Value → CSV
Communication agreement 281
Communication scenario 279
Communication system 280
Communication user 280
Company code 471, 488
   migration 477
   transfer 458, 476
Compatibility matrix 507
Compatibility packages 107
Compound employee API 518
Configuration
   self-service 168
   test 169

Index

Configuration application 210
Configuration item 210
Consolidation 42
Consolidation, systems 458
Contact, SAP Hybris Marketing Cloud 290
Content 419
Content activation 320
Controlling 50
Controlling area 477, 491
Conversion 419, 474
Conversion path 339
Conversion → System conversion
Conversion scenario → Migration scenario
Conversion table 232, 419
Cookbook 318
Core business processes 76
Core Data Services → CDS
Core process, business 76
Cost accounting 491
Cost center 496
  attributes 496
Cost element
  primary 494
  secondary 495
Cost/benefit analysis 462
Counter-deletion 477
Country 487
Credit management 330, 341
Credit Risk Analyzer 51
Crowdfunding 30
Crowdsourcing 30
CSV 234, 285, 296
Custom code check 132, 150
Custom Code Lifecycle Management toolset 350
Custom code migration worklist 150, 331, 349, 352
Custom development 348, 473
Custom development, automatic check 150
Custom developments 348, 548
Customer field 450
Customer master 396
Customer Vendor Integration 396

Customizing 123
  client-dependent 473
  client-independent 473
  data migration 395
  SAP S/4HANA Cloud 210
  transfer 474
Cut-over 175, 336, 464, 466
CVI 396
cXML 506

D

Dashboard, marketing manager 72
Data aging 147
Data analysis 380
Data cleansing 386, 395, 475
Data comparison 396
Data conversion 87, 366
Data flow 403
Data footprint 138, 146
Data governance 396
Data harmonization 468
Data import 430
  simulation 236
Data lineage 391
Data management object 296
Data migration
  content 393, 396
  Convert Values 233
  field mapping 412
  fixed values 235
  implementation phase 383
  monitoring 432
  performance 434
  phases 378
  platform 394
  Rapid Data Migration 390
  SAP S/4HANA migration cockpit 437
  starter system 203
  template 412
  validation function 428
Data Migration Server 486
Data model, simplification 84
Data quality 475
Data replication 153
Data replication monitoring 516

557

Index

Data security 101
Data Services Designer 398, 401, 426
Data Services → SAP Data Services
Data storage, architecture 86
Data structure, simplification 40
Data validation 384, 426
Data volume, development 76
Data, historical 540
Database
   integration 405
   migration 368
   migration, custom developments .. 351
   server 392
   sizing 362
   traditional 81
   view 85
Database Migration Option 151, 364, 368
Database Migration Option, Migration
   Control Center 369
DataSift 302
Datastore 405, 430
Decommissioning Cockpit 350
Deduplication 391
Delta reconciliation 396
Deploy phase 175, 208
Deployment option → Operating model
Development 62
Development system
   conversion 334
   system configuration 319
   transformation 467
Dialog process 436
Digital core 37, 78, 106
Digital farming 32
Digital native 79
Digital platform 33
Digital transformation 25
Digitalization 27
Discount management 246
Discover phase 139, 194
Disruptive transformation 30
Distribution model 511
DMO → Database Migration Option
Document exchange 244
Download Basket 313

Downtime 335, 366
Downtime-optimized procedure 370
Dual-stack system 338

E

eCATT 320
E-learning 34, 62
Electronic Data Interchange 521
Embedded analytics 96
Emergency patch 116
Employee data 277
   import 205, 275
   synchronization 519
Employee self-services 60
End user, training 337
End-to-end process 78
End-user extensibility 126
Enhancement option 120
Enhancement, side-by-side 124
Enterprise Services 521
Environment, Health, and Safety (EHS) 56
EPS 286
ERP → SAP ERP
ETL 391
Event Stream Processor 286
EWM 53, 342
Execution of Program After Import 87
Execution phase 346
Explore phase 174, 195, 203, 380
Explore phase → Explore phase
Extensibility
   business objects 130
   business processes 125
   calculation logic 130
   custom 122
   fields 129
   in-app approach 124, 126
   key user 126
   side-by-side approach 124
   tables 129
   traditional 131
   user interfaces 125

F

(F1) help	172
FaaS	325
Facebook	286
marketing	71
Fact sheet	89
Fan page	305
FES	322
Field mapping	382, 403, 411, 450
Field, custom	129
Fieldglass	64, 67
File interface	406
Final trial run	386
Financial closing	48, 111
Financial planning	49
Fiori as a Service	325
Fiori Cloud → SAP Fiori Cloud	
Fiori Launchpad → SAP Fiori Launchpad	
Fiori → SAP Fiori	
Fiscal year variant	489
Fit gap workshop	174, 189, 322, 382
Fit standard analysis	189
Fixed value	235
Flat file	405
Frontend server	90
add-on deployment	323
central hub deployment	323
deployment options	323
installation	325
SAP Fiori Cloud	323
Fully-Activated Appliance	182
Function module	398, 441
Function module, wrapper	441

G

Gateway → SAP Gateway	
General test	465
Gigya	302
Global availability check	53
Global Available-to-Promise	542
Global system	532, 545
Global variable	412, 420, 430
Golden record	392
Go-live	175, 467

Google	71
Google AdWords	287
Greenfield	99, 121, 329, 377
Guided buying	66
Guided configuration	110, 165
Guided process	231

H

Hard disk	83
Hardware	83, 116, 468
requirement	313
Harmonization	531
HCM	509
HEC	113, 311
Help text	212
Hotfix	116
HR	57
HTML5 total	125
Human capital	34
Human Capital Management	509
Human resources	57
Hybrid cloud	103
Hybrid operating model	103
Hybrid scenario	99

I

IaaS → Infrastructure as a Service	
Identity provider	200
IDoc	126, 291, 391, 398
background processing	435
basic type	399
control record	431
enhancement	399
HCM connection	511
import	430
inbound	431
message type	399
monitoring	434
parallel processing	436
performance	434
status	399, 434
transfer	430
type	399

Index

IDP 200
IFlow 282, 513
Implementation
 method 158
 process-oriented 136
 technical 135
Implementation Guide, Central
 Finance 483
Industry 4.0 25
Information Steward 391
Infrastructure as a Service . 102, 114, 180, 311
Infrastructure service 33
Initial situation 527
In-memory database 83
Innovation Strategy & Roadmap 529
Innovation Strategy & Roadmap
 service 529
In-place migration 368
Inspection run 356
Instagram 287
Installation 313
Installation guide 315
Integration 61, 95
Integration flow 282, 513
Integration package, SAP
 SuccessFactors 519
Integration, native 505
Interaction, SAP Hybris Marketing Cloud 290
Interface 126
Intermediate Document → IDoc
Internet of Things 25, 31, 37
Inventory management 52
 simplification 41
Invoice processing 65
IoT → Internet of Things
ISO code 423

J

Jam 178
Job 402
 validation 427

K

Key performance indicator 72
Key user 205
Key-user extensibility 93, 126
KPI 72

L

Landscape Management Database 345
Landscape strategy 532
Landscape transformation   140, 153, 457, 527, 539
 pre-analysis 462
 project phases 459
 scenarios 458
 system group 467
 testing 464
Launchpad → SAP Fiori Launchpad
Learning Hub → SAP Learning Hub
Ledger 489
Legacy System Migration Workbench 143, 454
License 120, 185
Lifecycle management 157
Live tile 92
LMDB 345
Load test, productive 384
Load, productive 386
Local Object Library 401
Localization 186
Logical system 485, 510
Logical Unit of Work 436
Lookup field 419
Lookup table 419
Loyalty program 72
LSMW 143, 454
LUW 436

M

Maintenance 31, 120, 468
Maintenance cycle 116
Maintenance plan 344

Index

Maintenance Planner .. 150, 313, 331, 344
   landscape data 345
   SAP Fiori 371
Managed cloud 113
Mandatory field 412
Mandatory structure 229
Manufacturing cloud 110
Manufacturing execution system 55
Mapping
   on paper 403, 412
   rules 474
   SAP Data Services Designer 413
   template 403
Market Risk Analyzer 51
Marketing calendar 72
Marketing Lead Management 72
Marketing resource management 72
Mass load ID 221
Massive Open Online Course 34, 172
Master client 187, 318
Master data 380
   Central Finance 493
   cleansing 494
   employee 196
   harmonization 474
   human resources 510
Master Data Governance → SAP Master Data Governance
Master system 154
Master system → Master system
Material group 497
Material master 497
Material number field 341
Material requirements planning 55
MDG 483, 494
Memory 83
Message type 244, 511
Metadata 392, 405
Methodology 173
Microsoft Azure 181
Microsoft Excel XML Spreadsheet 2003 ... 216, 226
Middleware 506
Migration 18
   content 390, 396
   landscape transformation 140

Migration (Cont.)
   new implementation 140
   scenarios 139
   system conversion 140
Migration Cockpit → SAP S/4HANA Migration Cockpit
Migration object 141, 214, 380, 387
   adapt 441
   copy 225
   determine 381
Migration Object Modeler → SAP S/4HANA Migration Object Modeler
Migration project 133
Migration scenario 139, 527
Migration services 419, 424
Migration template 226, 440
   add fields 445
   file extension 227
   release 227
   view 447
Migration tool 213
Migration Workbench 213, 216, 451
Model company 179
   clients 187
   structure 188
Modification 348, 473
Modification adjustment 318
MOOC 34, 172
Multi-client system 469
Multi-core processor 83
Multi-system landscape 204
MWB → Migration Workbench

N

Naming convention 497
Near-zero downtime 151
New implementation   140, 377, 527, 535, 539
   Rapid Data Migration 390
   SAP S/4HANA Cloud 194
   SAP S/4HANA migration cockpit ... 437
New installation 313
Non-SAP system 528
Number range 471

Index

O

OData	126, 284, 291, 518
OData service	323
ODBC	405
Offset	474
OLAP	82
OLTP	82
One-step procedure	332, 338, 537
One-tier system	111
Online Analytical Processing	82
Online Transaction Processing	82
On-premise	99
On-premise edition	104
Open Campaign Channel	287
Open Data Protocol → OData	
Open Database Connectivity	405
openSAP	172
Operating concern	492
Operating model	100, 134
cloud	100
hybrid	103
on-premise	100
Operation	115
ORDER BY statement	351
Organization derivation	478
Organizational unit	486, 492
transfer	476
Out of the box	291

P

PaaS	102, 124
Paid search	71
Paid search campaign	71
Parallel accounting	48
Payroll	60
Phased rollout	225, 235
PI → SAP Process Integration	
Planned data	50
Planning	49
Planning phase	460
Platform as a Service	102, 124
Platform, digital	33
Plausibility check	429
PLT	384
PoC	182, 184
Portal	88
Post	303
PP/DS	39
Pre-check	149, 331, 346
asset accounting	348
Pre-check → Pre-check	
Predictive analytics	31
Prefix	474
Prepare phase	174, 380
pre-checks	346
Prepare phase → Prepare phase	
Pre-Transition Check → Pre-check	
Principle of one	38
Private cloud	70, 103, 311
Private managed cloud solution	105
Process	
standardize	468
test	169
Process diagram	163, 251
Process Orchestration → SAP Process Orchestration	
Procurement	64
Product hierarchy	497
Product recommendation	72
Production	55
Production conversion	461, 466
monitoring	466
simulation	465
Production planning and detailed scheduling	39
Production system	204, 320
global	532
regional	532
strategy	530
transformation	466
Productive load	386
Profiling	391, 395
columns	408
relationships	410
Profit center	496
Profit center accounting	491
Profitability analysis, account-based	492
Program variant	475
Project management	111
Project plan	462

Index

Project planning 133
Project team 461
Proof of concept 182, 184
Provisioning framework 516
Public API 302
Public cloud 102, 116, 193, 311
Purchase order 244
Purchase requisition 243
Purchasing, operative 64

Q

Quality assurance system 204, 320
conversion 334
Quick Sizer 363
Quote automation 246
Quote, spot 246

R

RAM 88
Random-Access Memory 88
sizing 88
Rapid Data Migration 388, 390, 437
Rapid Data Migration, API 385
Rapid Deployment Solution (RDS) 69, 161
Rapid Deployment Solution, package ... 393
RDS → Rapid Deployment Solution
Realize phase 175, 204, 384
Regional system 532, 545
Relevance analysis 372
Remittance advice 246
Remote function call → RFC
Replication server 108, 482
Reporting 45
Repository 392
Representational State Transfer (REST) 126, 285
Request for quotation 243
Required field 412
Research and development 55
RFC 284, 430, 435
RFC connection 485
Roadmap 530, 543

Roadmap Viewer 176, 529
Role 92, 205
key user 199
SAP S/4HANA Cloud, starter system 199
SAP_BR_ADMINISTRATOR 199
SAP_BR_BPC_EXPERT 203, 216
Runtime estimate 457

S

S user 345
S/4HANA → SAP S/4HANA
S4CORE total 364
S4HANA_READINESS total 355
SaaS → Software as a Service
Sales 54
Sales order fulfillment 54
Sandbox system 182, 184, 313
SAP Activate 157, 179, 195, 378
content 158
integration 249
methodology 173
modules 159
phases 174
SAP Adaptive Server Enterprise 395
SAP Advanced Planning and
  Optimization 39, 55
SAP API Business Hub 282, 292, 301
SAP Application Interface Framework 522
SAP Ariba 503
interfaces 503
message type 244
native integration 505
rapid deployment solution 273
scope items 256
subscription 249
transaction rule 269
SAP Ariba business relationship 271
SAP Ariba Collaborative Commerce .. 245
SAP Ariba Collaborative Finance 247
SAP Ariba Discount Management 247
SAP Ariba Network 51, 64, 67, 241
integration 507
invite suppliers 259

563

Index

SAP Ariba Solution Integration for SAP
   Business Suite 273
SAP Ariba Sourcing 243, 508
SAP Best Practices 160, 179, 393
   activation 319
   baseline 163
   building blocks 166
   Explorer 164, 397
   localization 163
   migration content 226
   Rapid Data Migration 390
   scope items 166
   system configuration 318
SAP Business All-in-One 161
SAP Business Planning and
   Consolidation 49
SAP Business Suite 78
SAP Business Suite 4 SAP HANA → SAP
   S/4HANA
SAP Business Warehouse 532
SAP BusinessObjects BI Platform 391,
   432
SAP BusinessObjects Planning and
   Consolidation 542
SAP BusinessObjects Web Intelligence ......
   391, 434
   reports 432
SAP BW 532
SAP CAL 180
SAP Cash Management 50
SAP Cloud Appliance Library 180
SAP Cloud Identity 200
SAP Cloud Platform 102, 120, 124, 323,
   325, 513
SAP Cloud Platform integration   275, 282,
   285, 294, 299, 301, 506, 513
SAP Cloud Platform OData
   Provisioning 326
SAP Consumer Insight 43
SAP Credit Management 38, 40, 51
SAP Data Services 143, 386, 390
   data flow 402
   Designer 398, 401
   import 397
   jobs 396
   license 398
   profiler 408

SAP Download Manager 313
SAP Engineering Control Center 55
SAP Enterprise Architecture Explorer ....
   324
SAP ERP 75, 286, 291, 295
SAP ERP 6.0 527
SAP ERP HCM 509
SAP ERP HCM, side-by-side operation ......
   513
SAP Event Stream Processor 286
SAP Extended Warehouse
   Management 53, 342
SAP Fieldglass 64, 67
SAP Fiori 43, 79, 88, 370
   2.0 370
   App Finder 374
   app reference library 372
   Best Practices 162
   documentation 93
   enhancements 93
   frontend server 322
   help 93
   installation 371
   library 326
   operating concept 91
   relevance analysis 370
   role 92
   role concept 374
   technology 90
   transition phase 373
   types of apps 89
   X-ray 93
SAP Fiori Cloud 323, 325
   demo 325
   deployment options 326
SAP Fiori Launchpad 91, 322, 374
   group 92, 198
   navigation 198
   provider 323
SAP Gateway 126, 322
SAP GUI 88, 322, 373
SAP HANA 83
SAP HANA Cloud Connector 126, 323,
   326
SAP HANA Cloud Platform → SAP Cloud
   Platform

564

Index

SAP HANA Enterprise Cloud 113, 311
SAP HANA Enterprise Cloud, Central Finance 483
SAP HANA, custom developments 351
SAP Hybris Cloud for Customer .. 70, 285, 306
SAP Hybris Cloud for Customer 2.0 integration with SAP ERP 293
SAP Hybris Cloud for Service 285
SAP Hybris Commerce 70, 286
SAP Hybris Data Hub 286
SAP Hybris Loyalty Management 285
SAP Hybris Marketing 68
SAP Hybris Marketing Cloud .. 68–69, 112
   contacts 290
   data model 289
   File Based Data Load 299
   integration 284
   interactions 290
SAP Information Steward 391
SAP Jam 178
SAP Landscape Transformation 154
   delete company code 477
   Migration Object Modeler 142
SAP Landscape Transformation Replication Server 108, 482
   trigger 486
SAP Launch 158
SAP Learning Hub 172–173
SAP LT → SAP Landscape Transformation
SAP Manufacturing Execution 55
SAP Master Data Governance (MDG) 483, 494
SAP Note
   business impact 343
   implement 318
SAP Portfolio and Project Management ... 55
SAP Process Integration 95, 294, 521
SAP Process Orchestration 95, 506, 521
SAP Product Lifecycle Management 55
SAP Project System 55
SAP Promotion Management for Retail ... 286
SAP Query 386

SAP S/4HANA 17, 75, 106
   accounting 47
   admin guide 319
   architecture 90
   Asset Management 56
   business functions 46
   compatibility packages 59, 107
   components 46
   configuration 165
   digital transformation 37
   extensibility 122
   frontend server 322
   global system 532
   guided configuration 110
   human resources 57, 59
   implementation 158
   installation 313
   integration with SAP Ariba 503
   logistics 52
   migration 18
   on-premise 105, 313, 503
   operating models 100
   operation 115
   procurement 64
   product family 104
   public cloud 109
   reference 179
   regional system 532
   requirements 75
   sales and marketing 68
   sizing 313
   trial system 160
SAP S/4HANA Central Finance → Central Finance
SAP S/4HANA Cloud 109
   configuration 203, 210
   customizing 210
   data migration 203, 207, 213–214, 216, 220, 229, 377, 383–385, 388, 390, 400, 411, 419, 437, 441, 528
   hardware 116
   human resources 275
   implementation checklist 209
   implementation phase 203
   maintenance cycles 116
   operation 115

565

Index

SAP S/4HANA Cloud (Cont.)
  production system 205
  starter system 195
  trial system 180, 194
  user interface 94
SAP S/4HANA Community 318, 455
SAP S/4HANA Cookbook 318
SAP S/4HANA Embedded Analytics 45, 96
SAP S/4HANA Enterprise Management 106
SAP S/4HANA Enterprise Management Cloud 105, 112
  private option 114
SAP S/4HANA Finance 106, 538
  cloud 111
  pre-checks 348
SAP S/4HANA Fully-Activated Appliance 181
SAP S/4HANA Installation Guide 315
SAP S/4HANA Manufacturing Cloud ... 110
SAP S/4HANA Marketing Cloud → SAP Hybris Marketing Cloud
SAP S/4HANA Migration Cockpit 110, 141, 171, 203, 207, 214, 216, 220, 229, 377, 383–385, 388, 390, 400, 411, 419, 437, 441, 528
SAP S/4HANA Migration Object Modeler 142, 377, 441
SAP S/4HANA Professional Services Cloud 111
SAP Simple Finance → SAP S/4HANA Finance
SAP Solution Manager 177
  guided configuration 166
  LMDB 345
  release 7.2 319
SAP SuccessFactors 58
  Compensation Management 61
  employee master data 202
  integration 509
  Learning 62
  Recruiting 60
  side-by-side operation 513
  Succession & Development 62
  Talent Management Suite 511
  Workforce Analytics 62

SAP SuccessFactors Employee Central 59, 274, 513
  Admin Center 515
  communication scenario 281
  integration packages 519
SAP Supplier Network Collaboration 273
SAP Supply Chain Management ... 52, 273
SAP Support Portal 345
SAP Treasury and Risk Management ... 51
SAP Web Dispatcher 90, 323
SAP Web IDE 44, 93, 326
SAP_APPL 364
SAP_CUST 318
SAP_UCUS 318
SAPUI5 total 125
Satellite system 193, 284
SCM 52, 273
Scope item 166, 243, 251, 320
Search, paid 71
Secure File Transfer Protocol 285, 299
Segment 398
SELECT statement 351
Self-service configuration 69, 168
Sensor data 31
Service 33
Service model 101
Service process, smart 31
Set up key user, user 196
SFTP 299
Shadow instance 365
Shared secret 266
Simple Finance → SAP S/4HANA Finance
Simple Object Access Protocol 126
Simplification 37, 79
  analyses 45
  data structure 40
  functionality 37
Simplification list 60, 80, 147, 330, 340, 507, 521
  categories 341
  items 340
Single-client system 469
Sizing 87, 146, 313, 363
Sizing report 363
SL Toolset 331
SLD 345
SLO 459

Index

SLT → SAP Landscape Transformation
Smart product 31
Smart services 31
SNC 273
SOA Manager 517
SOAP 126, 284
Soft financial close 111
Software as a Service 70, 101, 115, 193, 311
Software component 364
Software Download Center 316
Software Logistics Toolset 331
Software Provisioning Manager 317
Software Update Manager .. 150, 317, 333
   analysis file 367
   default procedure 368
   downtime 367
   downtime optimization 370
   system conversion 363, 368
Solution Builder 166, 319
Solution Manager → SAP Solution Manager
Solution scope file 320
Source structure
   display mapping 449
   edit 445
Source system, integration with SAP Data Services 405
Sourcing 243
   strategic 65
SPAM 316
SPAU adjustment 318
Spot quote 246
Sprinklr 286
SQL 351
SQL Monitor 351
SQLScript 351
Stack XML 345, 347, 364
Staging 438
Staging area 229, 394, 419
Standard software 189
Standardization 468
Starter system 195
Subscription 183
Subscription model 120
SuccessFactors → SAP SuccessFactors
SUM → Software Update Manager

Supplier invoice 244
Supplier quick enablement 259
Supply Chain Management 52, 273
Support 467
Support Package Manager 316
SurveyMonkey 286
SWPM 317
System
   global 532, 545
   logical 485, 510
   regional 532, 545
   transactional 532
System consolidation   154, 458, 467, 530, 539
System conversion 140, 146, 329, 527, 535, 539
   after company code deletion 481
   conversion paths 339
   downtime 335
   one-step procedure 332, 338
   project phases 332
   requirements 332, 338
   system group 334
   system landscape 334
   technical 151
System copy 478
System group 334
System group, landscape transformation 467
System landscape 334, 481
   data 345
   decentralized 533
   deployment options 541
   simplification 38
   strategy 532
System Landscape Directory 345
System Landscape Optimization 459
System requirement 332, 546
System switch upgrade procedure 365

T

Table
   ACTDOCA 42
   custom 129
   MATDOC 42

Index

Target architecture 107
Target landscape 530
TCO 138, 467
Template, global 532, 545
Test 169
Test case 480
Test concept 463
Test run 461, 464
Test script 163
Test system 207
   deployment 465
Test variant 355
Theming 93
Three-system landscape 334
Tile, live tile 92
Time recording 59
Time to value 548
TLS 109
Total Cost of Ownership 138, 467
Trade-off 138
Training 62
Transaction
   BD64 511
   BD87 434
   BDBG 394, 400
   FAGLF03 499
   GCAC 500
   KA23 495
   LSMW 454
   LTMC 438
   LTMOM 443
   SAINT 318
   SALE 510
   SCI 351, 355
   SM59 510
   SNOTE 318
   SPAM 318
   SPAU 318, 362
   SPDD 362
   STO3 372
   SYCM 354
   usage analysis 372
   WE02 434
   WE05 434
   WE20 .... 435, 511
   WE21 511

Transaction data 380
Transaction Manager 51
Transaction rule 269
Transactional app 89
Transfer structure 227
Transformation → Landscape transformation
Transport Layer Security 109
Transport route 320
Transport system 320
Trial system 160
   clients 187
   on-premise 180
   SAP S/4HANA Cloud 180, 194
   transformation 467
Troubleshooting 429
Twitter 286, 303
Two-step procedure 537
Two-system landscape 204
Type conversion 416

U

UI → User interface
UI technology 117
Unicode 338
Universal Journal 42, 48, 111, 490
Universal Journal, account assignment ... 491
Update Manager → Software Update Manager
Upgrade 81, 116
Usage analysis 372
Usage Procedure Logging (UPL) 350
User
   authentication 200
   harmonization 475
   technical 196
User administration, options 202
User exit 473
User experience 34, 43
User extensibility 126
User interface 79, 88, 117
   enhancement 125
   simplification 43
User interface → User interface

User maintenance, SAP S/4HANA Cloud,
 starter system 196
UX 43

V

Validation 426
 technical 464
Validation function 428
Validation rules 386
Value mapping 419, 474
Value mapping, Central Finance 487
Variable, global → Global variable
VDM 96
View 226
Virtual data model 96

W

Warehouse management 342
Waterfall model 157
Web Dispatcher 90, 323
Web Intelligence → SAP BusinessObjects
 Web Intelligence
Web servers 323, 393
Work process 435
Workload Monitor 372
World template 179
Wrapper function module 441

X

XPRA 87
X-Ray 93

- Learn what SAP S/4HANA offers your company for financials and logistics
- Get the scoop on SAP S/4HANA deployment options, implementation, extensibility, and more
- Reference customer case studies to see how other companies are transforming their businesses

Bardhan, Baumgartl, Chaadaev, Choi, Dudgeon, Lahiri, Meijerink, Worsley-Tonks

SAP S/4HANA

An Introduction

Making the jump to SAP S/4HANA? From finance to logistics, from on-premise to cloud implementations, and from industry solutions to reporting, see what SAP S/4HANA can offer! Understand its architecture, adoption scenarios, and how SAP Activate can facilitate your transformation. Learn about all-new functionality for warehousing, manufacturing, procurement, and more. Up to date for 1709!

approx. 550 pp., 2nd edition, pub. 10/2017
E-Book: $59.99 | **Print:** $69.95 | **Bundle:** $79.99

www.sap-press.com/4499

Rheinwerk
Publishing

- Implement SAP Fiori on AS ABAP, SAP HANA, and SAP S/4HANA
- Customize transactional, analytical, and fact sheet apps
- Upgrade to SAP Fiori 2.0 and develop your own apps from scratch

Anil Bavaraju

SAP Fiori Implementation and Development

The SAP Fiori 2.0 design concept is here. See how to take your UI to the next level with this all-in-one resource to implementing and developing analytical, transactional, and fact sheet apps. Get the low-down on SAP Fiori's all-new look, SAP S/4HANA support, and more. This guide to Fiori has your back—implement, create, and customize!

615 pages, 2nd edition, pub. 05/2017
E-Book: $69.99 | **Print:** $79.95 | **Bundle:** $89.99

www.sap-press.com/4401

- Explore the new data warehousing solution from SAP
- Learn about data modeling, reporting, analytics, and administration
- Discover what SAP BW/4HANA will mean for you

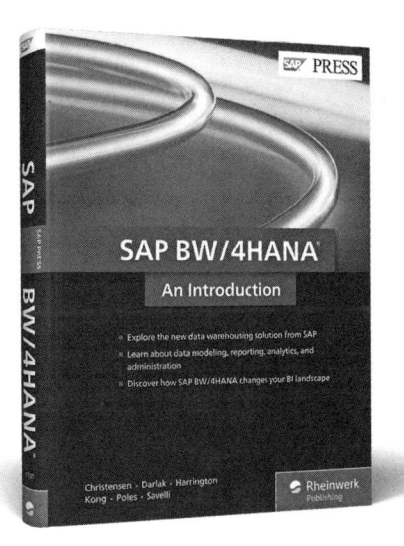

Christensen, Darlak, Harrington, Kong, Poles, Savelli

SAP BW/4HANA

An Introduction

What is SAP BW/4HANA? More importantly, what can it do for you? Between these pages, you'll explore the answers to these questions, from simplified data models and SAP BW/4HANA Analytics to automated data lifecycle management. You'll find step-by-step instructions for installation and setup, a guide to administrative tasks to keep your SAP BW/4HANA system in tip-top shape, and the low-down on security in your new system. Explore the data warehouse of the future!

427 pages, pub. 06/2017
E-Book: $59.99 | **Print:** $69.95 | **Bundle:** $79.99

www.sap-press.com/4377

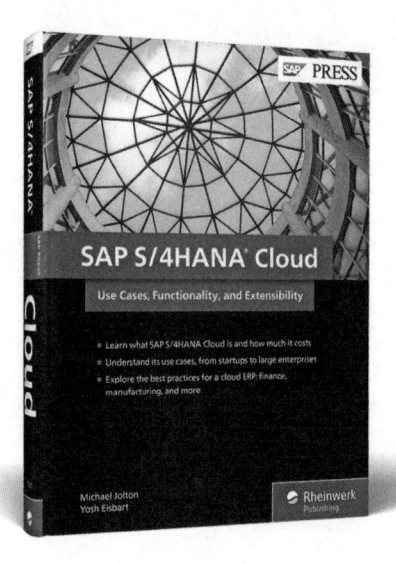

- Learn what SAP S/4HANA Cloud is and how much it costs
- Understand its use cases, from startups to large enterprises
- Explore the best practices for a cloud ERP: finance, manufacturing, and more

Michael Jolton, Yosh Eisbart

SAP S/4HANA Cloud

Use Cases, Functionality, and Extensibility

Is SAP S/4HANA Cloud right for you? Get the scoop on SAP S/4HANA Cloud, from implementation to extensibility. Find answers to your questions about use cases, costs, and maintenance requirements. Then dive into SAP S/4HANA Cloud's core processes: finance, inventory, production, sales, and more. Learn how you can tailor the system to grow with your business. Get the SAP S/4HANA Cloud big picture!

approx. 350 pp., pub. 10/2017
E-Book: $59.99 | **Print:** $69.95 | **Bundle:** $79.99

www.sap-press.com/4498

www.sap-press.com

- Learn what SAP S/4HANA offers for supply chain management: manufacturing, warehousing, procurement, and beyond
- Explore embedded analytics and key SAP Fiori applications for supply chain processes
- Preview your migration to SAP S/4HANA

Bhattacharjee, Monti, Perel, Vazquez

Logistics with SAP S/4HANA

An Introduction

Welcome to logistics in a digital world. From procurement to production and everything in between, see how SAP S/4HANA transforms your SAP Logistics landscape. Examine each supply chain line of business in SAP S/4HANA: sales order management, manufacturing, inventory management, plant maintenance, and more. Discover key innovations such as MRP Live and embedded SAP EWM. Explore the future of logistics with SAP!

approx. 500 pp., pub. 10/2017
E-Book: $59.99 | **Print:** $69.95 | **Bundle:** $79.99

www.sap-press.com/4485

Rheinwerk
Publishing

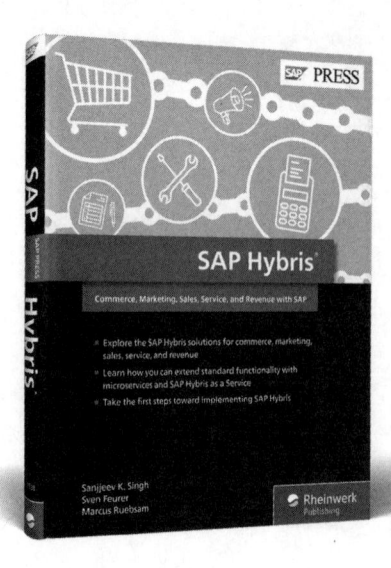

- Explore the SAP Hybris solutions for commerce, marketing, sales, service, and revenue

- Learn how you can extend standard functionality with microservices and SAP Hybris as a Service

- Take the first steps toward implementing SAP Hybris

Singh, Feurer, Ruebsam

SAP Hybris

Commerce, Marketing, Sales, Service, and Revenue with SAP

Looking to get the big picture on SAP Hybris? Want to learn what's available—on premise and in the cloud—and how it fits into your CRM landscape? With this guide, you'll begin by understanding the functionality of the five main SAP Hybris solutions: sales, service, commerce, marketing, and revenue. Then explore reporting and mobility options and see how each product integrates with existing SAP solutions. Connect better with your customers!

329 pages, pub. 05/2017
E-Book: $59.99 | **Print:** $69.95 | **Bundle:** $79.99

www.sap-press.com/4394

www.sap-press.com

Interested in reading more?

Please visit our website for all new book
and e-book releases from SAP PRESS.

www.sap-press.com

SAP PRESS